T0366237

Real Estate Modelling and Forecasting

As real estate forms a significant part of the asset portfolios of most investors and lenders, it is crucial that analysts and institutions employ sound techniques for modelling and forecasting the performance of real estate assets. Assuming no prior knowledge of econometrics, this book introduces and explains a broad range of quantitative techniques that are relevant for the analysis of real estate data. It includes numerous detailed examples, giving readers the confidence they need to estimate and interpret their own models. Throughout, the book emphasises how various statistical techniques may be used for forecasting and shows how forecasts can be evaluated. Written by a highly experienced teacher of econometrics and a senior real estate professional, both of whom are widely known for their research, *Real Estate Modelling and Forecasting* is the first book to provide a practical introduction to the econometric analysis of real estate for students and practitioners.

Chris Brooks is Professor of Finance and Director of Research at the ICMA Centre, University of Reading, United Kingdom, where he also obtained his PhD. He has published over sixty articles in leading academic and practitioner journals, including the *Journal of Business*, the *Journal of Banking and Finance*, the *Journal of Empirical Finance*, the *Review of Economics and Statistics* and the *Economic Journal*. He is associate editor of a number of journals, including the *International Journal of Forecasting*. He has also acted as consultant for various banks and professional bodies in the fields of finance, econometrics and real estate. He is the author of the best-selling textbook *Introductory Econometrics for Finance* (Cambridge University Press, 2009), now in its second edition.

Sotiris Tsolacos is Director of European Research at Property and Portfolio Research, a CoStar Group company. He has previously held positions with Jones Lang LaSalle Research and the University of Reading, where he also obtained his PhD. He has carried out extensive research work on modelling and forecasting real estate markets, with over forty papers published in major international real estate research and applied economics journals. He is also a regular commentator on topical themes in the real estate market, with numerous contributions to practitioner journals.

Real Estate Modelling and Forecasting

Chris Brooks
ICMA Centre, University of Reading

Sotiris Tsolacos
Property and Portfolio Research

CAMBRIDGE
UNIVERSITY PRESS

University Printing House, Cambridge CB2 8BS, United Kingdom

Cambridge University Press is part of the University of Cambridge.

It furthers the University's mission by disseminating knowledge in the pursuit of education, learning and research at the highest international levels of excellence.

www.cambridge.org
Information on this title: www.cambridge.org/9780521873390

First published 2010
4th printing 2014

A catalogue record for this publication is available from the British Library

Library of Congress Cataloguing in Publication data
Brooks, Chris
Real estate modelling and forecasting / Chris Brooks, Sotiris Tsolacos.
p. cm.
Includes bibliographical references and index.
ISBN 978-0-521-87339-0
1. Real estate investment – Statistical methods. I. Tsolacos, Sotiris. II. Title.
HD1382.5.B756 2010
332.63′2401 – dc22 2009054017

ISBN 978-0-521-87339-0 Hardback

Contents

Figures

Tables

Boxes

Preface

Motivations for the book

This book is designed to address the quantitative needs of students and practitioners of real estate analysis. Real estate is a truly multidisciplinary field. It combines specialities from urban economics, geography, land management, town planning, construction, valuations, surveying, finance, business economics and other areas in order to perform a range of tasks, including portfolio strategy, valuations, risk assessment and development feasibility. In performing these tasks, objective analysis, systematic relationships and greater sophistication are essential. The present book targets this fundamental need in the market.

The demand for modelling and forecasting work is expanding rapidly, with a direct requirement for insightful and well-informed processes to be in place. The growing number and larger size of forecasting teams within firms compared with just a few years ago, and the existence of forecasting-related research sponsored by industry organisations and of professional courses in this area, demonstrate the significance given by the industry to quantitative modelling and forecasting.

At the same time, undergraduate and postgraduate courses in real estate have increasingly introduced more quantitative analysis into their portfolios of modules. Such students rarely come from a statistics background, which is acknowledged in this book. With increasing demands from employers for their applicants to have received statistical training, academic institutions and other educational establishments need to introduce more formal quantitative analysis in their degrees. Given the greater availability of data, firms require that their intake will be able to analyse the data and to support valuations, fund management and other activities.

There is a dearth of textbooks specifically focused on the quantitative analysis of real estate markets, yet there has been an explosion of academic articles in the last ten years offering a variety of models, estimation methodologies and findings. Nevertheless, authors often use different criteria to evaluate their models, if they use any at all, and authors avoid discussing the factors that could invalidate their findings from a modelling point of view. This could lead to considerable confusion for readers who are not already familiar with the material. More importantly, just a handful of studies in this large literature will proceed to assess the model's adequacy and to engage in comparative analysis. This book aims to equip the reader with the knowledge to understand and evaluate empirical work in real estate modelling and forecasting.

Who should read this book?

The book is intended as an easy-to-read guide to using quantitative methods for solving problems in real estate that will be accessible to advanced undergraduate and Masters students, as well as practitioners who require knowledge of the econometric techniques commonly used in the real estate field. Use of the book may also extend to doctoral programmes in which students do not have strong backgrounds in econometric techniques but wish to conduct robust empirical research in real estate. The book can also be used by academic researchers whose work requires the undertaking of statistical analysis.

This book is also very much aimed at real estate practitioners. Analysts in research, investment, consultancy and other areas who require an introduction to the statistical tools employed to model real estate relationships and perform forecasting in practice will find this book relevant to their work. The book should also be useful for the growing number of professional education programmes in real estate modelling.

There are, of course, large numbers of econometrics textbooks, but the majority of these go through the introductory material in excruciating detail rather than being targeted at what really matters in real estate. Additionally, and more importantly, in such books, all the examples employed to illustrate the techniques are drawn from pure economics rather than real estate. Students of real estate who are required to learn some technical skills rapidly grow tired of such texts, and practitioners cannot relate to the examples, making it more difficult for them to see how the ideas could be applied.

Unique features of the book

(1) The reader can confidently claim an understanding of the methodologies used in real estate modelling. Great emphasis is put on regression analysis as the backbone of quantitative real estate analysis.

(2) Extensive examples: the range of international illustrations shows the reader the kind of relationships investigated in real estate market analysis. The examples are supported by a review of selected studies from the literature.
(3) The work on modelling in the book is extended to forecasting. The tone in the book is that forecasting in real estate is not, and should never be seen as, a black box. The detailed examples given in each chapter enable the reader to perform forecasting using all the methodologies we present.
(4) In much of the existing literature in real estate modelling and forecasting, there is a noticeable gap, in that diagnostic checking and forecast evaluation are overlooked. We examine these issues comprehensively and we devote a chapter to each of them. Our aim is to educate the reader to assess alternative theoretical propositions and/or the same proposition in different contexts and with diverse data.
(5) Hall (1994) argues that, 'while the technical aspects of forecasting are developing rapidly, there is still a need for the expert forecaster who blends a complex combination of real world institutional knowledge with formal academic modelling techniques to produce a credible view of the future' (p. iv). We devote a chapter to how real estate forecasting is carried out in practice and we highlight a host of practical issues of which the quantitative analyst, the expert and the final user should be aware. This chapter includes propositions as to how these parties can work more closely, make the forecast process more transparent and evaluate it.
(6) This book also studies the potential benefits of more complicated techniques, such as vector autoregressions, simultaneous systems and cointegration. We attempt to demystify these techniques and make them as accessible as possible. They are explained exhaustively and, again, the coverage extends to forecasting.
(7) All the data used in the examples are available on the book's companion website, www.cambridge.org/9780521873390.

Prerequisites for a good understanding of this material

In order to make this book as accessible as possible, the only background recommended in terms of quantitative techniques is that readers have an introductory-level knowledge of calculus, algebra (including matrices) and basic statistics. Even these are not necessarily prerequisites, however, since they are covered in the opening chapters of the book. The emphasis throughout the book is on a valid application of the techniques to real data and problems in real estate.

In the real estate area, it is assumed that the reader has basic knowledge of real estate theory, although, again, this is not strictly necessary. The aim of the book is to enable the reader to investigate and assess alternative theories in practice and in different contexts.

Our ambition

This book will be successful only if the reader is able to confidently carry out his/her own quantitative analysis, interpret conventional statistics encountered in similar studies in the fields of economics and finance, and conduct forecasting. We hope that the book achieves this aspiration.

Chris Brooks and Sotiris Tsolacos, April 2009

Acknowledgements

The authors are grateful to to Hilary Feltham for assistance with the material in chapter 2.

The publisher and authors have used their best endeavours to ensure that the URLs for external websites referred to in this book are correct and active at the time of going to press. The publisher and author have no responsibility for the websites, however, and can make no guarantee that a site will remain live or that the content is or will remain appropriate.

1 Introduction

Learning outcomes

In this chapter, you will learn how to

- outline key stages in the construction of econometric models;
- illustrate the principles of model building in real estate;
- explain the relationships and variables researchers most frequently model and forecast in the real estate market;
- broadly categorise quantitative and qualitative forecasting approaches;
- understand the objectives and usage of modelling and forecasting work; and
- compare the characteristics of real estate data with those of economic and financial data;
- you will also become acquainted with the use of econometrics software packages.

The focus of this book is econometric modelling and forecasting in the real estate field. The book tackles key themes in applied quantitative research in real estate and provides the basis for developing forecast models for this market. This chapter sets the scene for the book. It describes the rationale for this text and highlights the business areas in which real estate modelling is important. The econometric study of relationships in real estate and the forecasting process draw upon the general subjects of econometrics and economic forecasting. This chapter also touches on issues relating to the construction of general forecasting models with direct implications for real estate practice.

1.1 Motivation for this book

The complexity of the real estate market, its linkages to the economy and the importance of real estate in the credit and investment spheres have necessitated a closer study of the dynamics of the real estate market and the increasing use of quantitative analysis, to explore how adjustments take place within the market and to measure its relationship with the external environment. Researchers in both academia and industry are keen to identify systematic relationships in real estate and to formally study what shapes these relationships through time and across real estate sectors and locations, with the ultimate goal of forecasting the market. Quantitative work in real estate markets is now sizeable and has brought challenges. As real estate analysts are exposed to such work, there is an eagerness to understand the principles and to directly apply them in practice to inform decision making. A textbook treatment and application of econometric techniques to real estate is therefore appropriate. The present book aims to address this need by focusing on the key econometric methodologies that will facilitate quantitative modelling in the real estate market and help analysts to assess the empirical support for alternative a priori arguments and models.

In real estate courses at universities, modelling and forecasting analysis is now introduced. A number of real estate programmes have explicit streams in this subject area, and this component of the curriculum is expanding. The majority of these modules are conversion courses and are usually taken by students who do not have an economics or statistics background. Hence this book is intended to bring students with an interest in the quantitative analysis of the real estate market up to speed with the principles of econometric modelling and their application to real estate. The book provides structure to the development of these skills. Students will familiarise themselves with the most commonly used techniques in practice and will be well equipped to pursue the econometric analysis of real estate markets. The content of this book and the range of topics covered make it suitable for both undergraduate and postgraduate degrees.

The recognition of real estate as an asset class by the investment community is another motivation for this book, since it poses challenges to how analysis in real estate markets is conducted. Investors in other asset classes are accustomed to applying quantitative analysis to study market behaviour and they would like to see similar practices in the real estate market. This book illustrates to people who are not real estate industry analysts the range of techniques at their disposal to study relationships in this market. Forecasting is, of course, important for investment purposes. The methodologies we present in this book can all be used for forecasting. Through the key model diagnostics and forecast evaluation tests we describe, an investment analyst is able to assess how good the models are.

We focus on the areas that really matter in real estate modelling and forecasting and that have not been addressed due to the lack of such a textbook. For example, forecast evaluation and judgemental forecasting are topics with limited treatment in the real estate context. The book also highlights more advanced techniques and illustrates how these can be used for forecasting; most existing studies stop a step short of actually moving into forecasting. We emphasise diagnostic checking, as the standards of rigour within the industry differ. A key objective of this book is to allow readers to select between specifications and to equip the researcher with primary tools to construct a model, assess it, use it to forecast and assess the forecasts. We also identified a need to illustrate forecasting in practice with a large number of practical examples and with an emphasis on forecast production. In addition, our objective is to show students and professionals alike the potential and limitations of econometric modelling and forecasting. This will make communication between the various units involved in the forecast process and between producers and users of forecasts more effective. The book discusses both econometric model building and forecasting. These two areas are elaborated in subsequent sections in this chapter.

The demand for real estate analysts with at least basic skills in modelling is growing. Producers of forecasts are a source for this demand, but so are users or consumers of forecasts. Having the ability to understand how a model was built, how well it explains relationships between variables and how well it forecasts is itself a valuable skill. There is no doubt that we will see more emphasis on the quantitative analysis of the real estate market globally, especially as more data become available.

1.2 What is econometrics?

The literal meaning of the word 'econometrics' is 'measurement in economics'. The first four letters of the word suggest, correctly, that the origins of econometrics are rooted in economics. The main techniques employed for studying economic problems are of equal importance in real estate applications, however. We can define real estate econometrics as the application of statistical techniques to problems in the real estate market. Econometrics applied to real estate is useful for testing alternative theories of market adjustments, for determining income and returns, for examining the effect on real estate markets of changes in economic conditions, for studying the

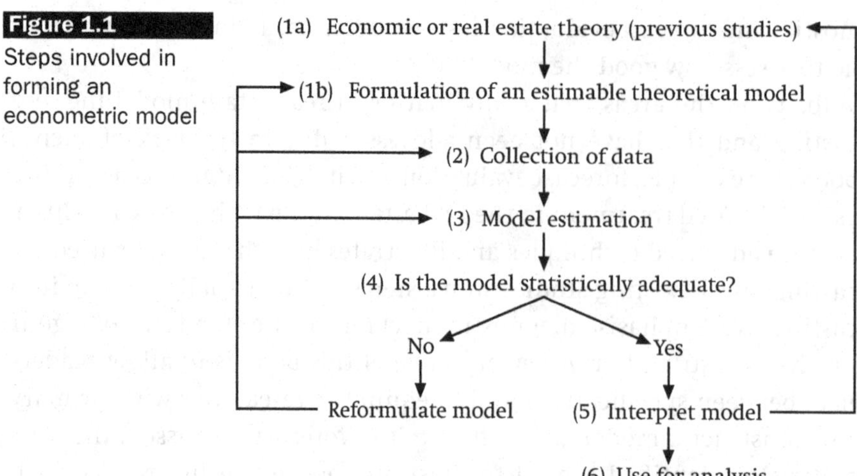

Figure 1.1 Steps involved in forming an econometric model

linkages of the real estate market with other investment markets and for investment decision making.

1.3 Steps in formulating an econometric model

Although there are of course many different ways to go about the process of model building, a logical and valid approach would be to follow the steps described in figure 1.1.

The steps involved in the model construction process are now listed and described. Further details on each stage are given in subsequent chapters of this book.

- *Steps 1a and 1b: general statement of the problem.* This will usually involve the formulation of a theoretical model, or intuition from real estate theory that two or more variables should be related to one another in a certain way. The model is unlikely to be able to completely capture every relevant real-world phenomenon, but it should present a sufficiently good approximation that it is useful for the purpose at hand.
- *Step 2: collection of data relevant to the model.* The real estate data required may be available through real estate firms or other data providers. The researcher may have to consult different sources of information depending on geography and sector. Government organisations may also hold real estate data.
- *Step 3: choice of estimation method relevant to the model proposed in step 1.* For example, is a single-equation or multiple-equation technique to be used?

- *Step 4: statistical evaluation of the model.* What assumptions were required to estimate the parameters of the model optimally? Were these assumptions satisfied by the data or the model? In addition, does the model adequately describe the data? If the answer is 'Yes', proceed to step 5; if not, go back to steps 1–3 and either reformulate the model, collect more data or select a different estimation technique that has less stringent requirements.
- *Step 5: evaluation of the model from a theoretical perspective.* Are the parameter estimates of the sizes and signs that the theory or intuition from step 1 suggested? If the answer is 'Yes', proceed to step 6; if not, again return to stages 1–3.
- *Step 6: use of model.* When a researcher is finally satisfied with the model, it can then be used for testing the theory specified in step 1, or for formulating forecasts or suggested courses of action. This suggested course of action might be for an investor to help reach a decision as to where and in which sector to buy or sell, for a developer to decide where and when to develop or for a lender wishing to underwrite risks from lending on real estate.

It is important to note that the process of building a robust empirical model is an iterative one, and it is certainly not an exact science. Often, the final preferred model may be very different from the one originally proposed, and need not be unique, in the sense that another researcher with the same data and the same initial theory could arrive at a different final specification.

1.4 Model building in real estate

Econometric models are driven by theory. Similarly, the building of econometric models for the real estate market requires us to have a good theoretical grasp of this market. Office, retail and industrial building structures are used for the production of services and goods. The demand for space is driven by the demand for goods and services (derived demand). Hence, in that respect, the market follows the principles of the factor of production market. Building construction is part of fixed capital investment, and therefore theories explaining fixed capital formation should be relevant for building construction. When real estate is seen as an asset class, general investment principles apply to this market. Real estate also comprises other characteristics that make the market unique, such as the impact of planning controls, the workings of the land market and institutional factors including the lease structure.

Apparently, there are several aspects of the market we can model utilising alternative theories. The particular characteristics of this market will affect model outcomes, and for this reason they should be well understood. There is a significant literature on the workings of the real estate market that should guide empirical modelling. The book does not intend to review this literature and the reader is referred to sources such as Ball, Lizieri and MacGregor (1998) and Di Pasquale and Wheaton (1996) and the references therein.

A simple framework of the real estate market is given by Keogh (1994). It breaks the market down into three major parts: the user or occupier market, the investment market and the development market. The three segments of the market interact. In each of the three components, demand and supply determine prices. In the occupier market, demand for space and the supply of buildings will affect metrics such as the vacancy rate, the rent level and the rent growth rate. Rent changes feed into both the investment and development markets. In the investment market, capital values and yields are established again by the demand and supply of investment interest in buildings. The investment market echoes trends in the occupier market but it also reflects wider asset market influences that determine the required rates of return. Both the occupier and investment markets send signals to the development market for new development, refurbishments, and so forth. The current and expected level of rents and building prices, along with other factors (e.g. land costs, borrowing costs), will determine the financial viability of supplying more space. The development market in turn supplies new space to the user and investment markets. Econometric analysis can be used to examine the relationships between the components in this framework, the adjustments within the components and the relationship of these components to influences outside the real estate market.

1.5 What do we model and forecast in real estate?

The discussion in this section focuses on the variables that are of most interest to real estate analysts. They represent all segments of the market and, hardly surprisingly, they are the focus of empirical modelling in the real estate market. There are, of course, more variables that are examined by analysts but the most common ones are briefly described below.

Demand variables

(1) *Take-up*. This is the amount of space taken up. It is not necessarily new demand, since the source could be firms already occupying premises in

the market (for example, vacating existing premises to move to a better specified building). Hence an occupier moving from an existing building into a newly completed building is recorded as 'take-up'. This variable is observable by real estate firms operating in the respective market and sector, especially in European markets.

(2) *Net absorption*, defined as the change in the occupied stock. Unlike take-up, it represents new demand, and as such it is appealing to investors and developers as a measure of demand strength in a market. This variable can be observed in some cases but, alternatively, it can be estimated from the vacancy rate, the stock and the occupied stock.

There exist other measures of demand, such as active demand (recording the number of enquiries for space), but this definition of demand is not as widely used as the previous two.

Supply variables

There are different definitions and measures of supply that analysts model. These measures depend on the level of aggregation or geographical coverage.

(1) *Stock*. This refers to the total amount of space in the market (both occupied and vacant). It is usually estimated by real estate firms or local government agencies.
(2) *Physical construction*. This is the amount of physical supply (in square metres or square feet). Data for physical construction are more common at the local level (city, metro). The completeness of the data set for this variable depends largely on the sector and location.
(3) *New orders*, new permits or value of building output. These series are encountered at the more aggregate level (say the national level), and they are usually compiled by government agencies.

Vacancy

Vacancy is either measured in physical terms (the amount of industrial space vacant in market A) or it is expressed as a percentage of total stock. These are measures usually produced by real estate consultancy firms.

Rents

There are different measures of rents, such as headline, effective, average, transaction and valuation-based rents. Transaction rents (either headline or average) are the levels achieved in transactions in the occupier market. The other source of rents is from valuations (to obtain measures such as the estimated rental values and sustainable rents). Valuation-based rent values are much more common than rents obtained from transactions. Given the availability of valuation-based rents, which can be headline or average, this source of rent data is often used in empirical modelling. Effective rents are constructed to take into account rent concessions. In this book we also encounter the concept of equilibrium rents.

Performance variables

These variables describe the performance of the real estate asset for the investment market segment.

(1) *Income return*. This refers to net operating income over value (or value from the previous period). Net operating income, when not observable, can be derived or modelled using changes in the vacancy rate, rent changes and lease structure information.
(2) *Yields*. These can be estimated directly or derived from capital values and income information. The focus of real estate researchers is mainly on initial yields and equivalent yields. The initial yield is the current income divided by price; it can be net or gross depending on the market environment. The net yield is the gross yield net of operating costs. The gross initial yield is the gross rent divided by price. The equivalent yield is an overall measure that is used to capitalise both the current and future cash flows after the rent review.[1]
(3) *Capital growth*. This is the change in the capital value of a building. It can either be observed (investment transactions) or estimated from rent or net operating income and yields.
(4) *Total returns*. This is the sum of income and capital returns.

1.6 Model categorisation for real estate forecasting

Real estate forecasting is in many respects not that different from economic forecasting, and the techniques used are similar. We summarise forecast approaches that can be used in real estate in figure 1.2.

The left-hand panel of figure 1.2 summarises the statistical approaches that are available to construct models and to produce forecasts. These techniques occupy the majority of the discussion in this book. Both econometric and pure time series techniques are explained. The right-hand panel of figure 1.2 brings a different dimension to forecasting, representing the qualitative approach. We explicitly discuss these approaches to real estate

[1] For more on yield definitions, see Baum and Crosby (2008), Wyatt (2007) and Brown and Matysiak (2000).

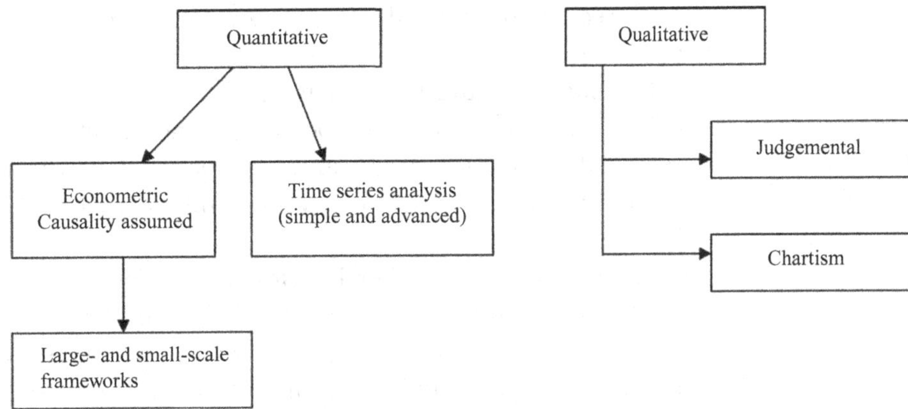

Figure 1.2 Summary of forecast approaches

forecasting, and this is the first textbook that makes a systematic attempt to bring the two approaches together in the real estate field. In economics, certain conditions may favour the one approach or the other, but in most cases the two can complement each other.

1.7 Why real estate forecasting?

Real estate forecasting has become a part of the larger process of business planning and strategic management. As in any industry, individuals in this market make decisions that affect the future performance of their business.

Investors in real estate, such as pension funds, insurance companies and real estate funds, will make allocations, which they might maintain for some time. They are therefore looking to forecast future asset performance across real estate sectors and locations. When investors and other participants take positions and make investments, they need to form a view and state their confidence in these decisions for their funders, banks, shareholders, etc. Investors need to know where rents, yields and prices will be within a predetermined time frame. Views about the future trajectory in rent growth are important to valuation departments. Will rent grow by the inflation rate or otherwise?

Real estate consultancies make plans about revenues based on forecasts for activity across their business lines. Leasing departments are interested in activity in the occupier markets as brokerage fees depend on the turnover in this segment. Using economic projections, they would like to know whether and to what extent firms are expected to expand or rationalise their space needs. Capital market departments are concerned with future events in the investment market and developments that might make real estate more attractive in relation to other assets. They would like to know what future economic and real estate market conditions will mean for investment transactions.

Developers would like to have estimates for future demand, rents and prices. Investors with loan portfolios, including those secured on real estate, demand objectivity and transparency in the analysis of future trends. Scenario analysis concerning future rent and cash flows is also important.

The pressure from **other investment classes** is apparent. Sophisticated investors accustomed to formal modelling and forecasting techniques will make similar demands if they are to enter the real estate asset class. These investors put particular focus on systematic relationships and predictions based on fundamentals – that is, the customary drivers of the market. In addition, they may explore other forecasting approaches, such as time series modelling and cointegration analysis, that are now completely standard tools in mainstream financial econometrics. As the real estate field attracts interest from the wider investment community, the pressure to apply well-recognised and transparent techniques to analyse markets and forecast will increase. As an illustration, consider the advent of real estate derivatives. With a range of investors being involved, including investment banks, real estate forecasting needs to live up to the standards demanded by these market participants. Overall, real estate forecasting that adheres to best practices in economics and finance increases the plausibility of the real estate field in the wider investment community.

Risk departments should also be interested in the impact of uncertainty on forecasts of future outcomes, and this represents another reason for the increasing sophistication of modelling work in real estate. The sensitivity of the predictions to the inputs is of great interest to both the producer and the consumer of the forecasts. Studying the accuracy of the forecasts, the gains from different models and producing confidence boundaries make the forecast process more acceptable to risk managers. Investors in real estate accept the location-specific influences on the risk–return profile of real estate. Many would argue that the value of a particular building structure does not follow general market trends, but that it has unique features that immunise it from a downturn. Investors and risk managers may be sceptical and may not accept that market risk is not relevant and that systematic risk is absent. Therefore a forecast about the market accompanied by scenario analysis provides comfort to the risk manager and sets a benchmark for the assessment of how immune individual assets are.

The location, building and lease characteristics that determine value at the building level or even at the market level created a tendency for 'bottom-up' real estate forecasting. Even so, many participants, such as those involved with acquisitions, will rely more on their knowledge of the locality and building to make a buy or sell decision. This has also given rise to so-called 'judgemental' forecasts. Real estate markets have gone through severe cycles not predicted by bottom-up analysis, however, and thus this approach to forecasting has been questioned. For many, the winning formula is now not just having good judgement about the future direction of the market, but also making a careful quantitative analysis explaining cyclical movements and the impact of broader trends. Therefore, consistent with evidence from other fields, a view that has increasingly gained popularity is that the optimal approach arises from a combination of judgemental and quantitative forecasting. Moreover, there is a more generic econometric and forecasting interest. Do quantitative techniques underperform judgemental approaches or is the combination of quantitative and judgemental forecasts the most successful formula in the real estate market? The book addresses this issue directly, and the tools presented will give the reader a framework to assess such quandaries.

Real estate forecasting can also be used for **model selection**. There are often competing theories available and it may be the case that there is more than one theory-consistent model that passes all the diagnostics tests set by the researcher. The past relative forecasting success of these models will guide model selection for future forecast production and other uses.

Finally, forecasting is the **natural progression** in real estate as more data become available for a larger number of markets. In scholarly activity, the issue of data availability is highlighted constantly. One would expect that, with more data and markets, interest in real estate forecasting will continue to grow. The key objectives of forecasting in real estate are presented in box 1.1.

Box 1.1 Objectives of forecasting work

(1) *Point forecasts*. The forecaster is seeking the actual forecast value for rent growth or capital growth in one, two, three quarters or years, etc.
(2) *Direction forecasts*. The forecaster is interested in the direction of the forecast and whether the trend is upward or downward (and perhaps an assessment can be made as to how steep this trend will be).
(3) *Turning point forecasts*. The aim in this kind of forecast is to identify turning points or the possibility of a turning point.
(4) *Confidence*. The modelling and forecasting process is used to attach a confidence interval to the forecast, how it can vary and with what probability.
(5) *Scenario analysis*. This is the sensitivity of the forecast to the drivers of the model.

The content of this book is more geared to help the reader to perform tasks one, two and five.

1.8 Econometrics in real estate, finance and economics: similarities and differences

The tools that we use when econometrics is applied to real estate are fundamentally the same as those in economic and financial applications. The sets of issues and problems that are likely to be encountered when analysing data are different, however. To an extent, real estate data are similar to economic data (e.g. gross domestic product [GDP], employment) in terms of their frequency, accuracy, seasonality and other properties. On the other hand, there are some important differences in how the data are generated. Real estate data can be generated through the valuation process rather than through surveys or government accounts, as is the case for economic data. There are some apparent differences with financial data, given their high frequency. A commonality with financial data, however, is that most real estate data are not subject to subsequent revisions, or, at least, not to the extent of economic data.

In economics, a serious problem is often a *lack of data to hand* for testing the theory or hypothesis of interest; this is often called a *small samples problem*. Such data may be annual and their method of estimation may have changed at some point in the past. For example, if the methods used to measure economic quantities changed twenty years ago then only twenty annual observations at most are usefully available. There is a similar problem in real estate markets. Here, though, the problem concerns not only changing methods of calculation but also the point at which the data were first collected. In the United Kingdom, data can be found back to 1966 or earlier, but only at the national level. Databases such as the United Kingdom's Investment Property Databank (IPD) and that of the United States' National Council of Real Estate Investment Fiduciaries (NCREIF) go back to the 1970s. In other regions, such as the Asia-Pacific retail markets, however, data are available only for about ten years. In general, the frequency differs by country, with monthly data very limited and available only in some locations.

As in finance, real estate data can come in many shapes and forms. Rents and prices that are recorded are usually the product of valuations that have been criticised as being excessively smooth and slow to adjust to changing market conditions. The problem arises from infrequent trading and trying to establish values where the size of the market is small. The industry has recognised this issue, and we see an increasing compilation of transactions data. We outlined in section 1.5 above that other real estate market data, such as absorption (a measure of demand), are constructed based on other market information. These data are subject to measurement error and revisions (e.g. absorption data are subject to stock and vacancy rate revisions unless they are observed). In general, measurement error affects most real estate series; data revisions can be less serious in the real estate context compared with economics, however.

Financial data are often considered 'noisy', which means that it is difficult to separate *underlying trends or patterns* from random and uninteresting features. Noise exists in real estate data as well, despite their smoothness, and sometimes it is transmitted from the financial markets. We would consider real estate data noisier than economic data. In addition, financial data are almost always not normally distributed in spite of the fact that most techniques in econometrics assume that they are. In real estate, normality is not always established and does differ by the frequency of the data.

The above features need to be considered in the model-building process, even if they are not directly of interest to the researcher. What should also be noted is that these issues are acknowledged by real estate researchers, valuers and investment analysts, so the model-building process is not happening in a vacuum or with ignorance of these data problems.

1.9 Econometric packages for modelling real estate data

As the title suggests, this section contains descriptions of various computer packages that may be employed to estimate econometric models. The number of available packages is large, and, over time, all packages have improved in the breadth of the techniques they offer, and they have also converged in terms of what is available in each package. Some readers may already be familiar with the use of one or more packages, and, if this is the case, this section may be skipped. For those who do not know how to use any econometrics software, or have not yet found a package that suits their requirements – read on.

1.9.1 *What packages are available?*

Although this list is by no means exhaustive, a set of widely used packages is given in table 1.1. The programmes can usefully be categorised according to whether they are fully interactive (menu-driven), command-driven (so that the user has to write mini-programmes) or somewhere in between. Menu-driven packages, which are usually based on a standard Microsoft Windows graphical user interface, are almost certainly the easiest for novices to get started with, for they require little knowledge of the structure of the package, and the menus can usually be negotiated simply. EViews is a package that falls into this category.

On the other hand, some such packages are often the least flexible, since the menus of available options are fixed by the developers, and hence, if one

Table 1.1 Econometric software packages for modelling financial data

	Package software supplier
EViews	QMS Software
Gauss	Aptech Systems
LIMDEP	Econometric Software
Matlab	The MathWorks
RATS	Estima
SAS	SAS Institute
Shazam	Northwest Econometrics
Splus	Insightful Corporation
SPSS	SPSS
Stata	StataCorp
TSP	TSP International

Note: Full contact details for all software suppliers can be found in the appendix at the end of this chapter.

wishes to build something slightly more complex or just different, one is forced to consider alternatives. EViews has a command-based programming language as well as a click-and-point interface, however, so it offers flexibility as well as user-friendliness.

1.9.2 *Choosing a package*

Choosing an econometric software package is an increasingly difficult task as the packages become more powerful but at the same time more homogeneous. For example, LIMDEP, a package originally developed for the analysis of a certain class of cross-sectional data, has many useful features for modelling financial time series. Moreover, many packages developed for time series analysis, such as TSP ('Time Series Processor'), can also now be used for cross-sectional or panel data. Of course, this choice may be made for you if your institution offers or supports only one or two of the above possibilities. Otherwise, sensible questions to ask yourself are as follows.

- Is the package suitable for your *intended applications* – for example, does the software have the capability for the models that you want to estimate? Can it handle sufficiently large databases?
- Is the package *user-friendly*?
- Is it *fast*?
- How much does it *cost*?

- Is it *accurate*?
- Is the package *discussed* or *supported* in a standard textbook?
- Does the package have *readable and comprehensive manuals*? Is help available online?
- Does the package come with *free technical support* so that you can e-mail the developers with queries?

A great deal of useful information can be obtained most easily from the web pages of the software developers. Additionally, many journals (including the *Journal of Applied Econometrics*, the *Economic Journal*, the *International Journal of Forecasting* and the *American Statistician*) publish software reviews that seek to evaluate and compare the packages' usefulness for a given purpose. Three reviews that the first author has been involved with are Brooks (1997) and Brooks, Burke and Persand (2001, 2003).

1.10 Outline of the remainder of this book

Chapter 2

This chapter aims to illustrate data transformation and computation, which are key to the construction of real estate series. The chapter also provides the mathematical foundations that are important for the computation of statistical tests in the following chapters. It begins by looking at how to index a single data series and produce a composite index from several series by different methods. The chapter continues by showing how to convert nominal data into real terms. The discussion explains why we log data and reminds the reader of the properties of logs. The calculation of simple and continuously compounded returns follows, a topic of much relevance in the construction of real estate series such as capital value (or price) and total returns. The last section of the chapter is devoted to matrix algebra. Key aspects of matrices are presented for the reader to help his/her understanding of the econometric concepts employed in the following chapters.

Chapter 3

This begins with a description of the types of data that may be available for the econometric analysis of real estate markets and explains the concepts of time series, cross-sectional and panel data. The discussion extends to the properties of cardinal, ordinal and nominal numbers. This chapter covers important statistical properties of data: measures of central tendency, such as the median and the arithmetic and geometric means; measures of spread, including range, quartiles, variance, standard deviation, semi-standard deviation and the coefficient of variation; higher moments – that is, skewness and kurtosis; and normal and skewed distributions. The reader is further introduced to the concepts of covariance and correlation and the metric of a correlation coefficient. This chapter also reviews probability distributions and hypothesis testing. It familiarises the reader with the *t*- and normal distributions and shows how to carry out hypothesis tests using the test of significance and confidence interval approaches. The chapter finishes by highlighting the implications of small samples and sampling error, trends in the data and spurious associations, structural breaks and data that do not follow the normal distribution. These data characteristics are crucially important to real estate analysis.

Chapter 4

This chapter introduces the classical linear regression model (CLRM). This is the first of four chapters we devote to regression models. The material brought into this chapter is developed and expanded upon in subsequent chapters. The chapter provides the general form of a single regression model and discusses the role of the disturbance term. The method of least squares is discussed in detail and the reader is familiarised with the derivation of the residual sum of squares, the regression coefficients and their standard errors. The discussion continues with the assumptions concerning disturbance terms in the CLRM and the properties of the least squares estimator. The chapter provides guidance to conduct tests of significance for variables in the regression model.

Chapter 5

Chapter 5 develops and extends the material of chapter 4 to multiple regression analysis. The coefficient estimates in multiple regression are discussed and derived. This chapter also presents measures of goodness of fit. It introduces the concept of non-nested hypotheses and provides a first view on model selection. In this chapter, the reader is presented with the F-test and its relationship to the t-test. With examples, it is illustrated how to run the F-test and determine the number of restrictions when running this test. The F-test is subsequently used in this chapter to assess whether a statistically significant variable is omitted from the regression model or a non-significant variable is included.

Chapter 6

This focuses on violations of the assumptions of the CLRM. The discussion provides the causes of these violations and highlights the implications for the robustness of the models. It shows the reader how to conduct diagnostic checks and interpret the results. With detailed examples, the concepts of heteroscedasticity, residual autocorrelation, non-normality of the residuals, functional form and multicollinearity are examined in detail. Within the context of these themes, the role of lagged terms in a regression is studied. The exposition of diagnostic checks continues with the presentation of parameter stability tests, and examples are given. The chapter finishes by critically reviewing two key approaches to model building.

Chapter 7

This chapter is devoted to two examples of regression analysis: a time series specification and a cross-sectional model. The aim is to illustrate further practical issues in building a model. The time series model is a rent growth model. This section begins by considering the data transformations required to address autocorrelation and trends in the data. Correlation analysis then informs the specification of a general model, which becomes specific by applying a number of tests. The diagnostics studied in the previous chapter are applied to two competing models of rent growth to illustrate comparisons. The second example of the chapter has a focus on international yields and seeks to identify cross-sectional effects on yields. This part of the chapter shows that the principles that are applied to build and assess a time series model can extend to a cross-sectional regression model.

Chapter 8

This presents an introduction to pure time series models. The chapter begins with a presentation of the features of some standard models of stochastic processes (white noise, moving average (MA), autoregressive (AR) and mixed ARMA processes). It shows how the appropriate model can be chosen for a set of actual data with emphasis on selecting the order of the ARMA model. The most common information criteria are discussed, which can, of course, be used to select terms in regression analysis as well. Forecasting from ARMA models is illustrated with a practical application to cap rates. The issue of seasonality in real estate data is also treated in the context of ARMA model estimation and forecasting.

Chapter 9

This chapter is wholly devoted to the assessment of forecast accuracy and educates the reader about the process of and tests for assessing forecasts. It presents key contemporary approaches adopted for forecast evaluation, including mean error measures, measures based on the mean squared error and Theil's metrics. The material in this chapter goes further to cover the principles of forecast efficiency and encompassing. It also examines more complete tools for forecast evaluation, such as the evaluation of rolling forecasts. Detailed examples are given throughout to help the application of the suite of tests proposed in this chapter. The chapter also reviews studies that show how forecast evaluation has been applied in the real estate field.

Chapter 10

Chapter 10 moves the analysis from regression models to more general forms of modelling, in which the segments of the real estate market are simultaneously modelled and estimated. These multivariate, multi-equation models are motivated by way of explanation of the possible existence of bidirectional causality in real estate relationships, and the simultaneous equations bias that results if this is ignored. The reader is familiarised with identification testing and the estimation of simultaneous models. The chapter makes the distinction between recursive and simultaneous models. Exhaustive examples help the reader to absorb the concept of multi-equation models. The analysis finally goes a step further to show how forecasts are obtained from these models.

Chapter 11

This chapter relaxes the intrinsic restrictions of simultaneous equations models and focuses on vector autoregressive (VAR) models, which have become quite popular in the empirical literature. The chapter focuses on how such models are estimated and how restrictions are imposed and tested. The interpretation of VARs is explained by way of joint tests of restrictions, causality tests, impulse responses and variance decompositions. The application of Granger causality tests is illustrated within the VAR context. Again, the last part of the chapter is devoted to a detailed example of obtaining forecasts from VARs for a REIT (real estate investment trust) series.

Chapter 12

The first section of the chapter discusses the concepts of stationarity, types of non-stationarity and unit root processes. It presents several procedures for unit root tests. The concept of and tests for cointegration, and the formulation of error correction models, are then studied within both the univariate framework of Engle–Granger and the multivariate framework of Johansen. Practical examples to illustrate these frameworks are given in the context of an office market and tests for cointegration between international REIT markets. These frameworks are also used to generate forecasts.

Chapter 13

Having reviewed frameworks for simple and more complex modelling in the real estate field and the process of obtaining forecasts from these frameworks in the previous chapters, the focus now turns to how this knowledge is applied in practice. The chapter begins with a review on how forecasting takes place in real estate in practice and highlights that intervention occurs to bring in judgement. It explains the reasons for such intervention and how the intervention operates, and brings to the reader's attention issues with judgemental forecasting. The reader benefits from the discussion on how judgement and model-based forecasts can be combined and how the relative contributions can be assessed. Ways to combine model-based with judgemental forecasts are critically presented. Finally, tips are given on how to make both intervention and the forecast process more acceptable to the end user.

Chapter 14

This summarises the book and concludes. Some recent developments in the field, which are not covered elsewhere in the book, are also mentioned. Some tentative suggestions for possible growth areas in the modelling of real estate series are also given in this short chapter.

Key concepts

The key terms to be able to define and explain from this chapter are

- real estate econometrics
- occupier market
- development market
- net absorption
- physical construction
- vacancy
- effective rent
- initial yield
- capital growth
- quantitative models
- point forecasts
- turning point forecasts
- data smoothness
- econometric software packages
- model building
- investment market
- take-up
- stock
- new orders
- prime and average rent
- income return
- equivalent yield
- total returns
- qualitative models
- direction forecasts
- scenario analysis
- small samples problem

Appendix: Econometric software package suppliers

Package	Contact information
EViews	QMS Software, 4521 Campus Drive, Suite 336, Irvine, CA 92612–2621, United States. Tel: (+1) 949 856 3368; Fax: (+1) 949 856 2044; Web: www.eviews.com.
Gauss	Aptech Systems Inc, PO Box 250, Black Diamond, WA 98010, United States. Tel: (+1) 425 432 7855; Fax: (+1) 425 432 7832; Web: www.aptech.com.
LIMDEP	Econometric Software, 15 Gloria Place, Plainview, NY 11803, United States. Tel: (+1) 516 938 5254; Fax: (+1) 516 938 2441; Web: www.limdep.com.
Matlab	The MathWorks Inc., 3 Apple Hill Drive, Natick, MA 01760-2098, United States. Tel: (+1) 508 647 7000; Fax: (+1) 508 647 7001; Web: www.mathworks.com.
RATS	Estima, 1560 Sherman Avenue, Evanson, IL 60201, United States. Tel: (+1) 847 864 8772; Fax: (+1) 847 864 6221; Web: www.estima.com.
SAS	SAS Institute, 100 Campus Drive, Cary, NC 27513–2414, United States. Tel: (+1) 919 677 8000; Fax: (+1) 919 677 4444; Web: www.sas.com.
Shazam	Northwest Econometrics Ltd, 277 Arbutus Reach, Gibsons, BC V0N 1V8, Canada. Tel: (+1) 604 608 5511; Fax: (+1) 707 317 5364; Web: shazam.econ.ubc.ca.
Splus	Insightful Corporation, 1700 Westlake Avenue North, Suite 500, Seattle, WA 98109–3044, United States. Tel: (+1) 206 283 8802; Fax: (+1) 206 283 8691; Web: www.splus.com.
SPSS	SPSS Inc, 233 S. Wacker Drive, 11th Floor, Chicago, IL 60606–6307, United States. Tel: (+1) 312 651 3000; Fax: (+1) 312 651 3668; Web: www.spss.com.
Stata	StataCorp, 4905 Lakeway Drive, College Station, Texas 77845, United States. Tel: (+1) 800 782 8272; Fax: (+1) 979 696 4601; Web: www.stata.com.
TSP	TSP International, PO Box 61015 Station A, Palo Alto, CA 94306, United States. Tel: (+1) 650 326 1927; Fax: (+1) 650 328 4163; Web: www.tspintl.com.

2 Mathematical building blocks for real estate analysis

Learning outcomes

In this chapter, you will learn how to

- construct price indices;
- compare nominal and real series and convert one to the other;
- use logarithms and work with matrices; and
- construct simple and continuously compounded returns from asset prices.

2.1 Introduction

This chapter provides the mathematical foundations for the quantitative techniques examined in the following chapters. These concepts are, in the opinions of the authors, fundamental to a solid understanding of the remainder of the material in this book. They are presented fairly briefly, however, since it is anticipated that the majority of readers will already have some exposure to the techniques, but may require some revision.

2.2 Constructing price index numbers

Index numbers are a useful way to present a series so that it is easy to see how it has changed over time, and they facilitate comparisons of series with different units of measurement (for example, if one is expressed in US dollars and another in euros per square metre). They are widely used in economics, real estate and finance – to display series for GDP, consumer prices, exchange rates, aggregate stock values, house prices, and so on. They are helpful in part because the original series may comprise numbers that are large and therefore not very intuitive. For example, the average UK house price according to the Halifax was £132,589 in 2004 rising to £165,807 in

2006.[1] Does this represent a large increase? It is hard to tell simply by glancing at the figures.

Index numbers also make comparisons of the rates of change between series easier to comprehend. To illustrate, suppose that the average house price in Greater London rose from £224,305 in 2004 to £247,419 in 2006. Was the increase in prices for London larger than for the country as a whole? These two questions can easily be answered by constructing an index for each series. The simplest way to do this is to construct a set of price relatives. This is usually achieved by establishing a 'base period', for which the index is given a notional value of 100, and then the other values of the index are defined relative to this and are calculated by the formula

$$I_t = \frac{p_t}{p_0} \times 100 \tag{2.1}$$

where p_0 is the initial value of the series in the base year, p_t is the value of the series in year t and I_t is the calculated value of the index at time t. The base figure is usually set to 100 by convention but of course any other value (e.g. 1 or 1,000 could be chosen). Applying this formula to the two examples above, both the United Kingdom overall and the Greater London average house prices would be given a value of 100 in 2004, and the figures for 2006 would be

$$I_{2006,UK} = \frac{p_{2006}}{p_{2004}} \times 100 = \frac{165807}{132589} \times 100 = 125.1 \tag{2.2}$$

and

$$I_{2006,London} = \frac{247419}{224305} \times 100 = 110.3 \tag{2.3}$$

respectively. Thus the rise in average house prices in Greater London (of 10.3 per cent) over the period failed to keep pace with that of the country as a whole (of 25.1 per cent). Indices can also be constructed in the same way for quantities rather than prices, or for the total value of an entity (e.g. the total market capitalisation of all stocks on an exchange).

An arguably more important use of index numbers is to represent the changes over time in the values of groups of series together. This would be termed an aggregate or composite index number – for example, a stock market index, an index of consumer prices or a real estate market index. In all three cases, the values of a number of series are combined or weighted at each point in time and an index formed on the aggregate measure. An important choice is of the weighting scheme employed to combine the

[1] Halifax have produced a number of house price series at the local, regional and national level dating back to 1983. These are freely available on their website: see www.hbosplc.com/economy/housingresearch.asp.

component series, and there are several methods that are commonly used for this, including:

- equal weighting of the components;
- base period weighting by quantity, also known as *Laspeyres* weighting; and
- current period weighting by quantity, also known as *Paasche* weighting.

Each of these three methods has its own relative advantages and disadvantages; the Laspeyres and Paasche methods are compared in box 2.1. Equal weighting evidently has simplicity and ease of interpretation on its side; it may be inappropriate, however, if some components of the series are viewed as more important than others. For example, if we wanted to compute a UK national house price index from a set of regional indices, equally weighting the regions would assign the same importance to Wales and to the south-east of England, even though the number of property transactions in the latter area is far higher. Thus an aggregate index computed in this way could give a misleading picture of the changing value of house prices in the country as a whole. Similarly, an equally weighted stock index would assign the same importance in determining the index value to a 'micro-cap' stock as to a vast multinational oil company.

Box 2.1 A comparison of the Laspeyres and Paasche methods

- The Laspeyres weighting scheme is simpler than the Paasche method and requires fewer data since the weights need to be calculated only once.
- Laspeyres indices may also be available earlier in the month or quarter for precisely this reason.
- The Laspeyres approach has the disadvantage, however, that the weights are fixed over time, and it does not take into account changes in market size or sector importance and technology that affect demand and prices. For example, a Laspeyres-weighted stock index constructed with a base year of 1998 would assign a high influence, which many researchers would consider inappropriate nowadays, to IT stocks whose prices fell considerably during the subsequent bursting of the technology bubble.
- On the other hand, the Paasche index will allow the weights to change over time, so it looks to be the superior method, since it uses the appropriate quantity figures for that period of time.
- This also means, however, that, under the Paasche approach, the group of entities being compared is not the same in all time periods.
- A Paasche index value could rise, therefore, either because the prices are rising or because the weights on the more expensive items within the data set are rising.
- These problems can lead to biases in the constructed index series that may be serious, and they have led to the development of what is known as the *Fisher ideal price index*, which is simply the geometric mean of the Laspeyres and Paasche approaches.

The following example illustrates how an index can be constructed using the various approaches. The data were obtained from tables 581 and 584 of the web pages of the Department for Communities and Local Government[2] and comprise annual house prices (shown in table 2.1) and numbers of property transactions (shown in table 2.2) for the districts of London for the period 1996 to 2005. The task is to form equally weighed, base-weighted, current-weighted and Fisher ideal price indices, assuming that the base year is 2000.[3] Clearly, given the amount of data involved, this task is best undertaken using a spreadsheet.

The equally weighted index

The easiest way to form an equally weighted index would be to first construct the average (i.e. unweighted or equally weighted) house price across the fourteen regions, which is given in table 2.3.

Effectively, the equal weighting method ignores the sales information in assigning equal importance to all the districts. Then we assign a value of 100 to the 2000 figure for the index (250,770), so that the figures for all other years are divided by 250,770 and multiplied by 100. Thus the 1996 figure would be $(124{,}719/250{,}770) \times 100 = 49.7$, and the 2005 figure would be $(350{,}549/250{,}770) \times 100 = 139.8$.

The base-weighted index

Turning now to the Laspeyres price index, this implies measuring the average value of a house in each year weighted by the base year quantities relative to the average price of the same set of houses at the base year. This translates for the current example into using the base level of house sales (the 2000 figures) to weight the regional house prices in forming the index. The relevant formula could be written as

$$I_t = \frac{\sum_{i=1}^{N} w_{i,0} p_{i,t}}{\sum_{i=1}^{N} w_{i,0} p_{i,0}} \times 100 \tag{2.4}$$

where $w_{i,0}$ is the weight assigned to each district i at the base year (2000), $p_{i,0}$ is the average price in each area at time 0 and $p_{i,t}$ is the price in district i at time t.

So, for this example, we first need to find for 2000 the total number (i.e. the sum) of sales across all districts, which turns out to be 63,592. Then we

[2] See www.communities.gov.uk/index.asp?id=1156110.

[3] Note that it does not have to be the case that the first year in the sample (1996 in this example) must be the base year, although it usually is.

Table 2.1 Mean house prices by district, British pounds

	1996	1997	1998	1999	2000	2001	2002	2003	2004	2005
Camden	170,030	198,553	225,966	246,130	319,793	340,971	377,347	387,636	414,538	444,165
City of London	136,566	219,722	324,233	290,773	359,332	310,604	272,664	326,592	311,574	326,496
Hackney	75,420	88,592	103,443	126,848	156,571	179,243	203,347	219,545	236,545	251,251
Hammersmith and Fulham	147,342	171,798	195,698	231,982	282,180	302,960	341,841	350,679	381,713	413,412
Haringey	101,971	106,539	124,106	141,050	171,660	193,083	224,232	236,324	259,604	274,531
Islington	123,425	146,684	171,474	206,023	249,636	263,086	290,018	294,163	321,507	332,866
Kensington and Chelsea	296,735	351,567	382,758	434,354	564,571	576,754	617,788	665,634	716,434	754,639
Lambeth	94,191	107,448	128,453	147,891	182,126	208,715	230,255	237,390	253,321	267,386
Lewisham	62,706	72,652	82,747	94,765	119,351	134,003	160,312	183,701	198,567	203,404
Newham	49,815	57,223	65,056	74,345	96,997	114,432	144,907	175,693	191,482	201,672
Southwark	87,057	104,555	123,644	142,527	189,468	208,728	220,433	238,938	252,454	271,614
Tower Hamlets	88,046	110,564	127,976	159,736	189,947	207,944	222,478	234,852	258,747	264,028
Wandsworth	118,767	137,335	155,833	190,309	234,190	252,773	284,367	298,519	335,431	348,870
Westminster	193,993	236,275	295,001	310,335	394,962	410,866	445,010	463,285	507,460	553,355

Table 2.2 Property sales by district

	1996	1997	1998	1999	2000	2001	2002	2003	2004	2005
Camden	3,877	4,340	3,793	4,218	3,642	3,765	3,932	3,121	3,689	3,283
City of London	288	329	440	558	437	379	374	468	307	299
Hackney	2,221	2,968	3,107	3,266	2,840	3,252	3,570	2,711	3,163	2,407
Hammersmith and Fulham	4,259	4,598	3,834	4,695	3,807	3,790	4,149	3,465	3,761	3,241
Haringey	3,966	4,662	4,248	4,836	4,238	4,658	4,534	3,765	4,233	3,347
Islington	2,516	3,243	3,347	3,935	3,075	3,407	3,365	2,776	2,941	2,900
Kensington and Chelsea	4,797	5,262	4,576	5,558	4,707	4,195	4,514	3,497	4,043	3,426
Lambeth	4,957	6,128	5,786	6,297	5,966	5,917	6,212	5,209	5,732	5,020
Lewisham	4,357	5,259	5,123	5,842	5,509	5,646	6,122	5,423	5,765	4,679
Newham	3,493	3,894	4,091	4,498	4,920	5,471	5,313	5,103	4,418	3,649
Southwark	3,223	4,523	4,525	5,439	5,191	5,261	4,981	4,441	5,012	4,204
Tower Hamlets	2,537	3,851	4,536	5,631	5,051	4,752	4,557	3,890	5,143	4,237
Wandsworth	7,389	8,647	7,793	9,757	7,693	8,187	8,485	6,935	8,156	7,072
Westminster	5,165	6,885	5,821	7,118	6,516	6,024	6,417	5,014	5,083	4,796

Table 2.3 Average house prices across all districts, British pounds

	1996	1997	1998	1999	2000	2001	2002	2003	2004	2005
Unweighted average	124,719	150,679	179,028	199,791	250,770	264,583	288,214	308,068	331,384	350,549

divide the number of sales in each region for 2000 by this total to get the weights. Note that, for this type of index, the weights are fixed for all time at the base period values. The weights are given in table 2.4.

The last row checks that the weights do indeed sum to 1 as they should. Now the formula in (2.4) can be applied as follows. For 2000 (the base period), the index value is set to 100 as before. For 1996, the calculation would be

$$I_t = \frac{(170,030 \times 0.057) + (136,566 \times 0.007) + (75,420 \times 0.045) + \cdots + (193,993 \times 0.102)}{(319,793 \times 0.057) + (359,332 \times 0.007) + (156,571 \times 0.045) + \cdots + (394,962 \times 0.102)} \times 100 \tag{2.5}$$

which is 100× (Camden price 1996 × Camden 2000 weight) +···+ (Westminster price 1996 × Westminster weight 2000) / (Camden price 2000 × Camden 2000 weight) +···+ (Westminster price 2000 × Westminster weight 2000).

Table 2.4 Laspeyres weights in index

Camden	0.057
City of London	0.007
Hackney	0.045
Hammersmith and Fulham	0.060
Haringey	0.067
Islington	0.048
Kensington and Chelsea	0.074
Lambeth	0.094
Lewisham	0.087
Newham	0.077
Southwark	0.082
Tower Hamlets	0.079
Wandsworth	0.121
Westminster	0.102
Sum of weights	1.000

The current-weighted index

The equivalent of equation (2.4) for the Paasche weighted index is

$$I_t = \frac{\sum_{i=1}^{N} w_{i,t}p_{i,t}}{\sum_{i=1}^{N} w_{i,t}p_{i,0}} \times 100 \tag{2.6}$$

with all notation as above.

Thus the first step in calculating the current weighted index is to calculate the weights as we did for 2000 above, but now for every year. This involves calculating the total number of sales across all districts separately for each year and then dividing the sales for the district by the total sales for all districts during that year. For example, the 1996 figure for Camden is $3{,}877/(3{,}877 + 288 + \cdots + 5{,}165) = 0.073$. The weights for all districts in each year are given in table 2.5.

Now that we have the weights for each district, equation (2.6) can be applied to get the index values for each year. For 1996, the calculation would be

$$I_t = \frac{(170,030 \times 0.073) + (136,566 \times 0.005) + (75,420 \times 0.042) + \cdots + (193,993 \times 0.097)}{(319,793 \times 0.073) + (359,332 \times 0.005) + (156,571 \times 0.042) + \cdots + (394,962 \times 0.097)} \times 100 \tag{2.7}$$

Table 2.5 Current weights for each year

	1996	1997	1998	1999	2000	2001	2002	2003	2004	2005
Camden	0.073	0.067	0.062	0.059	0.057	0.058	0.059	0.056	0.060	0.062
City of London	0.005	0.005	0.007	0.008	0.007	0.006	0.006	0.008	0.005	0.006
Hackney	0.042	0.046	0.051	0.046	0.045	0.050	0.054	0.049	0.051	0.046
Hammersmith and Fulham	0.080	0.071	0.063	0.066	0.060	0.059	0.062	0.062	0.061	0.062
Haringey	0.075	0.072	0.070	0.067	0.067	0.072	0.068	0.067	0.069	0.064
Islington	0.047	0.050	0.055	0.055	0.048	0.053	0.051	0.050	0.048	0.055
Kensington and Chelsea	0.090	0.081	0.075	0.078	0.074	0.065	0.068	0.063	0.066	0.065
Lambeth	0.093	0.095	0.095	0.088	0.094	0.091	0.093	0.093	0.093	0.096
Lewisham	0.082	0.081	0.084	0.082	0.087	0.087	0.092	0.097	0.094	0.089
Newham	0.066	0.060	0.067	0.063	0.077	0.085	0.080	0.091	0.072	0.069
Southwark	0.061	0.070	0.074	0.076	0.082	0.081	0.075	0.080	0.082	0.080
Tower Hamlets	0.048	0.060	0.074	0.079	0.079	0.073	0.069	0.070	0.084	0.081
Wandsworth	0.139	0.134	0.128	0.136	0.121	0.127	0.128	0.124	0.133	0.135
Westminster	0.097	0.107	0.095	0.099	0.102	0.093	0.096	0.090	0.083	0.091
Sum of weights	1.000	1.000	1.000	1.000	1.000	1.000	1.000	1.000	1.000	1.000

Table 2.6 Index values calculated using various methods

	1996	1997	1998	1999	2000	2001	2002	2003	2004	2005
Equally weighted	49.73	60.09	71.39	79.67	100.00	105.51	114.93	122.85	132.15	139.79
Base-weighted	50.79	59.89	69.59	79.48	100.00	107.41	118.77	126.10	137.03	145.04
Current-weighted	51.20	60.02	69.56	79.55	100.00	107.66	119.23	126.95	137.75	145.20
Fischer ideal	51.00	59.96	69.58	79.52	100.00	107.54	119.00	126.53	137.39	145.12

which is 100 × (Camden price 1996 × Camden 1996 weight) + · · · + (Westminster price 1996 × Westminster weight 1996) / (Camden price 2000 × Camden 1996 weight) + · · · + (Westminster price 2000 × Westminster weight 1996).

The final table of index values calculated using the four methods is given in table 2.6. As is evident, there is very little difference between the base and current weighted indices, since the relative number of sales in each district has remained fairly stable over the sample period. On the other hand, there is a slight tendency for the equally weighted index to rise more slowly in the second half of the period due to the relatively low weightings it gives to areas where prices were growing fast and where sales were large, such as Camden and Hammersmith. The Fisher index values were calculated by multiplying the square roots of the base (Laspeyres) and current weighted (Paasche) index values together. For example, the 1996 year Fisher value of 51.00 is given by $(50.79 \times 51.20)^{1/2}$, and so on.

Finally, it is worth noting that all the indices described above are aggregate price indices – that is, they measure how average prices change over time when the component prices are weighted by quantities. It is also possible, however, to construct quantity indices that measure how sales or transactions quantities vary over time when the prices are used as weights. Nonetheless, quantity indices are much less common than price indices, and so they are not discussed further here; interested readers are referred to Kazmier and Pohl (1984, pp. 468–9) or Watsham and Parramore (1997, pp. 74–5).

2.3 Real versus nominal series and deflating nominal series

If a newspaper headline suggests that 'house prices are growing at their fastest rate for more than a decade. A typical 3-bedroom house is now selling for £180,000, whereas in 1990 the figure was £120,000', it is important to appreciate that this figure is almost certainly in *nominal* terms. That is, the article is referring to the actual prices of houses that existed at those points in time. The general level of prices in most economies around the world has a general tendency to rise almost all the time, so we need to ensure that we compare prices on a like-for-like basis. We could think of part of the rise in house prices being attributable to an increase in demand for housing, and part simply arising because the prices of all goods and services are rising together. It would be useful to be able to separate the two effects, and to be able to answer the question 'How much have house prices risen when we remove the effects of general inflation?', or, equivalently, 'How much are houses worth now if we measure their values in 1990 terms?'. We can do this by *deflating* the nominal house price series to create a series of *real* house prices, which is then said to be in *inflation-adjusted terms* or *at constant prices*.

Deflating a series is very easy indeed to achieve: all that is required (apart from the series to deflate) is a *price deflator series*, which is a series measuring general price levels in the economy. Series such as the consumer price index (CPI), the producer price index (PPI) or the GDP implicit price deflator are often used. A more detailed discussion as to the most relevant general price index to use is beyond the scope of this book, but suffice to say that, if the researcher is interested only in viewing a broad picture of the real prices rather than a highly accurate one, the choice of deflator will be of little importance.

The real price series is obtained by taking the nominal series, dividing it by the price deflator index and multiplying by 100 (under the assumption that the deflator has a base value of 100):

$$real\ series_t = \frac{nominal\ series_t}{deflator_t} \times 100 \tag{2.8}$$

It is worth noting that deflation is a relevant process only for series that are measured in money terms, so it would make no sense to deflate a quantity-based series such as the number of houses rented or a series expressed as a proportion or percentage, such as vacancy or the rate of return on a stock.

Example 2.1

Take the series of annual prime office rents in Singapore expressed in local currency and the consumer price index for Singapore shown in table 2.7. In this example, we apply equation (2.8) and we conduct further calculations to help understand the conversion from nominal to real terms.

Column (i) gives the nominal rent series for Singapore offices taken from the Urban Redevelopment Authority and column (ii) the consumer price index for Singapore (values for December each year) taken from the Department of Statistics. We have rebased this index to take the value 100 in 1991. Column (iii) contains real rents calculated with equation (2.8). This series of real rents is also equivalent to rents in constant 1991 prices.

The remaining columns provide additional calculations that give exactly the same results as column (iii). We report the original Singapore CPI series (2004 = 100) in column (iv) and we use this series for further calculations. The results will not change, of course, if we use the rebased CPI (1991 = 100) series.

For the rent calculation in column (v), we use the formula real $rent_t$ = nominal $rent_t/CPI_t$ – that is, the value for 2007 is simply 1,274/106.6. This simple calculation makes the task of reflating the series more straightforward. Assume we wish to forecast this real index. In order to convert the forecast real rents to nominal values, we would need to multiply the real rent by the future CPI. If we wish to convert rents into a particular year's prices, we would apply equation (2.8), but instead of 100 we would have the CPI value that year. Consider that we wish to express nominal rents in 2007 prices (this is our last observation, and converting rents into today's prices

Table 2.7 Construction of a real rent index for offices in Singapore

	(i) Rent nominal[1]	(ii) CPI 1991 = 100	(iii) Rent real[1]	(iv) CPI 2004 = 100	(v) Rent real	(vi) Rent 2007 prices[1]	(vii) Rents index[2] nominal	(viii) real
1991	877	100.0	877.0	86.0	10.2	1,087.1	100.0	100.0
1992	720	101.7	708.0	87.5	8.2	877.2	82.1	80.7
1993	628	104.3	602.1	89.7	7.0	746.3	71.6	68.7
1994	699	107.3	651.4	92.3	7.6	807.3	79.7	74.3
1995	918	108.3	847.6	93.1	9.9	1,051.1	104.7	96.7
1996	933	110.5	844.3	95.0	9.8	1,046.9	106.4	96.3
1997	878	112.7	779.1	96.9	9.1	965.9	100.1	88.9
1998	727	111.0	655.0	95.5	7.6	811.5	82.9	74.7
1999	660	111.9	589.8	96.2	6.9	731.4	75.3	67.3
2000	743	114.2	650.6	98.2	7.6	806.6	84.7	74.2
2001	685	113.5	603.5	97.6	7.0	748.2	78.1	68.8
2002	600	114.0	526.3	98.0	6.1	652.7	68.4	60.0
2003	537	114.8	467.8	98.7	5.4	580.0	61.2	53.4
2004	556	116.3	478.1	100.0	5.6	592.7	63.4	54.5
2005	626	117.8	531.4	101.3	6.2	658.8	71.4	60.6
2006	816	118.7	687.4	102.1	8.0	852.0	93.0	78.4
2007	1,274	124.0	1,027.4	106.6	12.0	1,274.0	145.3	117.2

Notes: [1] Singapore dollars per square metre per year.
[2] Rents index, 1991 = 100.

is appealing). We would base the calculation on a variant of equation (2.8):

$$real\ rent_t = \frac{nominal\ rent_t}{CPI_t} CPI_{reference\ year} \tag{2.9}$$

Office rents in Singapore in 2007 prices are shown in column (vi). That is, for 2006, the value of rents in 2007 prices is given by (816/102.1) × 106.6 = 852. The value for 2007 is similar to the nominal value. The last two columns present a nominal index and a real rent index taking the value of 100 in 1991. This is a way to make some easy visual comparisons. Nominal rents were 45 per cent higher in 2007 than 1991. The values for the nominal and real indices in, say, 2005 are calculated as 71.4 = (626/877) × 100 and 60.6 = (6.2/10.2) × 100, respectively. For the real rent index, we use column (v) for real rents, but an identical result would be obtained if we used columns (iii) or (vi). A comparison of real and nominal rents is given in figure 2.1. Interestingly, office rents in real terms in Singapore recovered to their 1991 level only in 2007.

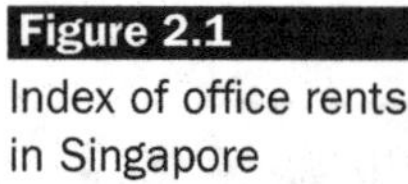

Figure 2.1
Index of office rents in Singapore

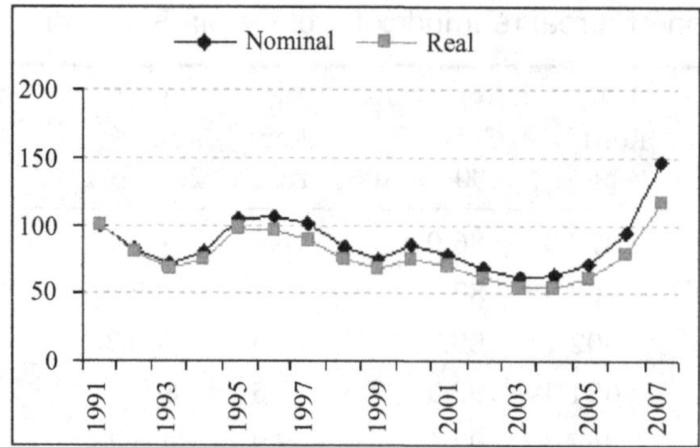

2.4 Properties of logarithms and the log transform

Logarithms were invented to simplify cumbersome calculations, since exponents can then be added or subtracted, which is easier than multiplying or dividing the original numbers. While making logarithmic transformations for computational ease is no longer necessary, they still have important uses in algebra and in data analysis. For the latter, there are at least three reasons why log transforms may be useful. First, taking a logarithm can often help to rescale the data so that their variance is more constant, which overcomes a common statistical problem. Second, logarithmic transforms can help to make a positively skewed distribution closer to a normal distribution. Third, taking logarithms can also be a way to make a non-linear, multiplicative relationship between variables into a linear, additive one. These issues are discussed in some detail in chapter 6.

Taking a logarithm is the inverse of taking an exponential. Natural logarithms, also known as logs to base e (where e is 2.71828...), are more commonly used and more useful mathematically than logs to any other base. A log to base e is known as a *natural* or *Naperian* logarithm, denoted interchangeably by $\ln(y)$ or $\log(y)$.

The properties of logarithms or 'laws of logs' describe the way that we can work with logs or manipulate expressions using them. These are presented in box 2.2.

Box 2.2 Laws of logs

For variables x and y:

- $\ln(x\,y) = \ln(x) + \ln(y)$;
- $\ln(x/y) = \ln(x) - \ln(y)$;
- $\ln(y^c) = c\ln(y)$;
- $\ln(1) = 0$; and
- $\ln(1/y) = \ln(1) - \ln(y) = -\ln(y)$.

2.5 Returns

In many of the problems of interest in real estate, especially when investment performance is studied, the starting point is a time series of income and prices (capital values). For a number of statistical reasons, it is preferable not to work directly with the price or index series, so raw price series are usually converted into series of returns. Additionally, returns have the added benefit that they are unit-free. So, for example, if an annualised return is 10 per cent, then investors know that they will get back £110 for a £100 investment, or £1,100 for a £1,000 investment, and so on.

There are essentially two methods used to calculate returns from a series of prices, and these involve the formation of *simple returns* or *continuously compounded returns*, which are achieved as follows:

Simple returns

$$R_t = \frac{p_t - p_{t-1}}{p_{t-1}} \times 100\% \qquad (2.10)$$

Continuously compounded returns

$$r_t = 100\% \times \ln\left(\frac{p_t}{p_{t-1}}\right) \qquad (2.11)$$

where R_t denotes the simple return at time t, r_t denotes the continuously compounded return at time t, p_t denotes the asset price at time t and ln denotes the natural logarithm.

If the asset under consideration is a building or portfolio of buildings, the total return to holding the asset is the sum of the capital gain and income received during the holding period. Returns in real estate could be income returns (that is, the change in income between time periods), capital returns (the change in the price of buildings) or total returns (income plus the value change). Box 2.3 shows two key reasons for applying the log-return formulation (also known as log-price relatives, as they are the log of the ratio of this period's price to the previous period's price) to calculate returns. There is also a disadvantage to using the log-returns, however. The simple return on a portfolio of assets is a weighted average of the simple returns on the individual assets:

$$R_{pt} = \sum_{i=1}^{N} w_i R_{it} \qquad (2.12)$$

This does not work for the continuously compounded returns, though, so that they are not additive across a portfolio. The fundamental reason why this is the case is that the log of a sum is not the same as the sum of a log, since the operation of taking a log constitutes a *non-linear transformation*. Calculating portfolio returns in this context must be conducted by first estimating the value of the portfolio at each time period and then determining the returns from the aggregate portfolio values.

Box 2.3 Two advantages of log returns

(1) Log-returns have the nice property that they can be interpreted as *continuously compounded returns* – so that the frequency of compounding of the return does not matter, and thus returns across assets can more easily be compared.
(2) Continuously compounded returns are *time-additive*. For example, suppose that a weekly returns series is required and daily log returns have been calculated for five days, numbered 1 to 5, representing the returns on Monday to Friday. It is valid to simply add up the five daily returns to obtain the return for the whole week:

Monday return	$r_1 = \ln(p_1/p_0) = \ln p_1 - \ln p_0$
Tuesday return	$r_2 = \ln(p_2/p_1) = \ln p_2 - \ln p_1$
Wednesday return	$r_3 = \ln(p_3/p_2) = \ln p_3 - \ln p_2$
Thursday return	$r_4 = \ln(p_4/p_3) = \ln p_4 - \ln p_3$
Friday return	$r_5 = \ln(p_5/p_4) = \ln p_5 - lnp_4$
Return over the week	$\ln p_5 - \ln p_0 = \ln(p_5/p_0)$

In the limit, as the frequency of the sampling of the data is increased, so that they are measured over a smaller and smaller time interval, the simple and continuously compounded returns will be identical.

2.6 Matrices

A matrix is simply a *collection* or *array of numbers*. The size of a matrix is given by its numbers of rows and columns. Matrices are very useful and important ways for organising sets of data together, making manipulating and transforming them much easier than it would be to work with each constituent of the matrix separately. Matrices are widely used in econometrics for deriving key results and for expressing formulae in a succinct way. Some useful features of matrices and explanations of how to work with them are described below.

- The size of a matrix is quoted as $R \times C$, which is the number of rows by the number of columns.
- Each element in a matrix is referred to using subscripts. For example, suppose a matrix M has two rows and four columns. The element in the second row and the third column of this matrix would be denoted m_{23}, so that m_{ij} refers to the element in the ith row and the jth column.
- If a matrix has only one row, it is known as a row vector, which will be of dimension $1 \times C$:

$$\text{e.g. } (2.7 \quad 3.0 \quad -1.5 \quad 0.3)$$

- A matrix having only one column is known as a column vector, which will be of dimension $R \times 1$:

$$\text{e.g. } \begin{pmatrix} 1.3 \\ -0.1 \\ 0.0 \end{pmatrix}$$

- When the number of rows and columns is equal (i.e. $R = C$), it is said that the matrix is square:

$$\text{e.g. } \begin{pmatrix} 0.3 & 0.6 \\ -0.1 & 0.7 \end{pmatrix}$$

- A matrix in which all the elements are zero is known as a zero matrix:

$$\text{e.g. } \begin{pmatrix} 0 & 0 & 0 \\ 0 & 0 & 0 \end{pmatrix}$$

- A symmetric matrix is a special type of square matrix that is symmetric about the leading diagonal (the diagonal line running through the matrix from the top left to the bottom right), so that $m_{ij} = m_{ji} \forall i, j$ (where $\forall$ denotes 'for all values of'):

$$\text{e.g. } \begin{pmatrix} 1 & 2 & 4 & 7 \\ 2 & -3 & 6 & 9 \\ 4 & 6 & 2 & -8 \\ 7 & 9 & -8 & 0 \end{pmatrix}$$

- A diagonal matrix is a square matrix that has non-zero terms on the leading diagonal and zeros everywhere else:

$$\text{e.g. } \begin{pmatrix} -3 & 0 & 0 & 0 \\ 0 & 1 & 0 & 0 \\ 0 & 0 & 2 & 0 \\ 0 & 0 & 0 & -1 \end{pmatrix}$$

- A diagonal matrix with one in all places on the leading diagonal and zero everywhere else is known as the identity matrix, denoted by I. By definition, an identity matrix must be symmetric (and therefore also square):

$$\text{e.g. } \begin{pmatrix} 1 & 0 & 0 & 0 \\ 0 & 1 & 0 & 0 \\ 0 & 0 & 1 & 0 \\ 0 & 0 & 0 & 1 \end{pmatrix}$$

- The identity matrix is essentially the matrix equivalent of the number one. Multiplying any matrix by the identity matrix of the appropriate size results in the original matrix being left unchanged:

$$\text{e.g. } MI = IM = M$$

- In order to perform operations with matrices (e.g. addition, subtraction or multiplication), the matrices concerned must be *conformable*. The dimensions of matrices required for them to be conformable depend on the operation.
- The addition and subtraction of matrices require the matrices concerned to be of the same order (i.e. to have the same number of rows and the same number of columns as one another). The operations are then performed element by element:

$$\text{e.g. if } A = \begin{pmatrix} 0.3 & 0.6 \\ -0.1 & 0.7 \end{pmatrix}, \quad \text{and} \quad B = \begin{pmatrix} 0.2 & -0.1 \\ 0 & 0.3 \end{pmatrix},$$

$$A + B = \begin{pmatrix} 0.5 & 0.5 \\ -0.1 & 1.0 \end{pmatrix}, \quad A - B = \begin{pmatrix} 0.1 & 0.7 \\ -0.1 & 0.4 \end{pmatrix}$$

- Multiplying or dividing a matrix by a scalar (that is, a single number), implies that every element of the matrix is multiplied by that number:

$$\text{e.g. } 2A = 2\begin{pmatrix} 0.3 & 0.6 \\ -0.1 & 0.7 \end{pmatrix} = \begin{pmatrix} 0.6 & 1.2 \\ -0.2 & 1.4 \end{pmatrix}$$

- It can also be stated that, for two matrices A and B of the same order and for c, a scalar:

$$A + B = B + A$$
$$A + 0 = 0 + A = A$$
$$cA = Ac$$
$$c(A + B) = cA + cB$$
$$A0 = 0A = 0$$

- Multiplying two matrices together requires the number of columns of the first matrix to be equal to the number of rows of the second matrix. Note also that the ordering of the matrices is important when multiplying them, so that, in general, $AB \neq BA$. When the matrices are multiplied together, the resulting matrix will be of size (number of rows of first matrix $\times$ number of columns of second matrix), e.g. $(3 \times 2) \times (2 \times 4) = (3 \times 4)$. It is as if the columns of the first matrix and the rows of the second cancel out. This rule also follows more generally, so that $(a \times b)\times (b \times c) \times(c \times d) \times (d \times e) = (a \times e)$, etc.
- The actual multiplication of the elements of the two matrices is done by multiplying along the rows of the first matrix and down the columns of

the second:

$$\text{e.g.} \begin{pmatrix} 1 & 2 \\ 7 & 3 \\ 1 & 6 \end{pmatrix} \begin{pmatrix} 0 & 2 & 4 & 9 \\ 6 & 3 & 0 & 2 \end{pmatrix}$$
$$(3 \times 2) \quad (2 \times 4)$$

$$= \begin{pmatrix} (1\times 0)+(2\times 6) & (1\times 2)+(2\times 3) & (1\times 4)+(2\times 0) & (1\times 9)+(2\times 2) \\ (7\times 0)+(3\times 6) & (7\times 2)+(3\times 3) & (7\times 4)+(3\times 0) & (7\times 9)+(3\times 2) \\ (1\times 0)+(6\times 6) & (1\times 2)+(6\times 3) & (1\times 4)+(6\times 0) & (1\times 9)+(6\times 2) \end{pmatrix}$$
$$(3 \times 4)$$

$$= \begin{pmatrix} 12 & 8 & 4 & 13 \\ 18 & 23 & 28 & 69 \\ 36 & 20 & 4 & 21 \end{pmatrix}$$
$$(3 \times 4)$$

- The transpose of a matrix, written A' or A^{T}, is the matrix obtained by transposing (switching) the rows and columns of a matrix:

$$\text{e.g. } A = \begin{pmatrix} 1 & 2 \\ 7 & 3 \\ 1 & 6 \end{pmatrix} \quad A' = \begin{pmatrix} 1 & 7 & 1 \\ 2 & 3 & 6 \end{pmatrix}$$

If A is $R \times C$, A' will be $C \times R$.
- The rank of a matrix A is given by the maximum number of linearly independent rows (or columns) contained in the matrix. For example, rank

$$\begin{pmatrix} 3 & 4 \\ 7 & 9 \end{pmatrix} = 2$$

since both rows and columns are (linearly) independent of one another, but rank

$$\begin{pmatrix} 3 & 6 \\ 2 & 4 \end{pmatrix} = 1$$

as the second column is not independent of the first (the second column is simply twice the first). A matrix with a rank equal to its dimension, as in the first of these two cases, is known as a *matrix of full rank*. A matrix that is less than of full rank is known as a *short rank matrix*, and such a matrix is also termed *singular*. Three important results concerning the rank of a matrix are:

$$\text{rank}\,(A) = \text{rank}\,(A')$$
$$\text{rank}\,(A\,B) \leq \min(\text{rank}\,(A),\ \text{rank}(B))$$
$$\text{rank}\,(A'\,A) = \text{rank}(A\,A') = \text{rank}\,(A)$$

- The inverse of a matrix A, denoted A^{-1}, where defined, is that matrix which, when pre-multiplied or post-multiplied by A, will result in the identity matrix:

  i.e. $AA^{-1} = A^{-1}A = I$

- The inverse of a matrix exists only when the matrix is square and non-singular – that is, when it is of full rank. The inverse of a 2×2 non-singular matrix whose elements are

$$\begin{pmatrix} a & b \\ c & d \end{pmatrix}$$

  will be given by

$$\frac{1}{ad - bc}\begin{pmatrix} d & -b \\ -c & a \end{pmatrix}$$

- The calculation of the inverse of an $N \times N$ matrix for $N > 2$ is more complex and beyond the scope of this text. Properties of the inverse of a matrix include:

$$I^{-1} = I$$
$$(A^{-1})^{-1} = A$$
$$(A')^{-1} = (A^{-1})'$$
$$(AB)^{-1} = B^{-1}A^{-1}$$

- The trace of a square matrix is the sum of the terms on its leading diagonal. For example, the trace of the matrix

$$A = \begin{pmatrix} 3 & 4 \\ 7 & 9 \end{pmatrix}$$

  written Tr(A), is $3 + 9 = 12$. Some important properties of the trace of a matrix are:

$$\text{Tr}(cA) = c\text{Tr}(A)$$
$$\text{Tr}(A') = \text{Tr}(A)$$
$$\text{Tr}(A + B) = \text{Tr}(A) + \text{Tr}(B)$$
$$\text{Tr}(I_N) = N$$

2.7 The eigenvalues of a matrix

The concept of the *eigenvalues* of a matrix is necessary for testing for long-run relationships between series, using what is known as the Johansen cointegration test (see chapter 12). Let Π denote a $p \times p$ square matrix, c

denote a $p \times 1$ non-zero vector and λ denote a scalar or set of scalars. λ is called a *characteristic root* or set of roots of the matrix Π if it is possible to write

$$\underset{p\times p}{\Pi}\,\underset{p\times 1}{c} = \underset{p\times 1}{\lambda c}$$

This equation can also be written as

$$\Pi c = \lambda I_p c$$

where I_p is an identity matrix, and hence

$$(\Pi - \lambda I_p)c = 0$$

Since $c \neq 0$ by definition, then, for this system to have a non-zero solution, the matrix $(\Pi - \lambda I_p)$ is required to be singular (i.e. to have zero determinant):

$$|\Pi - \lambda I_p| = 0$$

For example, let Π be the 2×2 matrix

$$\Pi = \begin{bmatrix} 5 & 1 \\ 2 & 4 \end{bmatrix}$$

Then the characteristic equation is

$$|\Pi - \lambda I_p| = \left| \begin{bmatrix} 5 & 1 \\ 2 & 4 \end{bmatrix} - \lambda \begin{bmatrix} 1 & 0 \\ 0 & 1 \end{bmatrix} \right| = 0$$

$$= \begin{vmatrix} 5-\lambda & 1 \\ 2 & 4-\lambda \end{vmatrix} = (5-\lambda)(4-\lambda) - 2 = \lambda^2 - 9\lambda + 18$$

This gives the solutions $\lambda = 6$ and $\lambda = 3$. The characteristic roots are also known as eigenvalues. The *eigenvectors* would be the values of c corresponding to the eigenvalues.

Some properties of the eigenvalues of any square matrix A are:

- the sum of the eigenvalues is the trace of the matrix;
- the product of the eigenvalues is the determinant; and
- the number of non-zero eigenvalues is the rank.

For a further illustration of the last of these properties, consider the matrix

$$\Pi = \begin{bmatrix} 0.5 & 0.25 \\ 0.7 & 0.35 \end{bmatrix}$$

Its characteristic equation is

$$\left| \begin{bmatrix} 0.5 & 0.25 \\ 0.7 & 0.35 \end{bmatrix} - \lambda \begin{bmatrix} 1 & 0 \\ 0 & 1 \end{bmatrix} \right| = 0$$

which implies that

$$\begin{vmatrix} 0.5-\lambda & 0.25 \\ 0.7 & 0.35-\lambda \end{vmatrix} = 0$$

This determinant can also be written $(0.5-\lambda)(0.35-\lambda) - (0.7 \times 0.25) = 0$ or

$$0.175 - 0.85\lambda + \lambda^2 - 0.175 = 0$$

or

$$\lambda^2 - 0.85\lambda = 0$$

which can be factorised to $\lambda\,(\lambda - 0.85) = 0$.

The characteristic roots are therefore 0 and 0.85. Since one of these eigenvalues is zero, it is obvious that the matrix Π cannot be of full rank. In fact, this is also obvious from just looking at Π, since the second column is exactly half the first.

Key concepts

The key terms to be able to define and explain from this chapter are

- price indices
- Laspeyres index
- Paasche index
- real and nominal series
- laws of logs
- continuously compounded returns
- simple returns
- matrix algebra
- eigenvalues

3 Statistical tools for real estate analysis

Learning outcomes

In this chapter, you will learn how to

- contrast time series, cross-sectional and panel data;
- calculate measures of central tendency, of dispersion, of skewness and of kurtosis for a given series;
- calculate measures of association between series;
- test hypotheses about the mean of a series by calculating test statistics and forming confidence intervals;
- interpret *p*-values; and
- discuss the most common pitfalls that can occur in the analysis of real estate data.

3.1 Types of data for quantitative real estate analysis

There are broadly three types of data that can be employed in quantitative analysis of real estate problems: time series data, cross-sectional data and panel data. Each of these types of data is now described, with examples of how and why they might be used.

3.1.1 *Time series data*

Time series data, as the name suggests, are data that have been collected over a period of time on one or more variables. Time series data have associated with them a particular frequency of observation or collection of data points. The frequency is simply a measure of the *interval over*, or the *regularity with which*, the data are collected or recorded. Box 3.1 shows some examples of time series data.

Box 3.1 Time series data in real estate

Series	*Frequency*
Rents	Monthly, quarterly or annually
Yields	Monthly, quarterly or annually
Absorption	Quarterly or annually

It is also generally a requirement that all data used in a model be of the same frequency of observation. So, for example, regressions that seek to estimate absorption (demand) using annual macroeconomic data for the region must also use annual observations on absorption, even if quarterly observations on the latter are available.

The data may be *quantitative* (absorption in thousands of square metres, or euros per square metre) or *qualitative* (e.g. surveys such as the Royal Institution of Chartered Surveyors [RICS] occupier surveys in the United Kingdom). The majority of data used in real estate are quantitative data.

Problems that can be tackled using time series data

- How office rent values in a country have varied with that country's macroeconomic fundamentals (GDP and interest rates).
- How REIT prices have varied with general stock market movements.
- How real estate value movements in one market are transmitted to other markets.

In all the above cases, it is clearly the time dimension that is the most important, and the regression will be conducted using the values of the variables over time.

3.1.2 *Cross-sectional data*

Cross-sectional data are data on one or more variables collected at a single point in time. For example, the data might be on:

- yields or cap rates for warehouses across European cities as at December 2008;
- a cross-section of office returns on US markets; or
- a sample of investment transactions in Asian markets in a particular year.

Problems that can be tackled using cross-sectional data

- How shopping centre rents vary with size, catchment area and local incomes in a country.
- The relationship between real estate yields and liquidity, transparency and economic dynamism measures.

3.1.3 Panel data

Panel data have the dimensions of both time series and cross-sections – e.g. the monthly prices of a number of REITs in the United Kingdom, France and the Netherlands over two years. The estimation of panel regressions is an interesting and developing area, but will not be considered further in this text. Interested readers are directed to chapter 10 of Brooks (2008) and the references therein.

Fortunately, virtually all the standard techniques and analysis in econometrics are equally valid for time series and cross-sectional data. This book concentrates mainly on time series data and applications, however, since these are more prevalent in real estate. For time series data, it is usual to denote the individual observation numbers using the index t and the total number of observations available for analysis by T. For cross-sectional data, the individual observation numbers are indicated using the index i and the total number of observations available for analysis by N. Note that there is, in contrast to the time series case, no natural ordering of the observations in a cross-sectional sample. For example, the observations i might be on city office yields at a particular point in time, ordered alphabetically by city name. So, in the case of cross-sectional data, there is unlikely to be any useful information contained in the fact that Los Angeles follows London in a sample of city yields, since it is purely by chance that their names both begin with the letter 'L'. On the other hand, in a time series context, the ordering of the data is relevant as the data are usually ordered chronologically. In this book, where the context is not specific to only one type of data or the other, the two types of notation (i and N or t and T) are used interchangeably.

3.1.4 Continuous and discrete data

As well as classifying data as being of the time series or cross-sectional type, we can also distinguish them as being either continuous or discrete, exactly as their labels would suggest. *Continuous* data can take on any value and are not confined to take specific numbers; their values are limited only by precision. For example, the initial yield on a real estate asset could be 6.2 per cent, 6.24 per cent, or 6.238 per cent, and so on. On the other hand, *discrete* data can take on only certain values, which are usually integers[1] (whole numbers), and are often defined to be count numbers – for instance, the number of people working in offices, or the number of industrial units

[1] Discretely measured data do not necessarily have to be integers. For example, until they became 'decimalised', many financial asset prices were quoted to the nearest 1/16th or 1/32nd of a dollar.

transacted in the last quarter. In these cases, having 2,013.5 workers or 6.7 units traded would not make sense.

3.1.5 *Cardinal, ordinal and nominal numbers*

Another way in which we can classify numbers is according to whether they are cardinal, ordinal or nominal. This distinction is drawn in box 3.2.

Box 3.2 Cardinal, ordinal and nominal numbers

- *Cardinal* numbers are those for which the actual numerical values that a particular variable takes have meaning, and for which there is an equal distance between the numerical values.
- On the other hand, *ordinal* numbers can be interpreted only as providing a position or an ordering. Thus, for cardinal numbers, a figure of twelve implies a measure that is 'twice as good' as a figure of six. Examples of cardinal numbers would be the price of a REIT or of a building, and the number of houses in a street. On the other hand, for an ordinal scale, a figure of twelve may be viewed as 'better' than a figure of six, but could not be considered twice as good. Examples include the ranking of global office markets that real estate research firms may produce. Based on measures of liquidity, transparency, risk and other factors, a score is produced. Usually, in this scoring, an office centre ranking second in transparency cannot be said to be twice as transparent as the office market that ranks fourth.
- The final type of data that can be encountered would be when there is no natural ordering of the values at all, so a figure of twelve is simply different from that of a figure of six, but could not be considered to be better or worse in any sense. Such data often arise when numerical values are arbitrarily assigned, such as telephone numbers or when codings are assigned to qualitative data (e.g., when describing the use of space, '1' might be used to denote offices, '2' to denote retail and '3' to denote industrial, and so on). Sometimes, such variables are called *nominal* variables.
- Cardinal, ordinal and nominal variables may require different modelling approaches or, at least, different treatments.

3.2 Descriptive statistics

When analysing a series containing many observations, it is useful to be able to describe the most important characteristics of the series using a small number of summary measures. This section discusses the quantities that are most commonly used to describe real estate and other series, which are known as *summary statistics* or *descriptive statistics*. Descriptive statistics are calculated from a sample of data rather than being assigned on the basis of theory. Before describing the most important summary statistics used in work with real estate data, we define the terms *population* and *sample*, which have precise meanings in statistics.

3.2.1 *The population and the sample*

The *population* is the total collection of all objects to be studied. For example, in the context of determining the relationship between risk and return for UK REITs, the population of interest would be all time series observations on all REIT stocks traded on the London Stock Exchange (LSE).

The population may be either finite or infinite, while a sample is a selection of *just some items from the population*. A population is finite if it contains a fixed number of elements. In general, either all the observations for the entire population will not be available, or they may be so many in number that it is infeasible to work with them, in which case a sample of data is taken for analysis. The sample is usually *random*, and it should be *representative* of the population of interest. A random sample is one in which each individual item in the population is equally likely to be drawn. A *stratified sample* is obtained when the population is split into *layers* or *strata* and the number of observations in each layer of the sample is set to try to match the corresponding number of elements in those layers of the population. The *size of the sample* is the number of observations that are available, or that the researcher decides to use, in estimating the parameters of the model.

3.2.2 *Measures of central tendency*

The average value of a series is sometimes known as its *measure of location* or *measure of central tendency*. The average value is usually thought to measure the 'typical' value of a series. There are a number of methods that can be used for calculating averages. The most well known of these is the *arithmetic mean* (usually just termed 'the mean'), which is simply calculated as the sum of all values in the series divided by the number of values.

The two other methods for calculating the average of a series are the mode and the median. The *mode* measures the most frequently occurring value in a series, which is sometimes regarded as a more representative measure of the average than the arithmetic mean. Finally, the *median* is the middle value in a series when the elements are arranged in an ascending order. For a symmetric distribution, the mean, mode and median will be coincident. For any non-symmetric distribution of points however, the three summary measures will in general be different.

Each of these measures of average has its relative merits and demerits. The mean is the most familiar method to most researchers, but can be unduly affected by extreme values, and, in such cases, it may not be representative of most of the data. The mode is, arguably, the easiest to obtain, but it is not suitable for continuous, non-integer data (e.g. returns or yields) or for distributions that incorporate two or more peaks (known as bimodal and multimodal distributions, respectively). The median is often considered to be a useful representation of the 'typical' value of a series, but it has the drawback that its calculation is based essentially on one observation. Thus if, for example, we had a series containing ten observations and we were to double the values of the top three data points, the median would be unchanged.

The geometric mean

There exists another method that can be used to estimate the average of a series, known as the *geometric mean*. It involves calculating the Nth root of the product of N numbers. In other words, if we want to find the geometric mean of six numbers, we multiply them together and take the sixth root (i.e. raise the product to the power of 1/6th).

In real estate investment, we usually deal with returns or percentage changes rather than actual values, and the method for calculating the geometric mean just described cannot handle negative numbers. Therefore we use a slightly different approach in such cases. To calculate the geometric mean of a set of N returns, we express them as proportions (i.e. on a $(-1, 1)$ scale) rather than percentages (on a $(-100, 100)$ scale), and we would use the formula

$$\overline{R}_G = [(1+r_1)(1+r_2)\ldots(1+r_N)]^{1/N} - 1 \tag{3.1}$$

where $r_1, r_2, \ldots, r_N$ are the returns and $\overline{R}_G$ is the calculated value of the geometric mean. Hence, what we would do would be to add one to each return, multiply the resulting expressions together, raise this product to the power $1/N$ and then subtract one right at the end.

Which method for calculating the mean should we use, therefore? The answer is, as usual, 'It depends.' Geometric returns give the fixed return on the asset or portfolio that would have been required to match the actual performance, which is not the case for the arithmetic mean. Thus, if you assumed that the arithmetic mean return had been earned on the asset every year, you would not reach the correct value of the asset or portfolio at the end! It could be shown that the geometric return is always less than or equal to the arithmetic return, however, and so the geometric return is a downward-biased predictor of future performance. Hence, if the objective is to forecast future returns, the arithmetic mean is the one to use. Finally, it is worth noting that the geometric mean is evidently less intuitive and less commonly used than the arithmetic mean, but it is less affected by extreme outliers than the latter. There is an approximate relationship that holds between the arithmetic and geometric means, calculated using the same set of returns:

$$\overline{R}_G \approx \overline{R}_A - \frac{1}{2}\sigma^2 \tag{3.2}$$

where $\overline{R}_G$ and $\overline{R}_A$ are the geometric and arithmetic means, respectively, and σ^2 is the variance of the returns.

3.2.3 *Measures of spread*

Usually, the average value of a series will be insufficient to characterise a data series adequately, since two series may have the same average but very different profiles because the observations on one of the series may be much more widely spread about the mean than the other. Hence another important feature of a series is how dispersed its values are. In finance theory, for example, the more widely spread returns are around their mean value the more risky the asset is usually considered to be, and the same principle applies in real estate. The simplest measure of spread is arguably the *range*, which is calculated by subtracting the smallest observation from the largest. While the range has some uses, it is fatally flawed as a measure of dispersion by its extreme sensitivity to an outlying observation.

A more reliable measure of spread, although it is not widely employed by quantitative analysts, is the *semi-interquartile range*, also sometimes known as the *quartile deviation*. Calculating this measure involves first ordering the data and then splitting the sample into four parts (*quartiles*)[2] with equal numbers of observations. The second quartile will be exactly at the halfway point, and is known as the median, as described above. The semi-interquartile range focuses on the first and third quartiles, however, which will be at the quarter and three-quarter points in the ordered series, and which can be calculated respectively by the following:

$$Q_1 = \left(\frac{N+1}{4}\right)^{\text{th}} \textit{value} \tag{3.3}$$

and

$$Q_3 = \frac{3}{4}(N+1)^{\text{th}} \textit{value} \tag{3.4}$$

The semi-interquartile range is then given by the difference between the two:

$$IQR = Q_3 - Q_1 \tag{3.5}$$

[2] Note that there are several slightly different formulae that can be used for calculating quartiles, each of which may provide slightly different answers.

This measure of spread is usually considered superior to the range, as it is not so heavily influenced by one or two extreme outliers that, by definition, would be right at the end of an ordered series and so would affect the range. The semi-interquartile range still only incorporates two of the observations in the entire sample, however, and thus another more familiar measure of spread, the *variance*, is very widely used. It is interpreted as the average squared deviation of each data point about its mean value, and is calculated using the usual formula for the variance of a sample:

$$\sigma^2 = \frac{\sum (y_i - \bar{y})^2}{N - 1} \tag{3.6}$$

Another measure of spread, the *standard deviation*, is calculated by taking the square root of equation (3.6):

$$\sigma = \sqrt{\frac{\sum (y_i - \bar{y})^2}{N - 1}} \tag{3.7}$$

The squares of the deviations from the mean are taken rather than the deviations themselves, in order to ensure that positive and negative deviations (for points above and below the average, respectively) do not cancel each other out.

While there is little to choose between the variance and the standard deviation, the latter is sometimes preferred since it will have the same units as the variable whose spread is being measured, whereas the variance will have units of the square of the variable. Both measures share the advantage that they encapsulate information from all the available data points, unlike the range and the quartile deviation, although they can also be heavily influenced by outliers, as for the range. The quartile deviation is an appropriate measure of spread if the median is used to define the average value of the series, while the variance or standard deviation will be appropriate if the arithmetic mean constitutes the adopted measure of central tendency.

Before moving on, it is worth discussing why the denominator in the formulae for the variance and standard deviation includes $N - 1$ rather than N, the sample size. Subtracting one from the number of available data points is known as a *degrees of freedom correction*, and this is necessary as the spread is being calculated about the mean of the series, and this mean has had to be estimated as well. Thus the spread measures described above are known as the *sample* variance and the *sample* standard deviation. Had we been observing the entire population of data rather than a mere sample from it, then the formulae would not need a degree of freedom correction and we would divide by N rather than $N - 1$.

A further measure of dispersion is the *negative semi-variance*, which also gives rise to the *negative semi-standard deviation*. These measures use identical formulae to those described above for the variance and standard deviation, but, when calculating their values, only those observations for which $y_i < \bar{y}$ are used in the sum, and N now denotes the number of such observations. This measure is sometimes useful if the observations are not symmetric about their mean value (i.e. if the distribution is *skewed*; see the next section).[3]

A final statistic that has some uses for measuring dispersion is the *coefficient of variation*, CV. This is obtained by dividing the standard deviation by the arithmetic mean of the series:

$$CV = \frac{\sigma}{\bar{y}} \tag{3.8}$$

CV is useful when we want to make comparisons between series. Since the standard deviation has units of the series under investigation, it will scale with that series. Thus, if we wanted to compare the spread of monthly apartment rental values in Manhattan with those in Houston, using the standard deviation would be misleading, as the average rental value in Manhattan will be much bigger. By *normalising* the standard deviation, the coefficient of variation is a unit-free (*dimensionless*) measure of spread, and so could be used more appropriately to compare the rental values.

Example 3.1

We calculate the measures of spreads described above for the annual office total return series in Frankfurt and Munich, which are presented in table 3.1. Annual total returns have ranged from −3.7 per cent to 11.3 per cent in Frankfurt and from −2.0 per cent to 13.3 per cent in Munich. Applying equation (3.3), the Q_1 observation is the fourth observation – hence 0.8 and 2.1 for Frankfurt and Munich, respectively. The third quartile value is the thirteenth observation – that is, 9.9 and 9.5. We observe that Frankfurt returns have a lower mean and higher standard deviation than those for Munich. On both the variance and standard deviation measures, Frankfurt exhibits more volatility than Munich. This is confirmed by the coefficient of variation. The higher value for Frankfurt indicates a more volatile market (the standard deviation is nearly as large as the mean return), whereas, for Munich, the standard deviation is only 0.7 times the mean return. Note that if the mean return in Frankfurt had been much higher (say 7 per cent), and all other metrics being equal, the coefficient of variation would have been lower than Munich's.

[3] Of course, we could also define the positive semi-variance, where only observations such that $y_i > \bar{y}$ are included in the sum.

Table 3.1 Summary statistics for Frankfurt and Munich returns

	Original data		Ordered data	
	Frankfurt	Munich	Frankfurt	Munich
1992	4.9	2.6	−3.7	−2.0
1993	5.8	−0.1	−2.5	−0.1
1994	3.4	2.0	−0.7	2.0
1995	−0.7	−2.0	0.8	2.1
1996	−2.5	7.3	2.6	2.6
1997	5.3	7.1	3.4	4.7
1998	6.2	10.1	4.0	5.4
1999	10.4	9.5	4.9	5.6
2000	11.1	11.7	5.3	5.7
2001	11.3	5.4	5.8	7.1
2002	4.0	5.6	6.2	7.3
2003	2.6	5.7	9.6	8.0
2004	−3.7	2.1	9.9	9.5
2005	0.8	4.7	10.4	10.1
2006	9.6	8.0	11.1	11.7
2007	9.9	13.3	11.3	13.3
Min			−3.7	−2.0
Max			11.3	13.3
N			16	16
Q_1			4.3 (4th) = 0.8	4.3 (4th) = 2.1
Q_3			12.8 (13th) = 9.9	12.8 (13th) = 9.5
IQR			9.1	7.4
μ			4.9	5.8
σ^2			23.0	17.8
σ			4.8	4.2
CV			0.98	0.73

Source: Authors' own estimates, based on Property and Portfolio Research (PPR) data.

3.2.4 *Higher moments*

If the observations for a given set of data follow a normal distribution, then the mean and variance are sufficient to describe the series entirely. In other words, it is impossible to have two different normal distributions with the same mean and variance. Most samples of data do not follow a normal distribution, however, and therefore we also need what are known as the *higher moments* of a series to characterise it fully. The mean and the variance are the first and second moments of a distribution, respectively, and the (standardised) third and fourth moments are known as the *skewness* and *kurtosis*, respectively. Skewness defines the shape of the distribution, and measures the extent to which it is not symmetric about its mean value. When the distribution of data is symmetric, the three methods for calculating the average (mean, mode and median) of the sample will be equal. If the distribution is positively skewed (when there is a long right-hand tail and most of the data are bunched over to the left), the ordering will be *mean > median > mode*, whereas, if the distribution is negatively skewed (a long left-hand tail and most of the data bunched on the right), the ordering will be the opposite. A normally distributed series has zero skewness (i.e. it is symmetric).

Kurtosis measures the fatness of the tails of the distribution and how peaked at the mean the series is. A normal distribution is defined to have a coefficient of kurtosis of three. It is possible to define a coefficient of excess kurtosis, equal to the coefficient of kurtosis minus three; a normal distribution will thus have a coefficient of excess kurtosis of zero. A normal distribution is said to be mesokurtic. Denoting the observations on a series by y_i and their variance by σ^2, it can be shown that the coefficients of skewness and kurtosis can be calculated respectively as[4]

$$skew = \frac{\frac{1}{N-1}\sum(y_i - \bar{y})^3}{\left(\sigma^2\right)^{3/2}} \tag{3.9}$$

and

$$kurt = \frac{\frac{1}{N-1}\sum(y_i - \bar{y})^4}{\left(\sigma^2\right)^{2}} \tag{3.10}$$

The kurtosis of the normal distribution is three, so its excess kurtosis $(b_2 - 3)$ is zero.

To give some illustrations of what a series having specific departures from normality may look like, consider figures 3.1 and 3.2. A normal distribution is symmetric about its mean, while a skewed distribution will not be, but will have one tail longer than the other. A leptokurtic distribution is one that

[4] There are a number of ways to calculate skewness (and kurtosis); the one given in the formula is sometimes known as the moment coefficient of skewness, but it could also be measured using the standardised difference between the mean and the median, or by using the quartiles of the data. Unfortunately, this implies that different software will give slightly different values for the skewness and kurtosis coefficients. For example, some packages make a 'degrees of freedom correction', as we do in equations (3.9) and (3.10), while others do not, so that the divisor in such cases would be N rather than $N - 1$ in the equations.

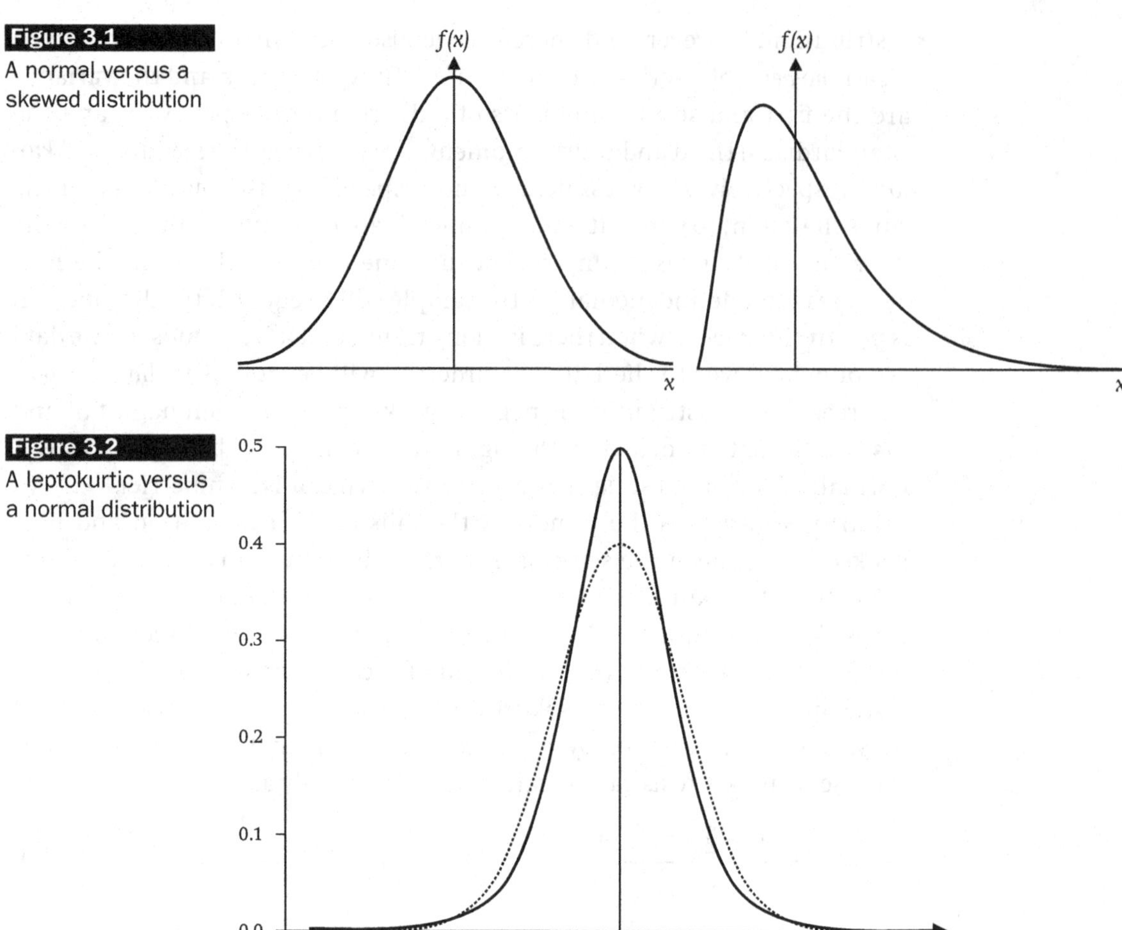

Figure 3.1 A normal versus a skewed distribution

Figure 3.2 A leptokurtic versus a normal distribution

has fatter tails and is more peaked at the mean than a normally distributed random variable with the same mean and variance, while a platykurtic distribution will be less peaked in the mean and will have thinner tails and more of the distribution in the shoulders than a normal. In practice, a leptokurtic distribution is more likely to characterise real estate (and economic) time series, and to characterise the residuals from a time series model. In figure 3.2, the leptokurtic distribution is shown by the bold line, with the normal by the dotted line. There is a formal test for normality, and this is described and discussed in chapter 6.

We now apply equations (3.9) and (3.10) to estimate the skewness and kurtosis for the Frankfurt and Munich office returns given in table 3.1 (see table 3.2). Munich returns show no skewness and Frankfurt slightly negative skewness. Therefore returns in Munich are symmetric about their mean; in Frankfurt, however, the tail tends to be a bit longer in the negative direction. Both series have a flatter peak around their mean and thinner tails than a

Table 3.2 Skewness and kurtosis for Frankfurt and Munich

	Skewness	Kurtosis
Frankfurt	−0.2	1.9
Munich	0.0	2.2

normal distribution – i.e. they are platykurtic. The flatness results from the data being less concentrated around their mean. Office returns in both cities are less concentrated around their means, and this is due to more volatility than usual. The values of 1.9 and 2.2 for the coefficient of kurtosis suggest that extreme values will not be highly likely, however.

3.2.5 *Measures of association*

There are two key descriptive statistics that are used for measuring the relationships between series: the covariance and the correlation.

Covariance

The *covariance* is a measure of linear association between two variables and represents the simplest and most common way to enumerate the relationship between them. It measures whether they on average move in the same direction (positive covariance) or in opposite directions (negative covariance), or have no association (zero covariance). The formula for calculating the covariance, $\sigma_{x,y}$, between two series, x_i and y_i, is given by

$$\sigma_{x,y} = \frac{\sum (x_i - \overline{x})(y_i - \overline{y})}{(N-1)} \tag{3.11}$$

Correlation

A fundamental weakness of the covariance as a measure of association is that it scales with the two variances, so it has units of $x \times y$. Thus, for example, multiplying all the values of series y by ten will increase the covariance tenfold, but it will not really increase the true association between the series since they will be no more strongly related than they were before the rescaling. The implication is that the particular numerical value that the covariance takes has no useful interpretation on its own and hence is not particularly useful. The *correlation*, therefore, takes the covariance and standardises or normalises it so that it is unit-free. The result of this standardisation is that the correlation is bounded to lie on the $(-1, 1)$ interval. A correlation of 1 (-1) indicates a perfect positive (negative) association between the series. The correlation measure, usually known as the *correlation coefficient*, is often denoted $\rho_{x,y}$, and is calculated as

$$\rho_{x,y} = \frac{\sum(x_i - \overline{x})(y_i - \overline{y})}{(N-1)\sigma_x\sigma_y} = \frac{\sigma_{x,y}}{\sigma_x\sigma_y} \tag{3.12}$$

where σ_x and σ_y are the standard deviations of x and y, respectively. This measure is more strictly known as *Pearson's product moment correlation.*

3.3 Probability and characteristics of probability distributions

The formulae presented above demonstrate how to calculate the mean and the variance of a given set of actual data. It is also useful to know how to work with the theoretical expressions for the mean and variance of a random variable, however. A *random variable* is one that can take on any value from a given set.

The mean of a random variable y is also known as its expected value, written $\text{E}(y)$. The properties of expected values are used widely in econometrics, and are listed below, referring to a random variable y.

- The expected value of a constant (or a variable that is non-stochastic) is the constant, e.g. $\text{E}(c) = c$.
- The expected value of a constant multiplied by a random variable is equal to the constant multiplied by the expected value of the variable: $\text{E}(cy) = c\,\text{E}(y)$. It can also be stated that $\text{E}(c\,y + d) = (c\,\text{E}(y)) + d$, where d is also a constant.
- For two independent random variables, y_1 and y_2, $\text{E}(y_1 y_2) = \text{E}(y_1)\,\text{E}(y_2)$.

The variance of a random variable y is usually written $\text{var}\,(y)$. The properties of the 'variance operator', var, are as follows.

- The variance of a random variable y is given by $\text{var}\,(y) = \text{E}[y - \text{E}(y)]^2$.
- The variance of a constant is zero: $\text{var}\,(c) = 0$.
- For c and d constants, $\text{var}\,(c\,y + d) = c^2\,\text{var}\,(y)$.
- For two independent random variables, y_1 and y_2, $\text{var}\,(c\,y_1 + dy_2) = c^2\,\text{var}\,(y_1) + d^2\,\text{var}\,(y_2)$.

The covariance between two random variables, y_1 and y_2, may be expressed as $\text{cov}\,(y_1, y_2)$. The properties of the 'covariance operator' are as follows.

- $\text{cov}\,(y_1, y_2) = \text{E}[(y_1 - \text{E}(y_1))(y_2 - \text{E}(y_2))]$.
- For two independent random variables, y_1 and y_2, $\text{cov}\,(y_1, y_2) = 0$.
- For four constants, c, d, e and f, $\text{cov}\,(c + dy_1, e + fy_2) = df\,\text{cov}\,(y_1, y_2)$.

It is often of interest to ask: 'What is the probability that a random variable will take on a value within a given range?' This information is given by a *probability distribution*. A *probability* is defined to lie between zero and one, with a probability of zero indicating an impossibility and one indicating a certainty.

There are many probability distributions, including the binomial, Poisson, log-normal, normal, exponential, *t*, Chi-squared and *F*. The most commonly used distribution to characterise a random variable is a *normal* or *Gaussian* (these terms are equivalent) distribution. The normal distribution is particularly useful, since it is symmetric, and the only pieces of information required to specify the distribution completely are its mean and variance, as discussed in section 3.2.4 above.

The probability density function for a normal random variable with mean μ and variance σ^2 is given by $f(y)$ in the following expression:

$$f(y) = \frac{1}{\sqrt{2\pi}} e^{-(y-\mu)^2/2\sigma^2} \tag{3.13}$$

Entering values of y into this expression would trace out the familiar 'bell' shape of the normal distribution, as shown in figure 3.3 below.

If a random sample of size N: $y_1, y_2, y_3, \ldots, y_N$ is drawn from a population that is normally distributed with mean μ and variance σ^2, the sample mean, $\bar{y}$, is also normally distributed, with mean μ and variance σ^2/N. In fact, an important rule in statistics, known as the *central limit theorem*, states that the sampling distribution of the mean of any random sample of observations will tend towards the normal distribution with mean equal to the population mean, μ, as the sample size tends to infinity. This theorem is a very powerful result, because it states that the sample mean, $\bar{y}$, will follow a normal distribution even if the original observations $(y_1, y_2, \ldots, y_N)$ did not. This means that we can use the normal distribution as a kind of benchmark when testing hypotheses, as described in the following section.

3.4 Hypothesis testing

Real estate theory and experience will often suggest that certain parameters should take on particular values, or values within a given range. It is therefore of interest to determine whether the relationships expected from real estate theory are upheld by the data to hand or not. For example, estimates of the mean (average) and standard deviation will have been obtained from the sample, but these values are not of any particular interest; the population values that describe the true mean of the variable would be of more interest, but are never available. Instead, inferences are made concerning the likely population values from the parameters that have been estimated using the sample of data. In doing this, the aim is to determine whether the differences between the estimates that are actually obtained and the expectations arising from real estate theory are a long way from one another, in a statistical sense. Thus we could use any of the descriptive statistic measures discussed above (mean, variance, skewness, kurtosis, correlation, etc.) that were calculated from sample data to test the plausible population parameters given these sample statistics.

3.4.1 *Hypothesis testing: some concepts*

In the hypothesis-testing framework, there are always two hypotheses that go together, known as the *null hypothesis* (denoted H_0, or occasionally H_N) and the *alternative hypothesis* (denoted H_1, or occasionally H_A). The null hypothesis is the statement or the statistical hypothesis that is actually being tested. The alternative hypothesis represents the remaining outcomes of interest.

For example, suppose that we have estimated the sample mean of the price of some houses to be £153,000, but prior research had suggested that the mean value ought to be closer to £180,000. It is of interest to test the hypothesis that the true value of μ – i.e. the true but unknown population average house price – is in fact 180,000. The following notation would be used:

$$H_0: \mu = 180{,}000$$
$$H_1: \mu \neq 180{,}000$$

This states that we are testing the hypothesis that the true but unknown value of μ is 180,000 against an alternative hypothesis that μ is not 180,000. This would be known as a *two-sided* test, since the outcomes of both $\mu <$ 180,000 and $\mu >$ 180,000 are subsumed under the alternative hypothesis.

Sometimes, some prior information may be available, suggesting for example that $\mu > 180{,}000$ would be expected rather than $\mu < 180{,}000$. In this case, $\mu < 180{,}000$ is no longer of interest to us, and hence a *one-sided* test would be conducted:

$$H_0: \mu = 180{,}000$$
$$H_1: \mu > 180{,}000$$

Here, the null hypothesis that the true value of μ is 180,000 is being tested against a one-sided alternative that μ is more than 180,000.

On the other hand, one could envisage a situation in which there is prior information that $\mu < 180{,}000$ was expected. In this case, the null and alternative hypotheses would be specified as

$$H_0: \mu = 180{,}000$$
$$H_1: \mu < 180{,}000$$

This prior information that leads us to conduct a one-sided test rather than a two-sided test should come from the real estate theory of the problem under consideration, and not from an examination of the estimated value of the coefficient. Note that there is always an equality under the null hypothesis. So, for example, $\mu < 180{,}000$ would not be specified under the null hypothesis.

There are two ways to conduct a hypothesis test: via the *test of significance approach* or via the *confidence interval approach*. Both approaches centre on a statistical comparison of the estimated value of a parameter and its value under the null hypothesis. In very general terms, if the estimated value is a long way away from the hypothesised value, the null hypothesis is likely to be rejected; if the value under the null hypothesis and the estimated value are close to one another, the null hypothesis is less likely to be rejected. For example, consider $\mu = 180{,}000$, as above. A hypothesis that the true value of μ is, say, 5,000 is more likely to be rejected than a null hypothesis that the true value of μ is 180,000. What is required now is a *statistical decision rule* that will permit the formal testing of such hypotheses.

In general, whether such null hypotheses are likely to be rejected will depend on three factors.

(1) The difference between the value under the null hypothesis, μ, and the estimated value, $\bar{y}$ (in this case 180,000 and 153,000, respectively).
(2) The variability of the estimates within the sample, measured by the sample standard deviation, $\hat{\sigma}$. In general, the larger this is the more uncertainty there would be surrounding the average value; by contrast, if all the sample estimates were within the range (148,000, 161,000), we could be more sure that the null hypothesis is incorrect.
(3) The number of observations in the sample, N; as stated above, the more data points are contained within the sample the more information we have, and the more reliable the sample average estimate will be. *Ceteris paribus*, the larger the sample size the less evidence we would need against a null hypothesis to reject it, and so the more likely such a rejection is to occur.

If we take repeated samples of size N from a population that has a mean μ and a standard deviation σ, then the sample mean will be distributed with mean μ and standard deviation $(\sigma/\sqrt{N})$. Suppose, for example, that we were interested in measuring the average transaction price of a three-bedroom

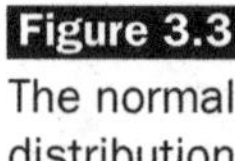

Figure 3.3
The normal distribution

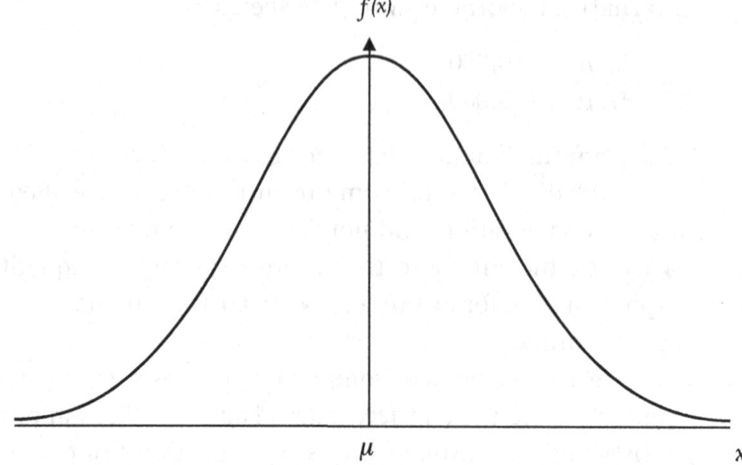

apartment in Hong Kong. We could take a sample of fifty apartments that had recently been sold and calculate the mean price from them, and then another sample of the same size to calculate the mean, and so on. If we did this repeatedly, we would get a distribution of mean values, with one observation (i.e. one estimate of the mean) for each of the samples. As we increased the number of fifty-apartment samples we took, the distribution of means would converge upon a normal distribution. This is an important definition, since it allows us to test hypotheses about the sample mean.

The way that we test hypotheses using the test of significance approach would be to form a *test statistic* and then compare it with a *critical value* from a statistical table. If we assume that the population standard deviation, σ, is known, the test statistic will follow a normal distribution and we would obtain the appropriate critical value from the normal distribution tables. This will never be the case in practice, however, and therefore the following discussion refers to the situation when we need to obtain an estimate of σ, which we usually denote by s (or sometimes by $\hat{\sigma}$). In this case, a different expression for the test statistic would be required, and the sample mean now follows a t-distribution with mean μ and variance $\sigma^2/(N-1)$ rather than a normal distribution. The test statistic would follow a t-distribution and the relevant critical value would be obtained from the t-tables.

3.4.2 A note on the t- and the normal distributions

The normal distribution, shown in figure 3.3, should be familiar to readers. Note its characteristic 'bell' shape and its symmetry around the mean. A normal variate can be scaled to have zero mean and unit variance by subtracting its mean and dividing by its standard deviation.

Table 3.3 Critical values from the standard normal versus t-distribution

Significance level	$N(0,1)$	t_{40}	t_4
50%	0	0	0
5%	1.64	1.68	2.13
2.5%	1.96	2.02	2.78
0.5%	2.57	2.70	4.60

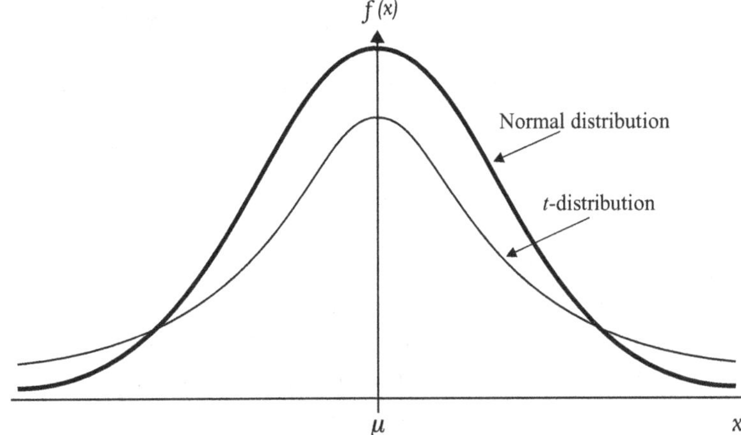

Figure 3.4 The t-distribution versus the normal

There is a specific relationship between the t- and the standard normal distribution, and the t-distribution has another parameter known as its *degrees of freedom*, which is defined below. What does the t-distribution look like? It looks similar to a normal distribution, but with fatter tails, and a smaller peak at the mean, as shown in figure 3.4. Some examples of the percentiles from the normal and t-distributions taken from the statistical tables are given in table 3.3. When used in the context of a hypothesis test, these percentiles become critical values. The values presented in table 3.3 would be those critical values appropriate for a one-sided test of the given significance level.

It can be seen that, as the number of degrees of freedom for the t-distribution increases from four to forty, the critical values fall substantially. In figure 3.4, this is represented by a gradual increase in the height of the distribution at the centre and a reduction in the fatness of the tails as the number of degrees of freedom increases. In the limit, a t-distribution with an infinite number of degrees of freedom is a standard normal – i.e. $t_\infty = N(0, 1)$ – so the normal distribution can be viewed as a special case of the t.

Putting the limit case, t_∞, aside, the critical values for the t-distribution are larger in absolute value than those for the standard normal. Thus, owing to the increased uncertainty associated with the situation in which the sample standard deviation must be estimated, when the t-distribution is used, for a given statistic to constitute the same amount of reliable evidence against the null, it has to be bigger in absolute value than in circumstances in which the normal distribution is applicable.

3.4.3 *The test of significance approach*

The steps involved in conducting a test of significance for testing a hypothesis about the mean value of a series are now given.

(1) Estimate the mean, $\overline{y}$, and the standard deviation, $\hat{\sigma}$, of the sample of data in the usual way.
(2) Calculate the test statistic. This is given by the formula

$$\textit{test statistic} = \frac{\overline{y} - \mu^*}{\hat{\sigma}/\sqrt{N-1}} \tag{3.14}$$

where μ^* is the value of μ under the null hypothesis. The null hypothesis is H_0: $\mu = \mu^*$ and the alternative hypothesis is H_1: $\mu \neq \mu^*$ (for a two-sided test). The denominator in this test statistic, $\hat{\sigma}/\sqrt{N-1}$, is known as the standard error of the sample mean, $\overline{y}$, and is denoted $SE(\overline{y})$.
(3) A tabulated distribution with which to compare the estimated test statistics is required. Test statistics derived in this way can be shown to follow a t-distribution with $N-1$ degrees of freedom.[5]
(4) Choose a 'significance level', often denoted α. It is conventional to use a significance level of 5 per cent, although 10 per cent and 1 per cent are also common. The choice of significance level is discussed below.
(5) Given a significance level, a *rejection region* and a *non-rejection region* can be determined. If a 5 per cent significance level is employed, this means that 5 per cent of the total distribution (5 per cent of the area under the curve) will be in the rejection region. That rejection region can either be split in half (for a two-sided test) or it can all fall on one side of the y-axis, as is the case for a one-sided test.

    For a two-sided test, the 5 per cent rejection region is split equally between the two tails, as shown in figure 3.5.

    For a one-sided test, the 5 per cent rejection region is located solely in one tail of the distribution, as shown in figures 3.6 and 3.7, for a

[5] $N-1$ degrees of freedom arise from the fact that one degree of freedom is 'used up' in estimating the mean, $\overline{y}$.

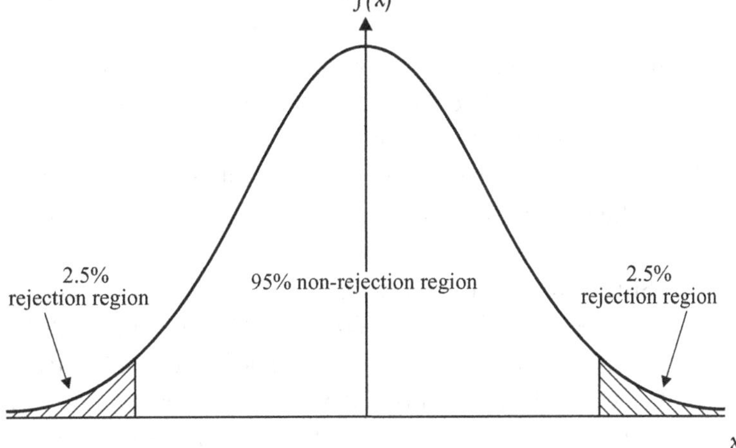

Figure 3.5 Rejection regions for a two-sided 5 per cent hypothesis test

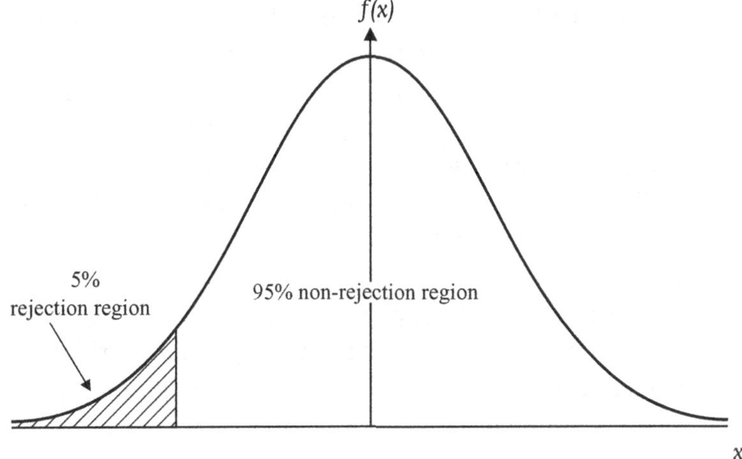

Figure 3.6 Rejection region for a one-sided hypothesis test of the form H_0: $\mu = \mu^*$, H_1: $\mu < \mu^*$

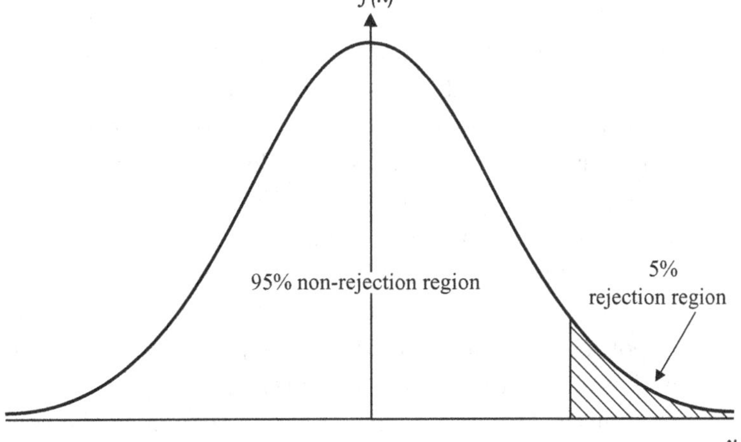

Figure 3.7 Rejection region for a one-sided hypothesis test of the form H_0: $\mu = \mu^*$, H_1: $\mu > \mu^*$

test in which the alternative is of the 'less than' form and in which the alternative is of the 'greater than' form, respectively.

(6) Use the t-tables to obtain a critical value or values with which to compare the test statistic. The critical value will be that value of x that puts 5 per cent into the rejection region.

(7) Finally perform the test. If the test statistic lies in the rejection region then reject the null hypothesis (H_0); otherwise, do not reject H_0.

Steps 2 to 7 require further comment. In step 2, the estimated value of μ is compared with the value that is subject to test under the null hypothesis, but this difference is 'normalised' or scaled by the standard error of the estimate of μ, which is the standard deviation divided by $\sqrt{N-1}$. The standard error is a measure of how confident one is in the estimate of the sample mean obtained in the first stage. If a standard error is small, the value of the test statistic will be large relative to the case in which the standard error is large. For a small standard error, it would not require the estimated and hypothesised values to be far away from one another for the null hypothesis to be rejected. Dividing by the standard error also ensures that the test statistic follows a tabulated distribution.

The significance level is also sometimes called the *size of the test* (note that this is completely different from the size of the sample), and it determines the region where the null hypothesis under test will be rejected or not rejected. Remember that the distributions in figures 3.5 to 3.7 are for a random variable. Purely by chance, a random variable will take on extreme values (either large and positive values or large and negative values) occasionally. More specifically, a significance level of 5 per cent means that a result as extreme as this or more extreme would be expected only 5 per cent of the time as a consequence of chance alone. To give one illustration, if the 5 per cent critical value for a one-sided test is 1.68, this implies that the test statistic would be expected to be greater than this only 5 per cent of the time by chance alone. There is nothing magical about the test; all that is done is to specify an arbitrary cut-off value for the test statistic that determines whether the null hypothesis would be rejected or not. It is conventional to use a 5 per cent size of test, but, as mentioned above, 10 per cent and 1 per cent are also widely used.

One potential problem with the use of a fixed (e.g. 5 per cent) size of test, however, is that, if the sample size is sufficiently large, virtually any null hypothesis can be rejected. This is particularly worrisome in finance, for which tens of thousands of observations or more are often available. What happens is that the standard errors reduce as the sample size increases, because $\hat{\sigma}$ is being divided by $\sqrt{N-1}$, thus leading to an increase in the value of all t-test statistics. This problem is frequently overlooked in empirical work, but some econometricians have suggested that a lower size of test (e.g. 1 per cent) should be used for large samples (see, for example, Leamer, 1978, for a discussion of these issues). In real estate, however, where samples are often very small, the 5 per cent significance level is widely used.

Note also the use of terminology in connection with hypothesis tests: it is said that the null hypothesis is either *rejected* or *not rejected*. It is incorrect to state that, if the null hypothesis is not rejected, it is 'accepted' (although this error is frequently made in practice), and it is never said that the alternative hypothesis is accepted or rejected. One reason why it is not sensible to say that the null hypothesis is 'accepted' is that it is impossible to know whether the null is actually true or not! In any given situation, many null hypotheses will not be rejected. For example, suppose that H_0: $\mu = 0.5$ and H_0: $\mu = 1$ are separately tested against the relevant two-sided alternatives and neither null is rejected. Clearly then it would not make sense to say that 'H_0: $\mu = 0.5$ is accepted' and 'H_0: $\mu = 1$ is accepted', since the true (but unknown) value of μ cannot be both 0.5 and 1. So, to summarise, the null hypothesis is either rejected or not rejected on the basis of the available evidence.

3.4.4 *The confidence interval approach*

The estimated mean, $\bar{y}$, of the sample values is sometimes known as a *point estimate* because it is a single quantity. It is often more useful not just to know the point estimate but to know how confident we are in the estimate, and this information is provided by a *confidence interval*. To give an example of its usage, one might estimate $\bar{y}$ to be 0.93, and a '95 per cent confidence interval' to be (0.77, 1.09). This means that in many repeated samples, 95 per cent of the time, the true value of the population parameter, μ, will be contained within this interval. Confidence intervals are almost invariably estimated in a two-sided form, although in theory a one-sided interval can be constructed such that either the upper or the lower limit in the interval will be infinity. Constructing a 95 per cent confidence interval is equivalent to using the 5 per cent level in a test of significance.

Carrying out a hypothesis test using confidence intervals

(1) Calculate the mean, $\bar{y}$, and the standard deviation, $\hat{\sigma}$, as above.
(2) Choose a significance level, α (again, the convention is 5 per cent). This is equivalent to choosing a $(1-\alpha)*100\%$ confidence interval – i.e. 5% significance level = 95% confidence interval.
(3) Use the t-tables to find the appropriate critical value, which will again have $N-1$ degrees of freedom.

(4) The confidence interval for $\bar{y}$ is given by

$$(\bar{y} - t_{crit} \cdot SE(\bar{y}), \bar{y} + t_{crit} \cdot SE(\bar{y}))$$

where $SE(\bar{y}) = \hat{\sigma}/\sqrt{N-1}$.

(5) Perform the test: if the hypothesised value of μ, i.e. μ^*, lies outside the confidence interval, then reject the null hypothesis that $\mu = \mu^*$, otherwise do not reject the null.

3.4.5 *The test of significance and confidence interval approaches always give the same conclusion*

Under the test of significance approach, the null hypothesis that $\mu = \mu^*$ will not be rejected if the test statistic lies within the non-rejection region – i.e. if the following condition holds:

$$-t_{crit} \leq \frac{\bar{y} - \mu^*}{\hat{\sigma}/\sqrt{N-1}} \leq +t_{crit}$$

Rearranging and denoting $= \hat{\sigma}/\sqrt{N-1}$ by $SE(\bar{y})$, the null hypothesis would not be rejected if

$$-t_{crit} \cdot SE(\bar{y}) \leq \bar{y} - \mu^* \leq +\, t_{crit} \cdot SE(\bar{y})$$

i.e. one would not reject if

$$\bar{y} - t_{crit} \cdot SE(\bar{y}) \leq \mu^* \leq \bar{y} + t_{crit} \cdot SE(\bar{y})$$

This is just the rule for non-rejection under the confidence interval approach, though, so it will always be the case that, for a given significance level, the test of significance and confidence interval approaches will provide the same conclusion by construction. One testing approach is simply an algebraic rearrangement of the other.

Example 3.2 Testing a hypothesis about the mean rental yield

A company holds a portfolio comprising twenty-five commercial properties in the XYZ market area, with an average initial yield of 6.2 per cent and a standard deviation of 6.37 per cent. The average yield from a number of sources for the whole market is 8 per cent. Is there evidence that the company's portfolio performs significantly differently from the market as a whole?

We could think of this as a test of whether the true but unknown population parameter initial yield, μ, is 8 per cent, with the data that the sample mean estimate, $\bar{y}$, is 6.2 per cent and the sample standard deviation, $\hat{\sigma}$, is 6.37 per cent. Therefore the standard error is $SE(\bar{y}) = \hat{\sigma}/\sqrt{N-1} = 6.37/\sqrt{24} = 1.3$. Since the question refers only to a 'difference in performance' rather than over-performance or underperformance specifically compared to the industry, the alternative hypothesis would be of the $\neq$ variety since both alternative outcomes, $<$ and $>$, are of interest. Hence the null and alternative hypotheses would be, respectively, H_0: $\mu = 8$ and H_1: $\mu \neq 8$.

The results of the test according to each approach are shown in box 3.3.

Box 3.3 The test of significance and confidence interval approaches compared in a regression context

Test of significance approach	Confidence interval approach
$\text{Test stat} = \dfrac{\bar{y} - \mu^*}{SE(\bar{y})} = \dfrac{6.2 - 8}{1.3} = -1.38$	Find $t_{crit} = t_{24;5\%} = \pm 2.064$
Find $t_{crit} = t_{24;5\%} = \pm 2.064$	$\bar{y} \pm t_{crit} \cdot SE(\bar{y}) = 6.2 \pm 2.064 \cdot 1.3 = (3.52, 8.88)$
Do not reject H_0, since test statistic lies within the non-rejection region.	Do not reject H_0, since eight lies within the confidence interval.

A couple of comments are in order. First, the required critical value from the t-distribution is for $N - 1 = 24$ degrees of freedom and at the 5 per cent level. This means that 5 per cent of the total distribution will be in the rejection region, and, since this is a two-sided test, 2.5 per cent of the distribution is required to be contained in each tail. Second, from the symmetry of the t-distribution around zero, the critical values in the upper and lower tails will be equal in magnitude, but opposite in sign, as shown in figure 3.5. The critical values are ± 2.064.

3.5 Pitfalls in the analysis of real estate data

While it is increasingly easy to generate results from even complex models at the click of a mouse, it is crucial to emphasise the importance of applying the statistical techniques validly, so that the results are reliable and robust rather than just being available. Specifically, the validity of the techniques for estimating parameters and for making hypothesis tests usually rests on a number of assumptions made about the model and the data, and if these assumptions are not fulfilled the results could be prone to misinterpretation, leading the researcher to draw the wrong conclusions. The statistical adequacy of the models used is a theme that runs continuously through this book, but, before proceeding to developing further the quantitative tools in the following chapter, we end this one by noting several of the most common difficulties that an empirical researcher in real estate is likely to run into.

3.5.1 Small samples and sampling error

A question that is often asked by those new to econometrics is: 'What is an appropriate sample size for model estimation?' Although there is no definitive answer to this question, it should be noted that most testing procedures in econometrics rely on *asymptotic theory*. That is, the results in theory hold only if there are an *infinite number of observations*. In practice, an infinite number of observations will never be available, but, fortunately, an infinite number of observations is not usually required to invoke the asymptotic theory! An approximation to the asymptotic behaviour of the test statistics can be obtained using finite samples, provided that they are large enough. In general, as many observations as possible should be used (although there are important caveats to this statement relating to 'structural stability', discussed later). The reason is that all the researcher has at his/her disposal is a sample of data from which to estimate parameter values and to infer their likely population counterparts. A sample may fail to deliver something close to the exact population values owing to sampling error. Even if the sample is randomly drawn from the population, some samples will be more representative of the behaviour of the population than others, purely because of the 'luck of the draw'. Sampling error is minimised by increasing the size of the sample, as the larger the sample the less likely it is that all the data points drawn will be unrepresentative of the population.

As the sample size used is reduced the estimates of the quantities of interest will become more and more unreliable, and it will become increasingly difficult to draw firm conclusions about the direction and strength of any relationships in the series. A rule of thumb that is sometimes used is to say that at least thirty observations are required to estimate even the simplest models, and at least 100 is desirable; the more complex the model, though, the more heavily it will rely on the available information, and the larger the quantity of data that will be required.

Small samples are a particular problem in real estate when analysing time series data compared with related areas of investigation such as macroeconomics and finance, since, for the former, often only annual, or at best quarterly, data are available. While it is not possible to create data artificially when there are none, and so a researcher can work only with what he/she has available, it is important to be highly cautious in interpreting the results from any study in which the sample size is very limited.

In addition to the small size of samples, there is an added problem with real estate data. The quality of the data may be poorer at the beginning of the sample, on account of less frequent transactions, limited valuations of buildings and a generally thin market. This problem is often particularly acute at the beginning of the production of a series, since evidence about rents, yields, prices and other real estate market series can be sparse.

In addition, the problem of smaller samples is accentuated by the diverse institutional contexts that exist internationally. In some markets, transaction details may not be disclosed, and hence the market evidence that can be used for valuations is limited; alternatively, the valuation processes may themselves be different, which will have an impact on the smoothness and volatility of real estate data.

3.5.2 *Trends in the series and spurious relationships*

In the context of time series data, if the series under examination contains a *trend* then the usual framework for making inferences from the sample to the population will not apply. In other words, it will not be possible to employ validly the techniques described above and in the following chapter for testing hypotheses in such circumstances. A more formal definition of a trend and a discussion of the different types of trends that may be present in data is presented in chapter 12, but for now it is sufficient to describe a series as trending if its average value is changing over time so that the series appears to 'wander' upwards or downwards for prolonged periods. Examples of two different types of trending series, and a series with no trend, are presented in figure 3.8. The distinction between the types of series represented by panels (a) and (b) (which show the index of US income returns for all real estate in nominal terms and the index of real office values in Tokyo, respectively) and panel (c) (which shows the all-property returns risk premium, calculated from total returns for all real estate minus returns on medium-term UK government bonds constructed using data from the IPD) is clearly evident. The series in panels (a) and (b) have upward and downward trends, respectively, while panel (c) has no trend.

If trending (also known as *non-stationary*) data are employed in their raw forms without being transformed appropriately, a number of undesirable consequences can arise. As well as any inferences from the sample to the population being invalid, the problem of *spurious regression* arises. If two stationary variables are generated as independent random series, the statistical

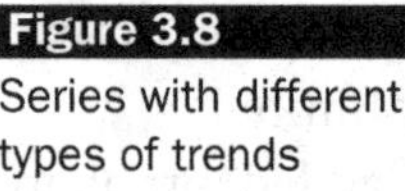

Figure 3.8 Series with different types of trends

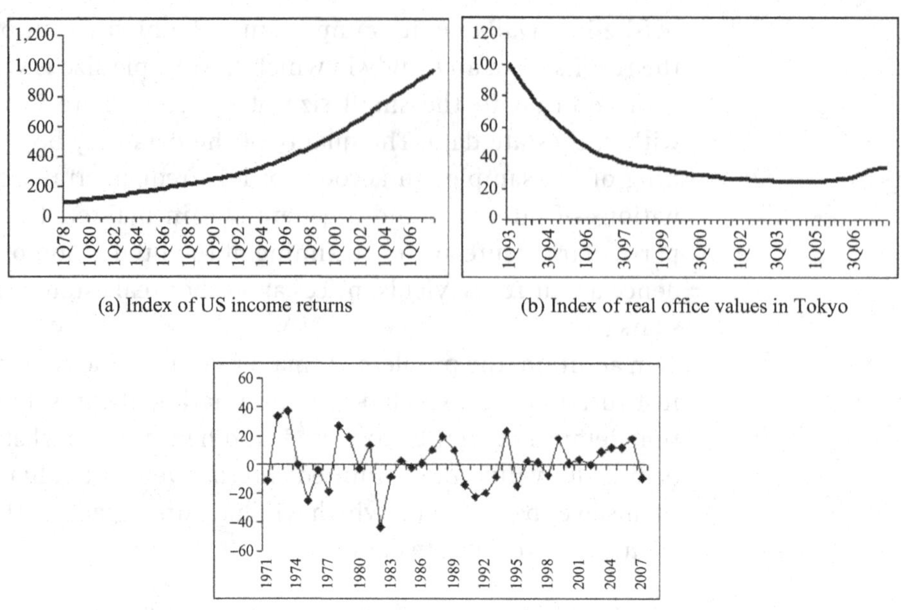

(a) Index of US income returns

(b) Index of real office values in Tokyo

(c) All-property risk premium

tests are likely to indicate, correctly, that the two variables are not related to one another. If the two variables are trending over time, however, the statistical techniques that we employ to determine whether there is a relationship between two series may indicate that the series are associated when in fact they are not. Thus the relationship that we appear to have observed between the two will be entirely spurious. This situation can be avoided by always ensuring that the time series employed for analysis are not trending (i.e. that they are *stationary*). Further details of this problem and how to solve it are the topic of chapter 12.

3.5.3 *Structural breaks*

Many time series in real estate seem to undergo episodes in which their behaviour changes quite dramatically compared to that exhibited previously. The behaviour of a series could change over time in terms of its mean value, its variability or the extent to which its current value is related to its previous value. The behaviour may change once and for all, usually known as a *structural break* in a series. Alternatively, it may change for a period of time before reverting to its original behaviour or switching to yet another style of behaviour, and the latter is typically termed a *regime shift* or *regime switch*.

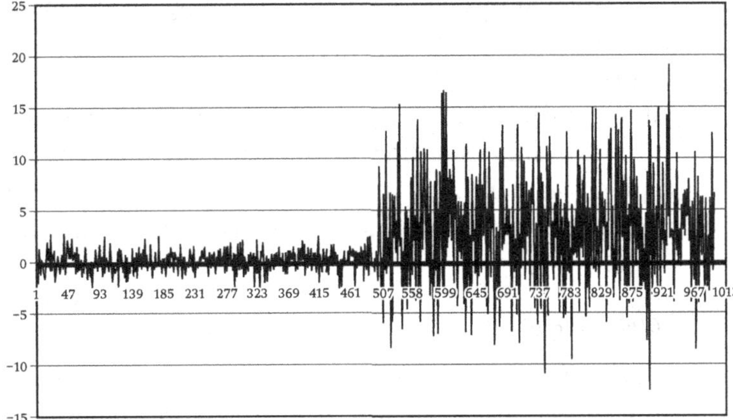

Figure 3.9 Sample time series plot illustrating a regime shift

Usually, very substantial changes in the properties of a series are attributed to large-scale events, such as wars, financial panics (e.g. a 'run on a bank'), significant changes in government policy (such as the introduction of an inflation target) or the relaxation of planning controls.

It is also true, however, that regime shifts can occur on a regular basis and at a higher frequency. Such changes may occur as a result of more subtle factors, but they can still lead to statistically important modifications in behaviour. An example would be the seasonal patterns often observed in housing market activity.

To give an illustration of the kind of shifts that may be seen to occur, figure 3.9 presents an extreme example. As can be seen from the figure, the behaviour of the series changes markedly at around observation 500. Not only does the series become much more variable than previously, its mean value is also substantially increased. Although this is a severe case that was generated using simulated data, clearly, in the face of such regime changes, a single model estimated over the whole sample covering the change would not be appropriate. One possible approach to this problem would be simply to split the data around the time of the change and to estimate separate models on each portion.

This method may be valid, but it is also likely to be wasteful of information. For example, even if there were enough observations in each sub-sample to estimate separate models, there would be an efficiency loss in having fewer observations in each of two samples than if all the observations were collected together. It may also be the case that only one characteristic of the series has changed – for example, the mean value of the series may have changed, leaving its other properties unaffected. In this case, it would be sensible to try to keep all the observations together, but to allow for the particular form of the structural change in the model-building process. Thus what is required is a set of models that allow all the observations in a series to be used for estimating a model, but also that the model is sufficiently flexible to allow different types of behaviour at different points in time. Examples of how to construct such models are presented in subsequent chapters, but suffice to say at this stage that structural breaks are a feature of series that need to be accounted for when building a valid model.

3.5.4 *Non-normality*

In order to test hypotheses about the underlying population parameters from the sample estimates, it is almost invariably necessary to make an assumption that the series under investigation[6] is normally distributed. The normality assumption is not only convenient in real estate theory (so that return and risk can be captured by the mean and variance, respectively, of returns) but also crucial in econometrics, so that the test statistics follow the required distributions. As highlighted above, an important result in statistics, known as *the central limit theorem* (CLT), shows that the sampling distribution of the mean will increasingly approximate a normal distribution as sample size increases, even if the original series (i.e. the y_i) are not normal. It therefore follows that, if we had made an assumption of normality but that this did not hold, we run the risk of making incorrect inferences if the sample size is not sufficiently large. Of course, this begs the question as to how big a sample has to be in order for it to be considered 'sufficiently large'; while there is no unique answer to this question, which would depend on the nature and characteristics of the underlying data, a sample in excess of around $N = 100$ observations is usually considered sufficient to invoke the central limit theorem. More detail on why the normality assumption is required, how to test for whether it holds or not and what to do if it does not is contained in chapter 6.

3.5.5 *Parametric and non-parametric statistics*

There are two types of testing methodologies commonly used in statistics, known as *parametric* and *non-parametric* approaches. All the tests described above and in subsequent chapters, which are based on assuming that a particular distribution holds, are examples of the former category. Non-parametric tests, on the other hand, are constructed quite differently and do not require any distributional assumptions. Thus such tests may be

[6] Actually, it is more commonly assumed that a *disturbance term* is normally distributed rather than the series under investigation, but this is discussed in the following chapter.

useful when the assumption of normality does not hold. Non-parametric approaches usually bring with them additional problems, however, and, most seriously, their lack of power (i.e. their lack of ability to reject the null hypothesis even when it is wrong) means that their usage is limited, and therefore they are not discussed further here. Interested readers are referred to the extensive but accessible treatment by Higgins (2003).

Key concepts

The key terms to be able to define and explain from this chapter are

- time series data
- continuous data
- cardinal, ordinal and nominal numbers
- arithmetic mean
- interquartile range
- correlation
- hypothesis test
- confidence interval
- cross-sectional data
- discrete data
- geometric mean
- variance
- covariance
- probability distribution
- test of significance

4 An overview of regression analysis

Learning outcomes

In this chapter, you will learn how to

- derive the OLS formulae for estimating parameters and their standard errors;
- explain the desirable properties that a good estimator should have;
- discuss the factors that affect the sizes of standard errors;
- test hypotheses using the test of significance and confidence interval approaches; and
- interpret *p*-values.

4.1 Chapter objectives

This chapter introduces the linear regression model and covers fundamental concepts in single-equation regression analysis. Regression analysis is important in itself for modelling and forecasting but it also lays the foundations to study and apply more complex methods, which we cover later in the book. In the real estate literature, regression analysis is used extensively. Problems with data availability have played a part in the continued popularity of linear regression modelling rather than more sophisticated procedures. In practice, regression analysis dominates the empirical modelling of real estate markets. The much-improved access to econometric packages, the ease they offer to run regressions and a greater availability of econometric skill in the real estate field have resulted in more quantitative modelling and a heavier use of single-equation regression models. Of course, data limitations (for example, long-term series may exist for rents but not for vacancy or measures of demand) have confined empirical investigations to standard regression models, which make lesser demands on the data than more general techniques. In addition, the ease of interpretation of the empirical results of single-equation regression models adds to their appeal with real estate analysts.

This chapter begins with the simple case of the bivariate regression. In a bivariate regression model, the variable we study is modelled by a single explanatory variable. Subsequently, we extend the analysis to multiple regression models, in which two or more variables explain the dependent variable. The estimation of bivariate or multiple variable models can provide valuable information to the analyst about the relationship of a real estate market series with economic, financial or other variables. Moreover, forecasting from a single-equation regression model can be less time-consuming than more complex approaches, and can give an analyst a benchmark forecast to assess the gains from more advanced techniques.

4.2 What is a regression model?

Regression analysis is almost certainly the most important tool at the real estate analyst's disposal. What is regression analysis, though? In very general terms, regression is concerned with describing and evaluating the *relationship between a given variable and one or more other variables.* More specifically, regression is an attempt to explain movements in a variable by reference to movements in one or more other variables.

To make this more concrete, denote the variable whose movements the regression seeks to explain by y and the variables that are used to explain those variations by $x_1, x_2, \ldots, x_k$. Hence, in this relatively simple set-up, it would be said that variations in k variables (the xs) cause changes in some other variable, y. This chapter limits itself to the case in which the model seeks to explain changes in only one variable y (although this restriction is removed in chapter 10).

There are various completely interchangeable names for y and the xs, and all these terms are used synonymously in this book (see box 4.1).

Box 4.1 Names for y and xs in regression models

Names for y	Names for the xs
Dependent variable	Independent variables
Regressand	Regressors
Effect variable	Causal variables
Explained variable	Explanatory variables
Left-hand side (LHS) variable	Right-hand side (RHS) variables

4.3 Regression versus correlation

All readers will be aware of the notion and definition of correlation, which was presented in the previous chapter. The correlation between two variables measures the *degree of linear association* between them. If it is stated that y and x are correlated, it means that y and x are being treated in a completely symmetrical way. Thus it is not implied that changes in x cause changes in y, or, indeed, that changes in y cause changes in x. Rather, it is simply stated that there is evidence for a linear relationship between the two variables, and that movements in the two are on average related, to an extent given by the correlation coefficient.

In regression, the dependent variable (y) and the independent variable(s) (xs) are treated very differently. The y variable is assumed to be random or 'stochastic' in some way – i.e. to have a *probability distribution*. The x variables are, however, assumed to have fixed ('non-stochastic') values in repeated samples. Regression as a tool is more flexible and more powerful than correlation.

4.4 Simple regression

For simplicity, suppose for now that it is believed that y depends on only one x variable. Again, of course, this is a severely restricted case, but the case of more explanatory variables is considered in the next chapter. Suppose that a researcher has some idea that there should be a relationship between two variables y and x, and that real estate theory suggests that an increase in x will lead to an increase in y. A sensible first stage to testing whether there is indeed an association between the variables would be to form a scatter plot of them. Suppose that the outcome of this plot is figure 4.1.

In this case, it appears that there is an approximate positive linear relationship between x and y, which means that increases in x are usually accompanied by increases in y, and that the relationship between them can be described approximately by a straight line. It would be possible to draw by hand onto the graph a line that appears to fit the data. The intercept and slope of the line fitted by eye could then be measured from the graph. In practice, however, such a method is likely to be laborious and inaccurate.

It would therefore be of interest to determine to what extent this relationship can be described by an equation that can be estimated using a defined procedure. It is possible to use the general equation for a straight line,

$$y = \alpha + \beta x \tag{4.1}$$

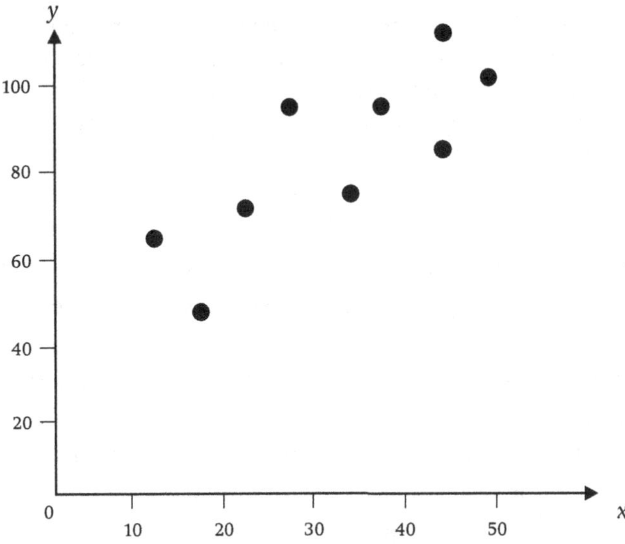

Figure 4.1 Scatter plot of two variables, y and x

to get the line that best 'fits' the data. The researcher would then be seeking to find the values of the parameters or coefficients, α and β, that would place the line as close as possible to all the data points taken together.

This equation ($y = \alpha + \beta x$) is an exact one, however. Assuming that this equation is appropriate, if the values of α and β had been calculated, then, given a value of x, it would be possible to determine with certainty what the value of y would be. Imagine – a model that says with complete certainty what the value of one variable will be given any value of the other.

Clearly this model is not realistic. Statistically, it would correspond to the case in which the model fitted the data perfectly – that is, all the data points lay exactly on a straight line. To make the model more realistic, a random disturbance term, denoted by u, is added to the equation, thus:

$$y_t = \alpha + \beta x_t + u_t \tag{4.2}$$

where the subscript $t\,(= 1, 2, 3, \ldots)$ denotes the observation number.

The disturbance term can capture a number of features (see box 4.2).

Box 4.2 Reasons for the inclusion of the disturbance term

- Even in the general case when there is more than one explanatory variable, some determinants of y_t will always in practice be omitted from the model. This might, for example, arise because the number of influences on y is too large to place in a single model, or because some determinants of y are unobservable or not measurable.
- There may be errors in the way that y is measured that cannot be modelled.

- There are bound to be random outside influences on y that, again, cannot be modelled. For example, natural disasters could affect real estate performance in a way that cannot be captured in a model and cannot be forecast reliably. Similarly, many researchers would argue that human behaviour has an inherent randomness and unpredictability!

How, then, are the appropriate values of α and β determined? α and β are chosen so that the (vertical) distances from the data points to the fitted lines are minimised (so that the line fits the data as closely as possible). The parameters are thus chosen to minimise collectively the (vertical) distances from the data points to the fitted line. This could be done by 'eyeballing' the data and, for each set of variables y and x, one could form a scatter plot and draw on a line that looks as if it fits the data well by hand, as in figure 4.2.

Note that it is the *vertical distances* that are usually minimised, rather than the horizontal distances or those taken perpendicular to the line. This arises as a result of the assumption that x is fixed in repeated samples, so that the problem becomes one of determining the appropriate model for y given (or conditional upon) the observed values of x.

This procedure may be acceptable if only indicative results are required, but of course this method, as well as being tedious, is likely to be imprecise. The most common method used to fit a line to the data is known as ordinary least squares (OLS). This approach forms the workhorse of econometric model estimation, and is discussed in detail in this and subsequent chapters.

Figure 4.2
Scatter plot of two variables with a line of best fit chosen by eye

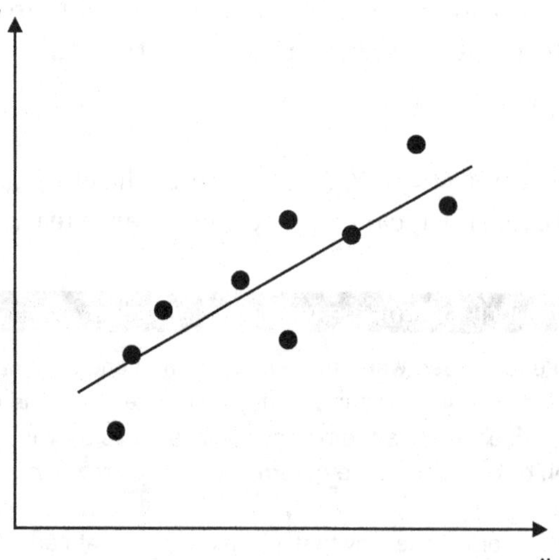

Figure 4.3
Method of OLS fitting a line to the data by minimising the sum of squared residuals

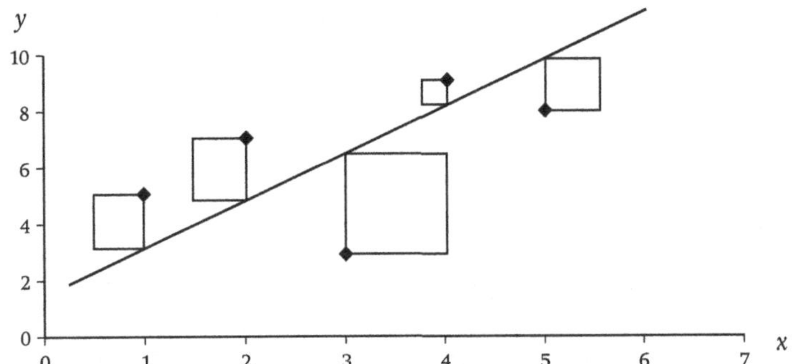

Two alternative estimation methods (for determining the appropriate values of the coefficients α and β) are the method of moments and the method of maximum likelihood. A generalised version of the method of moments, due to Hansen (1982), is popular, although the method of maximum likelihood is also widely employed.[1]

Suppose now, for ease of exposition, that the sample of data contains only five observations. The method of OLS entails taking each vertical distance from the point to the line, squaring it and then minimising the total sum of the areas of squares (hence 'least squares'), as shown in figure 4.3. This can be viewed as equivalent to minimising the sum of the areas of the squares drawn from the points to the line.

Tightening up the notation, let y_t denote the actual data point for observation t, $\hat{y}_t$ denote the fitted value from the regression line (in other words, for the given value of x of this observation t, $\hat{y}_t$ is the value for y which the model would have predicted; note that a hat [ˆ] over a variable or parameter is used to denote a value estimated by a model) and $\hat{u}_t$ denote the residual, which is the difference between the actual value of y and the value fitted by the model – i.e. $(y_t - \hat{y}_t)$. This is shown for just one observation t in figure 4.4.

What is done is to minimise the sum of the $\hat{u}_t^2$. The reason that the sum of the squared distances is minimised rather than, for example, finding the sum of $\hat{u}_t$ that is as close to zero as possible is that, in the latter case, some points will lie above the line while others lie below it. Then, when the sum to be made as close to zero as possible is formed, the points above the line would count as positive values, while those below would count as negatives. These distances will therefore in large part cancel each other out, which would mean that one could fit virtually any line to the data, so long as the sum of the distances of the points above the line and the sum of the distances of the points below the line were the same. In that case, there would not be

[1] Both methods are beyond the scope of this book, but see Brooks (2008, ch. 8) for a detailed discussion of the latter.

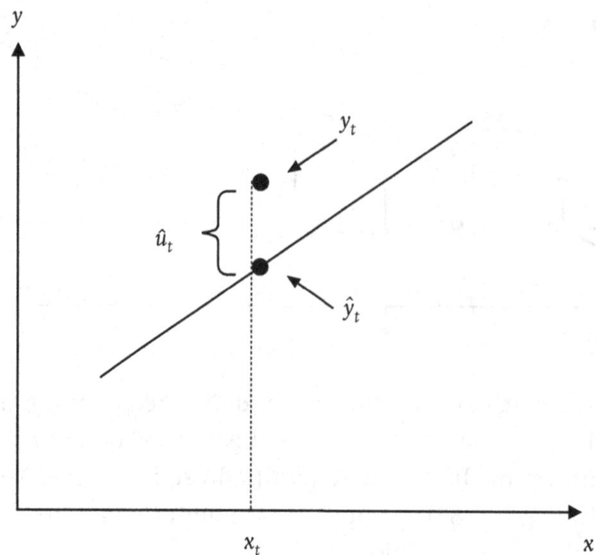

Figure 4.4
Plot of a single observation, together with the line of best fit, the residual and the fitted value

a unique solution for the estimated coefficients. In fact, any fitted line that goes through the mean of the observations (i.e. $\bar{x}$, $\bar{y}$) would set the sum of the $\hat{u}_t$ to zero. On the other hand, taking the squared distances ensures that all deviations that enter the calculation are positive and therefore do not cancel out.

Minimising the sum of squared distances is given by minimising $(\hat{u}_1^2 + \hat{u}_2^2 + \hat{u}_3^2 + \hat{u}_4^2 + \hat{u}_5^2)$, or minimising

$$\left(\sum_{t=1}^{5} \hat{u}_t^2\right)$$

This sum is known as the *residual sum of squares* (RSS) or the sum of squared residuals. What is $\hat{u}_t$, though? Again, it is the difference between the actual point and the line, $y_t - \hat{y}_t$. So minimising $\sum_t \hat{u}_t^2$ is equivalent to minimising $\sum_t (y_t - \hat{y}_t)^2$.

Letting $\hat{\alpha}$ and $\hat{\beta}$ denote the values of α and β selected by minimising the RSS, respectively, the equation for the fitted line is given by $\hat{y}_t = \hat{\alpha} + \hat{\beta} x_t$. Now let L denote the RSS, which is also known as a *loss function*. Take the summation over all the observations – i.e. from $t = 1$ to T, where T is the number of observations:

$$L = \sum_{t=1}^{T} (y_t - \hat{y}_t)^2 = \sum_{t=1}^{T} (y_t - \hat{\alpha} - \hat{\beta} x_t)^2 \tag{4.3}$$

L is minimised with respect to (w.r.t.) $\hat{\alpha}$ and $\hat{\beta}$, to find the values of α and β that minimise the residual sum of squares to give the line that is closest to the data. So L is differentiated w.r.t. $\hat{\alpha}$ and $\hat{\beta}$, setting the first derivatives to zero. A derivation of the ordinary least squares estimator is given in the appendix to this chapter. The coefficient estimators for the slope and the intercept are given by

$$\hat{\beta} = \frac{\sum x_t y_t - T\bar{x}\bar{y}}{\sum x_t^2 - T\bar{x}^2} \quad (4.4) \qquad \hat{\alpha} = \bar{y} - \hat{\beta}\bar{x} \quad (4.5)$$

Equations (4.4) and (4.5) state that, given only the sets of observations x_t and y_t, it is always possible to calculate the values of the two parameters, $\hat{\alpha}$ and $\hat{\beta}$, that best fit the set of data. To reiterate, this method of finding the optimum is known as OLS. It is also worth noting that it is obvious from the equation for $\hat{\alpha}$ that the regression line will go through the mean of the observations – i.e. that the point $(\bar{x}, \bar{y})$ lies on the regression line.

4.5 Some further terminology

4.5.1 *The data-generating process, the population regression function and the sample regression function*

The population regression function (PRF) is a description of the model that is thought to be generating the actual data and it represents the *true relationship between the variables*. The population regression function is also known as the data-generating process (DGP). The PRF embodies the true values of α and β, and is expressed as

$$y_t = \alpha + \beta x_t + u_t \quad (4.6)$$

Note that there is a disturbance term in this equation, so that, even if one had at one's disposal the entire population of observations on x and y, it would still in general not be possible to obtain a perfect fit of the line to the data. In some textbooks, a distinction is drawn between the PRF (the underlying true relationship between y and x) and the DGP (the process describing the way that the actual observations on y come about), but, in this book, the two terms are used synonymously.

The sample regression function (SRF) is the relationship that has been estimated using the sample observations, and is often written as

$$\hat{y}_t = \hat{\alpha} + \hat{\beta} x_t \quad (4.7)$$

Notice that there is no error or residual term in (4.7); all this equation states is that, given a particular value of x, multiplying it by $\hat{\beta}$ and adding $\hat{\alpha}$ will give the model fitted or expected value for y, denoted $\hat{y}$. It is also possible to write

$$y_t = \hat{\alpha} + \hat{\beta} x_t + \hat{u}_t \tag{4.8}$$

Equation (4.8) splits the observed value of y into two components: the fitted value from the model, and a residual term.

The SRF is used to infer likely values of the PRF. That is, the estimates $\hat{\alpha}$ and $\hat{\beta}$ are constructed, for the sample of data at hand, but what is really of interest is the true relationship between x and y – in other words, the PRF is what is really wanted, but all that is ever available is the SRF! What can be done, however, is to say how likely it is, given the figures calculated for $\hat{\alpha}$ and $\hat{\beta}$, that the corresponding population parameters take on certain values.

4.5.2 *Estimator or estimate?*

Estimators are the formulae used to *calculate the coefficients* – for example, the expressions given in (4.4) and (4.5) above, while the estimates, on the other hand, are the *actual numerical values for the coefficients* that are obtained from the sample.

Example 4.1

This example uses office rent and employment data of annual frequency. These are national series for the United Kingdom and they are expressed as growth rates – that is, the year-on-year (yoy) percentage change. The rent series is expressed in real terms – that is, the impact of inflation has been extracted. The sample period starts in 1979 and the end value is for 2005, giving twenty-seven annual observations. The national office data provide an 'average' picture in the growth of real rents in the United Kingdom. It is expected that regions and individual markets have performed around this growth path. The source of the rent series is constructed by the authors using UK office rent series from a number of real estate consultancies. The employment series is that for finance and business services published by the Office for National Statistics (ONS).

Assume that the analyst has some intuition that employment (in particular, employment growth) drives growth in real office rents. After all, in the existing literature, employment series (service sector employment or financial and business services employment) receive empirical support as a direct or indirect driver of office rents (see Giussani, Hsia and Tsolacos, 1993, D'Arcy, McGough and Tsolacos, 1997, and Hendershott, MacGregor and White, 2002). Employment in business and finance is a proxy for business conditions among firms occupying office space and their demand for office

Figure 4.5
Plot of the two variables

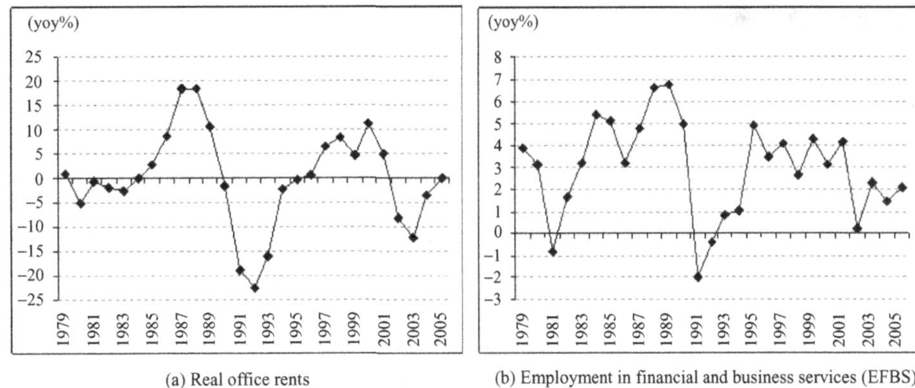

(a) Real office rents (b) Employment in financial and business services (EFBS)

space. Stronger employment growth will increase demand for office space and put upward pressure on rents. The relationship between economic drivers and rents is not as simple, however. Other influences can be important – for example, how quickly the vacancy rate adjusts to changes in the demand for office space, and, in turn, how rents respond to changing vacancy levels; how much more intensively firms utilise their space and what spare accommodation capacity they have; whether firms can afford a higher rent; and so forth. Nonetheless, a lack of good-quality data (for example, national office vacancy data in the United Kingdom) can necessitate the direct study of economic series and rents, as we discuss further in chapter 6.

A starting point to study the relationship between employment and real rent growth is a process of familiarisation with the path of the series through time (and possibly an examination of their statistical properties, although we do not do so in this example), and the two series are plotted in figure 4.5.

The growth rate of office rents fluctuated between nearly −25 per cent and 20 per cent during the sample period. This magnitude of variation in the growth rate is attributable to the severe cycle of the late 1980/early 1990s in the United Kingdom that also characterised office markets in other countries. The amplitude of the rent cycle in more recent years has lessened. Employment growth in financial and business services has been mostly positive in the United Kingdom, the exception being three years (1981, 1991 and 1992) when it was negative. The UK economy experienced a prolonged recession in the early 1990s. We observe greater volatility in employment growth in the early part of the sample than later. Panels (a) and (b) of figure 4.5 indicate that the two series have a general tendency to move together over time so that they follow roughly the same cyclical pattern. The scatter plot of employment and real rent growth, shown in figure 4.6, reveals a positive relationship that conforms with our expectations. This positive

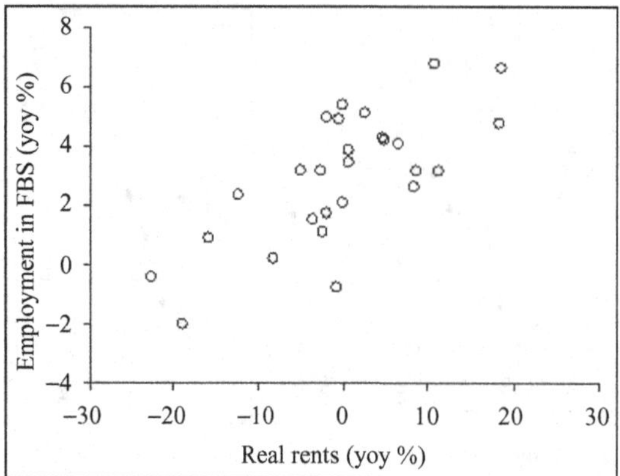

Figure 4.6 Scatter plot of rent and employment growth

relationship is also confirmed if we calculate the correlation coefficient, which is 0.72.

The population regression function in our example is

$$RRg_t = \alpha + \beta EFBSg_t + u_t \tag{4.9}$$

where RRg_t is the growth in real rents at time t and $EFBSg_t$ is the growth in employment in financial and business services at time t. Equation (4.9) embodies the true values of α and β, and u_t is the disturbance term. Estimating equation (4.9) over the sample period 1979 to 2005, we obtain the sample regression equation

$$R\hat{R}g_t = \hat{\alpha} + \hat{\beta} EFBSg_t = -9.62 + 3.27 EFBSg_t \tag{4.10}$$

The coefficients $\hat{\alpha}$ and $\hat{\beta}$ are computed based on the formulae (4.4) and (4.5) – that is,

$$\hat{\beta} = \frac{\sum x_t y_t - T\bar{x}\bar{y}}{\sum x_t^2 - T\bar{x}^2} = \frac{415.64 - 6.55}{363.60 - 238.37} = 3.27$$

and

$$\hat{\alpha} = 0.08 - 3.27 \times 2.97 = -9.62$$

The sign of the coefficient estimate for β (3.27) is positive. When employment growth is positive, real rent growth is also expected to be positive. If we examine the data, however, we observe periods of positive employment growth associated with negative real rent growth (e.g. 1980, 1993, 1994, 2004). Such inconsistencies describe a minority of data points in the sample, otherwise the sign on the employment coefficient would not have been positive. Thus it is worth noting that the regression estimate indicates that the relationship will be positive on average (loosely speaking, 'most of the time'), but not necessarily positive during every period.

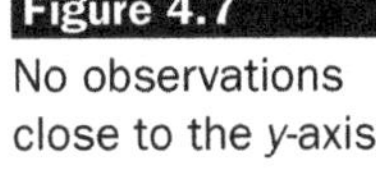
Figure 4.7 No observations close to the *y*-axis

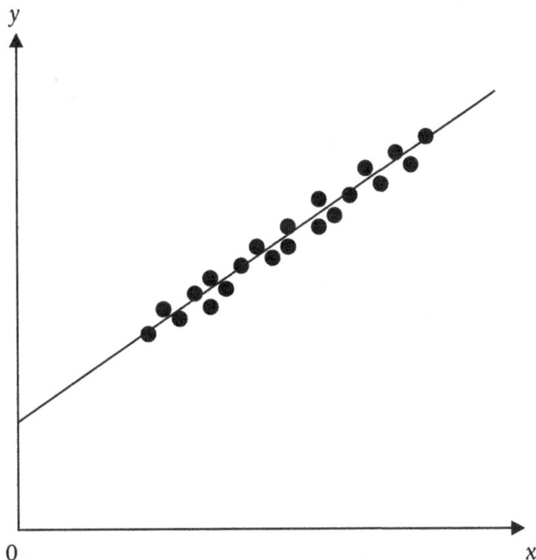

The coefficient estimate of 3.27 is interpreted as saying that, if employment growth changes by one percentage point (from, say, 1.4 per cent to 2.4 per cent – i.e. employment growth accelerates by one percentage point), real rent growth will tend to change by 3.27 percentage points (from, say, 2 per cent to 5.27 per cent). The computed value of 3.27 per cent is an average estimate over the sample period. In reality, when employment increases by 1 per cent, real rent growth will increase by over 3.27 per cent in some periods but less than 3.27 per cent in others. This is because all the other factors that affect rent growth do not remain constant from one period to the next. It is important to remember that, in our model, real rent growth depends on employment growth but also on the error term u_t, which embodies other influences on rents. The intercept term implies that employment growth of zero will tend on average to result in a fall in real rent growth by 9.62 per cent.

A word of caution is in order, however, concerning the reliability of estimates of the coefficient on the constant term. Although the strict interpretation of the intercept is indeed as stated above, in practice it is often the case that there are no values of x (employment growth, in our example) close to zero in the sample. In such instances, estimates of the value of the intercept will be unreliable. For example, consider figure 4.7, which demonstrates a situation in which no points are close to the y-axis.

In such cases, one could not expect to obtain robust estimates of the value of y when x is zero, as all the information in the sample pertains to the case in which x is considerably larger than zero.

Figure 4.8 Actual and fitted values and residuals for *RR* regression

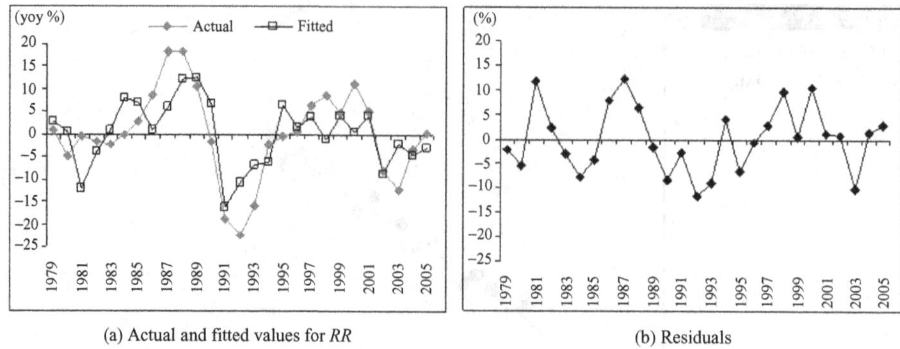

(a) Actual and fitted values for *RR* (b) Residuals

Similar caution should be exercised when producing predictions for y using values of x that are a long way outside the range of values in the sample. In example 4.1, employment growth takes values between −1.98 per cent and 6.74 per cent, only twice taking a value over 6 per cent. As a result, it would not be advisable to use this model to determine real rent growth if employment were to shrink by 4 per cent, for instance, or to increase by 8 per cent.

On the basis of the coefficient estimates of equation (4.10), we can generate the fitted values and examine how successfully the model replicates the actual real rent growth series. We calculate the fitted values for real rent growth as follows:

$$
\begin{aligned}
R\hat{R}g_{79} &= -9.62 + 3.27 \times EFBSg_{79} = -9.62 + 3.27 \times 3.85 = 2.96 \\
R\hat{R}g_{80} &= -9.62 + 3.27 \times EFBSg_{80} = -9.62 + 3.27 \times 3.15 = 0.68 \\
&\vdots \qquad\qquad\qquad\qquad \vdots \qquad\qquad\qquad\qquad \vdots \\
R\hat{R}g_{05} &= -9.62 + 3.27 \times EFBSg_{05} = -9.62 + 3.27 \times 2.08 = -2.83
\end{aligned} \tag{4.11}
$$

The plot of the actual and fitted values is given in panel (a) of figure 4.8. This figure also plots, in panel (b), the residuals – that is, the difference between the actual and fitted values.

The fitted values series replicates most of the important features of the actual values series. In particular years we observe a larger divergence – a finding that should be expected, as the environment (economic, real estate market) within which the relationship between rent growth and employment growth is studied, is changing. The difference between the actual and fitted values produces the estimated residuals. The properties of the residuals are of great significance in evaluating a model. Key misspecification tests are performed on these residuals. We study the properties of the residuals in detail in the following two chapters.

4.6 Linearity and possible forms for the regression function

In order to use OLS, a model that is *linear* is required. This means that, in the simple bivariate case, the relationship between x and y must be capable of being expressed diagramatically using a straight line. More specifically, the model must be *linear in the parameters* (α and β), but it does not necessarily have to be *linear in the variables* (y and x). By 'linear in the parameters', it is meant that the parameters are not multiplied together, divided, squared or cubed, etc.

Models that are not linear in the variables can often be made to take a linear form by applying a suitable transformation or manipulation. For example, consider the following exponential regression model:

$$Y_t = AX_t^{\beta} e^{u_t} \tag{4.12}$$

Taking logarithms of both sides, applying the laws of logs and rearranging the RHS gives

$$\ln\ Y_t = \ln(A) + \beta \ln X_t + u_t \tag{4.13}$$

where A and β are parameters to be estimated. Now let $\alpha = \ln(A)$, $y_t = \ln Y_t$ and $x_t = \ln X_t$:

$$y_t = \alpha + \beta x_t + u_t \tag{4.14}$$

This is known as an *exponential regression model*, since y varies according to some exponent (power) function of x. In fact, when a regression equation is expressed in 'double logarithmic form', which means that both the dependent and the independent variables are natural logarithms, the coefficient estimates are interpreted as elasticities. Thus a coefficient estimate of 1.2 for $\hat{\beta}$ in (4.13) or (4.14) is interpreted as stating that 'a rise in x of 1 per cent will lead on average, everything else being equal, to a rise in y of 1.2 per cent'. Conversely, for y and x in levels rather than logarithmic form (e.g. equation (4.6)), the coefficients denote unit changes as described above.

Similarly, if theory suggests that x should be inversely related to y according to a model of the form

$$y_t = \alpha + \frac{\beta}{x_t} + u_t \tag{4.15}$$

the regression can be estimated using OLS by setting

$$z_t = \frac{1}{x_t}$$

and regressing y on a constant and z. Clearly, then, a surprisingly varied array of models can be estimated using OLS by making suitable transformations to the variables. On the other hand, some models are intrinsically non-linear – e.g.

$$y_t = \alpha + \beta x_t^{\gamma} + u_t \tag{4.16}$$

Such models cannot be estimated using OLS, but might be estimable using a non-linear estimation method.[2]

4.7 The assumptions underlying the classical linear regression model

The model $y_t = \alpha + \beta x_t + u_t$ that has been derived above, together with the assumptions listed below, is known as the *classical linear regression model*. Data for x_t are observable, but, since y_t also depends on u_t, it is necessary to be specific about how the u_ts are generated. The set of assumptions shown in box 4.3 are usually made concerning the u_ts, the unobservable error or disturbance terms.

Box 4.3 Assumptions concerning disturbance terms and their interpretation

Technical notation	Interpretation
(1) $E(u_t) = 0$	The errors have zero mean.
(2) $\text{var}(u_t) = \sigma^2 < \infty$	The variance of the errors is constant and finite over all values of x_t.
(3) $\text{cov}(u_i, u_j) = 0$	The errors are statistically independent of one another.
(4) $\text{cov}(u_t, x_t) = 0$	There is no relationship between the error and corresponding x variable.

Note that no assumptions are made concerning their observable counterparts, the estimated model's residuals. As long as assumption (1) holds, assumption (4) can be equivalently written $E(x_t u_t) = 0$. Both formulations imply that the regressor is orthogonal to (i.e. unrelated to) the error term. An alternative assumption to (4), which is slightly stronger, is that the x_ts are non-stochastic or fixed in repeated samples. This means that there is no sampling variation in x_t, and that its value is determined outside the model.

A fifth assumption is required to make valid inferences about the population parameters (the actual α and β) from the sample parameters ($\hat{\alpha}$ and $\hat{\beta}$) estimated using a finite amount of data:

(5) $u_t \sim N(0, \sigma^2)$	u_t is normally distributed.

[2] See chapter 8 of Brooks (2008) for a discussion of one such method, maximum likelihood estimation.

4.8 Properties of the OLS estimator

If assumptions (1) to (4) hold, then the estimators $\hat{\alpha}$ and $\hat{\beta}$ determined by OLS will have a number of desirable properties; such an estimator is known as a best linear unbiased estimator (BLUE). What does this acronym represent?

- 'Estimator' means that $\hat{\alpha}$ and $\hat{\beta}$ are estimators of the true value of α and β.
- 'Linear' means that $\hat{\alpha}$ and $\hat{\beta}$ are linear estimators, meaning that the formulae for $\hat{\alpha}$ and $\hat{\beta}$ are linear combinations of the random variables (in this case, y).
- 'Unbiased' means that, on average, the actual values of $\hat{\alpha}$ and $\hat{\beta}$ will be equal to their true values.
- 'Best' means that the OLS estimator $\hat{\beta}$ has minimum variance among the class of linear unbiased estimators; the Gauss–Markov theorem proves that the OLS estimator is best by examining an arbitrary alternative linear unbiased estimator and showing in all cases that it must have a variance no smaller than the OLS estimator.

Under assumptions (1) to (4) listed above, the OLS estimator can be shown to have the desirable properties that it is consistent, unbiased and efficient. This is, essentially, another way of stating that the estimator is BLUE. These three properties will now be discussed in turn.

4.8.1 *Consistency*

The least squares estimators $\hat{\alpha}$ and $\hat{\beta}$ are consistent. One way to state this algebraically for $\hat{\beta}$ (with the obvious modifications made for $\hat{\alpha}$) is

$$\lim_{T\to\infty} \Pr\left[|\hat{\beta} - \beta| > \delta\right] = 0 \quad \forall\, \delta > 0 \tag{4.17}$$

This is a technical way of stating that the probability (Pr) that $\hat{\beta}$ is more than some arbitrary fixed distance δ away from its true value tends to zero as the sample size tends to infinity, for all positive values of δ. In the limit (i.e. for an infinite number of observations), the probability of the estimator being different from the true value is zero – that is, the estimates will converge to their true values as the sample size increases to infinity. Consistency is thus a large-sample, or asymptotic, property. The assumptions that $\mathrm{E}(x_t u_t) = 0$ and $\mathrm{var}(u_t) = \sigma^2 < \infty$ are sufficient to derive the consistency of the OLS estimator.

4.8.2 *Unbiasedness*

The least squares estimates of $\hat{\alpha}$ and $\hat{\beta}$ are unbiased. That is,

$$E(\hat{\alpha}) = \alpha \tag{4.18}$$

and

$$E(\hat{\beta}) = \beta \tag{4.19}$$

Thus, on average, the estimated values for the coefficients will be equal to their true values – that is, there is no systematic overestimation or underestimation of the true coefficients. To prove this also requires the assumption that $E(u_t) = 0$. Clearly, unbiasedness is a stronger condition than consistency, since it holds for small as well as large samples (i.e. for all sample sizes).

4.8.3 *Efficiency*

An estimator $\hat{\beta}$ of a parameter β is said to be efficient if no other estimator has a smaller variance. Broadly speaking, if the estimator is efficient, it will be minimising the probability that it is a long way off from the true value of β. In other words, if the estimator is 'best', the uncertainty associated with estimation will be minimised for the class of linear unbiased estimators. A technical way to state this would be to say that an efficient estimator would have a probability distribution that is narrowly dispersed around the true value.

4.9 Precision and standard errors

Any set of regression estimates $\hat{\alpha}$ and $\hat{\beta}$ are specific to the sample used in their estimation. In other words, if a different sample of data was selected from within the population, the data points (the x_t and y_t) will be different, leading to different values of the OLS estimates.

Recall that the OLS estimators ($\hat{\alpha}$ and $\hat{\beta}$) are given by (4.4) and (4.5). It would be desirable to have an idea of how 'good' these estimates of α and β are, in the sense of having some measure of the reliability or precision of the estimators ($\hat{\alpha}$ and $\hat{\beta}$). It is therefore useful to know whether one can have confidence in the estimates, and whether they are likely to vary much from one sample to another sample within the given population. An idea of the sampling variability and hence of the precision of the estimates can be calculated using only the sample of data available. This estimate of the precision of a coefficient is given by its *standard error*. Given assumptions (1) to (4) above, valid estimators of the standard errors can be shown to be given by

$$SE(\hat{\alpha}) = s\sqrt{\frac{\sum x_t^2}{T\sum (x_t - \bar{x})^2}} = s\sqrt{\frac{\sum x_t^2}{T\left(\left(\sum x_t^2\right) - T\bar{x}^2\right)}} \tag{4.20}$$

$$SE(\hat{\beta}) = s\sqrt{\frac{1}{\sum (x_t - \bar{x})^2}} = s\sqrt{\frac{1}{\sum x_t^2 - T\bar{x}^2}} \tag{4.21}$$

where s is the estimated standard deviation of the residuals (see below). These formulae are derived in the appendix to this chapter.

It is worth noting that the standard errors give only a general indication of the likely accuracy of the regression parameters. They do not show how accurate a particular set of coefficient estimates is. If the standard errors are small, it shows that the coefficients are likely to be precise on average, not how precise they are for this particular sample. Thus standard errors give a measure of the *degree of uncertainty* in the estimated values for the coefficients. It can be seen that they are a function of the actual observations on the explanatory variable, x, the sample size, T, and another term, s. The last of these is an estimate of the standard deviation of the disturbance term. The actual variance of the disturbance term is usually denoted by σ^2. How can an estimate of σ^2 be obtained?

4.9.1 *Estimating the variance of the error term (σ^2)*

From elementary statistics, the variance of a random variable u_t is given by

$$\text{var}(u_t) = \text{E}[(u_t) - \text{E}(u_t)]^2 \tag{4.22}$$

Assumption (1) of the CLRM was that the expected or average value of the errors is zero. Under this assumption, (4.22) above reduces to

$$\text{var}(u_t) = \text{E}\left[u_t^2\right] \tag{4.23}$$

What is required, therefore, is an estimate of the average value of u_t^2, which could be calculated as

$$s^2 = \frac{1}{T}\sum u_t^2 \tag{4.24}$$

Unfortunately, (4.24) is not workable, since u_t is a series of population disturbances, which is not observable. Thus the sample counterpart to u_t, which is $\hat{u}_t$, is used:

$$s^2 = \frac{1}{T}\sum \hat{u}_t^2 \tag{4.25}$$

This estimator is a biased estimator of σ^2, though. An unbiased estimator of s^2 is given by

$$s^2 = \frac{\sum \hat{u}_t^2}{T-2} \tag{4.26}$$

where $\sum \hat{u}_t^2$ is the residual sum of squares, so that the quantity of relevance for the standard error formulae is the square root of (4.26):

$$s = \sqrt{\frac{\sum \hat{u}_t^2}{T-2}} \tag{4.27}$$

s is also known as the standard error of the regression or the standard error of the estimate. It is sometimes used as a broad measure of the fit of the regression equation. Everything else being equal, the smaller this quantity is, the closer the fit of the line is to the actual data.

4.9.2 *Some comments on the standard error estimators*

It is possible, of course, to derive the formulae for the standard errors of the coefficient estimates from first principles using some algebra, and this is left to the appendix to this chapter. Some general intuition is now given as to why the formulae for the standard errors given by (4.20) and (4.21) contain the terms that they do and in the form that they do. The presentation offered in box 4.4 loosely follows that of Hill, Griffiths and Judge (1997), which is very clear.

Box 4.4 Standard error estimators

(1) The larger the sample size, T, the smaller the coefficient standard errors will be. T appears explicitly in SE($\hat{\alpha}$) and implicitly in SE($\hat{\beta}$). T appears implicitly as the sum $\sum (x_t - \bar{x})^2$ is from $t = 1$ to T. The reason for this is simply that, at least for now, it is assumed that every observation on a series represents a piece of useful information that can be used to help determine the coefficient estimates. Therefore, the larger the size of the sample the more information will have been used in the estimation of the parameters, and hence the more confidence will be placed in those estimates.
(2) Both SE($\hat{\alpha}$) and SE($\hat{\beta}$) depend on s^2 (or s). Recall from above that s^2 is the estimate of the error variance. The larger this quantity is, the more dispersed the residuals are, and so the greater the uncertainty is in the model. If s^2 is large, the data points are, collectively, a long way away from the line.

Figure 4.9 Effect on the standard errors of the coefficient estimates when $(x_t - \bar{x})$ are narrowly dispersed

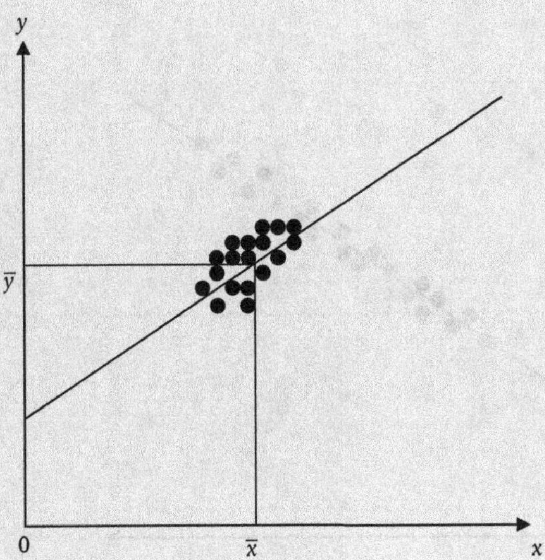

Figure 4.10 Effect on the standard errors of the coefficient estimates when $(x_t - \bar{x})$ are widely dispersed

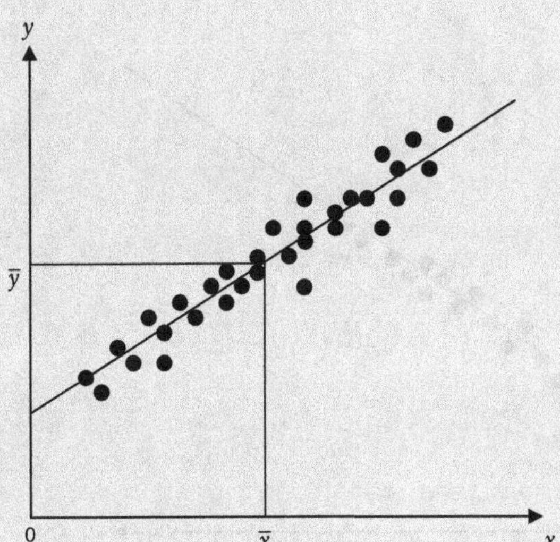

(3) The sum of the squares of the x_t about their mean appears in both formulae – since $\sum (x_t - \bar{x})^2$ appears in the denominators. The larger the sum of squares the smaller the coefficient variances. Consider what happens if $\sum (x_t - \bar{x})^2$ is small or large, as shown in figures 4.9 and 4.10, respectively.

In figure 4.9, the data are close together, so that $\sum (x_t - \bar{x})^2$ is small. In this first case, it is more difficult to determine with any degree of certainty exactly where the line should be. On the other hand, in figure 4.10, the points are widely dispersed across a long section of the line, so that one could hold more confidence in the estimates in this case.

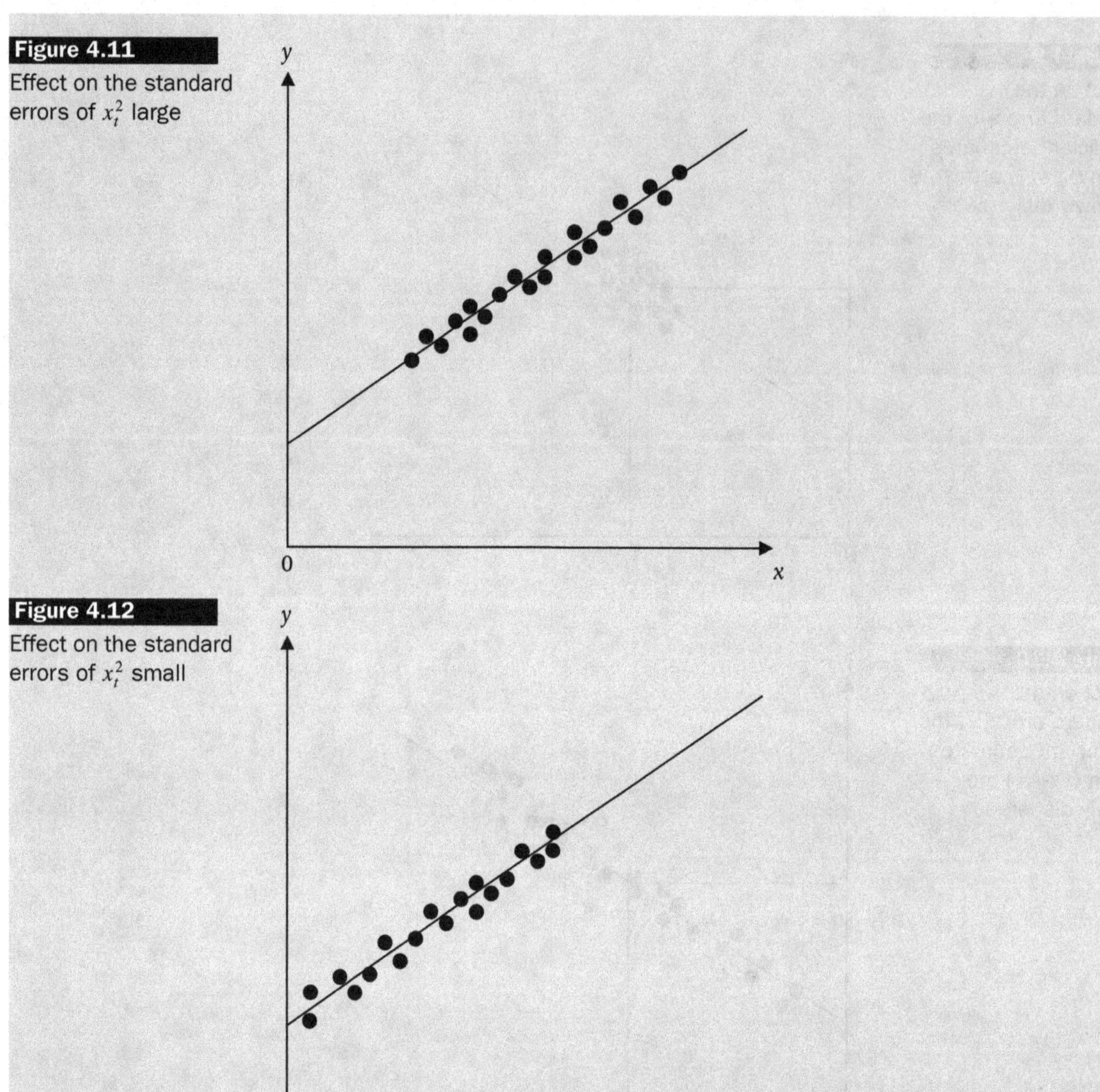

Figure 4.11 Effect on the standard errors of x_t^2 large

Figure 4.12 Effect on the standard errors of x_t^2 small

(4) The term $\sum x_t^2$ affects only the intercept standard error and not the slope standard error. The reason is that $\sum x_t^2$ measures how far the points are away from the y-axis. Consider figures 4.11 and 4.12.

In figure 4.11, all the points are bunched a long way away from the y-axis, which makes it more difficult to estimate accurately the point at which the estimated line crosses the y-axis (the intercept). In figure 4.12, the points collectively are closer to the y-axis, and hence it is easier to determine where the line actually crosses the axis. Note that this intuition will work only in the case in which all the x_t are positive!

Example 4.2

We now compute the standard error of the regression and the standard errors for the coefficients of equation (4.10). Based on the values $\sum \hat{u}_t^2 = 1214.20$ and $T = 27$, the standard error of this equation is

$$s = \sqrt{\frac{\sum \hat{u}_t^2}{T-2}} = 6.97$$

We use the estimate for the standard error of the regression (s) to calculate the standard error of the estimators $\hat{\alpha}$ and $\hat{\beta}$. For the calculation of $\text{SE}(\hat{\beta})$, we have $s = 6.97$, $\sum EFBS_t^2 = 363.60$, $T \times \overline{EFBS}^2 = 238.37$, and therefore $\text{SE}(\hat{\beta}) = 0.62$ and $\text{SE}(\hat{\alpha}) = 2.29$.

With the standard errors calculated, the results for equation (4.10) are written as

$$\begin{aligned} R\hat{R}g_t &= \underset{(2.29)}{-9.62} + \underset{(0.62)}{3.27}EFBSg_t \end{aligned} \tag{4.28}$$

The standard error estimates are usually placed in parentheses under the relevant coefficient estimates.

4.10 Statistical inference and the classical linear regression model

Chapter 3 has introduced the classical framework for inference from the sample to the population. Naturally, it will often also be of interest to undertake hypothesis tests in the context of the parameters in a regression model. While the underlying concepts are the same as in the previous chapter, we now proceed to explain how they operate in this slightly different environment. As a result, the steps involved in making inferences using the test of significance and the confidence interval approaches are described again, since the formulae involved are different. First, though, we need to discuss the distributions that the test statistics will follow in a regression-based framework, and therefore from where we can obtain the required critical values.

4.10.1 The probability distribution of the least squares estimators

In order to test hypotheses, assumption (5) of the CLRM must be used, namely that $u_t \sim \text{N}(0, \sigma^2)$ – i.e. that the error term is normally distributed. The normal distribution is a convenient one to use, for it involves only two parameters (its mean and variance). This makes the algebra involved in statistical inference considerably simpler than it otherwise would have been. Since y_t depends partially on u_t, it can be stated that, if u_t is normally distributed, y_t will also be normally distributed.

Further, since the least squares estimators are linear combinations of the random variables – i.e. $\hat{\beta} = \sum w_t y_t$, where w_t are effectively weights – and since the weighted sum of normal random variables is also normally distributed, it can be said that the coefficient estimates will also be normally distributed. Thus

$$\hat{\alpha} \sim \mathrm{N}(\alpha, \mathrm{var}(\alpha)) \quad \text{and} \quad \hat{\beta} \sim \mathrm{N}(\beta, \mathrm{var}(\beta))$$

Will the coefficient estimates still follow a normal distribution if the errors do not follow a normal distribution? Briefly, the answer is usually 'Yes', provided that the other assumptions of the CLRM hold, and the sample size is sufficiently large. The issue of non-normality, how to test for it, and its consequences is discussed further in chapter 6.

Standard normal variables can be constructed from $\hat{\alpha}$ and $\hat{\beta}$ by subtracting the mean and dividing by the square root of the variance:

$$\frac{\hat{\alpha} - \alpha}{\sqrt{\mathrm{var}(\alpha)}} \sim \mathrm{N}(0, 1) \quad \text{and} \quad \frac{\hat{\beta} - \beta}{\sqrt{\mathrm{var}(\beta)}} \sim \mathrm{N}(0, 1)$$

The square roots of the coefficient variances are the standard errors. Unfortunately, the standard errors of the true coefficient values under the PRF are never known; all that is available are their sample counterparts, the calculated standard errors of the coefficient estimates, $SE(\hat{\alpha})$ and $SE(\hat{\beta})$. Replacing the true values of the standard errors with the sample estimated versions induces another source of uncertainty, and also means that the standardised statistics follow a t-distribution with $T - 2$ degrees of freedom (defined below) rather than a normal distribution, so

$$\frac{\hat{\alpha} - \alpha}{SE(\hat{\alpha})} \sim t_{T-2} \quad \text{and} \quad \frac{\hat{\beta} - \beta}{SE(\hat{\beta})} \sim t_{T-2}$$

This result is not formally proved here. For a formal proof, see Hill, Griffiths and Judge (1997, pp. 88–90).

In this context, the number of degrees of freedom can be interpreted as the number of pieces of additional information beyond the minimum requirement. If two parameters are estimated (α and β – the intercept and the slope of the line, respectively), a minimum of two observations are required to fit this line to the data. As the number of degrees of freedom increases, the critical values in the tables decrease in absolute terms, as less caution is required and one can be more confident that the results

Box 4.5 Conducting a test of significance

Assume the regression equation is given by $y_t = \alpha + \beta x_t + u_t$, $t = 1, 2, \ldots, T$.

(1) Estimate $\hat{\alpha}$, $\hat{\beta}$ and $SE(\hat{\alpha})$, $SE(\hat{\beta})$.

(2) Calculate the test statistic. This is given by the formula

$$test\ statistic = \frac{\hat{\beta} - \beta^*}{SE(\hat{\beta})} \tag{4.29}$$

where β^* is the value of β under the null hypothesis. The null hypothesis is H_0: $\beta = \beta^*$ and the alternative hypothesis is H_1: $\beta \neq \beta^*$ (for a two-sided test).

(3) A tabulated distribution with which to compare the estimated test statistics is required. Test statistics derived in this way can be shown to follow a t-distribution with $T - 2$ degrees of freedom.

(4) Choose a 'significance level', often denoted α (note that this is *not* the same as the regression intercept coefficient). It is conventional to use a significance level of 5 per cent.

(5) Given a significance level, a *rejection region* and a *non-rejection region* can be determined.

(6) Use the t-tables to obtain a critical value or values with which to compare the test statistic.

(7) Finally, perform the test. If the test statistic lies in the rejection region, then reject the null hypothesis (H_0); otherwise, do not reject H_0.

Box 4.6 Carrying out a hypothesis test using confidence intervals

(1) Calculate $\hat{\alpha}$, $\hat{\beta}$ and $SE(\hat{\alpha})$, $SE(\hat{\beta})$ as before.

(2) Choose a significance level, α (again, the convention is 5 per cent).

(3) Use the t-tables to find the appropriate critical value, which will, again, have $T - 2$ degrees of freedom.

(4) The confidence interval for $\hat{\beta}$ is given by

$$(\hat{\beta} - t_{crit} \cdot SE(\hat{\beta}), \hat{\beta} + t_{crit} \cdot SE(\hat{\beta}))$$

(5) Perform the test: if the hypothesised value of $\beta(\beta^*)$ lies outside the confidence interval, then reject the null hypothesis that $\beta = \beta^*$; otherwise, do not reject the null.

are appropriate. Boxes 4.5 and 4.6 show how to conduct hypothesis tests using the test of significance and confidence interval approaches, respectively, in the context of a regression model.[3]

[3] While the approach to hypothesis testing that we describe here is evidently related to that outlined in chapter 3, the context is different, and so, for clarity, we explain the steps in detail here, even though this may imply some repetition.

Example 4.3

Suppose the following regression results have been calculated:

$$\hat{y}_t = 20.3 + 0.5091x_t \atop (14.38) \quad (0.2561) \tag{4.30}$$

Using both the test of significance and confidence interval approaches, test the hypothesis that $\beta = 1$ against a two-sided alternative. This hypothesis might be of interest, for a unit coefficient on the explanatory variable implies a 1:1 relationship between movements in x and movements in y. The null and alternative hypotheses are, respectively, H_0: $\beta = 1$ and H_1: $\beta \neq 1$. The results of the test according to each approach are shown in box 4.7.

Box 4.7 The test of significance and confidence interval approaches compared in a regression context

Test of significance approach	Confidence interval approach
$\text{Test stat} = \dfrac{\hat{\beta} - \beta^*}{SE(\hat{\beta})} = \dfrac{0.5091 - 1}{0.2561} = -1.917$	Find $t_{crit} = t_{20;5\%} = \pm 2.086$
Find $t_{crit} = t_{20;5\%} = \pm 2.086$	$\hat{\beta} \pm t_{crit} \cdot SE(\hat{\beta}) = 0.5091 \pm 2.086 \cdot 0.2561 = (-0.0251, 1.0433)$
Do not reject H_0, since test statistic lies within the non-rejection region.	Do not reject H_0, since one lies within the confidence interval.

A couple of comments are in order. First, the critical value from the t-distribution that is required is for twenty degrees of freedom and at the 5 per cent level. This means that 5 per cent of the total distribution will be in the rejection region, and, since this is a two-sided test, 2.5 per cent of the distribution is required to be contained in each tail. From the symmetry of the t-distribution around zero, the critical values in the upper and lower tail will be equal in magnitude, but opposite in sign, as shown in figure 4.13.

What if, instead, the researcher wanted to test H_0: $\beta = 0$ or H_0: $\beta = 2$? In order to test these hypotheses using the test of significance approach, the test statistic would have to be reconstructed in each case, although the critical value would be the same. On the other hand, no additional work would be required if the confidence interval approach is adopted, since it effectively permits the testing of an infinite number of hypotheses. So, for

Figure 4.13
Critical values and rejection regions for a $t_{20;5\%}$

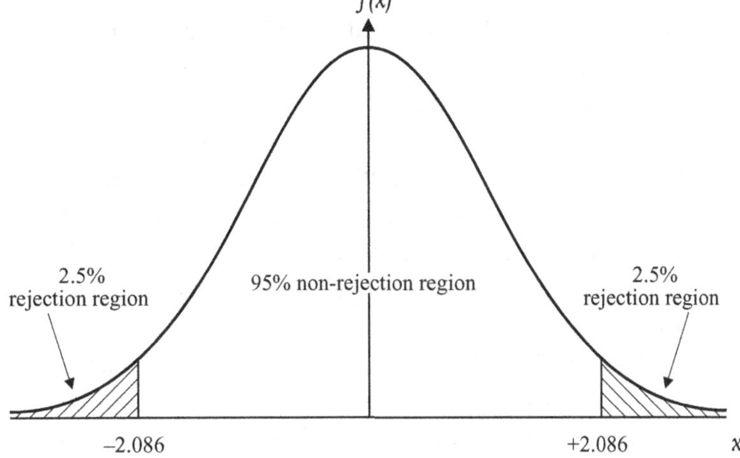

example, suppose that the researcher wanted to test

$$H_0\text{: } \beta = 0 \text{ versus } H_1\text{: } \beta \neq 0$$

and

$$H_0\text{: } \beta = 2 \text{ versus } H_1\text{: } \beta \neq 2$$

In the first case, the null hypothesis (that $\beta = 0$) would not be rejected, since zero lies within the 95 per cent confidence interval. By the same argument, the second null hypothesis (that $\beta = 2$) would be rejected, since two lies outside the estimated confidence interval.

On the other hand, note that this book has so far considered only the results under a 5 per cent size of test. In marginal cases (e.g. H_0: $\beta = 1$, where the test statistic and critical value are close together), a completely different answer may arise if a different size of test is used. This is when the test of significance approach is preferable to the construction of a confidence interval.

For example, suppose that now a 10 per cent size of test is used for the null hypothesis given in example 4.3. Using the test of significance approach,

$$\begin{aligned} \textit{test statistic} &= \frac{\hat{\beta} - \beta^*}{SE(\hat{\beta})} \\ &= \frac{0.5091 - 1}{0.2561} = -1.917 \end{aligned}$$

as above. The only thing that changes is the critical t-value. At the 10 per cent level (so that 5 per cent of the total distribution is placed in each of the tails for this two-sided test), the required critical value is

$t_{20;10\%} = \pm 1.725$. Now, therefore, as the test statistic lies in the rejection region, H_0 would be rejected. In order to use a 10 per cent test under the confidence interval approach, the interval itself would have to be re-estimated, since the critical value is embedded in the calculation of the confidence interval.

As can be seen, the test of significance and confidence interval approaches both have their relative merits. The testing of a number of different hypotheses is easier under the confidence interval approach, while a consideration of the effect of the size of the test on the conclusion is easier to address under the test of significance approach.

Caution should be used when placing emphasis on or making decisions in the context of marginal cases (i.e. in cases in which the null is only just rejected or not rejected). In this situation, the appropriate conclusion to draw is that the results are marginal and that no strong inference can be made one way or the other. A thorough empirical analysis should involve conducting a sensitivity analysis on the results to determine whether using a different size of test alters the conclusions. It is worth stating again that it is conventional to consider sizes of test of 10 per cent, 5 per cent and 1 per cent. If the conclusion (i.e. 'Reject' or 'Do not reject') is robust to changes in the size of the test, then one can be more confident that the conclusions are appropriate. If the outcome of the test is qualitatively altered when the size of the test is modified, the conclusion must be that there is no conclusion one way or the other!

It is also worth noting that, if a given null hypothesis is rejected using a 1 per cent significance level, it will also automatically be rejected at the 5 per cent level, so there is no need actually to state the latter. Dougherty (1992, p. 100), gives the analogy of a high jumper. If the high jumper can clear two metres, it is obvious that the jumper can also clear 1.5 metres. The 1 per cent significance level is a higher hurdle than the 5 per cent significance level. Similarly, if the null is not rejected at the 5 per cent level of significance, it will automatically not be rejected at any stronger level of significance (e.g. 1 per cent). In this case, if the jumper cannot clear 1.5 metres, there is no way he/she will be able to clear two metres.

4.10.2 *Some more terminology*

If the null hypothesis is rejected at the 5 per cent level, it can be said that the result of the test is 'statistically significant'. If the null hypothesis is not rejected, it can be said that the result of the test is 'not significant', or that it is 'insignificant'. Finally, if the null hypothesis is rejected at the 1 per cent level, the result is termed 'highly statistically significant'.

Table 4.1 Classifying hypothesis-testing errors and correct conclusions

		Reality	
		H_0 is true	H_0 is false
Result of test	Significant (reject H_0)	Type I error $= \alpha$	$\surd$
	Insignificant (do not reject H_0)	$\surd$	Type II error $= \beta$

Note that a statistically significant result may be of no practical significance. For example, if the estimated beta for a REIT under a capital asset pricing model (CAPM) regression is 1.05, and a null hypothesis that $\beta = 1$ is rejected, the result will be statistically significant. It may be the case, however, that a slightly higher beta will make no difference to an investor's choice as to whether to buy shares in the REIT or not. In that case, one would say that the result of the test was statistically significant but financially or practically insignificant.

4.10.3 *Classifying the errors that can be made using hypothesis tests*

H_0 is usually rejected if the test statistic is statistically significant at a chosen significance level. There are two possible errors that can be made.

(1) Rejecting H_0 when it is really true; this is called a *type I error*.
(2) Not rejecting H_0 when it is in fact false; this is called a *type II error*.

The possible scenarios can be summarised in tabular form, as in table 4.1. The probability of a type I error is just α, the significance level or size of test chosen. To see this, recall what is meant by 'significance' at the 5 per cent level: it is only 5 per cent likely that a result as extreme as or more extreme than this could have occurred purely by chance. Alternatively, to put it another way, it is only 5 per cent likely that this null will be rejected when it is in fact true.

Note that there is no chance for a free lunch (i.e. a costless gain) here! What happens if the size of the test is reduced (e.g. from a 5 per cent test to a 1 per cent test)? The chances of making a type I error would be reduced – but so would the probability of the null hypothesis being rejected at all, so increasing the probability of a type II error. The two competing effects of reducing the size of the test are shown in box 4.8.

Box 4.8 Type I and type II errors

				↗	Less likely to falsely reject	→ Lower chance of type I error of test
Reduce size (e.g. 5 per cent to 1 per cent)	→	More strict criterion for rejection	→	Reject null hypothesis less often		
				↘	More likely to incorrectly not reject	→ Higher chance of type II error

There always exists, therefore, a direct trade-off between type I and type II errors when choosing a significance level. The only way to reduce the chances of both is to increase the sample size, thus increasing the amount of information upon which the results of the hypothesis test are based. In practice, up to a certain level, type I errors are usually considered more serious, and hence a small size of test is usually chosen (5 per cent or 1 per cent are the most common).

The probability of a type I error is the probability of incorrectly rejecting a correct null hypothesis, which is also the size of the test. Another important piece of terminology in this area is the *power of a test*. The power of a test is defined as the probability of (appropriately) rejecting an incorrect null hypothesis. The power of the test is also equal to one minus the probability of a type II error.

An optimal test would be one with an actual test size that matched the nominal size and that had as high a power as possible. Such a test would imply, for example, that using a 5 per cent significance level would result in the null being rejected exactly 5 per cent of the time by chance alone, and that an incorrect null hypothesis would be rejected close to 100 per cent of the time.

4.10.4 *The exact significance level*

The exact significance level is also commonly known as the p-value. It gives the *marginal significance level* at which one would be indifferent between rejecting and not rejecting the null hypothesis. If the test statistic is 'large' in absolute value, the p-value will be small, and vice versa. For example, consider a test statistic that is distributed as a t_{62} and takes a value of 1.47. Would the null hypothesis be rejected? It would depend on the size of the test. Suppose that the p-value for this test is calculated to be 0.12.

- Is the null rejected at the 5 per cent level? No.
- Is the null rejected at the 10 per cent level? No.
- Is the null rejected at the 20 per cent level? Yes.

In fact, the null would have been rejected at the 12 per cent level or higher. To see this, consider conducting a series of tests with size 0.1 per cent, 0.2 per cent, 0.3 per cent, 0.4 per cent, ... 1 per cent, ... 5 per cent, ... 10 per cent, ... Eventually, the critical value and test statistic will meet, and this will be the p-value. Thus the decision rule for determining whether to reject or not reject a null hypothesis given a particular p-value and a particular significance level α would be

$$\text{reject } H_0 \text{ if } p\text{-value} < \alpha, \text{ otherwise do not reject}$$

software packages almost always provide p-values automatically. Note how useful they are. They provide all the information required to conduct a hypothesis test without requiring of the researcher the need to calculate a test statistic or to find a critical value from a table; both of these steps have already been taken by the package in producing the p-value. The p-value is also useful in that it avoids the requirement of specifying an arbitrary significance level (α). Sensitivity analysis of the effect of the significance level on the conclusion occurs automatically. The p-values produced for t-tests by computer packages almost always assume that a two-sided test is being conducted.

Informally, the p-value is also often referred to as the probability of being wrong when the null hypothesis is rejected. Thus, for example, if a p-value of 0.05 or less leads the researcher to reject the null (equivalent to a 5 per cent significance level), this is equivalent to saying that, if the probability of incorrectly rejecting the null is more than 5 per cent, do not reject it. The p-value has also been termed the 'plausibility' of the null hypothesis: the smaller the p-value is the less plausible the null hypothesis is.

Example 4.4

Consider the estimates for the rent model from equation (4.28), with standard errors in parentheses:

$$\underset{}{R\hat{R}g_t} = \underset{(2.29)}{-9.62} + \underset{(0.62)}{3.27}EFBSg_t \tag{4.31}$$

with $T = 27$.

Using both the test of significance and confidence interval approaches, test the hypothesis that $\beta = 1$ (that is, an exactly proportionate impact of employment growth on rent growth) against a two-sided alternative. This hypothesis may be of interest to the analyst for testing a lower degree of sensitivity of rent growth to employment growth. The null and alternative hypotheses are, respectively, H_0: $\beta = 1$ and H_1: $\beta \neq 1$. The results of the test according to the test of significance and confidence interval approach are as follows.

(1) Test of significance approach.
Test stat $= \frac{\hat{\beta}-\beta^*}{SE(\hat{\beta})} = \frac{3.27-1}{0.62} = 3.66$
Find $t_{crit} = t_{25;5\%} = \pm 2.060$.

We therefore reject H_0, since the test statistic lies within the rejection region.

(2) Confidence interval approach.
Find $t_{crit} = t_{25;5\%} = \pm 2.060$.

$$\hat{\beta} \pm t_{crit}.se(\hat{\beta}) = 3.27 \pm 2.060 \cdot 0.62 = (1.99, 4.55).$$

We therefore reject H_0, since one lies outside the confidence interval.

Example 4.5

In a study of office returns in the Helsinki market, McGough, Tsolacos and Olkkonen (2000) estimate alternative specifications, both simple and more general. The simple model of office returns in Helsinki takes the form of the following bivariate regression.

$$\Delta OFFRET_t = \alpha + \beta \Delta GDP_t + u_t \quad (4.32)$$

where Δ denotes the change in rents from one period to another, *OFFRET* is an index of office returns in Helsinki adjusted for inflation, and *GDP* is Finland's GDP at constant prices (adjusted for inflation). This relationship assumes that a buoyant Finnish economy is associated with increasing business activity in the Helsinki area (which is the region that dominates the Finnish economy) and greater demand for office space. Landlords will be able to charge higher rents (unless the market experiences an excessive supply of space) and will receive more income. Their income is also boosted by reduced vacancies, both at the building level and the overall market level. Hence income returns from office building investments improve. At the same time, the capital values of buildings increase, reflecting a more buoyant picture for future cash flows (which could push the discount rate down), further boosting total returns. Of course, this thinking may represent only a partial explanation of returns, as the supply side of the Helsinki office market is not considered. The authors acknowledge this, but the lack of a long historical supply series was the reason for omitting supply. In chapter 6, we study the implications of such omissions in a model by studying the properties of the residuals ($\hat{u}$).

The data available for this study were of annual frequency for the period 1970 to 1998. The empirical estimation of equation (4.32) resulted in

$$\Delta \widehat{OFFRET}_t = -24.5 + 20.0\Delta GDP_t \tag{4.33}$$

The intercept is negative, suggesting that if there is no change in GDP ($\Delta GDP_t = 0$) the real return index will fall by 24.5 units. The positive sign on the *GDP* coefficient denotes that positive (negative) changes in GDP result in positive (negative) changes in office returns. On average, over the sample period, a change in the *GDP* index by one unit will result in a change of twenty units in the index of real returns.

Key concepts

The key terms to be able to define and explain from this chapter are

- regression model
- disturbance term
- population
- sample
- linear model
- consistency
- unbiasedness
- efficiency
- standard error
- statistical inference
- null hypothesis
- alternative hypothesis
- *t*-distribution
- confidence interval
- test statistic
- rejection region
- type I error
- type II error
- size of a test
- power of a test
- *p*-value
- asymptotic

Appendix: Mathematical derivations of CLRM results for the bivariate case

4A.1 Derivation of the OLS coefficient estimator

$$L = \sum_{t=1}^{T}(y_t - \hat{y}_t)^2 = \sum_{t=1}^{T}(y_t - \hat{\alpha} - \hat{\beta}x_t)^2 \tag{4A.1}$$

It is necessary to minimise L w.r.t. $\hat{\alpha}$ and $\hat{\beta}$, to find the values of α and β that give the line that is closest to the data. L is therefore differentiated w.r.t. $\hat{\alpha}$ and $\hat{\beta}$, and the first derivatives are set to zero. The first derivatives are given by

$$\frac{\partial L}{\partial \hat{\alpha}} = -2\sum_t (y_t - \hat{\alpha} - \hat{\beta}x_t) = 0 \tag{4A.2}$$

$$\frac{\partial L}{\partial \hat{\beta}} = -2\sum_t x_t(y_t - \hat{\alpha} - \hat{\beta}x_t) = 0 \tag{4A.3}$$

The next step is to rearrange (4A.2) and (4A.3) in order to obtain expressions for $\hat{\alpha}$ and $\hat{\beta}$. From (4A.2),

$$\sum_t (y_t - \hat{\alpha} - \hat{\beta}x_t) = 0 \tag{4A.4}$$

Expanding the brackets and recalling that the sum runs from one to T so that there will be T terms in $\hat{\alpha}$,

$$\sum y_t - T\hat{\alpha} - \hat{\beta}\sum x_t = 0 \tag{4A.5}$$

$\sum y_t = T\bar{y}$ and $\sum x_t = T\bar{x}$, however, so it is possible to write (4A.5) as

$$T\bar{y} - T\hat{\alpha} - T\hat{\beta}\bar{x} = 0 \tag{4A.6}$$

or

$$\bar{y} - \hat{\alpha} - \hat{\beta}\bar{x} = 0 \tag{4A.7}$$

From (4A.3),

$$\sum_t x_t(y_t - \hat{\alpha} - \hat{\beta}x_t) = 0 \tag{4A.8}$$

From (4A.7),

$$\hat{\alpha} = \bar{y} - \hat{\beta}\bar{x} \tag{4A.9}$$

Substituting into (4A.8) for $\hat{\alpha}$ from (4A.9),

$$\sum_t x_t(y_t - \bar{y} + \hat{\beta}\bar{x} - \hat{\beta}x_t) = 0 \tag{4A.10}$$

$$\sum_t x_t y_t - \bar{y}\sum x_t + \hat{\beta}\bar{x}\sum x_t - \hat{\beta}\sum x_t^2 = 0 \tag{4A.11}$$

$$\sum_t x_t y_t - T\bar{x}\bar{y} + \hat{\beta}T\bar{x}^2 - \hat{\beta}\sum x_t^2 = 0 \tag{4A.12}$$

Rearranging for $\hat{\beta}$,

$$\hat{\beta}\left(T\bar{x}^2 - \sum x_t^2\right) = T\bar{x}\bar{y} - \sum x_t y_t \tag{4A.13}$$

Dividing both sides of (4A.13) by $(T\bar{x}^2 - \sum x_t^2)$ gives

$$\hat{\beta} = \frac{\sum x_t y_t - T\bar{x}\bar{y}}{\sum x_t^2 - T\bar{x}^2} \quad \textit{and} \quad \hat{\alpha} = \bar{y} - \hat{\beta}\bar{x} \tag{4A.14}$$

4A.2 Derivation of the OLS standard error estimators for the intercept and slope

Recall that the variance of the random variable $\hat{\alpha}$ can be written as

$$\text{var}(\hat{\alpha}) = E(\hat{\alpha} - E(\hat{\alpha}))^2 \tag{4A.15}$$

and, since the OLS estimator is unbiased,

$$\text{var}(\hat{\alpha}) = E(\hat{\alpha} - \alpha)^2 \tag{4A.16}$$

By similar arguments, the variance of the slope estimator can be written as

$$\text{var}(\hat{\beta}) = E(\hat{\beta} - \beta)^2 \tag{4A.17}$$

Working first with (4A.17), replacing $\hat{\beta}$ with the formula for it given by the OLS estimator,

$$\text{var}(\hat{\beta}) = E\left(\frac{\sum(x_t - \bar{x})(y_t - \bar{y})}{\sum(x_t - \bar{x})^2} - \beta\right)^2 \tag{4A.18}$$

Replacing y_t with $\alpha + \beta x_t + u_t$, and replacing $\bar{y}$ with $\alpha - \beta\bar{x}$ in (4A.18),

$$\text{var}(\hat{\beta}) = E\left(\frac{\sum(x_t - \bar{x})(\alpha + \beta x_t + u_t - \alpha - \beta\bar{x})}{\sum(x_t - \bar{x})^2} - \beta\right)^2 \tag{4A.19}$$

Cancelling α and multiplying the last β term in (4A.19) by $\dfrac{\sum(x_t - \bar{x})^2}{\sum(x_t - \bar{x})^2}$,

$$\text{var}(\hat{\beta}) = E\left(\frac{\sum(x_t - \bar{x})(\beta x_t + u_t - \beta\bar{x}) - \beta\sum(x_t - \bar{x})^2}{\sum(x_t - \bar{x})^2}\right)^2 \tag{4A.20}$$

Rearranging,

$$\text{var}(\hat{\beta}) = E\left(\frac{\sum (x_t - \bar{x})\beta(x_t - \bar{x}) + \sum u_t(x_t - \bar{x}) - \beta \sum (x_t - \bar{x})^2}{\sum (x_t - \bar{x})^2}\right)^2 \tag{4A.21}$$

$$\text{var}(\hat{\beta}) = E\left(\frac{\beta \sum (x_t - \bar{x})^2 + \sum u_t(x_t - \bar{x}) - \beta \sum (x_t - \bar{x})^2}{\sum (x_t - \bar{x})^2}\right)^2 \tag{4A.22}$$

Now the β terms in (4A.22) will cancel to give

$$\text{var}(\hat{\beta}) = E\left(\frac{\sum u_t(x_t - \bar{x})}{\sum (x_t - \bar{x})^2}\right)^2 \tag{4A.23}$$

Now let x_t^* denote the mean-adjusted observation for x_t – i.e. $(x_t - \bar{x})$. Equation (4A.23) can be written

$$\text{var}(\hat{\beta}) = E\left(\frac{\sum u_t x_t^*}{\sum x_t^{*2}}\right)^2 \tag{4A.24}$$

The denominator of (4A.24) can be taken through the expectations operator under the assumption that x is fixed or non-stochastic:

$$\text{var}(\hat{\beta}) = \frac{1}{\left(\sum x_t^{*2}\right)^2} E\left(\sum u_t x_t^*\right)^2 \tag{4A.25}$$

Writing the terms out in the numerator summation of (4A.25),

$$\text{var}(\hat{\beta}) = \frac{1}{\left(\sum x_t^{*2}\right)^2} E\left(u_1 x_1^* + u_2 x_2^* + \cdots + u_T x_T^*\right)^2 \tag{4A.26}$$

Now expanding the parentheses of the squared term in the expectations operator of (4A.26),

$$\text{var}(\hat{\beta}) = \frac{1}{\left(\sum x_t^{*2}\right)^2} E\left(u_1^2 x_1^{*2} + u_2^2 x_2^{*2} + \cdots + u_T^2 x_T^{*2} + \textit{cross-products}\right) \tag{4A.27}$$

where '*cross-products*' in (4A.27) denotes all the terms $u_i x_i^* u_j x_j^*$ $(i \neq j)$. These cross-products will have expectations of zero under the assumption that the error terms are uncorrelated with one another. Thus the '*cross-products*' term in (4A.27) will drop out. Recall also from the chapter text that $E(u_t^2)$ is the error variance, which is estimated using s^2:

$$\text{var}(\hat{\beta}) = \frac{1}{\left(\sum x_t^{*2}\right)^2} \left(s^2 x_1^{*2} + s^2 x_2^{*2} + \cdots + s^2 x_T^{*2}\right) \tag{4A.28}$$

which can also be written

$$\text{var}(\hat{\beta}) = \frac{s^2}{\left(\sum x_t^{*2}\right)^2} \left(x_1^{*2} + x_2^{*2} + \cdots + x_T^{*2}\right) = \frac{s^2 \sum x_t^{*2}}{\left(\sum x_t^{*2}\right)^2} \tag{4A.29}$$

A term in $\sum x_t^{*2}$ can be cancelled from the numerator and denominator of (4A.29), and, recalling that $x_t^* = (x_t - \bar{x})$, this gives the variance of the slope coefficient as

$$\text{var}(\hat{\beta}) = \frac{s^2}{\sum (x_t - \bar{x})^2} \tag{4A.30}$$

so that the standard error can be obtained by taking the square root of (4A.30):

$$SE(\hat{\beta}) = s\sqrt{\frac{1}{\sum (x_t - \bar{x})^2}} \tag{4A.31}$$

Turning now to the derivation of the intercept standard error, this is much more difficult than that of the slope standard error. In fact, both are very much easier using matrix algebra, as shown in the following chapter. This derivation is therefore offered in summary form.

It is possible to express $\hat{\alpha}$ as a function of the true α and of the disturbances, u_t:

$$\hat{\alpha} = \alpha + \frac{\sum u_t\left[\sum x_t^2 - x_t \sum x_t\right]}{\left[T\sum x_t^2 - \left(\sum x_t\right)^2\right]} \tag{4A.32}$$

Denoting all the elements in square brackets as g_t, (4A.32) can be written

$$\hat{\alpha} - \alpha = \sum u_t g_t \tag{4A.33}$$

From (4A.15), the intercept variance would be written

$$\text{var}(\hat{\alpha}) = E\left(\sum u_t g_t\right)^2 = \sum g_t^2 E\left(u_t^2\right) = s^2 \sum g_t^2 \tag{4A.34}$$

Writing (4A.34) out in full for g_t^2 and expanding the brackets,

$$\text{var}(\bar{\alpha}) = \frac{s^2\left[T\left(\sum x_t^2\right)^2 - 2\sum x_t\left(\sum x_t^2\right)\sum x_t + \left(\sum x_t^2\right)\left(\sum x_t\right)^2\right]}{\left[T\sum x_t^2 - \left(\sum x_t\right)^2\right]^2} \tag{4A.35}$$

This looks rather complex, but, fortunately, if we take $\sum x_t^2$ outside the square brackets in the numerator, the remaining numerator cancels with a term in the denominator to leave the required result:

$$SE(\hat{\alpha}) = s\sqrt{\frac{\sum x_t^2}{T\sum (x_t - \bar{x})^2}} \tag{4A.36}$$

5 Further issues in regression analysis

Learning outcomes

In this chapter, you will learn how to

- construct models with more than one explanatory variable;
- derive the OLS parameter and standard error estimators in the multiple regression context;
- determine how well the model fits the data;
- understand the principles of nested and non-nested models;
- test multiple hypotheses using an F-test;
- form restricted regressions; and
- test for omitted and redundant variables.

5.1 Generalising the simple model to multiple linear regression

Previously, a model of the following form has been used:

$$y_t = \alpha + \beta x_t + u_t \quad t = 1, 2, \ldots, T \tag{5.1}$$

Equation (5.1) is a simple bivariate regression model. That is, changes in the dependent variable are explained by reference to changes in one single explanatory variable x. What if the real estate theory or the idea that is sought to be tested suggests that the dependent variable is influenced by more than one independent variable, however? For example, simple estimation and tests of the capital asset pricing model can be conducted using an equation of the form of (5.1), but arbitrage pricing theory does not presuppose that there is only a single factor affecting stock returns. So, to give one illustration, REIT excess returns might be purported to depend on their sensitivity to unexpected changes in

(1) inflation;
(2) the differences in returns on short- and long-dated bonds;
(3) the dividend yield; or
(4) default risks.

Having just one independent variable would be no good in this case. It would, of course, be possible to use each of the four proposed explanatory factors in separate regressions. It is of greater interest, though, and it is also more valid, to have more than one explanatory variable in the regression equation at the same time, and therefore to examine the effect of all the explanatory variables together on the explained variable.

It is very easy to generalise the simple model to one with k regressors (independent variables). Equation (5.1) becomes

$$y_t = \beta_1 + \beta_2 x_{2t} + \beta_3 x_{3t} + \cdots + \beta_k x_{kt} + u_t, \quad t = 1, 2, \ldots, T \tag{5.2}$$

The variables $x_{2t}, x_{3t}, \ldots, x_{kt}$ are therefore a set of $k - 1$ explanatory variables that are thought to influence y, and the coefficient estimates $\beta_2, \beta_3, \ldots, \beta_k$ are the parameters that quantify the effect of each of these explanatory variables on y. The coefficient interpretations are slightly altered in the multiple regression context. Each coefficient is now known as a partial regression coefficient, interpreted as representing the partial effect of the given explanatory variable on the explained variable, after holding constant, or eliminating the effect of, all the other explanatory variables. For example, $\hat{\beta}_2$ measures the effect of x_2 on y after eliminating the effects of x_3, $x_4, \ldots, x_k$. Stating this in other words, each coefficient measures the average change in the dependent variable per unit change in a given independent variable, holding all other independent variables constant at their average values.

5.2 The constant term

In (5.2) above, astute readers will have noticed that the explanatory variables are numbered $x_2, x_3, \ldots$ – i.e. the list starts with x_2 and not x_1. So, where is x_1? In fact, it is the constant term, usually represented by a column of ones of length T:

$$x_1 = \begin{bmatrix} 1 \\ 1 \\ \vdots \\ 1 \end{bmatrix} \tag{5.3}$$

Thus there is a variable implicitly hiding next to β_1, which is a column vector of ones, the length of which is the number of observations in the sample. The x_1 in the regression equation is not usually written, in the same way that one unit of p and two units of q would be written as '$p + 2q$' and not '$1p + 2q$'. β_1 is the coefficient attached to the constant term (which was called α in the previous chapter). This coefficient can still be referred to as the *intercept*, which can be interpreted as the average value that y would take if all the explanatory variables took a value of zero.

A tighter definition of k, the number of explanatory variables, is probably now necessary. Throughout this book, k is defined as the number of 'explanatory variables' or 'regressors', including the constant term. This is equivalent to the number of parameters that are estimated in the regression equation. Strictly speaking, it is not sensible to call the constant an explanatory variable, since it does not explain anything and it always takes the same values. This definition of k will be employed for notational convenience, however.

Equation (5.2) can be expressed even more compactly by writing it in matrix form:

$$y = X\beta + u \tag{5.4}$$

where: y is of dimension $T \times 1$;
X is of dimension $T \times k$;
β is of dimension $k \times 1$; and
u is of dimension $T \times 1$.

The difference between (5.2) and (5.4) is that all the time observations have been stacked up in a vector, and also that all the different explanatory variables have been squashed together so that there is a column for each in the X matrix. Such a notation may seem unnecessarily complex, but, in fact, the matrix notation is usually more compact and convenient. So, for example, if k is two – i.e. there are two regressors, one of which is the constant term (equivalent to a simple bivariate regression $y_t = \alpha + \beta x_t + u_t$) – it is possible to write

$$\underset{T \times 1}{\begin{bmatrix} y_1 \\ y_2 \\ \vdots \\ y_T \end{bmatrix}} = \underset{T \times 2}{\begin{bmatrix} 1 & x_{21} \\ 1 & x_{22} \\ \vdots & \vdots \\ 1 & x_{2T} \end{bmatrix}} \underset{2 \times 1}{\begin{bmatrix} \beta_1 \\ \beta_2 \end{bmatrix}} + \underset{T \times 1}{\begin{bmatrix} u_1 \\ u_2 \\ \vdots \\ u_T \end{bmatrix}} \tag{5.5}$$

so that the x_{ij} element of the matrix X represents the jth time observation on the ith variable. Notice that the matrices written in this way are *conformable* – in other words, there is a valid matrix multiplication and addition on the RHS.[1]

5.3 How are the parameters (the elements of the β vector) calculated in the generalised case?

Previously, the residual sum of squares, $\sum \hat{u}_i^2$, was minimised with respect to α and β. In the multiple regression context, in order to obtain estimates of the parameters, $\beta_1, \beta_2, \ldots, \beta_k$, the RSS would be minimised with respect to all the elements of β. Now, the residuals can be stacked in a vector:

$$\hat{u} = \begin{bmatrix} \hat{u}_1 \\ \hat{u}_2 \\ \vdots \\ \hat{u}_T \end{bmatrix} \tag{5.6}$$

The RSS is still the relevant loss function, and would be given in a matrix notation by equation (5.7):

$$L = \hat{u}'\hat{u} = [\, \hat{u}_1 \quad \hat{u}_2 \quad \cdots \quad \hat{u}_T \,] \begin{bmatrix} \hat{u}_1 \\ \hat{u}_2 \\ \vdots \\ \hat{u}_T \end{bmatrix} = \hat{u}_1^2 + \hat{u}_2^2 + \cdots + \hat{u}_T^2 = \sum \hat{u}_t^2 \tag{5.7}$$

Using a similar procedure to that employed in the bivariate regression case – i.e. substituting into (5.7), and denoting the vector of estimated parameters as $\hat{\beta}$ – it can be shown (see the appendix to this chapter) that the coefficient estimates will be given by the elements of the expression

$$\hat{\beta} = \begin{bmatrix} \hat{\beta}_1 \\ \hat{\beta}_2 \\ \vdots \\ \hat{\beta}_k \end{bmatrix} = (X'X)^{-1}X'y \tag{5.8}$$

If one were to check the dimensions of the RHS of (5.8), it would be observed to be $k \times 1$. This is as required, since there are k parameters to be estimated by the formula for $\hat{\beta}$.

[1] The above presentation is the standard way to express matrices in the time series econometrics literature, although the ordering of the indices is different from that used in the mathematics of matrix algebra (as presented in chapter 2 of this book). In the latter case, x_{ij} would represent the element in row i and column j, although, in the notation used from this point of the book onwards, it is the other way around.

How are the standard errors of the coefficient estimates calculated, though? Previously, to estimate the variance of the errors, σ^2, an estimator denoted by s^2 was used:

$$s^2 = \frac{\sum \hat{u}_t^2}{T - 2} \tag{5.9}$$

The denominator of (5.9) is given by $T - 2$, which is the number of degrees of freedom for the bivariate regression model – i.e. the number of observations minus two. This applies, essentially, because two observations are effectively 'lost' in estimating the two model parameters – i.e. in deriving estimates for α and β. In the case in which there is more than one explanatory variable plus a constant, and using the matrix notation, (5.9) would be modified to

$$s^2 = \frac{\hat{u}'\hat{u}}{T - k} \tag{5.10}$$

where $k =$ the number of regressors including a constant. In this case, k observations are 'lost' as k parameters are estimated, leaving $T - k$ degrees of freedom. It can also be shown (see the appendix to this chapter) that the parameter variance–covariance matrix is given by

$$\text{var}(\hat{\beta}) = s^2(X'X)^{-1} \tag{5.11}$$

The leading diagonal terms give the coefficient variances while the off-diagonal terms give the covariances between the parameter estimates, so that the variance of $\hat{\beta}_1$ is the first diagonal element, the variance of $\hat{\beta}_2$ is the second element on the leading diagonal and the variance of $\hat{\beta}_k$ is the kth diagonal element. The coefficient standard errors are simply given therefore by taking the square roots of each of the terms on the leading diagonal.

Example 5.1

The following model with three regressors (including the constant) is estimated over fifteen observations,

$$y = \beta_1 + \beta_2 x_2 + \beta_3 x_3 + u \tag{5.12}$$

and the following data have been calculated from the original xs:

$$(X'X)^{-1} = \begin{bmatrix} 2.0 & 3.5 & -1.0 \\ 3.5 & 1.0 & 6.5 \\ -1.0 & 6.5 & 4.3 \end{bmatrix}, \quad (X'y) = \begin{bmatrix} -3.0 \\ 2.2 \\ 0.6 \end{bmatrix}, \quad \hat{u}'\hat{u} = 10.96$$

Calculate the coefficient estimates and their standard errors.

$$\hat{\beta} = \begin{bmatrix} \hat{\beta}_1 \\ \hat{\beta}_2 \\ \vdots \\ \hat{\beta}_k \end{bmatrix} = (X'X)^{-1}X'y = \begin{bmatrix} 2.0 & 3.5 & -1.0 \\ 3.5 & 1.0 & 6.5 \\ -1.0 & 6.5 & 4.3 \end{bmatrix} \times \begin{bmatrix} -3.0 \\ 2.2 \\ 0.6 \end{bmatrix} = \begin{bmatrix} 1.10 \\ -4.40 \\ 19.88 \end{bmatrix} \tag{5.13}$$

To calculate the standard errors, an estimate of σ^2 is required:

$$s^2 = \frac{RSS}{T-k} = \frac{10.96}{15-3} = 0.91 \tag{5.14}$$

The variance–covariance matrix of $\hat{\beta}$ is given by

$$s^2(X'X)^{-1} = 0.91(X'X)^{-1} = \begin{bmatrix} 1.82 & 3.19 & -0.91 \\ 3.19 & 0.91 & 5.92 \\ -0.91 & 5.92 & 3.91 \end{bmatrix} \tag{5.15}$$

The coefficient variances are on the diagonals, and the standard errors are found by taking the square roots of each of the coefficient variances.

$$\text{var}(\hat{\beta}_1) = 1.82 \qquad SE(\hat{\beta}_1) = 1.35 \tag{5.16}$$

$$\text{var}(\hat{\beta}_2) = 0.91 \Leftrightarrow SE(\hat{\beta}_2) = 0.95 \tag{5.17}$$

$$\text{var}(\hat{\beta}_3) = 3.91 \qquad SE(\hat{\beta}_3) = 1.98 \tag{5.18}$$

The estimated equation would be written

$$\begin{aligned} \hat{y} = {} & 1.10 - 4.40x_2 + 19.88x_3 \\ & (1.35) \quad (0.95) \qquad (1.98) \end{aligned} \tag{5.19}$$

In practice, fortunately, all econometrics software packages will estimate the coefficient values and their standard errors. Clearly, though, it is still useful to understand where these estimates came from.

5.4 A special type of hypothesis test: the t-ratio

Recall from equation (4.29) in the previous chapter that the formula under a test of significance approach to hypothesis testing using a t-test for variable i is

$$\textit{test statistic} = \frac{\hat{\beta}_i - \beta_i^*}{SE(\hat{\beta}_i)} \tag{5.20}$$

If the test is

$$H_0: \beta_i = 0$$
$$H_1: \beta_i \neq 0$$

i.e. a test that the population parameter is zero against a two-sided alternative – this is known as a t-ratio test. Since $\beta_i^* = 0$, the expression in (5.20) collapses to

$$test\ statistic = \frac{\hat{\beta}_i}{SE(\hat{\beta}_i)} \tag{5.21}$$

Thus the ratio of the coefficient to its standard error, given by this expression, is known as the t-ratio or t-statistic. In the last example above, the t-ratios associated with each of the three coefficients would be given by

	$\hat{\beta}_1$	$\hat{\beta}_2$	$\hat{\beta}_3$
Coefficient	1.10	−4.40	19.88
SE	1.35	0.95	1.98
t-ratio	0.81	−4.63	10.04

Note that, if a coefficient is negative, its t-ratio will also be negative. In order to test (separately) the null hypotheses that $\beta_1 = 0$, $\beta_2 = 0$ and $\beta_3 = 0$, the test statistics would be compared with the appropriate critical value from a t-distribution. In this case, the number of degrees of freedom, given by $T-k$, is equal to $15 - 3 = 12$. The 5 per cent critical value for this two-sided test (remember, 2.5 per cent in each tail for a 5 per cent test) is 2.179, while the 1 per cent two-sided critical value (0.5 per cent in each tail) is 3.055. Given these t-ratios and critical values, would the following null hypotheses be rejected?

$H_0: \beta_1 = 0?$ No.
$H_0: \beta_2 = 0?$ Yes.
$H_0: \beta_3 = 0?$ Yes.

If H_0 is rejected, it would be said that the test statistic is significant. If the variable is not 'significant' it means that, while the estimated value of the coefficient is not exactly zero (e.g. 1.10 in the example above), the coefficient is indistinguishable statistically from zero. If a zero was placed in the fitted equation instead of the estimated value, this would mean that, whatever happened to the value of that explanatory variable, the dependent variable would be unaffected. This would then be taken to mean that the variable is not helping to explain variations in y, and that it could therefore be removed from the regression equation. For example, if the t-ratio associated with x_3 had been 1.04 rather than 10.04, the variable would be classed as insignificant – i.e. not statistically different from zero). The only insignificant term in the above regression is the intercept. There are good statistical reasons for always retaining the constant, even if it is not significant; see chapter 6.

It is worth noting that, for degrees of freedom greater than around twenty-five, the 5 per cent two-sided critical value is approximately ± 2. So, as a rule of thumb (i.e. a rough guide), the null hypothesis would be rejected if the t-statistic exceeds two in absolute value.

Some authors place the t-ratios in parentheses below the corresponding coefficient estimates rather than the standard errors. Accordingly, one needs to check which convention is being used in each particular application, and also to state this clearly when presenting estimation results.

5.5 Goodness of fit statistics

5.5.1 R^2

It is desirable to have some measure of how well the regression model actually fits the data. In other words, it is desirable to have an answer to the question 'How well does the model containing the explanatory variables that was proposed actually explain variations in the dependent variable?'. Quantities known as *goodness of fit statistics* are available to test how well the sample regression function (SRF) fits the data – that is, how 'close' the fitted regression line is to all the data points taken together. Note that it is not possible to say how well the sample regression function fits the population regression function – i.e. how the estimated model compares with the true relationship between the variables – as the latter is never known.

What measures might therefore make plausible candidates to be goodness of fit statistics? A first response to this might be to look at the residual sum of squares. Recall that OLS selected the coefficient estimates that minimised this quantity, so the lower the minimised value of the RSS was, the better the model fitted the data. Consideration of the RSS is certainly one possibility, but the RSS is unbounded from above (strictly, it is bounded from above by the total sum of squares – see below) – i.e. it can take any (non-negative) value. So, for example, if the value of the RSS under OLS estimation was 136.4, what does this actually mean? It would be very difficult, by looking at this number alone, to tell whether the regression line fitted the data closely or not. The value of the RSS depends to a great extent on the scale of the dependent variable. Thus one way to reduce the RSS pointlessly would be to divide all the observations on y by ten!

In fact, a *scaled version* of the residual sum of squares is usually employed. The most common goodness of fit statistic is known as R^2. One way to define R^2 is to say that it is the square of the correlation coefficient between y and $\hat{y}$ – that is, the square of the correlation between the values of the dependent variable and the corresponding fitted values from the model. A correlation coefficient must lie between -1 and $+1$ by definition. Since R^2 (defined in this way) is the square of a correlation coefficient, it must lie between zero and one. If this correlation is high, the model fits the data well, while, if the correlation is low (close to zero), the model is not providing a good fit to the data.

Another definition of R^2 requires a consideration of what the model is attempting to explain. What the model is trying to do in effect is to explain variability of y about its mean value, $\bar{y}$. This quantity, $\bar{y}$, which is more specifically known as the unconditional mean of y, acts like a benchmark, since, if the researcher had no model for y, he/she could do no worse than to regress y on a constant only. In fact, the coefficient estimate for this regression would be the mean of y. So, from the regression

$$y_t = \beta_1 + u_t \tag{5.22}$$

the coefficient estimate, $\hat{\beta}_1$, will be the mean of y – i.e. $\bar{y}$. The total variation across all observations of the dependent variable about its mean value is known as the total sum of squares, TSS, which is given by

$$TSS = \sum_t (y_t - \bar{y})^2 \tag{5.23}$$

The TSS can be split into two parts: the part that has been explained by the model (known as the explained sum of squares, ESS) and the part that the model was not able to explain (the RSS). That is,

$$TSS = ESS + RSS \tag{5.24}$$

$$\sum_t (y_t - \bar{y})^2 = \sum_t (\hat{y}_t - \bar{y})^2 + \sum_t \hat{u}_t^2 \tag{5.25}$$

Recall that the residual sum of squares can also be expressed as

$$\sum_t (y_t - \hat{y}_t)^2$$

since a residual for observation t is defined as the difference between the actual and fitted values for that observation. The goodness of fit statistic is given by the ratio of the explained sum of squares to the total sum of squares,

$$R^2 = \frac{ESS}{TSS} \tag{5.26}$$

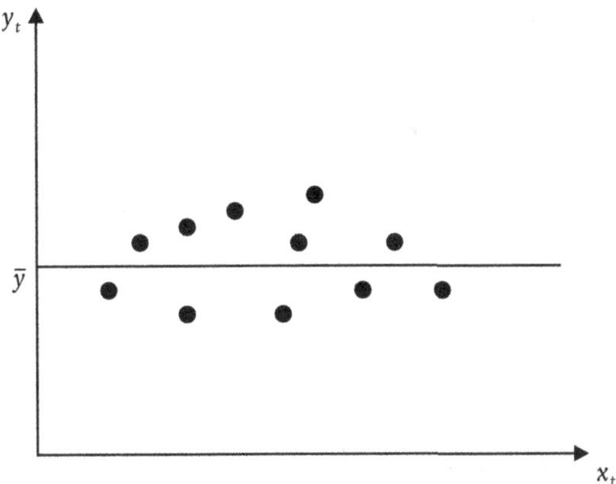

Figure 5.1
$R^2 = 0$ demonstrated by a flat estimated line

but, since $TSS = ESS + RSS$, it is also possible to write

$$R^2 = \frac{ESS}{TSS} = \frac{TSS - RSS}{TSS} = 1 - \frac{RSS}{TSS} \tag{5.27}$$

R^2 must always lie between zero and one (provided that there is a constant term in the regression). This is intuitive from the correlation interpretation of R^2 given above, but, for another explanation, consider two extreme cases:

$$\begin{array}{llll} RSS = TSS & \text{i.e. } ESS = 0 & \text{so} & R^2 = ESS/TSS = 0 \\ ESS = TSS & \text{i.e. } RSS = 0 & \text{so} & R^2 = ESS/TSS = 1 \end{array}$$

In the first case, the model has not succeeded in explaining any of the variability of y about its mean value, and hence the residual and total sums of squares are equal. This would happen only when the estimated values of all the coefficients were exactly zero. In the second case, the model has explained all the variability of y about its mean value, which implies that the residual sum of squares will be zero. This would happen only in the case in which all the observation points lie exactly on the fitted line. Neither of these two extremes is likely in practice, of course, but they do show that R^2 is bounded to lie between zero and one, with a higher R^2 implying, everything else being equal, that the model fits the data better.

To sum up, a simple way (but crude, as explained next) to tell whether the regression line fits the data well is to look at the value of R^2. A value of R^2 close to one indicates that the model explains nearly all the variability of the dependent variable about its mean value, while a value close to zero indicates that the model fits the data poorly. The two extreme cases, in which $R^2 = 0$ and $R^2 = 1$, are indicated in figures 5.1 and 5.2 in the context of a simple bivariate regression.

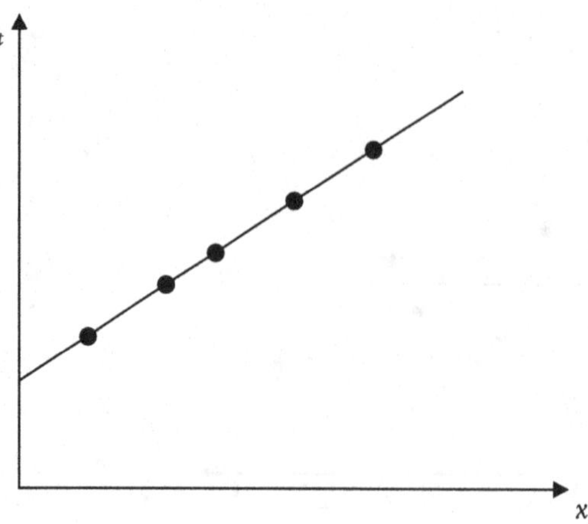

Figure 5.2
$R^2 = 1$ when all data points lie exactly on the estimated line

Example 5.2 Measuring goodness of fit

We now estimate the R^2 for equation (4.28) applying formula (5.27). RSS = 1214.20, TSS = 2550.59.

$$R^2 = 1 - \frac{RSS}{TSS} = 1 - \frac{1214.20}{2550.59} = 0.52$$

Equation (4.28) explains 52 per cent of the variability of rent growth. For a bivariate regression model, this would usually be considered a satisfactory performance.

5.5.2 *Problems with R^2 as a goodness of fit measure*

R^2 is simple to calculate and intuitive to understand, and provides a broad indication of the fit of the model to the data. There are a number of problems with R^2 as a goodness of fit measure, however, which are outlined in box 5.1.

Box 5.1 Disadvantages of R^2

(1) R^2 is defined in terms of variation about the mean of y, so, that if a model is reparameterised (rearranged) and the dependent variable changes, R^2 will change, even if the second model is a simple rearrangement of the first, with identical RSS. Thus it is not sensible to compare the value of R^2 between models with different dependent variables.

(2) R^2 never falls if more regressors are added to the regression. For example, consider the following two models:

$$\text{regression 1: } y = \beta_1 + \beta_2 x_2 + \beta_3 x_3 + u \quad (5.28)$$

$$\text{regression 2: } y = \beta_1 + \beta_2 x_2 + \beta_3 x_3 + \beta_4 x_4 + u \quad (5.29)$$

R^2 will always be at least as high for regression 2 relative to regression 1. The R^2 from regression 2 would be exactly the same as that for regression 1 only if the estimated value of the coefficient on the new variable were exactly zero – i.e. $\hat{\beta}_4 = 0$. In practice, $\hat{\beta}_4$ will always be non-zero, even if not significantly so, and thus in practice R^2 always rises as more variables are added to a model. This feature of R^2 essentially makes it impossible to use as a determinant of whether a given variable should be present in the model or not.

(3) R^2 quite often takes on values of 0.9 or higher for time series regressions, and hence it is not good at discriminating between models, as a wide array of models will frequently have broadly similar (and high) values of R^2.

5.5.3 *Adjusted R^2*

In order to get round the second of these three problems, a modification to R^2 is often made that takes into account the loss of degrees of freedom associated with adding extra variables. This is known as $\bar{R}^2$, or adjusted R^2, which is defined as

$$\bar{R}^2 = 1 - \left[\frac{T-1}{T-k}(1-R^2)\right] \tag{5.30}$$

where k is the number of parameters to be estimated in the model and T is the sample size. If an extra regressor (variable) is added to the model, k increases and, unless R^2 increases by a more than offsetting amount, $\bar{R}^2$ will actually fall. Hence $\bar{R}^2$ can be used as a decision-making tool for determining whether a given variable should be included in a regression model or not, with the rule being: include the variable if $\bar{R}^2$ rises and do not include it if $\bar{R}^2$ falls.

There are still problems with the maximisation of $\bar{R}^2$, however, as a criterion for model selection.

(1) It is a 'soft' rule, implying that, by following it, the researcher will typically end up with a large model, containing a lot of marginally significant or insignificant variables.

(2) There is no distribution available for $\bar{R}^2$ or R^2, so hypothesis tests cannot be conducted using them. The implication is that one can never tell whether the R^2 or the $\bar{R}^2$ from one model is significantly higher than that of another model in a statistical sense.

5.6 Tests of non-nested hypotheses

All the hypothesis tests conducted thus far in this book have been in the context of 'nested' models. This means that, in each case, the test involved imposing restrictions on the original model to arrive at a restricted formulation that would be a subset of, or nested within, the original specification.

Sometimes, however, it is of interest to compare between non-nested models. For example, suppose that there are two researchers working independently, each with a separate real estate theory for explaining the variation in some variable, y_t. The respective models selected by the researchers could be

$$y_t = \alpha_1 + \alpha_2 x_{2t} + u_t \tag{5.31}$$

$$y_t = \beta_1 + \beta_2 x_{3t} + v_t \tag{5.32}$$

where u_t and v_t are iid error terms. Model (5.31) includes variable x_2 but not x_3, while model (5.32) includes x_3 but not x_2. In this case, neither model can be viewed as a restriction of the other, so how then can the two models be compared as to which better represents the data, y_t? Given the discussion in the previous section, an obvious answer would be to compare the values of R^2 or adjusted R^2 between the models. Either would be equally applicable in this case, since the two specifications have the same number of RHS variables. Adjusted R^2 could be used even in cases in which the number of variables was different in the two models, since it employs a penalty term that makes an allowance for the number of explanatory variables. Adjusted R^2 is based upon a particular penalty function, however (that is, $T-k$ appears in a specific way in the formula). This form of penalty term may not necessarily be optimal.

Moreover, given the statement above that adjusted R^2 is a soft rule, it is likely on balance that use of it to choose between models will imply that models with more explanatory variables are favoured. Several other similar rules are available, each having more or less strict penalty terms; these are collectively known as 'information criteria'. These are explained in some detail in chapter 8, but suffice to say for now that a different strictness of the penalty term will in many cases lead to a different preferred model.

An alternative approach to comparing between non-nested models would be to estimate an encompassing or hybrid model. In the case of (5.31) and (5.32), the relevant encompassing model would be

$$y_t = \gamma_1 + \gamma_2 x_{2t} + \gamma_3 x_{3t} + w_t \tag{5.33}$$

where w_t is an error term. Formulation (5.33) contains both (5.31) and (5.32) as special cases when γ_3 and γ_2 are zero, respectively. Therefore a test for the best model would be conducted via an examination of the significances of γ_2 and γ_3 in model (5.33). There will be four possible outcomes (box 5.2).

Box 5.2 Selecting between models

(1) γ_2 is statistically significant but γ_3 is not. In this case, (5.33) collapses to (5.31), and the latter is the preferred model.
(2) γ_3 is statistically significant but γ_2 is not. In this case, (5.33) collapses to (5.32), and the latter is the preferred model.
(3) γ_2 and γ_3 are both statistically significant. This would imply that both x_2 and x_3 have incremental explanatory power for y, in which case both variables should be retained. Models (5.31) and (5.32) are both ditched and (5.33) is the preferred model.
(4) Neither γ_2 nor γ_3 is statistically significant. In this case, none of the models can be dropped, and some other method for choosing between them must be employed.

There are several limitations to the use of encompassing regressions to select between non-nested models, however. Most importantly, even if models (5.31) and (5.32) have a strong theoretical basis for including the RHS variables that they do, the hybrid model may be meaningless. For example, it could be the case that real estate theory suggests that y could either follow model (5.31) or model (5.32), but model (5.33) is implausible.

In adition, if the competing explanatory variables x_2 and x_3 are highly related – i.e. they are near-collinear – it could be the case that, if they are both included, neither γ_2 nor γ_3 is statistically significant, while each is significant in its separate regressions (5.31) and (5.32); see chapter 6 for an explanation of why this may happen.

An alternative approach is via the J-encompassing test due to Davidson and MacKinnon (1981). Interested readers are referred to their work or to Gujarati (2009) for further details.

Example 5.3 A multiple regression in real estate

Amy, Ming and Yuan (2000) study the Singapore office market and focus on obtaining empirical estimates for the natural vacancy rate and rents utilising existing theoretical frameworks. Their empirical analysis includes the estimation of different specifications for rents. For their investigation, quarterly data are available. One of the models they estimate is given by equation (5.34),

$$\%\Delta R_t = \beta_0 + \beta_1\%\Delta E_t - \beta_2 V_{t-1} \tag{5.34}$$

where $\%\Delta$ denotes a percentage change (over the previous quarter), R_t is the nominal rent (hence $\%\Delta R_t$ is the percentage change in nominal rent this quarter over the preceding one), E_t is the operating costs (due to data limitations, the authors approximate this variable with the consumer price index; the CPI reflects the cost-push elements in an inflationary environment as landlords push for higher rents to cover inflation and expenses) and V_{t-1} is the vacancy rate (in per cent) in the previous quarter. The fitted model is

$$\%\Delta\hat{R}_t = \underset{(2.7)}{6.21} + \underset{(2.5)}{2.07}(\%\Delta E_t) - \underset{(-3.0)}{0.54}V_{t-1} \tag{5.35}$$

Adjusted $\bar{R}^2 = 0.23$

According to the above results, if the vacancy rate in the previous quarter fell by 1 per cent, the rate of nominal growth will increase by 0.54 per cent. This is considered a rather small sensitivity. An increase in the CPI of 1 per cent will push up the rate of nominal rent growth by 2.07 per cent. The t-statistics in parentheses confirm that the parameters are statistically significant.

The above model explains approximately 23 per cent of the variation in nominal rent growth, which means that model (5.35) has quite low explanatory power. Both the low explanatory power and the small sensitivity of rents to vacancy are perhaps a result of model misspecification, which the authors detect and attempt to address in their paper. We consider such issues of model misspecification in the following chapter.

An alternative model that Amy, Ming and Yuan run is

$$\%\Delta RR_t = \beta_0 + \beta_2 V_t + u_t \tag{5.36}$$

This is a bivariate regression model; $\%\Delta RR_t$ is the quarterly percentage change in real rents (note that, in equation (5.34), nominal growth was used). The following equation is the outcome:

$$\%\Delta RR_t = \underset{(1.67)}{18.53} - \underset{(-3.3)}{1.50}V_t \tag{5.37}$$

Adjusted $R^2 = 0.21$

In equation (5.37), the vacancy takes the expected negative sign and the coefficient suggests that a 1 per cent rise in vacancy will, on average, reduce the rate of growth of real rents by 1.5 per cent. The sensitivity of rent growth to vacancy is greater than that in the previous model. The explanatory power remains low, however.

Although we have not completed the treatment of regression analysis, one may ask whether we can take a view as to which model is more appropriate to study office rents in Singapore.

This book equips the reader with the tools to answer this question, in particular by means of the tests we discuss in the next chapter and the evaluation of forecast performance in later chapters. On the basis of the information we have for these two models, however, some observations can be made.

(1) We would prefer the variables to be in real terms (adjusted for inflation), as for the rent series in equation (5.36).
(2) The models seem to have similar explanatory power but equation (5.34) has two drivers. Caution should be exercised, however. We said earlier that the adjusted R^2 can be used for comparisons only if the dependent variable is the same (which is not the case here, since the dependent variables differ). In this case, a comparison can tentatively be made, given that the dependent variables are not entirely different (which would have been the case if we had been modelling the percentage change in rents and the level of rents, for example).

Going back to our earlier point that more testing is required, the authors report misspecification problems in their paper, and hence none of the models scores particularly well. Based on this information, we would choose equation (5.36), because of point (1) above and the low adjusted R^2 of the multiple regression model (5.35).

5.7 Data mining and the true size of the test

Recall that the probability of rejecting a correct null hypothesis is equal to the size of the test, denoted α. The possibility of rejecting a correct null hypothesis arises from the fact that test statistics are assumed to follow a random distribution and hence take on extreme values that fall in the rejection region some of the time by chance alone. A consequence of this is that it will almost always be possible to find significant relationships between variables if enough variables are examined. For example, suppose that a dependent variable y_t and twenty explanatory variables $x_{2t}, \ldots, x_{21t}$ (excluding a constant term) are generated separately as independent normally distributed random variables. Then y is regressed separately on each of the twenty explanatory variables plus a constant, and the significance of each explanatory variable in the regressions is examined. If this experiment is repeated many times, on average one of the twenty regressions will have a slope coefficient that is significant at the 5 per cent level for each experiment. The implication is that, if enough explanatory variables are employed in a regression, often one or more will be significant by chance alone. More concretely, it could be stated that, if an α per cent size of test is used, on average one in every $(100/\alpha)$ regressions will have a significant slope coefficient by chance alone.

Trying many variables in a regression without basing the selection of the candidate variables on a real estate or economic theory is known as 'data mining' or 'data snooping'. The result in such cases is that the true significance level will be considerably greater than the nominal significance level assumed. For example, suppose that twenty separate regressions are conducted, of which three contain a significant regressor, and a 5 per cent nominal significance level is assumed; then the true significance level would be much higher (e.g. 25 per cent). Therefore, if the researcher then shows only the results for the regression containing the final three equations and states that they are significant at the 5 per cent level, inappropriate conclusions concerning the significance of the variables would result.

As well as ensuring that the selection of candidate regressors for inclusion in a model is made on the basis of real estate theory, another way to avoid data mining is by examining the forecast performance of the model in an 'out-of-sample' data set (see chapters 8 and 9). The idea, essentially, is that a proportion of the data is not used in model estimation but is retained for model testing. A relationship observed in the estimation period that is purely the result of data mining, and is therefore spurious, is very unlikely to be repeated for the out-of-sample period. Therefore models that are the product of data mining are likely to fit very poorly and to give very inaccurate forecasts for the out-of-sample period. This topic will be elaborated in subsequent chapters.

5.8 Testing multiple hypotheses: the *F*-test

The *t*-test was used to test single hypotheses – i.e. hypotheses involving only one coefficient. What if it is of interest to test more than one coefficient simultaneously, however? For example, what if a researcher wanted to determine whether a restriction that the coefficient values for β_2 and β_3 are both unity could be imposed, so that an increase in either one of the two variables x_2 or x_3 would cause y to rise by one unit? The *t*-testing framework is not sufficiently general to cope with this sort of hypothesis test. Instead, a more general framework is employed, centring on an F-test. Under the F-test framework, two regressions are required, known as the *unrestricted* and the *restricted regressions*. The unrestricted regression is the one in which the coefficients are freely determined by the data, as has been constructed previously. The restricted regression is the one in which the coefficients are restricted – i.e. the restrictions are imposed on some βs. Thus the F-test approach to hypothesis testing is also termed restricted least squares, for obvious reasons.

The residual sums of squares from each regression are determined, and the two residual sums of squares are 'compared' in the test statistic. The F-test statistic for testing multiple hypotheses about the coefficient estimates is given by

$$\textit{test statistic} = \frac{RRSS - URSS}{URSS} \times \frac{T - k}{m} \tag{5.38}$$

where the following notation applies:

URSS = residual sum of squares from unrestricted regression;
RRSS = residual sum of squares from restricted regression;
m = number of restrictions;
T = number of observations; and
k = number of regressors in unrestricted regression, including a constant.

The most important part of the test statistic to understand is the numerator expression, $RRSS - URSS$. To see why the test centres around a comparison of the residual sums of squares from the restricted and unrestricted regressions, recall that OLS estimation involves choosing the model that minimises the residual sum of squares, with no constraints imposed. If, after imposing constraints on the model, a residual sum of squares results that is not much higher than the unconstrained model's residual sum of squares, it would be concluded that the restrictions were supported by the data. On the other hand, if the residual sum of squares increased considerably after the restrictions were imposed, it would be concluded that the restrictions were not supported by the data and therefore that the hypothesis should be rejected.

It can be further stated that RRSS $\geq$ URSS. Only under a particular set of very extreme circumstances will the residual sums of squares for the restricted and unrestricted models be exactly equal. This would be the case when the restriction was already present in the data, so that it is not really a restriction at all (it would be said that the restriction is 'not binding' – i.e. it does not make any difference to the parameter estimates). So, for example, if the null hypothesis is H_0: $\beta_2 = 1$ and $\beta_3 = 1$, then RRSS = URSS only in the case in which the coefficient estimates for the unrestricted regression are $\hat{\beta}_2 = 1$ and $\hat{\beta}_3 = 1$. Of course, such an event is extremely unlikely to occur in practice.

Example 5.4

In the previous chapter, we estimated a bivariate model of real rent growth for UK offices (equation 4.10). The single explanatory variable was the growth in employment and financial and business services. We now extend this model to include GDP growth as another explanatory variable. There is an argument in the existing literature suggesting that employment is not the only factor that will affect rent growth but also an output measure that better captures turnover and profitability.[2]

The results of the multiple regression model of real office rent growth in the United Kingdom are given in equation (5.39) with *t*-statistics in parentheses. In this example of modelling UK office rents, we have also extended the sample by one more year, to 2006, compared with that in the previous chapter. From the results in this equation (estimated for the sample period 1979 to 2006), *GDPg* makes an incremental contribution to explain growth in real office rents:

$$\underset{}{R\hat{R}g_t} = \underset{(-4.9)}{-11.53} + \underset{(3.7)}{2.52}EFBSg_t + \underset{(2.1)}{1.75}GDPg_t \tag{5.39}$$

We would like to test the hypothesis that the coefficients on both GDP growth ($GDPg_t$) and employment growth ($EFBSg_t$) are zero. The unrestricted and restricted equations are, respectively,

$$RRg_t = \alpha + \beta_1 EFBSg_t + \beta_2 GDPg_t + u_t \tag{5.40}$$

$$RRg_t = \alpha + u_t \tag{5.41}$$

The RSS values for the unrestricted and restricted equation are 1,078.26 and 2,897.73, respectively. The number of observations, T, is twenty-eight. The number of restrictions, m, is two and the number of parameters to be estimated in the unrestricted equation, k, is three. Applying the formula (5.38), we get the value of 21.09 for the test statistic. The test statistic will follow an $F(m, T-k)$ or $F(2, 25)$, with critical value 3.39 at the 5 per cent significance level. The test statistic clearly exceeds the critical value at 5 per cent, and hence the null hypothesis is rejected. Therefore the coefficients are not jointly zero.

We would now like to test the hypothesis that the coefficients on *EFBS* and *GDP* are equal and thus that the two variables have the same impact on real rent growth – that is, $\beta_1 = \beta_2$. The unrestricted and restricted equations are, respectively,

$$RRg_t = \alpha + \beta_1 EFBSg_t + \beta_2 GDP_t + u_t \tag{5.42}$$

$$RRg_t = \alpha + \beta_1 (EFBSg_t + GDPg_t) + u_t \tag{5.43}$$

[2] The GDP data are taken from the Office for National Statistics.

The RSS for the unrestricted and restricted equation are 1,078.26 and 1,092.81, respectively. The number of observations, T, is twenty-eight. The number of restrictions, m, is two and the number of parameters to be estimated in the unrestricted equation is three. Applying the formula (5.38), we get the test statistic value of 0.46. The $F(m, T-k)$ or $F(1, 25)$ critical value is 4.24 at the 5 per cent significance level. The test statistic is considerably lower than the critical value, and hence the null hypothesis is not rejected. Therefore the coefficients on *EFBSg* and *GDPg* (the slopes) are not statistically significantly different from one another.

5.8.1 *The relationship between the t- and the F-distributions*

Any hypothesis that can be tested with a t-test could also have been tested using an F-test, but not the other way around. Accordingly, single hypotheses involving one coefficient can be tested using a t- or an F-test, but multiple hypotheses can be tested only using an F-test. For example, consider the hypothesis

$$H_0: \beta_2 = 0.5$$
$$H_1: \beta_2 \neq 0.5$$

This hypothesis could have been tested using the usual t-test,

$$test\ stat = \frac{\hat{\beta}_2 - 0.5}{SE(\hat{\beta}_2)} \tag{5.44}$$

or it could be tested in the framework above for the F-test. Note that the two tests always give the same conclusion, since the t-distribution is just a special case of the F-distribution, as demonstrated in box 5.3.

Box 5.3 The t- and F-distributions compared

- Consider any random variable Z that follows a t-distribution with $T-k$ degrees of freedom, and square it. The square of the t is equivalent to a particular form of the F-distribution:

$$Z^2 \sim t^2\ (T-k) \text{ then also } Z^2 \sim F(1, T-k)$$

- Thus the square of a t-distributed random variable with $T-k$ degrees of freedom also follows an F-distribution with one and $T-k$ degrees of freedom.
- This relationship between the t- and the F-distributions will always hold.
- The F-distribution has only positive values and is not symmetrical.
- Therefore the null is rejected only if the test statistic exceeds the critical F-value, although the test is a two-sided one in the sense that rejection will occur if $\hat{\beta}_2$ is significantly bigger or significantly smaller than 0.5.

5.8.2 *Determining the number of restrictions, m*

How is the appropriate value of m decided in each case? Informally, the number of restrictions can be seen as 'the number of equality signs under the null hypothesis'. To give some examples:

H_0: hypothesis	number of restrictions, m
$\beta_1 + \beta_2 = 2$	1
$\beta_2 = 1$ and $\beta_3 = -1$	2
$\beta_2 = 0$, $\beta_3 = 0$ and $\beta_4 = 0$	3

At first glance, you may have thought that, in the first of these cases, the number of restrictions was two. In fact, there is only one restriction that involves two coefficients. The number of restrictions in the second two examples is obvious, as they involve two and three separate component restrictions, respectively.

The last of these three examples is particularly important. If the model is

$$y = \beta_1 + \beta_2 x_2 + \beta_3 x_3 + \beta_4 x_4 + u \tag{5.45}$$

then the null hypothesis of

$$\mathrm{H}_0: \beta_2 = 0 \quad \text{and} \quad \beta_3 = 0 \quad \text{and} \quad \beta_4 = 0$$

is tested by 'the' regression F-statistic. It tests the null hypothesis that all the coefficients except the intercept coefficient are zero. This test is sometimes called a test for 'junk regressions', since, if this null hypothesis cannot be rejected, it would imply that none of the independent variables in the model was able to explain variations in y.

Note the form of the alternative hypothesis for all tests when more than one restriction is involved:

$$\mathrm{H}_1: \beta_2 \neq 0 \quad \text{or} \quad \beta_3 \neq 0 \quad \text{or} \quad \beta_4 \neq 0$$

In other words, 'and' occurs under the null hypothesis and 'or' under the alternative, so that it takes only one part of a joint null hypothesis to be wrong for the null hypothesis as a whole to be rejected.

5.8.3 *Hypotheses that cannot be tested with either an* F- *or a* t-*test*

It is not possible to test hypotheses that are not linear or that are multiplicative using this framework; for example, H_0: $\beta_2\beta_3 = 2$, or H_0: $\beta_2^2 = 1$, cannot be tested.

5.9 Omission of an important variable

What would the effects be of excluding from the estimated regression a variable that is a determinant of the dependent variable? For example, suppose that the true, but unknown, data-generating process is represented by

$$y_t = \beta_1 + \beta_2 x_{2t} + \beta_3 x_{3t} + \beta_4 x_{4t} + \beta_5 x_{5t} + u_t \quad (5.46)$$

but that the researcher estimates a model of the form

$$y_t = \beta_1 + \beta_2 x_{2t} + \beta_3 x_{3t} + \beta_4 x_{4t} + u_t \quad (5.47)$$

– i.e. with the variable x_{5t} omitted from the model. The consequence would be that the estimated coefficients on all the other variables will be biased and inconsistent unless the excluded variable is uncorrelated with all the included variables. Even if this condition is satisfied, the estimate of the coefficient on the constant term will be biased, which would imply that any forecasts made from the model would be biased. The standard errors will also be biased (upwards), and hence hypothesis tests could yield inappropriate inferences. Further intuition is offered by Dougherty (1992, pp. 168–73).

Example 5.5

Tests for omitted variables are very difficult to conduct in practice because we will usually not be able to observe the omitted variables, or we may not even be aware of their relevance. For illustration of what we would do if we did have a candidate omitted variable, however, in the context of our previous example of modelling real office rent growth, we now test whether we have omitted output in the financial and business services sectors (*OFBS*).[3] One could argue that GDP is a more general measure of activity in those business sectors that require office space whereas output in financial and business services is more relevant to examine activity and occupier demand in office-using industries. We run an F-test based on the sum of squared residuals in the restricted and unrestricted equations.

Before presenting the results, a note should be made about the sample size. For our reference equation (5.39), the sample period is 1979 to 2006, which comprises twenty-eight observations. When we examine the significance of the omitted *OFBS* series, the sample size shrinks, since official data for *OFBS* start only in 1983 and, since we use growth rates, the sample commences in 1984. Hence the estimations and tests below take place for the

[3] The data are from the Office for National Statistics.

sample period 1984 to 2006, which leads to different parameter estimates. Admittedly, this is a restricted sample period, but the objective here is more to illustrate the application of the test.

Unrestricted equation (1984–2006):

$$R\hat{R}g_t = \underset{(6.35)}{-17.68} + \underset{(3.76)}{2.45}EFBSg_t + \underset{(1.92)}{2.71}GDPg_t + \underset{(0.87)}{0.79}OFBSg_t \quad (5.48)$$

where $OFBSg$ is the annual percentage growth in $OFBS$, $R^2 = 0.76$, adj. $R^2 = 0.72$, URSS $= 619.46$, k (number of regressors) $= 4$ and m (number of added variables) $= 1$.

Restricted equation (1984–2006):

$$R\hat{R}g_t = \underset{(6.37)}{-17.06} + \underset{(3.96)}{2.53}EFBSg_t + \underset{(3.61)}{3.58}GDPg_t \quad (5.49)$$

$R^2 = 0.75$, adj. $R^2 = 0.72$, RRSS $= 643.98$, $T = 23$.

Before conducting the F-test, we make the following observations.

- The value of the intercept parameter estimate has not changed much, which provides an indication that the added variable does not bring further information into the model.
- The coefficient that is most affected is that of *GDPg*. Hence *OFBSg* very probably conveys similar information to that of *GDPg*. Indeed, their correlation is strong (the correlation coefficient is 0.78), whereas *OFBSg* is more moderately correlated with *EFBSg* (correlation coefficient = 0.48). Therefore *GDPg* and *OFBSg* are collinear, and this is why their t-ratios are not significant; this issue is discussed in detail in the following chapter.
- We observe no impact on the coefficients of determination, and in fact the adjusted R^2 of the unrestricted model is lower – a signal that the added variable does not contribute anything.

The F-test statistic is $\frac{643.98-619.46}{619.46} \times \frac{23-4}{1} = 0.75$. The critical value for $F(1{,}19)$ at the 5 per cent level is 4.38. Since the computed value is less than the critical value, we do not reject the null hypothesis that *OFBSg* does not belong to the equation at the 5 per cent significance level.

5.10 Inclusion of an irrelevant variable

Suppose now that the researcher makes the opposite error to that in section 5.9 – i.e. the true DGP is represented by

$$y_t = \beta_1 + \beta_2 x_{2t} + \beta_3 x_{3t} + \beta_4 x_{4t} + u_t \quad (5.50)$$

but the researcher estimates a model of the form

$$y_t = \beta_1 + \beta_2 x_{2t} + \beta_3 x_{3t} + \beta_4 x_{4t} + \beta_5 x_{5t} + u_t \tag{5.51}$$

thus incorporating the superfluous or irrelevant variable x_{5t}. As x_{5t} is irrelevant, the expected value of β_5 is zero, although, in any practical application, its estimated value is very unlikely to be exactly zero. The consequence of including an irrelevant variable would be that the coefficient estimators would still be consistent and unbiased, but the estimators would be inefficient. This would imply that the standard errors for the coefficients are likely to be inflated relative to the values that they would have taken if the irrelevant variable had not been included. Variables that would otherwise have been marginally significant may no longer be so in the presence of irrelevant variables. In general, it can also be stated that the extent of the loss of efficiency will depend positively on the absolute value of the correlation between the included irrelevant variable and the other explanatory variables.

Summarising the last two sections, it is evident that, when trying to determine whether to err on the side of including too many or too few variables in a regression model, there is an implicit trade-off between inconsistency and efficiency. Many researchers would argue that, while, in an ideal world, the model will incorporate precisely the correct variables – no more and no less – the former problem is more serious than the latter, and therefore, in the real world, one should err on the side of incorporating marginally significant variables.

Example 5.6

In our model for UK office rents, we test whether *GDPg* is irrelevant by computing an F-test. The null hypothesis is that *GDPg* does not belong to the equation (5.39) or that the coefficient on GDP_g is zero. Similar to example 5.5 above, we run the unrestricted and restricted equations. The unrestricted equation is equation (5.39). For that equation, the following statistics were obtained: $R^2 = 0.58$, adj. $R^2 = 0.55$, RRSS $= 1{,}078.26$.

Restricted equation:

$$\underset{}{R\hat{R}g_t} = \underset{(1.80)}{-9.54} + \underset{(5.18)}{3.25EFBSg_t} \tag{5.52}$$

$R^2 = 0.51$, adj. $R^2 = 0.49$, RRSS $= 1{,}268.38$. We observe that the adj. R^2 has not dropped much in the restricted equation and that the size of the coefficient on $EFBSg_t$ has increased, as it now picks up more influences that were previously explained by $GDPg_t$. The F-test statistic is $\frac{1268.38-1078.26}{1078.26} \times \frac{28-3}{1} = 4.41$.

The critical value for $F(1, 25)$ at the 5 per cent level is 4.24. Since the computed value is just higher than the critical value, we reject the null hypothesis at the 5 per cent significance level that *GDPg* does not belong to the equation. If we now repeat the analysis and test *EFBSg* as a redundant variable, the results will clearly indicate that this variable strongly belongs to equation (5.49). The computed F-test statistic is 22.08, which is comfortably higher than the critical $F(1, 25)$ value at the 5 per cent level of significance.

Key concepts

The key terms to be able to define and explain from this chapter are

- multiple regression model
- unrestricted regression
- restricted regression
- total sum of squares
- R^2
- adjusted R^2
- non-nested hypotheses
- encompassing regression
- data mining
- F-test
- restrictions
- omitted variable
- irrelevant variable

Appendix: Mathematical derivations of CLRM results for the multiple regression case

5A.1 Derivation of the OLS coefficient estimator

In the multiple regression context, in order to obtain estimates of the parameters, $\beta_1, \beta_2, \ldots, \beta_k$, the RSS would be minimised with respect to all the elements of β. Now the residuals are expressed in a vector:

$$\hat{u} = \begin{bmatrix} \hat{u}_1 \\ \hat{u}_2 \\ \vdots \\ \hat{u}_T \end{bmatrix} \tag{5A.1}$$

The RSS is still the relevant loss function, and would be given in a matrix notation by expression (5A.2):

$$L = \hat{u}'\hat{u} = [\,\hat{u}_1\,\hat{u}_2\,\ldots\,\hat{u}_T\,] \begin{bmatrix} \hat{u}_1 \\ \hat{u}_2 \\ \vdots \\ \hat{u}_T \end{bmatrix} = \hat{u}_1^2 + \hat{u}_2^2 + \cdots + \hat{u}_T^2 = \sum \hat{u}_t^2 \tag{5A.2}$$

Denoting the vector of estimated parameters as $\hat{\beta}$, it is also possible to write

$$L = \hat{u}'\hat{u} = (y - X\hat{\beta})'(y - X\hat{\beta}) = y'y - \hat{\beta}'X'y - y'X\hat{\beta} + \hat{\beta}'X'X\hat{\beta} \tag{5A.3}$$

It turns out that $\hat{\beta}'X'y$ is $(1 \times k) \times (k \times T) \times (T \times 1) = 1 \times 1$, and also that $y'X\hat{\beta}$ is $(1 \times T) \times (T \times k) \times (k \times 1) = 1 \times 1$, so in fact $\hat{\beta}'X'y = y'X\hat{\beta}$. Thus (5A.3) can be written

$$L = \hat{u}'\hat{u} = (y - X\hat{\beta})'(y - X\hat{\beta}) = y'y - 2\hat{\beta}'X'y + \hat{\beta}'X'X\hat{\beta} \tag{5A.4}$$

Differentiating this expression with respect to $\hat{\beta}$ and setting it to zero in order to find the parameter values that minimise the residual sum of squares would yield

$$\frac{\partial L}{\partial \hat{\beta}} = -2X'y + 2X'X\hat{\beta} = 0 \tag{5A.5}$$

This expression arises since the derivative of $y'y$ is zero with respect to $\hat{\beta}$, and $\hat{\beta}'X'X\hat{\beta}$ acts like a square of $X\hat{\beta}$, which is differentiated to $2X'X\hat{\beta}$. Rearranging,

$$2X'y = 2X'X\hat{\beta} \tag{5A.6}$$

$$X'y = X'X\hat{\beta} \tag{5A.7}$$

Pre-multiplying both sides of (5A.7) by the inverse of $X'X$,

$$\hat{\beta} = (X'X)^{-1}X'y \tag{5A.8}$$

Thus the vector of OLS coefficient estimates for a set of k parameters is given by

$$\hat{\beta} = \begin{bmatrix} \hat{\beta}_1 \\ \hat{\beta}_2 \\ \vdots \\ \hat{\beta}_k \end{bmatrix} = (X'X)^{-1}X'y \tag{5A.9}$$

5A.2 Derivation of the OLS standard error estimator

The variance of a vector of random variables $\hat{\beta}$ is given by the formula $E[(\hat{\beta} - \beta)(\hat{\beta} - \beta)']$. Since $y = X\beta + u$, it can also be stated, given (5A.8), that

$$\hat{\beta} = (X'X)^{-1}X'(X\beta + u) \tag{5A.10}$$

Expanding the parentheses,

$$\hat{\beta} = (X'X)^{-1}X'X\beta + (X'X)^{-1}X'u \tag{5A.11}$$

$$\hat{\beta} = \beta + (X'X)^{-1}X'u \tag{5A.12}$$

Thus it is possible to express the variance of $\hat{\beta}$ as

$$E[(\hat{\beta} - \beta)(\hat{\beta} - \beta)'] = E[(\beta + (X'X)^{-1}X'u - \beta)(\beta + (X'X)^{-1}X'u - \beta)'] \tag{5A.13}$$

Cancelling the β terms in each set of parentheses,

$$E[(\hat{\beta} - \beta)(\hat{\beta} - \beta)'] = E[((X'X)^{-1}X'u)((X'X)^{-1}X'u)'] \tag{5A.14}$$

Expanding the parentheses on the RHS of (5A.14) gives

$$E[(\hat{\beta} - \beta)(\hat{\beta} - \beta)'] = E[(X'X)^{-1}X'uu'X(X'X)^{-1}] \tag{5A.15}$$

$$E[(\hat{\beta} - \beta)(\hat{\beta} - \beta)'] = (X'X)^{-1}X'E[uu']X(X'X)^{-1} \tag{5A.16}$$

Now $E[uu'] = s^2 I$, so that

$$E[(\hat{\beta} - \beta)(\hat{\beta} - \beta)'] = (X'X)^{-1}X's^2 IX(X'X)^{-1} \tag{5A.17}$$

where I is a $k \times k$ identity matrix. Rearranging further,

$$E[(\hat{\beta} - \beta)(\hat{\beta} - \beta)'] = s^2(X'X)^{-1}X'X(X'X)^{-1} \tag{5A.18}$$

The $X'X$ and the last $(X'X)^{-1}$ term cancel out, to leave

$$\text{var}(\hat{\beta}) = s^2(X'X)^{-1} \tag{5A.19}$$

as the expression for the parameter variance–covariance matrix. This quantity, $s^2(X'X)^{-1}$, is known as the variance–covariance matrix of the coefficients. The leading diagonal terms give the coefficient variances while the off-diagonal terms give the covariances between the parameter estimates. The variance of $\hat{\beta}_1$ is the first diagonal element, the variance of $\hat{\beta}_2$ is the second element on the leading diagonal, ..., and the variance of $\hat{\beta}_k$ is the kth diagonal element, etc., as discussed in the body of the chapter.

6 Diagnostic testing

Learning outcomes

In this chapter, you will learn how to

- describe the steps involved in testing regression residuals for heteroscedasticity and autocorrelation;
- explain the impact of heteroscedasticity or autocorrelation on the optimality of OLS parameter and standard error estimation;
- distinguish between the Durbin–Watson and Breusch–Godfrey tests for autocorrelation;
- highlight the advantages and disadvantages of dynamic models;
- test for whether the functional form of the model employed is appropriate;
- determine whether the residual distribution from a regression differs significantly from normality;
- investigate whether the model parameters are stable; and
- appraise different philosophies of how to build an econometric model.

6.1 Introduction

Chapters 4 and 5 introduced the classical linear regression model and discussed key statistics in the estimation of bivariate and multiple regression models. The reader will have begun to build knowledge about assessing the goodness of fit and robustness of a regression model. This chapter continues the discussion of model adequacy by examining diagnostic tests that will help the real estate analyst to determine how reliable the model is and to recognise the circumstances under which OLS may run into problems. These tests enable an assessment of the quality of a model, the selection between models and, in particular, an assessment of the suitability of the chosen model to be used for forecasting.

6.2 Violations of the assumptions of the classical linear regression model

Recall that five assumptions were made relating to the CLRM. These were required to show that the estimation technique, ordinary least squares, had a number of desirable properties, and also so that hypothesis tests regarding the coefficient estimates could be conducted validly. Specifically, the following assumptions were made.

(1) $E(u_t) = 0$
(2) $\text{var}(u_t) = \sigma^2 < \infty$
(3) $\text{cov}(u_i, u_j) = 0$ for $i \neq j$
(4) $\text{cov}(u_t, x_t) = 0$
(5) $u_t \sim N(0, \sigma^2)$

These assumptions will now be studied further, looking in particular at the following points.

- How can violations of the assumptions be detected?
- What are the most likely causes of the violations in practice?
- What are the consequences for the model if an assumption is violated but this fact is ignored and the researcher proceeds regardless?

The answer to the last of these questions is that, in general, the model could encounter any combination of three problems:

- the coefficient estimates ($\hat{\beta}$s) are wrong;
- the associated standard errors are wrong; and/or
- the distributions that were assumed for the test statistics are inappropriate.

A pragmatic approach to 'solving' problems associated with the use of models in which one or more of the assumptions is not supported by the data is then adopted. Such solutions usually operate such that:

- the assumptions are no longer violated; or
- the problems are sidestepped, and alternative techniques are used that are still valid.

6.3 Statistical distributions for diagnostic tests

The text below discusses various regression diagnostic (misspecification) tests that are based on the calculation of a test statistic. These tests can be constructed in several ways, and the precise approach to constructing the test statistic will determine the distribution that the test statistic is assumed to follow. Two particular approaches are in common usage, and their results are given by the statistical packages: the LM (Lagrange multiplier) test and the Wald test. All that readers need to know concerning the operation of these testing procedures is that LM test statistics in the context of the diagnostic tests presented here follow a χ^2 distribution with degrees of freedom equal to the number of restrictions placed on the model, and denoted m. The Wald version of the test follows an F-distribution with $(m, T-k)$ degrees of freedom.

Asymptotically, these two tests are equivalent, although their results differ somewhat in small samples. They are equivalent as the sample size increases towards infinity, since there is a direct relationship between the χ^2 and F-distributions. Taking a χ^2 variate and dividing by its degrees of freedom asymptotically gives an F-variate:

$$\frac{\chi^2(m)}{m} \rightarrow F(m, T-k) \quad \text{as} \quad T \rightarrow \infty$$

Computer packages typically present results using both approaches, though only one of the two is illustrated for each test below. They usually give the same conclusion, although, if they do not, the F-version is usually considered preferable for finite samples, since it is sensitive to sample size (one of its degrees of freedom parameters depends on sample size) in a way that the χ^2 version is not.

6.4 Assumption 1: $E(u_t) = 0$

The first assumption required is that the average value of the errors is zero. In fact, if a constant term is included in the regression equation, this assumption will never be violated. What if real estate theory suggests, however, that, for a particular application, there should be no intercept and therefore the regression line is forced through the origin? If the regression did not include an intercept, and the average value of the errors was non-zero, several undesirable consequences could arise. First, R^2, defined as ESS/TSS, can be negative, implying that the sample average, $\bar{y}$, 'explains' more of the variation in y than the explanatory variables. Second, and more fundamentally, a regression with no intercept parameter could lead to potentially severe biases in the slope coefficient estimates. To see this, consider figure 6.1.

The solid line shows the regression line estimated including a constant term, while the dotted line shows the effect of suppressing – i.e. setting to zero – the constant term. The effect is that the estimated line, in this case, is

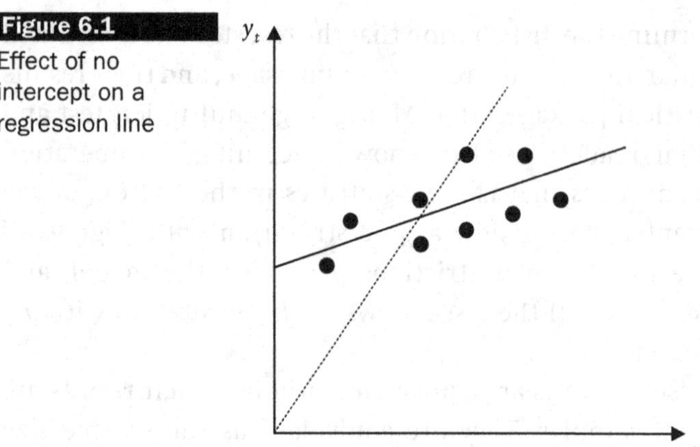

Figure 6.1 Effect of no intercept on a regression line

forced through the origin, so that the estimate of the slope coefficient ($\hat{\beta}$) is biased. Additionally, R^2 and $\bar{R}^2$ are usually meaningless in such a context. This arises because the mean value of the dependent variable, $\bar{y}$, is not equal to the mean of the fitted values from the model – i.e. the mean of $\hat{y}$ if there is no constant in the regression.

6.5 Assumption 2: $\text{var}(u_t) = \sigma^2 < \infty$

It has been assumed thus far that the variance of the errors is constant, σ^2; this is known as the *assumption of homoscedasticity*. If the errors do not have a constant variance, they are said to be *heteroscedastic*. To consider one illustration of heteroscedasticity, suppose that a regression had been estimated and the residuals, $\hat{u}_t$, have been calculated and then plotted against one of the explanatory variables, x_{2t}, as shown in figure 6.2.

It is clearly evident that the errors are heteroscedastic – that is, although their mean value is roughly constant, their variance is increasing systematically with x_{2t}.

6.5.1 *Detection of heteroscedasticity*

How can one tell whether the errors are heteroscedastic or not? It is possible to use a graphical method, as in figure 6.2, but, unfortunately, one rarely knows the cause or the form of the heteroscedasticity, so a plot is likely to reveal nothing. For example, if the variance of the errors was an increasing function of x_{3t}, and the researcher had plotted the residuals against x_{2t}, he/she would be unlikely to see any pattern, and would thus wrongly conclude that the errors had constant variance. It is also possible that the variance of the errors changes over time rather than systematically with one

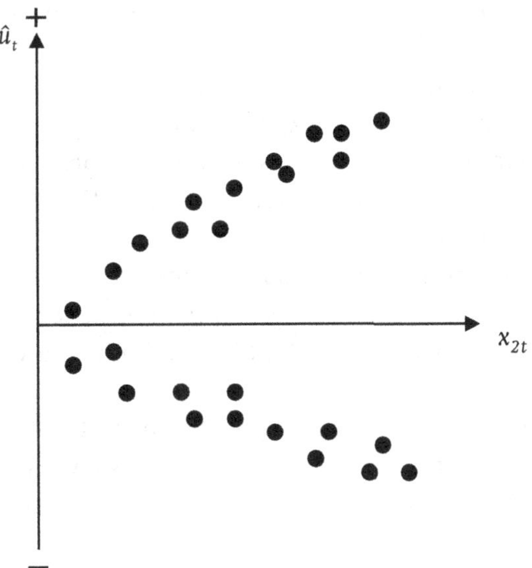

Figure 6.2 Graphical illustration of heteroscedasticity

of the explanatory variables; this phenomenon is known as autoregressive conditional heteroscedasticity (ARCH).

Fortunately, there are a number of formal statistical tests for heteroscedasticity, and one of the simplest such methods is the Goldfeld–Quandt (1965) test. Their approach is based on splitting the total sample of length T into two subsamples of length T_1 and T_2. The regression model is estimated on each subsample and the two residual variances are calculated as $s_1^2 = \hat{u}_1'\hat{u}_1/(T_1 - k)$ and $s_2^2 = \hat{u}_2'\hat{u}_2/(T_2 - k)$, respectively. The null hypothesis is that the variances of the disturbances are equal, which can be written H_0: $\sigma_1^2 = \sigma_2^2$, against a two-sided alternative. The test statistic, denoted GQ, is simply the ratio of the two residual variances, for which the larger of the two variances must be placed in the numerator (i.e. s_1^2 is the higher sample variance for the sample with length T_1, even if it comes from the second subsample):

$$GQ = \frac{s_1^2}{s_2^2} \tag{6.1}$$

The test statistic is distributed as an $F(T_1 - k, T_2 - k)$ under the null hypothesis, and the null of a constant variance is rejected if the test statistic exceeds the critical value.

The GQ test is simple to construct but its conclusions may be contingent upon a particular, and probably arbitrary, choice of where to split the sample. Clearly, the test is likely to be more powerful when this choice is made on theoretical grounds – for example, before and after a major structural event.

Suppose that it is thought that the variance of the disturbances is related to some observable variable z_t (which may or may not be one of the regressors); a better way to perform the test would be to order the sample according to values of z_t (rather than through time), and then to split the reordered sample into T_1 and T_2.

An alternative method that is sometimes used to sharpen the inferences from the test and to increase its power is to omit some of the observations from the centre of the sample so as to introduce a degree of separation between the two subsamples.

A further popular test is White's (1980) general test for heteroscedasticity. The test is particularly useful because it makes few assumptions about the likely form of the heteroscedasticity. The test is carried out as in box 6.1.

Box 6.1 Conducting White's test

(1) Assume that the regression model estimated is of the standard linear form – e.g.

$$y_t = \beta_1 + \beta_2 x_{2t} + \beta_3 x_{3t} + u_t \tag{6.2}$$

To test var(u_t) $= \sigma^2$, estimate the model above, obtaining the residuals, $\hat{u}_t$.

(2) Then run the auxiliary regression

$$\hat{u}_t^2 = \alpha_1 + \alpha_2 x_{2t} + \alpha_3 x_{3t} + \alpha_4 x_{2t}^2 + \alpha_5 x_{3t}^2 + \alpha_6 x_{2t} x_{3t} + v_t \tag{6.3}$$

where v_t is a normally distributed disturbance term independent of u_t.

This regression is of the squared residuals on a constant, the original explanatory variables, the squares of the explanatory variables and their cross-products. To see why the squared residuals are the quantity of interest, recall that, for a random variable u_t, the variance can be written

$$\text{var}(u_t) = \text{E}[(u_t - \text{E}(u_t))^2] \tag{6.4}$$

Under the assumption that E(u_t) $= 0$, the second part of the RHS of this expression disappears:

$$\text{var}(u_t) = \text{E}\left[u_t^2\right] \tag{6.5}$$

Once again, it is not possible to know the squares of the population disturbances, u_t^2, so their sample counterparts, the squared residuals, are used instead.

The reason that the auxiliary regression takes this form is that it is desirable to investigate whether the variance of the residuals (embodied in $\hat{u}_t^2$) varies systematically with any known variables relevant to the model. Relevant variables will include the original explanatory variables, their squared values and their cross-products. Note also that this regression should include a constant term, even if the original regression did not. This is as a result of the fact that $\hat{u}_t^2$ will always have a non-zero mean, even if $\hat{u}_t$ has a zero mean.

(3) Given the auxiliary regression, as stated above, the test can be conducted using two different approaches. First, it is possible to use the F-test framework described in chapter 5. This would involve estimating (6.3) as the unrestricted regression and then running a restricted regression of $\hat{u}_t^2$ on a constant only. The RSS from each specification would then be used as inputs to the standard F-test formula.

With many diagnostic tests, an alternative approach can be adopted that does not require the estimation of a second (restricted) regression. This approach is known as a Lagrange multiplier test, which centres around the value of R^2 for the auxiliary regression. If one or more coefficients in (6.3) is statistically significant the value of R^2 for that equation will be relatively high, whereas if none of the variables is significant R^2 will be relatively low. The LM test would thus operate by obtaining R^2 from the auxiliary regression and multiplying it by the number of observations, T. It can be shown that

$$TR^2 \sim \chi^2(m)$$

where m is the number of regressors in the auxiliary regression (excluding the constant term), equivalent to the number of restrictions that would have to be placed under the F-test approach.

(4) The test is one of the joint null hypothesis that $\alpha_2 = 0$ and $\alpha_3 = 0$ and $\alpha_4 = 0$ and $\alpha_5 = 0$ and $\alpha_6 = 0$. For the LM test, if the χ^2 test statistic from step 3 is greater than the corresponding value from the statistical table then reject the null hypothesis that the errors are homoscedastic.

Example 6.1

Consider the multiple regression model of office rents in the United Kingdom that we estimated in the previous chapter. The empirical estimation is shown again as equation (6.6), with t-ratios in parentheses underneath the coefficients.

$$\begin{aligned} \widehat{RRg}_t &= -11.53 + 2.52EFBSg_t + 1.75GDPg_t \\ &\quad\;(-4.9) \qquad (3.7) \qquad\qquad (2.1) \end{aligned} \tag{6.6}$$

$R^2 = 0.58$; adj. $R^2 = 0.55$; residual sum of squares = 1,078.26.

We apply the White test described earlier to examine whether the residuals of this equation are heteroscedastic. We first use the F-test framework. For this, we run the auxiliary regression (unrestricted) – equation (6.7) – and the restricted equation on the constant only, and we obtain the residual sums of squares from each regression (the unrestricted RSS and the restricted RSS). The results for the unrestricted and restricted auxiliary regressions are given below.

Unrestricted regression:

$$\hat{u}_t^2 = 76.52 + 0.88EFBSg_t - 21.18GDPg_t - 3.79EFBSg_t^2 - 0.38GDPg_t^2 + 7.14EFBSGMKg_t \quad (6.7)$$

$R^2 = 0.24$; $T = 28$; URSS $= 61{,}912.21$. The number of regressors k including the constant is six.

Restricted regression (squared residuals regressed on a constant):

$$\hat{u}_t^2 = 38.51 \quad (6.8)$$

RRSS $= 81{,}978.35$. The number of restrictions m is five (all coefficients are assumed to equal zero except the coefficient on the constant). Applying the standard F-test formula, we obtain the test statistic $\frac{81978.35-61912.21}{61912.21} \times \frac{28-6}{5} = 1.41$.

The null hypothesis is that the coefficients on the terms $EFBSg_t$, $GDPg_t$, $EFBSg_t^2$, $GDPg_t^2$ and $EFBSGDPg_t$ are all zero. The critical value for the F-test with $m = 5$ and $T - k = 22$ at the 5 per cent level of significance is $F_{5,22} = 2.66$. The computed F-test statistic is clearly lower than the critical value at the 5 per cent level, and we therefore do not reject the null hypothesis (as an exercise, consider whether we would still reject the null hypothesis if we used a 10 per cent significance level).

On the basis of this test, we conclude that heteroscedasticity is not present in the residuals of equation (6.6). Some econometric software packages report the computed F-test statistic along with the associated probability value, in which case it is not necessary to calculate the test statistic manually. For example, suppose that we ran the test using a software package and obtained a p-value of 0.25. This probability is higher than 0.05, denoting that there is no pattern of heteroscedasticity in the residuals of equation (6.6). To reject the null, the probability should have been equal to or less than 0.05 if a 5 per cent significance level were used or 0.10 if a 10 per cent significance level were used.

For the chi-squared version of the test, we obtain $TR^2 = 28 \times 0.24 = 6.72$. This test statistic follows a $\chi^2(5)$ under the null hypothesis. The 5 per cent critical value from the χ^2 table is 11.07. The computed test statistic is clearly less than the critical value, and hence the null hypothesis is not rejected. We conclude, as with the F-test earlier, that there is no evidence of heteroscedasticity in the residuals of equation (6.6).

6.5.2 *Consequences of using OLS in the presence of heteroscedasticity*

What happens if the errors are heteroscedastic, but this fact is ignored and the researcher proceeds with estimation and inference? In this case, OLS estimators will still give unbiased (and also consistent) coefficient estimates, but they are no longer BLUE – that is, they no longer have the minimum variance among the class of unbiased estimators. The reason is that the error variance, σ^2, plays no part in the proof that the OLS estimator is consistent and unbiased, but σ^2 does appear in the formulae for the coefficient variances. If the errors are heteroscedastic, the formulae presented for the coefficient standard errors no longer hold. For a very accessible algebraic treatment of the consequences of heteroscedasticity, see Hill, Griffiths and Judge (1997, pp. 217–18).

The upshot is that, if OLS is still used in the presence of heteroscedasticity, the standard errors could be wrong and hence any inferences made could be misleading. In general, the OLS standard errors will be too large for the intercept when the errors are heteroscedastic. The effect of heteroscedasticity on the slope standard errors will depend on its form. For example, if the variance of the errors is positively related to the square of an explanatory variable (which is often the case in practice), the OLS standard error for the slope will be too low. On the other hand, the OLS slope standard errors will be too big when the variance of the errors is inversely related to an explanatory variable.

6.5.3 *Dealing with heteroscedasticity*

If the form – i.e. the cause – of the heteroscedasticity is known then an alternative estimation method that takes this into account can be used. One possibility is called generalised least squares (GLS). For example, suppose that the error variance was related to some other variable, z_t, by the expression

$$\operatorname{var}(u_t) = \sigma^2 z_t^2 \tag{6.9}$$

All that would be required to remove the heteroscedasticity would be to divide the regression equation through by z_t:

$$\frac{y_t}{z_t} = \beta_1 \frac{1}{z_t} + \beta_2 \frac{x_{2t}}{z_t} + \beta_3 \frac{x_{3t}}{z_t} + v_t \tag{6.10}$$

where $v_t = \dfrac{u_t}{z_t}$ is an error term.

Now, if $\operatorname{var}(u_t) = \sigma^2 z_t^2$, $\operatorname{var}(v_t) = \operatorname{var}\left(\dfrac{u_t}{z_t}\right) = \dfrac{\operatorname{var}(u_t)}{z_t^2} = \dfrac{\sigma^2 z_t^2}{z_t^2} = \sigma^2$ for known z. Therefore the disturbances from (6.10) will be homoscedastic. Note that this latter regression does not include a constant, since β_1 is multiplied by $(1/z_t)$. GLS can be viewed as OLS applied to transformed data that satisfy the OLS assumptions. GLS is also known as weighted least squares (WLS), since under GLS a weighted sum of the squared residuals is minimised, whereas under OLS it is an unweighted sum.

Researchers are typically unsure of the exact cause of the heteroscedasticity, however, and hence this technique is usually infeasible in practice. Two other possible 'solutions' for heteroscedasticity are shown in box 6.2.

Box 6.2 'Solutions' for heteroscedasticity

(1) *Transforming the variables into logs or reducing by some other measure of 'size'.* This has the effect of rescaling the data to 'pull in' extreme observations. The regression would then be conducted upon the natural logarithms or the transformed data. Taking logarithms also has the effect of making a previously multiplicative model, such as the exponential regression model discussed above (with a multiplicative error term), into an additive one. Logarithms of a variable cannot be taken in situations in which the variable can take on zero or negative values, however – for example, when the model includes percentage changes in a variable. The log will not be defined in such cases.

(2) *Using heteroscedasticity-consistent standard error estimates.* Most standard econometrics software packages have an option (usually called something such as 'robust') that allows the user to employ standard error estimates that have been modified to account for the heteroscedasticity following White (1980). The effect of using the correction is that, if the variance of the errors is positively related to the square of an explanatory variable, the standard errors for the slope coefficients are increased relative to the usual OLS standard errors, which would make hypothesis testing more 'conservative', so that more evidence would be required against the null hypothesis before it can be rejected.

6.6 Assumption 3: $\text{cov}(u_i, u_j) = 0$ for $i \neq j$

The third assumption that is made of the CLRM's disturbance terms is that the covariance between the error terms over time (or cross-sectionally, for this type of data) is zero. In other words, it is assumed that the errors are uncorrelated with one another. If the errors are not uncorrelated with one another, it would be stated that they are 'autocorrelated' or that they are 'serially correlated'. A test of this assumption is therefore required.

Again, the population disturbances cannot be observed, so tests for autocorrelation are conducted on the residuals, $\hat{u}$. Before one can proceed to see how formal tests for autocorrelation are formulated, the concept of the lagged value of a variable needs to be defined.

6.6.1 *The concept of a lagged value*

The lagged value of a variable (which may be y_t, x_t or u_t) is simply the value that the variable took during a previous period. So, for example, the value

Table 6.1 Constructing a series of lagged values and first differences

t	y_t	y_{t-1}	Δy_t
2006M09	0.8	–	–
2006M10	1.3	0.8	$(1.3 - 0.8) = 0.5$
2006M11	−0.9	1.3	$(-0.9 - 1.3) = -2.2$
2006M12	0.2	−0.9	$(0.2 - -0.9) = 1.1$
2007M01	−1.7	0.2	$(-1.7 - 0.2) = -1.9$
2007M02	2.3	−1.7	$(2.3 - -1.7) = 4.0$
2007M03	0.1	2.3	$(0.1 - 2.3) = -2.2$
2007M04	0.0	0.1	$(0.0 - 0.1) = -0.1$
.	.	.	.
.	.	.	.
.	.	.	.

of y_t lagged one period, written y_{t-1}, can be constructed by shifting all the observations forward one period in a spreadsheet, as illustrated in table 6.1.

The value in the 2006M10 row and the y_{t-1} column shows the value that y_t took in the previous period, 2006M09, which was 0.8. The last column in table 6.1 shows another quantity relating to y, namely the 'first difference'. The first difference of y, also known as the change in y, and denoted Δy_t, is calculated as the difference between the values of y in this period and in the previous period. This is calculated as

$$\Delta y_t = y_t - y_{t-1} \tag{6.11}$$

Note that, when one-period lags or first differences of a variable are constructed, the first observation is lost. Thus a regression of Δy_t using the above data would begin with the October 2006 data point. It is also possible to produce two-period lags, three-period lags, and so on. These are accomplished in the obvious way.

6.6.2 *Graphical tests for autocorrelation*

In order to test for autocorrelation, it is necessary to investigate whether any relationships exist between the current value of $\hat{u}$, $\hat{u}_t$, and any of its previous values, $\hat{u}_{t-1}, \hat{u}_{t-2}, \ldots$ The first step is to consider possible relationships between the current residual and the immediately previous one, $\hat{u}_{t-1}$, via a graphical exploration. Thus $\hat{u}_t$ is plotted against $\hat{u}_{t-1}$, and $\hat{u}_t$ is plotted over time. Some stereotypical patterns that may be found in the residuals are discussed below.

Figure 6.3 Plot of $\hat{u}_t$ against $\hat{u}_{t-1}$, showing positive autocorrelation

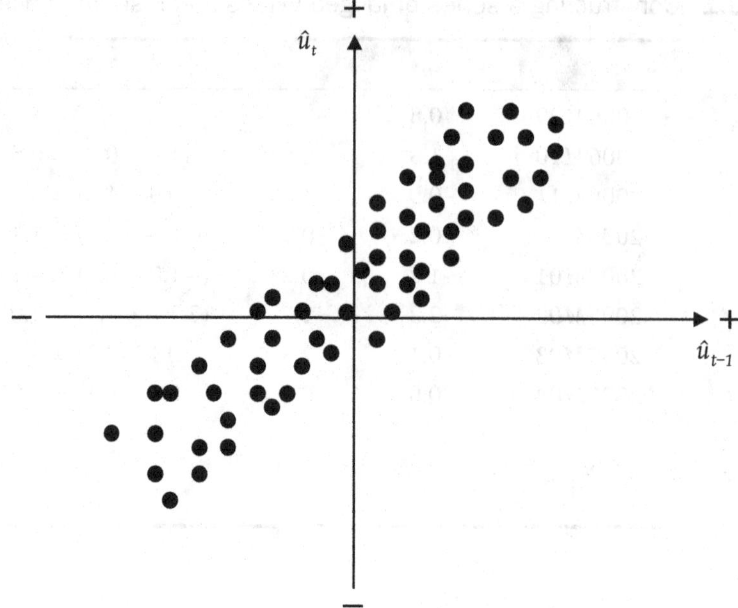

Figure 6.4 Plot of $\hat{u}_t$ over time, showing positive autocorrelation

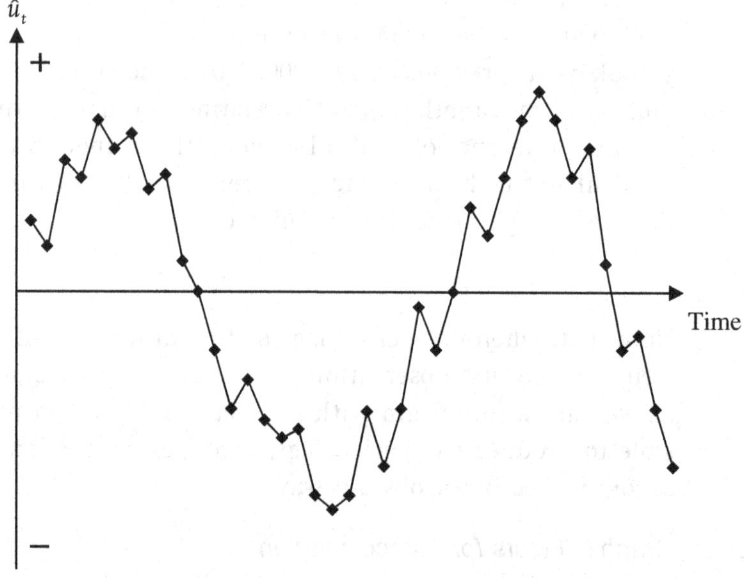

Figures 6.3 and 6.4 show positive autocorrelation in the residuals, which is indicated by a cyclical residual plot over time. This case is known as *positive autocorrelation*, since on average, if the residual at time $t-1$ is positive, the residual at time t is likely to be positive as well; similarly, if the residual at $t-1$ is negative, the residual at t is also likely to be negative. Figure 6.3 shows that most of the dots representing observations are in the first and

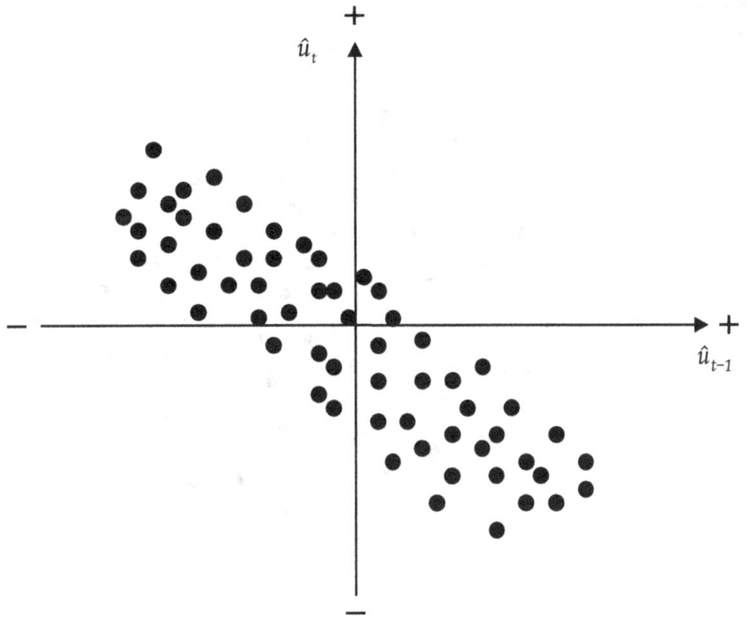

Figure 6.5
Plot of $\hat{u}_t$ against $\hat{u}_{t-1}$, showing negative autocorrelation

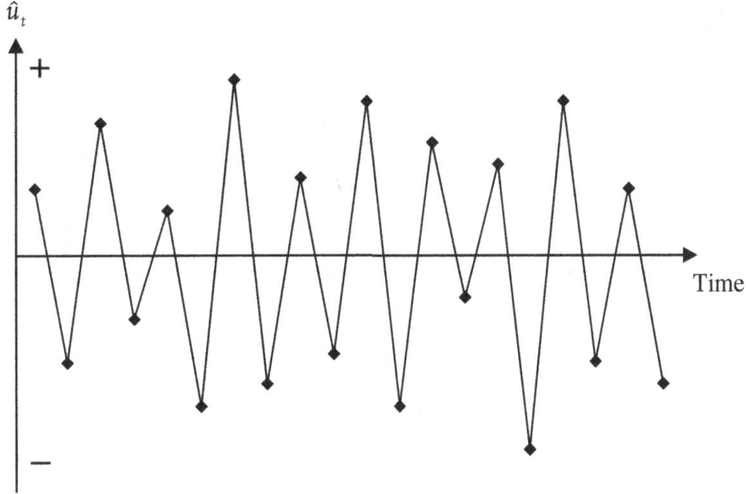

Figure 6.6
Plot of $\hat{u}_t$ over time, showing negative autocorrelation

third quadrants, while figure 6.4 shows that a positively autocorrelated series of residuals do not cross the time axis very frequently.

Figures 6.5 and 6.6 show *negative autocorrelation*, indicated by an alternating pattern in the residuals. This case is known as negative autocorrelation because on average, if the residual at time $t - 1$ is positive, the residual at time t is likely to be negative; similarly, if the residual at $t - 1$ is negative, the residual at t is likely to be positive. Figure 6.5 shows that most of the dots

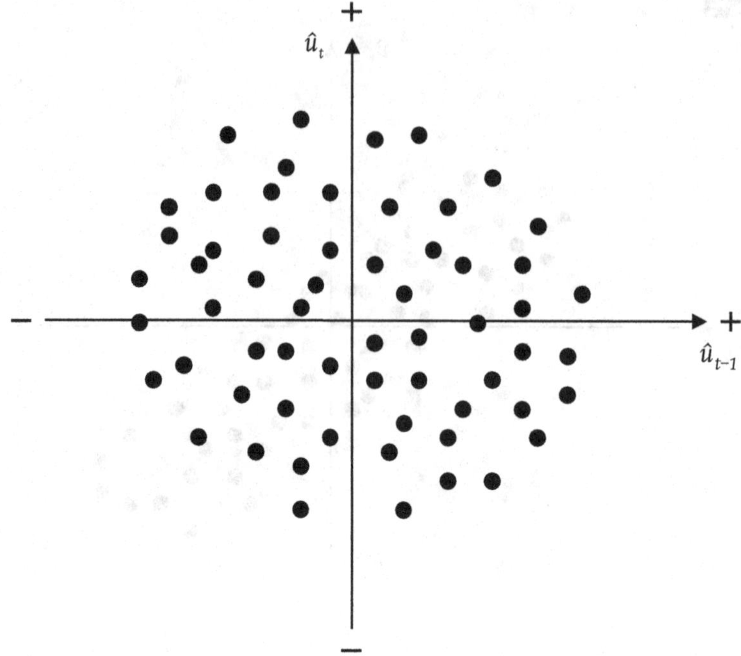

Figure 6.7 Plot of $\hat{u}_t$ against $\hat{u}_{t-1}$, showing no autocorrelation

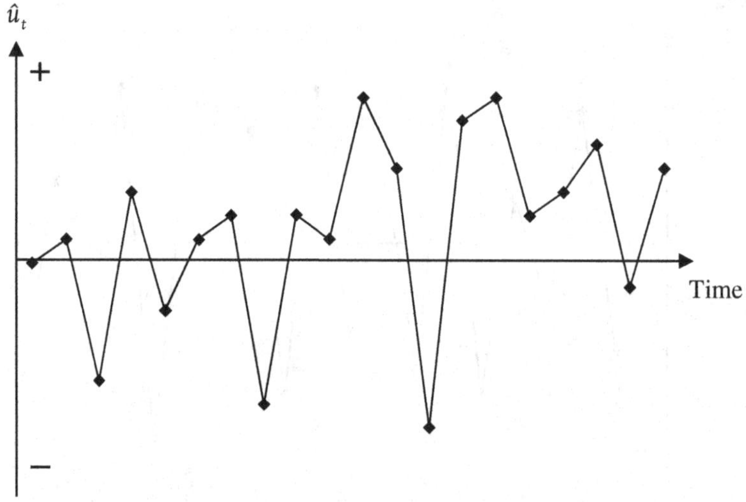

Figure 6.8 Plot of $\hat{u}_t$ over time, showing no autocorrelation

are in the second and fourth quadrants, while figure 6.6 shows that a negatively autocorrelated series of residuals cross the time axis more frequently than if they were distributed randomly.

Finally, figures 6.7 and 6.8 show no pattern in residuals at all: this is what is desirable to see. In the plot of $\hat{u}_t$ against $\hat{u}_{t-1}$ (figure 6.7), the points are randomly spread across all four quadrants, and the time series plot of the residuals (figure 6.8) does not cross the x-axis either too frequently or too little.

6.6.3 *Detecting autocorrelation: the Durbin–Watson test*

Of course, a first step in testing whether the residual series from an estimated model are autocorrelated would be to plot the residuals as above, looking for any patterns. Graphical methods may be difficult to interpret in practice, however, and hence a formal statistical test should also be applied. The simplest test is due to Durbin and Watson (1951).

DW is a test for first-order autocorrelation – i.e. it tests only for a relationship between an error and its immediately previous value. One way to motivate the test and to interpret the test statistic would be in the context of a regression of the time t error on its previous value,

$$u_t = \rho u_{t-1} + v_t \tag{6.12}$$

where $v_t \sim N(0, \sigma_v^2)$. The DW test statistic has as its null and alternative hypotheses

$$\text{H}_0\colon \rho = 0 \quad \text{and} \quad \text{H}_1\colon \rho \neq 0$$

Thus, under the null hypothesis, the errors at time $t-1$ and t are independent of one another, and if this null were rejected it would be concluded that there was evidence of a relationship between successive residuals. In fact, it is not necessary to run the regression given by (6.12), as the test statistic can be calculated using quantities that are already available after the first regression has been run:

$$DW = \frac{\sum_{t=2}^{T} (\hat{u}_t - \hat{u}_{t-1})^2}{\sum_{t=2}^{T} \hat{u}_t^2} \tag{6.13}$$

The denominator of the test statistic is simply (the number of observations $-$ 1)$\times$ the variance of the residuals. This arises since, if the average of the residuals is zero,

$$\text{var}(\hat{u}_t) = E(\hat{u}_t^2) = \frac{1}{T-1}\sum_{t=2}^{T} \hat{u}_t^2$$

so that

$$\sum_{t=2}^{T} \hat{u}_t^2 = \text{var}(\hat{u}_t) \times (T-1)$$

The numerator 'compares' the values of the error at times $t-1$ and t. If there is positive autocorrelation in the errors this difference in the numerator will be relatively small, while if there is negative autocorrelation, with the sign of the error changing very frequently, the numerator will be relatively large. No autocorrelation would result in a value for the numerator between small and large.

It is also possible to express the DW statistic as an approximate function of the estimated value of ρ:

$$DW \approx 2(1 - \hat{\rho}) \tag{6.14}$$

where $\hat{\rho}$ is the estimated correlation coefficient that would have been obtained from an estimation of (6.12). To see why this is the case, consider that the numerator of (6.13) can be written as the parts of a quadratic,

$$\sum_{t=2}^{T}(\hat{u}_t - \hat{u}_{t-1})^2 = \sum_{t=2}^{T}\hat{u}_t^2 + \sum_{t=2}^{T}\hat{u}_{t-1}^2 - 2\sum_{t=2}^{T}\hat{u}_t\hat{u}_{t-1} \tag{6.15}$$

Consider now the composition of the first two summations on the RHS of (6.15). The first of these is

$$\sum_{t=2}^{T}\hat{u}_t^2 = \hat{u}_2^2 + \hat{u}_3^2 + \hat{u}_4^2 + \cdots + \hat{u}_T^2$$

while the second is

$$\sum_{t=2}^{T}\hat{u}_{t-1}^2 = \hat{u}_1^2 + \hat{u}_2^2 + \hat{u}_3^2 + \cdots + \hat{u}_{T-1}^2$$

Thus the only difference between them is that they differ in the first and last terms in the summation:

$$\sum_{t=2}^{T}\hat{u}_t^2$$

contains $\hat{u}_T^2$ but not $\hat{u}_1^2$, while

$$\sum_{t=2}^{T}\hat{u}_{t-1}^2$$

contains $\hat{u}_1^2$ but not $\hat{u}_T^2$. As the sample size, T, increases towards infinity, the difference between these two will become negligible. Hence the expression in (6.15), the numerator of (6.13), is approximately

$$2\sum_{t=2}^{T}\hat{u}_t^2 - 2\sum_{t=2}^{T}\hat{u}_t\hat{u}_{t-1}$$

Replacing the numerator of (6.13) with this expression leads to

$$DW \approx \frac{2\sum_{t=2}^{T}\hat{u}_t^2 - 2\sum_{t=2}^{T}\hat{u}_t\hat{u}_{t-1}}{\sum_{t=2}^{T}\hat{u}_t^2} = 2\left(1 - \frac{\sum_{t=2}^{T}\hat{u}_t\hat{u}_{t-1}}{\sum_{t=2}^{T}\hat{u}_t^2}\right) \tag{6.16}$$

The covariance between u_t and u_{t-1} can be written as $\mathrm{E}[(u_t - \mathrm{E}(u_t))(u_{t-1} - E(u_{t-1}))]$. Under the assumption that $\mathrm{E}(u_t) = 0$ (and therefore that $\mathrm{E}(u_{t-1}) = 0$), the covariance will be $\mathrm{E}[u_t\, u_{t-1}]$. For the sample residuals, this covariance will be evaluated as

$$\frac{1}{T-1}\sum_{t=2}^{T}\hat{u}_t\hat{u}_{t-1}$$

The sum in the numerator of the expression on the right of (6.16) can therefore be seen as $T-1$ times the covariance between $\hat{u}_t$ and $\hat{u}_{t-1}$, while the sum in the denominator of the expression on the right of (6.16) can be seen from the previous exposition as $T-1$ times the variance of $\hat{u}_t$. Thus it is possible to write

$$\begin{aligned} DW &\approx 2\left(1 - \frac{T-1\,\mathrm{cov}(\hat{u}_t, \hat{u}_{t-1})}{T-1\,\mathrm{var}(\hat{u}_t)}\right) = 2\left(1 - \frac{\mathrm{cov}(\hat{u}_t, \hat{u}_{t-1})}{\mathrm{var}(\hat{u}_t)}\right) \\ &= 2\,(1 - \mathrm{corr}(\hat{u}_t, \hat{u}_{t-1})) \end{aligned} \tag{6.17}$$

so that the DW test statistic is approximately equal to $2(1 - \hat{\rho})$. Since $\hat{\rho}$ is a correlation, it implies that $-1 \leq \hat{\rho} \leq 1$. That is, $\hat{\rho}$ is bounded to lie between -1 and $+1$. Substituting in these limits for $\hat{\rho}$ to calculate DW from (6.17) would give the corresponding limits for DW as $0 \leq DW \leq 4$. Consider now the implication of DW taking one of three important values (zero, two and four):

- $\hat{\rho} = 0$, $DW = 2$. This is the case in which there is no autocorrelation in the residuals. Roughly speaking, therefore, the null hypothesis would not be rejected if DW is near two – i.e. there is little evidence of autocorrelation.
- $\hat{\rho} = 1$, $DW = 0$. This corresponds to the case in which there is perfect positive autocorrelation in the residuals.
- $\hat{\rho} = -1$, $DW = 4$. This corresponds to the case in which there is perfect negative autocorrelation in the residuals.

The DW test does not follow a standard statistical distribution, such as a t, F or χ^2. DW has two critical values – an upper critical value (d_U) and a lower critical value (d_L) – and there is also an intermediate region in which

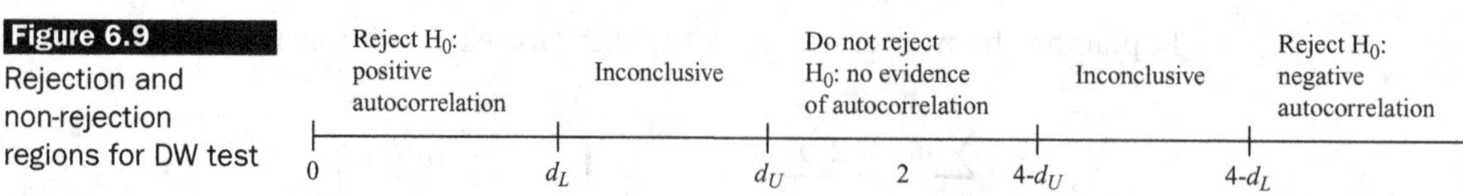

Figure 6.9 Rejection and non-rejection regions for DW test

the null hypothesis of no autocorrelation can neither be rejected nor not rejected! The rejection, non-rejection and inconclusive regions are shown on the number line in figure 6.9.

To reiterate, therefore, the null hypothesis is rejected and the existence of positive autocorrelation presumed if DW is less than the lower critical value; the null hypothesis is rejected and the existence of negative autocorrelation presumed if DW is greater than four minus the lower critical value; the null hypothesis is not rejected and no significant residual autocorrelation is presumed if DW is between the upper and four minus the upper limits.

6.7 Causes of residual autocorrelation

- Omitted variables. A key reason for autocorrelation is the omission of systematic influences that are reflected in the errors. The exclusion of an explanatory variable that conveys important information for the dependent variable and that is not allowed by the other explanatory variables causes autocorrelation. In the real estate market, the analyst may not have at his/her disposal all the variables required for modelling – for example, economic variables at the local (city or metropolitan area) level – leading to residual autocorrelation.
- Model misspecification. We may have adopted the wrong functional form for the relationship we examine. For example, we assume a linear model but the model should be expressed in log form. We may also have models in levels but the relationship may be of a cyclical nature. Hence we should transform the variables to allow for the cyclicality in the series. Residuals from models using strongly trended variables are likely to exhibit autocorrelated patterns in particular if the true relationship is more cyclical.
- Data smoothness and trends. These can be a major cause for residual autocorrelation in the real estate market. The real estate data we use are often smoothed and frequently also involve some interpolation. There has been much discussion about the smoothness in valuation data, which becomes more acute in markets with less frequent transactions and with data of lower frequency. Slow adjustments in the real estate market also give rise to autocorrelation. Smoothness and slow adjustments average the true disturbances over successive periods of time. Hence successive

values of the error term become interrelated. For example, a large change in GDP or employment growth in our example could be reflected by the residuals for several periods as the successive rent values carry this effect due to smoothness and slow adjustment.

- Misspecification of the true random error. The assumption $E(u_i u_j) = 0$ may not represent the true pattern of the errors. Major events such as a prolonged economic downturn or the cycles that the real estate market seems to go through (for example, it took several years for the markets to recover from the early 1990 crash) are likely to have an impact on the market that will persist for some time.

What is important from the above discussion is that the remedy for residual autocorrelation really depends on its cause.

Example 6.2

We test for first-order serial correlation in the residuals of equation (6.6) and compute the DW statistic using equation (6.14). The value of $\hat{\rho}$ is 0.37 and the sign suggests positive first-order autocorrelation in the residuals. Applying formula (6.14), we get $DW \approx 2 \times (1 - 0.37) = 1.26$.

Equation (6.6) was estimated with twenty-eight observations ($T = 28$) and the number of regressors including the constant term is three ($k = 3$). The critical values for the test are $d_L = 1.181$ and $d_U = 1.650$ at the 1 per cent level of significance.

The computed DW statistic falls into the inconclusive region and so we cannot tell with any reasonable degree of confidence whether to reject or not to reject the null hypothesis of no autocorrelation. Therefore we have no evidence as to whether our equation is misspecified on the basis of the DW test. For example, we do not know whether we have omitted systematic influences in our rent growth model. In such situations, the analyst can perform additional tests for serial correlation to generate further and perhaps more conclusive evidence. One such test is the Breusch–Godfrey approach, which we present subsequently and then apply.

For illustration purposes, suppose that the value of $\hat{\rho}$ in the above equation were not 0.37 but −0.37, indicating negative first-order autocorrelation. Then DW would take the value of 2.74. From the DW tables with $k = 3$ and $T = 28$, we compute the critical regions:

$$4 - d_U = 4 - 1.650 = 2.35 \quad \text{and} \quad 4 - d_L = 4 - 1.181 = 2.82.$$

Again, the test statistic of 2.74 falls into the indecisive region. If it were higher than 2.82 we would have rejected the null hypothesis in favour of the alternative of first-order serial correlation, and if it were lower than 2.35 we would not have rejected it.

6.7.1 *Conditions that must be fulfilled for DW to be a valid test*

In order for the DW test to be valid for application, three conditions must be fulfilled, as described in box 6.3.

Box 6.3 Conditions for DW to be a valid test

(1) There must be a constant term in the regression.
(2) The regressors must be non-stochastic – as assumption 4 of the CLRM (see chapter 10).
(3) There must be no lags of the dependent variable (see below) in the regression.

If the test were used in the presence of lags of the dependent variable or otherwise stochastic regressors, the test statistic would be biased towards two, suggesting that in some instances the null hypothesis of no autocorrelation would not be rejected when it should be.

6.7.2 *Another test for autocorrelation: the Breusch–Godfrey test*

Recall that DW is a test only of whether consecutive errors are related to one another: not only can the DW test not be applied if a certain set of circumstances is not fulfilled, there will also be many forms of residual autocorrelation that DW cannot detect. For example, if $\text{corr}(\hat{u}_t, \hat{u}_{t-1}) = 0$, but $\text{corr}(\hat{u}_t, \hat{u}_{t-2}) \neq 0$, DW as defined above will not find any autocorrelation. One possible solution would be to replace $\hat{u}_{t-1}$ in (6.13) with $\hat{u}_{t-2}$. Pairwise examination of the correlations $(\hat{u}_t, \hat{u}_{t-1})$, $(\hat{u}_t, \hat{u}_{t-2})$, $(\hat{u}_t, \hat{u}_{t-3})$, ... will be tedious in practice, however, and is not coded in econometrics software packages, which have been programmed to construct DW using only a one-period lag. In addition, the approximation in (6.14) will deteriorate as the difference between the two time indices increases. Consequently, the critical values should also be modified somewhat in these cases.

As a result, it is desirable to examine a joint test for autocorrelation that will allow examination of the relationship between $\hat{u}_t$ and several of its lagged values at the same time. The Breusch–Godfrey test is a more general test for autocorrelation up to the rth order. The model for the errors under this test is

$$u_t = \rho_1 u_{t-1} + \rho_2 u_{t-2} + \rho_3 u_{t-3} + \cdots + \rho_r u_{t-r} + v_t, \quad v_t \sim N\left(0, \sigma_v^2\right) \qquad (6.18)$$

The null and alternative hypotheses are

$$H_0: \rho_1 = 0 \text{ and } \rho_2 = 0 \text{ and} \ldots \text{and } \rho_r = 0$$
$$H_1: \rho_1 \neq 0 \text{ or } \rho_2 \neq 0 \text{ or} \ldots \text{or } \rho_r \neq 0$$

Under the null hypothesis, therefore, the current error is not related to any of its r previous values. The test is carried out as in box 6.4.

Box 6.4 Conducting a Breusch–Godfrey test

(1) Estimate the linear regression using OLS and obtain the residuals, $\hat{u}_t$.

(2) Regress $\hat{u}_t$ on all the regressors from stage 1 (the xs) plus $\hat{u}_{t-1}, \hat{u}_{t-2}, \ldots, \hat{u}_{t-r}$; the regression will thus be

$$\hat{u}_t = \gamma_1 + \gamma_2 x_{2t} + \gamma_3 x_{3t} + \gamma_4 x_{4t} + \rho_1 \hat{u}_{t-1} + \rho_2 \hat{u}_{t-2} + \rho_3 \hat{u}_{t-3} + \cdots + \rho_r \hat{u}_{t-r} + v_t,\ v_t \sim N\left(0, \sigma_v^2\right) \quad (6.19)$$

Obtain R^2 from this auxiliary regression.

(3) Letting T denote the number of observations, the test statistic is given by

$$(T - r)R^2 \sim \chi_r^2$$

Note that $(T - r)$ pre-multiplies R^2 in the test for autocorrelation rather than T (as was the case for the heteroscedasticity test). This arises because the first r observations will effectively have been lost from the sample in order to obtain the r lags used in the test regression, leaving $(T - r)$ observations from which to estimate the auxiliary regression. If the test statistic exceeds the critical value from the chi-squared statistical tables, reject the null hypothesis of no autocorrelation. As with any joint test, only one part of the null hypothesis has to be rejected to lead to rejection of the hypothesis as a whole. Thus the error at time t has to be significantly related only to one of its previous r values in the sample for the null of no autocorrelation to be rejected. The test is more general than the DW test, and can be applied in a wider variety of circumstances as it does not impose the DW restrictions on the format of the first-stage regression.

One potential difficulty with Breusch–Godfrey, however, is in determining an appropriate value of r, the number of lags of the residuals, to use in computing the test. There is no obvious answer to this, so it is typical to experiment with a range of values, and also to use the frequency of the data to decide. Therefore, for example, if the data are monthly or quarterly, set r equal to twelve or four, respectively. For annual data, which is often the case for real estate data, r could be set to two. The argument would then be that errors at any given time would be expected to be related only to those errors in the previous two years. Obviously, if the model is statistically adequate, no evidence of autocorrelation should be found in the residuals whatever value of r is chosen.

Example 6.3

We apply the Breusch–Godfrey test to detect whether the errors of equation (6.6) are serially correlated since the computed DW statistic fell in the inconclusive region. We first run the Breusch–Godfrey test to detect for the possible presence of first-order serial correlation. We obtain the residuals from equation (6.6) and run the unrestricted regression

$$\hat{u}_t = 0.74 - 0.38EFBSg_t + 0.23GDPg_t + 0.40\hat{u}_{t-1} \tag{6.20}$$

$R^2 = 0.14$; the number of observations (T) in this auxiliary regression is now twenty-seven, since the sample starts a year later due to the inclusion of the first lag of the residuals ($r = 1$). The estimated LM version of the test statistic for first-order serial correlation is

$$(T - r)R^2 = (28 - 1) \times 0.14 = 3.78 \sim \chi^2_r$$

From the statistical tables, the critical value for a χ^2_1 is 3.84 at the 5 per cent level of significance. The computed statistic is just lower than the critical value, indicating no serial correlation at this level of significance (the null was not rejected). This was a close call, as was expected from the inconclusive DW test result.

We also run the F-version of the Breusch–Godfrey test.

Unrestricted: this is equation (6.20). URSS = 918.90; the number of regressors k including the constant is three; $T = 27$.

Restricted:

$$\hat{u}_t = 0.000001 - 0.00004EFBSg_t + 0.00004GDPg_t \tag{6.21}$$

RRSS = 1,078.24. The number of restrictions m is one (the order of serial correlation we test for). Hence the F-test statistic is $\frac{1078.24-918.90}{918.90} \times \frac{27-4}{1} = 3.99$. The null hypothesis of no first-order residual autocorrelation is not rejected, as the critical F for $m = 1$ and $T - k = 23$ at the 5 per cent level of significance is $F_{1,23} = 4.30$.

We also examine equation (6.6) for second-order serial correlation:

$$\hat{u}_t = 0.06 - 0.61EFBSg_t + 0.70GDPg_t + 0.50\hat{u}_{t-1} - 0.18\hat{u}_{t-2} \tag{6.22}$$

$R^2 = 0.19$; the number of observations in this auxiliary regression is now twenty-six, due to the two lags of the residuals used in equation (6.22) with $r = 2$. Hence $T - r = 26$. The estimated χ^2 statistic is

$$(T - r)R^2 = (28 - 2) \times 0.19 = 4.94 \sim \chi^2_2$$

The χ_2^2 critical value is 5.99 at the 5 per cent level of significance. Hence the null hypothesis of no residual autocorrelation is not rejected.

The conclusion is the same as that we reach with the F-version of the test. The unrestricted equation is equation (6.22); URSS = 862.57; and the restricted equation is (6.21); RRSS = 1,078.24. With $T = 26$, $k = 5$ and $m = 2$, the computed F-statistic is $F_{2,21} = 2.63$, which is lower than the critical value of 3.43 at the 5 per cent level of significance. Again, therefore, the conclusion is of no serial correlation.

6.7.3 *Dealing with autocorrelation*

As box 6.5 shows, if autocorrelation is present but not accounted for, there can be important ramifications. So what can be done about it? An approach to dealing with autocorrelation that was once popular, but that has fallen out of favour, is known as the Cochrane–Orcutt iterative procedure. This is detailed in the appendix to this chapter.

Box 6.5 Consequences of ignoring autocorrelation if it is present

- In fact, the consequences of ignoring autocorrelation when it is present are similar to those of ignoring heteroscedasticity.
- The coefficient estimates derived using OLS are still unbiased, but they are inefficient – i.e. they are not BLUE, even at large sample sizes – so the standard error estimates could be wrong.
- There thus exists the possibility that the wrong inferences could be made about whether a variable is or is not an important determinant of variations in y.
- In the case of positive serial correlation in the residuals, the OLS standard error estimates will be biased downwards relative to the true standard errors – that is, OLS will understate their true variability. This would lead to an increase in the probability of type I error – i.e. a tendency to reject the null hypothesis sometimes when it is correct. Furthermore, R^2 is likely to be inflated relative to its 'correct' value if positive autocorrelation is present but ignored, since residual autocorrelation will lead to an underestimate of the true error variance (for positive autocorrelation).

An alternative approach is to modify the parameter standard errors to allow for the effect of the residual autocorrelation. The White variance–covariance matrix of the coefficients (that is, calculation of the standard errors using the White correction for heteroscedasticity) is appropriate when the residuals of the estimated equation are heteroscedastic but serially uncorrelated. Newey and West (1987) have developed a variance–covariance estimator that is consistent in the presence of both heteroscedasticity and autocorrelation. An alternative approach to dealing with residual autocorrelation, therefore, would be to use appropriately modified standard error estimates.

While White's correction to standard errors for heteroscedasticity as discussed above does not require any user input, the Newey–West procedure requires the specification of a truncation lag length to determine the number of lagged residuals used to evaluate the autocorrelation. Some software packages use INTEGER[$4(T/100)^{2/9}$]. The Newey–West procedure in fact produces 'HAC' (heteroscedasticity- and autocorrelation-consistent) standard errors that correct for both autocorrelation and heteroscedasticity that may be present.

A more 'modern' view concerning autocorrelation however, is that it presents an opportunity rather than a problem! This view, associated with Sargan, Hendry and Mizon, suggests that serial correlation in the errors arises as a consequence of 'misspecified dynamics'. For another explanation of the reason why this stance is taken, recall that it is possible to express the dependent variable as the sum of the parts that can be explained using the model, and a part that cannot (the residuals),

$$y_t = \hat{y}_t + \hat{u}_t \tag{6.23}$$

where $\hat{y}_t$ are the fitted values from the model ($= \hat{\beta}_1 + \hat{\beta}_2 x_{2t} + \hat{\beta}_3 x_{3t} + \cdots + \hat{\beta}_k x_{kt}$). Autocorrelation in the residuals is often caused by a dynamic structure in y that has not been modelled and so has not been captured in the fitted values. In other words, there exists a richer structure in the dependent variable y and more information in the sample about that structure than has been captured by the models previously estimated. What is required is a dynamic model that allows for this extra structure in y, and this approach is detailed in the following subsection.

6.7.4 *Dynamic models*

All the models considered so far have been static in nature, e.g.

$$y_t = \beta_1 + \beta_2 x_{2t} + \beta_3 x_{3t} + \beta_4 x_{4t} + \beta_5 x_{5t} + u_t \tag{6.24}$$

In other words, these models have allowed for only a *contemporaneous relationship* between the variables, so that a change in one or more of the explanatory variables at time t causes an instant change in the dependent variable at time t. This analysis can easily be extended though, to the case in which the current value of y_t depends on previous values of y or on previous values of one or more of the variables, e.g.

$$y_t = \beta_1 + \beta_2 x_{2t} + \beta_3 x_{3t} + \beta_4 x_{4t} + \beta_5 x_{5t} + \gamma_1 y_{t-1} + \gamma_2 x_{2t-1} + \cdots + \gamma_k x_{kt-1} + u_t \tag{6.25}$$

It is of course possible to extend the model even more by adding further lags – e.g. x_{2t-2}, y_{t-3}. Models containing lags of the explanatory variables (but no lags of the explained variable) are known as *distributed lag models*. Specifications with lags of both explanatory and explained variables are known as *autoregressive distributed lag* (ADL) models.

How many lags, and of which variables, should be included in a dynamic regression model? This is a tricky question to answer, but, hopefully, recourse to real estate and economic theory will help to provide an answer.

Another potential 'remedy' for autocorrelated residuals would be to switch to a model in first differences rather than in levels. As explained previously, the first difference of y_t (i.e. $y_t - y_{t-1}$) is denoted Δy_t; similarly, one can construct a series of first differences for each of the explanatory variables – e.g. $\Delta x_{2t} = x_{2t} - x_{2t-1}$, etc. Such a model has a number of other useful features (see chapter 12 for more details) and could be expressed as

$$\Delta y_t = \beta_1 + \beta_2 \Delta x_{2t} + \beta_3 \Delta x_{3t} + u_t \tag{6.26}$$

Sometimes the change in y is purported to depend on previous values of the level of y or $x_i (i = 2, \ldots, k)$ as well as changes in the explanatory variables,

$$\Delta y_t = \beta_1 + \beta_2 \Delta x_{2t} + \beta_3 \Delta x_{3t} + \beta_4 x_{2t-1} + \beta_5 y_{t-1} + u_t \tag{6.27}$$

6.7.5 *Why might lags be required in a regression?*

Lagged values of the explanatory variables or of the dependent variable (or both) can capture important dynamic structure in the dependent variable that might be caused by a number of features in the real estate market. These relate to the very nature of the market, the institutional environment and the way that data are generated. Below are representative examples.

- A classic example of slow response in the market is the long gestation period in the development and delivery of new buildings. Developers will not react immediately to changing economic circumstances but they will assess conditions over a period of time. When feasibility studies show that a new development should go ahead, actual construction will not start immediately, as the developer will have to obtain planning permission, secure finance, overcome physical site constraints, and so on. Even when these issues do not introduce delays (planning permission is outstanding, finance is available), other steps in the development process, such as finalising plans, may take some time. In addition, of course, the actual construction period represents a lag in putting new space into the market. This discussion suggests that the decision for buildings that are delivered today was made some time ago and was based on expectations about the economy, market, cost of finance and cost of construction over the past two, three or even four years. Hence lagged economic, real estate and financial variables (independent variables) are justified in an equation of new construction or new completions (dependent variable).

- Consider also an example of market take-up or absorption. A quarterly figure that is published at the end of each quarter comprises the space occupied in the course of that quarter. Firms had made that decision a while ago, however, and perhaps it took them some time to search and find space. Hence, when we explain take-up or absorption, lagged observations on economic variables are justified by the time it took firms to decide to search for and take up new space.
- The institutional characteristics of the market introduce lagged responses. Although conditions change in the occupier market, rents may not adjust due to lease contracts. Rents will adjust in the next rent review, but previous conditions in the market are relevant.
- Occupiers may decide to downsize or release space in the market on account of weakening business conditions. Although this decision has been made, occupiers will be able to vacate space (hence vacancy rises) only at the time of the next lease break. Of course, not all lease breaks and rent reviews take place at the same time, but, when such adjustments are under way, current rents or vacancy (dependent variable) reflect (i) the changing conditions over some period in the past (captured by lagged independent variables) and (ii) past rents and vacancy that have adjusted to an extent, as some rent reviews and lease breaks have already occurred.
- The effect of government policies and regulation (for example, planning policies) may take a few months or years to work through, since market participants may initially be unsure of what the implications are for the real estate market. This impact will reveal itself to the market, and past rents in a model capture these adjustments.
- It is argued that inertia in rents or yields (dependent variable) originates in the valuation process, which makes the inclusion of past values both of rents and yields relevant as well as that of the explanatory variables. It is argued that valuers do not incorporate new economic information quickly into their valuations and, therefore, rents and yields adjust slowly. This slow reaction to news can be the result of testing the resilience of the market, however, and it is also unclear how the market will react (will the news trigger an over- or underreaction, in which case the valuers will have to adjust pricing to take into account this kind of collective behaviour?). Moreover, valuers may adopt the principle of adaptive expectations, which suggests that an unweighted or weighted average

of past influences on rents or yields is examined to assess near-future trends.

- Valuers may anchor their current valuation to previous ones. This occurs when valuations are quarterly, or even monthly, but there has been no fresh news to change the valuation. In some contexts, the previous rent or yield may be given greater weight; this depends on the valuation practices across countries. Again, this points to the use of lagged values of the reference variable.
- When we model a rent series, the valuations used to construct the index do not take place at the same time. A quarterly index for a particular quarter may comprise valuations conducted over the previous and following one and a half months, and hence it represents an average over time of valuations carried out. This smoothness will be reflected in a lagged dependent variable.
- Finally, the data for independent variables may themselves be autocorrelated. This is particularly the case with regional economic data. Depending on the way that such data are constructed, strong smoothness can be present.

Moving from a purely static model to one that allows for lagged effects is likely to reduce, and possibly remove, serial correlation that was present in the static model's residuals. Other problems with the regression could cause the null hypothesis of no autocorrelation to be rejected, however, and these would not be remedied by adding lagged variables to the model.

- **The omission of relevant variables that are themselves autocorrelated.** In other words, if there is a variable that is an important determinant of movements in y, but that has not been included in the model and that itself is autocorrelated, this will induce the residuals from the estimated model to be serially correlated. To give a context in which this may arise, it is often assumed that investors assess one-step-ahead expected REIT returns using a linear relationship,

$$r_t = \alpha_0 + \alpha_1 \Omega_{t-1} + u_t \tag{6.28}$$

where Ω_{t-1} is a set of lagged information variables – i.e. Ω_{t-1} is a vector of observations on a set of variables at time $t-1$. Equation (6.28) cannot be estimated, however, since the actual information set used by investors to form their expectations of returns is not known. Ω_{t-1} is therefore proxied with an assumed subset of that information, Z_{t-1}. For example, investors will use insight from popular arbitrage pricing specifications, in which the information set used in the estimated model includes unexpected changes in the dividend yield, the term structure of interest rates, inflation and default risk premia. Such a model is bound to omit some informational variables used by actual investors in forming expectations of returns, and, if these are autocorrelated, it will induce the residuals of the estimated model to be autocorrelated as well.

- **Autocorrelation owing to unparameterised seasonality**. Suppose that the dependent variable contains seasonal or cyclical patterns, in which certain features occur periodically. This may arise, for example, in the context of end-of-year quarterly valuations that may be based on a larger sample than those in the rest of the year. Such phenomena are likely to lead to a positively autocorrelated residual structure that is cyclical in shape, such as that of figure 6.4, unless the seasonal patterns are captured by the model. See section 8.10 for a discussion of seasonality and how to deal with it.
- **If a 'misspecification' error has been committed by using an inappropriate functional form.** For example, if the relationship between y and the explanatory variables was a non-linear one, but the researcher had specified a linear regression model, this may again induce the residuals from the estimated model to be serially correlated.

6.7.6 *The long-run static equilibrium solution*

Once a general model of the form given in (6.27) has been found, it may contain many differenced and lagged terms that make it difficult to interpret from a theoretical perspective. For example, if the value of x_2 were to increase in period t, what would the effect be on y in periods $t, t+1, t+2$, and so on? One interesting property of a dynamic model that can be calculated is its long-run or static equilibrium solution.

The relevant definition of 'equilibrium' in this context is that a system has reached equilibrium if the variables have attained some steady state values and are no longer changing – i.e., if y and x are in equilibrium, it is possible to write

$$y_t = y_{t+1} = \ldots = y \quad \text{and} \quad x_{2t} = x_{2t+1} = \ldots = x_2$$

and so on. Consequently, $\Delta y_t = y_t - y_{t-1} = y - y = 0$, $\Delta x_{2t} = x_{2t} - x_{2t-1} = x_2 - x_2 = 0$, etc. since the values of the variables are no longer changing. Therefore the way to obtain a long-run static solution from a given empirical model such as (6.27) is as follows.

(1) Remove all time subscripts from the variables.
(2) Set error terms equal to their expected values of zero – i.e. $E(u_t) = 0$.

(3) Remove differenced terms (e.g. Δy_t) altogether.
(4) Gather terms in x together and gather terms in y together.
(5) Rearrange the resulting equation if necessary so that the dependent variable y is on the left-hand side and is expressed as a function of the independent variables.

Example 6.4

Calculate the long-run equilibrium solution for the following model:

$$\Delta y_t = \beta_1 + \beta_2 \Delta x_{2t} + \beta_3 \Delta x_{3t} + \beta_4 x_{2t-1} + \beta_5 y_{t-1} + u_t \tag{6.29}$$

Applying first steps 1 to 3 above, the static solution would be given by

$$0 = \beta_1 + \beta_4 x_2 + \beta_5 y \tag{6.30}$$

Rearranging (6.30) to bring y to the LHS,

$$\beta_5 y = -\beta_1 - \beta_4 x_2 \tag{6.31}$$

and finally, dividing through by β_5,

$$y = -\frac{\beta_1}{\beta_5} - \frac{\beta_4}{\beta_5} x_2 \tag{6.32}$$

Equation (6.32) is the long-run static solution to (6.29). Note that this equation does not feature x_3, since the only term that contained x_3 was in first-differenced form, so x_3 does not influence the long-run equilibrium value of y.

6.7.7 *Problems with adding lagged regressors to 'cure' autocorrelation*

In many instances, a move from a static model to a dynamic one will result in a removal of residual autocorrelation. The use of lagged variables in a regression model does bring with it additional problems, however.

- **The inclusion of lagged values of the dependent variable violates the assumption that the explanatory variables are non-stochastic** (assumption 4 of the CLRM), since by definition the value of y is determined partly by a random error term, and so its lagged values cannot be non-stochastic. In small samples, the inclusion of lags of the dependent variable can lead to biased coefficient estimates, although they are still consistent, implying that the bias will disappear asymptotically – that is, as the sample size increases towards infinity.
- **What does an equation with a large number of lags actually mean?** A model with many lags may have solved a statistical problem – autocorrelated residuals – at the expense of creating an interpretational

one: the empirical model containing many lags or differenced terms is difficult to interpret and may not test the original real estate theory that motivated the use of regression analysis in the first place.

Note that if there is still autocorrelation in the residuals of a model including lags, the OLS estimators will not even be consistent. To see why this occurs, consider the following regression model,

$$y_t = \beta_1 + \beta_2 x_{2t} + \beta_3 x_{3t} + \beta_4 y_{t-1} + u_t \tag{6.33}$$

in which the errors, u_t, follow a first-order autoregressive process:

$$u_t = \rho u_{t-1} + v_t \tag{6.34}$$

Substituting into (6.33) for u_t from (6.34),

$$y_t = \beta_1 + \beta_2 x_{2t} + \beta_3 x_{3t} + \beta_4 y_{t-1} + \rho u_{t-1} + v_t \tag{6.35}$$

Clearly, y_t depends upon y_{t-1}. Taking (6.35) and lagging it one period (i.e. subtracting one from each time index),

$$y_{t-1} = \beta_1 + \beta_2 x_{2t-1} + \beta_3 x_{3t-1} + \beta_4 y_{t-2} + u_{t-1} \tag{6.36}$$

It is clear from (6.36) that y_{t-1} is related to u_{t-1}, as they both appear in that equation. Thus the assumption that $\mathrm{E}(X'u) = 0$ is not satisfied for (6.36), nor, therefore, for (6.33). The OLS estimator will therefore not be consistent, so that, even with an infinite quantity of data, the coefficient estimates will be biased.

Example 6.5

Based on the Breusch–Godfrey test, we have concluded that the autocorrelation pattern in the residuals of equation (6.6) does not misspecify the model. In order to illustrate one of the remedies for residual autocorrelation, however, we investigate whether adding lags both of employment and GDP growth eliminates any remaining (albeit insignificant) autocorrelation from the residuals and improves the explanatory power of the rent growth equation. We augment equation (6.6) with the first lag of *EFBSg* and *GDPg* ($EFBSg_{t-1}$ and $GDPg_{t-1}$). This means that we test the proposition that rent growth in the current period reflects employment and *GDP* growth from a year ago. This dynamic could be the result of several factors. For example, in rent negotiations the parties may use both current and past economic information to better establish trends and test the resilience of the economy, as noted earlier. Furthermore, weight may be given to past economic data since the current data are to a larger degree subject to revisions.

The results are given in equation (6.37), with t-ratios in parentheses:

$$\underset{}{R\hat{R}g_t} = \underset{(-5.95)}{-15.31} + \underset{(2.32)}{2.03EFBSg_t} + \underset{(2.93)}{2.54GDPg_t} + \underset{(2.73)}{1.86EFBSg_{t-1}} - \underset{(-0.77)}{0.94GDPg_{t-1}} \quad (6.37)$$

$T = 27$; $R^2 = 0.69$; adj. $R^2 = 0.63$. We make a number of observations for the results of this estimation and in comparison with equation (6.6).

- The first lag of *EFBSg* is statistically significant but not that of *GDPg*; as a matter of fact, the coefficient on $GDPg_{t-1}$ takes a negative sign, which is at odds with our expectation. In the next chapter, we discuss possible reasons for such a finding. Therefore, unlike GDP growth, both employment growth terms are significant. These results may be due to the characteristics of the economic data and behavioural factors. For example, agents may be placing more attention on employment than GDP to assess the impact of economic conditions on the real estate market. This is particularly the case at the city level, whereby city-based employment figures are more real to market participants than city-based output. In our example, employment figures capture the rise in economic activity earlier than GDP, even though employment is usually considered a lagging indicator in economic research. The definition of the data may be another reason. Employment refers to the financial and business services sector, which is the main office-using sector, whereas GDP refers to overall economic activity.
- The sizes of the coefficients on *EFBS* and *GDP* are smaller in equation (6.37) than equation (6.6), as more terms are included, taking away explanatory power from the existing terms. For example, the significant $EFBSg_{t-1}$ term takes away from both $EFBSg_t$ and $GDPg_t$. This implies that these terms are to an extent related – a subject that we address later in this chapter (multicollinearity). The sizes of the coefficients on *EFBSg* in equation (6.37) suggest that the contemporaneous term has a slightly greater influence on rental growth than the lagged term. Hence the contemporaneous growth in employment has more bearing on rent determination (negotiations, valuations) than last year's – a plausible finding.
- The explanatory power of (6.37) in terms of $\bar{R}^2$ has improved a little, from 0.55 to 0.63; apparently, the additional terms did not bring much more explanatory power over and above the original regressors.

We revisit equation (6.37) and exclude the insignificant term $GDPg_{t-1}$, which results in equation (6.38):

$$\begin{array}{lllll} R\hat{R}g_t = & -15.02 & +1.64EFBSg_t & +2.27GDPg_t & +1.63EFBSg_{t-1} \\ & (-5.96) & (2.33) & (2.90) & (2.67) \end{array} \quad (6.38)$$

$T = 27$; $R^2 = 0.68$; adj. $R^2 = 0.64$. The explanatory power has increased a little further to $\bar{R}^2 = 0.64$, as the penalty for excluding an insignificant term is removed. R^2 has dropped marginally, as expected. We now test for first-order autocorrelation in the residuals with the Breusch–Godfrey test. The R^2 of the auxiliary regression is 0.29. Hence

$$(T - r)R^2 = (27 - 1) \times 0.29 = 7.54 \sim \chi^2_1$$

The χ^2_1 critical value is 3.84 at the 5 per cent level of significance. Therefore the inclusion of $EFBSg_{t-1}$ introduces stronger autocorrelation in the residuals, although it increases the explanatory power of the model. The F-version of the test also points to first-order serial correlation. The computed F-statistic is $\frac{817.75-571.16}{571.16} \times \frac{27-4}{1} = 9.93$. The critical F for $m = 1$ and $T - k = 23$ at the 5 per cent level of significance is $F_{1,23} = 4.28$.

A plausible explanation for this finding relates to estimation problems that may have arisen from the relationships between the explanatory variables; this issue is discussed later, in this and subsequent chapters. In such a situation, it would be better to stick with the original model; additional diagnostics will guide the decision on the final specification, however.

6.8 Assumption 4: the x_t are non-stochastic ($\text{cov}(u_t, x_t) = 0$)

Fortunately, it turns out that the OLS estimator is consistent and unbiased in the presence of stochastic regressors, provided that the regressors are not correlated with the error term of the estimated equation. To see this, recall that

$$\hat{\beta} = (X'X)^{-1}X'y \quad \text{and} \quad y = X\beta + u \quad (6.39)$$

Thus

$$\hat{\beta} = (X'X)^{-1}X'(X\beta + u) \quad (6.40)$$

$$\hat{\beta} = (X'X)^{-1}X'X\beta + (X'X)^{-1}X'u \quad (6.41)$$

$$\hat{\beta} = \beta + (X'X)^{-1}X'u \quad (6.42)$$

Taking expectations, and provided that X and u are independent,[1]

$$E(\hat{\beta}) = E(\beta) + E((X'X)^{-1}X'u) \tag{6.43}$$

$$E(\hat{\beta}) = \beta + E[(X'X)^{-1}X']E(u) \tag{6.44}$$

Since $E(u) = 0$, this expression is zero and therefore the estimator is still unbiased, even if the regressors are stochastic.

If one or more of the explanatory variables is contemporaneously correlated with the disturbance term, however, the OLS estimator will not even be consistent. This results from the estimator assigning explanatory power to the variables when in reality it is arising from the correlation between the error term and y_t. Suppose, for illustration, that x_{2t} and u_t are positively correlated. When the disturbance term happens to take a high value, y_t will also be high (because $y_t = \beta_1 + \beta_2 x_{2t} + \cdots + u_t$). If x_{2t} is positively correlated with u_t, however, then x_{2t} is also likely to be high. Thus the OLS estimator will incorrectly attribute the high value of y_t to a high value of x_{2t}, when in reality y_t is high simply because u_t is high, which will result in biased and inconsistent parameter estimates and a fitted line that appears to capture the features of the data much better than it does in reality.

6.9 Assumption 5: the disturbances are normally distributed

Recall that the normality assumption ($u_t \sim \mathrm{N}(0, \sigma^2)$) is required in order to conduct single or joint hypothesis tests about the model parameters.

6.9.1 *Testing for departures from normality*

One of the most commonly applied tests for normality is the BJ test (Bera and Jarque, 1981). The BJ test uses the property of a normally distributed random variable that the entire distribution is characterised by the first two moments – the mean and the variance. The standardised third and fourth moments of a distribution are known as its *skewness* and *kurtosis*, as discussed in chapter 3. These ideas are formalised by testing whether the coefficient of skewness and the coefficient of excess kurtosis are jointly zero. Denoting the errors by u and their variance by σ^2, it can be proved that the coefficients of skewness and kurtosis can be expressed, respectively, as

$$b_1 = \frac{E[u^3]}{\left(\sigma^2\right)^{3/2}} \quad \text{and} \quad b_2 = \frac{E[u^4]}{\left(\sigma^2\right)^2} \tag{6.45}$$

[1] A situation in which X and u are not independent is discussed at length in chapter 10.

The kurtosis of the normal distribution is three, so its excess kurtosis $(b_2 - 3)$ is zero.

The Bera–Jarque test statistic is given by

$$BJ = T\left[\frac{b_1^2}{6} + \frac{(b_2 - 3)^2}{24}\right] \tag{6.46}$$

where T is the sample size. The test statistic asymptotically follows a $\chi^2(2)$ under the null hypothesis that the distribution of the series is symmetric and mesokurtic.

b_1 and b_2 can be estimated using the residuals from the OLS regression, $\hat{u}$. The null hypothesis is of normality, and this would be rejected if the residuals from the model were either significantly skewed or leptokurtic/platykurtic (or both).

Example 6.6

We revert to equation (6.6) and we compute the BJ test for normality based on these residuals. The calculated higher moments are

$$\text{skewness} = 0.22$$
$$\text{kurtosis} = 2.97$$

and the BJ test statistic is

$$BJ = 28\left[\frac{0.22^2}{6} + \frac{(2.97 - 3)^2}{24}\right] = 0.23$$

The $\chi^2(2)$ critical value at the 5 per cent level of significance is 5.99. The computed value for the Bera-Jarque test is 0.23, and therefore we do not reject the null hypothesis that the disturbances corresponding to equation (6.6) follow the normal distribution.[2]

6.9.2 *What should be done if evidence of non-normality is found?*

The first point to make is that it is not obvious what should be done! It is, of course, possible to employ an estimation method that does not assume normality, but such a method may be difficult to implement, and one can be less sure of its properties. It is therefore desirable to stick with OLS if possible, as its behaviour in a variety of circumstances has been well researched. For sample sizes that are sufficiently large, violation of the normality assumption is virtually inconsequential. Appealing to a central

[2] Note that some packages, such as Microsoft Excel, purport to present a kurtosis value when they really mean excess kurtosis. To test for normality in such cases, we need to remember not to subtract three from the second part of the expression, as this would have already been done in calculating the excess kurtosis.

limit theorem, the test statistics will asymptotically follow the appropriate distributions even in the absence of error normality.[3]

In economic and real estate modelling, it is quite often the case that one or two very extreme residuals cause a rejection of the normality assumption. Such observations would appear in the tails of the distribution, and would therefore lead u^4, which enters into the definition of kurtosis, to be very large. Such observations that do not fit in with the pattern of the remainder of the data are known as *outliers*. If this is the case, one way to improve the chances of error normality is to use dummy variables or some other method to effectively remove those observations.

In the time series context, suppose that an annual model of all property returns from 1984 to 2007 had been estimated with UK data and the residuals plotted, and that a particularly large 'outlier' had been observed for 1987, as shown in figure 6.10. The model was unable to replicate the very high return achieved that year.

A new variable, called $D87_t$, could be defined as $D87_t = 1$ for the 1987 observation and zero otherwise. The data points for the dummy variable would appear as in box 6.6.

Box 6.6 Observations for the dummy variable

Time	Value of dummy variable $D87_t$
1986	0
1987	1
1988	0
⋮	⋮
1989	0
1990	0
⋮	⋮

The dummy variable would then be used just like any other variable in the regression model – e.g.

$$y_t = \beta_1 + \beta_2 x_{2t} + \beta_3 x_{3t} + \beta_4 D87_t + u_t \tag{6.47}$$

This type of dummy variable, which takes the value one for only a single observation, has an effect exactly equivalent to knocking out that observation from the sample altogether, by forcing the residual for that observation

[3] The law of large numbers states that the average of a sample (which is a random variable) will converge to the population mean (which is fixed), and the central limit theorem states that the sample mean converges to a normal distribution.

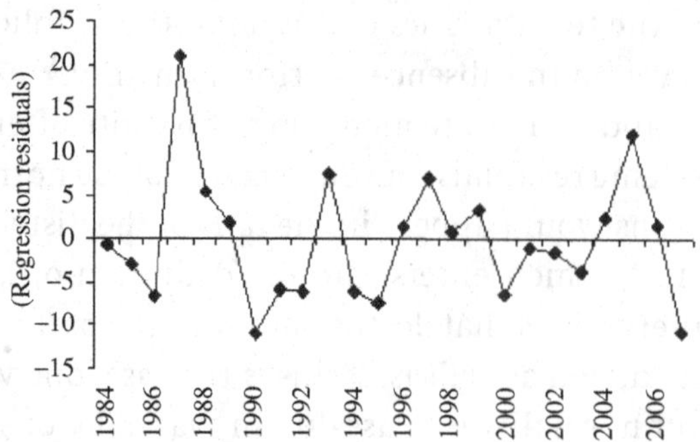

Figure 6.10
Regression residuals showing a large outlier

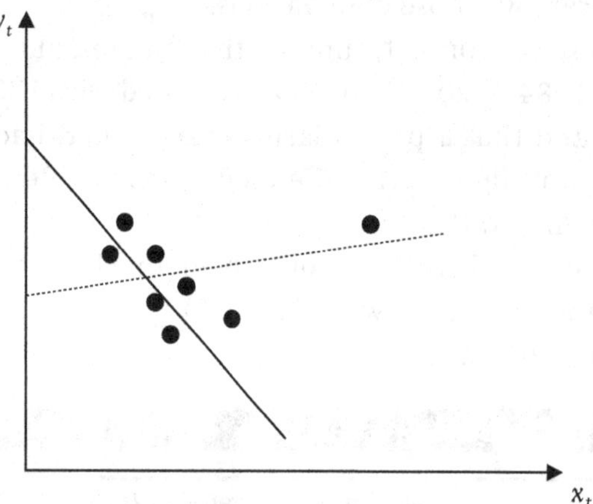

Figure 6.11
Possible effect of an outlier on OLS estimation

to zero. The estimated coefficient on the dummy variable will be equal to the residual that the dummied observation would have taken if the dummy variable had not been included.

Many econometricians would argue, however, that dummy variables to remove outlying residuals can be used to improve the characteristics of the model artificially – in essence fudging the results. Removing outlying observations will reduce standard errors, reduce the RSS and therefore increase R^2, thus improving the apparent fit of the model to the data. The removal of observations is also hard to reconcile with the notion in statistics that each data point represents a useful piece of information.

The other side of this argument is that observations that are 'a long way away' from the rest, and seem not to fit in with the general pattern of the rest of the data, are known as *outliers*. Outliers can have a serious effect on coefficient estimates, since, by definition, OLS will receive a big penalty, in the form of an increased RSS, for points that are a long way away from the fitted line. Consequently, OLS will try extra hard to minimise the distances of points that would have otherwise been a long way away from the line. A graphical depiction of the possible effect of an outlier on OLS estimation is given in figure 6.11.

In this figure, one point is a long way away from the rest. If this point is included in the estimation sample, the fitted line will be the dotted one, which has a slight positive slope. If this observation were removed, the full line would be the one fitted. Clearly, the slope is now large and negative. OLS will not select this line if the outlier is included since the observation is a long way from the others, and hence, when the residual (the distance from the point to the fitted line) is squared, it will lead to a big increase in the RSS. Note that outliers could be detected by plotting y against x only in the context of a bivariate regression. In the case in which there are more explanatory variables, outliers are identified most easily by plotting the residuals over time, as in figure 6.10.

It can be seen, therefore, that a trade-off potentially exists between the need to remove outlying observations that could have an undue impact on the OLS estimates and cause residual non-normality, on the one hand, and the notion that each data point represents a useful piece of information, on the other. The latter is coupled with the fact that removing observations at will could artificially improve the fit of the model. A sensible way to proceed is by introducing dummy variables to the model only if there is both a statistical need to do so and a theoretical justification for their inclusion. This justification would normally come from the researcher's knowledge of the historical events that relate to the dependent variable and the model over the relevant sample period. Dummy variables may be justifiably used to remove observations corresponding to 'one-off' or extreme events that are considered highly unlikely to be repeated, and the information content of which is deemed of no relevance for the data as a whole. Examples may include real estate market crashes, economic or financial crises, and so on.

Non-normality in the data could also arise from certain types of heteroscedasticity, known as ARCH. In this case, the non-normality is intrinsic to all the data, and therefore outlier removal would not make the residuals of such a model normal.

Another important use of dummy variables is in the modelling of seasonality in time series data, and accounting for so-called 'calendar anomalies', such as end-of-quarter valuation effects. These are discussed in section 8.10.

6.10 Multicollinearity

An implicit assumption that is made when using the OLS estimation method is that the explanatory variables are not correlated with one another. If there is no relationship between the explanatory variables, they would be said to be *orthogonal* to one another. If the explanatory variables were orthogonal to one another, adding or removing a variable from a regression equation would not cause the values of the coefficients on the other variables to change.

In any practical context, the correlation between explanatory variables will be non-zero, although this will generally be relatively benign, in the sense that a small degree of association between explanatory variables will almost always occur but will not cause too much loss of precision. A problem occurs when the explanatory variables are very highly correlated with each other, however, and this problem is known as *multicollinearity*. It is possible to distinguish between two classes of multicollinearity: perfect multicollinearity and near-multicollinearity.

Perfect multicollinearity occurs when there is an exact relationship between two or more variables. In this case, it is not possible to estimate all the coefficients in the model. Perfect multicollinearity will usually be observed only when the same explanatory variable is inadvertently used twice in a regression. For illustration, suppose that two variables were employed in a regression function such that the value of one variable was always twice that of the other (e.g. suppose $x_3 = 2x_2$). If both x_3 and x_2 were used as explanatory variables in the same regression, then the model parameters cannot be estimated. Since the two variables are perfectly related to one another, together they contain only enough information to estimate one parameter, not two. Technically, the difficulty would occur in trying to invert the $(X'X)$ matrix, since it would not be of full rank (two of the columns would be linearly dependent on one another), meaning that the inverse of $(X'X)$ would not exist and hence the OLS estimates $\hat{\beta} = (X'X)^{-1}X'y$ could not be calculated.

Near-multicollinearity is much more likely to occur in practice, and will arise when there is a non-negligible, but not perfect, relationship between two or more of the explanatory variables. Note that a high correlation between the dependent variable and one of the independent variables is not multicollinearity.

Visually, we could think of the difference between near- and perfect mutlicollinearity as follows. Suppose that the variables x_{2t} and x_{3t} were highly correlated. If we produced a scatter plot of x_{2t} against x_{3t}, then perfect multicollinearity would correspond to all the points lying exactly on a straight line, while near-multicollinearity would correspond to the points lying close to the line, and the closer they were to the line (taken altogether), the stronger the relationship between the two variables would be.

6.10.1 *Measuring near-multicollinearity*

Testing for multicollinearity is surprisingly difficult, and hence all that is presented here is a simple method to investigate the presence or otherwise of the most easily detected forms of near-multicollinearity. This method simply involves looking at the matrix of correlations between the individual variables. Suppose that a regression equation has three explanatory variables (plus a constant term), and that the pairwise correlations between these explanatory variables are

corr	x_2	x_3	x_4
x_2	–	0.2	0.8
x_3	0.2	–	0.3
x_4	0.8	0.3	–

Clearly, if multicollinearity was suspected, the most likely culprit would be a high correlation between x_2 and x_4. Of course, if the relationship involves three or more variables that are collinear – e.g. $x_2 + x_3 \approx x_4$ – then multicollinearity would be very difficult to detect.

In our example (equation (6.6)), the correlation between *EFBSg* and *GDPg* is 0.51, suggesting a moderately strong relationship. We do not think multicollinearity is completely absent from our rent equation, but, on the other hand, it probably does not represent a serious problem.

Another test is to run auxiliary regressions in which we regress each independent variable on the remaining independent variables and examine whether the R^2 values are zero (which would suggest that the variables are not collinear). In equations with several independent variables, this procedure is time-consuming, although, in our example, there it is only one auxiliary regression that we can run:

$$\underset{}{E\hat{F}BSg_t} = \underset{(2.54)}{1.55} + \underset{(2.99)}{0.62GDPg_t} \qquad (6.48)$$

$R^2 = 0.26$; adj. $R^2 = 0.23$; $T = 28$. We observe that *GDPg* is significant in the $EFBSg_t$ equation, which is indicative of collinearity. The square of the coefficient of determination is not high but neither is it negligible.

6.10.2 *Problems if near-multicollinearity is present but ignored*

First, R^2 will be high, but the individual coefficients will have high standard errors, so the regression 'looks good' as a whole,[4] but the individual variables are not significant. This arises in the context of very closely related

[4] Note that multicollinearity does not affect the value of R^2 in a regression.

explanatory variables as a consequence of the difficulty in observing the individual contribution of each variable to the overall fit of the regression. Second, the regression becomes very sensitive to small changes in the specification, so that adding or removing an explanatory variable leads to large changes in the coefficient values or significances of the other variables. Finally, near-multicollinearity will make confidence intervals for the parameters very wide, and significance tests might therefore give inappropriate conclusions, thus making it difficult to draw clear-cut inferences.

6.10.3 *Solutions to the problem of multicollinearity*

A number of alternative estimation techniques have been proposed that are valid in the presence of multicollinearity – for example, ridge regression, or principal component analysis (PCA). PCA is a technique that may be useful when explanatory variables are closely related, and it works as follows. If there are k explanatory variables in the regression model, PCA will transform them into k uncorrelated new variables. These components are independent linear combinations of the original data. Then the components are used in any subsequent regression model rather than the original variables. Many researchers do not use these techniques, however, as they can be complex, their properties are less well understood than those of the OLS estimator and, above all, many econometricians would argue that multicollinearity is more a problem with the data than with the model or estimation method.

Other, more ad hoc methods for dealing with the possible existence of near-multicollinearity include the following.

- **Ignore it**, if the model is otherwise adequate – i.e. statistically and in terms of each coefficient being of a plausible magnitude and having an appropriate sign. Sometimes the existence of multicollinearity does not reduce the t-ratios on variables that would have been significant without the multicollinearity sufficiently to make them insignificant. It is worth stating that the presence of near multicollinearity does not affect the BLUE properties of the OLS estimator – i.e. it will still be consistent, unbiased and efficient – as the presence of near-multicollinearity does not violate any of the CLRM assumptions 1 to 4. In the presence of near-multicollinearity, however, it will be hard to obtain small standard errors. This will not matter if the aim of the model-building exercise is to produce forecasts from the estimated model, since the forecasts will be unaffected by the presence of near-multicollinearity so long as this relationship between the explanatory variables continues to hold over the forecast sample.

- **Drop one of the collinear variables,** so that the problem disappears. This may be unacceptable to the researcher, however, if there are strong a priori theoretical reasons for including both variables in the model. Moreover, if the removed variable is relevant in the data-generating process for y, an omitted variable bias would result (see section 5.9).
- **Transform the highly correlated variables into a ratio and include only the ratio and not the individual variables in the regression.** Again, this may be unacceptable if real estate theory suggests that changes in the dependent variable should occur following changes in the individual explanatory variables, and not a ratio of them.
- Finally, as stated above, it is also often said that near-multicollinearity is more a problem with the data than with the model, with the result that there is insufficient information in the sample to obtain estimates for all the coefficients. This is why near-multicollinearity leads coefficient estimates to have wide standard errors, which is exactly what would happen if the sample size were small. An increase in the sample size will usually lead to an increase in the accuracy of coefficient estimation and, consequently, a reduction in the coefficient standard errors, thus enabling the model to better dissect the effects of the various explanatory variables on the explained variable. A further possibility, therefore, is for the researcher to go out and collect more data – for example, by taking a longer run of data, or switching to a higher frequency of sampling. Of course, it may be infeasible to increase the sample size if all available data are being utilised already. Another method of increasing the available quantity of data as a potential remedy for near-multicollinearity would be to use a pooled sample. This would involve the use of data with both cross-sectional and time series dimensions, known as a *panel* (see Brooks, 2008, ch. 10).

6.11 Adopting the wrong functional form

A further implicit assumption of the classical linear regression model is that the appropriate 'functional form' is linear. This means that the appropriate model is assumed to be linear in the parameters, and that, in the bivariate case, the relationship between y and x can be represented by a straight line. This assumption may not always be upheld, however. Whether the model should be linear can be formally tested using Ramsey's (1969) RESET test, which is a general test for misspecification of functional form. Essentially, the method works by using higher-order terms of the fitted values (e.g. $\hat{y}_t^2$, $\hat{y}_t^3$, etc.) in an auxiliary regression. The auxiliary regression is thus one in which y_t, the dependent variable from the original regression, is regressed on powers of the fitted values together with the original explanatory variables:

$$y_t = \alpha_1 + \alpha_2 \hat{y}_t^2 + \alpha_3 \hat{y}_t^3 + \cdots + \alpha_p \hat{y}_t^p + \sum \beta_i x_{it} + v_t \quad (6.49)$$

Higher-order powers of the fitted values of y can capture a variety of non-linear relationships, since they embody higher-order powers and cross-products of the original explanatory variables – e.g.

$$\hat{y}_t^2 = (\hat{\beta}_1 + \hat{\beta}_2 x_{2t} + \hat{\beta}_3 x_{3t} + \cdots + \hat{\beta}_k x_{kt})^2 \quad (6.50)$$

The value of R^2 is obtained from the regression (6.49), and the test statistic, given by TR^2, is distributed asymptotically as a $\chi^2(p-1)$. Note that the degrees of freedom for this test will be $(p-1)$ and not p. This arises because p is the highest-order term in the fitted values used in the auxiliary regression, and thus the test will involve $p-1$ terms: one for the square of the fitted value, one for the cube, ..., one for the pth power. If the value of the test statistic is greater than the χ^2 critical value, reject the null hypothesis that the functional form was correct.

6.11.1 *What if the functional form is found to be inappropriate?*

One possibility would be to switch to a non-linear model, but the RESET test presents the user with no guide as to what a better specification might be! In addition, non-linear models in the parameters typically preclude the use of OLS, and require the use of a non-linear estimation technique. Some non-linear models can still be estimated using OLS, provided that they are linear in the parameters. For example, if the true model is of the form

$$y_t = \beta_1 + \beta_2 x_{2t} + \beta_3 x_{2t}^2 + \beta_4 x_{2t}^3 + u_t \quad (6.51)$$

– that is, a third-order polynomial in x – and the researcher assumes that the relationship between y_t and x_t is linear (i.e. x_{2t}^2 and x_{2t}^3 are missing from the specification), this is simply a special case of omitted variables, with the usual problems (see section 5.9) and obvious remedy.

The model may be multiplicatively non-linear, however. A second possibility that is sensible in this case would be to transform the data into logarithms. This will linearise many previously multiplicative models into additive ones. For example, consider again the exponential growth model

$$y_t = \beta_1 x_t^{\beta_2} u_t \quad (6.52)$$

Taking logs, this becomes

$$\ln(y_t) = \ln(\beta_1) + \beta_2 \ln(x_t) + \ln(u_t) \quad (6.53)$$

or

$$Y_t = \alpha + \beta_2 X_t + v_t \tag{6.54}$$

where $Y_t = \ln(y_t)$, $\alpha = \ln(\beta_1)$, $X_t = \ln(x_t)$ and $v_t = \ln(u_t)$. A simple logarithmic transformation therefore makes this model a standard linear bivariate regression equation that can be estimated using OLS.

Loosely following the treatment given in Stock and Watson (2006), the following list shows four different functional forms for models that are either linear or can be made linear following a logarithmic transformation to one or more of the dependent variables, examining only a bivariate specification for simplicity. Care is needed when interpreting the coefficient values in each case.

(1) Linear: $y_t = \beta_1 + \beta_2 x_{2t} + u_t$; a one-unit increase in x_{2t} causes a β_2-unit increase in y_t.

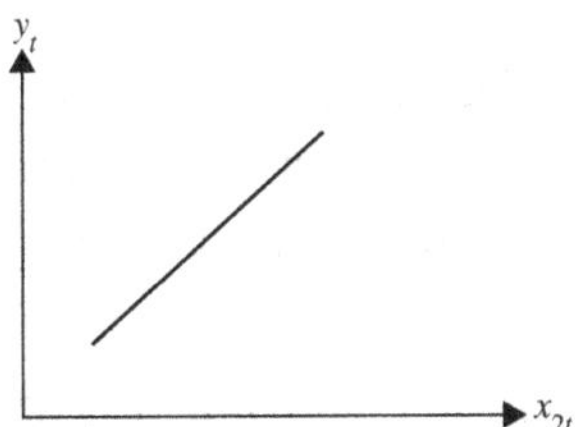

(2) Log-linear: $ln(y_t) = \beta_1 + \beta_2 x_{2t} + u_t$; a one-unit increase in x_{2t} causes a $100 \times \beta_2$ per cent increase in y_t.

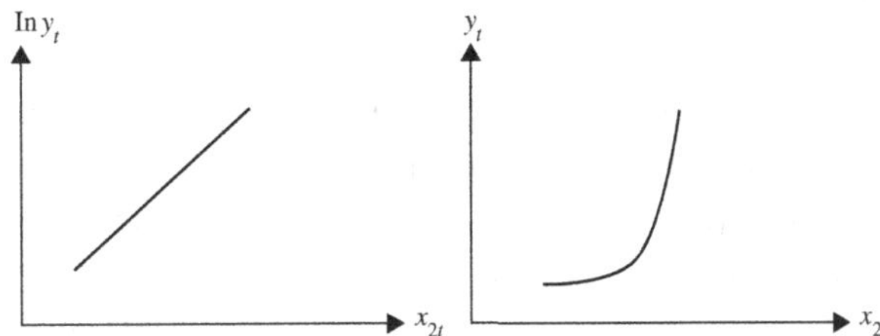

(3) Linear-log: $y_t = \beta_1 + \beta_2 ln(x_{2t}) + u_t$; a 1 per cent increase in x_{2t} causes a $0.01 \times \beta_2$-unit increase in y_t.

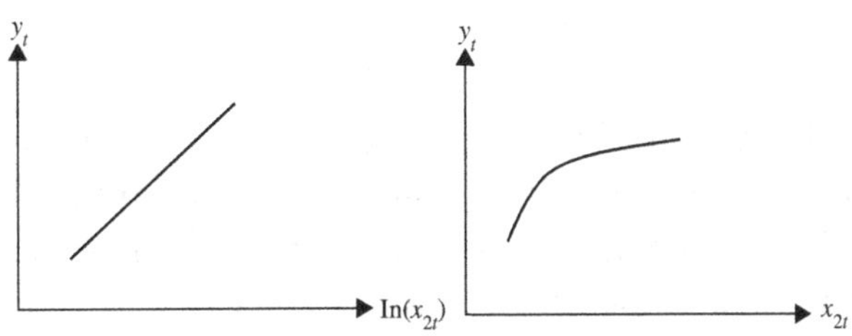

(4) Double log: $ln(y_t) = \beta_1 + \beta_2 ln(x_{2t}) + u_t$; a 1 per cent increase in x_{2t} causes a β_2 per cent increase in y_t. Note that to plot y against x_2 would be more complex, as the shape would depend on the size of β_2.

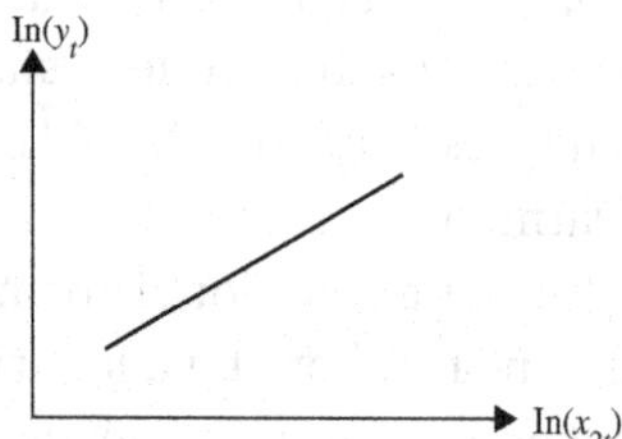

Note also that we cannot use R^2 or adjusted R^2 to determine which of these four types of model is most appropriate, since the dependent variables are different in some of the models.

Example 6.7

We follow the procedure described in equation (6.49) to test whether equation (5.39) has the correct functional form. Equation (5.39) is the restricted regression. The unrestricted (auxiliary) regression contains the square of the fitted value:

$$R\hat{R}g_t = -14.41 + 2.68EFBSg_t + 2.24GDPg_t + 0.02FITTED^2$$

RRSS = 1,078.26; URSS = 1,001.73; $T = 28$; $m = 1$; and $k = 4$. The F-statistic is

$$\frac{1078.26 - 1001.72}{1001.72} \times \frac{28 - 4}{1} = 1.83$$

The $F(1,24)$ critical value is 4.26 at the 5 per cent significance level. The computed test statistic is lower than the critical value, and hence we do not reject the null hypothesis that the functional form is correct, so we would conclude that the linear model is appropriate.

6.12 Parameter stability tests

So far, regressions of a form such as

$$y_t = \beta_1 + \beta_2 x_{2t} + \beta_3 x_{3t} + u_t \tag{6.55}$$

have been estimated. These regressions embody the implicit assumption that the parameters (β_1, β_2 and β_3) are constant for the entire sample, both for the data period used to estimate the model and for any subsequent period used in the construction of forecasts.

This implicit assumption can be tested using parameter stability tests. The idea is, essentially, to split the data into sub-periods and then to estimate up to three models, for each of the sub-parts and for all the data, and then to 'compare' the RSS of each of the models. There are two types of test that will be considered, namely the Chow (analysis of variance) test and the predictive failure test.

6.12.1 *The Chow test*

The steps involved are shown in box 6.7.

Box 6.7 Conducting a Chow test

(1) *Split the data into two sub-periods.* Estimate the regression over the whole period and then for the two sub-periods separately (three regressions). Obtain the RSS for each regression.

(2) *The restricted regression is now the regression for the whole period,* while the 'unrestricted regression' comes in two parts: one for each of the sub-samples. It is thus possible to form an F-test, which is based on the difference between the RSSs. The statistic is

$$\textit{test statistic} = \frac{RSS - (RSS_1 + RSS_2)}{RSS_1 + RSS_2} \times \frac{T - 2k}{k} \tag{6.56}$$

where RSS = residual sum of squares for the whole sample;
RSS_1 = residual sum of squares for sub-sample 1;
RSS_2 = residual sum of squares for sub-sample 2;
T = number of observations;
$2k$ = number of regressors in the 'unrestricted' regression (as it comes in two parts), each including a constant; and
k = number of regressors in (each) 'unrestricted' regression, including a constant.

The unrestricted regression is the one in which the restriction has not been imposed on the model. Since the restriction is that the coefficients are equal across the sub-samples, the restricted regression will be the single regression for the whole sample. Thus the test is one of how much the residual sum of squares for the whole sample (RSS) is bigger than the sum of the residual sums of squares for the two sub-samples ($RSS_1 + RSS_2$). If the coefficients do not change much between the samples, the residual sum of squares will not rise much upon imposing the restriction.

The test statistic in (6.56) can therefore be considered a straightforward application of the standard F-test formula discussed in chapter 5. The restricted residual sum of squares in (6.56) is RSS, while the unrestricted residual sum of squares is ($RSS_1 + RSS_2$). The number of restrictions is equal to the number of coefficients that are estimated for each of the regressions – i.e. k. The number of regressors in the unrestricted regression (including the constants) is $2k$, since the unrestricted regression comes in two parts, each with k regressors.

(3) *Perform the test.* If the value of the test statistic is greater than the critical value from the F-distribution, which is an $F(k, T - 2k)$, then reject the null hypothesis that the parameters are stable over time.

Note that it is also possible to use a dummy variables approach to calculating both Chow and predictive failure tests. In the case of the Chow test, the unrestricted regression would contain dummy variables for the intercept and for all the slope coefficients (see also section 8.10). For example, suppose that the regression is of the form

$$y_t = \beta_1 + \beta_2 x_{2t} + \beta_3 x_{3t} + u_t \tag{6.57}$$

If the split of the total of T observations is made so that the sub-samples contain T_1 and T_2 observations (where $T_1 + T_2 = T$), the unrestricted regression would be given by

$$y_t = \beta_1 + \beta_2 x_{2t} + \beta_3 x_{3t} + \beta_4 D_t + \beta_5 D_t x_{2t} + \beta_6 D_t x_{3t} + v_t \tag{6.58}$$

where $D_t = 1$ for $t \in T_1$ and zero otherwise. In other words, D_t takes the value one for observations in the first sub-sample and zero for observations in the second sub-sample. The Chow test viewed in this way would then be a standard F-test of the joint restriction H_0: $\beta_4 = 0$ and $\beta_5 = 0$ and $\beta_6 = 0$, with (6.58) and (6.57) being the unrestricted and restricted regressions, respectively.

Example 6.8

The application of the Chow test using equation (6.6) is restricted by the fact that we have only twenty-eight observations, and therefore if we split the sample we are left with a mere fourteen observations in each sub-sample. These are very small samples to run regressions, but we do so in this example for the sake of illustrating an application of the Chow test.

We split the sample into two sub-samples: 1979 to 1992 and 1993 to 2006. We compute the F-statistic (as described in equation (6.56)) and test for the null hypothesis that the parameters are stable over time.

The restricted equation is (6.6) and thus the RRSS is 1,078.26.

Unrestricted equation 1 (first sub-sample):

$$R\hat{R}g_t = -10.14 + 2.21EFBSg_t + 1.86GDPg_t \tag{6.59}$$

$R^2 = 0.66$; adj. $R^2 = 0.60$; $URSS_1 = 600.83$.

Unrestricted equation 2 (second sub-sample):

$$R\hat{R}g_t = -23.92 + 3.36EFBSg_t + 5.00GDPg_t \tag{6.60}$$

$R^2 = 0.52$; adj. $R^2 = 0.43$; $URSS_2 = 385.31$.

The following observations can be made, subject, of course, to the small sample periods. The explanatory power has fallen in the second sub-period, despite the fact that two variables are now used in the model to explain rent growth. With larger samples, perhaps the model would have been more stable over time. We should also remind readers, however, that with such very small sub-samples the tests will lack power, and so this result should perhaps have been expected in spite of the fairly large changes in the parameter estimates that we observe.

The F-test statistic is $\frac{1078.26-(600.83+385.31)}{(600.83+385.31)} \times \frac{28-6}{3} = 0.69$. The critical value for an $F(3,22)$ at the 5 per cent significance level is 3.05. Hence we do not reject the null hypothesis of parameter stability over the two sample periods despite the observations we made. The changes that have affected the model are not strong enough to constitute a break according to the Chow test.

6.12.2 *The predictive failure test*

We noted that a problem with the Chow test is that it is necessary to have enough data to do the regression on both sub-samples – i.e. $T_1 \gg k$, $T_2 \gg k$. This may not hold in the situation in which the total number of observations available is small. Even more likely is the situation in which the researcher would like to examine the effect of splitting the sample at some point very close to the start or very close to the end of the sample.

An alternative formulation of a test for the stability of the model is the predictive failure test, which requires estimation for the full sample and one of the sub-samples only. The predictive failure test works by estimating the regression over a 'long' sub-period – i.e. most of the data – and then using those coefficient estimates for predicting values of y for the other period. These predictions for y are then implicitly compared with the actual values. Although it can be expressed in several different ways, the null hypothesis for this test is that the prediction errors for all the forecasted observations are zero.

To calculate the test it is necessary to follow this procedure.

- **Run the regression for the whole period** (the restricted regression) and obtain the RSS.
- **Run the regression for the 'large' sub-period** and obtain the RSS (called RSS_1). Note that, in this book, the number of observations for the long-estimation sub-period will be denoted by T_1 (even though it may come second). The test statistic is given by

$$test\ statistic = \frac{RSS - RSS_1}{RSS_1} \times \frac{T_1 - k}{T_2} \tag{6.61}$$

where T_2 = number of observations that the model is attempting to 'predict'. The test statistic will follow an $F(T_2, T_1 - k)$.

Example 6.9

We estimate equation (6.6) for the period 1979 to 2000 (which gives us twenty-two observations) and we reserve the last six observations (2001 to 2006) to run the predictive failure test (hence the number of observations that the model is attempting to predict is six).

The restricted equation is again (6.6), with an RRSS of 1,078.26.

Unrestricted equation (sub-sample 1979 – 2000):

$$\hat{RRg}_t = \underset{(4.15)}{-10.95} + \underset{(3.01)}{2.35}EFBSg_t + \underset{(2.09)}{1.91}GDPg_t \tag{6.62}$$

$R^2 = 0.61$; adj. $R^2 = 0.56$; URSS $= 897.87$; T_1 (the number of observations) $=$ 22; T_2 (the number of observations that the model is attempting to predict) $=$ 6; k (the number of regressors) $= 3$. The F-test statistic is $\frac{1078.26-897.87}{897.87} \times \frac{22-3}{6} =$ 0.64. The critical value for $F(6,19)$ at the 5 per cent significance level is 2.63. The computed value is lower than the critical value, and therefore this test does not indicate predictive failure (we do not reject the null hypothesis that the predictive errors are zero).

Example 6.10 The predictive failure test with dummy variables

For an intuitive interpretation of the predictive failure test statistic formulation, consider an alternative way to test for predictive failure using a regression containing dummy variables. A separate dummy variable would be used for each observation that was in the prediction sample. The unrestricted regression would then be the one that includes the dummy variables, which will be estimated using all T observations, and will have $(k + T_2)$ regressors (the k original explanatory variables, and a dummy variable for each prediction observation – i.e. a total of T_2 dummy variables). The numerator of the last part of (6.61) would therefore be the total number of observations (T) minus the number of regressors in the unrestricted regression $(k + T_2)$. Noting also that $T - (k + T_2) = (T_1 - k)$, since $T_1 + T_2 = T$, this gives the numerator of the last term in (6.61). The restricted regression would then be the original regression containing the explanatory variables but none of the dummy variables (equation (6.6)). Thus the number of restrictions would be the number of observations in the prediction period, which would be equivalent to the number of dummy variables included in the unrestricted regression, T_2.

Unrestricted equation:

$$\begin{array}{llllll} R\hat{R}g_t = & -10.95 & +2.35EFBSg_t & +1.91GDPg_t & +1.59D01_t & -1.57D02_t \\ & (1.81) & (3.01) & (2.09) & (0.23) & (0.21) \\ & -12.17D03_t & -2.99D04_t & -1.37D05_t & +4.92D06_t & \\ & (1.71) & (0.42) & (0.19) & (0.69) & \end{array} \quad (6.63)$$

$R^2 = 0.65$; adj. $R^2 = 0.50$; URSS $= 897.87$. The sample period is 1979 to 2006 (twenty-eight observations), with $D01_t = 1$ for observation for 2001 and zero otherwise, $D02_t = 1$ for 2002 and zero otherwise, and so on. In this case, $k = 3$ and $T_2 = 6$. The null hypothesis for the predictive failure test in this regression is that the coefficients on all the dummy variables are zero (i.e. H_0: $\gamma_1 = 0$ and $\gamma_2 = 0$ and ... and $\gamma_6 = 0$), where $\gamma_1, \ldots, \gamma_6$ represent the parameters on the six dummy variables.

The F-test statistic is $\frac{1078.26-897.87}{897.87} \times \frac{28-9}{6} = 0.64$. This value is lower than the $F(6,19)$ critical value at the 5 per cent significance level (2.63), and therefore the dummy variable test confirms the finding of the version of the predictive failure test based on estimating two regressions.

Both approaches to conducting the predictive failure test described above are equivalent, although the dummy variable regression is likely to take more time to set up. For both the Chow and the predictive failure tests, however, the dummy variables approach has the one major advantage that it provides the user with more information. This additional information comes from the fact that one can examine the significances of the coefficients on the individual dummy variables to see which part of the joint null hypothesis is causing a rejection. For example, in the context of the Chow regression, is it the intercept or the slope coefficients that are significantly different between the two sub-samples? In the context of the predictive failure test, use of the dummy variables approach would show for which period(s) the prediction errors are significantly different from zero.

6.12.3 *Backward versus forward predictive failure tests*

There are two types of predictive failure tests: forward tests and backward tests. Forward predictive failure tests are those in which the last few observations are kept back for forecast testing. For example, suppose that observations for 1980Q1 to 2008Q4 are available. A forward predictive failure test could involve estimating the model over 1980Q1 to 2007Q4 and forecasting 2008Q1 to 2008Q4. Backward predictive failure tests attempt to 'backcast' the first few observations – e.g., if data for 1980Q1 to 2008Q4 are available, and the model is estimated over 1981Q1 to 2008Q4, the backcast could be

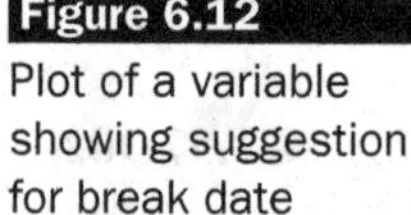

Figure 6.12
Plot of a variable showing suggestion for break date

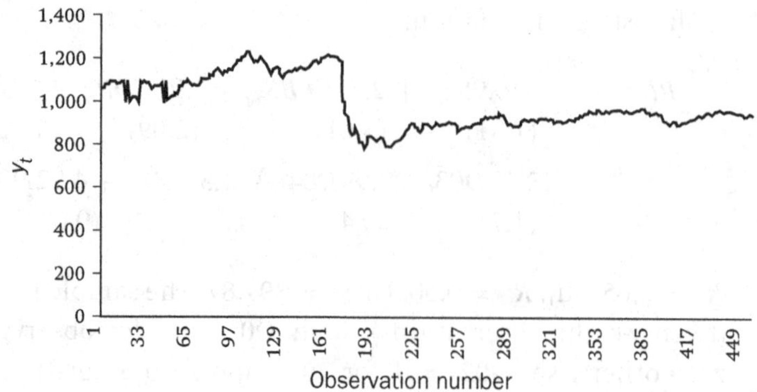

for 1980Q1 to 1980Q4. Both types of test offer further evidence on the stability of the regression relationship over the whole sample period, although in practice the forward test is more commonly used.

6.12.4 *How can the appropriate sub-parts to use be decided?*

As a rule of thumb, some or all of the following methods for selecting where the overall sample split occurs could be used.

- Plot the dependent variable over time and split the data according to *any obvious structural changes in the series*, as illustrated in figure 6.12.
  It is clear that y in figure 6.12 underwent a large fall in its value around observation 175, and it is possible that this may have caused a change in its behaviour. A Chow test could be conducted with the sample split at this observation.
- Split the data according to *any known important historical events* – e.g. a real estate market crash, new planning policies or inflation targeting. The argument is that a major change in the underlying environment in which y is measured is more likely to cause a structural change in the model's parameters than a relatively trivial change.
- Use all but the last few observations and do a *forward predictive failure test* on them.
- Use all but the first few observations and do a *backward predictive failure test* on them.

If a model is good it will survive a Chow or predictive failure test with any break date. If the Chow or predictive failure tests are failed, two approaches can be adopted. Either the model is respecified, for example by including additional variables, or separate estimations are conducted for each of the sub-samples. On the other hand, if the Chow and predictive failure tests show no rejections, it is empirically valid to pool all the data together in a single regression. This will increase the sample size and therefore the number of degrees of freedom relative to the case in which the sub-samples are used in isolation.

6.12.5 *The QLR test*

The Chow and predictive failure tests work satisfactorily if the date of a structural break in a time series can be specified. It is more often the case, however, that a researcher will not know the break date in advance, or may know only that it lies within a given range (subset) of the sample period. In such circumstances, a modified version of the Chow test, known as the Quandt likelihood ratio (QLR) test, named after Quandt (1960), can be used instead. The test works by automatically computing the usual Chow F-test statistic repeatedly with different break dates, and then the break date giving the largest F-statistic value is chosen. Although the test statistic is of the F-variety it will follow a non-standard distribution rather than an F-distribution, since we are selecting the largest from a number of F-statistics as opposed to examining a single one.

The test is well behaved only when the range of possible break dates is sufficiently far from the end points of the whole sample, so it is usual to 'trim' the sample by (typically) 15 per cent at each end. To illustrate, suppose that the full sample comprises 200 observations; then we would test for a structural break between observations 31 and 170 inclusive. The critical values will depend on how much of the sample is trimmed away, the number of restrictions under the null hypothesis (the number of regressors in the original regression, as this is effectively a Chow test) and the significance level.

6.12.6 *Stability tests based on recursive estimation*

An alternative to the QLR test for use in the situation in which a researcher believes that a series may contain a structural break but is unsure of the date is to perform a recursive estimation. This is sometimes known as recursive least squares (RLS). The procedure is appropriate only for time series data or cross-sectional data that have been ordered in some sensible way (such as a sample of yields across cities, ordered from lowest to highest). Recursive estimation simply involves starting with a sub-sample of the data, estimating the regression and then sequentially adding one observation at a time and rerunning the regression until the end of the sample is reached. It is common to begin the initial estimation with the very minimum number of observations possible, which will be $k+1$. At the first step, therefore, the model is estimated using observations 1 to $k+1$; at the second step, observations 1 to $k+2$ are used; and so on; at the final step, observations 1 to T

are used. The final result will be the production of $T - k$ separate estimates of every parameter in the regression model.

It is to be expected that the parameter estimates produced near the start of the recursive procedure will appear rather unstable, since these estimates are being produced using so few observations, but the key question is whether they then gradually settle down or whether the volatility continues throughout the whole sample. Seeing the latter would be an indication of parameter instability.

It should be evident that RLS in itself is not a statistical test for parameter stability as such but, rather, that it provides qualitative information that can be plotted and can thus give a very visual impression of how stable the parameters appear to be. Nevertheless, two important stability tests, known as the CUSUM and CUSUMSQ tests, are derived from the residuals of the recursive estimation (known as the recursive residuals).[5] The CUSUM statistic is based on a normalised – i.e. scaled – version of the cumulative sum of the residuals. Under the null hypothesis of perfect parameter stability, the CUSUM statistic is zero however many residuals are included in the sum (because the expected value of a disturbance is always zero). A set of ± 2 standard error bands is usually plotted around zero, and any statistic lying outside the bands is taken as evidence of parameter instability.

The CUSUMSQ test is based on a normalised version of the cumulative sum of squared residuals. The scaling is such that, under the null hypothesis of parameter stability, the CUSUMSQ statistic will start at zero and end the sample with a value of one. Again, a set of ± 2 standard error bands is usually plotted around zero, and any statistic lying outside these is taken as evidence of parameter instability.

6.13 A strategy for constructing econometric models

This section provides a discussion of two important model-building philosophies that have shaped the way applied researchers think about the process. The objective of many econometric model-building exercises is to build a statistically adequate empirical model that satisfies the assumptions of the CLRM, is parsimonious, has the appropriate theoretical interpretation and has the right 'shape' – i.e. all signs on coefficients are 'correct' and all sizes of coefficients are 'correct'.

[5] Strictly, the CUSUM and CUSUMSQ statistics are based on the one-step-ahead prediction errors – i.e. the differences between y_t and its predicted value based on the parameters estimated at time $t - 1$. See Greene (2002, ch. 7) for full technical details.

How might a researcher go about achieving this objective? A common approach to model building is the 'LSE' or 'general-to-specific' methodology associated with Sargan and Hendry. This approach essentially involves starting with a large model that is statistically adequate and restricting and rearranging the model to arrive at a parsimonious final formulation. Hendry's approach (see Gilbert, 1986) argues that a good model is consistent with the data and with theory. A good model will also encompass rival models, which means that it can explain all that rival models can and more. The Hendry methodology proposes the extensive use of diagnostic tests to ensure the statistical adequacy of the model.

An alternative philosophy of econometric model building, which predates Hendry's research, is that of starting with the simplest model and adding to it sequentially so that it gradually becomes more complex and a better description of reality. This approach, associated principally with Koopmans (1937), is sometimes known as a 'specific-to-general' or 'bottom-up' modelling approach. Gilbert (1986) terms this the 'average economic regression', since most applied econometric work has been tackled in that way. This term was also indended to have a joke at the expense of a top economics journal that published many papers using such a methodology.

Hendry and his co-workers have severely criticised this approach, mainly on the grounds that diagnostic testing is undertaken, if at all, almost as an afterthought and in a very limited fashion. If diagnostic tests are not performed, or are performed only at the end of the model-building process, however, all earlier inferences are potentially invalidated. Moreover, if the specific initial model is generally misspecified, the diagnostic tests themselves are not necessarily reliable in indicating the source of the problem. For example, if the initially specified model omits relevant variables that are themselves autocorrelated, introducing lags of the included variables would not be an appropriate remedy for a significant DW test statistic. Thus the eventually selected model under a specific-to-general approach could be suboptimal, in the sense that the model selected using a general-to-specific approach might represent the data better. Under the Hendry approach, diagnostic tests of the statistical adequacy of the model come first, with an examination of inferences for real estate theory drawn from the model left until after a statistically adequate model has been found.

According to Hendry and Richard (1982), a final acceptable model should satisfy several criteria (adapted slightly here). The model should:

- be logically plausible;
- be consistent with underlying real estate theory, including satisfying any relevant parameter restrictions;

- have regressors that are uncorrelated with the error term;
- have parameter estimates that are stable over the entire sample;
- have residuals that are white noise (i.e. completely random and exhibiting no patterns); and
- be capable of explaining the results of all competing models and more.

The last of these is known as the *encompassing principle*. A model that nests within it a smaller model always trivially encompasses it. A small model is particularly favoured, however, if it can explain all the results of a larger model; this is known as *parsimonious encompassing*.

The advantages of the general-to-specific approach are that it is statistically sensible and that the theory on which the models are based usually has nothing to say about the lag structure of a model. Therefore the lag structure incorporated in the final model is determined largely by the data themselves. Furthermore, the statistical consequences from excluding relevant variables are usually considered more serious than those from including irrelevant variables.

The general-to-specific methodology is conducted as follows. The first step is to form a 'large' model with many variables on the RHS. This is known as a generalised unrestricted model (GUM), which should originate from economic or real estate theory and which should contain all variables thought to influence the dependent variable. At this stage the researcher is required to ensure that the model satisfies all the assumptions of the CLRM. If the assumptions are violated, appropriate actions should be taken to address or allow for this – e.g. taking logs, adding lags or adding dummy variables.

It is important that the steps above are conducted prior to any hypothesis testing. It should also be noted that the diagnostic tests presented above should be interpreted cautiously, as general rather than specific tests. In other words, the rejection of a particular diagnostic test null hypothesis should be interpreted as showing that there is something specific wrong with the model. Thus, for example, if the RESET test or White's test show a rejection of the null, such results should not be immediately interpreted as implying that the appropriate response is to find a solution for inappropriate functional form or heteroscedastic residuals, respectively. It is quite often the case that one problem with the model can cause several assumptions to be violated simultaneously. For example, an omitted variable could cause failures of the RESET, heteroscedasticity and autocorrelation tests. Equally, a small number of large outliers could cause non-normality and residual autocorrelation (if they occur close together in the sample) or heteroscedasticity (if the outliers occur for a narrow range of the explanatory variables). Moreover, the diagnostic tests themselves do not operate optimally in the presence of other types of misspecification, as they assume, essentially, that the model is correctly specified in all other respects; for example, it is not clear that tests for heteroscedasticity will behave well if the residuals are autocorrelated.

Once a model that satisfies the assumptions of the CLRM has been obtained, it could be very big, with large numbers of lags and independent variables. The next stage, therefore, is to reparameterise the model by knocking out very insignificant regressors. Additionally, some coefficients may be insignificantly different from each other, so they can be combined. At each stage it should be checked whether the assumptions of the CLRM are still upheld. If this is the case, the researcher should have arrived at a statistically adequate empirical model that can be used for testing underlying financial theories, for forecasting future values of the dependent variable or for formulating policies.

Needless to say, however, the general-to-specific approach also has its critics. For small or moderate sample sizes it may be impractical. In such instances, the large number of explanatory variables will imply a small number of degrees of freedom. This could mean that none of the variables is significant, especially if they are highly correlated. This being the case, it would not be clear which of the original long list of candidate regressors should subsequently be dropped. In any case, moreover, the decision as to which variables to drop could have profound implications for the final specification of the model. A variable whose coefficient was not significant might have become significant at a later stage if other variables had been dropped instead.

In theory, the sensitivity of the final specification to the many possible paths of variable deletion should be checked carefully. This could imply checking many (perhaps even hundreds) of possible specifications, however. It could also lead to several final models, none of which appears noticeably better than the others.

The hope is that the general-to-specific approach, if followed faithfully to the end, will lead to a statistically valid model that passes all the usual model diagnostic tests and contains only statistically significant regressors. The final model could also turn out to be a bizarre creature that is devoid of any theoretical interpretation, however. There would also be more than just a passing chance that such a model could be the product of a statistically vindicated data-mining exercise. Such a model would closely fit the sample of data at hand, but could fail miserably when applied to other samples if it is not based soundly on theory.

Key concepts

The key terms to be able to define and explain from this chapter are

- homoscedasticity
- heteroscedasticity
- autocorrelation
- dynamic model
- equilibrium solution
- robust standard errors
- skewness
- kurtosis
- outlier
- functional form
- multicollinearity
- omitted variable
- irrelevant variable
- parameter stability
- recursive least squares
- general-to-specific approach

Appendix: Iterative procedures for dealing with autocorrelation

If the form of the autocorrelation is known, it would be possible to use a GLS procedure. One approach, which was once fairly popular, is known as the Cochrane–Orcutt procedure (see box 6.8). Such methods work by assuming a particular form for the structure of the autocorrelation (usually a first-order autoregressive process; see chapter 8 for a general description of these models). The model would thus be specified as follows:

$$y_t = \beta_1 + \beta_2 x_{2t} + \beta_3 x_{3t} + u_t, \qquad u_t = \rho u_{t-1} + v_t \tag{6A.1}$$

Note that a constant is not required in the specification for the errors since $\mathrm{E}(u_t) = 0$. If this model holds at time t, it is assumed also to hold for time $t-1$, so that the model in (6A.1) is lagged one period:

$$y_{t-1} = \beta_1 + \beta_2 x_{2t-1} + \beta_3 x_{3t-1} + u_{t-1} \tag{6A.2}$$

Multiplying (6A.2) by ρ,

$$\rho y_{t-1} = \rho\beta_1 + \rho\beta_2 x_{2t-1} + \rho\beta_3 x_{3t-1} + \rho u_{t-1} \tag{6A.3}$$

Subtracting (6A.3) from (6A.2) gives

$$y_t - \rho y_{t-1} = \beta_1 - \rho\beta_1 + \beta_2 x_{2t} - \rho\beta_2 x_{2t-1} + \beta_3 x_{3t} - \rho\beta_3 x_{3t-1} + u_t - \rho u_{t-1} \tag{6A.4}$$

Factorising, and noting that $v_t = u_t - \rho u_{t-1}$,

$$(y_t - \rho y_{t-1}) = (1-\rho)\beta_1 + \beta_2(x_{2t} - \rho x_{2t-1}) + \beta_3(x_{3t} - \rho x_{3t-1}) + v_t \tag{6A.5}$$

Setting $y_t^* = y_t - \rho y_{t-1}$, $\beta_1^* = (1-\rho)\beta_1$, $x_{2t}^* = (x_{2t} - \rho x_{2t-1})$ and $x_{3t}^* = (x_{3t} - \rho x_{3t-1})$, the model in (6A.5) can be written

$$y_t^* = \beta_1^* + \beta_2 x_{2t}^* + \beta_3 x_{3t}^* + v_t \tag{6A.6}$$

Since the final specification, equation (6A.6), contains an error term that is free from autocorrelation, OLS can be directly applied to it. This procedure is effectively an application of GLS. Of course, the construction of y_t^* etc. requires ρ to be known. In practice, this will never be the case, so ρ has to be estimated before (6A.6) can be used.

A simple method would be to use the ρ obtained from rearranging the equation for the DW statistic given in (6.14). This is only an approximation, however, as the related algebra shows. This approximation may be poor in the context of small samples. The Cochrane–Orcutt procedure is an alternative, which operates as in box 6.8.

Box 6.8 The Cochrane–Orcutt procedure

(1) Assume that the general model is of the form (6A.1) above. Estimate the equation in (6A.1) using OLS, ignoring the residual autocorrelation.
(2) Obtain the residuals, and run the regression

$$\hat{u}_t = \rho \hat{u}_{t-1} + v_t \tag{6A.7}$$

(3) Obtain $\hat{\rho}$ and construct y_t^* etc. using this estimate of $\hat{\rho}$.
(4) Run the GLS regression (6A.6).

This could be the end of the process. Cochrane and Orcutt (1949) argue that better estimates can be obtained by going through steps 2 to 4 again, however. That is, given the new coefficient estimates, $\beta_1^*, \beta_2, \beta_3$, etc., construct again the residual and regress it on its previous value to obtain a new estimate for $\hat{\rho}$. This is then used to construct new values of the variables $y_t^*, x_{2t}^*, x_{3t}^*$, and a new (6A.6) is estimated. This procedure is repeated until the change in $\hat{\rho}$ between one iteration and the next is less than some fixed amount – e.g. 0.01. In practice, a small number of iterations (no more than five) will usually suffice.

It is worth noting, however, that the Cochrane–Orcutt procedure and similar approaches require a specific assumption to be made concerning the form of the model for the autocorrelation. Consider again (6A.5). This can be rewritten taking ρy_{t-1} over to the RHS:

$$y_t = (1-\rho)\beta_1 + \beta_2(x_{2t} - \rho x_{2t-1}) + \beta_3(x_{3t} - \rho x_{3t-1}) + \rho y_{t-1} + v_t \tag{6A.8}$$

Expanding the brackets around the explanatory variable terms gives

$$y_t = (1-\rho)\beta_1 + \beta_2 x_{2t} - \rho\beta_2 x_{2t-1} + \beta_3 x_{3t} - \rho\beta_3 x_{3t-1} + \rho y_{t-1} + v_t \tag{6A.9}$$

Now, suppose that an equation containing the same variables as (6A.9) were estimated using OLS:

$$y_t = \gamma_1 + \gamma_2 x_{2t} + \gamma_3 x_{2t-1} + \gamma_4 x_{3t} + \gamma_5 x_{3t-1} + \gamma_6 y_{t-1} + v_t \tag{6A.10}$$

It can be seen that (6A.9) is a restricted version of (6A.10), with the restrictions imposed that the coefficient on x_{2t} in (6A.9) multiplied by the negative of the coefficient on y_{t-1} gives the coefficient on x_{2t-1}, and that the coefficient on x_{3t} multiplied by the negative of the coefficient on y_{t-1} gives the coefficient on x_{3t-1}. The restrictions implied for (6A.10) to get (6A.9) are therefore

$$\gamma_2\gamma_6 = -\gamma_3 \text{ and } \gamma_4\gamma_6 = -\gamma_5$$

These are known as the *common factor restrictions*, and they should be tested before the Cochrane–Orcutt procedure or a similar one is implemented. If the restrictions hold, Cochrane–Orcutt can be validly applied. If not, however, Cochrane–Orcutt and similar techniques would be inappropriate, and the appropriate step would be to estimate an equation such as (6A.10) directly using OLS. Note that in general there will be a common factor restriction for every explanatory variable (excluding a constant) $x_{2t}, x_{3t}, \ldots, x_{kt}$ in the regression. Hendry and Mizon (1978) argue that the restrictions are likely to be invalid in practice and therefore a dynamic model that allows for the structure of y should be used rather than a residual correction on a static model; see also Hendry (1980).

7 Applications of regression analysis

Learning outcomes

In this chapter, you will learn how to

- undertake all the stages involved in designing, building and evaluating an empirical econometric model in real estate through two detailed examples.

The regression analysis topics of chapters 4 to 6 are fundamental to conducting empirical research in real estate. Given the importance of regression in real estate analysis, we devote this chapter to more examples of multiple regression. We give two detailed illustrations, with the aim of further familiarising the reader with key tasks in the empirical estimation of a multiple regression model and particularly in model construction and selection. In chapters 4 to 6, we examined regressions with time series data, the most common form of data in real estate modelling. This chapter also presents an example with cross-sectional data. The estimation principles are identical but the focus of the illustration is also on the interpretation and usage of cross-section analysis.

7.1 Frankfurt office rents: constructing a multiple regression model

We focus on modelling office rents using a multiple regression model and use data for the Frankfurt office market. Our specification is guided by theory, as any good empirical model of the real estate market should be. Hence the empirical model of Frankfurt office rents in this example is driven by the a priori treatment of office rent determination originating in theoretical frameworks of real estate market dynamics put forward in a number of studies (e.g. DiPasquale and Wheaton, 1992; Clapp, 1993; RICS [Royal Institution of Chartered Surveyors], 1994; Ball, Lizieri and MacGregor,

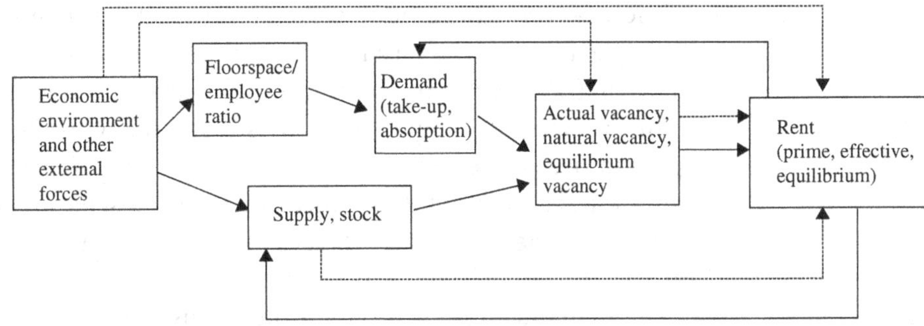

Figure 7.1
A theoretical structure for the determination of rents

Source: Authors.

1998). A conceptual framework that captures the key relationships in the empirical modelling of office rents is presented in figure 7.1.

The arrows in the figure illustrate paths that the analyst can follow to develop empirical models of office rents. In real estate modelling, however, the availability of data plays a significant role in the form of the model. In markets in which there is an abundance of data (in terms of both the existence and the history of series describing the occupier and investment markets), the solid black arrows show that a model of rents is part of a more general model within which demand, vacancy, rent and supply are determined. In markets with data limitations, office rents can be modelled on economic variables directly or through vacancy (as the dotted lines in figure 7.1 illustrate). The models specified for the relationships shown by the dotted lines are examples of so-called 'reduced-form' models. In chapter 10, we deal with more general frameworks, such as the set of relationships described by the solid lines, in which we allow for feedback effects. Our example in this chapter focuses on the estimation of a reduced-form model of office rents.

We estimate a specification that is based on the premise that real rents move through time in response to the vacancy rate (defined as vacant stock over total stock, expressed as a percentage) and an economic output variable. The argument is straightforward: vacancy is considered an indicator of the demand and supply balance in the real estate market – i.e. it reflects demand and supply conditions. As business conditions strengthen and firms need to take on more space, the level of vacant stock in the market should fall. The amount of actual vacant stock will also reflect the quantity of building supply, however. Newly constructed buildings may come on to the market along with second-hand space resulting from lease termination, sub-letting, and so forth. If these demand and supply forces result in falling vacancy, the market becomes a 'landlords' market'. Landlords will push for higher rents in new leases or rent reviews. Valuers will also be taking account of these developments, and estimated rental values should rise.

There is also an argument in the literature that rent growth is determined by the deviation of the actual vacancy rate from the natural or structural rate in the market. For example, if the actual amount of vacant space is higher than the natural vacancy level, it is a sign of weak demand and surplus space in the market. Rents would be expected to fall and new development to slow down. Clapp (1993) provides a critical discussion of this view, which extends to the important issue of how to measure the natural vacancy rate.

The demand influence on vacancy is usually captured by employment trends. What is concealed here, of course, are other adjustments that may affect the transmission of employment growth to vacancy. Figure 7.1, for example, highlights the floorspace/employee ratio. Although employment levels increase, this ratio may fall in a market (hence fewer square metres per employee), reducing the effective impact of employment on new demand for office space.

In addition, we can argue that the vacancy series on its own will not fully account for business conditions that impact on rents. As we noted earlier, vacancy reflects business conditions and demand for space largely through employment changes. Vacancy does not effectively allow for the impact on rents from the profitability and affordability of occupiers. Firms can become more profitable even if they expand their workforce moderately. Measures relating to the profitability of the firm can give us an insight as to the rent that firms are prepared to pay. Of course, in a market with a high vacancy rate (an 'occupiers' market'), firms will not pay the highest rent they can afford. Moreover, the vacancy data in a market may not be of good quality, which means that a model using solely vacancy as a determinant will not be well specified due to a paucity of data.

For the model of Frankfurt rents, we consider direct influences on rents that arise from the local economic environment. The measure of local economic conditions that we use is *output in the services sector* in the Frankfurt region. This variable is taken to provide an indication of the turnover and profitability of rents in Frankfurt. Therefore we would like to test the proposition that local economic conditions affect Frankfurt rents and that the information contained in output in services is not adequately conveyed by the vacancy series. If this conjecture is true, we would expect to find output a significant influence on office rents. The computation of diagnostic tests will, of course, tell us whether this contention will receive empirical support in Frankfurt or whether the only variable affecting rents is vacancy.

The following specification summarises the above discussion:

$$RR_t = f(VAC_t, OFS_t) \tag{7.1}$$

where RR_t is real rent (in levels) at time t, VAC_t is vacant space at time t and OFS_t is output in Frankfurt services sector at time t. More specifically, rents are expressed in constant 2005 euro prices (real rents), vacancy is in per cent and output is a volume measure of service sector activity in the Frankfurt region. Our data sample available to estimate equation (7.1) spans the period from 1980 to 2007, giving us twenty-eight annual observations. We have compiled the data for rents and vacancy from different sources; the economic data come from Eurostat and Cambridge Econometrics.

An implicit assumption in (7.1) is that both vacancy and output affect real rents contemporaneously – that is, in the course of the year. This could be seen as a restrictive assumption (in particular, if we were using quarterly data). In rent negotiations and rent valuations, recent past vacancy rates and output may be relevant. If this is the case, we should also allow for and test the possible influence of past values of vacancy and output on rents. We do so by introducing lags in the model. How far back should we look? This is largely an empirical question. We may expect rents to reflect trends in vacancy and output within, say, two years. Quantitative techniques as well as intuition could be used to guide the choice of lag length, however. A number of tests (including the t-ratio and the variable omission test) will show whether longer lags convey influences on the series we model. Equation (7.1) can therefore be rewritten to allow for such lagged effects from the determinants of rents:

$$RR_t = f\left(\sum_0^n VAC_{t-i} + \sum_0^m OFS_{t-i}\right) \tag{7.2}$$

where $t - i$ represents the lagged effects and n and m are the maximum lag lengths of the vacancy and output variables, respectively – which can, of course, vary with the variable.

Another decision we need to make is whether (7.2) should be estimated in levels or growth rates (or, alternatively, in first differences). Theory might guide this decision, and sometimes we can put forward a theoretical argument in real estate for modelling either in levels or in growth rates. Assuming that the analyst is interested in modelling short-term cyclical movements, significant weight is given to the statistical properties of the data. Historical data that contain trends, or data series that are smoothed and hence highly autocorrelated (a major area of debate about valuations data), may need transformation in order to perform any meaningful regression analysis. These are characteristics that are more pronounced in levels series (for example, the actual rent series or an index of rents) but less so when we take their first differences or growth rates. We address this topic further in chapter 12, in which we discuss the concept of stationarity.

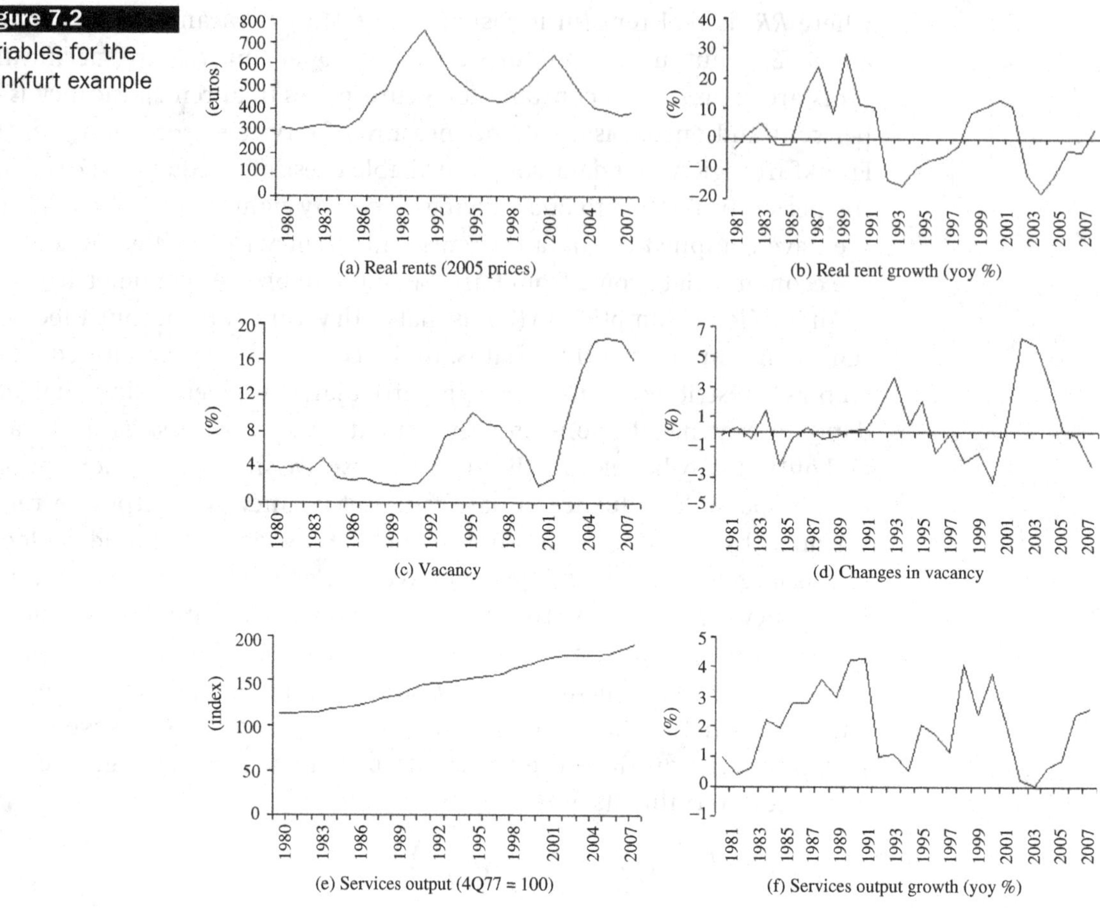

Figure 7.2 Variables for the Frankfurt example

7.1.1 *Features of data in the Frankfurt example*

We plot the data we use in our example both in levels and in growth rates (first differences in the case of the vacancy series) in figure 7.2 to obtain a visual familiarisation with the history of the data.

The real rent series in levels (panel (a)) exhibits two major cycles and looks quite smooth. In growth rates (panel (b)) the rent data are more volatile, but there are still long periods when rent growth remains positive or negative. The vacancy series (panel (c)) was fairly steady in the 1980s. Since 1990 two cycles can be discerned, the last of which has seen vacancy rising to over 16 per cent in this market. Nonetheless, despite this recent cycle, there is little short-term volatility. In first differences, vacancy exhibits more short-term variation (panel (d)).

The service sector output data have a strong upward trend (panel (e)). This is common in most output series, as they capture the size of the local economy and rising levels of business activity, which usually increase with

Table 7.1 Autocorrelation coefficients

Lag	*RR*	*RRg*	*VAC*	ΔVAC	*OFS*	*OFSg*
1	0.85	0.60	0.86	0.48	0.91	0.51
2	0.57	0.29	0.60	0.12	0.81	0.14
3	0.25	−0.05	0.32	−0.34	0.73	−0.23
Sample period	1980–2007	1981–2007	1980–2007	1981–2007	1980–2007	1981–2007

Notes: *RR* is the level of real office rents; *RRg* is the annual percentage growth in real rents; *VAC* is the vacancy rate; ΔVAC is the change in the vacancy rate; *OFS* is output in services in Frankfurt; *OFSg* is the annual percentage growth in output.

time. In growth rates (panel (f)), the volatility of the series increases and cycles become more apparent. An interesting feature of output growth is the accelerating upward trend that lasted for nearly ten years in the 1980s. Similarly, from 2003 to 2007 service sector output growth in Frankfurt was on a rising trend.

A visual inspection of the series in levels points to smooth data whereas, when taking growth rates or first differences, this is less apparent. We examine this smoothness and degree of autocorrelation more formally and calculate the values of the autocorrelation coefficients up to third order, with the results given in table 7.1.

All series in levels are strongly associated with their previous values (first-order autocorrelation). The size of the second-order autocorrelation coefficients (association of contemporaneous values with those two years ago) is lower but is still high for *OFS* (0.81) and moderate to strong for *RR* and *VAC*. In growth rates or first differences, the degree of autocorrelation decreases across the board. The first-order autocorrelation is still on the strong side for *RRg* (0.60) and moderate for the other two series. The transformed series, unlike the levels data, do not exhibit second-order autocorrelation. Of course, a highly autocorrelated rent series will limit the influence of vacancy and output, since rent values will be dependent on their own recent past values. Does it matter if vacancy and output are strongly autocorrelated? The answer is 'Yes', because positive autocorrelation restricts the short-term variation in the data so that current values mostly reflect past behaviour and not new developments that may be important for rents.

Cross-correlations facilitate an initial assessment of how strong the relationships between rent and our chosen drivers (vacancy and output) are. We estimate cross-correlations with two lags in table 7.2 – that is, we study past effects from vacancy and output on rents. In addition, we compute correlations between rents and lead values of vacancy and output. This is to

Table 7.2 Cross-correlations with annual data for RRg_t

(a) RR_t with lags/leads of VAC				(b) RRg_t with lags/leads of VAC			
VAC_t	−0.28	VAC_t	−0.28	VAC_t	−0.58	VAC_t	−0.58
VAC_{t-1}	−0.37	VAC_{t+1}	−0.05	VAC_{t-1}	−0.34	VAC_{t+1}	−0.68
VAC_{t-2}	−0.33	VAC_{t+2}	0.23	VAC_{t-2}	−0.08	VAC_{t+2}	−0.59
(c) RRg_t with lags/leads of ΔVAC							
ΔVAC_t	−0.60	ΔVAC_t	−0.60				
ΔVAC_{t-1}	−0.64	ΔVAC_{t+1}	−0.21				
ΔVAC_{t-2}	−0.37	ΔVAC_{t+2}	0.15				
(d) RR_t with lags/leads of OFS				(e) RRg_t with lags/leads of $OFSg$			
OFS_t	0.33	OFS_t	0.33	$OFSg_t$	0.71	$OFSg_t$	0.71
OFS_{t-1}	0.23	OFS_{t+1}	0.38	$OFSg_{t-1}$	0.52	$OFSg_{t+1}$	0.59
OFS_{t-2}	0.11	OFS_{t+2}	0.41	$OFSg_{t-2}$	0.13	$OFSg_{t+2}$	0.31

show whether vacancy or output movements precede rent movements, in which case rents should be more strongly correlated with lagged vacancy and output.[1]

Panel (a) shows that correlations between the real rent levels series and the level of vacancy (vacancy rate) are negative, as we would expect, but they are relatively weak. The strongest is at lag one (−0.37). In panel (b) we see a stronger correlation between real rent growth and the vacancy rate (the contemporaneous correlation coefficient is −0.58). We discern an interesting pattern, however. The contemporaneous real rent growth is more strongly correlated with future values of the vacancy than the immediately preceding ones, which is really not an appealing feature. It is desirable for the explanatory variable to contain leading information for the variable we model, although, modelling with annual data in real estate, the contemporaneous association tends to be the strongest. Conversely, the results in panel (c) demonstrate that lagged changes in vacancy correlate more strongly with contemporaneous real rent growth than lead values of vacancy changes, and therefore this variable is taken to contain leading information (on the basis of these cross-correlations) for the variation in real rent growth. The strongest correlation is achieved with ΔVAC lagged one year (−0.64).

[1] We should note that a formal examination of such lead–lag relationships requires the data to have certain properties (for example, to be stationary – see chapter 12) and the computation of formal tests (see chapter 11).

On the basis of these results, the impact of vacancy should be examined in a real rent growth model. The vacancy series should then be expressed in first differences to ensure its leading properties. Our model of rent growth can include and test the vacancy rate purely on theoretical or behavioural grounds, however. We assume that the level of the vacancy rate does influence market participants' expectations of rent movements. In practice, you may hear among market participants that there will be no rental growth if vacancy goes above a certain level. For Frankfurt, though, the cross-correlation results reveal that changes in the vacancy rate *are* useful to gauge the future direction in rents, and therefore this variable cannot be excluded from the regression analysis.

Real rent growth and service output growth correlate strongly, which is not the case when the series are in levels. Judging from the lead and lag correlation coefficients, the variation of the two series seems to be coincident, although output growth tends to lag rent growth at the margin. This should not be too surprising as real estate data at the regional level may be compiled and published more quickly than economic data.

7.1.2 *Regression models for Frankfurt rents*

On the basis of the cross-correlation results, we estimate the following general models:

$$RRg_t = \alpha_0 + \alpha_{1,0}\Delta VAC_t + \alpha_{1,1}\Delta VAC_{t-1} + \alpha_{2,0}OFSg_t + \alpha_{2,1}OFSg_{t-1} + \varepsilon_t \tag{7.3}$$

$$RRg_t = \beta_0 + \beta_{1,0}VAC_t + \beta_{1,1}VAC_{t-1} + \beta_{2,0}OFSg_t + \beta_{2,1}OFSg_{t-1} + u_t \tag{7.4}$$

The maximum lag length is determined by the size of the cross-correlation coefficients. Since we did not find strong correlations at lag 2, we truncate the lag length to one year. We acknowledge that *VAC* is a smoothed (and perhaps non-stationary – see chapter 12) series in (7.4), but we specify this model on assessments observed in practice. Table 7.3 contains the estimation results. We report the coefficients, the t-statistics and the associated p-values.

In model A (equation (7.3)), the terms ΔVAC_{t-1} and $OFSg_t$ are statistically significant at the 10 per cent and 5 per cent levels, respectively. In model B (equation (7.4)), the statistically significant terms are VAC_t and $OFSg_t$. The explanatory variables take the expected signs with the exception of VAC_{t-1}, which implies a positive impact on rent growth. This result is perhaps due to collinearity with VAC_t. If we were to run the regression on VAC_{t-1} only, we would have obtained a negative sign. Both models explain around 58 per cent of the variation in real rent growth according to the adjusted R^2 values.

Table 7.3 Regression models for Frankfurt rents

	Model A (equation (7.3))		Model B (equation (7.4))	
	Coefficient	t-ratio (p-value)	Coefficient	t-ratio (p-value)
Constant	−5.69	−1.3 (0.21)	−2.23	−0.4 (0.70)
ΔVAC_t	−1.03	−1.2 (0.26)	–	–
ΔVAC_{t-1}	−1.71	−1.8 (0.09)	–	–
VAC_t	–	–	−1.91	−2.2 (0.04)
VAC_{t-1}	–	–	1.28	1.6 (0.13)
$OFSg_t$	3.48	2.1 (0.05)	3.80	2.4 (0.02)
$OFSg_{t-1}$	0.86	0.6 (0.58)	0.57	0.3 (0.71)
Adjusted R^2	0.58		0.58	
DW statistic	1.53		1.79	
Sample period	1982–2007 (26 obs.)		1981–2007 (27 obs.)	

Note: The dependent variable is RRg.

Table 7.4 Respecified regression models for Frankfurt rents

	Model A (equation (7.3))		Model B (equation (7.4))	
	Coefficient	t-ratio (p-value)	Coefficient	t-ratio (p-value)
Constant	−6.39	−1.9 (0.08)	−3.53	−0.8 (0.42)
ΔVAC_{t-1}	−2.19	−2.7 (0.01)	–	–
VAC_t	–	–	−0.74	−2.4 (0.02)
$OFSg_t$	4.55	3.3 (0.00)	5.16	4.0 (0.00)
Adjusted R^2	0.59		0.57	
DW statistic	1.81		1.82	
Sample period	1982–2007 (26 obs.)		1981–2007 (27 obs.)	

Note: The dependent variable is RRg.

We continue by excluding the non-significant terms, starting with $OFSg_{t-1}$. The exclusion of this term does not affect the results already obtained for the other regressors in both models – that is, the same terms remain statistically significant. Subsequently, we drop the non-significant ΔVAC_t from model A and VAC_{t-1} from model B. The resulting fitted models are presented in table 7.4.

The models now contain only the statistically significant variables, and the p-values indicate high levels of significance. Despite dropping two terms from each of the models, the explanatory power remains virtually

Figure 7.3
Actual, fitted and residual values of rent growth regressions

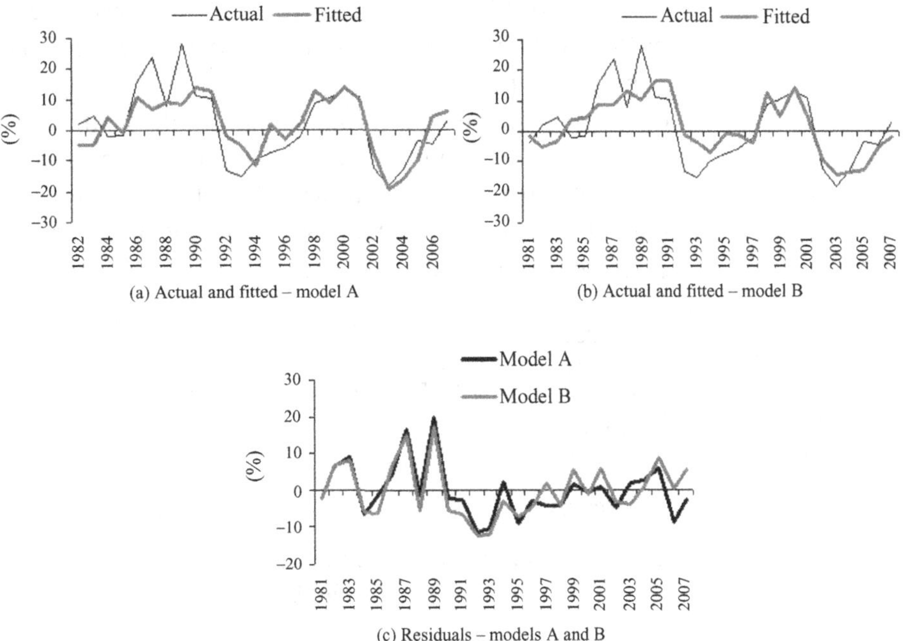

unchanged. The DW statistic in both models takes a value that denotes the absence of first-order correlation in the residuals of the equations.

The coefficient on $OFSg_t$ suggests that, if we use model A, a 1 per cent rise in $OFSg_t$ will on average push real rent growth up by 4.55 per cent, whereas, according to model B, it would rise by 5.16 per cent. One may ask what the real sensitivity of *RRg* to *OFSg* is. In reality, *OFSg* is not the only variable affecting real rent growth in Frankfurt. By accounting for other effects, in our case for vacancy and changes in vacancy, the sensitivity of *RRg* to *OFSg* changes. If we run a regression of *RRg* on *OFSg* only, the sensitivity is 6.48 per cent. *OFSg* on its own will certainly encompass influences from other variables, however – that is, the influence of other variables on rents is occurring indirectly through *OFSg*. This happens because the variables that have an influence on rent growth are to a degree correlated. The presence of other statistically significant variables takes away from *OFSg* and affects the size of its coefficient.

The coefficient on vacancy in model B implies that, if vacancy rises by 1 per cent, it will push real rent growth down by 0.74 per cent in the same year. The interpretation of the coefficient on ΔVAC_{t-1} is less straightforward. If the vacancy change declines by one percentage point – that is, from, say, a fall of 0.5 per cent to a fall of 1.5 per cent – rent growth will respond by rising 2.4 per cent after a year (due to the one-year lag). The actual and fitted values are plotted along with the residuals in figure 7.3.

The fitted values replicate to a degree the upward trend of real rent growth in the 1980s, but certainly not the volatility of the series; the models completely miss the two spikes. Since 1993 the fit of the models has improved considerably. Their performance is also illustrated in the residuals graph (panel (c)). The larger errors are recorded in the second half of the 1980s. After 1993 we discern an upward trend in the absolute values of the residuals of both models, which is not a welcome feature, although this was corrected after 1998.

7.1.3 *Diagnostics*

This section computes the key diagnostics we described in the previous chapters.

Normality

	Model A	Model B
Skewness	0.89	0.54
Kurtosis	3.78	2.71

The Bera–Jarque test statistic for the normality of the residuals of each model is

$$BJ_A = 26\left[\frac{0.89^2}{6} + \frac{(3.78-3)^2}{24}\right] = 4.09$$

$$BJ_B = 27\left[\frac{0.54^2}{6} + \frac{(2.71-3)^2}{24}\right] = 1.41$$

The computed values of 4.09 and 1.41 for models A and B, respectively, are lower than 5.99, the $\chi^2(2)$ critical value at the 5 per cent level of significance. Hence both these equations pass the normality test. Interestingly, despite the two misses of the actual values in the 1980s, which resulted in two large errors, and the small sample period, the models produce approximately normally distributed residuals.

Serial correlation

Table 7.5 presents the results of a Breusch–Godfrey test for autocorrelation in the model residuals. The tests confirm the findings of the DW test that the residuals do not exhibit first-order serial correlation. Similarly, the tests do not detect second-order serial correlation. In all cases, the computed

Table 7.5 Tests for first- and second-order serial correlation

	Model A		Model B	
	Order			
	First	Second	First	Second
Constant	−1.02	−2.07	1.04	−0.08
ΔVAC_{t-1}	0.19	0.29	–	–
VAC_t	–	–	−0.03	0.04
$OFSg_t$	0.31	0.54	−0.35	−0.18
$RESID_{t-1}$	0.07	0.00	0.10	0.09
$RESID_{t-2}$	–	0.20	–	0.17
R^2	0.009	0.062	0.009	0.035
T	25	24	25	25
r	1	2	1	
$T-r$	24	22		
Computed test stat. $\chi^2(r)$	$\chi^2(1) = 0.22$	$\chi^2(2) = 1.36$	$\chi^2(1) = 0.23$	$\chi^2(2) = 0.81$
Critical $\chi^2(r)$	$\chi^2(1) = 3.84$		$\chi^2(2) = 5.99$	

Notes: The dependent variable is $RESID_t$; T is the number of observations in the main equation; r is the number of lagged residuals (order of serial correlation) in the test equation; the computed χ^2 statistics are derived from $(T-r)R^2 \sim \chi^2_r$.

χ^2 statistic is lower than the critical value, and hence the null of no autocorrelation in the disturbances is not rejected at the 5 per cent level of significance.

When we model in growth rates or in first differences, we tend to remove serial correlation unless the data are still smoothed and trending or important variables are omitted. In levels, with trended and highly smoothed variables, serial correlation would certainly have been a likely source of misspecification.

Heteroscedasticity test

We run the White test with cross-terms, although we acknowledge the small number of observations for this version of the test. The test is illustrated and the results presented in table 7.6.[2] All computed test statistics take a value lower than the χ^2 critical value at the 5 per cent significance level, and hence no heteroscedasticity is detected in the residuals of either equation.

[2] The results do not change if we run White's test without the cross-terms, however.

Table 7.6 White's test for heteroscedasticity

Model A		Model B	
Constant	0.44	Constant	63.30
ΔVAC_{t-1}	47.70	VAC_t	−12.03
$\Delta VAC_{t-1}{}^2$	−8.05	$VAC_t{}^2$	0.53
$OFSg_t$	84.18	$OFSg_t$	69.41
$OFSg_t{}^2$	−19.35	$OFSg_t{}^2$	−15.21
$\Delta VAC_{t-1} \times OFSg_t$	−22.34	$VAC_t \times OFSg_t$	−1.73
R^2	0.164		0.207
T	26		27
r	5		5
Computed $\chi^2(r)$	$\chi^2(5) = 4.26$		$\chi^2(5) = 5.59$
Critical at 5%		$\chi^2(5) = 11.07$	

Notes: The dependent variable is $RESID_t{}^2$; the computed χ^2 statistics are derived from: $T * R^2 \sim \chi^2_r$.

The RESET test

Table 7.4 gives the restricted forms for models A and B. Table 7.7 contains the unrestricted equations. The models clear the RESET test, since the computed values of the test statistic are lower than the critical values, suggesting that our assumption about a linear relationship linking the variables is the correct specification according to this test.

Structural stability tests

We next apply the Chow breakpoint tests to examine whether the models are stable over two sub-sample periods. In the previous chapter, we noted that events in the market will guide the analyst to establish the date (or dates) and generate two (or more) sub-samples in which the equation is tested for parameter stability. In our example, due to the small number of observations, we simply split the sample in half, giving us thirteen observations in each of the sub-samples. The results are presented in table 7.8.

The calculations are as follows.

$$\text{Model A: } F\text{-test} = \frac{1383.86 - (992.91 + 209.81)}{(992.91 + 209.81)} \times \frac{26 - 6}{3} = 1.00$$

$$\text{Model B: } F\text{-test} = \frac{1460.02 - (904.87 + 289.66)}{(904.87 + 289.66)} \times \frac{27 - 6}{3} = 1.56$$

Table 7.7 RESET results

	Model A (unrestricted)		Model B (unrestricted)	
	Coefficient	p-value	Coefficient	p-value
Constant	−6.55	0.07	−3.67	0.41
ΔVAC_{t-1}	−2.83	0.01	–	–
VAC_t	–	–	−0.72	0.03
$OFSg_t$	3.88	0.02	5.45	0.00
$Fitted^2$	0.02	0.32	0.01	0.71
URSS	1,322.14		1,450.95	
RRSS	1,383.86		1,460.02	
F-statistic	1.03		0.14	
F-critical (5%)	$F(1,22) = 4.30$		$F(1,23) = 4.28$	

Note: The dependent variable is RRg_t.

Table 7.8 Chow test results for regression models

	Model A				Model B		
Variables	(i) Full	(ii) First half	(iii) Second half		(i) Full	(ii) First half	(iii) Second half
Constant	−6.39	−3.32	−7.72	Constant	−3.53	13.44	−4.91
	(0.08)	(0.60)	(0.03)		(0.42)	(0.25)	(0.37)
ΔVAC_{t-1}	−2.19	−4.05	−1.78	VAC_t	−0.74	−3.84	−0.60
	(0.01)	(0.11)	(0.01)		(0.02)	(0.05)	(0.07)
$OFSg_t$	4.55	4.19	4.13	$OFSg_t$	5.16	2.38	5.29
	(0.00)	(0.10)	(0.01)		(0.00)	(0.36)	(0.00)
Adj. R^2	0.59	0.44	0.80		0.57	0.51	0.72
DW	1.81	2.08	1.82		1.82	2.12	2.01
RSS	1,383.86	992.91	209.81		1,460.02	904.87	289.66
Sample	1982–2007	1982–94	1995–2007		1981–2007	1981–94	1995–2007
T	26	13	13		27	14	13
F-statistic	1.00				1.56		
Crit. F(5%)	F(3,20) at 5% ≈ 3.10				F(3,21) at 5% ≈ 3.07		

Notes: The dependent variable is RRg_t; cell entries are coefficients (p-values).

Table 7.9 Regression model estimates for the predictive failure test

	Model A		Model B	
	Coefficient	t-ratio (p-value)	Coefficient	t-ratio (p-value)
Constant	−6.81	−1.8 (0.08)	5.06	0.86 (0.40)
ΔVAC_{t-1}	−3.13	−2.5 (0.02)	–	–
VAC_t	–	–	−2.06	−2.9 (0.01)
$OFSg_t$	3.71	3.2 (0.01)	3.83	2.6 (0.02)
Adjusted R^2	0.53		0.57	
DW statistic	1.94		1.91	
Sample period	1982–2002 (21 obs.)		1981–2002 (22 obs.)	
RSS1	1,209.52		1,124.10	
RSS (full sample)	1,383.61		1,460.02	

Note: The dependent variable is *RRg*.

The Chow break point tests do not detect parameter instability across the two sub-samples for either model. From the estimation of the models over the two sample periods, a pattern emerges. Both models have a higher explanatory power in the second half of the sample. This is partly because they both miss the two spikes in real rent growth in the 1980s, which lowers their explanatory power. The DW statistic does not point to misspecification in either of the sub-samples. The coefficients on *OFSg* become significant at the 1 per cent level in the second half of the sample (this variable was not statistically significant even at the 10 per cent level in the first half for model A). As *OFSg* becomes more significant in the second half of the sample, it takes away from the sensitivity of rent growth to the vacancy terms. Even with these changes in the significance of the regressors between the two sample periods, the Chow test did not establish parameter instability, and does not therefore provide any motivation to examine different model specifications for the two sample periods

In addition to the Chow break point test, we run the Chow forecast (predictive failure) test, since our sample is small. As a cut-off date we take 2002 – that is, we reserve the last five observations to check the predictive ability of the two specifications. The results are presented in table 7.9.

The computed F-test statistics are as follows.

$$\text{Model A: } F\text{-test} = \frac{1383.61 - 1209.52}{1209.52} \times \frac{21-3}{5} = 0.52$$

$$\text{Model B: } F\text{-test} = \frac{1460.02 - 1124.10}{1124.10} \times \frac{22-3}{5} = 1.14$$

Table 7.10 Regression results for models with lagged rent growth terms

Models	A	B	C
Constant	−5.82 (0.12)	−3.36 (0.48)	−0.69 (0.89)
ΔVAC_{t-1}	−1.92 (0.05)	–	
VAC_t	–	−0.67 (0.11)	
VAC_{t+1}	–	–	−0.89 (0.02)
$OFSg_t$	4.12 (0.01)	4.79 (0.01)	4.31 (0.01)
RRg_{t-1}	0.12 (0.51)	0.08 (0.70)	–
Adj. R^2	0.57	0.55	0.58
Sample	1982–2007	1982–2007	1981–2006

Notes: The dependent variable is RRg_t; *p*-values in parentheses.

The test statistic values are lower than the critical $F(5, 18)$ and $F(5, 19)$ values at the 5 per cent level of significance, which are 2.77 and 2.74, respectively. These results do not indicate predictive failure in either of the equations. It is also worth noting the sensitivity of the intercept estimate to changes in the sample period, which is possibly caused by the small sample size.

7.1.4 *Additional regression models*

In the final part of our example, we illustrate three other specifications that one could construct. The first is related to the influence of past rents on current rents. Do our specifications account for the information from past rents given the fact that rents, even in growth rates, are moderately autocorrelated? This smoothness and autocorrelation in the real rent data invite the use of past rents in the equations. We test the significance of lagged rent growth even if the DW and the Breusch–Godfrey tests did not detect residual autocorrelation. In table 7.10, we show the estimations when we include lagged rent growth. In the rent growth specifications (models A and B), real rent growth lagged by one year takes a positive sign, suggesting that rent growth in the previous year impacts positively on rent growth in the current year. It is not statistically significant in either model, however. This is a feature of well-specified models. We would have reached similar conclusions if we had run the variable omission test described in the previous chapter, in which the omitted variable would have been rent growth or its level lagged by one year.

One may also ask whether it would be useful to model real rent growth with a lead of vacancy – that is, replacing the *VAC* term in model B above with VAC_{t+1}. In practice, this is adopted in order to bring forward-looking information into the model. An example is the study by RICS (1994), in which the yield model has next year's rent as an explanatory variable. We do so in our example, and the results are shown as model C in table 7.10. VAC_{t+1} is statistically significant, although the gain in explanatory power is very small. This model passes the diagnostics we computed above. Note also that the sample period is truncated to 2006 now as the last observation for vacancy is consumed to run the model including the lead term. The estimation for this model to 2007 would require a forecast for vacancy in 2008, which could be seen as a limitation of this approach. The models do well based on the diagnostic tests we performed. Our first preference is model A, since ΔVAC_{t-1} has a high correlation with real rent growth.

7.2 Time series regression models from the literature

Example 7.1 Sydney office rents

Hendershott (1996) constructs a rent model for the Sydney office market that uses information from estimated equilibrium rents and vacancy rates. The starting point is the traditional approach that relates rent growth to changes in the vacancy rate or to the difference between the equilibrium vacancy and the actual vacancy rate,

$$\Delta g_{t+j}/g_{t+j-1} = \lambda(\upsilon^* - \upsilon_{t+j-1}) \tag{7.5}$$

where g is the actual gross rent (effective) and υ^* and υ are the equilibrium and actual vacancy rates, respectively. This relationship is augmented with the inclusion of the difference between the equilibrium and actual rent,

$$\Delta g_{t+j}/g_{t+j-1} = \lambda(\upsilon^* - \upsilon_{t+j-1}) + \beta(g^*_{t+j}/g_{t+j-1}) \tag{7.6}$$

where g^* is the equilibrium gross rent.

Hendershott argues that a specification with only the term $(\upsilon^* - \upsilon_{t+j-1})$ is insufficient on a number of grounds. One criticism he advances is that the traditional approach (equation (7.5)) cannot hold for leases of different terms (multi-period leases). What he implies is that effective rents may start adjusting even before the actual vacancy rate reaches its natural level. Key to this argument is the fact that the rent on multi-period leases will be an average of the expected future rents on one-period leases. An analogy is given from the bond market, in which rational expectations imply that long-term bond rates are averages of future expected one-period bond rates – hence expectations that one-period rents will rise in the future will turn rents on multi-period leases upward before the actual rent moves and reaches its equilibrium level. In this way, the author introduces a more dynamic structure to the model and makes it more responsive to changing expectations of future one-period leases.

Another feature that Hendershott highlights in equation (7.6) is that rents adjust even if the disequilibrium between actual and equilibrium vacancy persists. A supply-side shock that is not met by the level of demand will result in a high vacancy level. After high vacancy rates have pushed rents significantly below equilibrium, the market knows that, eventually, rents and vacancy will return to equilibrium. As a result, rents begin to adjust (rising towards equilibrium) while vacancy is still above its equilibrium rate. The actual equation that Hendershott estimates is

$$\Delta g_{t+j}/g_{t+j-1} = \lambda \upsilon^* - \lambda \upsilon_{t+j-1} + \beta(g^*_{t+j}/g_{t+j-1}) \tag{7.7}$$

The estimation of this equation requires the calculation of the following.

- The real effective rent g (the headline rent adjusted for rent-free periods and tenant improvements and adjusted for inflation).
- The equilibrium vacancy rate υ^*.
- The equilibrium rent g^*.
- The real effective rent: data for rent incentives (which, over this study's period, ranged from less than four months' rent-free period to almost twenty-three months') and tenant improvement estimates are provided by a property consultancy. The same source computes effective real rents by discounting cash flows with a real interest rate. Hendershott makes the following adjustment. He discounts the value of rent incentives over the period of the lease and not over the life of the building. The percentage change in the resultant real effective rent is the dependent variable in equation (7.7).
- The equilibrium vacancy rate υ^* is treated as constant through time and is estimated from equation (7.7). The equilibrium vacancy rate will be the intercept in equation (7.7) divided by the estimated coefficient on υ_{t+j-1}.
- The equilibrium real gross rent rate g^* is given by the following expression:

$$g^* = \textit{real risk} - \textit{free rate} + \textit{risk premium} + \textit{depreciation rate} + \textit{expense ratio} \tag{7.8}$$

- Real risk-free rate: using the ten-year Treasury rate as the risk-free rate (r_f) and a three-period average of annualised percentage changes in the deflator for private final consumption expenditures as the expected inflation proxy (π), the real risk-free rate is given by $(1 + r_f)/(1 + \pi) - 1$.
- The risk premium and depreciation rate are held constant, with the respective values of 0.035 (3.5 per cent) and 0.025 (2.5 per cent).
- The expense ratio, to our understanding, is also constant, at 0.05 (5 per cent).

As a result, the equilibrium real rent varies through time with the real risk-free rate. The author also gives examples of the equilibrium rent:

$$g^*_{1970} = 0.02 + 0.035 + 0.025 + 0.05 = 0.13 \quad (7.9)$$
$$g^*_{82-92} = 0.06 + 0.035 + 0.025 + 0.05 = 0.17 \quad (7.10)$$

This gross real rent series is converted to dollars per square metre by multiplying it by the real rent level at which equilibrium and actual rents appear to have been equal. The author observes a steadiness of both actual and equilibrium rents during the 1983–5 period and he picks June 1986 as the point in time when actual and equilibrium rents coincided.

Now that a series of changes in real effective rents and a series of equilibrium rents are available, and with the assumption of a constant equilibrium vacancy rate, Hendershott estimates a number of models.

Two of the estimations are based on the theoretical specification (7.7) above. The inclusion of the term $g^* - g_{t-1}$ doubles the explanatory power of the traditional equation, which excludes this term. All regressors are statistically significant and υ^* is estimated at 6.4 per cent. In order to better explain the sharp fall in real rents in the period June 1989 to June 1992, the author adds the forward change in vacancy. This term is not significant and it does not really change the results much.

The equation including $g^* - g_{t-1}$ fits the actual data very well (a graph is provided in the original paper). According to the author, this is due to annual errors being independent.[3] Forecasts are also given for the twelve years to 2005. Our understanding is that, in calculating this forecast, the future path for vacancy was assumed.

Example 7.2 Helsinki office capital values

Karakozova (2004) models and forecasts capital values in the Helsinki office market. The theoretical treatment of capital values is based on the following discounted cash flow (DCF) model,

$$CV_t = \frac{E_0[CF_1]}{1+r} + \frac{E_0[CF_2]}{(1+r)^2} + \cdots + \frac{E_0[CF_{T-1}]}{(1+r)^{T-1}} + \frac{E_0[CF_T]}{(1+r)^T} \quad (7.11)$$

where CV_t is the capital value of the property at the end of period t, $E_0(CF_t)$ is the net operating income generated by the property in period t, and r is the appropriate discount rate or the required rate of return. T is the terminal period in the investment holding period and CF_T includes the resale value of the property at that time in addition to normal operating cash flow.

[3] This statement implies that the author carried out diagnostics, although it is not reported in the paper.

From equation (7.11) and based on a literature review, the author identifies different proxies for the above variables and she specifies the model as

$$CV = \phi(EA, GY, VOL, SSE, GDP, NOC) \tag{7.12}$$

where EA stands for three economic activity variables – SSE (service sector employment), GDP (gross domestic product) and OFB (output of financial and business services), all of which are expected to have a positive influence on capital values and are used as a partial determinant of net operating income; NOC is new office building completions, and it is also a partial determinant of income (the author notes a limitation of this proxy variable, which is the exclusion of supply from existing buildings; the required rate of return r consists of the risk-free rate, which is determined by the capital market, and the required risk premium is that determined by information from both space and capital markets); GY represents the proxy for the risk free component of r; and VOL is a measure of uncertainty in the wider investment markets, which captures the risk premium on all assets generally.

The empirical estimation of equation (7.12) is based on different modelling techniques. One of the techniques that the author deploys is regression analysis, which involves the estimation of equation (7.13),

$$\Delta cv_t = \alpha_0 + \sum_{i=0}^{K_1} \alpha_{1i} \Delta ea_{t-i} + \sum_{i=0}^{K_2} \alpha_{2i} \Delta cm_{t-i} + \sum_{i=0}^{K_3} \alpha_{3i} noc_{t-i} + \varepsilon_t \tag{7.13}$$

where Δcv_t is the change in the logarithm of real capital values (the capital value data refer to the Helsinki central business district [CBD] and are provided by KTI); Δea represents the changes in the logarithm of the values of each of the alternative economic activity variables Δsse, Δgdp and Δofb; Δcm denotes the first differences in the capital market variables Δgy (the absolute first differences) and Δvol, the absolute change in the volatility measure;[4] noc is the logarithm of the NOC (NOC is the total amount); and ε_t is a normally distributed error term; the subscript $t-i$ illustrates past effects on capital growth. Equation (7.13) is estimated with annual data from 1971 to 2001.

The author does not include the alternative economic variables simultaneously due to multicollinearity. The two risk premia variables are included concurrently, however, as they are seen to be different and, to an extent, independent components of risk premia. The supply-side variable (noc) is significant only at the 10 per cent level. The lag pattern in these equations

[4] No further information is given as to the precise definition of volatility that is employed.

is determined by Akaike's information criterion (AIC) – a metric that is discussed in detail in the following chapter.

All economic variables are statistically significant. The fact that *GDP* is lagged by one year in one of the models can be seen as *GDP* providing signals about capital growth in advance of the other two economic variables. Changes in the volatility of the stock market and changes in the government bond yield are both significant in all specifications. The negative sign of the volatility of stock returns means that increased uncertainty in the stock market leads to a higher risk premium in the office market in Helsinki (and a negative impact on capital values).

The author also carries out a number of diagnostic checks. All estimated p-values for the test statistics are above 0.10, and therefore all models seem to be well specified. It is difficult to select the best of the three models that the author estimates. The fact that *GDP* leads capital growth is an attractive feature of that model. The author subsequently assesses the forecast performance of these models in the last four years of the sample.

7.3 International office yields: a cross-sectional analysis

A significant area of research has concerned the fair value of yields in international markets. Global real estate investors welcome analysis that provides evidence on this issue. There is no single method to establish fair values in different markets, which is why the investor needs to consult alternative routes and apply different methodologies. Cross-sectional analysis is one of the methodologies that can be deployed for this purpose.

In our example, we attempt to explain the cross-sectional differences of office yields in 2006. A number of factors determine yield differentials between office centres in the existing literature. Sivitanidou and Sivitanides (1999), in their study of office capitalisation rates in US centres, identify both time-varying and time-invariant variables. In the latter category, they include the share of CBD office inventory in a particular year, the diversity of office tenant demand, the ratio of government employment over the sum of the financial, insurance and real estate and service office tenants and the level of occupied stock. McGough and Tsolacos (2002), who examine office yields in the United Kingdom, find significant impacts on the share of office-using employment from total employment and rents lagged one year.

In this chapter, the geographical differences in yields are examined with respect to

(1) the size of the market;
(2) rent growth over the course of the previous year;

Table 7.11 Office yields

City	Office yield	City	Office yield
United States (14 cities)		Europe (13 cities)	
Atlanta	6.7	Amsterdam	5.8
Boston	5.9	Athens	7.4
Charlotte	6.9	Budapest	6.9
Chicago	6.3	Frankfurt	5.8
Cincinnati	7.6	Lisbon	7.0
Dallas–Fort Worth	6.3	London, City of	4.4
Denver	6.2	Madrid	4.4
Los Angeles	5.5	Milan	5.8
Miami	5.9	Moscow	9.4
New York	5.0	Paris	4.5
Phoenix	5.8	Prague	6.5
San Francisco	5.3	Stockholm	4.8
Seattle	5.8	Warsaw	6.3
Washington–NoVA–MD	5.7		
Asia-Pacific (6 cities)			
Tokyo	3.7		
Sydney	6.5		
Beijing	8.0		
Mumbai	6.1		
Shanghai	8.6		
Seoul	6.7		

Notes: NoVA stands for northern Virginia and MD for Maryland.

(3) office-using employment growth over the previous year; and
(4) interest rates in the respective countries.

We use two measures for the size of the market: total employment and the stock of offices. We argue that the larger the market the more liquid it will be, as there is more and a greater variety of product for investors and more transactions for price discovery purposes. It follows, therefore, that the larger the market the lower the yield, as investors will be less exposed to liquidity risk and so will be willing to accept a lower premium. Hence the expected sign is negative. Table 7.11 gives the range of yields in the thirty-three office centres as at December 2006.

The first equation we estimate is

$$Y_j = \beta_0 + \beta_1 INT_j + \beta_2 INTRAT_j + \beta_3 RREg_j + \beta_4 EMPg_j + \beta_5 EMP_j + \beta_6 STOCK_j + \varepsilon_j \quad (7.14)$$

where Y = office yield as at the end of 2006; j = denotes location; INT = the long-term interest rate measured by the ten-year government bond series (it is used as the risk-free rate to which office yields are connected; hence the assumption is that different office yields in two office centres may partially reflect corresponding differences in long-term interest rates); $INTRAT$ = the ratio of the long-term interest rate over the short-term rate (this variable is constructed as an alternative measure to bring in the influence of interest rates. We use the ratio of interest rates following the suggestion by Lizieri and Satchell, 1997. When the rate ratio takes on a value of 1.0, long-term interest rates are equal to short-term interest rates [a flat yield curve]. Ratios higher than 1.0 indicate higher long-term interest rates [higher future spot rates], which may influence investors' estimates of the risk-free rate. Hence, if the ratio is 1.0 in one centre but in another centre it is higher than 1.0, investors may expect a higher risk-free rate in the latter that will push office yields somewhat higher); $RREg$ = real office rent growth between 2005 and 2006 (a gauge of buoyancy in the leasing market); $EMPg$ = office-using employment growth between 2005 and 2006, which indicates the strength of potential demand for office space; EMP = the level of office-using employment in the market (a proxy for the size of the market and the diversity of the office occupier base: the larger the market the larger and deeper the base of business activity; and $STOCK$ = office inventory, which provides a more direct measure of the size of the market; this variable captures, to a degree, similar influences to the EMP variable.

The estimation of equation (7.14) results in the following equation[5] (t-statistics are shown in parentheses):[6]

$$\begin{aligned}\hat{Y}_j = &\underset{(9.2)}{5.86} + \underset{(0.1)}{0.01} INT_j + \underset{(1.5)}{0.27} INTRAT_j - \underset{(-2.3)}{0.05} RREg_j + \underset{(3.8)}{0.20} EMPg_j \\ &- \underset{(-2.3)}{0.001} EMP_j + \underset{(0.7)}{0.01} STOCK_j \end{aligned} \quad (7.15)$$

Adj. $R^2 = 0.62$; F-statistic = 9.76; AIC = 2.426; sample = 33 observations.

[5] The real estate and employment data in this example are estimates derived from PPR's figures, and interest rates are taken from the national statistical offices of the respective countries.

[6] We also report the value of AIC, aiming to minimise its value in the model-building process. This is discussed extensively in the next chapter.

The intercept estimate suggests that the yield across global office centres will be around 5.9 per cent if all drivers are assumed to be zero. The mean (unweighted) yield in our sample is 6.2 per cent. The figure of 5.9 per cent reflects the base yield for investors from which they will calculate the effects of the factors in each location. The interest rate positively affects the yield, as expected, but it does not have a significant coefficient. The interest rate ratio is not significant either, even at the 10 per cent level. It takes the expected positive sign, however. Real rent growth has a negative impact on yields, which is in accord with our expectations, and the coefficient on this variable is statistically significant. Employment growth, which is assumed to capture similar effects to rent growth, is statistically significant but the sign is positive, the opposite from what we would expect. The size of the market as measured by the level of employment has the expected negative effect and it is significant at the 10 per cent level, whereas the more direct measure of the size of the market is not statistically significant and it takes a positive sign, which contradicts our a priori expectation.

A well-known problem with cross-sectional models is that of heteroscedasticity, and the above results may indeed be influenced by the presence of heteroscedasticity, which affects the standard errors and t-ratios. For this purpose, we carry out White's test. Due to the small number of observations and the large number of regressors, we do not include cross-terms (the products of pairs of regressors). The test is presented below.

Unrestricted regression:

$$\begin{aligned}\hat{u}_t^2 &= 1.50 - 0.48INT_j + 0.95INTRAT_j + 0.004RREg_j + 0.13EMPg_j \\ &\quad + 0.002EMP_j - 0.08STOCK_j + 0.01INT_j^2 - 0.10INTRAT_j^2 \\ &\quad + 0.00RREg_j^2 - 0.01EMPg_j^2 - 0.00EMP_j^2 + 0.001STOCK_j^2 \qquad (7.16)\end{aligned}$$

$R^2 = 0.30$; $T = 33$; residual sum of squares in unrestricted equation ($URSS$) $= 10.50$; the number of regressors, k, including the constant $= 13$.

Restricted regression:

$$\hat{u}_t^2 = 0.43 \qquad (7.17)$$

Residual sum of squares of restricted equation ($RRSS$) $= 15.10$; the number of restrictions, m, is twelve (all coefficients are assumed to equal zero apart from the constant).

$$F\text{-test statistic} = \frac{15.10 - 10.50}{10.50} \times \frac{33 - 13}{12} = 0.73.$$

Recall that the null hypothesis is that the coefficients on all slope terms in equation (7.16) are zero. The critical value for the F-test with $m = 12$ and $T - k = 20$ at the 5 per cent level of significance is $F_{12,20} = 2.28$. The value of the computed F-test is lower than the critical value, and therefore we do not reject the null hypothesis. The alternative χ^2 test also yields the same result (the computed test statistic is lower than the critical value): $TR^2 \sim \chi^2(m)$; $TR^2 = 33 \times 0.30 = 9.90$; critical $\chi^2(12) = 21.03$. Both versions of the White test therefore demonstrate that the errors of equation (7.15) are not heteroscedastic. The standard errors and t-ratios are not invalidated and we now proceed to refine the model by excluding the terms that are not statistically significant. In this case, removing insignificant variables and re-estimating the model is a worthwhile exercise to save valuable degrees of freedom, given the very modest number of observations.

We first exclude $STOCK$. The results are given as equation (7.18):

$$\begin{aligned}\hat{Y}_j = \underset{(9.4)}{5.90} + \underset{(0.1)}{0.01}INT_j + \underset{(1.5)}{0.26}INTRAT_j - \underset{(-2.5)}{0.05}RREg_j + \underset{(3.9)}{0.20}EMPg_j \\ - \underset{(-2.6)}{0.001}EMP_j \end{aligned} \quad (7.18)$$

Adj. $R^2 = 0.63$; F-statistic $= 11.83$; AIC $= 2.384$; $T = 33$; White's heteroscedasticity test (χ^2 version): $TR^2 = 33 \times 0.25 = 8.25$; critical $\chi^2(10) = 18.31$.

The residuals of equation (7.18) remain homoscedastic when we exclude the term *STOCK*. The AIC value falls from 2.426 to 2.384. The coefficients on the other terms barely change and the explanatory power (adjusted R^2) has marginally improved. Dropping *STOCK* from the equation does not really affect the results, therefore. We continue by re-estimating equation (7.18) without *INT*, which is highly insignificant.

$$\hat{Y}_j = \underset{(19.4)}{5.94} + \underset{(2.2)}{0.26}INTRAT_j - \underset{(-2.6)}{0.05}RREg_j + \underset{(4.0)}{0.20}EMPg_j - \underset{(-2.9)}{0.001}EMP_j \quad (7.19)$$

Adj. $R^2 = 0.64$; F-statistic $= 15.33$; AIC $= 2.324$; $T = 33$; White's heteroscedasticity test (χ^2 version): $TR^2 = 33 \times 0.12 = 3.96$; critical $\chi^2(8) = 15.51$.

Again, the exclusion of the interest rate variable *INT* has not affected the equation. The AIC has fallen further, suggesting that this variable was superfluous. The absence of *INT* has now made *INTRAT* significant; collinearity with *INT* may explain why it was not significant previously.

Equation (7.19) looks like the final equation; the sign for the employment growth variable (*EMPg*) is not as expected a priori, however. In markets in which employment growth is stronger, we expect yields to fall, reflecting greater demand for office space. Perhaps this expected effect on yields occurs with a lag. Unless there is a good argument to support a positive relationship between employment growth and yields in this sample of cities, the analyst should drop this variable. By doing so, we get the following estimation:

$$\underset{(21.2)}{\hat{Y}_j = 6.63} \quad \underset{(2.5)}{+\,0.37INTRAT_j} - \underset{(-0.5)}{0.01RREg_j} - \underset{(-4.3)}{0.001EMP_j} \tag{7.20}$$

Adj. $R^2 = 0.46$; F-statistic $= 9.94$; AIC $= 2.716$; $T = 33$; White's heteroscedasticity test (χ^2 version): $TR^2 = 33 \times 0.11 = 3.63$; critical $\chi^2(6) = 12.59$.

The omission of the employment growth variable has affected the explanatory power of the model, which dropped from 0.64 to 0.46. The AIC value has risen, since a statistically significant variable was omitted. Theory should ultimately drive the specification of the model, however. The new empirical specification does not fail the heteroscedasticity test.

In equation (7.20), growth in real rents also loses its significance when employment growth is omitted. Perhaps we would expect these variables to be collinear but their correlation is weak to moderate (0.37). We drop *RREg* and derive equation (7.21).

$$\underset{(21.7)}{\hat{Y}_j = 6.60} \quad \underset{(2.8)}{+\,0.39INTRAT_j} - \underset{(-4.6)}{0.001EMP_j} \tag{7.21}$$

Adj. $R^2 = 0.47$; F-statistic $= 15.13$; AIC $= 2.665$; $T = 33$; White's heteroscedasticity test (χ^2 version): $TR^2 = 33 \times 0.09 = 2.97$; critical $\chi^2(4) = 9.49$.

As expected, the specification of the equation was not affected much. Again, the new equation's residuals do not suffer from heteroscedasticity. This seems to be the final equation for our sample of thirty-three cities. The interpretation of the coefficients is straightforward for employment but not so for the interest rate ratio. Employment is expressed in thousands. If employment in the office centre is 100,000 higher than in another otherwise identical centre, the impact on the yield will be $-0.001 \times 100 = -0.1\%$ or a ten basis points (bps) fall on average. Thus, if the yield is 6.9 in one centre, it will be 6.8 in the other. With respect to the interest rate ratio, if it rises by 0.1 (from, say, 1.0 to 1.1), the impact on the yield will be $0.39 \times 0.1 = 0.039$. Hence, considering two centres with similar employment, if one has an interest ratio of 1.0 and the other of 1.1, the yield differential will only be around four bps.

We now conduct further diagnostics checks for equation (7.21). We examine whether the residuals are normally distributed (the Bera–Jarque test) and the form of the equation with the RESET test.

Normality test:

$$BJ = 33\left[\frac{0.15^2}{6} + \frac{(3.42-3)^2}{24}\right] = 0.37$$

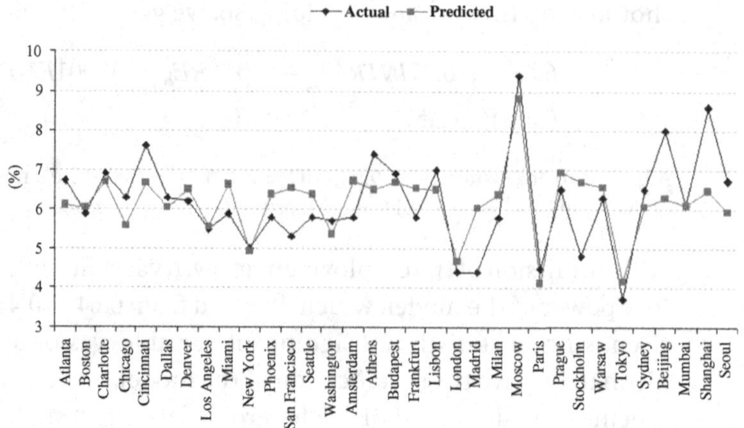

Figure 7.4 Actual and fitted values for international office yields

The $\chi^2(2)$ critical value is 5.99, and therefore we do not detect non-normality problems.

The unrestricted regression for the RESET test is

$$y_j = -10.49 - 2.02INTRAT_j + 0.004EMP_j + 0.41FITTED_j^2 \tag{7.22}$$

RRSS = 23.14; URSS = 22.00; $T = 33$; $m = 1$; $k = 4$, computed F-statistic = 1.50; critical $F(1, 29) = 4.17$ at the 5 per cent level.

The RESET test (equation (7.22)) does not identify any problems with the functional form of the model. The actual and fitted values are shown in figure 7.4. Equation (7.21) replicates the yields in a number of cities but, in others, it suggests that yields should have been lower or higher. Of the US cities, the model predicts lower yields in Atlanta, Chicago and Cincinnati and higher yields in Miami, Phoenix and San Francisco. In our sample of European cities, it is only Athens for which the model suggests a lower yield and, to an extent, Lisbon. For a number of other markets, such as Amsterdam, Frankfurt, Madrid, and Stockholm, equation (7.21) points to higher yields. It is interesting to note that the 'emerging European' markets (Budapest, Moscow and Prague) are fairly priced according to this model. Madrid and Stockholm are two cities where the model identifies significant mispricing.

It is also worth noting the performance of the model for Moscow. The Moscow office yield is the highest in our sample, and it can be argued that it represents an outlier. The global model of yields suggests that this yield is explained however, and also points to a small fall. The predicted values of our model for the Asia–Pacific cities show significant mispricing in Beijing and Shanghai, where yields should be lower. Moreover, for Seoul, there is a similar indication, but the magnitude of mispricing is smaller than for the other two cities.

Are these definite signs of mispricing that can guide investors' buy/sell decisions? How can we use the approach of cross-sectional analysis? The short answer to these questions is that cross-sectional analysis should be seen as another tool at the analyst's disposal for studying pricing in different locations. Here are some points that should be kept in mind when considering the use of cross-sectional analysis.

(1) The final model in this example contains two variables even though we initially examined several variables. This does not mean that other variables could not be included. For example, supply, future rent growth or an indication of investment confidence could be argued to be relevant.

(2) In our analysis, we found that employment growth took the opposite sign to what we were expecting. This impact may differ by geographical region, however. Our sample was too small to run the equation separately for US, European or Asian cities simply in order to check whether the impact of employment growth on yields is uniform globally. Hence the market context, leasing environment, data transparency, and so forth are important parameters that can make a more general (global) study less appropriate.

(3) There are many factors particular to certain cities (in the same way that events can occur in specific years in time series analyses) that are not picked up by the model, but the impact of these factors is, of course, identified in the plot of the residuals. Our suggestion is that the results of the cross-sectional analysis should be used as a guide for further action. For example, the residual analysis suggested that yields in Miami should be higher. Is this a selling opportunity for investors? The researcher needs to study this market more closely, and if there is no other evidence that justifies a lower yield than that predicted (for example, weak future rent growth) then it should be interpreted as a sell signal.

(4) In order for the results of the cross-sectional analysis to be more robust, one should replicate the analysis in consecutive years and see whether there has been a correction along the lines of the model predictions. That is, re-estimate the model with more or less recent data and compare the predictions with the actual adjustments in the market. Of course, if we have data for a number of years (say three to four years) and for several markets, we will be able to run panel regression models. Such market characteristics may not change in a market overnight or may change very slowly, and therefore the findings of the impact from a cross-sectional study are relevant.

Table 7.12 Variable description for global office yield model

Variable	Description
Mid-point yield	This refers to the prime yield.
Consumer price index	The all-items consumer price index.
Long-term government bonds	The long-term government bond rate (most likely the ten-year Treasury rate).
Short-term interest rates	Policy interest rates.
Nominal prime rent	
GDP per capita	GDP per capita in US dollars.
Average lease length	Calculated in years as an average of the typical lease length; in markets in which a range is given, the mid-point is used.
Transparency index	This is an index that ranges from 1 to 5, with a lower number indicating a more transparent market. This index has five components: legal system status, listed vehicles, market fundamentals, performance indicators and regulation.
Liquidity index	This index takes values from 1 to 10, with a lower number indicating a more liquid market. Investment volumes are an input to the construction of this index.

7.4 A cross-sectional regression model from the literature

A similar analysis to the example above was conducted by Hollies (2007). Hollies conducted empirical analysis to explain yield differences between global markets, examining the factors that were responsible for higher or lower yields between locations. The author notes that certain questions we ask can be better addressed through a cross-sectional analysis than a time series analysis, such as whether lease lengths impact on yields or whether more transparent markets command a lower premium than less transparent markets. The variables that are assumed to explain yields across countries are presented in table 7.12.

These data are available to the author over a five-year period and for forty-eight global markets, so this is not a truly cross-sectional analysis but a panel sample. The principles and, in particular, the variables and findings are relevant for cross-sectional studies in this area, however. The author runs bivariate regressions estimated for 2003 to assess the explanatory ability of the host of determinant variables on yields; the results of these are summarised below.

$$\hat{y} = 6.1767 + 49.458 \text{ inflation} \qquad R^2 = 0.47$$
$$\hat{y} = 4.1572 + 0.5691 \text{ long-term government bond} \qquad R^2 = 0.27$$
$$\hat{y} = 5.5034 + 0.4612 \text{ short-term interest rates} \qquad R^2 = 0.76$$
$$\hat{y} = 7.9197 + -0.1176 \text{ rent} \qquad R^2 = 0.002$$
$$\hat{y} = 10.551 - 0.0001 \text{ GDP per capita} \qquad R^2 = 0.48$$
$$\hat{y} = 8.8814 - 0.1229 \text{ lease length} \qquad R^2 = 0.12$$
$$\hat{y} = 4.4117 + 1.453 \text{ transparency} \qquad R^2 = 0.34$$
$$\hat{y} = 3.2739 + 0.7607 \text{ liquidity} \qquad R^2 = 0.41$$

All the variables are signed as expected. Higher inflation is associated with higher yields, which are expected intuitively, with investors asking for a higher premium to invest in higher-inflation markets. The author also removes outliers – countries with high inflation – but the positive sign remains. The highest explanatory power is achieved by the short-term interest rate variable, which outperforms the long-term rate by a significant margin (in terms of R^2). The author notes, however, that in the estimations there were more data points available for short-term interest rates, which may partly account for this difference in explanatory power. Interestingly, rent is an insignificant variable, with no contribution at all. The author re-estimated this equation across markets over different time periods but the results were disappointing. Hollies also introduced the ratio of the rent over the past volatility of the rent series (taking the standard deviation), but, again, the explanatory power was virtually zero. She points to the fact that a forecast of rent could have been more relevant.

The use of GDP per capita in this study measures economic strength and is a proxy for the general level of development of a country. More developed nations (with a higher GDP per capita) have better-operating business environments, with legal, insurance and banking facilities established and functioning well. The implied negative relationship between the level of yield and GDP per capita is confirmed by the findings. GDP per capita explains a satisfactory 48 per cent of the variation in yields. The negative sign between yields and lease length supports the expectation of higher yields in locations with shorter leases that introduce uncertainty on the part of landlords. The linear relationship estimated explains only 12 per cent of the yield variation. Both the transparency and liquidity indices affect yields positively (lower index values, which denote more transparent and liquid markets, are associated with lower yields).

The author does not estimate a cross-sectional regression model with all these variables included but, since data are available for five years, a panel estimation is pursued – a topic not covered in this book. Another point in this paper that is relevant for cross-sectional studies is the finding and the implication that the fit of the multiple panel regression model in the higher-yield locations was not as good as in the lower-yield locations. This may reflect the fact that yields are higher in these locations due to greater uncertainty. There also appears to be an increasing size to the error as yields become higher, a sign of heteroscedasticity. The author attributes this to (i) omitted explanatory variables and/or (ii) an incorrect method of estimation. The author addresses this issue in two ways. First, other (non-OLS) methods of estimation were deployed. Second, the data set was split into different pools: a transparent market pool, a non-transparent market pool and a European pool. The discussion of the results requires familiarity with panel concepts and is therefore not pursued here.

Key concepts

The key terms to be able to define and explain from this chapter are

- rent frameworks
- autocorrelation
- lagged and leading values
- lagged dependent variable
- equilibrium vacancy
- office yields
- reduced-form regression models
- cross-correlations
- level and growth variables
- equilibrium rents
- office capital values
- cross-sectional analysis

8 Time series models

Learning outcomes

In this chapter, you will learn how to

- explain the defining characteristics of various types of stochastic processes;
- identify the appropriate time series model for a given data series;
- distinguish between AR and MA processes;
- specify and estimate an ARMA model;
- address seasonality within the regression or ARMA frameworks; and
- produce forecasts from ARMA and exponential smoothing models.

8.1 Introduction

Univariate time series models constitute a class of specifications in which one attempts to model and to predict financial variables using only information contained in their own past values and current and, possibly, past values of an error term. This practice can be contrasted with *structural models*, which are multivariate in nature, and attempt to explain changes in a variable by reference to the movements in the current or past values of other (explanatory) variables. Time series models are usually atheoretical, implying that their construction and use is not based upon any underlying theoretical model of the behaviour of a variable. Instead, time series models are an attempt to capture empirically relevant features of the observed data that may have arisen from a variety of different (but unspecified) structural models.

An important class of time series models is the family of autoregressive integrated moving average (ARIMA) models, usually associated with Box and

Jenkins (1976). Time series models may be useful when a structural model is inappropriate. For example, suppose that there is some variable y_t whose movements a researcher wishes to explain. It may be that the variables thought to drive movements of y_t are not observable or not measurable, or that these forcing variables are measured at a lower frequency of observation than y_t. For example, y_t might be a series of quarterly real estate returns in a metropolitan area, where possible explanatory variables could be macroeconomic indicators that are available only annually. Additionally, structural models are often not useful for out-of-sample forecasting. These observations motivate the consideration of pure time series models, which are the focus of this chapter.

The approach adopted for this topic is as follows. In order to define, estimate and use ARIMA models, one first needs to specify the notation and to define several important concepts. The chapter then considers the properties and characteristics of a number of specific models from the ARIMA family. The chapter endeavours to answer the following question: 'For a specified time series model with given parameter values, what will its defining characteristics be?' Following this, the problem is turned round, so that the reverse question is asked: 'Given a set of data, with characteristics that have been determined, what is a plausible model to describe these data?'

8.2 Some notation and concepts

The following subsections define and describe several important concepts in time series analysis. Each is elucidated and drawn upon later in the chapter. The first of these concepts is the notion of whether a series is *stationary* or not. Determining this is very important, for the stationarity or otherwise of a series can strongly influence its behaviour and properties. Further detailed discussion of stationarity, testing for it, and the implications of its not being present are covered in chapter 12.

8.2.1 A strictly stationary process

A strictly stationary process is one in which, for any $t_1, t_2, \ldots, t_T \in Z$, any $k \in Z$ and $T = 1, 2, \ldots$

$$Fy_{t_1}, y_{t_2}, \ldots, y_{t_T}(y_1, \ldots, y_T) = Fy_{t_1+k}, y_{t_2+k}, \ldots, y_{t_T+k}(y_1, \ldots, y_T) \tag{8.1}$$

where F denotes the joint distribution function of the set of random variables (Tong, 1990, p. 3). It can also be stated that the probability measure for the sequence $\{y_t\}$ is the same as that for $\{y_{t+k}\}\forall k$ (where '$\forall k$' means 'for all values of k'). In other words, a series is strictly stationary if the distribution of its values remains the same as time progresses, implying that the probability that y falls within a particular interval is the same now as at any time in the past or the future.

8.2.2 A weakly stationary process

If a series satisfies (8.2) to (8.4) for $t = 1, 2, \ldots, \infty$, it is said to be weakly or covariance stationary:

$$E(y_t) = \mu \tag{8.2}$$

$$E(y_t - \mu)(y_t - \mu) = \sigma^2 < \infty \tag{8.3}$$

$$E(y_{t_1} - \mu)(y_{t_2} - \mu) = \gamma_{t_2 - t_1} \quad \forall\, t_1, t_2 \tag{8.4}$$

These three equations state that a stationary process should have a constant mean, a constant variance and a constant autocovariance structure, respectively. Definitions of the mean and variance of a random variable are probably well known to readers, but the autocovariances may not be.

The autocovariances determine how y is related to its previous values, and for a stationary series they depend only on the difference between t_1 and t_2, so that the covariance between y_t and y_{t-1} is the same as the covariance between y_{t-10} and y_{t-11}, etc. The moment

$$E(y_t - E(y_t))(y_{t-s} - E(y_{t-s})) = \gamma_s,\ s = 0, 1, 2, \ldots \tag{8.5}$$

is known as the *autocovariance function*. When $s = 0$, the autocovariance at lag zero is obtained, which is the autocovariance of y_t with y_t – i.e. the variance of y. These covariances, γ_s, are also known as autocovariances because they are the covariances of y with its own previous values. The autocovariances are not a particularly useful measure of the relationship between y and its previous values, however, since the values of the autocovariances depend on the units of measurement of y_t, and hence the values that they take have no immediate interpretation.

It is thus more convenient to use the autocorrelations, which are the autocovariances normalised by dividing by the variance

$$\tau_s = \frac{\gamma_s}{\gamma_0}, \quad s = 0, 1, 2, \ldots \tag{8.6}$$

The series τ_s now has the standard property of correlation coefficients that the values are bounded to lie between -1 and $+1$. In the case that $s = 0$, the autocorrelation at lag zero is obtained – i.e. the correlation of y_t with y_t, which is of course one. If τ_s is plotted against $s = 0, 1, 2, \ldots$, a graph known as the *autocorrelation function* (acf) or *correlogram* is obtained.

8.2.3 A white noise process

Roughly speaking, a white noise process is one with no discernible structure. A definition of a white noise process is

$$E(y_t) = \mu \tag{8.7}$$

$$\text{var}(y_t) = \sigma^2 \tag{8.8}$$

$$\gamma_{t-r} = \begin{cases} \sigma^2 & \text{if} \quad t = r \\ 0 & \textit{otherwise} \end{cases} \tag{8.9}$$

Thus a white noise process has constant mean and variance, and zero autocovariances, except at lag zero. Another way to state this last condition would be to say that each observation is uncorrelated with all the other values in the sequence. The autocorrelation function for a white noise process will therefore be zero apart from a single peak of one at $s = 0$. If $\mu = 0$, and the three conditions hold, the process is known as zero-mean white noise.

If it is further assumed that y_t is distributed normally, then the sample autocorrelation coefficients are also approximately normally distributed,

$$\hat{\tau}_s \sim \textit{approx. } N(0, 1/T)$$

where T is the sample size and $\hat{\tau}_s$ denotes the autocorrelation coefficient at lag s estimated from a sample. This result can be used to conduct significance tests for the autocorrelation coefficients by constructing a non-rejection region (like a confidence interval) for an estimated autocorrelation coefficient to determine whether it is significantly different from zero. For example, a 95 per cent non-rejection region would be given by

$$\pm 1.96 \times \frac{1}{\sqrt{T}}$$

for $s \neq 0$. If the sample autocorrelation coefficient, $\hat{\tau}_s$, falls outside this region for a given value of s, then the null hypothesis that the true value of the coefficient at that lag s is zero is rejected.

It is also possible to test the joint hypothesis that all m of the τ_k correlation coefficients are simultaneously equal to zero using the Q-statistic developed by Box and Pierce (1970),

$$Q = T \sum_{k=1}^{m} \hat{\tau}_k^2 \tag{8.10}$$

where T = sample size, m = maximum lag length.

The correlation coefficients are squared so that the positive and negative coefficients do not cancel each other out. Since the sum of the squares of independent standard normal variates is itself a χ^2 variate with degrees of freedom equal to the number of squares in the sum, it can be stated that the Q-statistic is asymptotically distributed as a χ^2_m under the null hypothesis that all m autocorrelation coefficients are zero. As for any joint hypothesis test, only one autocorrelation coefficient needs to be statistically significant for the test to result in a rejection.

The Box–Pierce test has poor small-sample properties, however, implying that it leads to the wrong decision too frequently for small samples. A variant of the Box–Pierce test with better small-sample properties has been developed. The modified statistic is known as the Ljung–Box (1978) statistic:

$$Q^* = T(T+2)\sum_{k=1}^{m} \frac{\hat{\tau}_k^2}{T-k} \sim \chi^2_m \tag{8.11}$$

It should be clear from the form of the statistic that, asymptotically (that is, as the sample size increases towards infinity), the $(T+2)$ and $(T-k)$ terms in the Ljung–Box formulation will cancel out, so that the statistic is equivalent to the Box–Pierce test. This statistic is very useful as a portmanteau (general) test of linear dependence in time series.

Example 8.1

Suppose that a researcher had estimated the first five autocorrelation coefficients using a series consisting of 100 observations, and found them to be

Lag	1	2	3	4	5
Autocorrelation coefficient	0.207	−0.013	0.086	0.005	−0.022

Test each of the individual correlation coefficients for significance, and test all five jointly using the Box–Pierce and Ljung–Box tests.

A 95 per cent band can be constructed for each coefficient using

$$\pm 1.96 \times \frac{1}{\sqrt{T}}$$

where $T = 100$ in this case. The decision rule is thus to reject the null hypothesis that a given coefficient is zero in the cases in which the coefficient lies outside of the range (−0.196, +0.196). For this example, it would be concluded that only the first autocorrelation coefficient is significantly different from zero at the 5 per cent level.

Turning to the joint tests, the null hypothesis is that all the first five autocorrelation coefficients are jointly zero – i.e.

$$H_0\colon \tau_1 = 0,\ \tau_2 = 0,\ \tau_3 = 0,\ \tau_4 = 0,\ \tau_5 = 0$$

The test statistics for the Box–Pierce and Ljung–Box tests are given respectively as

$$Q = 100 \times (0.207^2 + -0.013^2 + 0.086^2 + 0.005^2 + -0.022^2) = 5.09 \tag{8.12}$$

$$Q^* = 100 \times 102 \times \left(\frac{0.207^2}{100-1} + \frac{-0.013^2}{100-2} + \frac{0.086^2}{100-3} + \frac{0.005^2}{100-4} + \frac{-0.022^2}{100-5}\right) = 5.26 \tag{8.13}$$

The relevant critical values are from a χ^2 distribution with five degrees of freedom, which are 11.1 at the 5 per cent level and 15.1 at the 1 per cent level. Clearly, in both cases, the joint null hypothesis that all the first five autocorrelation coefficients are zero cannot be rejected. Note that, in this instance, the individual test caused a rejection while the joint test did not. This is an unexpected result, which may have arisen as a result of the low power of the joint test when four of the five individual autocorrelation coefficients are insignificant. The effect of the significant autocorrelation coefficient is thus diluted in the joint test by the insignificant coefficients.

8.3 Moving average processes

The simplest class of time series models that one could entertain is that of the moving average process. Let u_t $(t = 1, 2, 3, \ldots)$ be a white noise process with $\mathrm{E}(u_t) = 0$ and $\mathrm{var}(u_t) = \sigma^2$. Then

$$y_t = \mu + u_t + \theta_1 u_{t-1} + \theta_2 u_{t-2} + \cdots + \theta_q u_{t-q} \tag{8.14}$$

is a qth order moving average mode, denoted MA(q). This can be expressed using sigma notation as

$$y_t = \mu + \sum_{i=1}^{q} \theta_i u_{t-i} + u_t \tag{8.15}$$

A moving average model is simply a linear combination of white noise processes, so that y_t depends on the current and previous values of a white noise disturbance term. Equation (8.15) will later have to be manipulated, and such a process is most easily achieved by introducing the lag operator notation. This would be written $Ly_t = y_{t-1}$ to denote that y_t is lagged once. In order to show that the ith lag of y_t is being taken (that is, the value that y_t took i periods ago), the notation would be $L^i y_t = y_{t-i}$. Note that, in some books and studies, the lag operator is referred to as the 'backshift operator', denoted by B. Using the lag operator notation, (8.15) would be written as

$$y_t = \mu + \sum_{i=1}^{q} \theta_i L^i u_t + u_t \tag{8.16}$$

or as

$$y_t = \mu + \theta(L)u_t \tag{8.17}$$

where $\theta(L) = 1 + \theta_1 L + \theta_2 L^2 + \cdots + \theta_q L^q$.

In much of what follows, the constant (μ) is dropped from the equations. Removing μ considerably eases the complexity of algebra involved, and is inconsequential, for it can be achieved without loss of generality. To see this, consider a sample of observations on a series, z_t, that has a mean, $\bar{z}$. A zero-mean series, y_t, can be constructed by simply subtracting $\bar{z}$ from each observation z_t.

The three distinguishing properties of the moving average process of order q given above are

$$\mathrm{E}(y_t) = \mu \tag{8.18}$$

$$\mathrm{var}(y_t) = \gamma_0 = \left(1 + \theta_1^2 + \theta_2^2 + \cdots + \theta_q^2\right)\sigma^2 \tag{8.19}$$

covariances γ_s

$$= \begin{cases} (\theta_s + \theta_{s+1}\theta_1 + \theta_{s+2}\theta_2 + \cdots + \theta_q\theta_{q-s})\sigma^2 & \textit{for} \quad s = 1, 2, \ldots, q \\ 0 & \textit{for} \quad s > q \end{cases} \tag{8.20}$$

A moving average process therefore has constant mean, constant variance and autocovariances that may be non-zero to lag q and will always be zero thereafter. Each of these results is derived in section 8A.1 of the appendix to this chapter.

8.4 Autoregressive processes

An autoregressive model is one in which the current value of a variable, y, depends upon only the values that the variable took in previous periods plus an error term. An autoregressive model of order p, denoted an AR(p), can be expressed as

$$y_t = \mu + \phi_1 y_{t-1} + \phi_2 y_{t-2} + \cdots + \phi_p y_{t-p} + u_t \tag{8.21}$$

where u_t is a white noise disturbance term. A manipulation of expression (8.21) will be required to demonstrate the properties of an autoregressive model. This expression can be written more compactly using sigma notation,

$$y_t = \mu + \sum_{i=1}^{p} \phi_i y_{t-i} + u_t \tag{8.22}$$

or, using the lag operator, as

$$y_t = \mu + \sum_{i=1}^{p} \phi_i L^i y_t + u_t \tag{8.23}$$

or

$$\phi(L)y_t = \mu + u_t \tag{8.24}$$

where $\phi(L) = (1 - \phi_1 L - \phi_2 L^2 - \cdots - \phi_p L^p)$. The characteristics of autoregressive models (mean, variance and autocorrelation function) are derived in section 8A.2 of the appendix to this chapter.

8.4.1 *The stationarity condition*

Stationarity is a desirable property of an estimated AR model, for several reasons. One important reason is that a model whose coefficients are non-stationary will exhibit the unfortunate property that previous values of the error term will have a non-declining effect on the current value of y_t as time progresses. This is arguably counter-intuitive and empirically implausible in many cases. More discussion on this issue is presented in chapter 12. Box 8.1 defines the stationarity condition algebraically.

Box 8.1 The stationarity condition for an AR(p) model

Setting μ to zero in (8.24), for a zero mean AR(p) process, y_t, given by

$$\phi(L)y_t = u_t \tag{8.25}$$

it would be stated that the process is stationary if it is possible to write

$$y_t = \phi(L)^{-1} u_t \tag{8.26}$$

with $\phi(L)^{-1}$ converging to zero. This means that the autocorrelations will decline eventually as the lag length is increased. When the expansion $\phi(L)^{-1}$ is calculated it will contain an infinite number of terms, and can be written as an MA(∞) – e.g. $a_1 u_{t-1} + a_2 u_{t-2} + a_3 u_{t-3} + \cdots + u_t$. If the process given by (8.25) is stationary, the coefficients in the MA(∞) representation will decline eventually with lag length, On the other hand, if the process is non-stationary, the coefficients in the MA(∞) representation will not converge to zero as the lag length increases.

The condition for testing for the stationarity of a general AR(p) model is that the roots of the 'characteristic equation',

$$1 - \phi_1 z - \phi_2 z^2 - \cdots - \phi_p z^p = 0 \tag{8.27}$$

all lie outside the unit circle. The notion of a characteristic equation is so-called because its roots determine the characteristics of the process y_t – for example, the acf for an AR process will depend on the roots of this characteristic equation, which is a polynomial in z.

Example 8.2

Is the following model stationary?

$$y_t = y_{t-1} + u_t \tag{8.28}$$

In order to test this, first write y_{t-1} in lag operator notation (i.e. as Ly_t), take this term over to the LHS of (8.28) and factorise

$$y_t = Ly_t + u_t \tag{8.29}$$

$$y_t - Ly_t = u_t \tag{8.30}$$

$$y_t(1 - L) = u_t \tag{8.31}$$

Then the characteristic equation is

$$1 - z = 0 \tag{8.32}$$

having the root $z = 1$, which lies on, not outside, the unit circle. In fact, the particular AR(p) model given by (8.28) is a non-stationary process known as a random walk (see chapter 12).

This procedure can also be adopted for autoregressive models with longer lag lengths and when the stationarity or otherwise of the process is less obvious. For example, is the following process for y_t stationary?

$$y_t = 3y_{t-1} - 2.75y_{t-2} + 0.75y_{t-3} + u_t \tag{8.33}$$

Again, the first stage is to express this equation using the lag operator notation, and then take all the terms in y over to the LHS:

$$y_t = 3Ly_t - 2.75L^2 y_t + 0.75L^3 y_t + u_t \tag{8.34}$$

$$(1 - 3L + 2.75L^2 - 0.75L^3)y_t = u_t \tag{8.35}$$

The characteristic equation is

$$1 - 3z + 2.75z^2 - 0.75z^3 = 0 \tag{8.36}$$

which, fortunately, factorises to

$$(1 - z)(1 - 1.5z)(1 - 0.5z) = 0 \tag{8.37}$$

so that the roots are $z = 1, z = 2/3$ and $z = 2$. Only one of these lies outside the unit circle, and hence the process for y_t described by (8.33) is not stationary.

8.5 The partial autocorrelation function

The partial autocorrelation function, or pacf (denoted τ_{kk}), measures the correlation between an observation k periods ago and the current observation, after controlling for observations at intermediate lags (that is, all lags $< k$) – i.e. the correlation between y_t and y_{t-k}, after removing the effects of $y_{t-k+1}, y_{t-k+2}, \ldots, y_{t-1}$. For example, the pacf for lag 3 would measure the correlation between y_t and y_{t-3} after controlling for the effects of y_{t-1} and y_{t-2}.

At lag 1, the autocorrelation and partial autocorrelation coefficients are equal, since there are no intermediate lag effects to eliminate. Thus $\tau_{11} = \tau_1$, where τ_1 is the autocorrelation coefficient at lag 1.

At lag 2,

$$\tau_{22} = \left(\tau_2 - \tau_1^2\right)/\left(1 - \tau_1^2\right) \tag{8.38}$$

where τ_1 and τ_2 are the autocorrelation coefficients at lags 1 and 2, respectively. For lags greater than two, the formulae are more complex, and hence a presentation of these is beyond the scope of this book. There now proceeds, however, an intuitive explanation of the characteristic shape of the pacf for a moving average and for an autoregressive process.

In the case of an autoregressive process of order p, there will be direct connections between y_t and y_{t-s} for $s \leq p$, but no direct connections for $s > p$. For example, consider the following AR(3) model:

$$y_t = \phi_0 + \phi_1 y_{t-1} + \phi_2 y_{t-2} + \phi_3 y_{t-3} + u_t \tag{8.39}$$

There is a direct connection through the model between y_t and y_{t-1}, between y_t and y_{t-2} and between y_t and y_{t-3}, but not between y_t and y_{t-s}, for $s \geq 4$. Hence the pacf will usually have non-zero partial autocorrelation coefficients for lags up to the order of the model, but will have zero partial autocorrelation coefficients thereafter. In the case of the AR(3), only the first three partial autocorrelation coefficients will be non-zero.

What shape would the partial autocorrelation function take for a moving average process? One would need to think about the MA model as being transformed into an AR in order to consider whether y_t and y_{t-k}, $k = 1, 2, \ldots$, are directly connected. In fact, so long as the MA(q) process is invertible, it can be expressed as an AR(∞). A definition of invertibility is therefore now required.

8.5.1 *The invertibility condition*

An MA(q) model is typically required to have roots of the characteristic equation $\theta(z) = 0$ greater than one in absolute value. The invertibility condition is mathematically the same as the stationarity condition, but is different in the sense that the former refers to MA rather than AR processes. This condition prevents the model from exploding under an AR(∞) representation, so that $\theta^{-1}(L)$ converges to zero. Box 8.2 shows the invertibility condition for an MA(2) model.

Box 8.2 The invertibility condition for an MA(2) model

In order to examine the shape of the pacf for moving average processes, consider the following MA(2) process for y_t:

$$y_t = u_t + \theta_1 u_{t-1} + \theta_2 u_{t-2} = \theta(L)u_t \tag{8.40}$$

Provided that this process is invertible, this MA(2) can be expressed as an AR(∞):

$$y_t = \sum_{i=1}^{\infty} c_i L^i y_{t-i} + u_t \tag{8.41}$$

$$y_t = c_1 y_{t-1} + c_2 y_{t-2} + c_3 y_{t-3} + \cdots + u_t \tag{8.42}$$

It is now evident when expressed in this way that, for a moving average model, there are direct connections between the current value of y and all its previous values. Thus the partial autocorrelation function for an MA(q) model will decline geometrically, rather than dropping off to zero after q lags, as is the case for its autocorrelation function. It could therefore be stated that the acf for an AR has the same basic shape as the pacf for an MA, and the acf for an MA has the same shape as the pacf for an AR.

8.6 ARMA processes

By combining the AR(p) and MA(q) models, an ARMA(p, q) model is obtained. Such a model states that the current value of some series y depends linearly on its own previous values plus a combination of the current and previous values of a white noise error term. The model can be written

$$\phi(L)y_t = \mu + \theta(L)u_t \tag{8.43}$$

where

$$\phi(L) = 1 - \phi_1 L - \phi_2 L^2 - \cdots - \phi_p L^p \quad \text{and}$$

$$\theta(L) = 1 + \theta_1 L + \theta_2 L^2 + \cdots + \theta_q L^q$$

or

$$y_t = \mu + \phi_1 y_{t-1} + \phi_2 y_{t-2} + \cdots + \phi_p y_{t-p} + \theta_1 u_{t-1} + \theta_2 u_{t-2} + \cdots + \theta_q u_{t-q} + u_t \tag{8.44}$$

with

$$\mathrm{E}(u_t) = 0; E(u_t^2) = \sigma^2; E(u_t u_s) = 0, t \neq s$$

The characteristics of an ARMA process will be a combination of those from the autoregressive and moving average parts. Note that the pacf is particularly useful in this context. The acf alone can distinguish between a pure autoregressive and a pure moving average process. An ARMA process will have a geometrically declining acf, however, as will a pure AR process. The pacf is therefore useful for distinguishing between an AR(p) process and an ARMA(p, q) process; the former will have a geometrically declining autocorrelation function, but a partial autocorrelation function, that cuts off to zero after p lags, while the latter will have both autocorrelation and partial autocorrelation functions that decline geometrically.

We can now summarise the defining characteristics of AR, MA and ARMA processes.

An autoregressive process has:

- a geometrically decaying acf; and
- number of non-zero points of pacf = AR order.

A moving average process has:

- number of non-zero points of acf = MA order; and
- a geometrically decaying pacf.

A combination autoregressive moving average process has:

- a geometrically decaying acf; and
- a geometrically decaying pacf.

In fact, the mean of an ARMA series is given by

$$E(y_t) = \frac{\mu}{1 - \phi_1 - \phi_2 - \cdots - \phi_p} \tag{8.45}$$

The autocorrelation function will display combinations of behaviour derived from the AR and MA parts, but, for lags beyond q, the acf will simply be identical to the individual AR(p) model, with the result that the AR part will dominate in the long term. Deriving the acf and pacf for an ARMA process requires no new algebra but is tedious, and hence it is left as an exercise for interested readers.

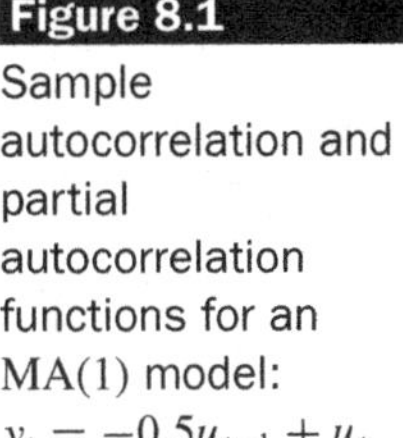

Figure 8.1
Sample autocorrelation and partial autocorrelation functions for an MA(1) model: $y_t = -0.5u_{t-1} + u_t$

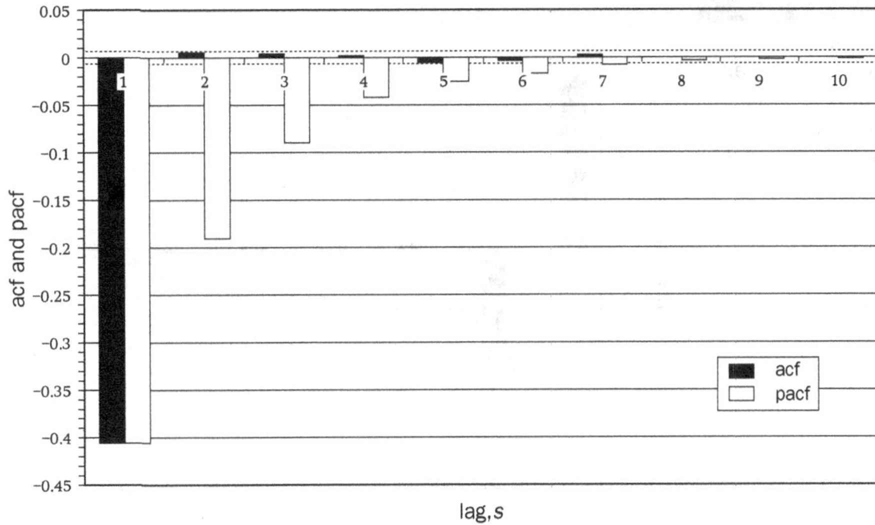

8.6.1 *Sample acf and pacf plots for standard processes*

Figures 8.1 to 8.7 give some examples of typical processes from the ARMA family, with their characteristic autocorrelation and partial autocorrelation functions. The acf and pacf are not produced analytically from the relevant formulae for a model of this type but, rather, are estimated using 100,000 simulated observations with disturbances drawn from a normal distribution. Each figure also has 5 per cent (two-sided) rejection bands represented by dotted lines. These are based on $(\pm 1.96/\sqrt{100000}) = \pm 0.0062$, calculated in the same way as given above. Notice how, in each case, the acf and pacf are identical for the first lag.

In figure 8.1, the MA(1) has an acf that is significant only for lag 1, while the pacf declines geometrically, and is significant until lag 7. The acf at lag 1 and all the pacfs are negative as a result of the negative coefficient in the MA-generating process.

Again, the structures of the acf and pacf in figure 8.2 are as anticipated for an MA(2). The first two autocorrelation coefficients only are significant, while the partial autocorrelation coefficients are geometrically declining. Note also that, since the second coefficient on the lagged error term in the MA is negative, the acf and pacf alternate between positive and negative. In the case of the pacf, we term this alternating and declining function a 'damped sine wave' or 'damped sinusoid'.

For the autoregressive model of order 1 with a fairly high coefficient – i.e. relatively close to one – the autocorrelation function would be expected to die away relatively slowly, and this is exactly what is observed here in figure 8.3. Again, as expected for an AR(1), only the first pacf

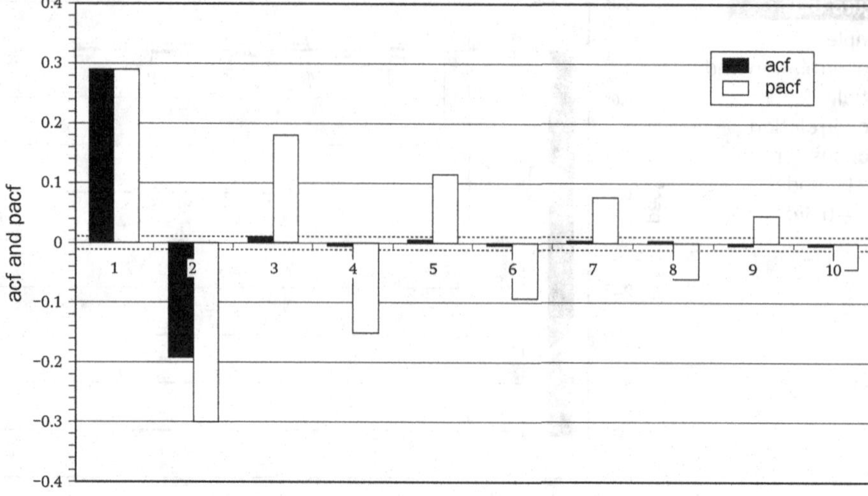

Figure 8.2 Sample autocorrelation and partial autocorrelation functions for an MA(2) model: $y_t = 0.5u_{t-1} - 0.25u_{t-2} + u_t$

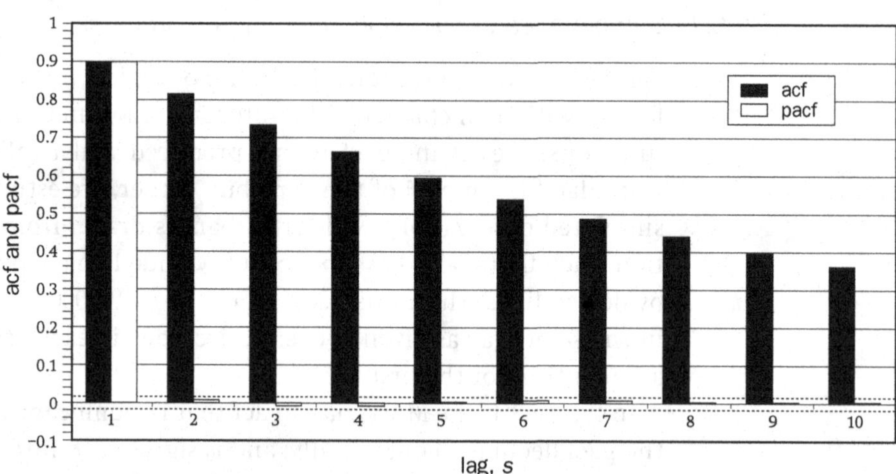

Figure 8.3 Sample autocorrelation and partial autocorrelation functions for a slowly decaying AR(1) model: $y_t = 0.9y_{t-1} + u_t$

coefficient is significant, while all the others are virtually zero and are not significant.

Figure 8.4 plots an AR(1) that was generated using identical error terms but a much smaller autoregressive coefficient. In this case, the autocorrelation function dies away much more quickly than in the previous example, and in fact becomes insignificant after around five lags.

Figure 8.5 shows the acf and pacf for an identical AR(1) process to that used for figure 8.4, except that the autoregressive coefficient is now negative. This results in a damped sinusoidal pattern for the acf, which again becomes insignificant after around lag 5. Recalling that the autocorrelation

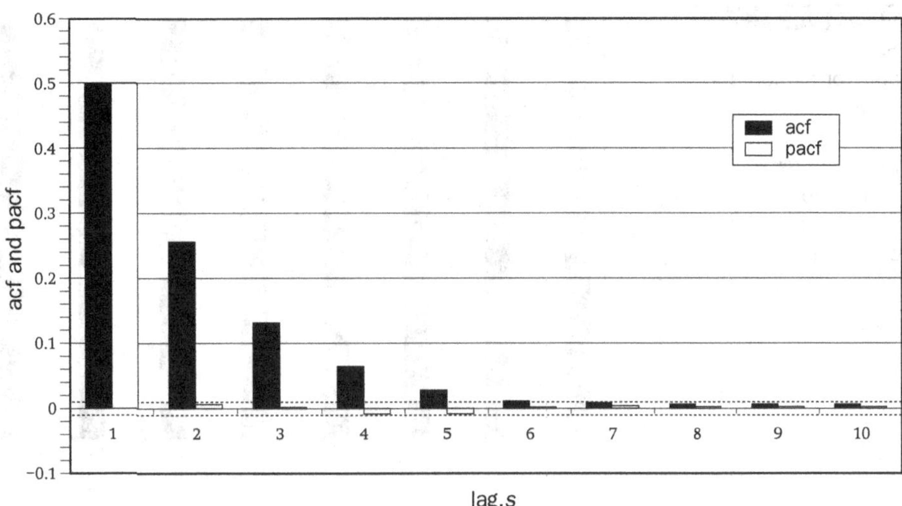

Figure 8.4 Sample autocorrelation and partial autocorrelation functions for a more rapidly decaying AR(1) model: $y_t = 0.5y_{t-1} + u_t$

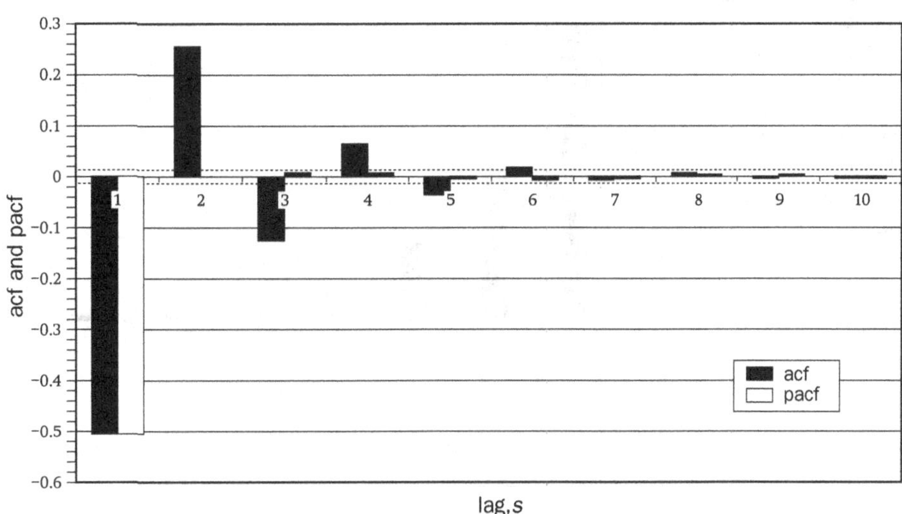

Figure 8.5 Sample autocorrelation and partial autocorrelation functions for a more rapidly decaying AR(1) model with negative coefficient: $y_t = -0.5y_{t-1} + u_t$

coefficient for this AR(1) at lag s is equal to $(-0.5)^s$, this will be positive for even s and negative for odd s. Only the first pacf coefficient is significant (and negative).

Figure 8.6 plots the acf and pacf for a non-stationary series (see chapter 12 for an extensive discussion) that has a unit coefficient on the lagged dependent variable. The result is that shocks to y never die away, and persist indefinitely in the system. Consequently, the acf function remains relatively flat at unity, even up to lag 10. In fact, even by lag 10, the autocorrelation coefficient has fallen only to 0.9989. Note also that, on some occasions, the

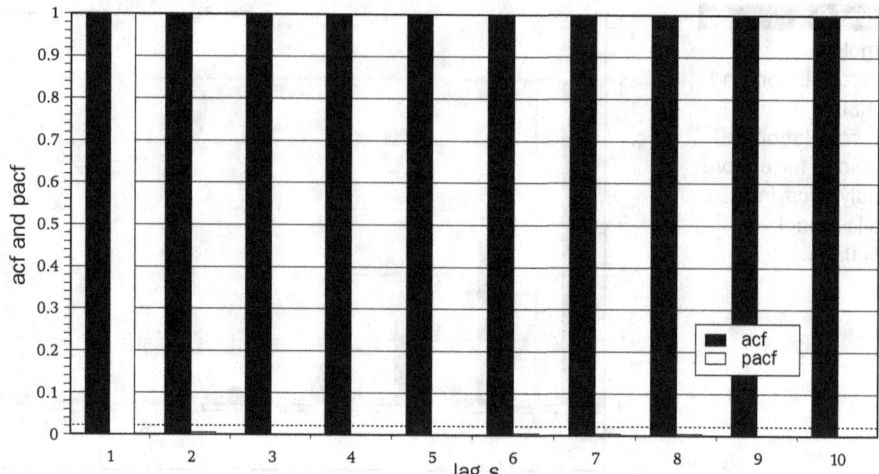

Figure 8.6 Sample autocorrelation and partial autocorrelation functions for a non-stationary model (i.e. a unit coefficient):
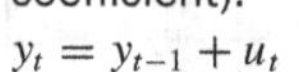
$y_t = y_{t-1} + u_t$

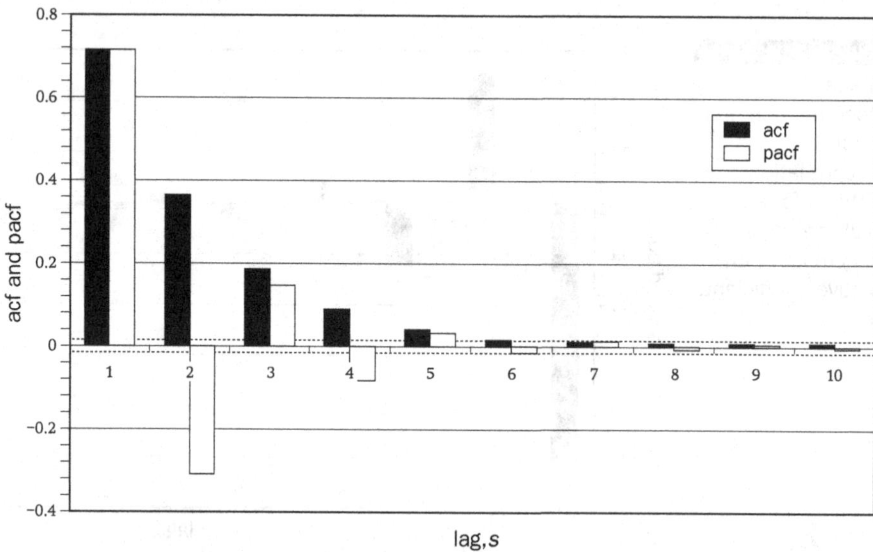

Figure 8.7 Sample autocorrelation and partial autocorrelation functions for an ARMA(1, 1) model: $y_t = 0.5y_{t-1} + 0.5u_{t-1} + u_t$

acf does die away, rather than looking like figure 8.6, even for such a non-stationary process, owing to its inherent instability combined with finite computer precision. The pacf is significant only for lag 1, however, correctly suggesting that an autoregressive model with no moving average term is most appropriate.

Finally, figure 8.7 plots the acf and pacf for a mixed ARMA process. As one would expect of such a process, both the acf and the pacf decline geometrically – the acf as a result of the AR part and the pacf as a result of the MA part. The coefficients on the AR and MA are, however, sufficiently small that both acf and pacf coefficients have become insignificant by lag 6.

8.7 Building ARMA models: the Box–Jenkins approach

Although the existence of ARMA models pre-dates them, Box and Jenkins (1976) were the first to approach the task of estimating an ARMA model in a systematic manner. Their approach was a practical and pragmatic one, involving three steps:

(1) identification;
(2) estimation; and
(3) diagnostic checking.

These steps are now explained in greater detail.

Step 1

This involves *determining the order of the model required* to capture the dynamic features of the data. Graphical procedures are used (plotting the data over time and plotting the acf and pacf) to determine the most appropriate specification.

Step 2

This involves *estimating the parameters of the model* specified in step 1. This can be done using least squares or another technique, known as maximum likelihood, depending on the model.

Step 3

This involves *model checking* – i.e. determining whether the model specified and estimated is adequate. Box and Jenkins suggest two methods: overfitting and residual diagnostics. *Overfitting* involves deliberately fitting a larger model than that required to capture the dynamics of the data as identified in step 1. If the model specified at step 1 is adequate, any extra terms added to the ARMA model would be insignificant. *Residual diagnostics* implies checking the residuals for evidence of linear dependence, which, if present, would suggest that the model originally specified was inadequate to capture the features of the data. The acf, pacf or Ljung–Box tests can all be used.

It is worth noting that 'diagnostic testing' in the Box–Jenkins world essentially involves only autocorrelation tests rather than the whole barrage of tests outlined in chapter 6. In addition, such approaches to determining the adequacy of the model would reveal only a model that is under-parameterised ('too small') and would not reveal a model that is over-parameterised ('too big').

Examining whether the residuals are free from autocorrelation is much more commonly used than overfitting, and this may have arisen partly because, for ARMA models, it can give rise to common factors in the overfitted model that make estimation of this model difficult and the statistical tests ill-behaved. For example, if the true model is an ARMA(1,1) and we deliberately then fit an ARMA(2,2), there will be a common factor so that not all the parameters in the latter model can be identified. This problem does not arise with pure AR or MA models, only with mixed processes.

It is usually the objective to form a *parsimonious model*, which is one that describes all the features of the data of interest using as few parameters – i.e. as simple a model – as possible. A parsimonious model is desirable for the following reasons.

- The residual sum of squares is *inversely proportional* to the number of degrees of freedom. A model that contains irrelevant lags of the variable or of the error term (and therefore unnecessary parameters) will usually lead to increased coefficient standard errors, implying that it will be more difficult to find significant relationships in the data. Whether an increase in the number of variables – i.e. a reduction in the number of degrees of freedom – will actually cause the estimated parameter standard errors to rise or fall will obviously depend on how much the RSS falls, and on the relative sizes of T and k. If T is very large relative to k, then the decrease in the RSS is likely to outweigh the reduction in $T - k$, so that the standard errors fall. As a result 'large' models with many parameters are more often chosen when the sample size is large.
- Models that are profligate might be inclined to fit to data specific features that would not be replicated out of the sample. This means that the models may appear to fit the data very well, with perhaps a high value of R^2, but would give very inaccurate forecasts. Another interpretation of this concept, borrowed from physics, is that of the distinction between 'signal' and 'noise'. The idea is to fit a model that *captures the signal* (the important features of the data, or the underlying trends or patterns) but that does not try to fit a spurious model to the noise (the completely random aspect of the series).

8.7.1 Information criteria for ARMA model selection

Nowadays, the identification stage would typically not be done using graphical plots of the acf and pacf. The reason is that, when 'messy' real data are used, they rarely exhibit the simple patterns of figures 8.1 to 8.7, unfortunately. This makes the acf and pacf very hard to interpret, and thus it is difficult to specify a model for the data. Another technique, which removes some of the subjectivity involved in interpreting the acf and pacf, is to use what are known as *information criteria*. Information criteria embody two factors: a term that is a function of the residual sum of squares, and some penalty for the loss of degrees of freedom from adding extra parameters. As a consequence, adding a new variable or an additional lag to a model will have two competing effects on the information criteria: the RSS will fall but the value of the penalty term will increase.

The object is to choose the number of parameters that minimises the value of the information criteria. Thus adding an extra term will reduce the value of the criteria only if the fall in the RSS is sufficient to more than outweigh the increased value of the penalty term. There are several different criteria, which vary according to how stiff the penalty term is. The three most popular information criteria are Akaike's (1974) information criterion, Schwarz's (1978) Bayesian information criterion (SBIC) and the Hannan–Quinn information criterion (HQIC). Algebraically, these are expressed, respectively, as

$$\text{AIC} = \ln(\hat{\sigma}^2) + \frac{2k}{T} \tag{8.46}$$

$$\text{SBIC} = \ln(\hat{\sigma}^2) + \frac{k}{T}\ln T \tag{8.47}$$

$$\text{HQIC} = \ln(\hat{\sigma}^2) + \frac{2k}{T}\ln(\ln(T)) \tag{8.48}$$

where $\hat{\sigma}^2$ is the residual variance (also equivalent to the residual sum of squares divided by the number of observations, T), $k = p + q + 1$ is the total number of parameters estimated and T is the sample size. The information criteria are actually minimised subject to $p \leq \bar{p}, q \leq \bar{q}$ – i.e. an upper limit is specified on the number of moving average ($\bar{q}$) and/or autoregressive ($\bar{p}$) terms that will be considered.

SBIC embodies a much stiffer penalty term than AIC, while HQIC is somewhere in between. The adjusted R^2 measure can also be viewed as an information criterion, although it is a very soft one, which would typically select the largest models of all. It is worth noting that there are several other possible criteria, but these are less popular and are mainly variants of those described above.

8.7.2 *Which criterion should be preferred if they suggest different model orders?*

SBIC is strongly consistent, but inefficient, and AIC is not consistent, but is generally more efficient. In other words, SBIC will asymptotically deliver the correct model order, while AIC will deliver on average too large a model, even with an infinite amount of data. On the other hand, the average variation in selected model orders from different samples within a given population will be greater in the context of SBIC than AIC. Overall, then, no criterion is definitely superior to others.

8.7.3 *ARIMA modelling*

ARIMA modelling, as distinct from ARMA modelling, has the additional letter 'I' in the acronym, standing for 'integrated'. An *integrated autoregressive process* is one whose characteristic equation has a root on the unit circle. Typically, researchers difference the variable as necessary and then build an ARMA model on those differenced variables. An ARMA(p, q) model in the variable differenced d times is equivalent to an ARIMA(p, d, q) model on the original data (see chapter 12 for further details). For the remainder of this chapter, it is assumed that the data used in model construction are stationary, or have been suitably transformed to make them stationary. Thus only ARMA models are considered further.

8.8 Exponential smoothing

Exponential smoothing is another modelling technique (not based on the ARIMA approach) that uses only a linear combination of the previous values of a series for modelling it and for generating forecasts of its future values. Given that only previous values of the series of interest are used, the only question remaining is how much weight to attach to each of the previous observations. Recent observations would be expected to have the most power in helping to forecast future values of a series. If this is accepted, a model that places more weight on recent observations than those further in the past would be desirable. On the other hand, observations a long way in the past may still contain some information useful for forecasting future values of a series, which would not be the case under a centred moving average. An exponential smoothing model will achieve this, by imposing a geometrically declining weighting scheme on the lagged values of a series. The equation for the model is

$$S_t = \alpha y_t + (1 - \alpha) S_{t-1} \tag{8.49}$$

where α is the smoothing constant, with $0 < \alpha < 1$, y_t is the current realised value and S_t is the current smoothed value.

Since $\alpha + (1 - \alpha) = 1$, S_t is modelled as a weighted average of the current observation y_t and the previous smoothed value. The model above can be rewritten to express the exponential weighting scheme more clearly. By lagging (8.49) by one period, the following expression is obtained,

$$S_{t-1} = \alpha y_{t-1} + (1-\alpha)S_{t-2} \tag{8.50}$$

and, lagging again,

$$S_{t-2} = \alpha y_{t-2} + (1-\alpha)S_{t-3} \tag{8.51}$$

Substituting into (8.49) for S_{t-1} from (8.50),

$$S_t = \alpha y_t + (1-\alpha)(\alpha y_{t-1} + (1-\alpha)S_{t-2}) \tag{8.52}$$

$$S_t = \alpha y_t + (1-\alpha)\alpha y_{t-1} + (1-\alpha)^2 S_{t-2} \tag{8.53}$$

Substituting into (8.53) for S_{t-2} from (8.51),

$$S_t = \alpha y_t + (1-\alpha)\alpha y_{t-1} + (1-\alpha)^2(\alpha y_{t-2} + (1-\alpha)S_{t-3}) \tag{8.54}$$

$$S_t = \alpha y_t + (1-\alpha)\alpha y_{t-1} + (1-\alpha)^2 \alpha y_{t-2} + (1-\alpha)^3 S_{t-3} \tag{8.55}$$

T successive substitutions of this kind would lead to

$$S_t = \left(\sum_{i=0}^{T} \alpha(1-\alpha)^i y_{t-i}\right) + (1-\alpha)^{T+1} S_{t-1-T} \tag{8.56}$$

Since $\alpha > 0$, the effect of each observation declines geometrically as the variable moves another observation forward in time. In the limit as $T \to \infty$, $(1-\alpha)^T S_0 \to 0$, so that the current smoothed value is a geometrically weighted infinite sum of the previous realisations.

The forecasts from an exponential smoothing model are simply set to the current smoothed value, for any number of steps ahead, s:

$$f_{t,s} = S_t,\ s = 1, 2, 3, \ldots \tag{8.57}$$

The exponential smoothing model can be seen as a special case of a Box–Jenkins model, an ARIMA(0,1,1), with MA coefficient $(1-\alpha)$ – see Granger and Newbold (1986, p. 174).

The technique above is known as single or simple exponential smoothing, and it can be modified to allow for trends (Holt's method) or to allow for seasonality (Winter's method) in the underlying variable. These augmented models are not pursued further in this text, as there is a much better way to model the trends (using a unit root process – see chapter 12) and the seasonalities (see later in this chapter) of the form that are typically present in real estate data.

Exponential smoothing has several advantages over the slightly more complex ARMA class of models discussed above. First, exponential smoothing is obviously very simple to use. Second, there is no decision to be made on how many parameters to estimate (assuming only single exponential

Figure 8.8
Cap rates first quarter 1978–fourth quarter 2007

smoothing is considered). Thus it is easy to update the model if a new realisation becomes available.

Among the disadvantages of exponential smoothing is the fact that it is excessively simplistic and inflexible. Exponential smoothing models can be viewed as but one model from the ARIMA family, which may not necessarily be optimal for capturing any linear dependence in the data. Moreover, the forecasts from an exponential smoothing model do not converge on the long-term mean of the variable as the horizon increases. The upshot is that long-term forecasts are overly affected by recent events in the history of the series under investigation and will therefore be suboptimal.

8.9 An ARMA model for cap rates

We apply an ARMA model to the NCREIF appraisal-based cap rates for the 'all real estate' category. The capitalisation (cap) refers to the going-in cap rate series (or initial yield) and is the net operating income in the first year over the purchase price. This series is available from 1Q1978 and the last observation in our sample is 4Q2007. We plot the series in figure 8.8. The cap rate fell steeply from 2001, with the very last observation of the sample indicating a reversal. Cap rates had also shown a downward trend in the 1980s and up to the mid-1990s, but the latest decreasing trend was steeper (apart from a few quarters in 1999 to 2000). Certainly, by the end of 2007, cap rates had reached their lowest level in our sample.

Applying an ARMA model to the original cap rates may be problematic, as the series exhibits low variation and trends are apparent over several years – e.g. a downward trend from 1995. The series is also smoothed and strongly autocorrelated, as the correlogram in figure 8.9 panel (a) demonstrates. Panel (b) shows the partial autocorrelation function.

Figure 8.9 Autocorrelation and partial autocorrelation functions for cap rates

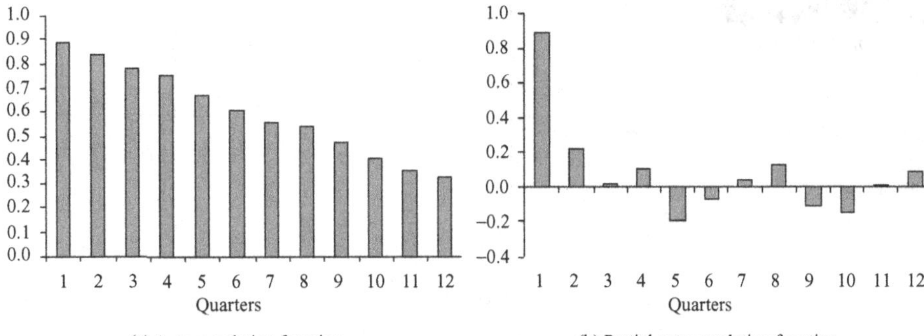

Figure 8.10 Cap rates in first differences

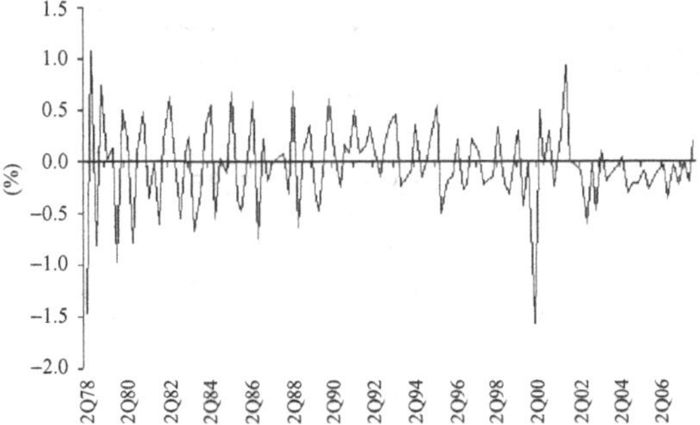

The values of the acf are gradually declining from a first-order autocorrelation coefficient of 0.89. Even after eight quarters, the autocorrelation coefficient is still 0.54. The computed Ljung Box Q^* statistic with twelve lags takes a value of 600.64 (p-value $= 0.00$), which is highly significant, confirming the strong autocorrelation pattern. The partial autocorrelation function shows a large peak at lag 1 with a rapid decline thereafter, which is indicative of a highly persistent autoregressive structure in the series.

The cap rate series in levels does not have the appropriate properties to fit an ARMA model, therefore, and a transformation to first differences is required (see chapter 12, where this issue is discussed in detail). The new series of differences of the cap rate is given in figure 8.10.

The cap rate series in first differences appears to have very different properties from that in levels, and we again compute the acf and pacf for the transformed series, which are shown in figure 8.11.

The first-order autocorrelation coefficient is now negative, at −0.30. Both the second- and third-order coefficients are small, indicating that the transformation has made the series much less autocorrelated compared with the levels data. The Ljung–Box statistic using twelve lags is now reduced to

Figure 8.11 Autocorrelation and partial autocorrelation functions for cap rates in first differences

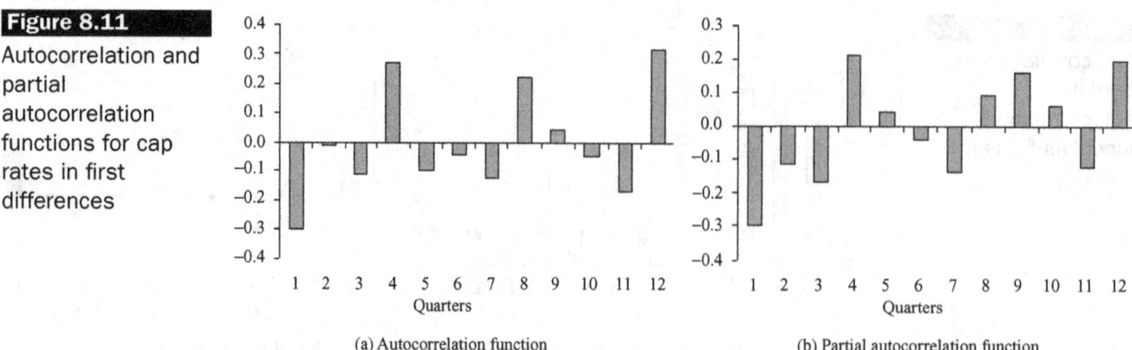

(a) Autocorrelation function

(b) Partial autocorrelation function

Table 8.1 Selecting the ARMA specification for cap rates

Order of AR, MA terms	AIC	SBIC
1,1	−1.94	−1.87
1,2	−1.95	−1.85
1,3	−1.98	−1.89
1,4	−1.97	−1.83
2,1	−1.92	−1.83
2,2	−1.92	−1.80
2,3	−1.95	−1.81
2,4	−1.93	−1.77
3,1	−1.97	−1.85
3,2	−1.95	−1.81
3,3	**−2.18**	**−2.02**
3,4	−2.15	−1.96
4,1	−1.98	−1.84
4,2	−2.16	−1.99
4,3	−2.17	−1.98
4,4	−2.15	−1.93

49.42, although it is still significant at the 1 per cent level ($p = 0.00$). We also observe a seasonal pattern at lags 4, 8 and 12, when the size of the autocorrelation coefficients increases. This is also the case for the pacf. For the moment we ignore this characteristic of the data (the strong autocorrelation at lags 4, 8 and 12), and we proceed to fit an ARMA model to the first differences of the cap rate series. We apply AIC and SBIC to select the model order. Table 8.1 shows different combinations of ARMA specifications and the estimated AIC and SBIC values.

Table 8.2 Estimation of ARMA (3,3)

ARMA terms	Coefficient	*t*-ratio
Constant	−0.03	−1.04
AR(1)	−0.72	−7.69***
AR(2)	−0.95	−65.33***
AR(3)	−0.68	−7.92***
MA(1)	0.57	4.40***
MA(2)	1.01	52.88***
MA(3)	0.52	4.13***
Adj. R^2	0.31	
Sample period	1Q79–4Q07	

Note: *** denotes statistical significance at the 1 per cent level.

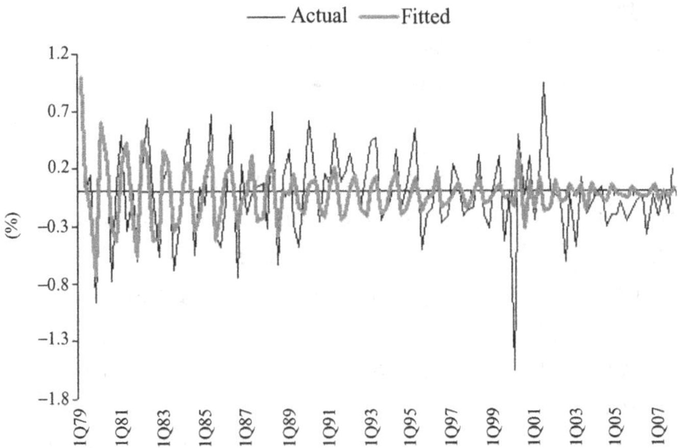

Figure 8.12 Actual and fitted values for cap rates in first differences

Interestingly, both AIC and SBIC select an ARMA(3,3). Despite the fact that AIC often tends to select higher order ARMAs, in our example there is a consensus across the two criteria. The estimated ARMA(3,3) is presented in table 8.2.

All the AR and MA terms are highly significant at the 1 per cent level. This ARMA model explains approximately 31 per cent of the changes in the cap rate. This is a satisfactory performance if we consider the quarterly volatility of the changes in the cap rate. Figure 8.12 illustrates this volatility and gives the actual and fitted values.

The fitted series exhibit some volatility, which tends to match that of the actual series in the 1980s. The two spikes in 1Q2000 and 3Q2001

Table 8.3 Actual and forecast cap rates

	Actual	Forecast	ΔCAP forecast
Forecast period 1Q07–4Q07			
4Q06	5.47	5.47	
1Q07	5.25	5.42	−0.053
2Q07	5.25	5.44	0.021
3Q07	5.07	5.38	−0.061
4Q07	5.28	5.34	−0.037
Forecast period 1Q06–4Q06			
4Q05	5.96	5.96	
1Q06	5.89	5.95	−0.011
2Q06	5.87	5.95	−0.002
3Q06	5.50	5.90	−0.043
4Q06	5.47	5.86	−0.044

are not captured. In the last four years of the sample the model tends to under-predict the negative changes in the cap rate. During this period the actual series becomes less volatile, and so do the fitted values.

The forecast performance of the ARMA(3,3) is examined next. There are, of course, different ways to evaluate the model's forecast, as we outline in chapter 9. The application of ARMA models in economics and finance suggests that they are good predictors in the short run. We use the ARMA model in our example to produce two sets of four-quarter forecasts. We obtain the forecasts from this model for the four-quarters of 2006 and the next four quarters (that is, for 2006 and for 2007). In the first case we estimate the full sample specification up to 4Q2005 and we generate forecast for 1Q2006 to 4Q2006. We then repeat the analysis for the next four-quarter period – i.e. we estimate the ARMA to 4Q2006 and we produce forecasts for the period 1Q2007 to 4Q2007. From the ARMA model we obtain forecasts for the first differences in the cap rate, which we then use to obtain the forecast for the actual level of the cap rates. Table 8.3 summarises the forecasts and figure 8.13 plots them.

Before discussing the forecasts, it is worth noting that all the terms in the ARMA(3,3) over the two estimation periods retain their statistical significance at the 1 per cent level. In the first three quarters of 2007 cap rates fell by over forty bps (figure 8.13, panel (a)). The ARMA model produces a

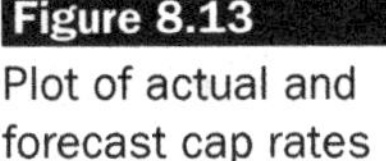
Figure 8.13
Plot of actual and forecast cap rates

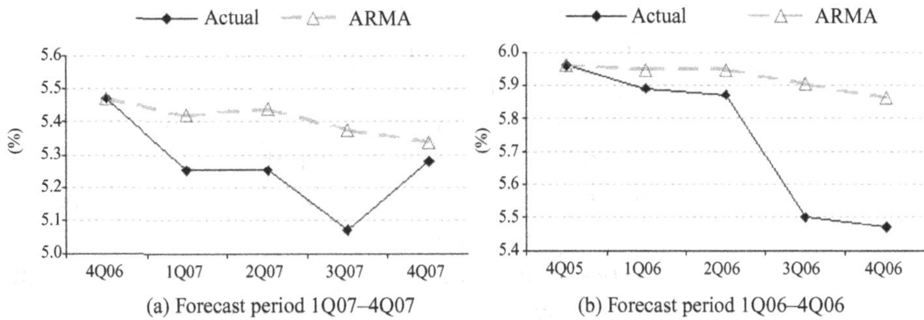

(a) Forecast period 1Q07–4Q07
(b) Forecast period 1Q06–4Q06

forecast for declining cap rates in the first three quarters but only by ten bps. Subsequently, in the fourth quarter, actual yields turn and show a rise of twenty bps, which the ARMA misses as it predicts a further small fall. If we ignore the path of the forecast and that of the actual values, however, the ARMA model would have provided a very accurate forecast for the level of cap rates four-quarters in advance at the end of 2007.

Focusing on the forecasts for the previous four-quarter period (figure 8.13, panel (b)), the ARMA model does a good job in predicting the pattern of the actual values in the first two quarters of 2006. The forecast is flat and the actual cap rates fell by ten bps. In the third quarter the actual cap rate fell by thirty-seven bps, while the forecast points to a fall, but only a marginal one. The small decline in the cap rate for the last quarter of 2006 is predicted well. The overall level forecast for the cap rate in 4Q06 made four quarters in advance is inaccurate, however, due to the 3Q miss. An argument can be made here that abrupt quarterly changes in cap rates are not captured by the ARMA forecasts. Another observation is that, in a period when cap rates followed a downward trend with the exception of the last quarter of 2007, the ARMA model tended to under-predict the fall.

8.10 Seasonality in real estate data

In the NCREIF cap rate series we observed spikes in both the acf and pacf at regular quarters, for which seasonality could be the cause. Calendar effects may be loosely defined as the tendency of time series to display systematic patterns at certain times of the month, quarter or year.

If any of these calendar phenomena are present in the data but ignored by the model-building process, the result is likely to be a misspecified model. For example, ignored seasonality in y_t is likely to lead to residual autocorrelation of the order of the seasonality – e.g. fourth-order residual autocorrelation in our example above.

One very simple method for coping with seasonality and examining the degree to which it is present is the inclusion of dummy variables in regression equations. These dummies can be included both in standard regression models based on exogenous explanatory variables ($x_{2t}, x_{3t}, \ldots, x_{kt}$) and in pure time series models. The number of dummy variables that can sensibly be constructed to model the seasonality would depend on the frequency of the data. For example, four dummy variables would be created for quarterly data, twelve for monthly data, and so on. In the case of quarterly data, the four dummy variables would be defined as follows:

$D1_t = 1$ in quarter 1 and zero otherwise;
$D2_t = 1$ in quarter 2 and zero otherwise;
$D3_t = 1$ in quarter 3 and zero otherwise;
$D4_t = 1$ in quarter 4 and zero otherwise.

Box 8.3 shows how intercept dummy variables operate. How many dummy variables can be placed in a regression model? If an intercept term is used in the regression, the number of dummies that can also be included would be one fewer than the 'seasonality' of the data. To see why this is the case, consider what happens if all four dummies are used for the quarterly series. The following gives the values that the dummy variables would take for a period during the mid-1980s, together with the sum of the dummies at each point in time, presented in the last column.

		$D1$	$D2$	$D3$	$D4$	Sum
1986	Q1	1	0	0	0	1
	Q2	0	1	0	0	1
	Q3	0	0	1	0	1
	Q4	0	0	0	1	1
1987	Q1	1	0	0	0	1
	Q2	0	1	0	0	1
	Q3	0	0	1	0	1
		etc.				

The sum of the four dummies would be one in every time period. Unfortunately, this sum is, of course, identical to the variable that is implicitly attached to the intercept coefficient. Thus, if the four dummy variables and the intercept were both included in the same regression, the problem would be one of perfect multicollinearity, so that $(X'X)^{-1}$ would not exist and none of the coefficients could be estimated. This problem is known as the *dummy variable trap*. The solution would be either to use just three dummy variables plus the intercept or to use the four dummy variables with no intercept.

The seasonal features in the data would be captured using either of these, and the residuals in each case would be identical, although the interpretation of the coefficients would be changed. If four dummy variables were used (and assuming that there were no explanatory variables in the regression), the estimated coefficients could be interpreted as the average value of the dependent variable during each quarter. In the case in which a constant and three dummy variables were used, the interpretation of the estimated coefficients on the dummy variables would be that they represented the average deviations of the dependent variables for the included quarters from their average values for the excluded quarter, as discussed in the example in box 8.3.

Box 8.3 How do dummy variables work?

The dummy variables as described above operate by *changing the intercept*, so that the average value of the dependent variable, given all the explanatory variables, is permitted to change across the seasons. This is shown in figure 8.14.

Consider the following regression:

$$y_t = \beta_1 + \gamma_1 D1_t + \gamma_2 D2_t + \gamma_3 D3_t + \beta_2 x_{2t} + \cdots + u_t \tag{8.58}$$

During each period the intercept will be changed. The intercept will be:

- $\hat{\beta}_1 + \hat{\gamma}_1$ in the first quarter, since $D1 = 1$ and $D2 = D3 = 0$ for all quarter 1 observations;
- $\hat{\beta}_1 + \hat{\gamma}_2$ in the second quarter, since $D2 = 1$ and $D1 = D3 = 0$ for all quarter 2 observations;
- $\hat{\beta}_1 + \hat{\gamma}_3$ in the third quarter, since $D3 = 1$ and $D1 = D2 = 0$ for all quarter 3 observations; and
- $\hat{\beta}_1$ in the fourth quarter, since $D1 = D2 = D3 = 0$ for all quarter 4 observations.

8.10.1 *Slope dummy variables*

As well as, or instead of, intercept dummies, slope dummy variables can be used. These operate by changing the slope of the regression line, leaving the intercept unchanged. Figure 8.15 gives an illustration in the context of just one slope dummy (i.e. two different 'states'). Such a set-up would apply if, for example, the data were biannual (twice yearly). Then D_t would be defined as $D_t = 1$ for the first half of the year and zero for the second half.

In the above case, the intercept is fixed at α, while the slope varies over time. For periods when the value of the dummy is zero the slope will be β, while for periods when the dummy is one the slope will be $\beta + \gamma$.

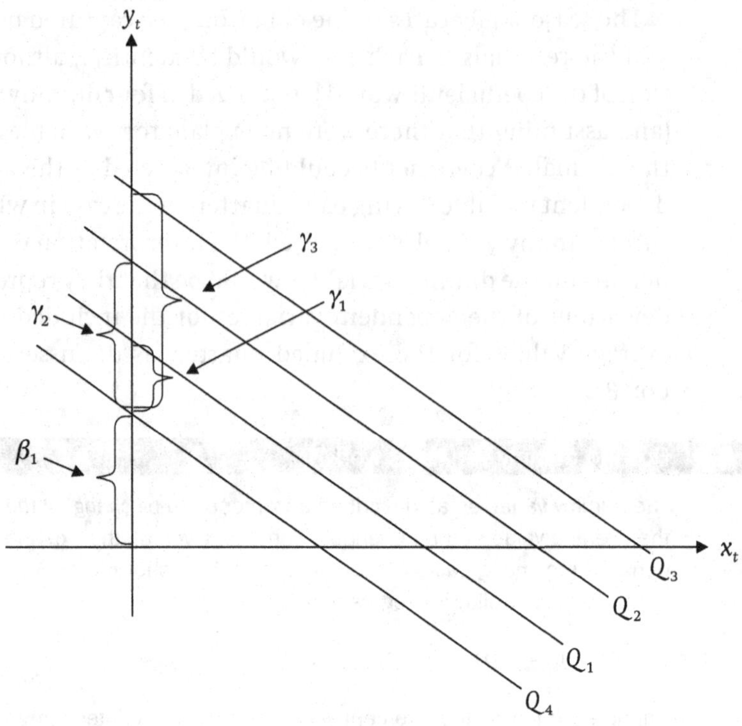

Figure 8.14
Use of intercept dummy variables for quarterly data

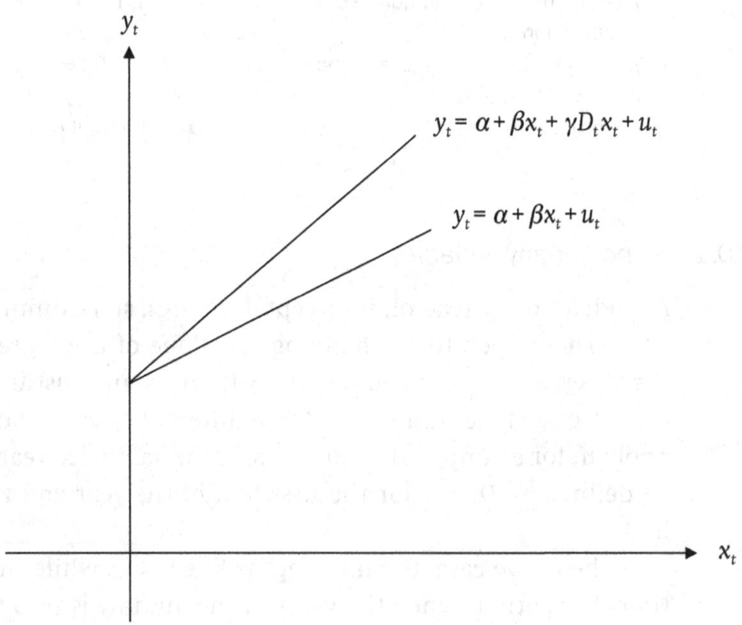

Figure 8.15
Use of slope dummy variables

Table 8.4 ARMA with seasonal dummies

ARMA terms	Coefficient	t-ratio
Constant	−0.05	−0.94
SDUM(2Q)	0.29	3.53***
SDUM(3Q)	−0.21	−2.69***
AR(1)	−0.38	−1.54
AR(2)	−0.27	−1.05
AR(3)	−0.54	−3.23***
MA(1)	0.33	1.43
MA(2)	0.05	0.20
MA(3)	0.71	3.95***
Adj. R^2	0.33	
Sample period	1Q79–4Q07	

Note: *** denotes statistical significance at the 1 per cent level.

Of course, it is also possible to use more than one dummy variable for the slopes. For example, if the data were quarterly, the following set-up could be used, with $D1_t \ldots D3_t$ representing quarters 1 to 3.

$$y_t = \alpha + \beta x_t + \gamma_1 D1_t x_t + \gamma_2 D2_t x_t + \gamma_3 D3_t x_t + u_t \tag{8.59}$$

In this case, since there is also a term in x_t with no dummy attached, the interpretation of the coefficients on the dummies (γ_1 etc.) is that they represent the deviation of the slope for that quarter from the average slope over all quarters. On the other hand, if the four slope dummy variables were included (and not βx_t), the coefficients on the dummies would be interpreted as the average slope coefficients during each quarter. Again, it is important not to include four quarterly slope dummies and the βx_t in the regression together; otherwise perfect multicollinearity would result.

8.10.2 *An example of the use of seasonal dummy variables*

We test for seasonality effects in the ARMA specification and construct seasonal dummies as described earlier. We leave the intercept in the model and we add seasonal dummies for quarters 1 to 3. We find that the seasonal dummy for quarter 1 is not statistically significant but the seasonal dummies for quarters 2 and 3 are significant at the 1 per cent level. In table 8.4, we report the results after excluding the insignificant dummy for 1Q.

Table 8.5 Actual and forecast cap rates including seasonal dummies

		Forecast	
Actual		Levels	First differences
Forecast period 1Q07–4Q07			
4Q06	5.47	5.47	
1Q07	5.25	5.37	−0.098
2Q07	5.25	5.63	0.253
3Q07	5.07	5.32	−0.308
4Q07	5.28	5.31	−0.004
Forecast period 1Q06–4Q06			
4Q05	5.96	5.96	
1Q06	5.89	5.85	−0.107
2Q06	5.87	6.14	0.290
3Q06	5.50	5.87	−0.277
4Q06	5.47	5.86	−0.009

The quarter 2 seasonal effect has a positive influence on yield changes (that is, it tends to push the actual cap rate higher), and the third-quarter dummy has a negative effect on changes in cap rates. We also observe that the AR and MA terms of order 1 and 2 have lost their significance, since the seasonal dummies appear to capture some of the information that these terms carry. The overall explanatory power of the model has marginally risen.

We repeat the forecast exercise we performed earlier, with the results shown in table 8.5. Figure 8.16 presents the forecasts from the ARMA model with and without the seasonal dummies for the two forecast periods.

For both forecast evaluation periods, the second-quarter dummy pushes the cap rate higher and results in an inaccurate forecast for that quarter. The inclusion of the third-quarter dummy does not seem to have such a noticeable effect on changes in cap rates and their levels. With the exception of the second quarter, the ARMAs with the seasonal dummies do not perform distinctly differently from the plain ARMA, although, at the margin, the former do better in some quarters.

Running the ARMA with only the 3Q dummy produces different results, as all the AR and MA terms are significant (unlike the case in which the

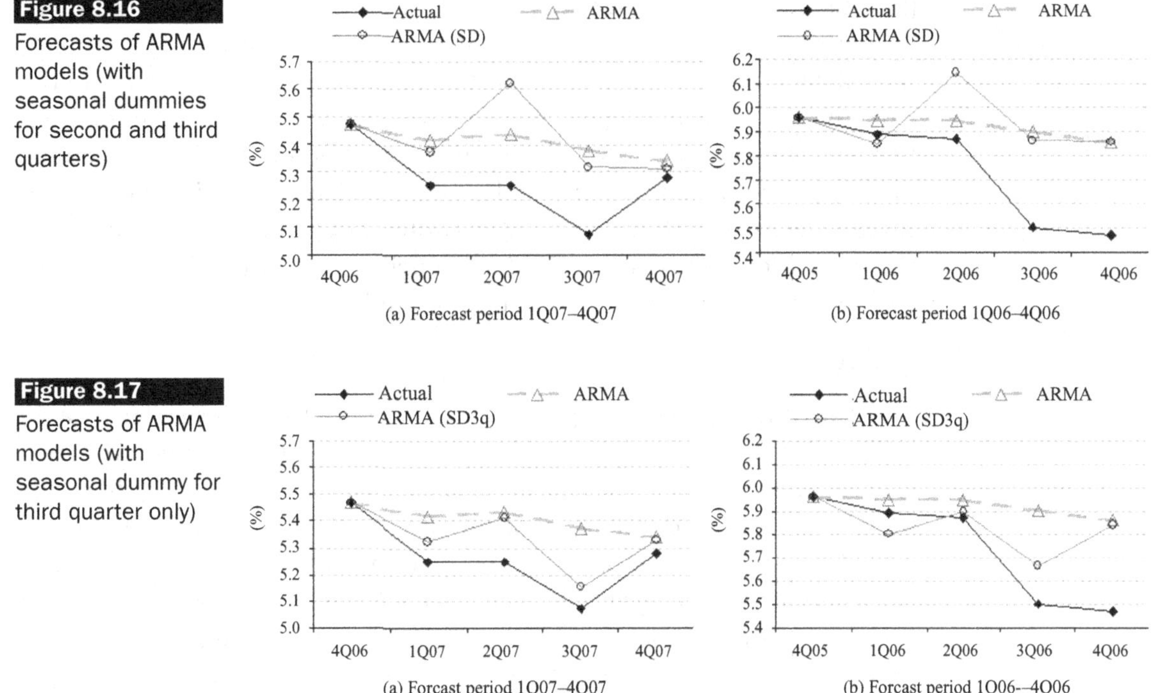

Figure 8.16 Forecasts of ARMA models (with seasonal dummies for second and third quarters)

Figure 8.17 Forecasts of ARMA models (with seasonal dummy for third quarter only)

quarter 2 dummy was present). The forecasts differ as well. We reproduce the graphs, but now with the new forecasts from the seasonal ARMA model that incorporates only the third-quarter dummy, in figure 8.17.

In the 1Q07 to 4Q07 period the ARMA with the seasonal dummy produces good forecasts, with the exception of the second quarter, when actual cap rates remained flat whereas the forecast yield decreased. Interestingly, it captures the turn in cap rates in the last quarter quite accurately. If we repeat the forecast analysis for 2006, the forecasts from the seasonal dummy ARMA are good for three quarters, especially for 3Q, when it replicates the fall in actual cap rates. In 4Q, however, it predicts a rise in the cap rate (unlike the plain ARMA forecast), with cap rates falling marginally further. It appears that the presence of the dummy variable in the model pushes the forecast in 3Q downwards, which then tends to bounce back in the following quarter.

8.11 Studies using ARMA models in real estate

In the real estate literature, ARMA models are used mainly for short-term forecasting and to provide a benchmark by which to judge structural models

(models that include exogenous variables). Tse (1997) focuses on the short-term movements of the office and industrial markets in Hong Kong, employing ARMA analysis to generate short-term forecasts for these sectors. In the study by Wilson *et al.* (2000), ARMA models are used to produce forecasts that are combined with those from different models to improve the out-of-sample predictive ability of individual models. Their study is conducted in three regions – the United States, the United Kingdom and Australia – and the focus is on securitised real estate returns. We now briefly discuss how time series models are employed in these studies.

Tse (1997)

Tse applies ARIMA models to price indices for office and industrial real estate in Hong Kong. The prices are for the direct market and are drawn from two sources: the *Property Review* and the *Hong Kong Monthly Digest of Statistics*. His sample consists of quarterly data for the period 1Q1980 to 2Q1995. Tse considers this sample of sixty-two observations sufficient to fit such models as are founded on those of Holden, Peel and Thompson (1990), who indicate that a sample of fifty observations enables ARIMA modelling. The office and industrial price series are deflated with the consumer price index.

For both the office and the industrial sectors, the best ARIMA model is of the order (2,1,1). The AR terms suggest that the cyclical effects generated in past information are transmitted endogenously to current prices. The author applies the Box–Pierce chi-squared test to examine whether the residuals are white noise. For both the office and industrial series, the ARIMA (2,1,1) passes the test, since there is no further pattern left in their residual series. The application of Chow tests for structural stability was not possible on account of the short sample period (or, rather, the short sub-periods when the original sample had to be split). Nevertheless, Tse reiterates the contention of Clements and Hendry (1996) that ARIMAs can be less susceptible to structural breaks. He argues that ARIMA models may do better in periods of unforeseen structural breaks than causal econometric models, because the former are adaptive models that are updated all the time to establish patterns in the data.

Tse examines the forecast accuracy over a three-quarter period 3Q1995 to 1Q1996. The ARIMAs indicate a fall in the office and industrial prices of 18.3 per cent and 24.6 per cent, respectively, which, according to Tse, is the right direction and very close to the actual prices. Tse also uses several other forecast evaluation metrics (defined in the following chapter) to examine the in-sample improvement of the ARIMA to the naive 'no change' forecast. On the basis of this analysis of the forecast errors, he also concludes that the ARIMA models fit industrial values better than office values.

Wilson *et al.* (2000)

Wilson *et al.* investigate the ability of time series models to predict turning points in securitised real estate indices. The ARIMA class is one of the time series techniques that these authors apply. Wilson *et al.* fit ARIMA models to quarterly price return series. The price return series are derived from monthly price databases. In the United States, the All REIT (equity and mortgage REITs) index series is available from January 1972 to November 1998. In the absence of a comparable securitised real estate series in the United Kingdom, they splice two *Financial Times* real estate indices and derive a series that starts in January 1969 and ends in February 1999. For Australia, they take the Listed Property Trust Index from January 1973 to February 1999. The authors collapse the monthly data into quarterly observations by taking a simple average of the monthly data. The quarterly series thus obtained maintain the shape of the original series but are smoother. The authors use quarterly data in order to compare the results of this study with those of econometric models (in a separate study), in which economic indicators of quarterly frequency are used.

Wilson *et al.* point to the following requirements in the diagnostic checking of the tentatively identified ARIMA models: (i) all the parameters are statistically significant, (ii) all the models are invertible (that is, the series can be represented by a convergent autoregressive process) and (iii) no more parameters can be added to the model. These diagnostic checks guarantee that the tentatively identified model is adequate, but they do not guarantee the best ARIMA model (the one that best fits the data, and perhaps produces the most accurate forecasts).

The ARIMA models that were selected are as follows.

- For the United States and the United Kingdom: the All REIT and the UK securitised series are differenced once. The ARIMA model does not contain MA terms but it includes four AR terms: AR(1), AR(4), AR(8) and AR(12). All four AR terms are statistically significant.
- For Australia: the ARIMA model is of the form (1,1,0) – that is, it contained only an AR(1) term.

The authors examine the performance of the models from both in-sample and out-of-sample perspectives. For the out-of-sample exercise, they generate dynamic (out-of-sample) forecasts for the eight-quarter period 4Q1996 to 3Q1998 for the US data and 1Q1997 to 4Q1998 for the UK and Australian data.

In the United States and the United Kingdom, the ARIMA model forecasts are quite similar. In both cases, the models do not predict the significant increase in prices by June 1998 and the subsequent fall to the end of the out-of-sample period. By the end of the forecast period, however, the models are fairly accurate in closely predicting the value of the indices, but they have missed the path of the sharp rise in prices and their subsequent steep fall. In Australia, over the out-of-sample period, the index is rising. The model predicts this constant rising trend, but it under-predicts the magnitude. Based on the actual and forecast values that the authors report in the paper, we calculate positive mean errors (actual minus forecast values), which are the result of model under-prediction. The UK ARIMA yields the lowest absolute forecast errors.

Key concepts

The key terms to be able to define and explain from this chapter are

- ARIMA models
- invertible MA
- autocorrelation function
- Box–Jenkins methodology
- exponential smoothing
- multi-step forecast
- Ljung–Box test
- Wold's decomposition theorem
- partial autocorrelation function
- information criteria
- out-of-sample

Appendix: Some derivations of properties of ARMA models

8A.1 Deriving the autocorrelation function for an MA process

Consider the following MA(2) process,

$$y_t = u_t + \theta_1 u_{t-1} + \theta_2 u_{t-2} \tag{8A.1}$$

where u_t is a zero mean white noise process with variance σ^2.

(1) Calculate the mean and variance of y_t.
(2) Derive the autocorrelation function for this process – i.e. express the autocorrelations, $\tau_1, \tau_2, \ldots$, as functions of the parameters θ_1 and θ_2.
(3) If $\theta_1 = -0.5$ and $\theta_2 = 0.25$, sketch the acf of y_t.

Solution

(1) If $\text{E}(u_t) = 0$, then $\text{E}(u_{t-i}) = 0 \ \forall \ i$.
The expected value of the error term is therefore zero for all time periods. Taking expectations of both sides of (8A.1) gives

$$\begin{aligned} \text{E}(y_t) &= \text{E}(u_t + \theta_1 u_{t-1} + \theta_2 u_{t-2}) \\ &= \text{E}(u_t) + \theta_1 \text{E}(u_{t-1}) + \theta_2 \text{E}(u_{t-2}) = 0 \qquad (8\text{A}.2) \\ \text{var}(y_t) &= \text{E}[y_t - \text{E}(y_t)][y_t - \text{E}(y_t)] \qquad (8\text{A}.3) \end{aligned}$$

but $\text{E}(y_t) = 0$, so that the last component in each set of square brackets in (8A.3) is zero, and this reduces to

$$\text{var}(y_t) = \text{E}[(y_t)(y_t)] \tag{8A.4}$$

Replacing y_t in (8A.4) with the RHS of (8A.1),

$$\text{var}(y_t) = \text{E}[(u_t + \theta_1 u_{t-1} + \theta_2 u_{t-2})(u_t + \theta_1 u_{t-1} + \theta_2 u_{t-2})] \tag{8A.5}$$

$$\text{var}(y_t) = \text{E}\left[u_t^2 + \theta_1^2 u_{t-1}^2 + \theta_2^2 u_{t-2}^2 + \textit{cross-products}\right] \tag{8A.6}$$

$\text{E}[\textit{cross-products}] = 0$, however, since $\text{cov}(u_t, u_{t-s}) = 0$ for $s \neq 0$. '*Cross-products*' is thus a catch-all expression for all the terms in u that have different time subscripts, such as $u_{t-1}, u_{t-2}, u_{t-5}, u_{t-20}$, etc. Again, one does not need to worry about these cross-product terms, as they are effectively the autocovariances of u_t, which will all be zero by definition since u_t is a random error process, which will have zero autocovariances (except at lag 0). Therefore

$$\text{var}(y_t) = \gamma_0 = E\left[u_t^2 + \theta_1^2 u_{t-1}^2 + \theta_2^2 u_{t-2}^2\right] \tag{8A.7}$$

$$\text{var}(y_t) = \gamma_0 = \sigma^2 + \theta_1^2\sigma^2 + \theta_2^2\sigma^2 \tag{8A.8}$$

$$\text{var}(y_t) = \gamma_0 = \left(1 + \theta_1^2 + \theta_2^2\right)\sigma^2 \tag{8A.9}$$

γ_0 can also be interpreted as the autocovariance at lag 0.

(2) Calculating now the acf of y_t, first determine the autocovariances and then the autocorrelations by dividing the autocovariances by the variance.

The autocovariance at lag 1 is given by

$$\gamma_1 = \text{E}[y_t - E(y_t)][y_{t-1} - E(y_{t-1})] \tag{8A.10}$$

$$\gamma_1 = \text{E}[y_t][y_{t-1}] \tag{8A.11}$$

$$\gamma_1 = \text{E}[(u_t + \theta_1 u_{t-1} + \theta_2 u_{t-2})(u_{t-1} + \theta_1 u_{t-2} + \theta_2 u_{t-3})] \tag{8A.12}$$

Again, ignoring the cross-products, (8A.12) can be written as

$$\gamma_1 = \text{E}\left[\left(\theta_1 u_{t-1}^2 + \theta_1\theta_2 u_{t-2}^2\right)\right] \tag{8A.13}$$

$$\gamma_1 = \theta_1\sigma^2 + \theta_1\theta_2\sigma^2 \tag{8A.14}$$

$$\gamma_1 = (\theta_1 + \theta_1\theta_2)\sigma^2 \tag{8A.15}$$

The autocovariance at lag 2 is given by

$$\gamma_2 = \text{E}[y_t - E(y_t)][y_{t-2} - E(y_{t-2})] \tag{8A.16}$$

$$\gamma_2 = \text{E}[y_t][y_{t-2}] \tag{8A.17}$$

$$\gamma_2 = \text{E}[(u_t + \theta_1 u_{t-1} + \theta_2 u_{t-2})(u_{t-2} + \theta_1 u_{t-3} + \theta_2 u_{t-4})] \tag{8A.18}$$

$$\gamma_2 = \text{E}[(\theta_2 u_{t-2}^2)] \tag{8A.19}$$

$$\gamma_2 = \theta_2\sigma^2 \tag{8A.20}$$

The autocovariance at lag 3 is given by

$$\gamma_3 = \text{E}[y_t - \text{E}(y_t)][y_{t-3} - \text{E}(y_{t-3})] \tag{8A.21}$$

$$\gamma_3 = \text{E}[y_t][y_{t-3}] \tag{8A.22}$$

$$\gamma_3 = \text{E}[(u_t + \theta_1 u_{t-1} + \theta_2 u_{t-2})(u_{t-3} + \theta_1 u_{t-4} + \theta_2 u_{t-5})] \tag{8A.23}$$

$$\gamma_3 = 0 \tag{8A.24}$$

Therefore $\gamma_s = 0$ for $s > 2$. All autocovariances for the MA(2) process will be zero for any lag length, s, greater than two.
The autocorrelation at lag 0 is given by

$$\tau_0 = \frac{\gamma_0}{\gamma_0} = 1 \tag{8A.25}$$

The autocorrelation at lag 1 is given by

$$\tau_1 = \frac{\gamma_1}{\gamma_0} = \frac{(\theta_1 + \theta_1\theta_2)\sigma^2}{(1 + \theta_1^2 + \theta_2^2)\sigma^2} = \frac{(\theta_1 + \theta_1\theta_2)}{(1 + \theta_1^2 + \theta_2^2)} \tag{8A.26}$$

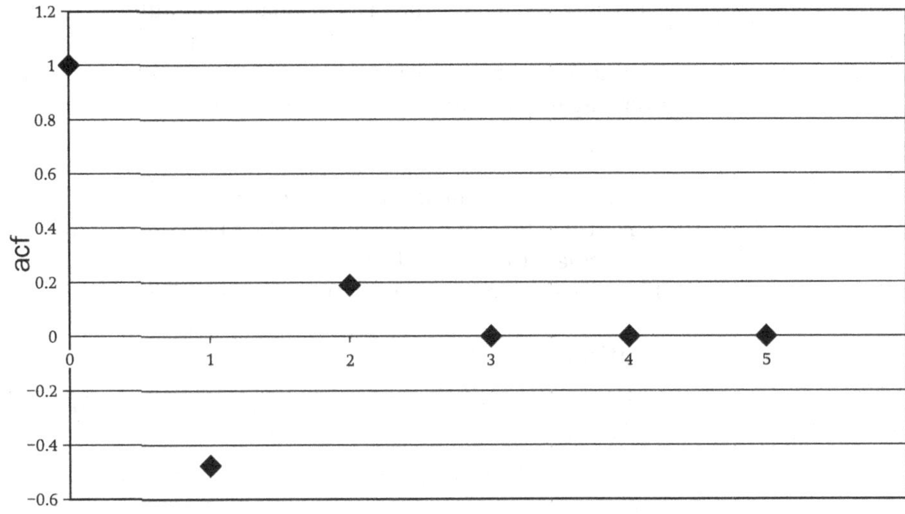

Figure 8.18 Autocorrelation function for sample MA(2) process

The autocorrelation at lag 2 is given by

$$\tau_2 = \frac{\gamma_2}{\gamma_0} = \frac{(\theta_2)\sigma^2}{(1+\theta_1^2+\theta_2^2)\sigma^2} = \frac{\theta_2}{(1+\theta_1^2+\theta_2^2)} \tag{8A.27}$$

The autocorrelation at lag 3 is given by

$$\tau_3 = \frac{\gamma_3}{\gamma_0} = 0 \tag{8A.28}$$

The autocorrelation at lag s is given by

$$\tau_s = \frac{\gamma_s}{\gamma_0} = 0 \ \forall \ s > 2 \tag{8A.29}$$

(3) For $\theta_1 = -0.5$ and $\theta_2 = 0.25$, substituting these into the formulae above gives the first two autocorrelation coefficients as $\tau_1 = -0.476$, $\tau_2 = 0.190$. Autocorrelation coefficients for lags greater than two will all be zero for an MA(2) model. Thus the acf plot will appear as in figure 8.18.

8A.2 Deriving the properties of AR models

Wold's decomposition theorem states that any stationary series can be decomposed into the sum of two unrelated processes, a purely deterministic part and a purely stochastic part, which will be an MA(∞). A simpler way of stating this in the context of AR modelling is that any stationary autoregressive process of order p with no constant and no other terms can be expressed as an infinite-order moving average model. This result is important for deriving the autocorrelation function for an autoregressive process.

The characteristics of an autoregressive process are as follows. The (unconditional) mean of y is given by

$$E(y_t) = \frac{\mu}{1-\phi_1-\phi_2-\cdots-\phi_p} \tag{8A.30}$$

For any AR model that is stationary, the autocorrelation function will decay geometrically to zero.[1] These characteristics of an autoregressive process are now derived from first principles below using an illustrative example. Consider the following AR(1) model:

$$y_t = \mu + \phi_1 y_{t-1} + u_t \tag{8A.31}$$

(1) Calculate the (unconditional) mean y_t.
For the remainder of the question, set the constant to zero ($\mu = 0$) for simplicity.
(2) Calculate the (unconditional) variance of y_t.
(3) Derive the autocorrelation function for this process.

Solution

(1) The unconditional mean will be given by the expected value of expression (8A.31),

$$E(y_t) = E(\mu + \phi_1 y_{t-1}) \tag{8A.32}$$
$$E(y_t) = \mu + \phi_1 E(y_{t-1}) \tag{8A.33}$$

but also by

$$y_{t-1} = \mu + \phi_1 y_{t-2} + u_{t-1} \tag{8A.34}$$

So, replacing y_{t-1} in (8A.33) with the RHS of (8A.34),

$$E(y_t) = \mu + \phi_1(\mu + \phi_1 E(y_{t-2})) \tag{8A.35}$$
$$E(y_t) = \mu + \phi_1 \mu + \phi_1^2 E(y_{t-2}) \tag{8A.36}$$

Lagging (8A.34) by a further one period,

$$y_{t-2} = \mu + \phi_1 y_{t-3} + u_{t-2} \tag{8A.37}$$

Repeating the steps given above one more time,

$$E(y_t) = \mu + \phi_1 \mu + \phi_1^2(\mu + \phi_1 E(y_{t-3})) \tag{8A.38}$$
$$E(y_t) = \mu + \phi_1 \mu + \phi_1^2 \mu + \phi_1^3 E(y_{t-3}) \tag{8A.39}$$

It is hoped that readers will by now be able to see a pattern emerging. Making n such substitutions would give

$$E(y_t) = \mu(1 + \phi_1 + \phi_1^2 + \cdots + \phi_1^{n-1}) + \phi_1^t E(y_{t-n}) \tag{8A.40}$$

So long as the model is stationary – i.e. $|\phi_1| < 1$ – then $\phi_1^\infty = 0$. Therefore, taking limits as $n \rightarrow \infty$, then $lim_{n\rightarrow\infty} \phi_1^t E(y_{t-n}) = 0$, and so

$$E(y_t) = \mu(1 + \phi_1 + \phi_1^2 + \cdots) \tag{8A.41}$$

Recall the rule of algebra that the finite sum of an infinite number of geometrically declining terms in a series is given by 'first term in series divided by (one minus common difference)', where the common difference is the quantity that

[1] Note that the autocorrelation function will not follow an exact geometric sequence but, rather, the absolute value of the autocorrelation coefficients is bounded by a geometric series. This means that the autocorrelation function does not have to be monotonically decreasing and may change sign.

each term in the series is multiplied by to arrive at the next term. It can thus be stated from (8A.41) that

$$E(y_t) = \frac{\mu}{1 - \phi_1} \tag{8A.42}$$

Thus the expected or mean value of an autoregressive process of order one is given by the intercept parameter divided by one minus the autoregressive coefficient.

(2) Calculating now the variance of y_t, with μ set to zero,

$$y_t = \phi_1 y_{t-1} + u_t \tag{8A.43}$$

This can be written equivalently as

$$y_t(1 - \phi_1 L) = u_t \tag{8A.44}$$

From Wold's decomposition theorem, the AR(p) can be expressed as an MA(∞),

$$y_t = (1 - \phi_1 L)^{-1} u_t \tag{8A.45}$$

$$y_t = (1 + \phi_1 L + \phi_1^2 L^2 + \cdots) u_t \tag{8A.46}$$

or

$$y_t = u_t + \phi_1 u_{t-1} + \phi_1^2 u_{t-2} + \phi_1^3 u_{t-3} + \cdots \tag{8A.47}$$

So long as $|\phi_1| < 1$ – i.e. so long as the process for y_t is stationary – this sum will converge.

From the definition of the variance of any random variable y, it is possible to write

$$\text{var}(y_t) = \text{E}[y_t - \text{E}(y_t)][y_t - \text{E}(y_t)] \tag{8A.48}$$

but $\text{E}(y_t) = 0$, since μ is set to zero to obtain (8A.48) above. Therefore

$$\text{var}(y_t) = \text{E}[(y_t)(y_t)] \tag{8A.49}$$

$$\text{var}(y_t) = \text{E}[(u_t + \phi_1 u_{t-1} + \phi_1^2 u_{t-2} + \cdots)(u_t + \phi_1 u_{t-1} + \phi_1^2 u_{t-2} + \cdots)] \tag{8A.50}$$

$$\text{var}(y_t) = \text{E}\left[u_t^2 + \phi_1^2 u_{t-1}^2 + \phi_1^4 u_{t-2}^2 + \cdots + \textit{cross-products}\right] \tag{8A.51}$$

As discussed above, the 'cross-products' can be set to zero:

$$\text{var}(y_t) = \gamma_0 = \text{E}\left[u_t^2 + \phi_1^2 u_{t-1}^2 + \phi_1^4 u_{t-2}^2 + \cdots\right] \tag{8A.52}$$

$$\text{var}(y_t) = \sigma^2 + \phi_1^2 \sigma^2 + \phi_1^4 \sigma^2 + \cdots \tag{8A.53}$$

$$\text{var}(y_t) = \sigma^2 \left(1 + \phi_1^2 + \phi_1^4 + \cdots\right) \tag{8A.54}$$

Provided that $|\phi_1| < 1$, the infinite sum in (8A.54) can be written as

$$\text{var}(y_t) = \frac{\sigma^2}{\left(1 - \phi_1^2\right)} \tag{8A.55}$$

(3) Turning now to the calculation of the autocorrelation function, the autocovariances must first be calculated. This is achieved by following similar algebraic manipulations to those for the variance above, starting with the definition of the

autocovariances for a random variable. The autocovariances for lags 1, 2, 3, ..., s, will be denoted by $\gamma_1, \gamma_2, \gamma_3, \ldots, \gamma_s$, as previously.

$$\gamma_1 = \text{cov}(y_t, y_{t-1}) = \text{E}[y_t - E(y_t)][y_{t-1} - E(y_{t-1})] \tag{8A.56}$$

Since μ has been set to zero, $\text{E}(y_t) = 0$ and $\text{E}(y_{t-1}) = 0$, so

$$\gamma_1 = \text{E}[y_t y_{t-1}] \tag{8A.57}$$

under the result above that $\text{E}(y_t) = \text{E}(y_{t-1}) = 0$. Thus

$$\gamma_1 = \text{E}[(u_t + \phi_1 u_{t-1} + \phi_1^2 u_{t-2} + \cdots)(u_{t-1} + \phi_1 u_{t-2} + \phi_1^2 u_{t-3} + \cdots)] \tag{8A.58}$$

$$\gamma_1 = \text{E}[\phi_1 u_{t-1}^2 + \phi_1^3 u_{t-2}^2 + \cdots + \textit{cross-products}] \tag{8A.59}$$

Again, the cross-products can be ignored, so that

$$\gamma_1 = \phi_1\sigma^2 + \phi_1^3\sigma^2 + \phi_1^5\sigma^2 + \cdots \tag{8A.60}$$

$$\gamma_1 = \phi_1\sigma^2(1 + \phi_1^2 + \phi_1^4 + \cdots) \tag{8A.61}$$

$$\gamma_1 = \frac{\phi_1\sigma^2}{(1 - \phi_1^2)} \tag{8A.62}$$

For the second autocovariance,

$$\gamma_2 = \text{cov}(y_t, y_{t-2}) = \text{E}[y_t - \text{E}(y_t)][y_{t-2} - \text{E}(y_{t-2})] \tag{8A.63}$$

Using the same rules as applied above for the lag 1 covariance,

$$\gamma_2 = \text{E}[y_t, y_{t-2}] \tag{8A.64}$$

$$\gamma_2 = \text{E}[(u_t + \phi_1 u_{t-1} + \phi_1^2 u_{t-2} + \cdots)(u_{t-2} + \phi_1 u_{t-3} + \phi_1^2 u_{t-4} + \cdots)] \tag{8A.65}$$

$$\gamma_2 = \text{E}[\phi_1^2 u_{t-2}^2 + \phi_1^4 u_{t-3}^2 + \cdots + \textit{cross-products}] \tag{8A.66}$$

$$\gamma_2 = \phi_1^2\sigma^2 + \phi_1^4\sigma^2 + \cdots \tag{8A.67}$$

$$\gamma_2 = \phi_1^2\sigma^2(1 + \phi_1^2 + \phi_1^4 + \cdots) \tag{8A.68}$$

$$\gamma_2 = \frac{\phi_1^2\sigma^2}{(1 - \phi_1^2)} \tag{8A.69}$$

By now it should be possible to see a pattern emerging. If these steps were repeated for γ_3, the following expression would be obtained,

$$\gamma_3 = \frac{\phi_1^3\sigma^2}{(1 - \phi_1^2)} \tag{8A.70}$$

and, for any lag s, the autocovariance would be given by

$$\gamma_s = \frac{\phi_1^s\sigma^2}{(1 - \phi_1^2)} \tag{8A.71}$$

The acf can now be obtained by dividing the covariances by the variance, so that

$$\tau_0 = \frac{\gamma_0}{\gamma_0} = 1 \tag{8A.72}$$

$$\tau_1 = \frac{\gamma_1}{\gamma_0} = \frac{\left(\dfrac{\phi_1\sigma^2}{(1-\phi_1^2)}\right)}{\left(\dfrac{\sigma^2}{(1-\phi_1^2)}\right)} = \phi_1 \tag{8A.73}$$

$$\tau_2 = \frac{\gamma_2}{\gamma_0} = \frac{\left(\dfrac{\phi_1^2\sigma^2}{(1-\phi_1^2)}\right)}{\left(\dfrac{\sigma^2}{(1-\phi_1^2)}\right)} = \phi_1^2 \tag{8A.74}$$

$$\tau_3 = \phi_1^3 \tag{8A.75}$$

The autocorrelation at lag s is given by

$$\tau_s = \phi_1^s \tag{8A.76}$$

which means that $\text{corr}(y_t, y_{t-s}) = \phi_1^s$. Note that use of the Yule–Walker equations would have given the same answer.

9 Forecast evaluation

Learning outcomes

In this chapter, you will learn how to

- compute forecast evaluation tests;
- distinguish between and evaluate in-sample and out-of-sample forecasts;
- undertake comparisons of forecasts from alternative models;
- assess the gains from combining forecasts;
- run rolling forecast exercises; and
- calculate sign and direction predictions.

In previous chapters, we focused on diagnostic tests that the real estate analyst can compute to choose between alternative models. Once a model or competing models have been selected, we really want to know how accurately these models forecast. Forecast adequacy tests complement the diagnostic checking that we performed in earlier chapters and can be used as additional criteria to choose between two or more models that have satisfactory diagnostics. In addition, of course, assessing a model's forecast performance is also of interest in itself.

Determining the forecasting accuracy of a model is an important test of its adequacy. Some econometricians would go as far as to suggest that the statistical adequacy of a model, in terms of whether it violates the CLRM assumptions or whether it contains insignificant parameters, is largely irrelevant if the model produces accurate forecasts.

This chapter presents commonly used forecast evaluation tests. The literature on forecast accuracy is large and expanding. In this chapter, we draw upon conventional forecast adequacy tests, the application of which generates useful information concerning the forecasting ability of different models.

At the outset we should point out that forecast evaluation can take place with a number of different tests. The choice of which to use depends largely on the objectives of the forecast evaluation exercise. These objectives and tasks to accomplish in the forecast evaluation process are illustrated in this chapter. In addition, we review a number of studies that undertake forecast evaluation so as to illustrate alternative aspects of and approaches to the evaluation process, all of which have practical value.

The computation of the forecast metrics we present below revolves around the forecast errors. We define the forecast error as the actual value minus the forecast value (although, in the literature, the forecast error is sometimes specified as the forecast value minus the actual value). We can categorise four influences that determine the size of the forecast error.

(1) Poor specification on the part of the model.
(2) Structural events: major events that change the nature of the relationship between the variables permanently.
(3) Inaccurate inputs to the model.
(4) Random events: unpredictable circumstances that are short-lived.

The forecast evaluation analysis in this chapter aims to expose poor model specification that is reflected in the forecast error. We neutralise the impact of inaccurate inputs on the forecast error by assuming perfect information about the future values of the inputs. Our analysis is still subject to structural impacts and random events on the forecast error, however. Unfortunately, there is not much that can be done – at least, not quantitatively – when these occur out of the sample.

9.1 Forecast tests

An object of crucial importance in measuring forecast accuracy is the loss function, defined as $L(A_{t+n}, F_{t+n,t})$ or $L(\hat{e}_{t+n,t})$, where A is the realisations (actual values), F is the forecast series, $\hat{e}_{t+n,t}$ is the forecast error $A_{t+n} - F_{t+n,t}$ and n is the forecast horizon. A_{t+n} is the realisation at time $t+n$ and $F_{t+n,t}$ is the forecast for time $t+n$ made at time t (n periods beforehand). The loss function charts the 'loss' or 'cost' associated with the forecasts and realisations (see Diebold and Lopez, 1996). Loss functions differ, as they depend on the situation at hand (see Diebold, 1993). The loss function of the forecast by a government agency will differ from that of a company forecasting the economy or forecasting real estate. A forecaster may be interested in volatility or mean accuracy or the contribution of alternative models to more accurate forecasting. Thus the appropriate accuracy measure arises from the loss function that best describes the utility of the forecast user regarding the forecast error.

In the literature on forecasting, several measures have been proposed to describe the loss function. These measures of forecast quality can be grouped into a number of categories, including forecast bias, sign predictability, forecast accuracy with emphasis on large errors, forecast efficiency and encompassing. The evaluation of the forecast performance on these measures takes place through the computation of the appropriate statistics.

The question frequently arises as to whether there is systematic bias in a forecast. It is obviously a desirable property that the forecast is not biased. The null hypothesis is that the model produces forecasts that lead to errors with a zero mean. A t-test can be calculated to determine whether there is a statistically significant negative or positive bias in the forecasts. For simplicity of exposition, letting the subscript i now denote each observation for which the forecast has been made and the error calculated, the mean error ME or mean forecast error MFE is defined as

$$ME = \frac{1}{n}\sum_{i=1}^{n}\hat{e}_i \tag{9.1}$$

where n is the number of periods that the model forecasts.

Another conventional error measure is the mean absolute error MAE, which is the average of the differences between the actual and forecast values in absolute terms, and it is also sometimes termed the mean absolute forecast error MAFE. Thus an error of −2 per cent or +2 per cent will have the same impact on the MAE of 2 per cent. The MAE formula is

$$MAE = \frac{1}{n}\sum_{i=1}^{n}|\hat{e}_i| \tag{9.2}$$

Since both ME and MAE are scale-dependent measures (i.e. they vary with the scale of the variable being forecast), a variant often reported is the mean absolute percentage error MAPE:

$$MAPE = \frac{100\%}{n}\sum_{i=1}^{n}\left|\frac{A_i - F_i}{A_i}\right| \tag{9.3}$$

The mean absolute error and the mean absolute percentage error both use absolute values of the forecast errors, which prevent positive and negative errors from cancelling each other out. The above measures are used to assess how closely individual predictions track their corresponding real data figures. In practice, when the series under investigation is already expressed in percentage terms, the MAE criterion is sufficient. Therefore, if we forecast rent growth (expressed as a percentage), MAE is used. If we forecast the actual rent or a rent index, however, MAPE facilitates forecast comparisons.

Another set of tests commonly used in forecast comparisons builds on the variance of the forecast errors. An important statistic from which other metrics are computed is the mean squared error MSE or, equivalently, the mean squared forecast error MSFE:

$$MSE = \frac{1}{n}\sum_{i=1}^{n} \hat{e}_i^2 \tag{9.4}$$

MSE will have units of the square of the data – i.e. of $A_t{}^2$. In order to produce a statistic that is measured on the same scale as the data, the root mean squared error RMSE is proposed:

$$RMSE = \sqrt{MSE} \tag{9.5}$$

The MSE and RMSE measures have been popular methods to aggregate the deviations of the forecasts from their actual trajectory. The smaller the values of the MSE and RMSE, the more accurate the forecasts. Due to its similar scale with the dependent variable, the RMSE of a forecast can be compared to the standard error of the model. An RMSE higher than, say, twice the standard error does not suggest a good set of forecasts. The RMSE and MSE are useful when comparing different methods applied to the same set of data, but they should not be used when comparing data sets that have different scales (see Chatfield, 1988, and Collopy and Armstrong, 1992).

The MSE and RMSE impose a greater penalty for large errors. The RMSE is a better performance criterion than measures such as MAE and MAPE when the variable of interest undergoes fluctuations and turning points. If the forecast misses these large changes, the RMSE will disproportionately penalise the larger errors. If the variable follows a steadier path, then other measures such as the mean absolute error may be preferred. It follows that the RMSE heavily penalises forecasts with a few large errors relative to forecasts with a large number of small errors. This is important for samples of the small size that we often encounter in real estate. A few large errors will produce higher RMSE and MSE statistics and may lead to the conclusion that the model is less fit for forecasting. Since these measures are sensitive to outliers, some authors (such as Armstrong, 2001) have recommended caution in their use for forecast accuracy evaluation.

Given that the RMSE is scale-dependent, the root mean squared percentage error (RMSPE) can also be used:

$$RMSPE = \sqrt{\frac{100\%}{n}\sum_{i=1}^{n}\left(\frac{A_i - F_i}{A_i}\right)^2} \tag{9.6}$$

As for MAE versus MAPE, if the series we forecast is in percentage terms, the RMSE suffices to illustrate comparisons and use of the RMSPE is unnecessary.

Theil (1966, 1971) utilises the RMSE metric to propose an inequality coefficient that measures the difference between the predicted and actual values in terms of change. An appropriate scalar in the denominator restricts the variations of the coefficient between zero and one:

$$U1 = \frac{RMSE}{\sqrt{\frac{1}{n}\sum A_i^2} + \sqrt{\frac{1}{n}\sum F_i^2}} \tag{9.7}$$

Theil's $U1$ coefficient ranges between zero and one; the closer the computed $U1$ for the forecast is to zero, the better the prediction.

The MSE can be decomposed as the sum of three components that collectively explain 100 per cent of its variation. These components are the bias proportion, the variance proportion and the covariance proportion. These components are defined as

$$\textit{Bias proportion:} \quad \frac{(\bar{F} - \bar{A})^2}{MSE} \tag{9.8}$$

$$\textit{Variance proportion:} \quad \frac{(\sigma_F - \sigma_A)^2}{MSE} \tag{9.9}$$

$$\textit{Covariance proportion:} \quad \frac{2\sigma_F\sigma_A[1 - \rho(F, A)]}{MSE} \tag{9.10}$$

where $\bar{F}$ is the mean of the forecast values in the forecast period, $\bar{A}$ is the mean of the actual values in the forecast period, σ is the standard deviation and ρ is the correlation coefficient between A and F in the forecast period.

The bias proportion indicates the part of the systematic error in the forecasts that arises from the discrepancy of the average value of the forecast path from the mean of the actual path of the variable. Pindyck and Rubinfeld (1998) argue that a value above 0.1 or 0.2 is troubling. The variance proportion is an indicator of how different the variability of the forecasts is from that of the observed variable over the forecast horizon. Too large a value is also troubling. Finally, the covariance proportion measures the unsystematic error in the forecasts. The larger this component the better, since this would imply that most of the error is due to random events and does not arise from the inability of the model to replicate the mean of the actual series or its variance.

The second metric proposed by Theil, the $U2$ coefficient, assesses the contribution of the forecast against a naive rule (such as 'no change' – that is, the future values are forecast as the last available observed value) or, more generally, an alternative model:

$$U2 = \left(\frac{MSE}{MSE^{NAIVE}}\right)^{1/2} \tag{9.11}$$

Theil's $U2$ coefficient measures the adequacy of the forecast by the quadratic loss criterion. The $U2$ statistic takes a value of less than one if the model under investigation outperforms the naive one (since the MSE of the naive will be higher than the MSE of the model). If the naive model produces more accurate forecasts, the value of the $U2$ metric will be higher than one. Of course, the naive approach here does not need to be the 'no change' extrapolation or a random walk, but other methods such as an exponential smoothing or an MA model could be used. This criterion can be generalised in order to assess the contributions of an alternative model relative to a base model or an existing model that the forecaster has been using. Again, if $U2$ is less than one, the model under study (the MSE of which is shown in the numerator) is doing better than the base or existing model.

An alternative statistic to illustrate the gains from using one model instead of an alternative is a measure that is explored by Diebold and Kilian (1997) and Galbraith (2003). This metric is also based on the variance of the forecast error and measures the gain in reducing the value of the MSE from not using the forecasts from a competing model. In essence, this is another way to report results. This statistic is given by

$$C = \frac{MSE}{MSE_{ALT}} - 1 \tag{9.12}$$

where C, the proposed measure, compares the MSE of two forecasts.

Turning to the category of forecast efficiency, the conventional test involves running a regression of the form

$$\hat{e}_i = \alpha + \beta A_i + u_i \tag{9.13}$$

where A is the series of actual values. Forecast efficiency requires that $\alpha = \beta = 0$ (see Mincer and Zarnowitz, 1969). Equation (9.13) also provides the baseline for rationality. The right-hand side can be augmented with explanatory variables that the forecaster believes the forecasts do not capture. Forecast rationality implies that all coefficients should be zero in any such regression. According to Mincer and Zarnowitz, equation (9.13) can also be used to test for bias. If a forecast is unbiased then $\alpha = 0$.

Tsolacos and McGough (1999) apply similar tests to examine rationality in office construction in the United Kingdom. They test whether their model of UK office construction efficiently incorporates all available information, including that contained in the past values of construction and whether multi-span forecasts are obtained recursively. It is found that the estimated model incorporates all available information, and that this information is consistently applied to future time periods.

A regression-based test can also be used to examine forecast encompassing – that is, to examine whether the forecasts of a model encompass the forecasts of other models. A formal framework in the case of two competing forecasting models will require the estimation of a model by regressing the realised values on a constant and the two competing series of forecasts. If one forecast set encompasses the other, its regression coefficient will be one, and that of the other zero, with an intercept that also takes a value of zero. Hence the test equation is

$$A_i = \alpha_0 + \alpha_1 F_{1t} + \alpha_2 F_{2t} + u_i \tag{9.14}$$

where F_{1t} and F_{2t} are the two competing forecasts. If forecast F_{1t} encompasses forecast F_{2t}, α_1 should be statistically significant and close to one, whereas the coefficient α_2 will not be significantly different from zero.

9.1.1 *The difference between in-sample and out-of-sample forecasts*

These important concepts are defined and contrasted in box 9.1.

Box 9.1 Comparing in-sample and out-of-sample forecasts

- *In-sample forecasts* are those generated for the same set of data that was used to estimate the model's parameters. Essentially, in-sample forecasts are the fitted values from a regression model.
- One would expect the 'forecasts' of a model to be relatively good within the sample, for this reason.
- Therefore a sensible approach to model evaluation through an examination of forecast accuracy is not to use all the observations in estimating the model parameters but, rather, to hold some observations back.
- The latter sample, sometimes known as a *hold-out sample*, would be used to construct out-of-sample forecasts.

9.2 Application of forecast evaluation criteria to a simple regression model

9.2.1 *Forecast evaluation for Frankfurt rental growth*

Our objective here is to evaluate forecasts from the model we constructed for Frankfurt rent growth in chapter 7 for a period of five years, which is a commonly used horizon in real estate forecasting. It is the practice in

Table 9.1 Regression models for Frankfurt office rents

Independent variables	1982–2002 Coefficient	1982–2002 t-ratio	1982–2007 Coefficient	1982–2007 t-ratio
C	−6.81	−1.8	−6.39	−1.9
ΔVAC_{t-1}	−3.13	−2.5	−2.19	−2.7
$OFSg_t$	4.72	3.2	4.55	3.3
Adjusted R^2	0.53		0.59	
Durbin–Watson statistic	1.94		1.81	

Notes: The dependent variable is RRg, which is real rent growth; ΔVAC is the change in vacancy; $OFSg$ is services output growth in Frankfurt.

empirical work in real estate to evaluate the forecasts at the end of the sample, particularly in markets with small data samples, since it is usually thought that the most recent forecast performance best describes the immediate future performance. Examining forecast adequacy over successive other periods provides a more robust picture of the model's ability to forecast, however.

We evaluate the forecast accuracy of model A in table 7.4 in the five-year period 2003 to 2007. We estimate the model until 2002 and we forecast the remaining five years in the sample. Table 9.1 presents the model estimates over the shorter sample period, along with the results we presented in table 7.4 for the whole sample period.

We observe that the sensitivity of rent growth to vacancy falls when we include the last five years of the sample. In the last five years rent growth appears to have become more sensitive to $OFSg_t$. Adding five years of data therefore changes some of the characteristics of the model, which is to some extent a consequence of the small size of the sample in the first place.

For the computation of forecasts, the analyst has two options as to which coefficients to use. First, to use the sub-sample coefficients (for the period 1982 to 2002) or to apply those estimated for the whole sample. We would expect coefficients estimated over a longer sample to 'win' over coefficients obtained from shorter samples, as the model is trained with additional and more recent data and therefore the forecasts using the latter should be more accurate. This does not replicate the real-time forecasting process, however, since we use information that was not available at that time. If we use the full-sample coefficients, we obtain the fitted values we presented in chapter 7 (in-sample forecasts – see box 9.1). The data to calculate the

Table 9.2 Data and forecasts for rent growth in Frankfurt

				Sample for estimation	
	RRg	ΔVAC	*OFSg*	1982–2002	1982–2007
2002	−12.37	6.3	0.225		
2003	−18.01	5.7	0.056	−26.26	−19.93
2004	−13.30	3.4	0.618	−21.73	−16.06
2005	−3.64	0.1	0.893	−13.24	−9.77
2006	−4.24	−0.2	2.378	4.10	4.21
2007	3.48	−2.3	2.593	6.05	5.85

Note: The forecasts are for the period 2003–7.

Table 9.3 Calculation of forecasts for Frankfurt office rents

	Sample for estimation	
	1982–2002	1982–2007
2003	$-6.81 - 3.13 \times 6.3 + 4.72 \times 0.056 = -26.26$	$-6.39 - 2.19 \times 6.3 + 4.55 \times 0.056 = -19.93$
2004	$-6.81 - 3.13 \times 5.7 + 4.72 \times 0.618 = -21.73$	$-6.39 - 2.19 \times 5.7 + 4.55 \times 0.618 = -16.06$
⋮	⋮	⋮
2007	$-6.81 - 3.13 \times -0.2 + 4.72 \times 2.593 = 6.05$	$-6.39 - 2.19 \times -0.2 + 4.55 \times 2.593 = 5.85$

forecasts are given in table 9.2, and table 9.3 demonstrates how to perform the calculations.

Hence the forecasts from the two models are calculated using the following formulae:

$$\text{sub-sample coefficients (1982–2002): } RRg_{03} = -6.81 - 3.13 \times \Delta VAC_{02} + 4.72 \times OFSg_{03} \quad (9.15)$$

$$\text{full-sample coefficients (1982–2007): } RRg_{03} = -6.39 - 2.19 \times \Delta VAC_{02} + 4.55 \times OFSg_{03} \quad (9.16)$$

For certain years the forecast from the sub-sample is more accurate than the full-sample model's – for example, in 2003. Overall, however, we would expect the full-sample coefficients to yield more accurate forecasts. A comparison of the forecasts with the actual values confirms this (e.g. in 2003 and 2005). From this comparison, we can obtain an idea of the size of the error, which is fairly large in 2005 and 2006 in particular. We proceed with the calculation of the forecast evaluation tests and undertake a formal assessment of forecast performance.

Table 9.4 shows the results of the forecast evaluation and their computation in detail. It should be easy for the reader to follow the steps and to see how the forecast test formulae of the previous section are applied. There are two panels in the table: panel (a) presents the forecasts with coefficients for the sample period 1982 to 2002 whereas panel (b) shows the forecasts computed with the coefficients estimated for the period 1982 to 2007. An observation to make before discussing the forecast test values is that both models predict the correct sign in four out of five years, which is certainly a good feature in terms of direction prediction. The mean error of model A is positive – that is, the forecast values tend to be lower than the actual values. Hence, on average, the model tends to under-predict the growth in rents (for example, rent growth was −18.01 per cent in 2003 but the model predicted −26.26 per cent). The mean error of the full sample coefficient model (model B) is zero – undoubtedly a desirable feature. This means that positive and negative errors (errors from under-predicting and over-predicting) cancel out and sum to zero. The absolute error is 7.4 per cent for the shorter sample model and 4.3 per cent for the full sample model. A closer examination of the forecast errors shows that the better performance of the latter is owed to more accurate forecasts for four of the five years.

The mean squared errors of the forecast take the values 61.49 per cent and 25.18 per cent, respectively. As noted earlier, these statistics in themselves cannot help us to evaluate the variance of the forecast error, and are used to compare with forecasts obtained from other models. Hence the full sample model scores better, and, as a consequence, it does so on the RMSE measure too. The RMSE metric, which is the square root of MSE, can be compared with the standard error of the regression. For the shorter period, the RMSE value is 7.84 per cent. The standard error of the model is 8.2 per cent. The RMSE is lower and comfortably beats the rule of thumb (that an RMSE around two or more times higher than the standard error indicates a weak forecasting performance).

Theil's $U1$ statistic takes the value of 0.29, which is closer to zero than to one. This value suggests that the predictive performance of the model is moderate. A value of around 0.20 or less would have been preferred.

Finally, we assess whether the forecasts we obtained from the rent growth equation improve upon a naive alternative. As the naive alternative, we take the previous year's growth for the forecast period.[1] The real rent growth was −12.37 per cent in 2002, so this is the naive forecast for the next five years. Do the models outperform it? The computation of the $U2$ coefficient for the forecasts from the first model results in a value of 0.85, leading us to

[1] We could have taken the historical average as another naive forecast.

Table 9.4 Evaluation of forecasts for Frankfurt rent growth

(a) Sample coefficients for 1982–2002

(i)	(ii) A	(iii) F	(iv) $A-F$	(v) Abs $A-F$	(vi) Squ $A-F$	(vii) Squ A	(viii) Squ F	(ix) F^{Naive}	(x) Squ $A-F^{Naive}$
2003	−18.01	−26.26	8.25	8.25	68.06	324.36	689.59	−12.37	31.81
2004	−13.30	−21.73	8.43	8.43	71.06	176.89	472.19	−12.37	0.86
2005	−3.64	−13.24	9.60	9.60	92.16	13.25	175.30	−12.37	76.21
2006	−4.24	4.10	−8.34	−8.34	69.56	17.98	16.81	−12.37	66.10
2007	3.48	6.05	−2.57	−2.57	6.60	12.11	36.60	−12.37	251.22
Sum of column			15.37	37.19	307.45	544.59	1390.49		426.21
Forecast periods			5	5	5	5	5		5
Average of column			3.07	7.44	61.49	108.92	278.10		85.24
Square root of average of column					7.84	10.44	16.68		

Mean forecast error	3.07%	ME = 15.37/5
Mean absolute error	7.44%	MAE = 37.19/5
Mean squared error	61.49%	MSE = 307.45/5
Root mean squared error	7.84%	RMSE = $61.49^{1/2}$
Theil's $U1$ inequality coefficient	0.29	$U1 = 7.84/(10.44 + 16.68)$
Theil's $U2$ coefficient	0.85	$U2 = (61.49/85.24)^{1/2}$
C-statistic	−0.28	$C = (61.49/85.24) - 1$

(b) Sample coefficients for 1982–2007

(i)	(ii) A	(iii) F	(iv) $A-F$	(v) Abs $A-F$	(vi) Squ $A-F$	(vii) Squ A	(viii) Squ F	(ix) F^{Naive}	(x) Squ $A-F^{Naive}$
2003	−18.01	−19.93	1.92	1.92	3.69	324.36	397.20	−12.37	31.81
2004	−13.30	−16.06	2.76	2.76	7.62	176.89	257.92	−12.37	0.88
2005	−3.64	−9.77	6.13	6.13	37.58	13.25	95.45	−12.37	76.21
2006	−4.24	4.21	−8.45	−8.45	71.40	17.98	17.72	−12.37	66.05
2007	3.48	5.85	−2.37	−2.37	5.62	12.11	34.22	−12.37	251.16
Sum of column			−0.01	21.63	125.90	544.59	802.53		426.11
Forecast periods			5	5	5	5	5		5
Average of column			0.00	4.33	25.18	108.92	160.51		85.22
Square root of average of column					5.02	10.44	12.67		9.23

Mean forecast error	0.00%	ME = −0.01/5
Mean absolute error	4.33%	MAE = 21.63/5
Mean squared error	25.18%	MSE = 125.9/5
Root mean squared error	5.02%	RMSE = $25.18^{1/2}$
Theil's $U1$ inequality coefficient	0.22	$U1 = 5.02/(10.44 + 12.67)$
Theil's $U2$ coefficient	0.54	$U2 = (25.18/85.22)^{1/2}$
C-statistic	−0.70	$C = (25.18/85.22) - 1$

Notes: A: actual values; F: forecast values; $A-F$: actual minus forecast; Abs $A-F$: absolute actual minus forecast; *Squ*, A: squared actual, etc.; N denotes the naive forecast of −12.37 per cent (rent growth in the previous year, 2002).

Table 9.5 Estimates for an alternative model for Frankfurt rents

	1981–2002		1981–2007	
	Coefficient	t-ratio	Coefficient	t-ratio
Constant	5.06	0.9	−3.53	−0.8
VAC_t	−2.06	−2.9	−0.74	−2.4
$OFSg_t$	3.83	2.6	5.16	4.0
Adjusted R^2	0.57		0.57	
DW statistic	1.91		1.82	

Note: The dependent variable is *RRg*.

conclude that this model improves upon the naive model. A similar result is obtained from the C-metric. Since this statistic is negative, it denotes a better performance. The value of the $U1$ statistic for the full-sample model of 0.22 suggests better forecast performance. Theil's $U2$ value is less than one, and hence this model improves upon the forecasts of the naive approach. Similarly, the negative value of the C-statistic (−0.70) says that the model MSE is smaller than that of the naive forecast (70 per cent lower).

It should be made clear that the forecasts are produced assuming *complete knowledge* of the future values (post-2002) for both the changes in vacancy and output growth. In practice, of course, we will not know their future values when we forecast. What we do know with certainty, however, is that any errors in the forecasts for vacancy and output growth will be reflected in the error of the model. By assuming full knowledge, we eliminate this source of forecast error. The remaining error is largely related to model specification and random events.

9.2.2 *Comparative forecast evaluation*

In chapter 7, we presented another model of real rent growth that included the vacancy rate instead of changes in vacancy (model B in table 7.4). As we did with our main model for Frankfurt rents, we evaluate the forecast capacity of this model over the last five years of the sample and compare its forecasts with those from the main model (table 9.4). We first present estimates of model B for the shorter sample period and the whole period in table 9.5.

The estimation of the models over the two sample periods does not affect the explanatory power, whereas in both cases the DW statistic is within the non-rejection region, pointing to no serial correlation. The observation we made of the previous model regarding the coefficients on vacancy and output can also be made in the case of this one. By adding five observations (2003 to 2007), the vacancy coefficient more than halves, suggesting a lower impact on real rent growth. On the other hand, the coefficient on $OFSg_t$ denotes a higher sensitivity.

Using the coefficients estimated for the sample period 1981 to 2002, we obtain forecasts for 2003 to 2007. We also examine the in-sample forecast adequacy of the model – that is, generating the forecasts using the whole-sample coefficients. By now, the reader should be familiar with how the forecasts are calculated, but we present these for model B of Frankfurt rents in table 9.6.

When model B is used for the out-of-sample forecasting, it performs very poorly. It under-predicts by a considerable margin every single year. The mean absolute error is 17.9 per cent, compared with 7.4 per cent from the main model. Every forecast measure is worse than the main model's (model A in (7.4)): the MSE, RMSE and $U1$ statistics for the model B forecasts all take higher values. Theil's $U2$ statistic is higher than one and the C-statistic is positive, both suggesting that this model performs worse than the naive forecast.

This weak forecast performance is linked to the fact that the model attached a high weight to vacancy (coefficient value −2.06) whereas, from the full-sample estimations, the magnitude of this coefficient was −0.74. With vacancy rates remaining high, a coefficient of −2.06 damped rent growth significantly. One may ask why this significant change in coefficient happened. It is quite a significant adjustment indeed, which we attribute largely to the increase in the structural vacancy rate. It could also be a data issue.

The in-sample forecasts from model B improve upon the accuracy of the out-of-sample forecasts, as would be expected, given that we have used all the information in the sample to build the model. Nontheless, it does not predict the positive rent growth in 2007, but it does forecast negative growth in 2006 whereas the main model predicted positive growth. The MAE, RMSE and $U1$ criteria suggest that the in-sample forecasts from model B are marginally better than the main model's. A similar observation is made for the improvement in the naive forecasts.

Does this mean that the good in-sample forecast of model B will be reflected in the out-of-sample performance from now on? Over the 2003 to 2007 period the Frankfurt office market experienced adjustments that reduced the sensitivity of rent growth to vacancy. If these conditions continue to prevail, then our second model is liable to large errors. It is likely, however, that the coefficient on the second model has gravitated to a more stable value, based on the assumption that some influence from the yield

Table 9.6 Evaluating the forecasts from the alternative model for Frankfurt office rents

(a) Sample coefficients for 1982–2002

(i)	(ii)	(iii)	(iv)	(v)	(vi)	(vii)	(viii)	(ix)	(x)
				Abs	*Squ*	*Squ*	*Squ*		*Squ*
	A	F	$A-F$	$A-F$	$A-F$	A	F	F^{Naive}	$A-F^{Naive}$
2003	−18.01	−25.21	7.20	7.20	51.89	324.36	635.72	−12.37	31.81
2004	−13.30	−30.07	16.77	16.77	281.07	176.89	903.91	−12.37	0.86
2005	−3.64	−29.22	25.58	25.58	654.22	13.25	853.68	−12.37	76.21
2006	−4.24	−23.12	18.88	18.88	356.39	17.98	534.45	−12.37	66.10
2007	3.48	−17.56	21.04	21.04	442.55	12.11	308.24	−12.37	251.22
Sum of column			89.46	89.46	1786.12	544.59	3236.01		426.21
Forecast periods			5	5	5	5	5		5
Average of column			17.89	17.89	357.22	108.92	647.20		85.24
Square root of average of column					18.90	10.44	25.44		

Mean forecast error	17.89%	ME = 89.46/5
Mean absolute error	17.89%	MAE = 89.46/5
Mean squared error	357.22%	MSE = 1786.12/5
Root mean squared error	18.90%	RMSE = $357.22^{1/2}$
Theil's $U1$ inequality coefficient	0.53	$U1 = 18.90/(10.44 + 25.44)$
Theil's $U2$ coefficient	2.05	$U2 = (357.22/85.24)^{1/2}$
C-statistic	3.19	$C = (357.22/85.24) - 1$

(b) Sample coefficients for 1982–2007

(i)	(ii)	(iii)	(iv)	(v)	(vi)	(vii)	(viii)	(ix)	(x)
				Abs	*Squ*	*Squ*	*Squ*		*Squ*
	A	F	$A-F$	$A-F$	$A-F$	A	F	F^{Naive}	$A-F^{Naive}$
2003	−18.01	−14.19	−3.82	3.82	14.57	324.36	201.44	−12.37	31.81
2004	−13.30	−13.81	0.51	0.51	0.26	176.89	190.69	−12.37	0.86
2005	−3.64	−12.46	8.82	8.82	77.87	13.25	155.35	−12.37	76.21
2006	−4.24	−4.65	0.41	0.41	0.17	17.98	21.66	−12.37	66.10
2007	3.48	−1.84	5.32	5.32	28.32	12.11	3.39	−12.37	251.22
Sum of column			11.25	18.89	121.19	544.59	572.54		426.11
Forecast periods			5	5	5	5	5		5
Average of column			2.25	3.78	24.24	108.92	114.51		85.22
Square root of average of column					4.92	10.44	10.70		9.23

Mean forecast error	2.25%	ME = 11.25/5
Mean absolute error	3.78%	MAE = 18.89/5
Mean squared error	24.24%	MSE = 121.19/5
Root mean squared error	4.92%	RMSE = $24.24^{1/2}$
Theil's $U1$ inequality coefficient	0.23	$U1 = 4.92/(10.44 + 10.70)$
Theil's $U2$ coefficient	0.53	$U2 = (24.24/85.24)^{1/2}$
C-statistic	−0.72	$C = (24.24/85.24) - 1$

Notes: A: actual values; F: forecast values; $A - F$: actual minus forecast; Abs $A - F$: absolute actual minus forecast; Squ, A: squared actual, etc.; N denotes the naive forecast of −12.37 per cent (rent growth in the previous year, 2002).

on real rent growth should be expected. The much-improved in-sample forecast evaluation statistics suggest that the adjustment in sensitivity has run its course. Research will be able to test this as more observations become available.

From the results of the diagnostic checks in chapter 7 and the forecast evaluation analysis in this chapter, our preferred model remains the one that includes changes in the vacancy rate.

It is important to highlight again that forecast evaluation with five observations in the prediction sample can be misleading (a single large error in an otherwise good run of forecasts will affect particularly significantly the values of the quadratic forecast criteria: MSE, RMSE, $U1$, $U2$ and C). With a larger sample, we could have performed the tests over longer forecast horizons or employed rolling forecasts, which are described below. Reflecting the lack of data in real estate markets, however, we will still have to consider forecast test results obtained from small samples.

It is also worth exploring whether using a combination of models improves forecast accuracy. Usually, a combination of models is sought when models produce forecasts with different biases, so that, by combining the forecasts, the errors cancel (rather like the diversification benefit from holding a portfolio of stocks). In other words, there are possible gains from merging forecasts that consistently over-predict and under-predict the actual values. In our case, however, such gains do not emerge, since all the specifications under-predict on average.

Consider the in-sample forecasts of the two models for Frankfurt office rent growth. Table 9.7 combines the forecasts even if the bias in both sets of forecasts is positive. In some years, however, the two models tend to give a different forecast. For example, in 2007 the main model over-predicts (5.85 per cent compared to the actual 3.48 per cent) and model B under-predicts (−1.84 per cent). A similar tendency, albeit not as evident, is observed in 2003 and 2006.

We evaluate the combined forecasts in the final section of table 9.7. By combining the forecasts, there is still positive bias. The mean absolute error has fallen to 3.1 per cent, from (4.3 per cent and 3.8 per cent from the main model and model B, respectively). Moreover, an improvement is recorded on all other criteria. The combination of the forecasts from these two models is therefore worth considering for future out-of-sample forecasts.

On the topic of forecast combination in real estate, the reader is also referred to the paper by Wilson and Okunev (2001), who combine negatively correlated forecasts for securitised real estate returns in the United States, the United Kingdom and Australia and assess the improvement over

Table 9.7 Evaluating the combination of forecasts for Frankfurt office rents

(i)	(ii) A	(iii) F	(iv) $A-F$	(v) Abs $A-F$	(vi) Squ $A-F$	(vii) Squ A	(viii) Squ F	(ix) F^{Naive}	(x) Squ $A-F^{Naive}$
2003	−18.01	−17.06	−0.95	0.95	0.90	324.36	291.10	−12.37	31.81
2004	−13.30	−14.93	1.63	1.63	2.67	176.89	223.04	−12.37	0.86
2005	−3.64	−11.12	7.48	7.48	55.91	13.25	123.59	−12.37	76.21
2006	−4.24	−0.22	−4.02	4.02	16.15	17.98	0.05	−12.37	66.10
2007	3.48	2.00	1.48	1.48	2.18	12.11	4.02	−12.37	251.22
Sum of column			5.62	15.55	77.80	544.59	641.79		426.21
Forecast periods			5	5	5	5	5		5
Average of column			1.12	3.11	15.56	108.92	128.36		85.24
Square root of average of column					3.94	10.44	11.33		
Mean forecast error					1.12%	ME = 5.62/5			
Mean absolute error					3.11%	MAE = 15.55/5			
Mean squared error					15.56%	MSE = 77.80/5			
Root mean squared error					3.94%	RMSE = $15.56^{1/2}$			
Theil's $U1$ inequality coefficient					0.18	$U1 = 3.94/(10.44 + 11.33)$			
Theil's $U2$ coefficient					0.43	$U2 = (15.56/85.24)^{1/2}$			
C-statistic					−0.82	$C = (15.56/85.24) - 1$			

Notes: A: actual values; F: forecast values; $A - F$: actual minus forecast; Abs $A - F$: absolute actual minus forecast; Squ, A: squared actual, etc.; N denotes the naive forecast of −12.37 per cent (rent growth in the previous year, 2002).

benchmark forecasts. This study also provides a good account on the subject of forecast combination.

The additional tests we discuss in section 9.1 are those for efficiency and encompassing. These tests require us to run regressions, and therefore the five-year forecast horizon in our example is far too short. For the purpose of illustrating these tests, consider the data in table 9.8. They show actual quarterly real rent growth in Frankfurt offices and the in-sample forecast values and errors of the three models we constructed for Frankfurt quarterly rents (quarterly rent growth). The exact specification is not relevant to this discussion, but, for information, the models are also based on the vacancy and output variables.

We apply equation (9.13) to study forecast efficiency for all three forecast models, in this case using a t subscript to denote each observation, since

Table 9.8 Data on real rent growth for forecast efficiency and encompassing tests

		Forecast values			Forecast errors		
	Actual	RM1	RM2	RM3	RM1	RM2	RM3
1Q02	−1.41	−2.01	−0.92	−1.27	0.60	−0.49	−0.14
2Q02	−3.15	−3.70	−1.80	−3.14	0.55	−1.35	−0.01
3Q02	−4.16	−5.45	−2.46	−5.02	1.29	−1.70	0.86
4Q02	−4.24	−6.18	−2.78	−6.40	1.94	−1.46	2.16
1Q03	−4.34	−7.32	−3.06	−7.29	2.98	−1.28	2.95
2Q03	−5.00	−8.51	−3.35	−7.66	3.51	−1.65	2.66
3Q03	−5.24	−8.94	−3.62	−7.54	3.70	−1.62	2.30
4Q03	−4.79	−8.25	−3.55	−7.09	3.46	−1.24	2.30
1Q04	−4.15	−7.13	−3.50	−6.52	2.98	−0.65	2.37
2Q04	−3.81	−6.56	−3.36	−5.91	2.75	−0.45	2.10
3Q04	−3.35	−6.09	−3.51	−5.22	2.74	0.16	1.87
4Q04	−2.71	−5.44	−3.62	−4.45	2.73	0.91	1.74
1Q05	−1.69	−4.31	−3.68	−3.55	2.62	1.99	1.86
2Q05	−0.84	−3.19	−3.68	−2.62	2.35	2.84	1.78
3Q05	−0.46	−2.54	−3.40	−1.77	2.08	2.94	1.31
4Q05	−0.69	−1.55	−2.81	−0.92	0.86	2.12	0.23
1Q06	−1.01	−0.45	−2.23	−0.24	−0.56	1.22	−0.77
2Q06	−1.04	1.01	−1.64	0.36	−2.05	0.60	−1.40
3Q06	−1.11	1.52	−1.07	0.71	−2.63	−0.04	−1.82
4Q06	−1.15	1.87	−0.79	1.07	−3.02	−0.36	−2.22

we are dealing with a continuous time series of forecasts (with t-ratios in parentheses).

$$\hat{e}_t^{RM1} = \underset{(-1.0)}{-0.73} - \underset{(-3.6)}{0.80} RRg_t \tag{9.17}$$

$$\hat{e}_t^{RM2} = \underset{(5.1)}{2.04} + \underset{(5.9)}{0.74} RRg_t \tag{9.18}$$

$$\hat{e}_t^{RM3} = \underset{(-1.5)}{-0.76} - \underset{(-4.0)}{0.65} RRg_t \tag{9.19}$$

Both the intercept and the slope coefficients on RRg_t are different from zero and statistically significant. Therefore we do not establish forecast efficiency for any of the models. The rent variation still explains the error, and misspecification could be part of the reason for these findings – for example, if the models have strong serial correlation, which is the case for all three error series.

The estimation of equation (9.14) to study whether RM3 encompasses RM1 or RM2 yields the following results:

$$R\hat{R}g_t = \underset{(-3.5^{***})}{-0.78} \; + \underset{(3.8^{***})}{1.17F_t^{RM3}} - \underset{(-2.1^{**})}{0.58F_t^{RM1}} \tag{9.20}$$

$$R\hat{R}g_t = \underset{(-7.6^{***})}{-2.17} \; + \underset{(15.8^{***})}{0.69F_t^{RM3}} - \underset{(-5.6^{***})}{0.74F_t^{RM2}} \tag{9.21}$$

where F represents the forecast of the respective model, ** denotes significance at the 5 per cent level and *** denotes significance at the 1 per cent level.

Clearly, RM3 does not encompass either RM1 or RM2, since the coefficients on these forecast series are statistically significantly different from zero. The negative sign on the RM1 forecast variable is slightly counter-intuitive, but means that, after allowing for the impact of RM3 on RRg, RM1 forecasts are negatively related to the actual values. The forecast encompassing test here is for illustrative purposes. Let us not ignore the fact that regressions (9.17) to (9.21) above are run with twenty observations, and this could imply that the results are neither reliable nor realistic.

9.2.3 *Rolling forecasts*

We now consider the case in which the analyst is interested in evaluating the adequacy of the model when making predictions for a certain number of years (1, 2, 3, etc.) or quarters (say 4, 8, 12, etc.). Let us assume that, at the beginning of each year, we are interested in forecasting rent growth at the end of the year – that is, one year ahead. We make these predictions with models A and B for Frankfurt office rents. We initially estimate the model until 2002 and we forecast rent growth in 2003. Then the models are estimated until 2003 and we produce a forecast for 2004, and so forth, until the models are estimated to 2006 and we produce a forecast for 2007. In this way, we obtain five one-year forecasts. These are compared with the actual values under the assumption of perfect foresight again, and we run the forecast evaluation tests. Table 9.9 contains the coefficients for the forecasts, the data and the forecasts.

In panel (a), we observe the changing coefficients through time. As we have noted already, the most notable one is the declining value of the coefficient on vacancy – i.e. rents are becoming less sensitive to vacancy. The calculation of the forecasts should be straightforward. As another example, the forecast of -19.43 (model B for 2005) is obtained as: $0.90 - 1.32 \times 18.3 + 4.28 \times 0.893$.

Table 9.9 Coefficient values from rolling estimations, data and forecasts

(a) Rolling regression coefficients

	Sample ends in				
	2002	2003	2004	2005	2006
Model A					
Intercept	−6.81	−6.47	−6.41	−6.12	−6.35
ΔVAC_{t-1}	−3.13	−2.57	−2.34	−2.20	−2.19
$OFSg_t$	4.72	4.68	4.70	4.65	4.58
Model B					
Intercept	5.06	3.79	0.90	−1.87	−2.51
VAC_t	−2.06	−1.78	−1.32	−0.91	−0.85
$OFSg_t$	3.83	3.87	4.28	4.72	4.88

(b) Data

	VAC	ΔVAC	$OFSg$
2002		6.3	
2003	14.8	5.7	0.056
2004	18.2	3.4	0.618
2005	18.3	0.1	0.893
2006	18.1	−0.2	2.378
2007	15.8		2.593

(c) Forecasts

	Actual rent growth	Forecasts by model		
		A	B	naive
2002	−12.37			
2003	−18.01	−26.26	−25.21	−12.37
2004	−13.30	−18.23	−26.21	−18.01
2005	−3.64	−10.17	−19.43	−13.30
2006	−4.24	4.72	−7.12	−3.64
2007	3.48	5.96	7.52	−4.24

Note: Naive forecast is the previous year's forecast.

The forecast evaluation measures shown in table 9.10 illustrate the dominance of model A across all criteria. The only unsatisfactory finding is that it does not win over the naive model. On average, over the five-year horizon their performance is at par. It is worth observing the success of model B

Table 9.10 Forecast evaluation

Model	A	B
Mean error	1.65	6.95
Mean absolute error	6.23	8.56
Mean squared error	44.29	98.49
Root mean squared error	6.65	9.92
Theil's $U1$ inequality coefficient	0.26	0.34
Theil's $U2$ coefficient	1.03	1.54
C-metric	0.07	1.38

in capturing the changing direction in rent growth (from negative to positive). Model A had indicated positive rent growth in 2006, which did not materialise, but the model continued to predict positive growth for 2007. Another remark we should make relates to the future values of the independent variables required for these one-year forecasts. Model A requires only the forecast for output growth, since its impact on real rent growth is contemporaneous. For model B, we need a forecast for the vacancy rate as well as for output growth in one-year forecasts.

The forecast horizon can of course change to two, three or more periods (years, in our example) ahead. In this case, for assessing two-year forecasts, we would estimate the models until, say, 2002 and obtain the forecast for 2004, then roll the estimation forward to 2003 and make the forecast for 2005, and so forth. The sample of two-year-ahead forecasts is then compared to the actual values.

9.2.4 *Statistical versus 'economic' loss functions*

Many econometric forecasting studies evaluate models' success using statistical loss functions such as those described above. It is not necessarily the case, however, that models classed as accurate because they have small mean squared forecast errors are useful in practical situations. To give one specific illustration, it has been shown (Gerlow, Irwin and Liu, 1993) that the accuracy of forecasts according to traditional statistical criteria may give little guide to the potential profitability of employing those forecasts in a market trading strategy. Accordingly, models that perform poorly on statistical grounds may still yield a profit if they are used for trading, and vice versa.

On the other hand, models that can accurately forecast the sign of future returns, or can predict turning points in a series, have been found to be more profitable (Leitch and Tanner, 1991). Two possible indicators of the ability of a model to predict direction changes irrespective of their magnitude are those suggested by Pesaran and Timmerman (1992) and by Refenes (1995). Defining the actual value of the series at time $t+s$ as A_{t+s} and the forecast for that series s steps ahead made at time t as $F_{t,s}$, the relevant formulae to compute these measures are, respectively,

$$\%\text{ correct sign predictions} = \frac{1}{T-(T_1-1)}\sum_{t=T_1}^{T} z_{t+s} \tag{9.22}$$

$$\text{where } z_{t+s} = 1 \text{ if } (A_{t+s}F_{t,s}) > 0$$
$$z_{t+s} = 0 \text{ otherwise}$$

and

$$\%\text{ correct direction change predictions} = \frac{1}{T-(T_1-1)}\sum_{t=T_1}^{T} z_{t+s} \tag{9.23}$$

$$\text{where } z_{t+s} = 1 \text{ if } (A_{t+s}-A_t)(F_{t,s}-A_t) > 0$$
$$z_{t+s} = 0 \text{ otherwise}$$

In these equations, T is the total sample size, T_1 is the first out-of-sample forecast observation and the total number of observations in the hold-out sample is $T-(T_1-1)$. In each case, the criteria give the proportion of correctly predicted signs and directional changes for some given lead time s, respectively.

Considering how strongly the MSE, MAE and proportion of correct sign prediction criteria penalise large errors relative to small ones, they can be ordered as follows:

penalises large errors least → penalises large errors most heavily
sign prediction → *MAE* → *MSE*

The MSE penalises large errors disproportionately more heavily than small errors, MAE penalises large errors proportionately equally as heavily as small errors while the sign prediction criterion does not penalise large errors any more than small errors. Let us now estimate the model until 2000 and examine its performance for sign and direction predictions. Table 9.11 illustrates the calculations.

The coefficients from estimating the model until 2000 are given in panel (a). We also report the values for *OFSg* and ΔVAC, the independent variables, for the reader to compute the forecasts shown in the forecasts column (column headed F in panel (b)). We apply formulae (9.22) and (9.23) to calculate

Table 9.11 Example of sign and direction predictions

(a) Parameter estimates and standard errors

	Coef.	Prob.
Cons	−5.61	0.22
OFSg	4.34	0.02
ΔVAC	−3.37	0.04

(b) Forecasts, actual values and calculations

	OFSg	ΔVAC	*A*	*F*	z_t	$A_{t+s} - A_t$	$F_{t+s} - A_t$	$A_{t+s} - A_t \times F_{t+s} - A_t$	z_t
2000		−3.3	13.19						
2001	2.010	0.9	10.93	14.23	1	−2.26	1.04	−2.4	0
2002	0.225	6.3	−12.37	−7.67	1	−25.56	−20.86	533.1	1
2003	0.056	5.7	−18.00	−26.60	1	−31.20	−39.79	1241.4	1
2004	0.618	3.4	−13.30	−22.14	1	−26.49	−35.33	935.8	1
2005	0.893	0.1	−3.64	−13.19	1	−16.83	−26.38	444.0	1
2006	2.378	−0.2	−4.24	4.37	0	−17.43	−8.82	153.7	1
2007	2.593	−2.3	3.48	6.32	1	−9.71	−6.87	66.7	1

(c) Sign and direct prediction statistics

	Sign prediction	Direction prediction
Sum z_t	6	6
Holding periods	7	7
% correct predictions	87(6/7)	87(6/7)

how successful the model is in predicting the sign and direction of rent growth in the period 2001 to 2007.

The calculation of z_t values for sign predictions shows that, in six out of seven cases, z takes the value of one. That is, the proportion of correctly predicted signs for real rent growth (positive or negative rent growth) is 87 per cent. In our example, the model failed to predict the correct sign in 2006, when the actual value was −4.24 per cent whereas the model predicted +4.37 per cent.

Similarly, the model predicts the observed direction of real rent growth in six out of seven years. The exception is the first year. The forecast indicated a marginal pick-up in growth in relation to the previous year but the actual outcome was a slowdown from 13.19 per cent to 10.93 per cent. In every other year in our out-of-sample period (but assuming perfect foresight) the model predicts the correct direction change in relation to 2000. For example, in 2005 the actual real rent growth in Frankfurt was −3.64 per cent (a slowdown in relation to the 13.19 per cent outturn in 2000) and the model also predicted a much lower rate of growth (of −13.19 per cent). We should, of course, note the success of the model to predict sign and direction in the context that perfect foresight has been assumed.

The above rules can be adapted for other objectives in forecasting. For example, in a rolling forecast framework, the analyst may wish to check the correctness of sign and direction predictions for rolling two-year forecasts. Assume that we use the above Frankfurt rent growth model to obtain rolling two-year forecasts: we estimate the model until 1998, 1999, 2000, 2001, 2002, 2003, 2004 and 2005 to generate eight two-year-ahead forecasts (respectively for 2000, 2001, 2002, 2003, 2004, 2005, 2006 and 2007). This set of forecasts is used to calculate the zs for the sign and direction formulae. The holding period is now the number of the rolling forecasts, which in this case is eight years.

9.3 Forecast accuracy studies in real estate

Forecast evaluation in the real estate literature is relatively new. Recent studies focus on *ex post* valuation and out-of-sample forecasting conditional on perfect information. A part of the literature focuses on examining the performance of different models. One such study is that by D'Arcy, McGough and Tsolacos (1999), who compare the predictions of a regression model of Dublin office rents to the forecasts obtained from two exponential smoothing approaches for a three-year period. The latter were taken to be the naive model. The forecast evaluation is based on a comparison of the forecasts with the realised values for only two years: 1996 and 1997. The regression model over-predicted by 3.6 percentage points in 1996 and by three percentage points in 1997. The naive methods, which are variants of the exponential smoothing approach, under-predict by larger margins of 5.3 and 17.9 percentage points, respectively. The authors also examine the regression model forecast performance by comparing the values of the regression standard error (for the full-sample period) with the value of the RMSE for the forecast period. The latter is found to be only 0.3 times higher than the former, and the authors conclude that this is an encouraging indication of the model's forecast ability.

Matysiak and Tsolacos (2003) use the mean error and mean squared error measures to examine whether the forecasts for rents obtained from regression models that contain leading economic indicators outperform those of simpler models. They find that not all leading indicators improve upon the forecasts of naive specifications, and that forecasting with leading indicators is more successful for office and industrial rents than retail rents.

The study by Karakozova (2004), which was reviewed in chapter 7, also adopts formal evaluation tests to examine the forecast performance of the different models that she uses. Karakozova evaluates the forecast performance of three alternative models: a regression model, an error correction model and an ARIMAX model. The latter is an ARIMA model of the type we examined in chapter 8 but with predetermined variables included. This author uses the percentage error, the mean absolute percentage error and the root mean squared error to compare the forecasts. Perfect foresight is also assumed in constructing the out-of-sample forecasts. All models produce small percentage errors, but the computed MAPE and RMSE values clearly suggest that, for both short and long predictive horizons (that is, up to three years using annual data), the ARIMAX model has a better forecasting performance than the other two approaches.

9.3.1 *Evaluating central London forecasts*

In the remainder of this chapter, we review in more detail three studies that illustrate different angles in forecast evaluation. The first of these is by Stevenson and McGrath (2003), who compare the forecasting ability of four alternative models of office rents in central London offices. Their database, comprising semi-annual data, spans the period May 1977 to May 1999. These authors estimate their models for the period up to May 1996, holding the data for the next three years (six observations) to assess out-of-sample forecast performance.

The authors examine four models.

(1) An ARIMA specification that is finally reduced to an AR(1) – a form selected by the Akaike and Schwarz information criteria.
(2) A single-equation model; the theoretical version of this model includes variables that had been given support in prior research. These variables are changes in real GDP, changes in (real) service sector GDP, new construction (volume), real interest rates, service sector employment, building costs, the number of property transactions, gross company trading profits (adjusted for inflation) and shorter and longer leading indicators. The authors apply stepwise regression, which entails the search for the variables (or terms) from among the above list that maximise the explanatory power of the model. The final specification of this model includes three employment terms (contemporaneous employment and

employment at lags 1 and 3), new construction lagged five periods and the longer leading indicator.

(3) A Bayesian VAR model (BVAR). This is a reduced form of the VAR model we discuss in chapter 11. The BVAR contains the variables that are used for the general form of the single-equation model above.

(4) A simultaneous equations model, the structure of which is discussed in chapter 10 in this book. The simultaneous model is based on the Wheaton, Torto and Evans (1997) model for Greater London. It contains an absorption equation, an equilibrium rent equation, an equation of first differences in rents and a construction equation.

The forecast performance of the models is examined for the three years (six steps) from November 1996 to May 1999. A characteristic of this study is that the authors construct real-time forecasts – that is, they use only information available in May 1996.

Of the four forecasting models, the AR(1) and BVAR models are dynamic. This is apparent with the AR(1) model. The forecasts for all variables in the BVAR arise from the system itself. Hence rents and their drivers are forecast within the system. For the single-regression model and the simultaneous equation system the situation is different, and the future values of some of the variables are required. Stevenson and McGrath make use of both independent forecasts and exponential smoothing. The latter is guided by the findings of Makridakis, Wheelwright and Hyndman (1998), who suggest that an exponential smoothing method provides better results than alternative forecasting techniques. More specifically, they suggest the following.

(1) As new construction is lagged by five periods, the actual values are used. Exponential smoothing is used for the sixth period forecast.

(2) Employment forecasts. The authors had available forecasts from the National Institute of Economic and Social Research (NIESR) until 4Q98. They use the 3Q96 NIESR forecast for 1996H2, the 1Q97 for 1997H1 and the 3Q97 for 1997H2. For the remaining three periods the authors obtained future employment values using the double exponential smoothing method.

A simple comparison of the actual and forecast values points to the impressive results of the BVAR, followed by the single-equation model; in this case, the AR(1) is the worst model. The forecast evaluation is achieved using five tests. All models over-predict (producing forecast values higher than actual values), with the BVAR having the lowest – i.e. closest to zero – mean error. The BVAR also provides the lowest mean absolute error. On the other metrics, this model clearly outperforms all the other models, as the statistics take the smallest values.

9.3.2 Model-based versus consensus forecasts

Tsolacos (2006) assesses whether consensus forecasts in the United Kingdom, compiled by the Investment Property Forum (IPF), outperform those from a simple regression model and a benchmark AR(1) model. The IPF conducts a survey of professional forecasters (property consultancies, property funds and fund managers) and compiles their forecasts for rents, capital growth and total returns. The series forecast are the standard IPD series for all UK office, retail and industrial properties. Hence all the forecasts are for the same series. The survey began in October 1998, and it is published quarterly. The forecast horizon has been one and two years, and more recently a five-year average has been added. These forecasts are widely circulated in the industry and are also published in the *Estates Gazette*, a popular industry magazine in the United Kingdom. Given the number of respondents to this survey (over thirty forecast houses), the IPF consensus forecasts are taken to represent the base case scenario for near-future real estate market conditions in the United Kingdom.

The AR(1) model in this study for both rent growth and total returns is

$$y_t = a + by_{t-1} + \varepsilon_t \tag{9.24}$$

where y_t represents a series of rents or returns and ε_t is the random error at time t.

The rent regression models are specified using gross domestic product (*GDP*) or household spending (*SPEND*). Gross domestic product is used as a broad indicator of economic activity that impacts on the occupier market and rent growth. Household spending is an alternative aggregate variable. The general specifications of the two rent regression models are

$$\Delta lRENT_t = a + \sum_{i=1}^{k} \beta_i \Delta lGDP_{t-i} + \Delta lRENT_{t-1} + \varepsilon_t \tag{9.25}$$

$$\Delta lRENT_t = a + \sum_{i=1}^{k} \beta_i \Delta lSPEND_{t-i} + \Delta lRENT_{t-1} + \varepsilon_t \tag{9.26}$$

where *RENT* is the IPD all-property rent index (annual database) adjusted for inflation using the all-items retail price index (ONS data). The indices are logged and the first differences are taken (denoted by Δl). In equations (9.25) and (9.26), slow adjustments in the market and the weight of previous rents on current rents are allowed through rents lagged by one year ($\Delta lRENT_{t-1}$). The most significant lags of the terms $\Delta lGDP_{t-i}$ and $\Delta lSPEND_{t-i}$ were selected by minimising the value of the Schwarz information criterion.

Table 9.12 Empirical forms of equations (9.25) to (9.28)

Equations	Adj. R^2	Diagnostics
Rent		
RM1: $\Delta l\hat{RENT}_t = -0.04 + 1.80\Delta lGDP_t + 0.61\Delta lRENT_{t-1}$	0.76	$BJ = 0.83$; $LB(1) = 0.18$
RM2: $\Delta l\hat{RENT}_t = -0.08 + 2.58\Delta lSPEND_t$	0.60	$BJ = 0.79$; $LB(1) = 0.19$
Total Returns		
TRM1: $\Delta T\hat{RET}_t = -0.07 + 1.12E - 05\Delta GDP_t$	0.51	$BJ = 0.79$; $LB(1) = 0.34$
TRM2: $\Delta T\hat{RET}_t = 0.47 - 0.04INT_{t-1}$	0.42	$BJ = 0.88$; $LB(1) = 0.08$

Notes: All coefficients on regressors (excluding the intercept) are significant at the 1 per cent level. BJ is the probability value for the estimated Bera–Jarque test statistic for normality. LB(1) is the probability value for the computed Ljung–Box *Q*-test (one lag). The total return models are not in logged form. The use of logs results in failing the BJ test – that is, the residuals are not normally distributed. The estimation period in all regressions is 1971 to 2004.

The total return regressions are run on GDP and on interest rates (*INT*) in separate regressions – i.e. two separate modelling frameworks are used. GDP growth also enters investors' assessments about the strength of the property market and the economic risks to returns. Interest rates capture the discount rate and the risk-free rate, which impact on property yields and capital growth and therefore determine total returns. The general forms of the total return regressions are

$$\Delta lTRET_t = a + \sum_{i=1}^{k} \beta_i \Delta lGDP_{t-i} + \Delta lTRET_{t-1} + \varepsilon_t \tag{9.27}$$

$$\Delta lTRET_t = a + \sum_{i=1}^{k} \beta_i INT_{t-i} + \Delta lTRET_{t-1} + \varepsilon_t \tag{9.28}$$

TRET is the total return index adjusted for inflation using the ONS retail price index. *INT* is represented by the official rate (repo rate) taken from the Bank of England. The December value is taken for each year to coincide with the end-of-year valuations from which the annual rent and return data are produced. The estimation of equations (9.25) to (9.28) results in the following models, which are subsequently used to predict rents and total returns one and two years ahead, as shown in table 9.12.

The forecasts are evaluated over two time horizons: one year and two years. The sample of one-year forecasts for rent and returns contains six observations (1999 to 2004). This set is based on the forecasts reported in the first IPF survey each year: April 1999, February 2000, . . . , February 2004 (the forecast for rents and returns for 1999 are taken from the survey published in April 1999 and for 2004 are those reported in February 2004). The sample of two-year rent/return forecasts contains one observation fewer. The start year for this set of forecasts is 2000, which corresponds to the forecast published in April 1999 for 2000. The last observation is for 2004, reported in the survey of February 2003.

The one- and two-year forecasts based on the models described earlier are real-time forecasts. This means that the models contain information available to the analyst at the time of the forecast. The benchmark AR(1) specifications for real rent and real returns are initially estimated up to 1998 and forecasts are produced for 1999 and 2000. These real forecasts are converted into nominal terms using the predictions for inflation reported in the monthly Treasury publication *Forecasts for the UK Economy: A Comparison of Independent Forecasts* ('Treasury Survey') in April 1999. The April 1999 issue is chosen to correspond to the publication date of the IPF survey from which the consensus views for 1999 and 2000 are taken. Subsequently, the sample period for estimation of the AR(1) model extends to 1999, and the one- and two-year forecasts (for real rents and returns) for 2000 and 2001 are obtained. The real forecasts are also converted into nominal figures using the forecast for inflation reported in the 'Treasury Survey' in February 1999 (again, to coincide with the publication date of the IPF survey that year). The procedure continues until the sample is exhausted.

Turning to the regression models, the first observations for the one- and two-year real rent and return forecasts are generated by estimating the models up to 1998 and making predictions for 1999 and 2000. The sample then increases by one observation and the regression models are re-estimated to make further one-step- and two-step-ahead forecasts (for 2000 and 2001, respectively). This recursive process continues until the sample extends to 2002 for the final two-year forecast and to 2003 for the final one-year forecast (that for 2004 in both cases). Throughout this process, future values of GDP and consumer expenditure growth (one and two years forward) are required, since there are no lagged terms in the equation. We take GDP and consumer spending forecasts from the 'Treasury Survey' publications. The issues of the 'Treasury Survey' are those used for inflation. In the case of the interest rate variable, the presence of one year's lag requires just a one-year forecast for interest rates to predict real returns two years ahead. The forecasts for the base rate are taken from two different sources: the Bank of England's *Inflation Report* for 1999, 2000 and 2001 (published in February) and from the 'Treasury Survey' for the subsequent years (February

Table 9.13 Evaluation of two-year-ahead forecasts of all-property rents

		Actual	IPF	AR(1)	RM1	RM2	Comb 1
2000		7.0	2.4	5.0*	2.0	−0.3	2.4
2001		3.4	4.1*	4.7	5.5	1.0	2.9
2002		−0.8	3.7	5.0	4.3	0.1*	2.6
2003		−1.6	1.9	4.6	4.0	0.9*	2.8
2004		2.3	0.8	1.1	1.3*	−0.3	0.4
Tests							
ME (%)			−0.5	−1.7	−1.4	1.5	−0.4
MAE (%)			2.97	2.76	3.77	2.87	2.69
RMSE (%)			3.37	3.65	4.19	3.30	3.01
Theil $U1$			0.23	0.20	0.25	0.38	0.24
	Bias		0.02	0.31	0.10	0.20	0.02
	Variance		0.32	0.16	0.14	0.45	0.43
	Covariance		0.66	0.53	0.76	0.35	0.55
C-measure (%)				−15	−35	4	26

Notes: Comb 1 = average of AR(1) and RM(2). See also notes to table 9.12. Forecasts and actual values are all expressed as percentages. The asterisks represent the model that gives the most accurate forecast for the year in question.

publication). The real forecasts are turned into nominal terms using the inflation forecasts from the 'Treasury Survey'.

Therefore, in this process, the structure of the model is the same but the model parameters are continually updated and real-time information is used for GDP, consumer expenditure, interest rates and inflation. The forecast process therefore resembles reality. The criteria for evaluation of the forecasts are the mean error, the mean absolute error, the root mean squared error, Theil's $U1$ statistic, its bias, variance and covariance proportions and the *C*-measure.

In table 9.13, rent forecasts are evaluated over the two-year horizon. The survey (consensus) forecasts are positively biased (they over-predict on average). The survey forecasts under-perform the AR(1) model and RM2 forecasts on the mean absolute error criterion. It should be noted, however, that, although the AR(1) specification has a lower mean absolute error than the consensus, it is poor in predicting rent growth for 2002 and 2003. The sizes of the errors in these two years inflate the value of the RMSE for the AR(1) forecasts. On the RMSE measure, RM2 performs marginally better than the consensus view, but the latter is slightly better on the $U1$ metric.

Table 9.14 Evaluation of two-year-ahead forecasts of all-property total returns

		Actual	IPF	AR(1)	RM1	RM2
2000		10.5	10.4*	5.7	5.8	9.2
2001		6.8	11.6	6.4	7.4*	7.6
2002		9.6	10.0*	6.1	7.1	8.8
2003		10.9	9.4*	6.6	7.4	9.2
2004		18.3	7.9	7.8	7.2	9.4*
Tests						
ME (%)			1.4	5.5	4.2	2.4
MAE (%)			3.42	5.50	4.48	2.71
RMSE (%)			5.18	6.61	5.74	4.16
Theil $U1$			0.11	0.15	0.14	0.09
	Bias		0.07	0.69	0.55	0.33
	Variance		0.26	0.30	0.32	0.59
	Covariance		0.68	0.01	0.14	0.08
C-measure (%)				−39	−19	55

Note: See notes to tables 9.12 and 9.13.

Such conflicting results from alternative criteria are not uncommon when the call is close and the sample is small. This is illustrated by just a slight gain of 4 per cent (on the C-measure) from using RM2 over the consensus forecasts. It is evident, however, that the performance of the latter can be at least matched by one of the regression models and there is no extra gain from using the consensus forecast. Further clear gains are made when AR(1) and RM2 are combined.

Table 9.14 reports the assessment results for the two-year predictions of total returns. A comparison of the realised total returns with the consensus forecasts reveals the impressive accuracy of the latter in 2000, 2002 and, to a degree, 2003. This good performance is reflected in the lowest mean error. Again, as was the case for the one-year forecast sample, all methods under-predict (forecast values lower than actual values). When considering the other metrics, the winning model is again the regression model with interest rates (RM2), demonstrated by the lowest MAE, RMSE and $U1$ values. A clear gain (55 per cent) is also recorded by the C-metric.

The consistency of the performance of the univariate regression for total returns (RM2) over both forecast horizons should be highlighted. Clearly, recent past information about interest rates is not efficiently incorporated in the consensus forecasts. The fact that the IPF forecasts have been very accurate for three out of the five years considered makes this survey an important source of total return forecasts, however.

9.3.3 *Evaluation of rolling forecasts for different horizons*

The last study we review (Brooks and Tsolacos, 2000) focuses on retail rent forecasts in the United Kingdom. This study evaluates the performance of different models using a large sample of forecast points with a rolling window to run the tests, and also using two different indices of retail rents to illustrate the sensitivities of the results to the series used.

This research adopts four methodologies to forecast retail rents. The first framework is an ARIMA model, which the authors fit to each of the retail rent series. A second specification is an AR(2) model. The third specification is a VAR model that contains variables that a priori determine retail rents: consumer spending, retail sales, disposable income, gross domestic product and new retail orders. This class of models is described at length in chapter 11. For the purposes of this chapter on forecast evaluation, the VAR approach can be thought of as simply another class of models that can be used to make comparative predictions.

The two series of retail rents are the LaSalle Investment Management (LIM) and CB Hillier Parker (CBHP) indices. The LIM series represents an overall retail rent index with a higher weight in standard shop units covering all geographical regions in the United Kingdom, and is based on the performance of a portfolio of actual properties. The CBHP index in the United Kingdom is also an overall index of retail rents covering all geographical regions in the country. Rental values in this index apply to shops in the 100 per cent trading position in a high street or a shopping centre measuring 20ft frontage by 60ft depth with 300 sq ft of storage or staff accommodation let on a full repairing and insuring lease. Rental values also apply to units located in the adjacent trading areas of high streets and shopping centres.

All approaches are used to make eight out-of-sample (dynamic) quarterly forecasts. These forecasts are made recursively and the start date is 1988 quarter one. This means that the VAR and AR models are fitted to the rent series for the period 2Q77 to 4Q87 and forecasts are made for eight quarters ahead: 1Q88 to 4Q89. Similarly, the long-term average of the rent series (estimated over the sub-sample 2Q77 to 4Q87) is used for the eight-quarter forecast. The forecasts from the random walk model for the period 1Q88 to 4Q89 are the value at 4Q87. Subsequently, the models are estimated up to 1Q88, and an eight-quarter forecast (2Q88 to 1Q90) is again computed. This procedure continues until the forecast sample period is exhausted (the last

Table 9.15 Mean forecast errors for the changes in rents series

	Steps ahead							
	1	2	3	4	5	6	7	8
(a) LaSalle Investment Management rents series								
VAR(1)	−1.141	−2.844	−3.908	−4.729	−5.407	−5.912	−6.158	−6.586
VAR(2)	−0.799	−1.556	−2.652	−3.388	−4.155	−4.663	−4.895	−5.505
AR(2)	−0.595	−0.960	−1.310	−1.563	−1.720	−1.819	−1.748	−1.876
Long-term mean	−2.398	−3.137	−3.843	−4.573	−5.093	−5.520	−5.677	−6.049
Random walk	0.466	−0.246	−0.923	−1.625	−2.113	−2.505	−2.624	−2.955
(b) CB Hillier Parker rents series								
VAR(1)	−1.447	−3.584	−5.458	−7.031	−8.445	−9.902	−11.146	−12.657
AR(2)	−1.845	−2.548	−2.534	−1.979	−1.642	−1.425	−1.204	−1.239
Long-term mean	−3.725	−5.000	−6.036	−6.728	−7.280	−7.772	−8.050	−8.481
Random walk	1.126	−0.108	−1.102	−1.748	−2.254	−2.696	−2.920	−3.292

forecast is made in 1Q97 for the period 2Q97 to 1Q99). In this way, forty-four one-quarter forecasts, forty-four two-quarter forecasts, and so forth are calculated.

The forty-four one-quarter forecasts are compared with the realised data for each of the four methodologies. This is repeated for the two-quarter-, three-quarter-, . . . , and eight-quarter-ahead computed values. This comparison reveals how closely rent predictions track the corresponding historical rent changes over the different lengths of the forecast horizon (one to eight quarters). The mean forecast error, the mean squared forecast error and the percentage of correct sign predictions are the criteria employed to select the best performing models.

Ex ante forecasts of retail rents based on all methods are also made for eight quarters from the last available observation at the time that the study was written. Forecasts of real retail rents are therefore made for the periods 1999 quarter two to 2001 quarter one. An evaluation of the forecasts obtained from the different methodologies is presented in tables 9.15 to 9.17. Table 9.15 reports the MFE.

As noted earlier, a good forecasting model should have a mean forecasting error of zero. The first observation that can be made is that, on average, all mean errors are negative for all models and forecast horizons. This means that all models over-predict, except for the one-quarter-ahead CBHP forecast using the random walk. This bias could reflect non-economic influences

Table 9.16 Mean squared forecast errors for the changes in rents series

	Steps ahead							
	1	2	3	4	5	6	7	8
(a) LaSalle Investment Management rents series								
VAR(1)	111.30	112.92	112.59	106.86	106.00	108.91	114.13	115.88
VAR(2)	67.04	69.69	75.39	71.22	87.04	96.64	103.89	115.39
AR(2)	77.16	84.10	86.17	76.80	79.27	86.63	84.65	86.12
Long-term mean	159.55	163.42	139.88	137.20	139.98	143.91	150.20	154.84
Random walk	138.16	132.86	162.95	178.34	184.43	196.55	202.22	198.42
(b) CB Hillier Parker rents series								
VAR(1)	78.69	117.28	170.41	236.70	360.34	467.90	658.41	867.72
AR(1)	75.39	88.24	84.32	92.18	88.44	89.15	80.03	87.44
Long-term mean	209.55	163.42	139.88	137.20	139.98	143.91	150.20	154.84
Random walk	198.16	132.86	123.71	149.78	132.94	148.79	149.62	158.13

during the forecast period. The continuous fall in rents in the period 1990 to 1995, which constitutes much of the out-of-sample period, may to some extent explain this over-prediction, however. Reasons that the authors put forward include the contention that supply increases had greater effects during this period when retailers were struggling than in the overall sample period and the fact that retailers benefited less than the growth in GDP at that time suggested, as people were indebted and seeking to save more to reduce indebtedness.

Of the two VAR models used for LIM rents, the VAR(2) model – i.e. a VAR with a lag length of two – produces more accurate forecasts. This is not surprising, given that the VAR(1) model of changes in LIM rents is a poor performer compared with the VAR(2) model. The forecasts produced by the random walk model appear to be the most successful when forecasts up to three quarters ahead are considered, however. Then the AR model becomes the best performer. The same conclusion can be reached for CBHP rents, but here the random walk model is superior to the AR(2) model for the first four quarter-ahead forecasts.

Table 9.16 shows the results based on the MSFE, an overall accuracy measure. The computations of the MSFE for all eight time horizons in the CBHP case show that the AR(2) model has the smallest MSFEs. The VAR model appears to be the second-best-performing methodology when forecasts up

Table 9.17 Percentage of correct sign predictions for the changes in rents series

	Steps ahead							
	1	2	3	4	5	6	7	8
(a) LaSalle Investment Management rents series								
VAR(1)	62	45	40	40	34	33	31	29
VAR(2)	80	75	72	67	61	63	56	47
AR(2)	80	80	79	81	73	75	74	71
Long-term mean	40	39	40	38	34	33	31	32
(b) CB Hillier Parker rents series								
VAR(1)	76	66	67	69	49	43	41	47
AR(2)	78	80	81	79	73	78	77	74
Long-term mean	42	41	42	40	34	35	33	34

Note: The random walk in levels model cannot, by definition, produce sign predictions, since the predicted change is always zero.

to two quarters ahead are considered, but, as the forecast time horizon lengthens, the performance of the VAR deteriorates. In the case of LIM retail rents, the VAR(2) model performs best up to four quarters ahead, but when longer-term forecasts are considered the AR process appears to generate the most accurate forecasts. Overall, the long-term mean procedure outperforms the random walk model in the first two quarters of the forecast period for both series, but this is reversed when the forecast period extends beyond four quarters. Therefore, based on the MSFE criterion, the VAR(2) is the most appropriate model to forecast changes in LIM rents up to four quarters but then the AR(2) model performs better. This criterion also suggests that changes in CBHP rents are best forecast using a pure autoregressive model across all forecasting horizons.

Table 9.17 displays the percentage of correct predictions of the sign for changes in rent from each model for forecasts up to eight periods ahead. While the VAR model's performance can almost match that of the AR specification for the shortest horizon, the latter model dominates as the models forecast further into the future. From these results, the authors conclude that rent changes have substantial memory for (at least) two periods. Hence useful information for predicting rents is contained in their own lags. The predictive capacity of the other aggregates within the VAR model is limited. There is some predictive ability for one period, but it quickly disappears thereafter. Overall, then, the autoregressive approach is to be preferred.

Key concepts

The key terms to be able to define and explain from this chapter are

- forecast error
- mean error
- mean absolute error
- mean squared error
- root mean squared error
- Theil's $U1$ statistic
- bias, variance and covariance proportions
- Theil's $U2$ statistic
- forecast efficiency
- forecast improvement
- rolling forecasts
- in-sample forecasts
- out-of-sample forecasts
- forecast encompassing

10 Multi-equation structural models

Learning outcomes

In this chapter, you will learn how to

- compare and contrast single-equation and systems-based approaches to building models;
- discuss the cause, consequence and solution to simultaneous equations bias;
- derive the reduced-form equations from a structural model;
- describe and apply several methods for estimating simultaneous equations models; and
- conduct a test for exogeneity.

All the structural models we have considered thus far are single-equation models of the general form

$$y = X\beta + u \tag{10.1}$$

In chapter 7, we constructed a single-equation model for rents. The rent equation could instead be one of several equations in a more general model built to describe the market, however. In the context of figure 7.1, one could specify four equations – for demand (absorption or take-up), vacancy, rent and construction. Rent variation is then explained within this system of equations. Multi-equation models represent alternative and competitive methodologies to single-equation specifications, which have been the main empirical frameworks in existing studies and in practice. It should be noted that, even if single equations fit the historical data very well, they can still be combined to construct multi-equation models when theory suggests that causal relationships should be bidirectional or multidirectional. Such systems are also used by private practices even though their performance may be poorer. This is because the dynamic structure of a multi-equation system may affect the ability of an individual equation to reproduce the properties of an historical series. Multi-equation systems are frameworks of importance to real estate forecasters.

Multi-equation frameworks usually take the form of simultaneous-equation structures. These simultaneous models come with particular conditions that need to be satisfied for their estimation and, in general, their treatment and estimation require the study of specific econometric issues. There is also another family of models that, although they resemble simultaneous-equations models, are actually not. These models, which are termed recursive or triangular systems, are also commonly encountered in the real estate field.

This chapter has four objectives. First, to explain the nature of simultaneous-equations models and to study the conditions that need to be fulfilled for their estimation. Second, to describe the available estimation techniques for these models. Third, to draw a distinction between simultaneous and recursive multi-equation models. Fourth, to illustrate the estimation of a systems model.

10.1 Simultaneous-equation models

Systems of equations constitute one of the important circumstances under which the assumption of non-stochastic explanatory variables can be violated. Remember that this is one of the assumptions of the classical linear regression model. There are various ways of stating this condition, differing slightly in terms of strictness, but they all have the same broad implication. It can also be stated that all the variables contained in the X matrix are assumed to be *exogenous* – that is, their values are determined outside the equation. This is a rather simplistic working definition of exogeneity, although several alternatives are possible; this issue is revisited later in this chapter. Another way to state this is that the model is 'conditioned on' the variables in X, or that the variables in the X matrix are assumed not to have a probability distribution. Note also that causality in this model runs from X to y, and not vice versa – i.e. changes in the values of the explanatory variables cause changes in the values of y, but changes in the value of y will not impact upon the explanatory variables. On the other hand, y is an *endogenous* variable – that is, its value is determined by (10.1).

To illustrate a situation in which this assumption is not satisfied, consider the following two equations, which describe a possible model for the demand and supply of new office space in a metropolitan area:

$$Q_{dt} = \alpha + \beta R_t + \gamma EMP_t + u_t \tag{10.2}$$

$$Q_{st} = \lambda + \mu R_t + \kappa INT_t + v_t \tag{10.3}$$

$$Q_{dt} = Q_{st} \tag{10.4}$$

where Q_{dt} = quantity of new office space demanded at time t, Q_{st} = quantity of new office space supplied (newly completed) at time t, R_t = rent level prevailing at time time t, EMP_t = office-using employment at time t, INT_t = interest rate at time t, and u_t and v_t are the error terms.

Equation (10.2) is an equation for modelling the demand for new office space, and (10.3) is a specification for the supply of new office space. (10.4) is an equilibrium condition for there to be no excess demand (firms requiring more new space to let but they cannot) and no excess supply (empty office space due to lack of demand for a given structural vacancy rate in the market).[1] Assuming that the market always clears – that is, that the market is always in equilibrium – (10.2) to (10.4) can be written

$$Q_t = \alpha + \beta R_t + \gamma EMP_t + u_t \tag{10.5}$$

$$Q_t = \lambda + \mu R_t + \kappa INT_t + v_t \tag{10.6}$$

Equations (10.5) and (10.6) together comprise a simultaneous structural form of the model, or a set of structural equations. These are the equations incorporating the variables that real estate theory suggests should be related to one another in a relationship of this form. The researcher may, of course, adopt different specifications that are consistent with theory, but any structure that resembles equations (10.5) and (10.6) represents a simultaneous multi-equation model. The point to emphasise here is that price and quantity are determined simultaneously: rent affects the quantity of office space and office space affects rent. Thus, in order to construct and rent more office space, everything else equal, the developers will have to lower the price. Equally, in order to achieve higher rents per square metre, developers need to construct and place in the market less floor space. R and Q are endogenous variables, while EMP and INT are exogenous.

[1] Of course, one could argue here that such contemporaneous relationships are unrealistic. For example, interest rates will have affected supply in the past when developers were making plans for development. This is true, although on several occasions the contemporaneous term appears more important even if theory supports a lag structure. To an extent, this owes to the linkages of economic and monetary data in successive periods. Hence the current interest rate gives an idea of the interest rate in the recent past. For the sake of illustrating simultaneous-equations models, however, let us assume the presence of relationships such as (10.2) and (10.3).

A set of reduced-form equations corresponding to (10.5) and (10.6) can be obtained by solving (10.5) and (10.6) for R and Q separately. There will be a reduced-form equation for each endogenous variable in the system, which will contain *only exogenous variables*.

Solving for Q,

$$\alpha + \beta R_t + \gamma EMP_t + u_t = \lambda + \mu R_t + \kappa INT_t + v_t \tag{10.7}$$

Solving for R,

$$\frac{Q_t}{\beta} - \frac{\alpha}{\beta} - \frac{\gamma EMP_t}{\beta} - \frac{u_t}{\beta} = \frac{Q_t}{\mu} - \frac{\lambda}{\mu} - \frac{\gamma INT_t}{\mu} - \frac{v_t}{\mu} \tag{10.8}$$

Rearranging (10.7),

$$\beta R_t - \mu R_t = \lambda - \alpha + \kappa INT_t - \gamma EMP_t + v_t - u_t \tag{10.9}$$

$$(\beta - \mu)R_t = (\lambda - \alpha) + \kappa INT_t - \gamma EMP_t + (v_t - u_t) \tag{10.10}$$

$$R_t = \frac{\lambda - \alpha}{\beta - \mu} + \frac{\kappa}{\beta - \mu} INT_t - \frac{\gamma}{\beta - \mu} EMP_t + \frac{v_t - u_t}{\beta - \mu} \tag{10.11}$$

Multiplying (10.8) through by $\beta\mu$ and rearranging,

$$\mu Q_t - \mu\alpha - \mu\gamma EMP_t - \mu u_t = \beta Q_t - \beta\lambda - \beta\kappa INT_t - \beta v_t \tag{10.12}$$

$$\mu Q_t - \beta Q_t = \mu\alpha - \beta\lambda - \beta\kappa INT_t + \mu\gamma EMP_t + \mu u_t - \beta v_t \tag{10.13}$$

$$(\mu - \beta)Q_t = (\mu\alpha - \beta\lambda) - \beta\kappa INT_t + \mu\gamma EMP_t + (\mu u_t - \beta v_t) \tag{10.14}$$

$$Q_t = \frac{\mu a - \beta\lambda}{\mu - \beta} - \frac{\beta\kappa}{\mu - \beta} INT_t + \frac{\mu\gamma}{\mu - \beta} EMP_t + \frac{\mu u_t - \beta v_t}{\mu - \beta} \tag{10.15}$$

(10.11) and (10.15) are the reduced-form equations for R_t and Q_t. They are the equations that result from solving the simultaneous structural equations given by (10.5) and (10.6). Notice that these reduced form equations have only exogenous variables on the RHS.

10.2 Simultaneous equations bias

It would not be possible to estimate (10.5) and (10.6) validly using OLS, as they are related to one another because they both contain R and Q, and OLS would require them to be estimated separately. What would have happened, however, if a researcher had estimated them separately using OLS? Both equations depend on R. One of the CLRM assumptions was that X and u are independent (when X is a matrix containing all the variables on the RHS of the equation), and, given the additional assumption that $E(u) = 0$, then $E(X'u) = 0$ (i.e. the errors are uncorrelated with the explanatory variables) It is clear from (10.11), however, that R is related to the errors in (10.5) and (10.6) – i.e. it is *stochastic*. This assumption has therefore been violated.

What would the consequences be for the OLS estimator, $\hat{\beta}$, if the simultaneity were ignored? Recall that

$$\hat{\beta} = (X'X)^{-1}X'y \tag{10.16}$$

and that

$$y = X\beta + u \tag{10.17}$$

Replacing y in (10.16) with the RHS of (10.17),

$$\hat{\beta} = (X'X)^{-1}X'(X\beta + u) \tag{10.18}$$

so that

$$\hat{\beta} = (X'X)^{-1}X'X\beta + (X'X)^{-1}X'u \tag{10.19}$$

$$\hat{\beta} = \beta + (X'X)^{-1}X'u \tag{10.20}$$

Taking expectations,

$$E(\hat{\beta}) = E(\beta) + E((X'X)^{-1}X'u) \tag{10.21}$$

$$E(\hat{\beta}) = \beta + E((X'X)^{-1}X'u) \tag{10.22}$$

If the Xs are non-stochastic (i.e. if the assumption had not been violated), $\mathrm{E}[(X'X)^{-1}X'u] = (X'X)^{-1}X'\mathrm{E}[u] = 0$, which would be the case in a single-equation system, so that $E(\hat{\beta}) = \beta$ in (10.22). The implication is that the OLS estimator, $\hat{\beta}$, would be unbiased.

If the equation is part of a system, however, then $\mathrm{E}[(X'X)^{-1}X'u] \neq 0$, in general, so the last term in (10.22) will not drop out, and it can therefore be concluded that the application of OLS to structural equations that are part of a simultaneous system will lead to biased coefficient estimates. This is known as *simultaneity bias* or *simultaneous equations bias*.

Is the OLS estimator still consistent, even though it is biased? No, in fact, the estimator is inconsistent as well, so that the coefficient estimates would still be biased even if an infinite amount of data were available, although proving this would require a level of algebra beyond the scope of this book.

10.3 How can simultaneous-equation models be estimated?

Taking (10.11) and (10.15) – i.e. the reduced-form equations – they can be rewritten as

$$R_t = \pi_{10} + \pi_{11}INT_t + \pi_{12}EMP_t + \varepsilon_{1t} \tag{10.23}$$

$$Q_t = \pi_{20} + \pi_{21}INT_t + \pi_{22}EMP_t + \varepsilon_{2t} \tag{10.24}$$

where the π coefficients in the reduced form are simply combinations of the original coefficients, so that

$$\pi_{10} = \frac{\lambda - \alpha}{\beta - \mu}, \pi_{11} = \frac{\kappa}{\beta - \mu}, \pi_{12} = \frac{-\gamma}{\beta - \mu}, \varepsilon_{1t} = \frac{v_t - u_t}{\beta - \mu}$$

$$\pi_{20} = \frac{\mu\alpha - \beta\lambda}{\mu - \beta}, \pi_{21} = \frac{-\beta\kappa}{\mu - \beta}, \pi_{22} = \frac{\mu\gamma}{\mu - \beta}, \varepsilon_{2t} = \frac{\mu u_t - \beta v_t}{\mu - \beta}$$

Equations (10.23) and (10.24) can be estimated using OLS as all the RHS variables are exogenous, so the usual requirements for consistency and unbiasedness of the OLS estimator will hold (provided that there are no other misspecifications). Estimates of the π_{ij} coefficients will thus be obtained. The values of the π coefficients are probably not of much interest, however; what we wanted were the original parameters in the structural equations – α, β, γ, λ, μ and κ. The latter are the parameters whose values determine how the variables are related to one another according to economic and real estate theory.

10.4 Can the original coefficients be retrieved from the πs?

The short answer to this question is 'Sometimes', depending upon whether the equations are identified. *Identification* is the issue of whether there is enough information in the reduced-form equations to enable the structural-form coefficients to be calculated. Consider the following demand and supply equations:

$$Q_t = \alpha + \beta R_t \quad \text{supply equation} \tag{10.25}$$

$$Q_t = \lambda + \mu R_t \quad \text{demand equation} \tag{10.26}$$

It is impossible to say which equation is which, so, if a real estate analyst simply observed some space rented and the price at which it was rented, it would not be possible to obtain the estimates of α, β, λ and μ. This arises because there is insufficient information from the equations to estimate four parameters. Only two parameters can be estimated here, although each would be some combination of demand and supply parameters, and so neither would be of any use. In this case, it would be stated that both equations are *unidentified* (or not identified or under-identified). Notice that this problem would not have arisen with (10.5) and (10.6), since they have different exogenous variables.

10.4.1 *What determines whether an equation is identified or not?*

Any one of three possible situations could arise, as shown in box 10.1.

Box 10.1 Determining whether an equation is identified

(1) An equation such as (10.25) or (10.26) is *unidentified*. In the case of an unidentified equation, structural coefficients cannot be obtained from the reduced-form estimates by any means.
(2) An equation such as (10.5) or (10.6) is *exactly identified (just identified)*. In the case of a just identified equation, unique structural-form coefficient estimates can be obtained by substitution from the reduced-form equations.
(3) If an equation is *over-identified*, more than one set of structural coefficients can be obtained from the reduced form. An example of this is presented later in this chapter.

How can it be determined whether an equation is identified or not? Broadly, the answer to this question depends upon how many and which variables are present in each structural equation. There are two conditions that can be examined to determine whether a given equation from a system is identified – the order condition and the rank condition.

- The *order condition* is a necessary but not sufficient condition for an equation to be identified. That is, even if the order condition is satisfied, the equation might still not be identified.
- The *rank condition* is a necessary and sufficient condition for identification. The structural equations are specified in a matrix form and the rank of a coefficient matrix of all the variables excluded from a particular equation is examined. An examination of the rank condition requires some technical algebra beyond the scope of this text.

Even though the order condition is not sufficient to ensure the identification of an equation from a system, the rank condition is not considered further here. For relatively simple systems of equations, the two rules would lead to the same conclusions. In addition, most systems of equations in economics and real estate are in fact over-identified, with the result that under-identification is not a big issue in practice.

10.4.2 *Statement of the order condition*

There are a number of different ways of stating the order condition; that employed here is an intuitive one (taken from Ramanathan, 1995, p. 666, and slightly modified):

> Let G denote the number of structural equations. An equation is just identified if the number of variables excluded from an equation is $G - 1$, where 'excluded' means the number of all endogenous and exogenous variables that are not present in this particular equation. If more than $G - 1$ are absent, it is over-identified. If less than $G - 1$ are absent, it is not identified.

One obvious implication of this rule is that equations in a system can have differing degrees of identification, as illustrated by the following example.

Example 10.1 Determining whether equations are identified

Let us determine whether each equation is over-identified, under-identified or just identified in the following system of equations.

$$ABS_t = \alpha_0 + \alpha_1 R_t + \alpha_2 Q_{st} + \alpha_3 EMP_t + \alpha_4 USG_t + u_{1t} \tag{10.27}$$

$$R_t = \beta_0 + \beta_1 Q_{st} + \beta_2 EMP_t + u_{2t} \tag{10.28}$$

$$Q_{st} = \gamma_0 + \gamma_1 R_t + u_{3t} \tag{10.29}$$

where ABS_t = quantity of office space absorbed at time t, R_t = rent level prevailing at time t, Q_{st} = quantity of new office space supplied at time t, EMP_t = office-using employment at time t, USG_t = is the usage ratio (that is, a measure of the square metres per employee) at time t and u_t, e_t and v_t are the error terms at time t.

In this case, there are $G = 3$ equations and three endogenous variables (Q, ABS and R). EMP and USG are exogenous, so we have five variables in total. According to the order condition, if the number of excluded variables is exactly two, the equation is just identified. If the number of excluded variables is more than two, the equation is over-identified. If the number of excluded variables is fewer than two, the equation is not identified.

Applying the order condition to (10.27) to (10.29) produces the following results.

- Equation (10.27): contains all the variables, with none excluded, so it is not identified.
- Equation (10.28): two variables (*ABS* and *USG*) are excluded, and so it is just identified.
- Equation (10.29): has variables *ABS*, *USG* and *EMP* excluded, hence it is over-identified.

10.5 A definition of exogeneity

Leamer (1985) defines a variable x as exogenous if the conditional distribution of y given x does not change with modifications of the process generating x. Although several slightly different definitions exist, it is possible to classify two forms of exogeneity: predeterminedness and strict exogeneity

- A *predetermined* variable is one that is independent of all contemporaneous and future errors in that equation.
- A *strictly exogenous* variable is one that is independent of all contemporaneous, future and past errors in that equation.

10.5.1 *Tests for exogeneity*

Consider again (10.27) to (10.29). Equation (10.27) contains R and Q – but are separate equations required for them, or could the variables R and Q be treated as exogenous? This can be formally investigated using a Hausman (1978) test, which is calculated as shown below.

(1) Obtain the reduced-form equations corresponding to (10.27) to (10.29), as follows.
Substituting in (10.28) for Q_{st} from (10.29),

$$R_t = \beta_0 + \beta_1(\gamma_0 + \gamma_1 R_t + u_{3t}) + \beta_2 EMP_t + u_{2t} \tag{10.30}$$

$$R_t = \beta_0 + \beta_1\gamma_0 + \beta_1\gamma_1 R_t + \beta_1 u_{3t} + \beta_2 EMP_t + u_{2t} \tag{10.31}$$

$$R_t(1-\beta_1\gamma_1) = (\beta_0 + \beta_1\gamma_0) + \beta_2 EMP_t + (u_{2t} + \beta_1 u_{3t}) \tag{10.32}$$

$$R_t = \frac{(\beta_0 + \beta_1\gamma_0)}{(1-\beta_1\gamma_1)} + \frac{\beta_2 EMP_t}{(1-\beta_1\gamma_1)} + \frac{(u_{2t} + \beta_1 u_{3t})}{(1-\beta_1\gamma_1)} \tag{10.33}$$

(10.33) is the reduced-form equation for R_t, since there are no endogenous variables on the RHS. Substituting in (10.27) for Q_{st} from (10.29),

$$ABS_t = \alpha_0 + \alpha_1 R_t + \alpha_2(\gamma_0 + \gamma_1 R_t + u_{3t}) + \alpha_3 EMP_t + \alpha_4 USG_t + u_{1t} \tag{10.34}$$

$$ABS_t = \alpha_0 + \alpha_1 R_t + \alpha_2\gamma_0 + \alpha_2\gamma_1 R_t + \alpha_2 u_{3t} + \alpha_3 EMP_t + \alpha_4 USG_t + u_{1t} \tag{10.35}$$

$$ABS_t = (\alpha_0 + \alpha_2\gamma_0) + (\alpha_1 + \alpha_2\gamma_1)R_t + \alpha_3 EMP_t + \alpha_4 USG_t + (u_{1t} + \alpha_2 u_{3t}) \tag{10.36}$$

Substituting in (10.36) for R_t from (10.33),

$$\begin{aligned} ABS_t = {} & (\alpha_0 + \alpha_2\gamma_0) + (\alpha_1 + \alpha_2\gamma_1) \\ & \times \left[\frac{(\beta_0 + \beta_1\gamma_0)}{(1-\beta_1\gamma_1)} + \frac{\beta_2 EMP_t}{(1-\beta_1\gamma_1)} + \frac{(u_{2t} + \beta_1 u_{3t})}{(1-\beta_1\gamma_1)}\right] \\ & + \alpha_3 EMP_t + \alpha_4 USG_t + (u_{1t} + \alpha_2 u_{3t}) \end{aligned} \tag{10.37}$$

$$\begin{aligned} ABS_t = {} & \left(\alpha_0 + \alpha_2\gamma_0 + (\alpha_1 + \alpha_2\gamma_1)\frac{(\beta_0 + \beta_1\gamma_0)}{(1-\beta_1\gamma_1)}\right) \\ & + \frac{(\alpha_1 + \alpha_2\gamma_1)\beta_2 EMP_t}{(1-\beta_1\gamma_1)} + \frac{(\alpha_1 + \alpha_2\gamma_1)(u_{2t} + \beta_1 u_{3t})}{(1-\beta_1\gamma_1)} \\ & + \alpha_3 EMP_t + \alpha_4 USG_t + (u_{1t} + \alpha_2 u_{3t}) \end{aligned} \tag{10.38}$$

$$ABS_t = \left(\alpha_0 + \alpha_2\gamma_0 + (\alpha_1 + \alpha_2\gamma_1)\frac{(\beta_0 + \beta_1\gamma_0)}{(1 - \beta_1\gamma_1)}\right) + \left(\frac{(\alpha_1 + \alpha_2\gamma_1)\beta_2}{(1 - \beta_1\gamma_1)} + \alpha_3\right) EMP_t + \alpha_4 USG_t + \left(\frac{(\alpha_1 + \alpha_2\gamma_1)(u_{2t} + \beta_1 u_{3t})}{(1 - \beta_1\gamma_1)}\right) + (u_{1t} + \alpha_2 u_{3t}) \tag{10.39}$$

(10.39) is the reduced-form equation for ABS_t. Finally, to obtain the reduced-form equation for Q_{st}, substitute in (10.29) for R_t from (10.33):

$$Q_{st} = \left(\gamma_0 + \frac{\gamma_1(\beta_0 + \beta_1\gamma_0)}{(1 - \beta_1\gamma_1)}\right) + \frac{\gamma_1\beta_2 EMP_t}{(1 - \beta_1\gamma_1)} + \left(\frac{\gamma_1(u_{2t} + \beta_1 u_{3t})}{(1 - \beta_1\gamma_1)} + u_{3t}\right) \tag{10.40}$$

Thus the reduced-form equations corresponding to (10.27) to (10.29) are, respectively, given by (10.39), (10.33) and (10.40). These three equations can also be expressed using π_{ij} for the coefficients, as discussed above:

$$ABS_t = \pi_{10} + \pi_{11}EMP_t + \pi_{12}USG_t + v_1 \tag{10.41}$$

$$R_t = \pi_{20} + \pi_{21}EMP_t + v_2 \tag{10.42}$$

$$Q_{st} = \pi_{30} + \pi_{31}EMP_t + v_3 \tag{10.43}$$

Estimate the reduced-form equations (10.41) to (10.43) using OLS, and obtain the fitted values, $\hat{ABS}_t^1$, $\hat{R}_t^1$, $\hat{Q}_{st}^1$, where the superfluous superscript[1] denotes the fitted values from the reduced-form equations.

(2) Run the regression corresponding to (10.27) – i.e. the structural-form equation – at this stage ignoring any possible simultaneity.

(3) Run the regression (10.27) again, but now also including the fitted values from the reduced-form equations, $\hat{R}_t^1$, $\hat{Q}_{st}^1$, as additional regressors.

$$ABS_t = \alpha_0 + \alpha_1 R_t + \alpha_2 Q_{st} + \alpha_3 EMP_t + \alpha_4 USG_t + \lambda_2\hat{R}_t^1 + \lambda_3\hat{Q}_{st}^1 + \varepsilon_{1t} \tag{10.44}$$

(4) Use an F-test to test the joint restriction that $\lambda_2 = 0$ and $\lambda_3 = 0$. If the null hypothesis is rejected, R_t and Q_{st} should be treated as endogenous. If λ_2 and λ_3 are significantly different from zero, there is extra important information for modelling ABS_t from the reduced-form equations. On the other hand, if the null is not rejected, R_t and Q_{st} can be treated as exogenous for ABS_t, and there is no useful additional information available for ABS_t from modelling R_t and Q_{st} as endogenous variables.

Steps 2 to 4 would then be repeated for (10.28) and (10.29).

10.6 Estimation procedures for simultaneous equations systems

Each equation that is part of a recursive system (see section 10.8 below) can be estimated separately using OLS. In practice, though, not all systems of equations will be recursive, so a direct way to address the estimation of equations that are from a true simultaneous system must be sought. In fact, there are potentially many methods that can be used, three of which – indirect least squares (ILS), two-stage least squares (2SLS or TSLS) and instrumental variables – are detailed here. Each of these are discussed below.

10.6.1 *Indirect least squares*

Although it is not possible to use OLS directly on the structural equations, it is possible to apply OLS validly to the reduced-form equations. If the system is just identified, ILS involves estimating the reduced-form equations using OLS, and then using them to substitute back to obtain the structural parameters. ILS is intuitive to understand in principle, but it is not widely applied, for the following reasons.

(1) *Solving back to get the structural parameters can be tedious.* For a large system, the equations may be set up in a matrix form, and to solve them may therefore require the inversion of a large matrix.
(2) *Most simultaneous equations systems are over-identified*, and ILS can be used to obtain coefficients only for just identified equations. For over-identified systems, ILS would not yield unique structural form estimates.

ILS estimators are consistent and asymptotically efficient, but in general they are biased, so that in finite samples ILS will deliver biased structural-form estimates. In a nutshell, the bias arises from the fact that the structural-form coefficients under ILS estimation are transformations of the reduced-form coefficients. When expectations are taken to test for unbiasedness, it is, in general, not the case that the expected value of a (non-linear) combination of reduced-form coefficients will be equal to the combination of their expected values (see Gujarati, 2009, for a proof).

10.6.2 *Estimation of just identified and over-identified systems using 2SLS*

This technique is applicable for the estimation of over-identified systems, for which ILS cannot be used. It can also be employed for estimating the coefficients of just identified systems, in which case the method would yield asymptotically equivalent estimates to those obtained from ILS.

Two-stage least squares estimation is done in two stages.

- *Stage 1.* Obtain and estimate the reduced-form equations using OLS. Save the fitted values for the dependent variables.
- *Stage 2.* Estimate the structural equations using OLS, but replace any RHS endogenous variables with their stage 1 fitted values.

Example 10.2

Suppose that (10.27) to (10.29) are required. 2SLS would involve the following two steps (with time subscripts suppressed for ease of exposition).

- *Stage 1.* Estimate the reduced-form equations (10.41) to (10.43) individually by OLS and obtain the fitted values, and denote them $\hat{ABS}^1$, $\hat{R}^1$, $\hat{Q}_S^1$, where the superfluous superscript[1] indicates that these are the fitted values from the first stage.
- *Stage 2.* Replace the RHS endogenous variables with their stage 1 estimated values:

$$ABS = \alpha_0 + \alpha_1 \hat{R}^1 + \alpha_3 \hat{Q}_S^1 + \alpha_4 EMP + \alpha_5 USG + u_1 \tag{10.45}$$

$$R = \beta_0 + \beta_1 \hat{Q}_S^1 + \beta_2 EMP + u_2 \tag{10.46}$$

$$Q_S = \gamma_0 + \gamma_1 \hat{R}^1 + u_3 \tag{10.47}$$

where $\hat{R}^1$ and $\hat{Q}_S^1$ are the fitted values from the reduced-form estimation. Now $\hat{R}^1$ and $\hat{Q}_S^1$ will not be correlated with u_1, $\hat{Q}_S^1$ will not be correlated with u_2, and $\hat{R}^1$ will not be correlated with u_3. The simultaneity problem has therefore been removed. It is worth noting that the 2SLS estimator is consistent, but not unbiased.

In a simultaneous equations framework, it is still of concern whether the usual assumptions of the CLRM are valid or not, although some of the test statistics require modifications to be applicable in the systems context. Most econometrics packages will automatically make any required changes. To illustrate one potential consequence of the violation of the CLRM assumptions, if the disturbances in the structural equations are autocorrelated, the 2SLS estimator is not even consistent.

The standard error estimates also need to be modified compared with their OLS counterparts (again, econometrics software will usually do this automatically), but, once this has been done, the usual *t*-tests can be used to test hypotheses about the structural-form coefficients. This modification arises as a result of the use of the reduced-form fitted values on the RHS rather than actual variables, which implies that a modification to the error variance is required.

10.6.3 *Instrumental variables*

Broadly, the method of instrumental variables (IV) is another technique for parameter estimation that can be validly used in the context of a simultaneous equations system. Recall that the reason that OLS cannot be used directly on the structural equations is that the endogenous variables are correlated with the errors.

One solution to this would be not to use R or Q_S but, rather, to use some other variables instead. These other variables should be (highly) correlated with R and Q_S, but not correlated with the errors; such variables would be known as *instruments*. Suppose that suitable instruments for R and Q_S were found and denoted z_2 and z_3, respectively. The instruments are not used in the structural equations directly but, rather, regressions of the following form are run:

$$R = \lambda_1 + \lambda_2 z_2 + \varepsilon_1 \tag{10.48}$$

$$Q_S = \lambda_3 + \lambda_4 z_3 + \varepsilon_2 \tag{10.49}$$

Obtain the fitted values from (10.48) and (10.49), $\hat{R}^1$ and $\hat{Q}_S^1$, and replace R and Q_S with these in the structural equation. It is typical to use more than one instrument per endogenous variable. If the instruments are the variables in the reduced-form equations, then IV is equivalent to 2SLS, so that the latter can be viewed as a special case of the former.

10.6.4 *What happens if IV or 2SLS are used unnecessarily?*

In other words, suppose that one attempted to estimate a simultaneous system when the variables specified as endogenous were in fact independent of one another. The consequences are similar to those of including irrelevant variables in a single-equation OLS model. That is, the coefficient estimates will still be consistent, but will be inefficient compared to those that just used OLS directly.

10.6.5 *Other estimation techniques*

There are, of course, many other estimation techniques available for systems of equations, including three-stage least squares (3SLS), full-information maximum likelihood (FIML) and limited-information maximum likelihood (LIML). Three-stage least squares provides a third step in the estimation process that allows for non-zero covariances between the error terms in the structural equations. It is asymptotically more efficient than 2SLS, since the latter ignores any information that may be available concerning the error covariances (and also any additional information that may be contained in the endogenous variables of other equations).

Full-information maximum likelihood involves estimating all the equations in the system simultaneously using maximum likelihood.[2] Thus, under FIML, all the parameters in all equations are treated jointly, and an appropriate likelihood function is formed and maximised. Finally, limited-information maximum likelihood involves estimating each equation separately by maximum likelihood. LIML and 2SLS are asymptotically equivalent. For further technical details on each of these procedures, see Greene (2002, ch. 15).

10.7 Case study: projections in the industrial property market using a simultaneous equations system

Thompson and Tsolacos (2000) construct a three-equation simultaneous system to model the industrial market in the United Kingdom. The system allows the interaction of the supply of new industrial space, industrial rents, construction costs, the availability of industrial floor space and macroeconomic variables. The supply of new industrial space, industrial real estate rents and the availability of industrial floor space are the variables that are simultaneously explained in the system. The regression forms of the three structural equations in the system are

$$NIBSUP_t = \alpha_0 + a_1 RENT_t + \alpha_2 CC_t + u_t \tag{10.50}$$

$$RENT_t = \beta_0 + \beta_1 RENT_{t-1} + \beta_2 AVFS_t + e_t \tag{10.51}$$

$$AVFS_t = \gamma_0 + \gamma_1 GDP_t + \gamma_2 GDP_{t-1} + \gamma_3 NIBSUP_t + \varepsilon_t \tag{10.52}$$

where *NIBSUP* is new industrial building supply, *RENT* is real industrial rents, *CC* is the construction cost, *AVFS* is the availability of industrial floor space (a measure of physical vacancy and not as a percentage of stock) and *GDP* is gross domestic product. The αs, βs and γs are the structural parameters to be estimated, and u_t, e_t and ε_t are the stochastic disturbances. Therefore, in this system, the three endogenous variables $NIBSUP_t$, $RENT_t$ and $AVFS_t$ are determined in terms of the exogenous variables and the disturbances.

In (10.50) it is assumed that the supply of new industrial space in a particular year is driven by rents and construction costs in that year. The inclusion of past values of rents and construction costs in (10.50) is also tested, however. Rents (equation 10.51) respond to the level of industrial floor space available. Available floor space reflects both new buildings, which have not been occupied previously, and the stock of the existing and previously

[2] See Brooks (2008) for a discussion of the principles of maximum likelihood estimation.

occupied buildings that came onto the market as the result of lease termination, bankruptcy, etc. A high level of available industrial space that is suitable for occupation will satisfy new demand and relieve pressures on rent increases. Recent past rents also have an influence on current rents.

The final equation (10.52) of the system describes the relationship for the availability of industrial floor space (or vacant industrial floor space) as a function both of demand (*GDP*) and supply-side (*NIBSUP*) factors. *GDP* lagged by a year enters the equation as well to allow for 'pent-up' demand (demand that was not satisfied in the previous period) on floor space availability. The sample period for this study is 1977 to 1998.

10.7.1 Results

Before proceeding to estimate the system, the authors address the identification and simultaneity conditions that guide the choice of the estimation methodologies. Based on the order condition for identification, which is a necessary condition for an equation to be identified, it is concluded that all equations in the system are over-identified. There are three equations in the system, and therefore, as we noted above, an equation is identified if at least two variables are missing from that equation. In the case of the first equation, $RENT_{t-1}$, $AVFS_t$, GDP_t and GDP_{t-1} are all missing; GDP_t, GDP_{t-1}, $NIBSUP_t$ and CC_t are missing from the second equation; and CC_t, $RENT_t$ and $RENT_{t-1}$ are missing from the third equation. Therefore there could be more than one value for each of the structural parameters of the equations when they are reconstructed from estimates of the reduced-form coefficients. This finding has implications for the estimation methodology – for example, the OLS methodology will not provide consistent estimates.

The simultaneity problem occurs when the endogenous variables included on the right-hand side of the equations in the system are correlated with the disturbance term of those equations. It arises from the interaction and cross-determination of the variables in a simultaneous-equation model. To test formally for possible simultaneity in the system, the authors apply the Hausman specification test to pairs of equations in the system as described above, and also as discussed by Nakamura and Nakamura (1981) and Gujarati (2009). It is found from these tests that simultaneity is present and, therefore, the system should be estimated with an approach other than OLS.

When the system of equations (10.50) to (10.52) is estimated, the errors in all equations are serially correlated. The inclusion of additional lags in the system does not remedy the situation. Another way to deal with the problem of serial correlation is to use changes (first differences) instead of levels for some or all of the variables; the inclusion of some variables in

Table 10.1 OLS estimates of system of equations (10.53) to (10.55)

	$NIBSUP_t$	$\Delta RENT_t$	$\Delta AVFS_t$
Constant	6,518.86	1.90	3,093.07
	(14.83)	(0.42)	(3.41)
$\Delta RENT_t$	24.66		
	(5.91)		
CC_t	−34.28		
	(−5.95)		
$\Delta RENT_{t-1}$		0.62	
		(4.12)	
$\Delta AVFS_t$		−0.01	
		(−3.10)	
ΔGDP_t			−102.28
			(−4.15)
ΔGDP_{t-1}			−77.39
			(−3.14)
$NIBSUP_t$			−0.12
			(−0.56)
Adj. R^2	0.79	0.57	0.76
DW statistic	$d = 1.73$	$h = 0.88$	$d = 1.40$

Notes: Numbers in parentheses are t-ratios. The h-statistic is a variant on DW that is still valid when lagged dependent variables are included in the model.

first differences helps to rectify the problem. Therefore, in order to remove the influence of trends in all equations and produce residuals that are not serially correlated, the first differences for *RENT*, *AVFS* and *GDP* are used. First differences of *NIBSUP* are not taken as this is a flow variable; CC_t in first differences is not statistically significant in the model and therefore the authors included this variable in levels form. The modified system that is finally estimated is given by equations (10.53) to (10.55).

$$NIBSUP_t = \alpha_0 + \alpha_1 \Delta RENT_t + \alpha_2 CC_t + u_t \tag{10.53}$$

$$\Delta RENT_t = \beta_0 + \beta_1 \Delta RENT_{t-1} + \beta_2 \Delta AVFS_t + e_t \tag{10.54}$$

$$\Delta AVFS_t = \gamma_0 + \gamma_1 \Delta GDP_t + \gamma_2 \Delta GDP_{t-1} + \gamma_3 NIBSUP_t + \varepsilon_t \tag{10.55}$$

where Δ is the first difference operator. Since first differences are used for some of the variables, the estimation period becomes 1978 to 1998.

Initially, for comparison, the system is estimated with OLS in spite of its inappropriateness, with the results presented in table 10.1. It can be seen that all the variables take the expected sign and all are statistically

Table 10.2 2SLS estimates of system of equations (10.53) to (10.55)

	$NIBSUP_t$	$\Delta RENT_t$	$\Delta AVFS_t$
Constant	6,532.45 (12.84)	2.40 (0.51)	2,856.02 (3.17)
$\Delta RENT_t$	25.07 (5.25)		
CC_t	−34.44 (−5.26)		
$\Delta RENT_{t-1}$		0.62 (4.01)	
$\Delta AVFS_t$		−0.01 (−3.70)	
ΔGDP_t			−94.43 (−4.17)
ΔGDP_{t-1}			−83.79 (−3.44)
$NIBSUP_t$			−0.05 (−0.21)
Adj. R^2	0.78	0.55	0.82
DW-statistic	$d = 1.72$	$h = 1.07$	$d = 0.99$

Notes: numbers in parentheses are t-ratios. The h-statistic is a variant on DW that is still valid when lagged dependent variables are included in the model.

significant, with the exception of $NIBSUP_t$ in equation (10.53). It is worth noting that all the coefficients are significant at the 1 per cent level (except, of course, for the coefficient on $NIBSUP_t$). The explanatory power of equations (10.53) to (10.55) is good. The specification for the rent equation has a lower $\bar{R}^2$ value of 0.57. (10.54) and (10.55) appear to be well specified based on the DW statistic (the d-statistic and h-statistic, respectively). The value of this statistic points to a potential problem of serial correlation in equation (10.54), however. This is further tested with an application of the Breusch–Godfrey test, which suggests that the errors are not serially correlated.

Although the overall results of the estimation of the system are considered good, the authors note that the use of OLS may lead to biased and inconsistent parameter estimates because the equations are over-identified and simultaneity is present. For this purpose, the system is estimated by the method of two-stage least squares, with the results shown in table 10.2. Interestingly, the results obtained from using 2SLS hardly change from those derived using OLS. The magnitudes of the structural coefficients and their levels of significance in all three equations are similar to those in

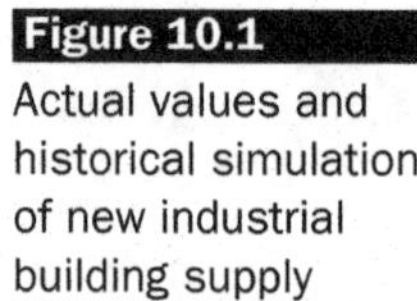
Figure 10.1
Actual values and historical simulation of new industrial building supply

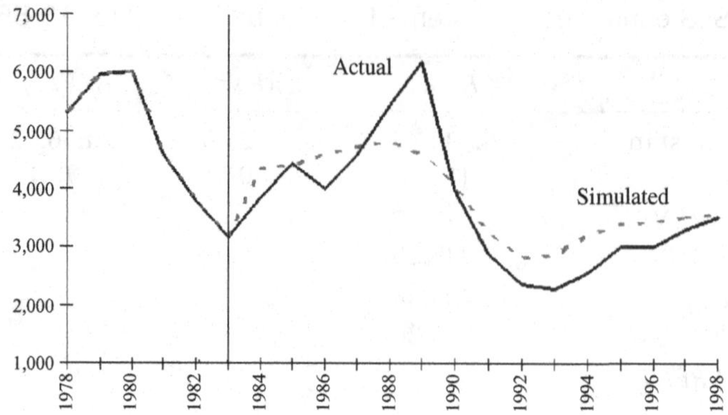

table 10.1. The explanatory power of the *NIBSUP* and $\Delta RENT$ equations shows a marginal fall. On the other hand, the adjusted R^2 is higher in the equation for $\Delta AVFS$, but the low DW d-statistic indicates problems of serial correlation. Overall, it can be seen that, in this particular example, the 2SLS procedure does not improve the OLS results, although the former approach is still superior from an econometric perspective.

10.7.2 *Simulations*

Evaluation of the estimated structural coefficients in the simultaneous model for the industrial property market takes place with an examination of the fit of the individual endogenous variables in a simulation context. The ability of the estimated coefficients to track the historical path of the endogenous variables *NIBSUP*, $\Delta RENT$ and $\Delta AVFS$ is thereby examined. The system that produces the simulations is that estimated with OLS but the authors exclude the term $NIBSUP_t$ from the last equation since it is not significant and does not add to the explanatory power of the system. The period for the simulations is 1984 to 1998. The starting point in the simulation period allows an evaluation of the performance of the system over the cycle of the late 1980s to the early 1990s. These simulations are dynamic. Therefore, over the simulation period, only the actual values of ΔGDP_t, ΔGDP_{t-1} and CC_t are used. The term $\Delta RENT_{t-1}$ in equation (10.54) is the simulation solution – that is, the value that the system predicted for the previous period. In these simulations, the structural coefficients estimated using the whole-sample period are employed. From the simulated values of $\Delta RENT$ and $\Delta AVFS$, the simulated series for *RENT* and *AVFS* are constructed. The simulated and actual series are given in figures 10.1 to 10.3.

Figure 10.1 shows the actual new industrial building supply and the simulated series (in millions of pounds, 1995 prices). The simulated series

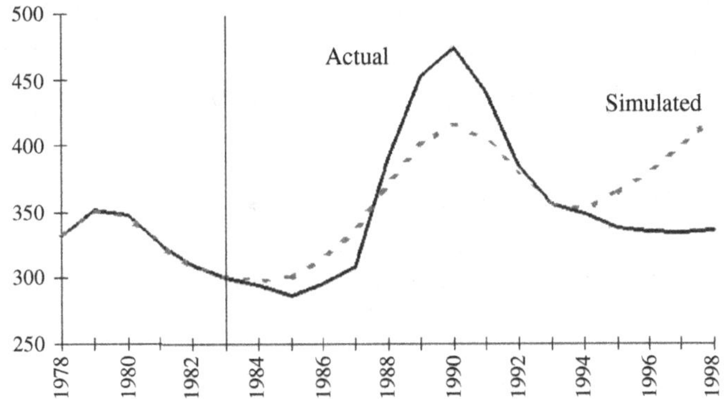

Figure 10.2 Actual values and historical simulation of real industrial rents

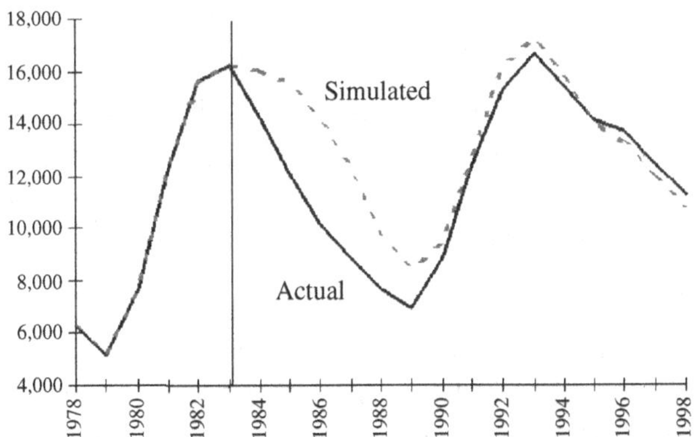

Figure 10.3 Actual values and historical simulation of industrial floor space availability

tracks the phases of the 1983 to 1998 cycle but it does not replicate the peak in 1989 and the drop during 1991 to 1993. In addition, the simulated series over-predicts the actual series during the period 1991 to 1997.

With regard to rents, the simulated series (measured in index values) reproduces the trend of the actual series well (figure 10.2) until 1993, but, again, the peak of 1990 is not replicated. Since 1993 the actual series of real rents has exhibited a slight fall, which seems to bottom out in 1997, but the model predicts a continuous growth in real rents. The authors attribute the deviation of the simulated series from the actual rent series to (1) fuller capacity utilisation, especially at the initial phases of an economic expansion; (2) the positive take-up rate in the period 1993 to 1998 (when the availability of floor space declined continuously); and (3) the higher output/floor space ratio caused by technological advances.

Finally, figure 10.3 illustrates the cycles of the availability of industrial floor space (measured in thousands of square metres). The availability of floor space has increased in periods of recession and low economic growth (the first half of the 1980s and the beginning of the 1990s) and has fallen in periods of economic expansion (the second half of the 1980s and after

1993). The simulated series tracks the actual series very well. The simulation fit has improved considerably since 1990 and reproduces the last cycle of available industrial space very accurately.

10.8 A special case: recursive models

Consider the following system of equations, with time subscripts omitted for simplicity:

$$Y_1 = \beta_{10} + \gamma_{11}X_1 + \gamma_{12}X_2 + u_1 \quad (10.56)$$

$$Y_2 = \beta_{20} + \beta_{21}Y_1 + \gamma_{21}X_1 + \gamma_{22}X_2 + u_2 \quad (10.57)$$

$$Y_3 = \beta_{30} + \beta_{31}Y_1 + \beta_{32}Y_2 + \gamma_{31}X_1 + \gamma_{32}X_2 + u_3 \quad (10.58)$$

Assume that the error terms from each of the three equations are not correlated with each other. Can the equations be estimated individually using OLS? At first sight, an appropriate answer to this question might appear to be 'No, because this is a simultaneous equations system'. Consider the following, though.

- Equation (10.56) contains no endogenous variables, so X_1 and X_2 are not correlated with u_1. OLS can therefore be used on (10.56).
- Equation (10.57) contains endogenous Y_1 together with exogenous X_1 and X_2. OLS can be used on (10.57) if all the RHS variables in (10.57) are uncorrelated with that equation's error term. In fact, Y_1 is not correlated with u_2, because there is no Y_2 term in (10.56). So OLS can indeed be used on (10.57).
- Equation (10.58) contains both Y_1 and Y_2; these are required to be uncorrelated with u_3. By similar arguments to the above, (10.56) and (10.57) do not contain Y_3. OLS can therefore be used on (10.58).

This is known as a *recursive* or *triangular system*, which is really a special case – a set of equations that looks like a simultaneous equations system, but is not. There is no simultaneity problem here, in fact, as the dependence is not bidirectional; for each equation it all goes one way.

10.9 Case study: an application of a recursive model to the City of London office market

Hendershott, Lizieni and Matysiak (1999) develop a recursive multi-equation model to track the cyclical nature of the City of London office market. The model incorporates the interlinked occupational, development and investment markets. This structural model has four identities and three equations. The identities (using the same notation as in the original paper) are

$$S = (1 - dep)S(-1) + complete \tag{10.59}$$

$$D = D(-1) + absorp \tag{10.60}$$

$$v = 100\frac{S - D}{S} \tag{10.61}$$

where S is supply or total stock, *dep* refers to the depreciation rate, *complete* is completions, D is demand (that is, space occupied), *absorp* is net absorptions and v is the vacancy rate.

The fourth identity specifies the equilibrium rent,

$$R^* = (r + dep + oper)RC \tag{10.62}$$

where r is the real interest rate, *oper* is the operating expense ratio and RC is the replacement cost.

The rent specification is given by

$$\%\Delta R^* = f(v^* - v, R^* - R) \tag{10.63}$$

where * denotes an equilibrium value. The equilibrium vacancy v^* is the rate at which real rents will be constant when they equal their equilibrium value. More specifically, the rent equation the authors estimate is

$$\%\Delta R = \alpha + \beta_1 v_{t-1} + \beta_2(R_t^* - R_{t-1}) + u_t \tag{10.64}$$

with $\alpha = -\lambda v^*$.

The measure of rent modelled in this study is the real effective rent. The headline nominal values are converted into real figures using the GDP deflator. The resulting real rents are then adjusted to allow for varying tenant incentive packages. To estimate (10.64), we need a series for the equilibrium rent R^*, which is taken from (10.62). The authors assume that the operating expense ratio for property investors in the United Kingdom is low. It is assumed to be 1.5 per cent due to the full repairing and insuring terms of leases. To put this figure into context, in an earlier paper, Hendershott (1996) had assumed a figure of 5 per cent for the Sydney office market. The depreciation rate is assumed constant at 2 per cent. The real interest rate is estimated as

redemption yield on 20-year government bonds + 2% (risk premium)
− expected inflation

For the expected inflation rate, a number of different measures can be used. Based on Hendershott (1996), we believe that the expected inflation proxy used is a moving average of annualised percentage changes in the GDP deflator. Because of implausibly negative real interest rates during the 1975 to 1981 period, the authors make an amendment to the resulting real interest rate series. The real risk-free interest rate (the twenty-year government bond yield minus expected inflation) is set as the maximum of the above estimate and 1 per cent. Hence the lowest permissible value of the real risk-free rate is 1 per cent. The expression for the cash flow return is

$$\begin{aligned} r + dep + oper &= \textit{real risk-free rate} + premium + dep + oper \\ &= \textit{real risk-free rate} \; + 2\% + 2\% + 1.5\% \\ &= \textit{real risk-free rate} \; + 5.5\% \end{aligned}$$

Finally, an estimate is needed for the replacement cost (RC). The authors observe that, over the period 1977 to 1985, real effective rents changed very little. They therefore assume that real rents were in broad equilibrium during that period and that building values approximated replacement cost. The RC was determined by scaling down the required cash flow return (real risk-free rate + 0.055) to the effective rent in 1983. Hence the R^* series was the effective real rent in 1983 multiplied by the required cash flow return. It appears that the variable that determines R^* is the real risk-free rate through time, since everything else is constant.

The empirical estimation of the rent equation (with t-ratios in parentheses) is

$$\underset{}{\%\Delta\hat{R}_t} = \underset{(4.40)}{20.08} - \underset{(-5.25)}{2.83 vacancy_{t-1}} + \underset{(10.49)}{3.72(R_t^* - R_{t-1})} \tag{10.65}$$

Adj. $R^2 = 0.64$; the estimated υ^* is 7.10 per cent.

The theoretical specification for completions is broadly similar to that for rent growth:

$$complete = g(\upsilon^* - \upsilon, R - R^*) \tag{10.66}$$

Relatively low vacancy rates in relation to equilibrium vacancy and relatively high real effective rents relative to the equilibrium rent will therefore trigger new construction. The empirical estimations did not establish a positive influence of the vacancy gap ($\upsilon^* - \upsilon$) on construction. Accordingly, the vacancy gap was dropped. On the other hand, the rent gap had the expected positive influence on completions.

The completions equation specified on the rent gap was unable to replicate the rise in completions in 1989/90. The authors included a dummy (DUM) in 1989 to allow for the spike. The theoretical regression equation is

$$complete_t = \alpha_1 + \gamma_1(Gap_{t-1} + Gap_{t-2}) + \gamma_2 DUM_t + e_t \tag{10.67}$$

and the fitted specification is

$$\hat{complete}_t = \underset{(3.57)}{71.36} + \underset{(7.53)}{67.69}(Gap_{t-1} + Gap_{t-2}) + \underset{(4.56)}{309.67}DUM_t \qquad (10.68)$$

$R^2 = 0.82$.

Finally, the net absorption equation, or the percentage increase in space demanded, was taken as a positive function of the percentage change in employment in finance and business services and a negative function of the level of real effective rents. The theoretical specification is given by (10.69):

$$\frac{absorp}{D_{t-1}} = h(\%\Delta EMPL, R) \qquad (10.69)$$

Prior analysis by the authors revealed that demand for office space (D), employment (*EMPL*) and rents (R) form a long-run relationship, a subject that is covered in chapter 12. The estimated long-run equation was

$$\hat{D}_t = \underset{(4.40)}{2.80} + \underset{(5.78)}{22.95}EMPL_t - \underset{(-6.70)}{0.13}R_t \qquad (10.70)$$

Adj. $R^2 = 0.69$.

In (10.70), both employment and rent are signed as expected. The resulting error correction equation (see chapter 12) is

$$\hat{absor}_t = \underset{(3.06)}{0.50}\ absor_{t-1} - \underset{(-1.96)}{5.37}ECT_{t-1} - \underset{(-2.71)}{0.08}(\%\Delta R_{t-1}) \qquad (10.71)$$

Adj. $R^2 = 0.64$.

The error correction term (*ECT*) takes the expected negative sign (denoting the presence of an equilibrium adjustment process) and is statistically significant.

10.10 Example: a recursive system for the Tokyo office market

We further illustrate the estimation of a recursive system with identities using data from the Tokyo market. In order to link this example to the study by Hendershott, Lizieri and Matysiak (1999), we use the framework of that paper. The Tokyo data available are quarterly from 1Q1995 to 4Q2007.[3] For the estimation of the equilibrium rent series we take the yield on long-term bonds, and for the real yield (or real risk-free rate) we deduct the annual CPI inflation rate from the bond yield each quarter (hence we do not use an expected measure for inflation as Hendershott, Lizieri and Matysiak did).

[3] The data are heavily based on PPR's international database.

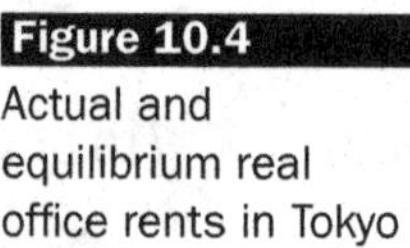
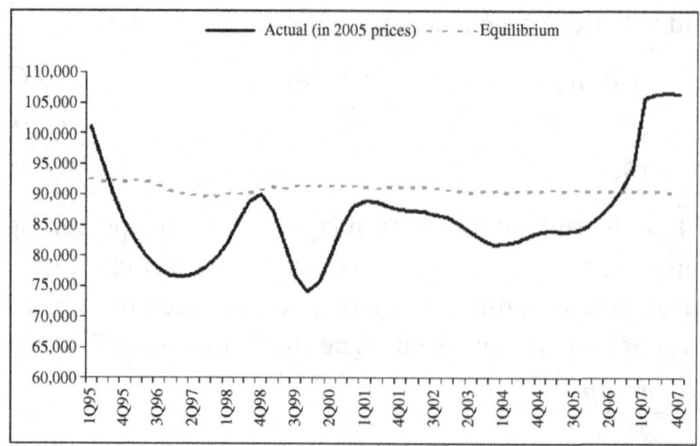

Figure 10.4 Actual and equilibrium real office rents in Tokyo

The risk premium is set at 1.5 per cent, the operating expense ratio at 2 per cent and the depreciation rate also at 2 per cent. The bond yield in 1Q1996 was 4.44 per cent and the annual inflation rate that quarter was −0.15 per cent. Hence the value for the cash flow return in that quarter is

$$\begin{aligned} & \textit{bond yield} - \textit{inflation} + \textit{premium} + \textit{depreciation} + \textit{operating expense rate} \\ & \quad = 3.23 - (-0.35) + 1.5 + 2 + 2.5 = 9.58. \end{aligned}$$

We scale the cash flow series with the level of real rent in 2Q2005, when real rents showed no change or, rather, they exhibited the lowest quarterly change in our sample (with the exception of 4Q2007, the last observation in our sample). The equilibrium rent series along with the real rent series are plotted in figure 10.4.

In relation to the actual rent, the equilibrium rent shows very little variation, reflecting the low volatility of the long-term bond yield and inflation. For most of the sample, the actual series is below this measure of equilibrium rent. On two occasions the actual series moved closer to and nearly matched the equilibrium series, but it moved away again. In 2006 the actual series broke through the equilibrium rent, remaining well above it by the end of 2007. Having established an equilibrium rent series, we now estimate the equations of the system.

Rent equation

$$\begin{aligned} \%\Delta \widehat{RENTR}_t = \; & \underset{(5.7^{***})}{6.657} + \underset{(3.1^{***})}{0.000163}(R_t^* - RENTR_{t-1}) - \underset{(-6.2^{***})}{1.463}VAC_{t-1} \end{aligned} \tag{10.72}$$

Adj. $R^2 = 0.42$, DW = 0.97. The three asterisks here (and subsequently) indicate significance at the 1 per cent level; t-ratios in parentheses.

All the coefficients are signed according to our expectations and they are significant at the 1 per cent level. As noted earlier, from the above coefficients we can derive an estimate for the natural vacancy rate in the Tokyo market:

$$-\lambda \upsilon^* = 6.657 \text{ with } \lambda = -1.463, \text{ hence } \upsilon^* = 6.657/(-(-1.463)) = 4.6\%.$$

Completions equation

$$\underset{}{\hat{COMPL}_t} = \underset{(7.8^{***})}{120.90} + \underset{(1.3)}{0.00243}(RENTR - R^*)_{t-6} \qquad (10.73)$$

Adj. $R^2 = 0.02$, DW $= 0.60$.

In the completions equation, the gap has a positive sign, and hence rents above equilibrium will trigger new construction. We use a similar lag length to Hendershott, Lizieri and Matysiak. The explanatory power of this equation is negligible; the rent gap explains close to nothing of the variation in completions. If we plot the actual and fitted values for this equation, we observe that the trend is captured but not the variation. The inclusion of different lags for the rent gap does not change the results.

Absorption equation

Estimation of the absorption equation requires two stages. In the first stage, we estimate the long-term relationship

$$\hat{D}_t = \underset{(-15.8^{***})}{-45100.1} + \underset{(20.00^{***})}{32.98}OFFEMP_t + \underset{(1.9^{*})}{0.02}RENTR_t \qquad (10.74)$$

Adj. $R^2 = 0.91$, DW $= 0.13$.

The level of real rent takes a positive sign, which is counter-intuitive and opposite to the result obtained by Hendershott, Lizieri and Matysiak for London. Although this represents a misspecification, for the sake of sticking to this methodology we proceed to estimate the absorption equation. The residuals of (10.74) become the error correction term series in (10.75). In (10.75), we follow the Hendershott, Lizieri and Matysiak specification

$$\hat{ABS}_t = \underset{(3.7^{***})}{79.94} + \underset{(2.3^{**})}{0.339}ABS_{t-1} - \underset{(-0.2)}{0.679}\%\Delta RENTR_{t-1} + \underset{(0.1)}{0.0017}ECT_{t-1} \qquad (10.75)$$

Adj. $R^2 = 0.06$. The two asterisks here (are subsequently) indicate significance at the 5 per cent level.

The absorption equation is not a promising one. The only significant term is absorption in the previous period. The error correction term takes a positive sign and is not significant. Similarly, past rent growth is not statistically significant, and the explanatory power is a mere 6 per cent.

Another option is to check for a long-term relationship between demand and employment only (so that the error correction term is based on this bivariate relationship), and then we could still add the lagged rent growth term.

Both the completions and absorption equations are far from well specified – a finding that sheds doubt on the applicability of this model for the Tokyo office market. The differences with Hendershott, Lizieri and Matysiak's London office model can be explained by several factors, however. First, in the Tokyo model, we use quarterly data. The variation of completions and in particular of absorption is much greater than when we estimate the model with annual data. A lower explanatory ability of the model is perhaps not surprising, therefore (although in our case two equations have no explanatory power at all). Second, the sample period is different. Third, the data are not from the same source, and this certainly introduces further variation in the results. Fourth, we do not use effective rents but rents not adjusted for rent concessions (such as rent-free periods). Fifth, we may not have the right equilibrium rent measure for Tokyo. Sixth, the system may not be appropriate.

Nevertheless, since one of our objectives in this chapter is to illustrate the estimation of such recursive models, and in this case with identities, we examine the performance of this system over the last four years of the sample. We re-estimate equations (10.74) to (10.75) for the period until 4Q2003. We then use the coefficients to forecast rents, completions and absorption for the remaining four years of the sample. Through the vacancy identity, we will obtain a forecast for vacancy. The computations are shown in table 10.3.

Columns (iv) and (x), in bold, represent the exogenous variables. Column (iv) is also an identity, but since we have calculated future values for this forecast we also consider it exogenous, as it is determined outside the system. The three equations we are estimating are in italics. To illustrate the workings, let us start with the rent equation (column (ii)). The estimation of (10.72) for the period until 4Q2003 gives

$$\%\Delta \widehat{RENTR}_t = \underset{(2.8^{***})}{5.128} + \underset{(2.6^{***})}{0.000194}(R_t^* - RENTR_{t-1}) - \underset{(-4.2^{***})}{1.279}VAC_{t-1} \qquad (10.76)$$

Adj. $R^2 = 0.44$, DW $= 0.50$.

The value of real rent growth in 1Q2004 is

$$\%\Delta RENTR_{4Q04} = 5.128 + 0.000194 \times (90271 - 81839) - 1.279 \times 7.0 = -2.19$$

Table 10.3 Simulations from the system of equations

(i)	(ii) %ΔR	(iii) R	(iv) R*	(v) VAC	(vi) S	(vii) Compl	(viii) D	(ix) ABS	(x) offemp	(xi) ECT
3Q02		86,793	**90,811**							
4Q02		86,207	**90,600**							
1Q03		85,206	**90,433**							
2Q03		83,866	**90,288**							
3Q03		82,594	**90,473**							
4Q03	*−0.91*	81,839	**90,425**	7.0	20,722	*220*	19,271	*225*	**1,910**	252.1
1Q04	*−2.19*	80,047	**90,271**	6.7	20,840	*118*	19,445	*174*	**1,909**	476.9
2Q04	*−1.43*	78,904	**90,403**	6.5	20,958	*118*	19,592	*147*	**1,908**	686.0
3Q04	*−0.97*	78,138	**90,459**	6.4	21,074	*116*	19,721	*129*	**1,907**	860.5
4Q04	*−0.69*	77,597	**90,477**	6.4	21,188	*114*	19,839	*118*	**1,908**	972.7
1Q05	*−0.50*	77,207	**90,563**	6.3	21,300	*111*	19,949	*111*	**1,911**	1,017.5
2Q05	*−0.40*	76,896	**90,499**	6.3	21,410	*110*	20,055	*106*	**1,915**	1,015.5
3Q05	*−0.31*	76,656	**90,564**	6.3	21,517	*107*	20,158	*103*	**1,920**	984.9
4Q05	*−0.26*	76,453	**90,488**	6.3	21,622	*105*	20,260	*102*	**1,925**	954.5
1Q06	*−0.21*	76,289	**90,441**	6.3	21,725	*103*	20,361	*101*	**1,930**	925.0
2Q06	*−0.15*	76,176	**90,496**	6.3	21,827	*102*	20,461	*100*	**1,936**	883.2
3Q06	*−0.12*	76,086	**90,396**	6.2	21,929	*101*	20,561	*100*	**1,941**	838.0
4Q06	*−0.06*	76,044	**90,481**	6.2	22,030	*101*	20,662	*100*	**1,947**	791.7
1Q07	*−0.01*	76,033	**90,485**	6.2	22,130	*100*	20,762	*100*	**1,952**	752.9
2Q07	*0.01*	76,043	**90,427**	6.2	22,230	*100*	20,863	*101*	**1,957**	713.7
3Q07	*0.02*	76,062	**90,300**	6.1	22,330	*100*	20,963	*101*	**1,962**	677.3
4Q07	*0.01*	76,068	**90,024**	6.1	22,430	*100*	21,065	*101*	**1,967**	646.8

Since (real) rent growth is now known (−2.19) for 1Q2004, we can calculate the real rent level in 1Q2004 by solving the following percentage growth formula for $RENT_t$:

$$\%\Delta R\hat{ENT}R_t = \left[\frac{RENTR_t}{RENTR_{t-1}} - 1\right] \times 100 = 2.19;$$

$$RENTR_t = (-2.19/100 + 1) \times 81839 = 80047$$

The completions equation is

$$CO\hat{M}PL_t = \underset{(7.3^{***})}{125.72} + \underset{(1.0)}{0.00182}(RENTR - R^*)_{t-6} \tag{10.77}$$

Adj. $R^2 = -0.002$, DW = 0.13.

As we can see, estimating the completions equations over the shorter period does not improve the results; on the contrary, the results become even worse. We can experiment with other lags, of course, but the performance of the equation hardly improves. Nevertheless, we use (10.77) to predict completions for 1Q2004:

$$\hat{COMPL}_t = 125.72 + 0.00182 \times (86793 - 90811) = 118$$

From identity (10.59), we estimate the supply, S, for 1Q2004. For simplicity, we ignore depreciation. Hence S in 1Q2004 is $20722 + 118 = 20840$.

The last equation to estimate is the absorption equation. Prior to this, we get the error correction term from (10.78):

$$\hat{D}_t = \underset{(-6.5^{***})}{-34179.85} + \underset{(10.2^{***})}{26.83 OFFEMP_t} + \underset{(1.5)}{0.024 RENTR_t} \tag{10.78}$$

Adj. $R^2 = 0.75$, DW $= 0.12$.

In the shorter estimation period, the sign on the rent coefficient remains positive (expected negative) and it is not significant. The ECT for 4Q2003 is

$$\begin{aligned} \hat{ECT}_{4Q03} &= D_{4Q03} - (-34179.85) - (+26.83 OFFEMP_{4Q03}) \\ &\quad - (+0.024 RENTR_{4Q03}) \qquad (10.79) \\ \hat{ECT}_{4Q03} &= 19271 - (-34179.85) - (+26.83 \times 1909.6) \\ &\quad - (+0.024 \times 81839) = 252.1 \end{aligned}$$

The absorption equation is

$$\hat{ABS}_t = \underset{(2.1^{**})}{48.55} + \underset{(3.3^{**})}{0.554 ABS_{t-1}} - \underset{(-0.5)}{1.929\% \Delta RENTR_{t-1}} - \underset{(-0.2)}{0.00479 ECT_{t-1}} \tag{10.80}$$

Adj. $R^2 = 0.20$.

Over this sample period the ECT is negatively signed but is not statistically significant. Using (10.80) to estimate absorption in 1Q2004, we obtain

$$\hat{ABS}_t = 48.55 + 0.554 \times 225 - 1.929 \times (-0.91) - 0.00479 \times 252.1 = 174$$

From identities (10.60) and (10.61), we obtain the demand and vacancy for 1Q2004: respectively, 19,445 and 6.7 per cent. Table 10.4 compares the simulations for the main real estate variables, real rent growth, vacancy, absorption and completions, with the actual figures.

If we start with completions, it is clear that the variation of the actual series is not replicated by the model. This was largely expected, given the very poor performance of the model. With annual data and less volatile completions, perhaps the results might have been different. Despite the

Table 10.4 Actual and simulated values for the Tokyo office market

	Rent growth		Vacancy		Absorption		Completions	
	Actual	Predicted	Actual	Predicted	Actual	Predicted	Actual	Predicted
1Q04	0.03	−2.19	6.0	6.7	356	174	159	118
2Q04	0.69	−1.43	6.0	6.5	117	147	124	118
3Q04	0.96	−0.97	5.7	6.4	202	129	148	116
4Q04	0.78	−0.69	5.7	6.4	42	118	44	114
1Q05	0.23	−0.50	5.1	6.3	186	111	62	111
2Q05	−0.07	−0.40	4.6	6.3	98	106	−9	110
3Q05	0.12	−0.31	4.0	6.3	154	103	28	107
4Q05	0.87	−0.26	3.6	6.3	221	102	140	105
1Q06	1.71	−0.21	2.9	6.3	240	101	93	103
2Q06	2.35	−0.15	2.7	6.3	69	100	26	102
3Q06	3.02	−0.12	2.4	6.2	144	100	82	101
4Q06	3.62	−0.06	2.3	6.2	−17	100	−40	101
1Q07	12.36	−0.01	1.8	6.2	213	100	107	100
2Q07	0.56	0.01	1.9	6.2	142	101	174	100
3Q07	0.12	0.02	2.1	6.1	113	101	162	100
4Q07	−0.07	0.01	2.3	6.1	88	101	123	100
	Average values over forecast horizon							
	1.70	−0.45	3.7	6.3	148	112	89	107
ME	2.16		−2.61		36		−18	
MAE	2.17		2.61		70		53	
RMSE	3.57		2.97		86		65	

performance of the completions equation, the average value over the four-year period is 107 compared with the average actual figure of eighty-nine. The system under-predicts absorption and, again, the quarterly volatility of the series is not reproduced. The higher predicted completions in relation to the actual values in conjunction with the under-prediction in absorption (in relation to the actual values, again) results in a vacancy rate higher than the actual figure. Actual vacancies follow a downward path all the way to 2Q2007, when they turn and rise slightly. The actual vacancy rate falls from 7 per cent in 4Q2003 to 1.8 per cent in 1Q2007. The prediction of the model is for vacancy falling to 6.1 per cent. Similarly, the forecasts for rent growth are off the mark despite a well-specified rent model. The measured quarterly rises (on average) in 2004 and 2005 are not allowed for and the system completely misses the acceleration in rent growth in 2006. Part of this has to do with the vacancy forecast, which is an input into the rent growth model. In turn, the vacancy forecast is fed by the misspecified models for absorption and completions. This highlights a major problem with systems of equations: a badly specified equation will have an impact on the rest of the system.

In table 10.4 we also provide the values for three forecast evaluation statistics, which are used to compare the forecasts from an alternative model later in this section. That the ME and MAE metrics are similar for the rent growth and vacancy simulations owes to the fact that the forecasts of rent growth are below the actual values in fourteen of sixteen quarters, whereas the forecast vacancy is consistently higher than the actual value.

What comes out of this analysis is that a particular model may not fit all markets. As a matter of fact, alternative empirical models can be based on a plausible theory of the workings of the real estate market, but in practice different data sets across markets are unlikely to support the same model. In these recursive models we can try to improve the individual equations, which are sources of error for other equations in the system. In our case, the rent equation is well specified, and therefore it can be left as is. We focus on the other two equations and try to improve them. After experimentation with different lags and drivers (we also included GDP as an economic driver alongside employment growth), we estimated the following equations for absorption and completions.

The revised absorption equation for the full-sample period (2Q1995 to 4Q2007) is

$$\hat{ABS}_t = \underset{(9.6^{***})}{102.80} + \underset{(4.8^{***})}{68.06}\%\Delta GDP_t \tag{10.81}$$

Adj. $R^2 = 0.30$, DW $= 1.88$.

For the sample period 2Q1995 to 4Q2003 it is

$$\hat{ABS}_t = \underset{(11.0^{***})}{107.77} + \underset{(5.9^{***})}{95.02}\%\Delta GDP_t \tag{10.82}$$

Adj. $R^2 = 0.50$, DW $= 1.68$.

GDP growth ($\%\Delta GDP_t$) is highly significant in both sample periods. Other variables, including office employment growth and the floor space/employment ratio, were not significant in the presence of $\%\Delta GDP$. Moreover, past values of absorption did not register an influence on current absorption. In this market, we found $\%\Delta GDP$ to be a major determinant of absorption. Hence the occupation needs for office space are primarily reflected in output series. Output series are also seen as proxies for revenue. GDP growth provides a signal to investors about better or worse times to follow. Two other observations are interesting. The inclusion of $\Delta\%GDP$ has eliminated the serial correlation and the DW statistic now falls within the non-rejection region for both samples. The second observation is that the impact of *GDP* weakens when the last four years are added. This is a development to watch.

In the model for completions, long lags of rent growth ($\%\Delta RENTR$) and vacancy (*VAC*) are found to be statistically significant. The results are, for the full-sample period (2Q1998 to 4Q2007),

$$\begin{aligned} \widehat{COMPL}_t = {} & \underset{(8.4^{***})}{312.13} + \underset{(3.6^{***})}{8.24}\%\Delta RENTR_{t-12} - \underset{(-5.3^{***})}{38.35} VAC_{t-8} \end{aligned} \tag{10.83}$$

Adj. $R^2 = 0.57$, DW $= 1.25$.

For the restricted-sample period (2Q1998 to 4Q2003), the results are

$$\begin{aligned} \widehat{COMPL}_t = {} & \underset{(7.1^{***})}{307.63} + \underset{(4.4^{***})}{8.37}\%\Delta RENTR_{t-12} - \underset{(-4.0^{***})}{35.97} VAC_{t-8} \end{aligned} \tag{10.84}$$

Adj. $R^2 = 0.67$, DW $= 0.35$.

Comparing the estimations over the two periods, we also see that, once we add the last four years, the explanatory power of the model again decreases. The sensitivities of completions to rent and vacancy do not change much, however. We should also note that, due to the long lags in the rent growth variable, we lose twelve degrees of freedom at the beginning of the sample. This results in estimation with a shorter sample of only twenty-three observations. Perhaps this is a reason for the low DW statistic, which improves as we add more observations.

We rerun the system to obtain the new forecasts. The calculations are found in table 10.5 (table 10.6 makes the comparison with the actual data).

Completions 1Q04: $307.63 + 8.374 \times 1.07 - 35.97 \times 4.4 = 158$
Absorption 1Q04: $107.77 + 95.02 \times 1.53 = 253$

The new models over-predict both completions and absorption but by broadly the same amount. The over-prediction of supply may reflect the fact that we have both rent growth and vacancy in the same equation. This could give excess weight to changing market conditions, or may constitute some kind of double-counting (as the vacancy was falling constantly and rent growth was on a positive path).

The forecast for vacancy is definitely an improvement on that of the previous model. It overestimates the prediction in the vacancy rate but it does

Table 10.5 Simulations from the system of revised equations

(i)	(ii) %ΔR	(iii) R	(iv) R*	(v) VAC	(vi) S	(vii) Compl	(viii) D	(ix) ABS	(x) %ΔGDP
1Q01	*1.07*								
2Q01	*−0.18*								
3Q01	*−0.73*								
4Q01	*−0.56*								
1Q02	*−0.22*			4.4					
2Q02	*−0.27*			4.9					
3Q02	*−0.42*			5.1					
4Q02	*−0.68*			6.1					
1Q03	*−1.16*			6.0					
2Q03	*−1.57*			6.7					
3Q03	*−1.52*			7.1					
4Q03	*−0.91*	81,839	**90,425**	7.0	20,722	*220*	19,271	*225*	**0.98**
1Q04	*−2.19*	80,047	**90,271**	6.5	20,880	*158*	19,524	*253*	**1.53**
2Q04	*−1.17*	79,111	**90,403**	5.7	21,010	*130*	19,818	*294*	**1.96**
3Q04	*0.07*	79,168	**90,459**	4.8	21,128	*118*	20,111	*293*	**1.95**
4Q04	*1.17*	80,091	**90,477**	4.0	21,212	*83*	20,359	*247*	**1.47**
1Q05	*2.02*	81,705	**90,563**	3.6	21,302	*90*	20,543	*185*	**0.81**
2Q05	*2.28*	83,568	**90,499**	3.1	21,366	*64*	20,694	*151*	**0.45**
3Q05	*2.46*	85,625	**90,564**	2.7	21,415	*49*	20,832	*138*	**0.32**
4Q05	*2.59*	87,844	**90,488**	2.3	21,465	*50*	20,982	*150*	**0.44**
1Q06	*2.75*	90,261	**90,441**	1.8	21,529	*64*	21,146	*164*	**0.59**
2Q06	*2.89*	92,873	**90,496**	1.4	21,620	*90*	21,314	*169*	**0.64**
3Q06	*2.84*	95,510	**90,396**	1.2	21,741	*122*	21,484	*170*	**0.65**
4Q06	*2.64*	98,027	**90,481**	1.1	21,897	*155*	21,650	*167*	**0.62**
1Q07	*2.23*	100,209	**90,485**	1.1	22,058	*161*	21,811	*161*	**0.56**
2Q07	*1.80*	102,012	**90,427**	1.2	22,243	*185*	21,970	*159*	**0.54**
3Q07	*1.29*	103,328	**90,300**	1.4	22,453	*210*	22,129	*159*	**0.54**
4Q07	*0.70*	104,056	**90,024**	1.8	22,689	*236*	22,290	*161*	**0.56**

capture the downward trend until 2007. The model also picks up the turning point in 1Q2007, which is a significant feature. The forecast for rent growth is good on average. It is hardly surprising that it does not allow for the big increase in 1Q2007, which most likely owes to random factors. It over-predicts rents in 2005, but it does a very good job in predicting the

Table 10.6 Evaluation of forecasts

	Rent growth		Vacancy		Absorption		Completions	
	Actual	Predicted	Actual	Predicted	Actual	Predicted	Actual	Predicted
1Q04	0.03	−2.19	6.0	6.5	356	253	158	158
2Q04	0.69	−1.17	6.0	5.7	117	294	124	130
3Q04	0.96	0.07	5.7	4.8	202	293	148	118
4Q04	0.78	1.17	5.7	4.0	42	247	44	83
1Q05	0.23	2.02	5.1	3.6	186	185	62	90
2Q05	−0.07	2.28	4.6	3.1	98	151	−8	64
3Q05	0.12	2.46	4.0	2.7	154	138	27	49
4Q05	0.87	2.59	3.6	2.3	221	150	141	50
1Q06	1.71	2.75	2.9	1.8	240	164	93	64
2Q06	2.35	2.89	2.7	1.4	69	169	26	90
3Q06	3.02	2.84	2.4	1.2	144	170	82	122
4Q06	3.62	2.64	2.3	1.1	−17	167	−40	155
1Q07	12.36	2.23	1.8	1.1	213	161	107	161
2Q07	0.56	1.80	1.9	1.2	142	159	174	185
3Q07	0.12	1.29	2.1	1.4	113	159	163	210
4Q07	−0.07	0.70	2.3	1.8	88	161	122	236
	Average values over forecast horizon							
	1.70	1.52	3.7	2.7	148	189	89	123
ME	0.18		1.00 (−0.80)		−41 (−2)		−34	
MAE	1.85		1.00 (0.90)		81 (67)		53	
RMSE	2.90		1.10 (1.11)		100 (83)		71	

acceleration of rent growth in 2006. This model also picks up the deceleration in rents in 2007, and, as a matter of fact, a quarter earlier than it actually happened. This is certainly a powerful feature of the model.

The forecast performance of this alternative system is again evaluated with the ME, MAE and RMSE metrics, and compared to the previous system, in table 10.6. The forecasts for vacancy and rent growth from the second system are more accurate than those from the first. For absorption and completions, however, the first system does better, especially for absorption. One suggestion, therefore, is that, depending on which variable we are interested in (say rent growth or absorption), we should use the system that better forecasts that variable. If the results resemble those of tables 10.4 and 10.6, it is advisable to monitor the forecasts from both models. Another feature of the forecasts from the two systems is that, for vacancy and absorption, the forecast bias is opposite (the first system over-predicts vacancy whereas the second under-predicts it). Possible benefits from combining the forecasts should then be investigated. These benefits are shown by the numbers in parentheses, which are the values of the respective metrics when the forecasts are combined. A marginal improvement is recorded on the ME and MAE criteria for vacancy and a more notable one for absorption (with a mean error of nearly zero and clearly smaller MAE and RMSE values).

One may ask how the model produces satisfactory vacancy and real rent growth forecasts when the forecasts for absorption and completions are not that accurate. The system over-predicts both the level of absorption and completions. The predicted average gap between absorption and completions is sixty-six (189 – 123), whereas the same (average) actual gap is fifty-nine (148 – 89). In the previous estimates, the system under-predicted absorption and over-predicted completions. The gap between absorption and completion levels was only five (112 – 107), and that is on average each quarter. Therefore this was not sufficient to drive vacancy down through time and predict stronger rent growth (see table 10.4). In the second case, the good results for vacancy and rent growth certainly arise from the accurate forecast of the relative values of absorption and completion (the gap of sixty-six). If one is focused on absorption only, however, the forecasts would not have been that accurate. Further work is therefore required in such cases to improve the forecasting ability of all equations in the system.

Key concepts

The key terms to be able to define and explain from this chapter are

- endogenous variable
- exogenous variable
- simultaneous equations bias
- identified equation
- order condition
- rank condition
- Hausman test
- reduced form
- structural form
- instrumental variables
- indirect least squares
- two-stage least squares

11 Vector autoregressive models

Learning outcomes

In this chapter, you will learn how to

- describe the general form of a VAR;
- explain the relative advantages and disadvantages of VAR modelling;
- choose the optimal lag length for a VAR;
- carry out block significance tests;
- conduct Granger causality tests;
- estimate impulse responses and variance decompositions;
- use VARs for forecasting; and
- produce conditional and unconditional forecasts from VARs.

11.1 Introduction

Vector autoregressive models were popularised in econometrics by Sims (1980) as a natural generalisation of univariate autoregressive models, discussed in chapter 8. A VAR is a systems regression model – i.e. there is more than one dependent variable – that can be considered a kind of hybrid between the univariate time series models considered in chapter 8 and the simultaneous-equation models developed in chapter 10. VARs have often been advocated as an alternative to large-scale simultaneous equations structural models.

The simplest case that can be entertained is a bivariate VAR, in which there are just two variables, y_{1t} and y_{2t}, each of whose current values depend on different combinations of the previous k values of both variables, and error terms

$$y_{1t} = \beta_{10} + \beta_{11} y_{1t-1} + \cdots + \beta_{1k} y_{1t-k} + \alpha_{11} y_{2t-1} + \cdots + \alpha_{1k} y_{2t-k} + u_{1t} \tag{11.1}$$

$$y_{2t} = \beta_{20} + \beta_{21} y_{2t-1} + \cdots + \beta_{2k} y_{2t-k} + \alpha_{21} y_{1t-1} + \cdots + \alpha_{2k} y_{1t-k} + u_{2t} \tag{11.2}$$

where u_{it} is a white noise disturbance term with $E(u_{it}) = 0$, $(i = 1, 2)$, $E(u_{1t}, u_{2t}) = 0$.

As should already be evident, an important feature of the VAR model is its flexibility and the ease of generalisation. For example, the model could be extended to encompass moving average errors, which would be a multivariate version of an ARMA model, known as a VARMA. Instead of having only two variables, y_{1t} and y_{2t}, the system could also be expanded to include g variables, $y_{1t}, y_{2t}, y_{3t}, \ldots, y_{gt}$, each of which has an equation.

Another useful facet of VAR models is the compactness with which the notation can be expressed. For example, consider the case from above in which $k = 1$, so that each variable depends only upon the immediately previous values of y_{1t} and y_{2t}, plus an error term. This could be written as

$$y_{1t} = \beta_{10} + \beta_{11} y_{1t-1} + \alpha_{11} y_{2t-1} + u_{1t} \tag{11.3}$$

$$y_{2t} = \beta_{20} + \beta_{21} y_{2t-1} + \alpha_{21} y_{1t-1} + u_{2t} \tag{11.4}$$

or

$$\begin{pmatrix} y_{1t} \\ y_{2t} \end{pmatrix} = \begin{pmatrix} \beta_{10} \\ \beta_{20} \end{pmatrix} + \begin{pmatrix} \beta_{11} & \alpha_{11} \\ \alpha_{21} & \beta_{21} \end{pmatrix} \begin{pmatrix} y_{1t-1} \\ y_{2t-1} \end{pmatrix} + \begin{pmatrix} u_{1t} \\ u_{2t} \end{pmatrix} \tag{11.5}$$

or, even more compactly, as

$$\underset{g \times 1}{y_t} = \underset{g \times 1}{\beta_0} + \underset{g \times g\, g \times 1}{\beta_1 y_{t-1}} + \underset{g \times 1}{u_t} \tag{11.6}$$

In (11.5), there are $g = 2$ variables in the system. Extending the model to the case in which there are k lags of each variable in each equation is also easily accomplished using this notation:

$$\underset{g \times 1}{y_t} = \underset{g \times 1}{\beta_0} + \underset{g \times g\, g \times 1}{\beta_1 y_{t-1}} + \underset{g \times g\; g \times 1}{\beta_2 y_{t-2}} + \cdots + \underset{g \times g\; g \times 1}{\beta_k y_{t-k}} + \underset{g \times 1}{u_t} \tag{11.7}$$

The model could be further extended to the case in which the model includes first difference terms and cointegrating relationships (a vector error correction model [VECM] – see chapter 12).

11.2 Advantages of VAR modelling

VAR models have several advantages compared with univariate time series models or simultaneous equations structural models.

- The researcher does not need to specify which variables are endogenous or exogenous, as *all are endogenous*. This is a very important point, since a requirement for simultaneous equations structural models to be estimable is that all equations in the system are identified. Essentially, this requirement boils down to a condition that some variables are treated as exogenous and that the equations contain different RHS variables. Ideally, this restriction should arise naturally from real estate or economic theory. In practice, however, theory will be at best vague in its suggestions as to which variables should be treated as exogenous. This leaves the researcher with a great deal of discretion concerning how to classify the variables. Since Hausman-type tests are often not employed in practice when they should be, the specification of certain variables as exogenous, required to form identifying restrictions, is likely in many cases to be invalid. Sims terms these identifying restrictions 'incredible'. VAR estimation, on the other hand, requires no such restrictions to be imposed.
- VARs allow the value of a variable to depend on more than just its own lags or combinations of white noise terms, so VARs are more flexible than univariate AR models; the latter can be viewed as a restricted case of VAR models. VAR models can therefore offer a very *rich structure*, implying that they may be able to capture more features of the data.
- Provided that there are no contemporaneous terms on the RHS of the equations, it is possible simply to *use OLS separately on each equation*. This arises from the fact that all variables on the RHS are predetermined – that is, at time t they are known. This implies that there is no possibility for feedback from any of the LHS variables to any of the RHS variables. Predetermined variables include all exogenous variables and lagged values of the endogenous variables.
- The forecasts generated by VARs are often *better than 'traditional structural' models*. It has been argued in a number of articles (see, for example, Sims, 1980) that large-scale structural models perform badly in terms of their out-of-sample forecast accuracy. This could perhaps arise as a result of the ad hoc nature of the restrictions placed on the structural models to ensure the identification discussed above. McNees (1986) shows that forecasts for some variables, such as the US unemployment rate and real GNP, among others, are produced more accurately using VARs than from several different structural specifications.

11.3 Problems with VARs

Inevitably, VAR models also have drawbacks and limitations relative to other model classes.

- VARs are *atheoretical* (as are ARMA models), since they use little theoretical information about the relationships between the variables to guide the specification of the model. On the other hand, valid exclusion restrictions that ensure the identification of equations from a simultaneous structural system will inform the structure of the model. An upshot of this is that VARs are less amenable to theoretical analysis and therefore to policy prescriptions. There also exists an increased possibility under the VAR approach that a hapless researcher could obtain an essentially spurious relationship by mining the data. Furthermore, it is often not clear how the VAR coefficient estimates should be interpreted.
- How should the appropriate *lag lengths* for the VAR be determined? There are several approaches available for dealing with this issue, which are discussed below.
- *So many parameters!* If there are g equations, one for each of g variables and with k lags of each of the variables in each equation, $(g + kg^2)$ parameters will have to be estimated. For example, if $g = 3$ and $k = 3$, there will be thirty parameters to estimate. For relatively small sample sizes, degrees of freedom will rapidly be used up, implying large standard errors and therefore wide confidence intervals for model coefficients.
- Should *all the components of the VAR be stationary*? Obviously, if one wishes to use hypothesis tests, either singly or jointly, to examine the statistical significance of the coefficients, then it is essential that all the components in the VAR are stationary. Many proponents of the VAR approach recommend that differencing to induce stationarity should not be done, however. They would argue that the purpose of VAR estimation is purely to examine the relationships between the variables, and that differencing will throw information on any long-run relationships between the series away. It is also possible to combine levels and first-differenced terms in a VECM; see chapter 12.

11.4 Choosing the optimal lag length for a VAR

Real estate theory will often have little to say on what an appropriate lag length is for a VAR and how long changes in the variables should take to work through the system. In such instances, there are basically two methods that can be used to arrive at the optimal lag length: cross-equation restrictions and information criteria.

11.4.1 Cross-equation restrictions for VAR lag length selection

A first (but incorrect) response to the question of how to determine the appropriate lag length would be to use the block F-tests highlighted in section 11.7 below. These are not appropriate in this case, however, as the F-test would be used separately for the set of lags in each equation, and what is required here is a procedure to test the coefficients on a set of lags on all variables for all equations in the VAR at the same time.

It is worth noting here that, in the spirit of VAR estimation (as Sims, for example, thought that model specification should be conducted), the models should be as unrestricted as possible. A VAR with different lag lengths for each equation could be viewed as a restricted VAR. For example, consider a bivariate VAR with three lags of both variables in one equation and four lags of each variable in the other equation. This could be viewed as a restricted model in which the coefficient on the fourth lags of each variable in the first equation have been set to zero.

An alternative approach would be to specify the same number of lags in each equation and to determine the model order as follows. Suppose that a VAR estimated using quarterly data has eight lags of the two variables in each equation, and it is desired to examine a restriction that the coefficients on lags 5 to 8 are jointly zero. This can be done using a likelihood ratio test (see chapter 8 of Brooks, 2008, for more general details concerning such tests). Denote the variance–covariance matrix of residuals (given by $\hat{u}\hat{u}'$) as $\hat{\Sigma}$. The likelihood ratio test for this joint hypothesis is given by

$$LR = T[\log|\hat{\Sigma}_r| - \log|\hat{\Sigma}_u|] \tag{11.8}$$

where $|\hat{\Sigma}_r|$ is the determinant of the variance–covariance matrix of the residuals for the restricted model (with four lags), $|\hat{\Sigma}_u|$ is the determinant of the variance–covariance matrix of residuals for the unrestricted VAR (with eight lags) and T is the sample size. The test statistic is asymptotically distributed as a χ^2 variate with degrees of freedom equal to the total number of restrictions. In the VAR case above, four lags of two variables are being restricted in each of the two equations – a total of $4 \times 2 \times 2 = 16$ restrictions. In the general case of a VAR with g equations, to impose the restriction that the last q lags have zero coefficients there would be $g^2 q$ restrictions altogether. Intuitively, the test is a multivariate equivalent to examining the extent to which the RSS rises when a restriction is imposed. If $\hat{\Sigma}_r$ and $\hat{\Sigma}_u$ are 'close together', the restriction is supported by the data.

11.4.2 *Information criteria for VAR lag length selection*

The likelihood ratio (LR) test explained above is intuitive and fairly easy to estimate, but it does have its limitations. Principally, one of the two VARs must be a special case of the other and, more seriously, only pairwise comparisons can be made. In the above example, if the most appropriate lag length had been seven or even ten, there is no way that this information could be gleaned from the LR test conducted. One could achieve this only by starting with a VAR(10), and successively testing one set of lags at a time.

A further disadvantage of the LR test approach is that the χ^2 test will, strictly, be valid asymptotically only under the assumption that the errors from each equation are normally distributed. This assumption may not be upheld for real estate data. An alternative approach to selecting the appropriate VAR lag length would be to use an information criterion, as defined in chapter 8 in the context of ARMA model selection. Information criteria require no such normality assumptions concerning the distributions of the errors. Instead, the criteria trade off a fall in the RSS of each equation as more lags are added, with an increase in the value of the penalty term. The univariate criteria could be applied separately to each equation but, again, it is usually deemed preferable to require the number of lags to be the same for each equation. This requires the use of multivariate versions of the information criteria, which can be defined as

$$MAIC = \log\left|\hat{\Sigma}\right| + 2k'/T \tag{11.9}$$

$$MSBIC = \log\left|\hat{\Sigma}\right| + \frac{k'}{T}\log(T) \tag{11.10}$$

$$MHQIC = \log\left|\hat{\Sigma}\right| + \frac{2k'}{T}\log(\log(T)) \tag{11.11}$$

where, again, $\hat{\Sigma}$ is the variance–covariance matrix of residuals, T is the number of observations and k' is the total number of regressors in all equations, which will be equal to $p^2k + p$ for p equations in the VAR system, each with k lags of the p variables, plus a constant term in each equation. As previously, the values of the information criteria are constructed for $0, 1, \ldots, \bar{k}$ lags (up to some pre-specified maximum $\bar{k}$), and the chosen number of lags is that number minimising the value of the given information criterion.

11.5 Does the VAR include contemporaneous terms?

So far, it has been assumed that the VAR specified is of the form

$$y_{1t} = \beta_{10} + \beta_{11} y_{1t-1} + \alpha_{11} y_{2t-1} + u_{1t} \tag{11.12}$$

$$y_{2t} = \beta_{20} + \beta_{21} y_{2t-1} + \alpha_{21} y_{1t-1} + u_{2t} \tag{11.13}$$

so that there are no contemporaneous terms on the RHS of (11.12) or (11.13) – i.e. there is no term in y_{2t} on the RHS of the equation for y_{1t} and no term in y_{1t} on the RHS of the equation for y_{2t}. What if the equations had a contemporaneous feedback term, however, as in the following case?

$$y_{1t} = \beta_{10} + \beta_{11} y_{1t-1} + \alpha_{11} y_{2t-1} + \alpha_{12} y_{2t} + u_{1t} \tag{11.14}$$

$$y_{2t} = \beta_{20} + \beta_{21} y_{2t-1} + \alpha_{21} y_{1t-1} + \alpha_{22} y_{1t} + u_{2t} \tag{11.15}$$

Equations (11.14) and (11.15) can also be written by stacking up the terms into matrices and vectors:

$$\begin{pmatrix} y_{1t} \\ y_{2t} \end{pmatrix} = \begin{pmatrix} \beta_{10} \\ \beta_{20} \end{pmatrix} + \begin{pmatrix} \beta_{11} & \alpha_{11} \\ \alpha_{21} & \beta_{21} \end{pmatrix} \begin{pmatrix} y_{1t-1} \\ y_{2t-1} \end{pmatrix} + \begin{pmatrix} \alpha_{12} & 0 \\ 0 & \alpha_{22} \end{pmatrix} \begin{pmatrix} y_{2t} \\ y_{1t} \end{pmatrix} + \begin{pmatrix} u_{1t} \\ u_{2t} \end{pmatrix} \tag{11.16}$$

This would be known as a *VAR in primitive form*, similar to the structural form for a simultaneous equation model. Some researchers have argued that the atheoretical nature of reduced-form VARs leaves them unstructured and their results difficult to interpret theoretically. They argue that the forms of VAR given previously are merely reduced forms of a more general structural VAR (such as (11.16)), with the latter being of more interest.

The contemporaneous terms from (11.16) can be taken over to the LHS and written as

$$\begin{pmatrix} 1 & -\alpha_{12} \\ -\alpha_{22} & 1 \end{pmatrix} \begin{pmatrix} y_{1t} \\ y_{2t} \end{pmatrix} = \begin{pmatrix} \beta_{10} \\ \beta_{20} \end{pmatrix} + \begin{pmatrix} \beta_{11} & \alpha_{11} \\ \alpha_{21} & \beta_{21} \end{pmatrix} \begin{pmatrix} y_{1t-1} \\ y_{2t-1} \end{pmatrix} + \begin{pmatrix} u_{1t} \\ u_{2t} \end{pmatrix} \tag{11.17}$$

or

$$\mathrm{A} y_t = \beta_0 + \beta_1 y_{t-1} + u_t \tag{11.18}$$

If both sides of (11.18) are pre-multiplied by A^{-1},

$$y_t = \mathrm{A}^{-1}\beta_0 + \mathrm{A}^{-1}\beta_1 y_{t-1} + \mathrm{A}^{-1} u_t \tag{11.19}$$

or

$$y_t = \mathrm{A}_0 + \mathrm{A}_1 y_{t-1} + e_t \tag{11.20}$$

This is known as a *standard-form VAR*, which is akin to the reduced form from a set of simultaneous equations. This VAR contains only predetermined values on the RHS (i.e. variables whose values are known at time t), and so there is no contemporaneous feedback term. This VAR can therefore be estimated equation by equation using OLS.

Equation (11.16), the structural or primitive-form VAR, is not identified, since identical predetermined (lagged) variables appear on the RHS of both equations. In order to circumvent this problem, a restriction that one of the coefficients on the contemporaneous terms is zero must be imposed. In (11.16), either α_{12} or α_{22} must be set to zero to obtain a triangular set of VAR equations that can be validly estimated. The choice of which of these two restrictions to impose is, ideally, made on theoretical grounds. For example, if real estate theory suggests that the current value of y_{1t} should affect the current value of y_{2t} but not the other way around, set $\alpha_{12} = 0$, and so on. Another possibility would be to run separate estimations, first imposing $\alpha_{12} = 0$ and then $\alpha_{22} = 0$, to determine whether the general features of the results are much changed. It is also very common to estimate only a reduced-form VAR, which is, of course, perfectly valid provided that such a formulation is not at odds with the relationships between variables that real estate theory says should hold.

One fundamental weakness of the VAR approach to modelling is that its atheoretical nature and the large number of parameters involved make the estimated models difficult to interpret. In particular, some lagged variables may have coefficients that change sign across the lags, and this, together with the interconnectivity of the equations, could render it difficult to see what effect a given change in a variable would have upon the future values of the variables in the system. In order to alleviate this problem partially, three sets of statistics are usually constructed for an estimated VAR model: block significance tests, impulse responses and variance decompositions. How important an intuitively interpretable model is will of course depend on the purpose of constructing the model. Interpretability may not be an issue at all if the purpose of producing the VAR is to make forecasts.

11.6 A VAR model for real estate investment trusts

The VAR application we examine draws upon the body of literature regarding the factors that determine the predictability of securitised real estate returns. Nominal and real interest rates, the term structure of interest rates, expected and unexpected inflation, industrial production, unemployment and consumption are among the variables that have received empirical support. Brooks and Tsolacos (2003) and Ling and Naranjo (1997), among other authors, provide a review of the studies in this subject area. A common characteristic in the findings of extant work, as Brooks and Tsolacos (2003) note, is that there is no universal agreement as to the variables that best predict real estate investment trust returns. In addition, diverse results arise from the different methodologies that are used to study securitised real estate returns. VAR models constitute one such estimation methodology. Clearly, this subject area will attract further research, which will be reinforced by the introduction of REIT legislation in more and more countries.

In this example, our reference series is the index of REIT returns in the United States. These trusts were established there in the 1960s, and researchers have long historical time series to carry out research on the predictability of REIT prices. In this study, we focus on the impact of dividend yields, long-term interest rates and the corporate bond yield on US REIT returns. These three variables have been found to have predictive power for securitised real estate. The predictive power of the dividend yield is emphasised in several studies (see Keim and Stambaugh, 1986, and Fama and French, 1988). Indeed, as the study by Kothari and Shanken (1997) reminds us, anything that increases or decreases the rate at which future cash flows are discounted has an impact on value. Changes in the dividend yield transmit the influence of the discount rate. The long-term interest rate is sometimes viewed as a proxy for the risk-free rate of return. Movements in the risk-free rate are expected to influence required returns and yields across asset classes. The corporate bond yield guides investors about the returns that can be achieved in other asset classes. This in turn affects their required return from investing in securitised real estate, and hence pricing. We therefore examine the contention that movements across a spectrum of yields are relevant for predicting REIT returns.

The data we use in this example are as follows.

- All REIT price returns (*ARPRET*): the return series is defined as the difference in the logs of the monthly price return index in successive months. The source is the National Association of Real Estate Investment Trusts (NAREIT).
- Changes in the S&P500 dividend yield (ΔSPY): this is the monthly absolute change in the Standard and Poor's dividend yield series. Source: S&P.
- Long-term interest rate ($\Delta 10Y$): the annual change in the ten-year Treasury bond yield. Source: Federal Reserve.
- Corporate bond yield change (ΔCBY): the annual change in the AAA corporate bond yield. Source: Federal Reserve.

We begin our analysis by testing these variables for unit roots in order to ensure that we are working with stationary data. The details are not presented here as the tests are not described until chapter 12, but suffice to say that we are able to conclude that the variables are indeed stationary and we can now proceed to construct the VAR model. Determining that the

Table 11.1 VAR lag length selection

Lag	AIC value: *ARPRET* equation	AIC value: system
1	**−3.397**	−6.574
2	−3.395	**−6.623**
3	−3.381	−6.611
4	−3.372	−6.587
8	−3.325	−6.430

Note: Bold entries denote optimal lag lengths.

variables are stationary (or dealing appropriately with the non-stationarity if that is the case) is an essential first step in building any model with time series data.

We select the VAR lag length on the basis of Akaike's information criterion. Since our interest is the *ARPRET* equation in the system, we could minimise the AIC value of this equation on its own and assume that this lag length is also relevant for other equations in the system. An alternative approach, however, would be to choose the lag length that minimises the AIC for the system as a whole (see equation (11.9) above). The latter approach is more in the spirit of VAR modelling, and the AIC values for both the whole system and for the *ARPRET* equation alone are given in table 11.1.

The AIC value for the whole system is minimised at lag 2 whereas the AIC value for the *ARPRET* equation alone is minimised with a single lag. If we select one lag, this may be insufficient to capture the effects of the variables on each other. Therefore we run the VAR with two lags, as suggested by the AIC value for the system. The results for the VAR estimation with two lags are given in table 11.2.

As we noted earlier, on account of the possible existence of multicollinearity and other factors, some of the coefficients in the VAR equations may not be statistically significant and take the expected signs. We observe these in the results reported in table 11.2, but this is not necessarily a problem if the model as a whole has the correct 'shape'. To determine this would require the use of joint tests on a number of coefficients together, or an examination of the impulse responses or variance decompositions. These will be considered in subsequent sections, but, for now, let us focus on the *ARPRET* equation, which is our reference equation. We expect a negative impact from all yield terms on *ARPRET*. This negative sign is taken only by the second lag of the Treasury bond yield and the corporate bond yield terms. Of the two corporate bond yields – i.e. lag 1 and lag 2 – it is the second

Table 11.2 VAR results

	Equation in VAR			
	$ARPRET_t$	ΔSPY_t	$\Delta 10Y_t$	ΔCBY_t
Constant	−0.00	−0.00	−0.00	−0.01
	(−1.17)	(−0.60)	(−0.28)	(−0.52)
$ARPRET_{t-1}$	0.05	−0.91	0.10	−0.30
	(1.00)	(−5.94)	(0.27)	(−1.05)
$ARPRET_{t-2}$	0.05	0.28	−0.22	−0.32
	(0.93)	(1.74)	(−0.56)	(−1.05)
ΔSPY_{t-1}	0.02	0.11	−0.23	−0.18
	(1.12)	(1.96)	(−1.69)	(−1.72)
ΔSPY_{t-2}	0.01	−0.03	−0.35	−0.27
	(0.73)	(−0.51)	(−2.78)	(−2.79)
$\Delta 10Y_{t-1}$	−0.03	0.08	0.44	0.26
	(−1.40)	(1.50)	(3.55)	(2.76)
$\Delta 10Y_{t-2}$	0.05	−0.07	−0.26	−0.17
	(2.71)	(−1.37)	(−2.13)	(−1.83)
ΔCBY_{t-1}	−0.01	−0.00	−0.07	0.13
	(−0.29)	(−0.01)	(−0.44)	(1.01)
ΔCBY_{t-2}	−0.06	0.12	0.13	0.02
	(−2.65)	(1.77)	(0.84)	(0.17)
$\bar{R}^2$	0.05	0.20	0.16	0.21

Notes: Sample period is March 1972 to July 2007. Numbers in parentheses are t-ratios.

lag (ΔCBY_{t-2}) that is statistically significant. The impact of lagged returns on the current returns is positive but not statistically significant.

11.7 Block significance and causality tests

The likelihood is that, when a VAR includes many lags of variables, it will be difficult to see which sets of variables have significant effects on each dependent variable and which do not. In order to address this issue, tests are usually conducted that restrict all the lags of a particular variable to zero. For illustration, consider the following bivariate VAR(3):

$$\begin{pmatrix} y_{1t} \\ y_{2t} \end{pmatrix} = \begin{pmatrix} \alpha_{10} \\ \alpha_{20} \end{pmatrix} + \begin{pmatrix} \beta_{11} & \beta_{12} \\ \beta_{21} & \beta_{22} \end{pmatrix} \begin{pmatrix} y_{1t-1} \\ y_{2t-1} \end{pmatrix} + \begin{pmatrix} \gamma_{11} & \gamma_{12} \\ \gamma_{21} & \gamma_{22} \end{pmatrix} \begin{pmatrix} y_{1t-2} \\ y_{2t-2} \end{pmatrix}$$

$$+ \begin{pmatrix} \delta_{11} & \delta_{12} \\ \delta_{21} & \delta_{22} \end{pmatrix} \begin{pmatrix} y_{1t-3} \\ y_{2t-3} \end{pmatrix} + \begin{pmatrix} u_{1t} \\ u_{2t} \end{pmatrix} \tag{11.21}$$

Table 11.3 Granger causality tests and implied restrictions on VAR models

	Hypothesis	Implied restriction
1	Lags of y_{1t} do not explain current y_{2t}	$\beta_{21} = 0$ and $\gamma_{21} = 0$ and $\delta_{21} = 0$
2	Lags of y_{1t} do not explain current y_{1t}	$\beta_{11} = 0$ and $\gamma_{11} = 0$ and $\delta_{11} = 0$
3	Lags of y_{2t} do not explain current y_{1t}	$\beta_{12} = 0$ and $\gamma_{12} = 0$ and $\delta_{12} = 0$
4	Lags of y_{2t} do not explain current y_{2t}	$\beta_{22} = 0$ and $\gamma_{22} = 0$ and $\delta_{22} = 0$

This VAR could be written out to express the individual equations as

$$\begin{aligned} y_{1t} &= \alpha_{10} + \beta_{11} y_{1t-1} + \beta_{12} y_{2t-1} + \gamma_{11} y_{1t-2} + \gamma_{12} y_{2t-2} \\ &\quad + \delta_{11} y_{1t-3} + \delta_{12} y_{2t-3} + u_{1t} \\ y_{2t} &= \alpha_{20} + \beta_{21} y_{1t-1} + \beta_{22} y_{2t-1} + \gamma_{21} y_{1t-2} + \gamma_{22} y_{2t-2} \\ &\quad + \delta_{21} y_{1t-3} + \delta_{22} y_{2t-3} + u_{2t} \end{aligned} \tag{11.22}$$

One might be interested in testing the hypotheses and their implied restrictions on the parameter matrices given in table 11.3. Assuming that all the variables in the VAR are stationary, the joint hypotheses can easily be tested within the F-test framework, since each individual set of restrictions involves parameters drawn from only one equation. The equations would be estimated separately using OLS to obtain the unrestricted RSS, then the restrictions would be imposed and the models re-estimated to obtain the restricted *RSS*. The F-statistic would then take the usual form as described in chapter 5. Evaluation of the significance of variables in the context of a VAR thus almost invariably occurs on the basis of joint tests on all the lags of a particular variable in an equation, rather than by the examination of individual coefficient estimates.

In fact, the tests described above could also be referred to as causality tests. Tests of this form have been described by Granger (1969), with a slight variant due to Sims (1972). Causality tests seek to answer simple questions of the type 'Do changes in y_1 cause changes in y_2?'. The argument follows that, if y_1 causes y_2, lags of y_1 should be significant in the equation for y_2. If this is the case and not vice versa, it can be said that y_1 'Granger-causes' y_2 or that there exists unidirectional causality from y_1 to y_2. On the other hand, if y_2 causes y_1, lags of y_2 should be significant in the equation for y_1. If both sets of lags are significant, it is said that there is 'bidirectional causality' or 'bidirectional feedback'. If y_1 is found to Granger-cause y_2, but not vice versa, it is said that variable y_1 is strongly exogenous (in the equation for

Table 11.4 Joint significance tests for yields

$ARPRET_t$ equation (unrestricted) RSS = 0.800 Restricted equations: lags of ΔSPY, $\Delta 10Y$ and ΔCBY do not explain $ARPRET_t$		
	RRSS	F-test
All coefficients on ΔSPY are zero	0.804	1.04
All coefficients on $\Delta 10Y$ are zero	0.816	4.16
All coefficients on ΔCBY are zero	0.814	3.64
F-critical: $F(2,416)$ at 5% $\approx$ 3.00		

Notes: See F-test formula and discussion in chapter 5. The number of observations is 425. The number of restrictions is two in each case. The number of regressors in unrestricted regression is nine (table 11.2).

y_2). If neither set of lags are statistically significant in the equation for the other variable, it is said that y_1 and y_2 are independent.

Finally, the word 'causality' is something of a misnomer, for Granger causality really means only a correlation between the *current* value of one variable and the *past* values of others; it does not mean that movements of one variable cause movements of another.

Example 11.1 Block F-tests and causality tests

We compute F-tests for the joint significance of yield terms in the return equation. It may be argued that not all yield series are required in the *ARPRET* equation since, to a degree, they convey similar signals to investors concerning REIT pricing. We investigate this proposition by conducting joint significance tests for the three groups of yield series. We therefore examine whether the two lagged terms of the changes in the dividend yield are significant when the Treasury and corporate bond yields are included in the *ARPRET* equation, and similarly with the other two groups of yields. For this, we carry out F-tests as described in chapter 5. The results are shown in table 11.4.

We observe that the blocks of lagged changes in S&P yields are not significant in the REIT return equation (*ARPRET*), unlike the two lags for the Treasury bond and corporate bond yields (the computed F-test values are higher than the corresponding critical values). Hence it is only the latter two yield series that carry useful information in explaining the REIT price returns in the United States.

Running the causality tests, in our case, it is interesting to study whether ΔSPY, $\Delta 10Y$ and ΔCBY lead $ARPRET$ and, if so, whether there are feedback effects. We initially have to identify the number of lags to be used in the test equations (the unrestricted and the restricted equations). For this particular example we use two lags, which is the optimum number in our VAR according to the AIC. It is also the practice to conduct the causality tests with a number of different lags to determine the robustness of the results. For example, for quarterly data, we could examine a VAR with two, four and eight quarters, or, for monthly data, use three, six and twelve months. The values of the AIC or another information criterion can also provide guidance, however, and, in the present example, two lags were selected. Below, we illustrate the process in the case of ΔSPY and $ARPRET$.

Step 1: Lags of ΔSPY do not cause $ARPRET$

Unrestricted equation:

$$\begin{aligned} \widehat{ARPRET}_t &= -0.002 + 0.10 ARPRET_{t-1} + 0.05 ARPRET_{t-2} \\ &\quad + 0.01 \Delta SPY_{t-1} + 0.01 \Delta SPY_{t-2} \end{aligned} \tag{11.23}$$

Restricted equation:

$$\widehat{ARPRET}_t = -0.002 + 0.09 ARPRET_{t-1} + 0.03 ARPRET_{t-2} \tag{11.24}$$

URSS: 0.844; RRSS: 0.846; $T = 425$; $k = 5$; $m = 2$; F-test statistic $= 0.50$; F-critical $= F(2,425)$ at 5% ≈ 3.00.

The null hypothesis is that lags of ΔSPY do not cause $ARPRET$, and hence the null is that the coefficients on the two lags of ΔSPY are jointly zero. In this example, the estimated value for the F-statistic (0.50) is considerably lower than the critical value of F at the 5 per cent significance level (3.00), and therefore we do not reject the null hypothesis. Similarly, we search for a relationship in the reverse direction by running the following unrestricted and restricted equations.

Step 2: Lags of $ARPRET$ do not cause ΔSPY

Unrestricted equation:

$$\begin{aligned} \Delta \widehat{SPY}_t &= -0.004 + 0.16 \Delta SPY_{t-1} - 0.02 \Delta SPY_{t-2} - 1.05 ARPRET_{t-1} \\ &\quad + 0.27 ARPRET_{t-2} \end{aligned} \tag{11.25}$$

Restricted equation:

$$\Delta \widehat{SPY}_t = -0.002 + 0.29 \Delta SPY_{t-1} - 0.08 \Delta SPY_{t-2} \tag{11.26}$$

URSS: 6.517; RRSS: 7.324; $T = 425$; $k = 5$; $m = 2$; F-test statistic $= 26.00$; F-critical $= F(2,420)$ at 5% ≈ 3.00.

Table 11.5 Granger causality tests between returns and yields

Null hypothesis		Lags	URSS / RRSS	*F*-test statistic; *F*-critical at 5%	Conclusion
Lags of	Do not cause				
ΔSPY	*ARPRET*	4	0.838 / 0.841	0.37; $(F_{4,414}) \approx 2.37$	Do not reject
ARPRET	ΔSPY	4	6.452 / 7.307	13.72; $(F_{4,414}) \approx 2.37$	Reject
$\Delta 10Y$	*ARPRET*	2	0.816 / 0.846	7.72; $(F_{2,420}) \approx 3.00$	Reject
ARPRET	$\Delta 10Y$	2	37.510 / 37.759	1.39; $(F_{2,420}) \approx 3.00$	Do not reject
$\Delta 10Y$	*ARPRET*	4	0.808 / 0.841	4.23; $(F_{4,414}) \approx 2.37$	Reject
ARPRET	$\Delta 10Y$	4	37.077 / 37.493	1.16; $(F_{4,414}) \approx 2.37$	Do not reject
ΔCBY	*ARPRET*	2	0.820 / 0.846	6.66; $(F_{2,420}) \approx 3.00$	Reject
ARPRET	ΔCBY	2	23.001 / 23.071	0.64; $(F_{2,420}) \approx 3.00$	Do not reject
ΔCBY	*ARPRET*	4	0.810 / 0.841	3.96; $(F_{4,414}) \approx 2.37$	Reject
ARPRET	ΔCBY	4	22.728 / 22.954	1.03; $(F_{4,414}) \approx 2.37$	Do not reject

The computed *F*-statistic is higher than the critical value at the 5 per cent significance level, and we therefore reject the null hypothesis that returns do not cause S&P dividend yield changes. Interestingly, the causal relationship runs in the opposite direction, suggesting that the appreciation in real estate prices precedes changes in S&P dividend yields. In table 11.5, we repeat the process with four lags and we run the tests to examine the causal relationship of price returns with both the Treasury and corporate bond yields.

The third column (URSS/RRSS) of the table gives the squared sum of residuals both for the unrestricted and restricted equations at a given lag length. We observe that changes in the S&P dividend yield do not cause returns at a lag length of four, but the opposite is not true. Hence the test results do not differ across the two lag lengths.

The results are also broadly the same for the government and corporate bond yields. Movements in the ten-year Treasury bond yield and the corporate yield do cause changes in annual REIT price returns. This finding is consistent over the two lag lengths we use. Hence both Treasury and corporate bond yields contain leading information for REIT returns. Unlike the feedback effect we established from *ARPRET* to changes in dividend yields, there are no causal effects running from *ARPRET* to either the Treasury bond or the corporate bond yield. Based on the findings presented in tables 11.4 and 11.5, we may consider excluding the S&P dividend yield from the VAR. The variable ΔSPY may contain useful information for the other variables, however, in which case it still belongs in the system, and for that reason we retain it.

11.8 VARs with exogenous variables

Consider the following specification for a VAR(1) in which X_t is a vector of exogenous variables and B is a matrix of coefficients

$$y_t = A_0 + A_1 y_{t-1} + BX_t + e_t \tag{11.27}$$

The components of the vector X_t are known as exogenous variables, since their values are determined outside the VAR system – in other words, there are no equations in the VAR with any of the components of X_t as dependent variables. Such a model is sometimes termed a VARX, although it could be viewed as simply a restricted VAR in which there are equations for each of the exogenous variables, but with the coefficients on the RHS in those equations restricted to zero. Such a restriction may be considered desirable if theoretical considerations suggest it, although it is clearly not in the true spirit of VAR modelling, which is not to impose any restrictions on the model but, rather, to 'let the data decide'.

11.9 Impulse responses and variance decompositions

Block F-tests and an examination of causality in a VAR will suggest which of the variables in the model have statistically significant impacts on the future values of each of the variables in the system. F-test results will not, by construction, be able to explain the sign of the relationship or how long these effects require to take place, however. That is, F-test results will not reveal whether changes in the value of a given variable have a positive or negative effect on other variables in the system, or how long it will take for the effect of that variable to work through the system. Such information will, however, be given by an examination of the VAR's impulse responses and variance decompositions.

Impulse responses trace out the responsiveness of the dependent variables in the VAR to shocks to each of the variables. So, for each variable from each equation separately, a unit shock is applied to the error, and the effects upon the VAR system over time are noted. Thus, if there are g variables in a system, a total of g^2 impulse responses can be generated. The way that this is achieved in practice is by expressing the VAR model as a VMA – that is, the vector autoregressive model is written as a vector moving average (in the same way as was done for univariate autoregressive models in chapter 8). Provided that the system is stable, the shock should gradually die away.

To illustrate how impulse responses operate, consider the following bivariate VAR(1):

$$y_t = A_1 y_{t-1} + u_t \tag{11.28}$$
$$\text{where } A_1 = \begin{bmatrix} 0.5 & 0.3 \\ 0.0 & 0.2 \end{bmatrix}$$

The VAR can also be written out using the elements of the matrices and vectors as

$$\begin{bmatrix} y_{1t} \\ y_{2t} \end{bmatrix} = \begin{bmatrix} 0.5 & 0.3 \\ 0.0 & 0.2 \end{bmatrix} \begin{bmatrix} y_{1t-1} \\ y_{2t-1} \end{bmatrix} + \begin{bmatrix} u_{1t} \\ u_{2t} \end{bmatrix} \tag{11.29}$$

Consider the effect at time $t = 0, 1, \ldots,$ of a unit shock to y_{1t} at time $t = 0$:

$$y_0 = \begin{bmatrix} u_{10} \\ u_{20} \end{bmatrix} = \begin{bmatrix} 1 \\ 0 \end{bmatrix} \tag{11.30}$$

$$y_1 = A_1 y_0 = \begin{bmatrix} 0.5 & 0.3 \\ 0.0 & 0.2 \end{bmatrix} \begin{bmatrix} 1 \\ 0 \end{bmatrix} = \begin{bmatrix} 0.5 \\ 0 \end{bmatrix} \tag{11.31}$$

$$y_2 = A_1 y_1 = \begin{bmatrix} 0.5 & 0.3 \\ 0.0 & 0.2 \end{bmatrix} \begin{bmatrix} 0.5 \\ 0 \end{bmatrix} = \begin{bmatrix} 0.25 \\ 0 \end{bmatrix} \tag{11.32}$$

and so on. It would thus be possible to plot the impulse response functions of y_{1t} and y_{2t} to a unit shock in y_{1t}. Notice that the effect on y_{2t} is always zero, since the variable y_{1t-1} has a zero coefficient attached to it in the equation for y_{2t}.

Now consider the effect of a unit shock to y_{2t} at time $t = 0$:

$$y_0 = \begin{bmatrix} u_{10} \\ u_{20} \end{bmatrix} = \begin{bmatrix} 0 \\ 1 \end{bmatrix} \tag{11.33}$$

$$y_1 = A_1 y_0 = \begin{bmatrix} 0.5 & 0.3 \\ 0.0 & 0.2 \end{bmatrix} \begin{bmatrix} 0 \\ 1 \end{bmatrix} = \begin{bmatrix} 0.3 \\ 0.2 \end{bmatrix} \tag{11.34}$$

$$y_2 = A_1 y_1 = \begin{bmatrix} 0.5 & 0.3 \\ 0.0 & 0.2 \end{bmatrix} \begin{bmatrix} 0.3 \\ 0.2 \end{bmatrix} = \begin{bmatrix} 0.21 \\ 0.04 \end{bmatrix} \tag{11.35}$$

and so on. Although it is probably fairly easy to see what the effects of shocks to the variables will be in such a simple VAR, the same principles can be applied in the context of VARs containing more equations or more lags, when it is much more difficult to see by eye what the interactions are between the equations.

Variance decompositions offer a slightly different method for examining VAR system dynamics. They give the proportion of the movements in the dependent variables that are due to their 'own' shocks as opposed to shocks to the other variables. A shock to the ith variable will of course directly affect that variable, but it will also be transmitted to all the other variables in the system through the dynamic structure of the VAR. Variance decompositions determine how much of the s-step-ahead forecast error variance of a given variable is explained by innovations to each explanatory variable for $s = 1, 2, \ldots$ In practice, it is usually observed that own-series shocks explain most of the (forecast) error variance of the series in a VAR. To some extent, impulse responses and variance decompositions offer very similar information.

For calculating impulse responses and variance decompositions, the ordering of the variables is important. To see why this is the case, recall that the impulse responses refer to a unit shock to the errors of one VAR equation alone. This implies that the error terms of all the other equations in the VAR system are held constant. This is not realistic, however, as the error terms are likely to be correlated across equations to some extent. Assuming that they are completely independent would therefore lead to a misrepresentation of the system dynamics. In practice, the errors will have a common component that cannot be associated with a single variable alone.

The usual approach to this difficulty is to generate *orthogonalised impulse responses*. In the context of a bivariate VAR, the whole of the common component of the errors is attributed somewhat arbitrarily to the first variable in the VAR. In the general case in which there are more than two variables in the VAR, the calculations are more complex but the interpretation is the same. Such a restriction in effect implies an 'ordering' of variables, so that the equation for y_{1t} would be estimated first and then that of y_{2t} – a bit like a recursive or triangular system.

Assuming a particular ordering is necessary to compute the impulse responses and variance decompositions, although the restriction underlying the ordering used may not be supported by the data. Again, ideally, real estate theory should suggest an ordering (in other words, that movements in some variables are likely to follow, rather than precede, others). Failing this, the sensitivity of the results to changes in the ordering can be observed by assuming one ordering, and then exactly reversing it and recomputing the impulse responses and variance decompositions. It is also worth noting that, the more highly correlated the residuals from an estimated equation are, the more the variable ordering will be important. When the residuals are almost uncorrelated, however, the ordering of the variables will make little difference (see Lütkepohl, 1991, ch. 2, for further details), and thus an examination of the correlation structure between the residual series will

Table 11.6 Residual correlations

	ARPRET	ΔSPY	$\Delta 10Y$	ΔCBY
ARPRET	1.00			
ΔSPY	−0.43	1.00		
$\Delta 10Y$	−0.26	0.27	1.00	
ΔCBY	−0.29	0.33	0.92	1.00

Table 11.7 Variance decompositions for *ARPRET* equation residuals

	Explained by innovations in			
Months ahead	*ARPRET*	ΔSPY	$\Delta 10Y$	ΔCBY
1	100.0	0.0	0.0	0.0
2	96.3	0.0	3.7	0.0
3	94.7	0.1	3.7	1.4
4	94.5	0.2	3.7	1.5
5	94.4	0.3	3.8	1.5
6	94.4	0.3	3.8	1.5

Note: Ordering is *ARPRET*, ΔSPY, $\Delta 10Y$, ΔCBY.

guide the choice as to how important it is to examine a variety of variable orderings.

Runkle (1987) argues that impulse responses and variance decompositions are both notoriously difficult to interpret accurately. He argues that confidence bands around the impulse responses and variance decompositions should always be constructed. He further states, however, that, even then, the confidence intervals are typically so wide that sharp inferences are impossible.

11.9.1 *Impulse responses and variance decompositions for the REIT VAR*

Table 11.6 shows the correlations between the residuals of the VAR equations in our example.

A fairly strong correlation is established between the residuals of the equations and $\Delta 10Y$ and ΔCBY (0.92). The residuals of the equations *ARPRET* and ΔSPY show moderate correlation of −0.43. Hence the ordering will have some impact on the computation of variance decompositions and impulse responses alike. Tables 11.7 and 11.8 present the variance decompositions.

Table 11.8 Variance decompositions for *ARPRET* equation residuals: alternative ordering

	Explained by innovations in			
Months ahead	*ARPRET*	$\Delta_{12}SPY$	$\Delta_{12}10Y$	$\Delta_{12}CBY$
1	91.8	0.0	6.7	1.5
2	87.8	0.3	10.4	1.4
3	86.3	0.6	10.4	2.7
4	86.1	0.8	10.4	2.7
5	86.1	0.8	10.4	2.7
6	86.0	0.8	10.5	2.7

Note: Ordering is $\Delta 10Y$, ΔCBY, *ARPRET*, ΔSPY.

The observation to make is that shocks to all yields barely influence the variation in REIT price returns. The impact of $\Delta 10Y$ after six months is only 3.8 per cent.

The results under a different ordering change slightly. Now $\Delta 10Y$ explains a greater proportion of the variance in *ARPRET*. There has been a very marginal rise in the impact of the other two yield series on REIT returns. With the second ordering, after six months, the Treasury bond yield accounts for 10.5 per cent of the variance of the residuals of the REIT price returns and the corporate bond yield accounts for about 2.7 per cent, leaving a large 86 per cent of the variance to be accounted for by own *ARPRET* lags. The impact of the Treasury bond yield is maximised after two months. This finding is in accordance with the short lag length selected for the VAR model. We would thus conclude that there is little evidence for external influences on *ARPRET* from other variables in the system. We could, of course, calculate and print the variance decompositions for the impacts on other variables in the system, but these are not of direct interest here. Figure 11.1 presents the impulse responses for *ARPRET* associated with unit shocks in each of the three yield series for a given order of the variables in the VAR. The dotted lines represent ± 1 standard deviation. The order of the variables for calculating the impulse responses is *ARPRET*, ΔSPY, $\Delta 10Y$, ΔAAA.

The response of returns to an own shock is absorbed within two months. Returns do not respond to S&P dividend yield shocks – a finding that confirms the results of the joint significance tests (table 11.5). A shock to the Treasury bill rate is dissipated in all REIT price returns within two months before it dies away. The impact of the corporate yield is weaker than that of the Treasury bond yield, with the strongest impact recorded after three months.

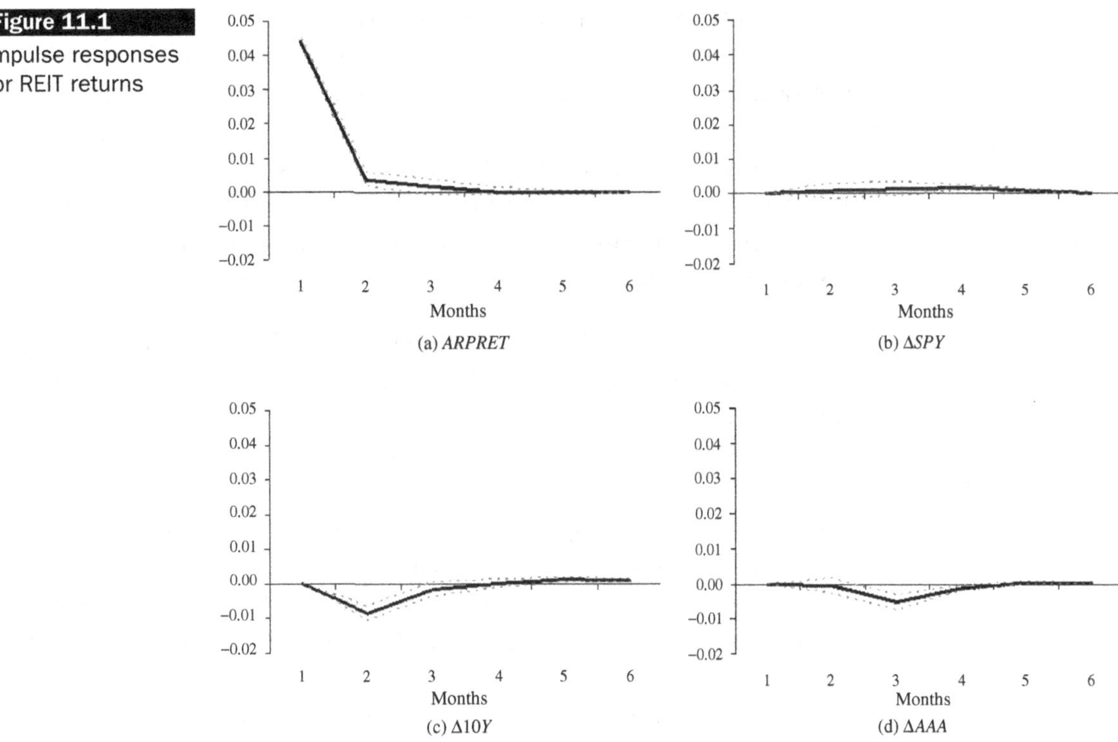

Figure 11.1 Impulse responses for REIT returns

11.10 A VAR for the interaction between real estate returns and the macroeconomy

11.10.1 *Background, data and variables*

Brooks and Tsolacos (1999) employ a VAR methodology to investigate the interaction between the UK real estate market and various macroeconomic variables. Monthly data, in logarithmic form, are used for the period from December 1985 to January 1998. The selection of the variables for inclusion in the VAR model is governed by the time series that are commonly included in studies of stock return predictability. It is assumed that stock returns are related to macroeconomic and business conditions, and hence time series that may be able to capture both current and future directions in the broad economy and the business environment are used in the investigation.

They elect to use the equity-based FTSE Property Total Return Index to construct real estate returns. In order to purge the real estate return series of its general stock market influences, it is common to regress property returns on a general stock market index returns (in this case the FTA All-Share Index is used), saving the residuals. These residuals are expected to reflect only the variation in real estate returns. This series, denoted *PROPRES*, is the real estate market return measure used in this study.

The variables included in the VAR, therefore, are the real estate returns (with general stock market effects removed), the rate of unemployment, nominal interest rates, the spread between the long- and short-term interest rates, unanticipated inflation and the dividend yield. The motivations for including these particular variables in the VAR, together with the property series, are as follows.

- *The growth rate of unemployment* (denoted *UNEM*) is included to indicate general economic conditions. In US research, authors tend to use aggregate consumption, a variable that has been built into asset-pricing models and examined as a determinant of stock returns. Data for this variable, and for alternative variables such as GDP, are not available on a monthly basis in the United Kingdom. As a result, the authors did not consider this series as a potential causal variable.
- *Short-term nominal interest rates* (*SIR*) are assumed to contain information about future economic conditions and to capture the state of investment opportunities.
- *Interest rate spreads* (*SPREAD*) are usually measured as the difference in the returns between long-term Treasury bonds (of maturity, say, ten or twenty years) and the one- or three-month Treasury bill rate.
- *Inflation rate* influences are also considered important in the pricing of stocks. For example, unanticipated inflation could be a source of economic risk, and, as a result, a risk premium will also be added if share prices have exposure to unanticipated inflation. The unanticipated inflation variable (denoted *UNINFL*) is defined as the difference between the realised inflation rate, computed as the percentage change in the retail price index (RPI), and an estimated series of expected inflation. The latter series was produced by fitting an ARMA model to the actual series and making a one-period(month)-ahead forecast, then rolling the sample forward one period, re-estimating the parameters and making another one-step-ahead forecast, and so on.
- *Dividend yields* (denoted *DIVY*) are widely used to model stock market returns, and also real estate returns, based on the assumption that movements in the dividend yield series are related to long-term business conditions and that they capture some predictable components of returns.

11.10.2 Methodology

Brooks and Tsolacos (1999) employ a reduced-form VAR, and hence each equation can be estimated separately using OLS. We noted earlier that, for a VAR to be unrestricted, it is required that the same number of lags of all the variables is used in all equations. The appropriate lag length is determined using the multivariate generalisation of Akaike's information criterion.

Within the framework of the VAR system of equations, the significance of all the lags of each of the individual variables is examined jointly with an F-test. The authors note that, since several lags of the variables are included in each of the equations of the system, the coefficients on individual lags may not appear significant for all the lags, and may have signs and degrees of significance that vary with the lag length. F-tests will be able to establish whether all the lags of a particular variable are jointly significant, however. In order to consider further the effect of the macroeconomy on the real estate returns index, the impact multipliers (orthogonalised impulse responses) are also calculated for the estimated VAR model. Two standard error bands are calculated using the Monte Carlo integration approach employed by McCue and Kling (1994), and based on Doan (1994). The forecast error variance is also decomposed to determine the proportion of the movements in the real estate series that are a consequence of its own shocks rather than shocks to other variables.

11.10.3 *Results*

The number of lags that minimises the value of Akaike's information criterion is fourteen, consistent with the fifteen lags used by McCue and Kling (1994). There are thus $(1 + 14 \times 6) = 85$ variables in each equation, implying fifty-nine degrees of freedom. The p-values associated with the F-tests for the null hypothesis that all the lags of a given variable are jointly insignificant in a given equation are presented in table 11.9.

In contrast to a number of US studies that have used similar variables, this study finds that it is difficult to explain the variation in the UK real estate returns index using macroeconomic factors, as the last row of table 11.9 shows. Of all the lagged variables in the real estate equation, only the lags of the real estate returns themselves are highly significant, and the dividend yield variable is significant only at the 20 per cent level. No other variables have any significant explanatory power for the real estate returns. One possible explanation for this might be that, in the United Kingdom, these variables do not convey the information about the macroeconomy and business conditions that is assumed to determine the intertemporal behaviour of real estate returns. It is possible that real estate returns may reflect real estate market influences, such as rents, yields or capitalisation rates, rather than macroeconomic or financial variables. The use of monthly data limits the set of both macroeconomic and real estate market variables

Table 11.9 Marginal significance levels associated with joint *F*-tests

Dependent variable	Lags of variable					
	SIR	*DIVY*	*SPREAD*	*UNEM*	*UNINFL*	*PROPRES*
SIR	0.0000	0.0091	0.0242	0.0327	0.2126	0.0000
DIVY	0.5025	0.0000	0.6212	0.4217	0.5654	0.4033
SPREAD	0.2779	0.1328	0.0000	0.4372	0.6563	0.0007
UNEM	0.3410	0.3026	0.1151	0.0000	0.0758	0.2765
UNINFL	0.3057	0.5146	0.3420	0.4793	0.0004	0.3885
PROPRES	0.5537	0.1614	0.5537	0.8922	0.7222	0.0000

Note: The test is that all fourteen lags have no explanatory power for that particular equation in the VAR.
Source: Brooks and Tsolacos (1999).

that can be used in the quantitative analysis of real estate returns in the United Kingdom, however.

This study finds that lagged values of the real estate variable have explanatory power for some other variables in the system. These results are shown in the last column of table 11.9. The real estate sector appears to help explain variations in the term structure and short-term interest rates, and, moreover, as these variables are not significant in the real estate index equation, it is possible to state further that the real estate residual series Granger-causes the short-term interest rate and the term spread. This is an interesting result. The fact that real estate returns are explained by own lagged values – i.e. there is interdependency between neighbouring data points (observations) – may reflect the way that real estate market information is produced and reflected in the real estate return indices.

Table 11.10 gives variance decompositions for the property returns index equation of the VAR for one, two, three, four, twelve and twenty-four steps ahead for the following two variable orderings.

Order I: *PROPRES, DIVY, UNINFL, UNEM, SPREAD, SIR*.
Order II: *SIR, SPREAD, UNEM, UNINFL, DIVY, PROPRES*.

The ordering of the variables is important in the decomposition. Two orderings are therefore applied that are the exact opposite of one another, and the sensitivity of the result is then considered.

It is clear that, by the two-year forecasting horizon, the variable ordering has become almost irrelevant in most cases. An interesting feature of the results is that shocks to the term spread and unexpected inflation together account for over 50 per cent of the variation in the real estate series. The

Table 11.10 Variance decompositions for property sector index residuals

	Explained by innovations in											
	SIR		*DIVY*		*SPREAD*		*UNEM*		*UNINFL*		*PROPRES*	
Months ahead	I	II	I	II	I	II	I	II	I	II	I	II
1	0.0	0.8	0.0	38.2	0.0	9.1	0.0	0.7	0.0	0.2	100.0	51.0
2	0.2	0.8	0.2	35.1	0.2	12.3	0.4	1.4	1.6	2.9	97.5	47.5
3	3.8	2.5	0.4	29.4	0.2	17.8	1.0	1.5	2.3	3.0	92.3	45.8
4	3.7	2.1	5.3	22.3	1.4	18.5	1.6	1.1	4.8	4.4	83.3	51.5
12	2.8	3.1	15.5	8.7	15.3	19.5	3.3	5.1	17.0	13.5	46.1	50.0
24	8.2	6.3	6.8	3.9	38.0	36.2	5.5	14.7	18.1	16.9	23.4	22.0

Source: Brooks and Tsolacos (1999).

short-term interest rate and dividend yield shocks account for only 10 to 15 per cent of the variance of this series. One possible explanation for the difference in results between the F-tests and the variance decomposition is that the former is a causality test and the latter is, effectively, an exogeneity test. Hence the latter implies the stronger restriction that neither current nor lagged shocks to the explanatory variables influence the current value of the dependent variable of the real estate equation. Another way of stating this is that the term structure and unexpected inflation have a contemporaneous rather than a lagged effect on real estate returns, which implies insignificant F-test statistics but explanatory power in the variance decomposition. Therefore, although the F-tests do not establish any significant effects, the error variance decompositions show evidence of a contemporaneous relationship between *PROPRES* and both *SPREAD* and *UNINFL*. The lack of lagged effects could be taken to imply speedy adjustment of the market to changes in these variables.

Figures 11.2 and 11.3 give the impulse responses for *PROPRES* associated with separate unit shocks to unexpected inflation and the dividend yield, as examples (as stated above, a total of thirty-six impulse responses could be calculated since there are six variables in the system).

Considering the signs of the responses, innovations to unexpected inflation (figure 11.2) always have a negative impact on the real estate index, since the impulse response is negative, and the effect of the shock does not die down, even after twenty-four months. Increasing stock dividend yields (figure 11.3) have a negative impact for the first three periods, but, beyond that, the shock appears to have worked its way out of the system.

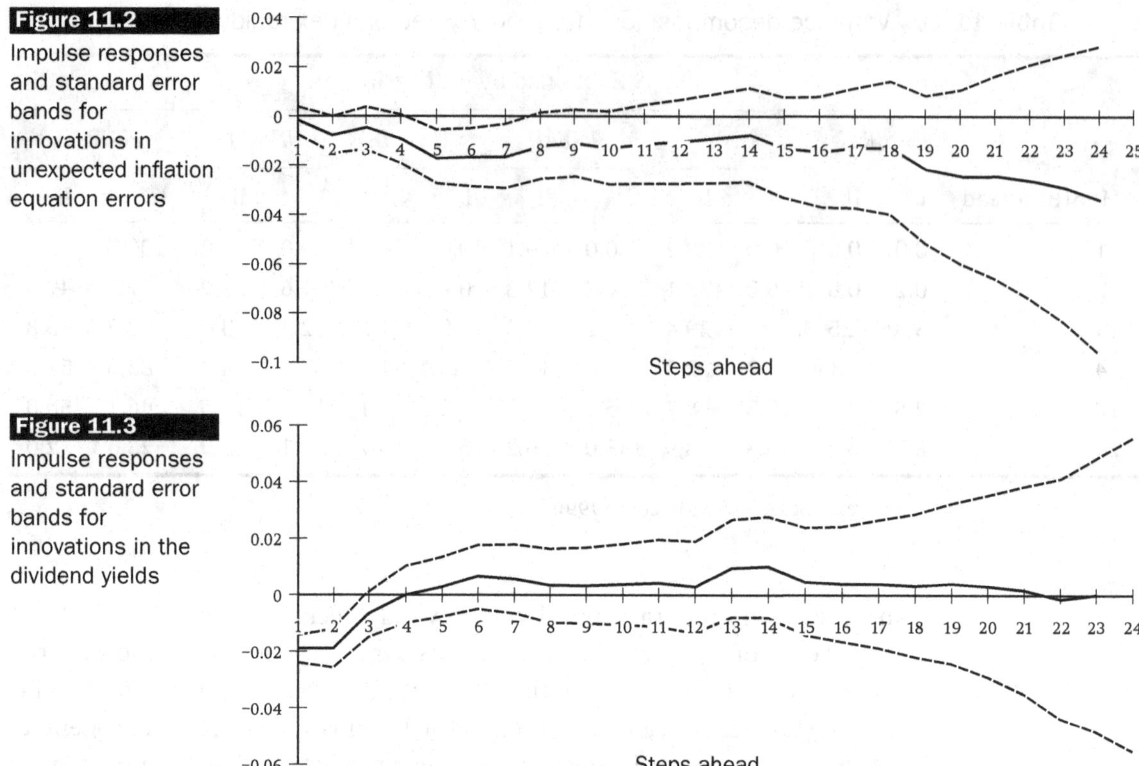

Figure 11.2 Impulse responses and standard error bands for innovations in unexpected inflation equation errors

Figure 11.3 Impulse responses and standard error bands for innovations in the dividend yields

11.10.4 *Conclusions*

The conclusion from the VAR methodology adopted in the Brooks and Tsolacos paper is that, overall, UK real estate returns are difficult to explain on the basis of the information contained in the set of the variables used in existing studies based on non-UK data. The results are not strongly suggestive of any significant influences of these variables on the variation of the filtered real estate returns series. There is some evidence, however, that the interest rate term structure and unexpected inflation have a contemporaneous effect on real estate returns, in agreement with the results of a number of previous studies.

11.11 Using VARs for forecasting

As we have pointed out, a key use of a VAR specification is for forecasting. Based on our VAR example for US REITs, we attempt to forecast REIT returns. We also evaluate the forecast performance of the VAR. Since the VAR contains only lags, the system can be used to forecast without any assumptions of the future values of any of the variables. All variables are forecast within

Table 11.11 Dynamic VAR forecasts

	Coefficients used in the forecast equation			
	$ARPRET_t$	ΔSPY_t	$\Delta 10Y_t$	ΔAAA_t
Constant	−0.0025	−0.0036	−0.0040	−0.0058
$ARPRET_{t-1}$	0.0548	−0.9120	0.0985	−0.3003
$ARPRET_{t-2}$	0.0543	0.2825	−0.2192	−0.3176
ΔSPY_{t-1}	0.0223	0.1092	−0.2280	−0.1792
ΔSPY_{t-2}	0.0136	−0.0263	−0.3501	−0.2720
$\Delta 10Y_{t-1}$	−0.0257	0.0770	0.4401	0.2644
$\Delta 10Y_{t-2}$	0.0494	−0.0698	−0.2612	−0.1739
ΔAAA_{t-1}	−0.0070	−0.0003	−0.0706	0.1266
ΔAAA_{t-2}	−0.0619	0.1158	0.1325	0.0202
	Forecasts			
	$ARPRET_t$	ΔSPY_t	$\Delta 10Y_t$	ΔAAA_t
May 07	−0.0087	−0.0300	0.0600	0.0000
Jun. 07	−0.1015	0.0000	0.3500	0.3200
Jul. 07	−0.0958	−0.0100	−0.1000	−0.0600
Aug. 07	**−0.0130**	**0.0589**	**−0.0777**	**−0.0314**
Sep. 07	**−0.0062**	**−0.0180**	**−0.0080**	**0.0123**
Oct. 07	**−0.0049**	**−0.0039**	**−0.0066**	**−0.0003**
Nov. 07	**−0.0044**	**0.0007**	**0.0050**	**0.0031**
Dec. 07	**−0.0035**	**0.0000**	**0.0015**	**0.0009**
Jan. 08	**−0.0029**	**−0.0015**	**−0.0039**	**−0.0038**

the system. Table 11.11 shows six months of forecasts and explains how we obtained them.

The top panel of the table shows the VAR coefficients estimated over the whole-sample period (presented to four decimal points so that the forecasts can be calculated with more accuracy). The lower panel shows the VAR forecasts for the six months August 2007 to January 2008. The forecast for *ARPRET* for August 2007 (−0.0130 or −1.3 per cent monthly return) is given by the following equation:

$$\begin{aligned}&-0.0025 + [0.0548 \times -0.0958 + 0.0543 \times -0.1015] + [0.0223 \times -0.0100 \\ &\quad + 0.0136 \times 0.0000] + [-0.0257 \times -0.1000 + 0.0494 \times 0.3500] \\ &\quad + [-0.0070 \times -0.0600 - 0.0619 \times 0.3200]\end{aligned}$$

The forecast for ΔSPY_t for August 2007 – that is, the change between July 2007 and August 2007 (0.0589 or 5.89 basis points) – is given by the following equation:

$$-0.0036 + [-0.9120 \times -0.0958 + 0.2825 \times -0.1015] + [0.1092 \times -0.0100 - 0.0263 \times 0.0000] + [0.0770 \times -0.1000 - 0.0698 \times 0.3500] + [-0.0003 \times -0.0600 + 0.1158 \times 0.3200]$$

The forecasts for August 2007 will enter the calculation of the September 2007 figure. This version of the VAR model is therefore a truly dynamic one, as the forecasts moving forward are generated within the system and are not conditioned by the future values of any of the variables. These are sometimes called unconditional forecasts (see box 11.1). In table 11.11, the VAR forecasts suggest continuously negative monthly REIT price returns for the six months following the last observation in July 2007. The negative growth is forecast to get smaller every month and to reach −0.29 per cent in January 2008 from −1.3 per cent in August 2007.

Box 11.1 Forecasting with VARs

- One of the main advantages of the VAR approach to modelling and forecasting is that, since only lagged variables are used on the right-hand side, forecasts of the future values of the dependent variables can be calculated using only information from within the system.
- We could term these *unconditional* forecasts, since they are not constructed conditional on a particular set of assumed values.
- Conversely, however, it may be useful to produce forecasts of the future values of some variables *conditional upon* known values of other variables in the system.
- For example, it may be the case that the values of some variables become known before the values of the others.
- If the known values of the former are employed, we would anticipate that the forecasts should be more accurate than if estimated values were used unnecessarily, thus throwing known information away.
- Alternatively, conditional forecasts can be employed for counterfactual analysis based on examining the impact of certain scenarios.
- For example, in a trivariate VAR system incorporating monthly REIT returns, inflation and GDP, we could answer the question 'What is the likely impact on the REIT index over the next one to six months of a two percentage point increase in inflation and a one percentage point rise in GDP?'.

Within the VAR, the three yield series are also predicted. It can be argued, however, that series such as the Treasury bond yield cannot be effectively forecast within this system, as they are determined exogenously. Hence we can make use of alternative forecasts for Treasury bond yields (from the conditional VAR forecasting methodology outlined in box 11.1). Assuming

Table 11.12 VAR forecasts conditioned on future values of $\Delta 10Y$

	$ARPRET_t$	ΔSPY_t	$\Delta 10Y_t$	ΔAAA_t
May 07	−0.0087	−0.0300	0.0600	0.0000
Jun. 07	−0.1015	0.0000	0.3500	0.3200
Jul. 07	−0.0958	−0.0100	−0.1000	−0.0600
Aug. 07	**−0.0130**	**0.0589**	**0.2200**	**−0.0314**
Sep. 07	**−0.0139**	**0.0049**	**0.3300**	**0.0911**
Oct. 07	**0.0006**	**0.0108**	**0.4000**	**0.0455**
Nov. 07	**−0.0028**	**0.0112**	**0.0000**	**0.0511**
Dec. 07	**0.0144**	**−0.0225**	**0.0000**	**−0.0723**
Jan. 08	**−0.0049**	**−0.0143**	**−0.1000**	**−0.0163**

that we accept this argument, we then obtain forecasts from a different source for the ten-year Treasury bond yield. In our VAR forecast, the Treasury bond yield was falling throughout the prediction period. Assume, however, that we have a forecast (from an economic forecasting house) of the bond yield rising and following the pattern shown in table 11.12. We estimate the forecasts again, although, for the future values of the Treasury bond yield, we do not use the VAR's forecasts but our own.

By imposing our own assumptions for the future values of the movements in the Treasury bill rate, we affect the forecasts across the board. With the unconditional forecasts, the Treasury bill rate was forecast to fall in the first three months of the forecast period and then rise, whereas, according to our own assumptions, the Treasury Bill rate rises immediately and it then levels off (in November 2007). The forecasts conditioned on the Treasury bill rate are given in table 11.12. The forecasts for August 2007 have not changed, since they use the actual values of the previous two months.

11.11.1 Ex post *forecasting and evaluation*

We now conduct an evaluation of the VAR forecasts. We estimate the VAR over the sample period March 1972 to January 2007, reserving the last six months for forecast assessment. We evaluate two sets of forecasts: dynamic VAR forecasts and forecasts conditioned by the future values of the Treasury and corporate bond yields. The parameter estimates are shown in table 11.13.

The forecast for *ARPRET* for February 2007 is produced in the same way as in table 11.11, although we are now computing genuine out-of-sample

Table 11.13 Coefficients for VAR forecasts estimated using data for March 1972 to January 2007

	$ARPRET_t$	ΔSPY_t	$\Delta 10Y_t$	ΔAAA_t
Constant	0.0442	−0.9405	0.0955	−0.3128
$ARPRET_{t-1}$	0.0552	0.2721	−0.205	−0.3119
$ARPRET_{t-2}$	0.0203	0.1037	−0.2305	−0.1853
ΔSPY_{t-1}	0.013	−0.0264	−0.3431	−0.2646
ΔSPY_{t-2}	−0.0251	0.0744	0.4375	0.2599
$\Delta 10Y_{t-1}$	0.0492	−0.0696	−0.2545	−0.1682
$\Delta 10Y_{t-2}$	−0.0072	0.0035	−0.0626	0.1374
ΔAAA_{t-1}	−0.0609	0.1145	0.1208	0.0086
ΔAAA_{t-2}	−0.0019	−0.0033	−0.0042	−0.0062

Table 11.14 *Ex post* VAR dynamic forecasts

	$ARPRET_t$		ΔSPY		$\Delta 10Y$		ΔCBY	
	Actual	Forecast	Actual	Forecast	Actual	Forecast	Actual	Forecast
Dec. 06	−0.0227		−0.0100		−0.0400		−0.0100	
Jan. 07	0.0718		0.0200		0.2000		0.0800	
Feb. 07	−0.0355	**−0.0067**	0.0100	**−0.0579**	−0.0400	**0.0976**	−0.0100	**0.0470**
Mar. 07	−0.0359	**0.0030**	0.0700	**0.0186**	−0.1600	**−0.0146**	−0.0900	**−0.0222**
Apr. 07	−0.0057	**0.0000**	−0.0500	**−0.0071**	0.1300	**−0.0111**	0.1700	**−0.0161**
May. 07	−0.0087	**−0.0006**	−0.0300	**−0.0061**	0.0600	**−0.0124**	0.0000	**−0.0136**
Jun. 07	−0.1015	**−0.0013**	0.0000	**−0.0052**	0.3500	**−0.0041**	0.3200	**−0.0064**
Jul. 07	−0.0958	**−0.0018**	−0.0100	**−0.0036**	−0.1000	**−0.0008**	−0.0600	**−0.0030**

forecasts as we would in real time. The forecasts for all series are compared to the actual values, shown in table 11.14.

In the six-month period February 2007 to July 2007, REIT returns were negative every single month. The VAR correctly predicts the direction for four of the six months. In these four months, however, the prediction for negative monthly returns is quite short of what actually happened.

We argued earlier that the Treasury bond yield is unlikely to be determined within the VAR in our example. For the purpose of illustration, we take the actual values of the Treasury yield and recalculate the VAR forecasts. We should expect an improvement in this conditional forecast, since we are

Table 11.15 Conditional VAR forecasts

	$ARPRET_t$		ΔSPY		$\Delta 10Y$	ΔCBY	
	Actual	Forecast	Actual	Forecast	Actual	Actual	Forecast
Dec. 06	−0.0227		−0.0100		−0.0400	−0.0100	
Jan. 07	0.0718		0.0200		0.2000	0.0800	
Feb. 07	−0.0355	**−0.0067**	0.0100	**−0.0579**	−0.0400	−0.0100	**0.0470**
Mar. 07	−0.0359	**0.0065**	0.0700	**0.0084**	−0.1600	−0.0900	**−0.0580**
Apr. 07	−0.0057	**−0.0030**	−0.0500	**−0.0128**	0.1300	0.1700	**−0.0348**
May. 07	−0.0087	**−0.0092**	−0.0300	**0.0138**	0.0600	0.0000	**0.0483**
Jun. 07	−0.1015	**0.0043**	0.0000	**−0.0021**	0.3500	0.3200	**−0.0015**
Jul. 07	−0.0958	**−0.0108**	−0.0100	**0.0170**	−0.1000	−0.0600	**0.0731**

Table 11.16 VAR forecast evaluation

	Dynamic	Conditional
Mean forecast error	−0.05	−0.04
Mean absolute error	0.05	0.04
RMSE	0.06	0.06
Theil's $U1$	0.93	0.87

now effectively assuming perfect foresight for one variable. The results are reported in table 11.15.

The *ARPRET* forecasts have not changed significantly and, in some months, the forecasts are worse than the unconditional ones. The formal evaluations of the dynamic and the conditional forecasts are presented in table 11.16.

The mean forecast error points to an under-prediction (error defined as the actual values minus the forecasted values) of 5 per cent on average per month. The mean absolute error confirms the level of under-prediction. When we use actual values for the Treasury bill rate, these statistics improve but only slightly. Both VAR forecasts have a similar RMSE but the Theil statistic is better for the conditional VAR. On both occasions, however, the Theil statistics indicate poor forecasts. To an extent, this is not surprising, given the low explanatory power of the independent variables in the *ARPRET* equation in the VAR. Moreover, the results both of the variance decomposition and the impulse response analysis did not demonstrate strong influences from any of the yield series we examined. Of course, these forecast evaluation results refer to a single period of six months during which REIT prices showed large falls. A better forecast assessment would involve conducting this analysis over a longer period or rolling six-month periods; see chapter 9.

Key concepts

The key terms to be able to define and explain from this chapter are

- VAR system
- likelihood ratio test
- optimal lag length
- variable ordering
- impulse response
- VAR forecasting
- contemporaneous VAR terms
- multivariate information criteria
- exogenous VAR terms (VARX)
- Granger causality
- variance decomposition
- conditional and unconditional VAR forecasts

12 Cointegration in real estate markets

Learning outcomes

In this chapter, you will learn how to

- highlight the problems that may occur if non-stationary data are used in their levels forms:
- distinguish between types of non-stationarity;
- run unit root and stationarity tests;
- test for cointegration;
- specify error correction models;
- implement the Engle–Granger procedure;
- apply the Johansen technique; and
- forecast with cointegrated variables and error correction models.

12.1 Stationarity and unit root testing

12.1.1 *Why are tests for non-stationarity necessary?*

There are several reasons why the concept of non-stationarity is important and why it is essential that variables that are non-stationary be treated differently from those that are stationary. Two definitions of non-stationarity were presented at the start of chapter 8. For the purpose of the analysis in this chapter, a stationary series can be defined as one with a *constant mean*, *constant variance* and *constant autocovariances* for each given lag. The discussion in this chapter therefore relates to the concept of weak stationarity. An examination of whether a series can be viewed as stationary or not is essential for the following reasons.

- The stationarity or otherwise of a series can *strongly influence its behaviour and properties*. To offer one illustration, the word 'shock' is usually used

Figure 12.1
Value of R^2 for 1,000 sets of regressions of a non-stationary variable on another independent non-stationary variable

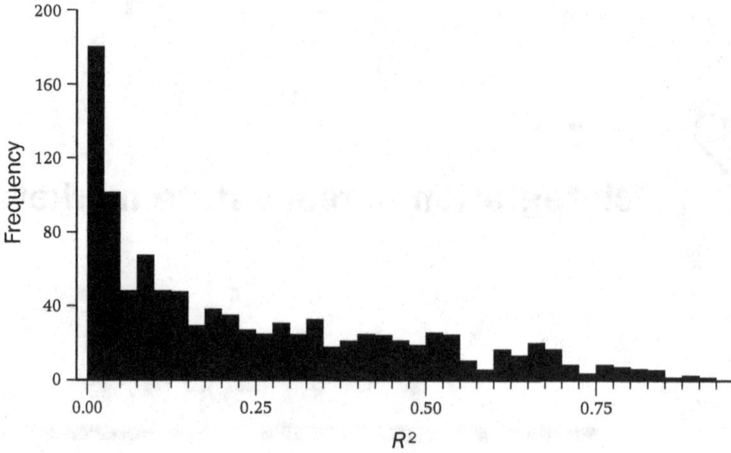

to denote a change or an unexpected change in a variable, or perhaps simply the value of the error term during a particular time period. For a stationary series, 'shocks' to the system will gradually die away. That is, a shock during time t will have a smaller effect in time $t+1$, a smaller effect still in time $t+2$, and so on. This can be contrasted with the case of non-stationary data, in which the persistence of shocks will always be infinite, so that, for a non-stationary series, the effect of a shock during time t will not have a smaller effect in time $t+1$, and in time $t+2$, etc.

- The use of non-stationary data can lead to *spurious regressions*. If two stationary variables are generated as independent random series, when one of those variables is regressed on the other the t-ratio on the slope coefficient would be expected not to be significantly different from zero, and the value of R^2 would be expected to be very low. This seems obvious, for the variables are not related to one another. If two variables are trending over time, however, a regression of one on the other could have a high R^2 even if the two are totally unrelated. If standard regression techniques are applied to non-stationary data, therefore, the end result could be a regression that 'looks' good under standard measures (significant coefficient estimates and a high R^2) but that is actually valueless. Such a model would be termed a 'spurious regression'.

  To give an illustration of this, two independent sets of non-stationary variables, y and x, were generated with sample size 500, one was regressed on the other and the R^2 was noted. This was repeated 1,000 times to obtain $1{,}000 R^2$ values. A histogram of these values is given in figure 12.1.

  As the figure shows, although one would have expected the R^2 values for each regression to be close to zero, since the explained and explanatory

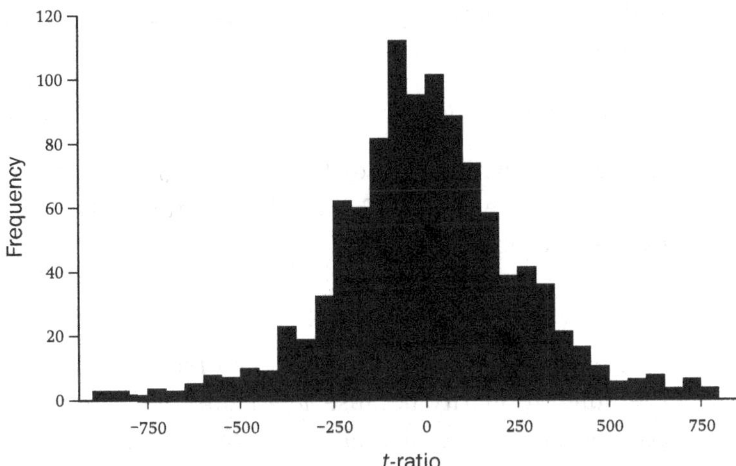

Figure 12.2 Value of t-ratio of slope coefficient for 1,000 sets of regressions of a non-stationary variable on another independent non-stationary variable

variables in each case are independent of one another, in fact R^2 takes on values across the whole range. For one set of data, R^2 is bigger than 0.9, while it is bigger than 0.5 over 16 per cent of the time!

- If the variables employed in a regression model are *not stationary* then it can be proved that the standard assumptions for asymptotic analysis will not be valid. In other words, the usual 't-ratios' will not follow a t-distribution, and the F-statistic will not follow an F-distribution, and so on. Using the same simulated data as used to produce figure 12.1, figure 12.2 plots a histogram of the estimated t-ratio on the slope coefficient for each set of data.

In general, if one variable is regressed on another unrelated variable, the t-ratio on the slope coefficient will follow a t-distribution. For a sample of size 500, this implies that, 95 per cent of the time, the t-ratio will lie between $+2$ and -2. As the figure shows quite dramatically, however, the standard t-ratio in a regression of non-stationary variables can take on enormously large values. In fact, in the above example, the t-ratio is bigger than two in absolute value over 98 per cent of the time, when it should be bigger than two in absolute value only around 5 per cent of the time! Clearly, it is therefore not possible to undertake hypothesis tests validly about the regression parameters if the data are non-stationary.

12.1.2 *Two types of non-stationarity*

There are two models that have been frequently used to characterise the non-stationarity: the *random walk model with drift*,

$$y_t = \mu + y_{t-1} + u_t \tag{12.1}$$

and the *trend-stationary process*, so-called because it is stationary around a linear trend,

$$y_t = \alpha + \beta t + u_t \tag{12.2}$$

where u_t is a white noise disturbance term in both cases.

Note that the model (12.1) can be generalised to the case in which y_t is an explosive process,

$$y_t = \mu + \phi y_{t-1} + u_t \tag{12.3}$$

where $\phi > 1$. Typically, this case is ignored, and $\phi = 1$ is used to characterise the non-stationarity because $\phi > 1$ does not describe many data series in economics, finance or real estate, but $\phi = 1$ has been found to describe accurately many financial, economic and real estate time series. Moreover, $\phi > 1$ has an intuitively unappealing property: not only are shocks to the system persistent through time, they are propagated, so that a given shock will have an increasingly large influence. In other words, the effect of a shock during time t will have a larger effect in time $t + 1$, a larger effect still in time $t + 2$, and so on.

To see this, consider the general case of an AR(1) with no drift:

$$y_t = \phi y_{t-1} + u_t \tag{12.4}$$

Let ϕ take any value for now. Lagging (12.4) one and then two periods,

$$y_{t-1} = \phi y_{t-2} + u_{t-1} \tag{12.5}$$
$$y_{t-2} = \phi y_{t-3} + u_{t-2} \tag{12.6}$$

Substituting into (12.4) from (12.5) for y_{t-1} yields

$$y_t = \phi(\phi y_{t-2} + u_{t-1}) + u_t \tag{12.7}$$
$$y_t = \phi^2 y_{t-2} + \phi u_{t-1} + u_t \tag{12.8}$$

Substituting again for y_{t-2} from (12.6),

$$y_t = \phi^2(\phi y_{t-3} + u_{t-2}) + \phi u_{t-1} + u_t \tag{12.9}$$
$$y_t = \phi^3 y_{t-3} + \phi^2 u_{t-2} + \phi u_{t-1} + u_t \tag{12.10}$$

T successive substitutions of this type lead to

$$y_t = \phi^{T+1} y_{t-(T+1)} + \phi u_{t-1} + \phi^2 u_{t-2} + \phi^3 u_{t-3} + \cdots + \phi^T u_{t-T} + u_t \tag{12.11}$$

There are three possible cases.

(1) $\phi < 1 \Rightarrow \phi^T \rightarrow 0$ as $T \rightarrow \infty$

The shocks to the system gradually die away; this is the *stationary case*.

(2) $\phi = 1 \Rightarrow \phi^T = 1 \forall T$
Shocks persist in the system and never die away. The following is obtained:

$$y_t = y_0 + \sum_{t=0}^{\infty} u_t \quad \text{as} \quad T \to \infty \tag{12.12}$$

So the current value of y is just an infinite sum of past shocks plus some starting value of y_0. This is known as the *unit root case*, for the root of the characteristic equation would be unity.

(3) $\phi > 1$
Now given shocks become more influential as time goes on, since, if $\phi > 1$, $\phi^3 > \phi^2 > \phi$, etc. This is the *explosive case*, which, for the reasons listed above, is not considered as a plausible description of the data.

Let us return to the two characterisations of non-stationarity, the random walk with drift,

$$y_t = \mu + y_{t-1} + u_t \tag{12.13}$$

and the trend-stationary process,

$$y_t = \alpha + \beta t + u_t \tag{12.14}$$

The two will require different treatments to induce stationarity. The second case is known as *deterministic non-stationarity*, and detrending is required. In other words, if it is believed that only this class of non-stationarity is present, a regression of the form given in (12.14) would be run, and any subsequent estimation would be done on the residuals from (12.14), which would have had the linear trend removed.

The first case is known as *stochastic non-stationarity*, as there is a stochastic trend in the data. Let $\Delta y_t = y_t - y_{t-1}$ and $Ly_t = y_{t-1}$ so that $(1 - L)\, y_t = y_t - Ly_t = y_t - y_{t-1}$. If (12.13) is taken and y_{t-1} subtracted from both sides,

$$y_t - y_{t-1} = \mu + u_t \tag{12.15}$$
$$(1 - L)\, y_t = \mu + u_t \tag{12.16}$$
$$\Delta\, y_t = \mu + u_t \tag{12.17}$$

There now exists a new variable, Δy_t, which will be stationary. It is said that stationarity has been induced by 'differencing once'. It should also be apparent from the representation given by (12.16) why y_t is also known as a *unit root process* – i.e. the root of the characteristic equation, $(1 - z) = 0$, will be unity.

Although trend-stationary and difference-stationary series are both 'trending' over time, the correct approach needs to be used in each case. If first differences of a trend-stationary series are taken, this will 'remove' the non-stationarity, but at the expense of introducing an MA(1) structure into the errors. To see this, consider the trend-stationary model

$$y_t = \alpha + \beta t + u_t \tag{12.18}$$

This model can be expressed for time $t-1$, which is obtained by removing one from all the time subscripts in (12.18):

$$y_{t-1} = \alpha + \beta(t-1) + u_{t-1} \tag{12.19}$$

Subtracting (12.19) from (12.18) gives

$$\Delta y_t = \beta + u_t - u_{t-1} \tag{12.20}$$

Not only is this a moving average in the errors that have been created, it is a non-invertible MA – i.e. one that cannot be expressed as an autoregressive process. Thus the series Δy_t would in this case have some very undesirable properties.

Conversely, if one tries to detrend a series that has a stochastic trend, the non-stationarity will not be removed. Clearly, then, it is not always obvious which way to proceed. One possibility is to nest both cases in a more general model and to test that. For example, consider the model

$$\Delta y_t = \alpha_0 + \alpha_1 t + (\gamma - 1)y_{t-1} + u_t \tag{12.21}$$

Again, of course, the t-ratios in (12.21) will not follow a t-distribution, however. Such a model could allow for both deterministic and stochastic non-stationarity. This book now concentrates on the stochastic stationarity model, though, as it is the model that has been found to best describe most non-stationary real estate and economic time series. Consider again the simplest stochastic trend model,

$$y_t = y_{t-1} + u_t \tag{12.22}$$

or

$$\Delta y_t = u_t \tag{12.23}$$

This concept can be generalised to consider the case in which the series contains more than one 'unit root' – that is, the first difference operator, Δ, would need to be applied more than once to induce stationarity. This situation is described later in this chapter.

Arguably the best way to understand the ideas discussed above is to consider some diagrams showing the typical properties of certain relevant types

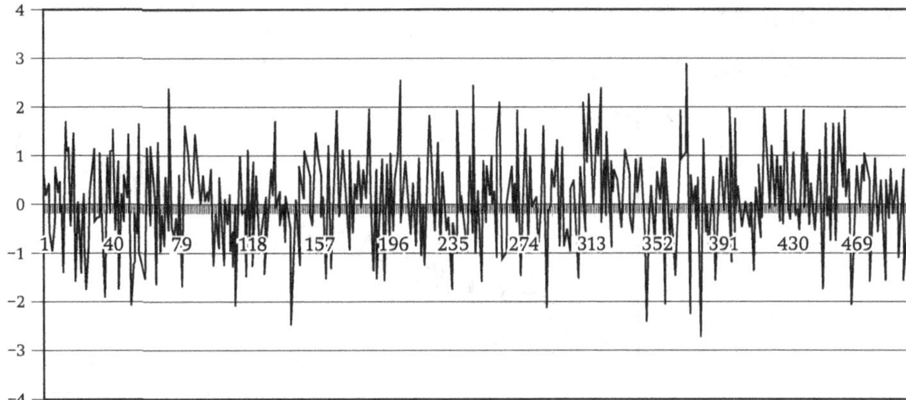

Figure 12.3
Example of a white noise process

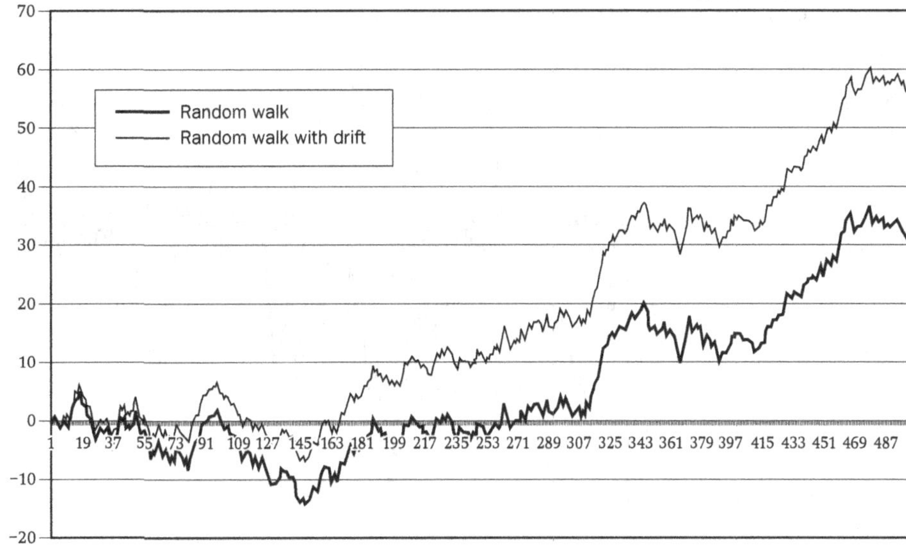

Figure 12.4
Time series plot of a random walk versus a random walk with drift

of processes. Figure 12.3 plots a white noise (pure random) process, while figures 12.4 and 12.5 plot a random walk versus a random walk with drift and a deterministic trend process, respectively.

Comparing these three figures gives a good idea of the differences between the properties of a stationary, a stochastic trend and a deterministic trend process. In figure 12.3, a white noise process visibly has no trending behaviour, and it frequently crosses its mean value of zero. The random walk (thick line) and random walk with drift (faint line) processes of figure 12.4 exhibit 'long swings' away from their mean value, which they cross very rarely. A comparison of the two lines in this graph reveals that the positive drift leads to a series that is more likely to rise over time than

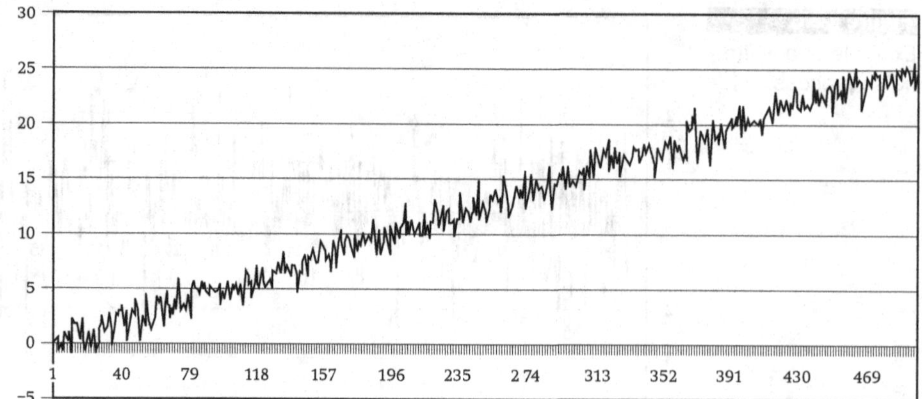

Figure 12.5 Time series plot of a deterministic trend process

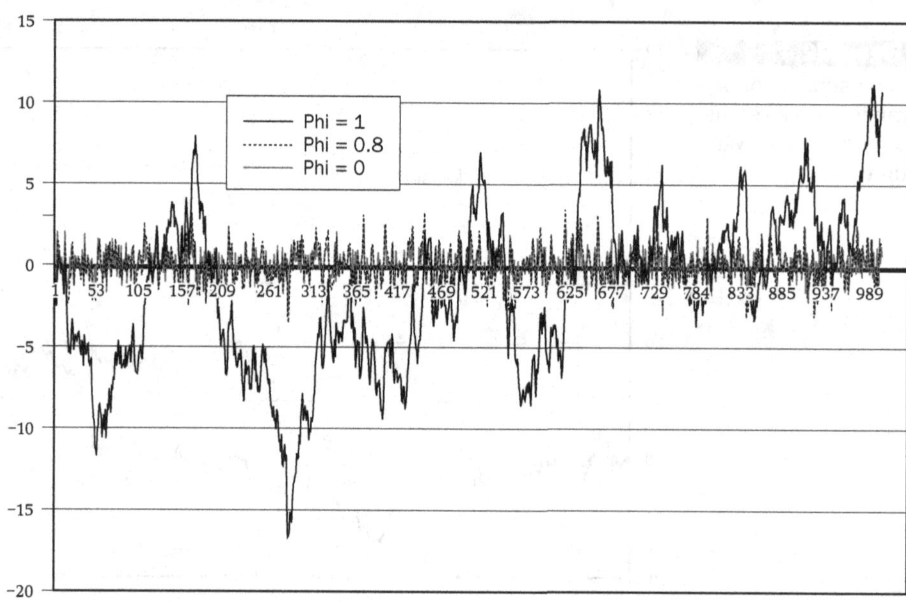

Figure 12.6 Autoregressive processes with differing values of ϕ (0, 0.8, 1)

to fall; obviously, the effect of the drift on the series becomes greater and greater the further the two processes are tracked. The deterministic trend process of figure 12.5 clearly does not have a constant mean, and exhibits completely random fluctuations about its upward trend. If the trend were removed from the series, a plot similar to the white noise process of figure 12.3 would result. It should be evident that more time series in real estate look like figure 12.4 than either figure 12.3 or 12.5. Consequently, as stated above, the stochastic trend model is the focus of the remainder of this chapter.

Finally, figure 12.6 plots the value of an autoregressive process of order 1 with different values of the autoregressive coefficient as given by (12.4).

Values of $\phi = 0$ (i.e. a white noise process), $\phi = 0.8$ (i.e. a stationary AR(1)) and $\phi = 1$ (i.e. a random walk) are plotted over time.

12.1.3 *Some more definitions and terminology*

If a non-stationary series, y_t, must be differenced d times before it becomes stationary then it is said to be integrated of order d. This would be written $y_t \sim \text{I}(d)$. So if $y_t \sim \text{I}(d)$ then $\Delta^d y_t \sim \text{I}(0)$. This latter piece of terminology states that applying the difference operator, Δ, d times leads to an I(0) process – i.e. a process with no unit roots. In fact, applying the difference operator more than d times to an I(d) process will still result in a stationary series (but with an MA error structure). An I(0) series is a stationary series, while an I(1) series contains one unit root. For example, consider the random walk

$$y_t = y_{t-1} + u_t \tag{12.24}$$

An I(2) series contains two unit roots and so would require differencing twice to induce stationarity. I(1) and I(2) series can wander a long way from their mean value and cross this mean value rarely, while I(0) series should cross the mean frequently.

The majority of financial and economic time series contain a single unit root, although some are stationary and with others it has been argued that they possibly contain two unit roots (series such as nominal consumer prices and nominal wages). This is true for real estate series too, which are mostly I(1) in their levels forms, although some are even I(2). The efficient markets hypothesis together with rational expectations suggest that asset prices (or the natural logarithms of asset prices) should follow a random walk or a random walk with drift, so that their differences are unpredictable (or predictable only to their long-term average value).

To see what types of data-generating process could lead to an I(2) series, consider the equation

$$y_t = 2y_{t-1} - y_{t-2} + u_t \tag{12.25}$$

Taking all the terms in y over to the LHS, and then applying the lag operator notation,

$$y_t - 2y_{t-1} + y_{t-2} = u_t \tag{12.26}$$

$$(1 - 2L + L^2)y_t = u_t \tag{12.27}$$

$$(1 - L)(1 - L)y_t = u_t \tag{12.28}$$

It should be evident now that this process for y_t contains two unit roots, and requires differencing twice to induce stationarity.

What would happen if y_t in (12.25) were differenced only once? Taking first differences of (12.25) – i.e. subtracting y_{t-1} from both sides –

$$y_t - y_{t-1} = y_{t-1} - y_{t-2} + u_t \quad (12.29)$$
$$y_t - y_{t-1} = (y_t - y_{t-1})_{-1} + u_t \quad (12.30)$$
$$\Delta y_t = \Delta y_{t-1} + u_t \quad (12.31)$$
$$(1 - L)\Delta y_t = u_t \quad (12.32)$$

First differencing would therefore remove one of the unit roots, but there is still a unit root remaining in the new variable, Δy_t.

12.1.4 Testing for a unit root

One immediately obvious (but inappropriate) method that readers may think of to test for a unit root would be to examine the autocorrelation function of the series of interest. Although shocks to a unit root process will remain in the system indefinitely, however, the acf for a unit root process (a random walk) will often be seen to decay away very slowly to zero. Such a process may therefore be mistaken for a highly persistent but stationary process. Thus it is not possible to use the acf or pacf to determine whether a series is characterised by a unit root or not. Furthermore, even if the true DGP for y_t contains a unit root, the results of the tests for a given sample could lead one to believe that the process is stationary. Therefore what is required is some kind of formal hypothesis-testing procedure that answers the question 'Given the sample of data to hand, is it plausible that the true data-generating process for y contains one or more unit roots?'.

The early and pioneering work on testing for a unit root in time series was done by Fuller and Dickey (Fuller, 1976; Dickey and Fuller, 1979). The basic objective of the test is to examine the null hypothesis that $\phi = 1$ in

$$y_t = \phi y_{t-1} + u_t \quad (12.33)$$

against the one-sided alternative $\phi < 1$. Thus the hypotheses of interest are

H_0: series contains a unit root
versus
H_1: series is stationary

In practice, the following regression is employed, rather than (12.33), for ease of computation and interpretation,

$$\Delta y_t = \psi y_{t-1} + u_t \quad (12.34)$$

so that a test of $\phi = 1$ is equivalent to a test of $\psi = 0$ (since $\phi - 1 = \psi$).

Table 12.1 Critical values for DF tests

Significance level	10%	5%	1%
CV for constant but no trend	−2.57	−2.86	−3.43
CV for constant and trend	−3.12	−3.41	−3.96

Dickey–Fuller (DF) tests are also known as τ-tests, and can be conducted allowing for an intercept, or an intercept and deterministic trend, or neither, in the test regression. The model for the unit root test in each case is

$$y_t = \phi y_{t-1} + \mu + \lambda t + u_t \tag{12.35}$$

The tests can also be written, by subtracting y_{t-1} from each side of the equation, as

$$\Delta y_t = \psi y_{t-1} + \mu + \lambda t + u_t \tag{12.36}$$

In another paper, Dickey and Fuller (1981) provide a set of additional test statistics and their critical values for joint tests of the significance of the lagged y, and the constant and trend terms. These are not examined further here. The test statistics for the original DF tests are defined as

$$test\ statistic = \frac{\hat{\psi}}{S\hat{E}(\hat{\psi})} \tag{12.37}$$

The test statistics do not follow the usual t-distribution under the null hypothesis, since the null is one of non-stationarity, but, rather, they follow a non-standard distribution. Critical values are derived from simulations experiments by, for example, Fuller (1976). Relevant examples of the distribution, obtained from simulations by the authors, are shown in table 12.1.

Comparing these with the standard normal critical values, it can be seen that the DF critical values are much bigger in absolute terms – i.e. more negative. Thus more evidence against the null hypothesis is required in the context of unit root tests than under standard t-tests. This arises partly from the inherent instability of the unit root process, the fatter distribution of the t-ratios in the context of non-stationary data (see figure 12.2 above) and the resulting uncertainty in inference. The null hypothesis of a unit root is rejected in favour of the stationary alternative in each case if the test statistic is more negative than the critical value.

The tests above are valid only if u_t is white noise. In particular, u_t is assumed not to be autocorrelated, but would be so if there was autocorrelation in the dependent variable of the regression (Δy_t), which has not been modelled. If this is the case, the test would be 'oversized', meaning that the true size of the test (the proportion of times a correct null hypothesis is incorrectly rejected) would be higher than the nominal size used (e.g. 5 per cent). The solution is to 'augment' the test using p lags of the dependent variable. The alternative model in the first case is now written

$$\Delta y_t = \psi y_{t-1} + \sum_{i=1}^{p} \alpha_i \Delta y_{t-i} + u_t \tag{12.38}$$

The lags of Δy_t now 'soak up' any dynamic structure present in the dependent variable, to ensure that u_t is not autocorrelated. The test is known as an augmented Dickey–Fuller (ADF) test and is still conducted on ψ, and the same critical values from the DF tables are used as beforehand.

A problem now arises in determining the optimal number of lags of the dependent variable. Although several ways of choosing p have been proposed, they are all somewhat arbitrary, and are thus not presented here. Instead, the following two simple rules of thumb are suggested. First, the *frequency of the data* can be used to decide. So, for example, if the data are monthly, use twelve lags; if the data are quarterly, use four lags; and so on. Second, an *information criterion* can be used to decide. Accordingly, choose the number of lags that minimises the value of an information criterion.

It is quite important to attempt to use an optimal number of lags of the dependent variable in the test regression, and to examine the sensitivity of the outcome of the test to the lag length chosen. In most cases, it is to be hoped, the conclusion will not be qualitatively altered by small changes in p, but sometimes it will. Including too few lags will not remove all the autocorrelation, thus biasing the results, while using too many will increase the coefficient standard errors. The latter effect arises because an increase in the number of parameters to estimate uses up degrees of freedom. Therefore, everything else being equal, the absolute values of the test statistics will be reduced. This will result in a reduction in the power of the test, implying that for a stationary process the null hypothesis of a unit root will be rejected less frequently than would otherwise have been the case.

12.1.5 Phillips–Perron (PP) tests

Phillips and Perron (1988) have developed a more comprehensive theory of unit root non-stationarity. The tests are similar to ADF tests, but they incorporate an automatic correction to the DF procedure to allow for autocorrelated residuals. The tests often give the same conclusions, and suffer from most of the same important limitations, as the ADF tests.

12.1.6 *Criticisms of Dickey–Fuller- and Phillips–Perron-type tests*

The most important criticism that has been levelled at unit root tests is that their power is low if the process is stationary but with a root close to the non-stationary boundary. So, for example, consider an AR(1) data-generating process with coefficient 0.95. If the true DGP is

$$y_t = 0.95y_{t-1} + u_t \tag{12.39}$$

the null hypothesis of a unit root should be rejected. It has been argued therefore that the tests are poor at deciding, for example, whether $\phi = 1$ or $\phi = 0.95$, especially with small sample sizes. The source of this problem is that, under the classical hypothesis-testing framework, the null hypothesis is never accepted; it is simply stated that it is either rejected or not rejected. This means that a failure to reject the null hypothesis could occur either because the null was correct or because there is insufficient information in the sample to enable rejection. One way to get around this problem is to use a stationarity test as well as a unit root test, as described in box 12.1.

Box 12.1 Stationarity tests

Stationarity tests have stationarity under the null hypothesis, thus reversing the null and alternatives under the Dickey–Fuller approach. Under stationarity tests, therefore the data will appear stationary by default if there is little information in the sample. One such stationarity test is the KPSS test, named after the authors of the Kwiatkowski *et al.*, 1992, paper. The computation of the test statistic is not discussed here but the test is available within many econometric software packages. The results of these tests can be compared with the ADF/PP procedure to see if the same conclusion is obtained. The null and alternative hypotheses under each testing approach are as follows:

ADF/PP	KPSS
H_0: $y_t \sim I(1)$	H_0: $y_t \sim I(0)$
H_1: $y_t \sim I(0)$	H_1: $y_t \sim I(1)$

There are four possible outcomes.

(1) Reject H_0 and do not reject H_0.
(2) Do not reject H_0 and reject H_0.
(3) Reject H_0 and reject H_0.
(4) Do not reject H_0 and do not reject H_0.

For the conclusions to be robust, the results should fall under outcomes 1 or 2, which would be the case when both tests concluded that the series is stationary or non-stationary, respectively. Outcomes 3 or 4 imply conflicting results. The joint use of stationarity and unit root tests is known as *confirmatory data analysis*.

12.2 Cointegration

In most cases, if two variables that are I(1) are linearly combined then the combination will also be I(1). More generally, if variables with differing orders of integration are combined, the combination will have an order of integration equal to the largest. If $X_{i,t} \sim \mathrm{I}(d_i)$ for $i = 1, 2, 3, \ldots, k$ so that there are k variables, each integrated of order d_i, and letting

$$z_t = \sum_{i=1}^{k} \alpha_i X_{i,t} \tag{12.40}$$

then $z_t \sim \mathrm{I}(\max d_i)$. z_t in this context is simply a linear combination of the k variables X_i. Rearranging (12.40),

$$X_{1,t} = \sum_{i=2}^{k} \beta_i X_{i,t} + z'_t \tag{12.41}$$

where $\beta_i = -\dfrac{\alpha_i}{\alpha_1}, z'_t = \dfrac{z_t}{\alpha_1}, i = 2, \ldots, k$. All that has been done is to take one of the variables, $X_{1,t}$, and to rearrange (12.40) to make it the subject. It could also be said that the equation has been normalised on $X_{1,t}$. Viewed another way, however, (12.41) is just a regression equation in which z'_t is a disturbance term. These disturbances can have some very undesirable properties: in general, z'_t will not be stationary and is autocorrelated if all the X_i are I(1).

As a further illustration, consider the following regression model containing variables y_t, x_{2t}, x_{3t} that are all I(1):

$$y_t = \beta_1 + \beta_2 x_{2t} + \beta_3 x_{3t} + u_t \tag{12.42}$$

For the estimated model, the SRF would be written

$$y_t = \hat{\beta}_1 + \hat{\beta}_2 x_{2t} + \hat{\beta}_3 x_{3t} + \hat{u}_t \tag{12.43}$$

Taking everything except the residuals to the LHS,

$$y_t - \hat{\beta}_1 - \hat{\beta}_2 x_{2t} - \hat{\beta}_3 x_{3t} = \hat{u}_t \tag{12.44}$$

Again, the residuals when expressed in this way can be considered a linear combination of the variables. Typically, this linear combination of I(1) variables will itself be I(1), but it would obviously be desirable to obtain residuals that are I(0). Under what circumstances will this be the case? The answer is that a linear combination of I(1) variables will be I(0) – in other words, stationary – if the variables are *cointegrated*.

12.2.1 *Definition of cointegration (Engle and Granger, 1987)*

Let w_t be a $k \times 1$ vector of variables; the components of w_t are integrated of order (d, b) if:

(1) all components of w_t are $\mathrm{I}(d)$;
(2) there is at least one vector of coefficients α such that

$$\alpha' w_t \sim \mathrm{I}(d - b)$$

In practice, many real estate variables contain one unit root, and are thus I(1), so the remainder of this chapter restricts analysis to the case in which $d = b = 1$. In this context, a set of variables is defined as cointegrated if a linear combination of them is stationary. Many time series are non-stationary but 'move together' over time – that is, there exist some influences on the series (for example, market forces), implying that the two series are bound by some relationship in the long run. A cointegrating relationship may also be seen as a long-term or equilibrium phenomenon, since it is possible that cointegrating variables may deviate from their relationship in the short run, but their association should return in the long run.

12.2.2 *Long-run relationships and cointegration in real estate*

The concept of cointegration and the implications of cointegrating relationships are very relevant in the real estate market. Real estate economic and investment theory often suggests that two or more variables would be expected to hold some long-run relationship with one another. Such relationships may hold both in the occupier (leasing) and investment markets. In a supply-constrained market, rents may in the long run move in proportion with demand-side forces measured by one or more economic variables. For example, high street retail rents may form a long-run relationship with consumer spending. In less supply-constrained markets, a long-run relationship can be identified both with economic variables and supply variables or vacancy. It may also be possible to find long-run relationships at the more aggregate level when local market influences are less important or cancel out.

In the capital market, expected rents and the discount rate affect capital values. These three variables could form a long-run relationship, since the former two variables represent the fundamentals driving capital values. Of course, investor sentiment changes, and other factors will affect risk premia and the discount rate, but, in the long run, some kind of equilibrium should be expected.

As more international markets offer assets for institutional investors, private equity, developers and others, the effects of globalisation and international movements in capital in the real estate markets should lead to greater linkages between markets through investors seeking to exploit arbitrage opportunities. Markets in which investor arbitrage is taking place may cointegrate – for example, international office markets such as London, Paris and New York. These are transparent and liquid markets that investors may consider switching money back and forth between if they feel that one of them is over- or underpriced relative to the others and that they have moved away from equilibrium.

The characteristic of cointegration between markets can be studied with different series, such as rents versus total return indices – two series that respond to different forces. If rent series cointegrate, it will imply similar demand–supply impacts on rents in the long run or that the markets are substitutes (occupiers will move between markets to ride out rent differentials). Cointegration on the basis of total return indices would mean similar pricing, similar shifts in the cap rate and a similar impact on capital growth in the long run, although diverse trends could be observed in the short run.

How long is the long run in practice in real estate, though? The study of the long-run relationships in real estate should, ideally, include a few real estate cycles and different market contexts (economic environment, capital markets). If full real estate cycles last for around eight to ten years then the inclusion of a few cycles would require a sample of forty to fifty years. This might still be considered a short period in economics research, in which the long run may be 100 years or more. Such long series are not available, particularly in commercial real estate, even in those countries with long histories. Data availability therefore limits the usefulness of cointegration in real estate. More and more real estate studies now use cointegration, however, and we expect this trend to continue.

On evidence of cointegration, investors will need to focus on short-term strategies. In the long run, diversification benefits will not be achieved, as the various markets will revert to their long-run relationship path and will deliver a similar risk-adjusted performance. These markets will be close substitutes over the long term. Divergence in the short run can make arbitrage profitable, but this strategy requires good information about the relative positions of these markets in relation to their long-run equilibrium trajectory (how far they have deviated from each other). Short-term deviations reflect market-specific events and volatility, which disturb the stochastic relationships of total returns in these markets. Therefore, in cointegrated markets, a return (absolute or risk-adjusted) maximisation strategy should aim to exploit short-run arbitrage opportunities.

Cointegration also represents another methodology for forecasting. Although forecasting from cointegrated relationships is still in its infancy in real estate, we expect this area to gain ground, leading to cointegration being used for signal extraction, direction forecasts and point forecasts. The analyst needs to adapt the model used to study short-term fluctuations of the variable of interest and forecast by taking into account information from the long-run relationship and assess its significance.

In the existing literature, authors have deployed cointegration analysis to examine relationships between markets. The work has concentrated primarily on the securitised real estate market and its linkages with the overall stock market. Tuluca, Myer and Webb (2000) use cointegration analysis to find that the capital values of treasury bills, bonds, stocks, securitised real estate and direct real estate are cointegrated, forming two long-run relationships. Liow (2000) also finds evidence of a long-run relationship between direct property, property stocks and macroeconomic variables in Singapore. More recently, the cointegration analysis of Liow and Yang (2005) establishes a contemporaneous linear long-run relationship between securitised real estate, the stock market and selected macroeconomic series in Japan, Hong Kong, Singapore and Malaysia, showing that the series interact and move together in the long run. Moreover, these authors conclude that securitised real estate stocks are substitutable in Hong Kong and Singapore, which appears to reduce the degree of diversification.

12.3 Equilibrium correction or error correction models

When the concept of non-stationarity was first considered, in the 1970s, a common response was to take the first differences of each of the I(1) variables independently and then to use these first differences in any subsequent modelling process. In the context of univariate modelling, such as the construction of ARMA models, this is entirely the correct approach. When the relationship between variables is important, however, such a procedure is inadvisable. Although the approach is statistically valid, it does have the problem that pure first difference models have no long-run solution.

For example, consider two series, y_t and x_t, that are both I(1). The model that one may consider estimating is

$$\Delta y_t = \beta \Delta x_t + u_t \tag{12.45}$$

One definition of the long run that is employed in econometrics implies that the variables have converged upon some long-term values and are no longer changing, thus $y_t = y_{t-1} = y$; $x_t = x_{t-1} = x$. Hence all the difference terms will be zero in (12.45) – i.e. $\Delta y_t = 0$; $\Delta x_t = 0$ – and thus everything in the equation cancels. Model (12.45) has no long-run solution and it therefore has nothing to say about whether x and y have an equilibrium relationship (see chapter 6).

Fortunately, there is a class of models that can overcome this problem by using combinations of first-differenced and lagged levels of cointegrated variables. For example, consider the following equation:

$$\Delta y_t = \beta_1 \Delta x_t + \beta_2(y_{t-1} - \gamma x_{t-1}) + u_t \tag{12.46}$$

This model is known as an *error correction model* (ECM) or an *equilibrium correction model*, and $(y_{t-1} - \gamma x_{t-1})$ is known as the *error correction term*. Provided that y_t and x_t are cointegrated with cointegrating coefficient γ, then $(y_{t-1} - \gamma x_{t-1})$ will be I(0) even though the constituents are I(1). It is thus valid to use OLS and standard procedures for statistical inference on (12.46). It is, of course, possible to have an intercept either in the cointegrating term (e.g. $y_{t-1} - \alpha - \gamma x_{t-1}$) or in the model for Δy_t (e.g. $\Delta y_t = \beta_0 + \beta_1 \Delta x_t + \beta_2(y_{t-1} - \gamma x_{t-1}) + u_t$), or both. Whether a constant is included or not can be determined on the basis of theory, considering the arguments on the importance of a constant discussed in chapter 6.

The two terms 'error correction model' and 'equilibrium correction model' are used synonymously for the purposes of this book. Error correction models are interpreted as follows. y is purported to change between $t-1$ and t as a result of changes in the values of the explanatory variable(s), x, between $t-1$ and t, and also in part to correct for any disequilibrium that existed during the previous period. Note that the error correction term $(y_{t-1} - \gamma x_{t-1})$ appears in (12.46) with a lag. It would be implausible for the term to appear without any lag (i.e. as $y_t - \gamma x_t$), as this would imply that y changes between $t-1$ and t in response to a disequilibrium at time t. γ defines the long-run relationship between x and y, while β_1 describes the short-run relationship between changes in x and changes in y. Broadly, β_2 describes the speed of adjustment back to equilibrium, and its strict definition is that it measures the proportion of the last period's equilibrium error that is corrected for.

Of course, an error correction model can be estimated for more than two variables. For example, if there were three variables, x_t, w_t, y_t, that were cointegrated, a possible error correction model would be

$$\Delta y_t = \beta_1 \Delta x_t + \beta_2 \Delta w_t + \beta_3(y_{t-1} - \gamma_1 x_{t-1} - \gamma_2 w_{t-1}) + u_t \tag{12.47}$$

The *Granger representation theorem* states that, if there exists a dynamic linear model with stationary disturbances and the data are I(1), the variables must be cointegrated of order (1, 1).

12.4 Testing for cointegration in regression: a residuals-based approach

The model for the equilibrium correction term can be generalised further to include k variables (y and the $k-1$ xs):

$$y_t = \beta_1 + \beta_2 x_{2t} + \beta_3 x_{3t} + \cdots + \beta_k x_{kt} + u_t \tag{12.48}$$

u_t should be I(0) if the variables $y_t, x_{2t}, \ldots x_{kt}$ are cointegrated, but u_t will still be non-stationary if they are not.

Thus it is necessary to test the residuals of (12.48) to see whether they are non-stationary or stationary. The DF or ADF test can be used on $\hat{u}_t$, using a regression of the form

$$\Delta\hat{u}_t = \psi\hat{u}_{t-1} + v_t \tag{12.49}$$

with v_t an independent and identically distributed (iid) error term.

Nonetheless, since this is a test on residuals of a model, $\hat{u}_t$, then the critical values are changed compared to a DF or an ADF test on a series of raw data. Engle and Granger (1987) have tabulated a new set of critical values for this application and hence the test is known as the Engle–Granger (EG) test. The reason that modified critical values are required is that the test is now operating on the residuals of an estimated model rather than on raw data. The residuals have been constructed from a particular set of coefficient estimates, and the sampling estimation error in these coefficients will change the distribution of the test statistic. Engle and Yoo (1987) tabulate a new set of critical values that are larger in absolute value – i.e. more negative – than the DF critical values. The critical values also become more negative as the number of variables in the potentially cointegrating regression increases.

It is also possible to use the Durbin–Watson test statistic or the Phillips–Perron approach to test for non-stationarity of $\hat{u}_t$. If the DW test is applied to the residuals of the potentially cointegrating regression, it is known as the cointegrating regression Durbin–Watson CRDW. Under the null hypothesis of a unit root in the errors, $CRDW \approx 0$, so the null of a unit root is rejected if the CRDW statistic is larger than the relevant critical value (which is approximately 0.5).

What are the null and alternative hypotheses for any unit root test applied to the residuals of a potentially cointegrating regression?

$$H_0: \hat{u}_t \sim I(1)$$
$$H_1: \hat{u}_t \sim I(0).$$

Thus under the null hypothesis, there is a unit root in the potentially cointegrating regression residuals, while, under the alternative, the residuals are stationary. Under the null hypothesis, therefore, a stationary linear combination of the non-stationary variables has not been found. Hence, if this null hypothesis is not rejected, there is no cointegration. The appropriate strategy for econometric modelling in this case would be to employ specifications in first differences only. Such models would have no long-run equilibrium solution, but this would not matter as no cointegration implies that there is no long-run relationship anyway.

On the other hand, if the null of a unit root in the potentially cointegrating regression's residuals is rejected, it would be concluded that a stationary linear combination of the non-stationary variables had been found. Therefore the variables would be classed as cointegrated. The appropriate strategy for econometric modelling in this case would be to form and estimate an error correction model, using a method described in the following section. Box 12.2 explains whether there will be only one cointegrating relationship between the variables or whether there could be more.

Box 12.2 Multiple cointegrating relationships

In the case in which there are only two variables in an equation, y_t and x_t, say, there can be at most only one linear combination of y_t, and x_t that is stationary – i.e. at most one cointegrating relationship. Suppose that there are k variables in a system (ignoring any constant term), however, denoted $y_t, x_{2t}, \ldots x_{kt}$. In this case, there may be up to r linearly independent cointegrating relationships (where $r \leq k - 1$). This potentially presents a problem for the OLS regression approach described above, which is capable of finding at most one cointegrating relationship no matter how many variables there are in the system.

If there are multiple cointegrating relationships, moreover, how can one know if there are others, or whether the 'best' or strongest cointegrating relationship has been found? An OLS regression will find the minimum-variance stationary linear combination of the variables, but there may be other linear combinations of the variables that have more intuitive appeal. The answer to this problem is to use a systems approach to cointegration, which will allow the determination of all r cointegrating relationships. One such approach is Johansen's method; see section 12.8.

12.5 Methods of parameter estimation in cointegrated systems

What should the modelling strategy be if the data at hand are thought to be non-stationary and possibly cointegrated? There are (at least) three methods that can be used: Engle–Granger, Engle–Yoo and Johansen. The first and third of these procedures are considered in some detail in the following sections.

12.5.1 *The Engle–Granger two-step method*

This is a single-equation technique, which is conducted as follows.

Step 1

Make sure that all the individual variables are I(1). Then estimate the cointegrating regression using OLS. Note that it is not possible to perform any inferences on the coefficient estimates in this regression; all that can be done is to estimate the parameter values. Save the residuals of the cointegrating regression, $\hat{u}_t$. Test these residuals to ensure that they are I(0). If they are I(0), proceed to step 2; if they are I(1), estimate a model containing only first differences.

Step 2

Use the step 1 residuals as one variable in the error correction model, such as

$$\Delta y_t = \beta_1 \Delta x_t + \beta_2(\hat{u}_{t-1}) + v_t \tag{12.50}$$

where $\hat{u}_{t-1} = y_{t-1} - \hat{\tau} x_{t-1}$. The stationary, linear combination of non-stationary variables is also known as the *cointegrating vector*. In this case, the cointegrating vector would be $[1 \quad -\hat{\tau}]$. Additionally, any linear transformation of the cointegrating vector will also be a cointegrating vector. So, for example, $-10y_{t-1} + 10\hat{\tau}x_{t-1}$ will also be stationary. In (12.44) above, the cointegrating vector would be $[1 \quad -\hat{\beta}_1 \quad -\hat{\beta}_2 \quad -\hat{\beta}_3]$. It is now valid to perform inferences in the second-stage regression – i.e. concerning the parameters β_1 and β_2 (provided that there are no other forms of misspecification, of course) – since all variables in this regression are stationary.

The Engle–Granger two-step method suffers from a number of problems.

(1) The usual finite-sample problem of a *lack of power in unit root and cointegration tests* discussed above.
(2) There could be a *simultaneous equations bias* if the causality between y and x runs in both directions, but this single-equation approach requires the researcher to normalise on one variable – i.e. to specify one variable as the dependent variable and the others as independent variables. The researcher is forced to treat y and x asymmetrically, even though there may have been no theoretical reason for doing so. A further issue is the following. Suppose that the specification in (12.51) has been estimated as a potential cointegrating regression:

$$y_t = \alpha_1 + \beta_1 x_t + u_{1t} \tag{12.51}$$

What if, instead, the following equation had been estimated?

$$x_t = \alpha_2 + \beta_2 y_t + u_{2t} \tag{12.52}$$

If it is found that $u_{1t} \sim$ I(0), does this imply automatically that $u_{2t} \sim$ I(0)? The answer in theory is 'Yes', but in practice different conclusions may be reached in finite samples. Furthermore, if there is an error in the model specification at stage 1, this will be carried through to the cointegration test at stage 2, as a consequence of the sequential nature of the computation of the cointegration test statistic.

(3) It is not possible to perform any *hypothesis tests* about the actual cointegrating relationship estimated at stage 1.

Problems 1 and 2 are small-sample problems that should disappear asymptotically. Problem 3 is addressed by another method due to Engle and Yoo. There is also another alternative technique, which overcomes problems 2 and 3 by adopting a different approach based on the estimation of a VAR system; see section 12.8.

12.6 Applying the Engle–Granger procedure: the Sydney office market

We apply the Engle–Granger procedure to study the possible existence of a long-run relationship and cointegration in the Sydney office market. We examine whether Sydney office rents form an equilibrium relationship with economic variables. Of course, we expect a number of factors to affect rent movements, as we explained in previous chapters, including supply and vacancy. In the long run, however, the economy should drive rent performance, although a combination of the economy and supply may still be relevant. In this example, we focus on rents and the economy. We relate rents to two variables that represent the general economy: gross domestic product and total employment. Both economic variables are for the New South Wales region. Figure 12.7 plots the real rents, GDP and total employment series. All series are given in the form of an index that takes the value 100 in 2Q1990, although note that the scales on the y-axes are different in panels (a) and (b).[1]

Real rents in Sydney showed sustained falls a couple of times in our sample period. In the early 1990s real rent falls are associated with stagnation in GDP and a small fall in the level of regional employment. In the period 2001 to 2003, when another fall in real rents is recorded, neither

[1] The rent data are primarily based on published reports by Colliers and the economic data are from the Australian Bureau of Statistics.

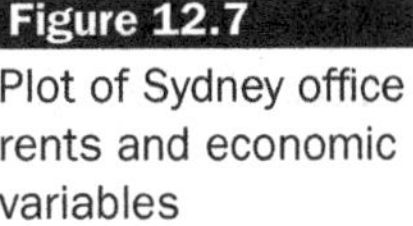

Figure 12.7 Plot of Sydney office rents and economic variables

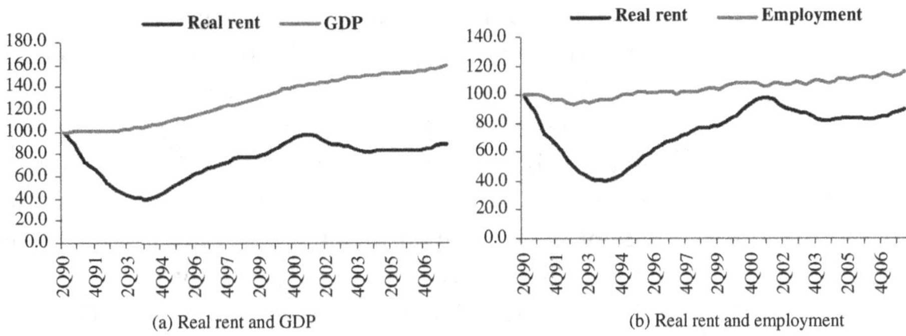

(a) Real rent and GDP

(b) Real rent and employment

Table 12.2 Unit root tests for office rents in Sydney

Level office rents (*RENT*)				Office rents in first differences ($\Delta RENT$)			
	Dependent: $\Delta RENT_t$				Dependent: $\Delta\Delta RENT_t$		
	(i)	(ii)	(iii)		(iv)	(v)	(vi)
	Coefficient *t*-ratio				Coefficient *t*-ratio		
Intercept	–	0.95	1.31	Intercept	–	0.10	0.20
	–	2.21	2.70		–	1.10	0.99
Trend	–	–	0.01	Trend	–	–	0.00
	–	–	1.56		–	–	−0.58
$RENT_{t-1}$	0.00	−0.01	−0.02	$\Delta RENT_{t-1}$	−0.12	−0.12	−0.12
	0.68	***−2.02***	***−2.50***		***−3.29***	***−3.33***	***−3.01***
$\Delta RENT_{t-1}$	1.46	1.37	1.34	$\Delta\Delta RENT_{t-1}$	0.59	0.57	0.56
	12.18	11.14	10.77		5.34	5.09	4.81
$\Delta RENT_{t-2}$	−1.12	−1.03	−1.01	$\Delta\Delta RENT_{t-2}$	−0.54	−0.54	−0.54
	−5.90	−5.43	−5.38		−4.84	−4.86	−4.84
$\Delta RENT_{t-3}$	0.85	0.77	0.74	$\Delta\Delta RENT_{t-3}$	0.32	0.31	0.29
	4.52	4.08	3.98		2.94	2.79	2.61
$\Delta RENT_{t-4}$	−0.32	−0.22	−0.20				
	−2.89	−1.93	−1.69				
Critical 5%	−1.95	−2.91	−3.48		−1.95	−2.91	−3.48

Notes: Dickey–Fuller test statistics are in bold italics.

economic variable experienced declines. Clearly, GDP and total employment exhibit an upward trend, but the real rent series also seems to exhibit a trend.

Table 12.2 details the ADF tests for real rents. We estimate the ADF regression with no intercept, including an intercept and with both an intercept and a deterministic trend. We set the lag length to four given our quarterly data, which should be sufficient to ensure that the residuals of the ADF regressions are free from serial correlation.

In the level-based tests for real rents, the intercept is significant in equation (ii). It is also significant in version (iii) of the ADF regression, but the trend is not. The null hypothesis of a unit root is not rejected as the sample value of the coefficient on $RENT_{t-1}$ is not more negative than the critical value at the 5 per cent level of −2.91 for version (ii). In first differences, the tests reject the null hypothesis of a unit root in representation (iv) since the parameter on the lagged first difference term is statistically significant in two variations of the ADF regression. Therefore Sydney real office rents are integrated of order one (I(1)).

A similar set of unit root tests applied to the two economic variables shows less clear-cut results, but the weight of evidence combined with our theoretical knowledge about the behaviour of such series suggests that they are also I(1).[2] On the basis of the confirmed stochastic non-stationarity of the three component series, we now test whether the property of cointegration is established between office rents and GDP and between office rents and total employment using the Engle–Granger procedure. We examine the series on a pair-wise basis rather than together, mainly for ease of illustration and interpretation. In a research context, however, if theory suggests that a number of variables should be related, they should all be included in the model together. The potentially cointegrating equations between rents and GDP or employment are

$$\widehat{RENT}_t = \underset{(-0.13)}{-1.276} + \underset{(8.14)}{0.590}GDP_t \tag{12.53}$$

Adj. $R^2 = 0.48$; DW $= 0.04$.

$$\widehat{RENT}_t = \underset{(-6.15)}{-153.07} + \underset{(9.17)}{2.180}EMP_t \tag{12.54}$$

Adj. $R^2 = 0.54$; DW $= 0.08$.

Table 12.3 presents the results of augmented Dickey–Fuller tests on the residuals from these equations.

Again, we observe a marginal result concerning the presence of a unit root. The form of the test that omits both the intercept and the trend shows test statistics of −2.64 and −2.59 for the regression with GDP and employment, respectively. Since these figures are more negative than the critical values, the null hypothesis of a unit root in the regression residuals

[2] The unit root test results for the GDP and employment variables are not shown, so as to avoid repetition.

Table 12.3 ADF tests on residuals of potentially cointegrating equations

Residuals of equation (12.53)				Residuals of equation (12.54)			
	GDP				Employment		
	(i)	(ii)	(iii)		(iv)	(v)	(vi)
	Coefficient *t*-ratio				Coefficient *t*-ratio		
Intercept	–	0.00	0.00	Intercept	–	−0.03	0.19
	–	*−0.05*^{ns}	*0.01*^{ns}		–	*−0.12*^{ns}	*0.31*^{ns}
Trend	–	–	0.00	Trend	–	–	−0.01
	–	–	*−0.03*^{ns}		–	–	*−0.40*^{ns}
RES_{t-1}	−0.03	−0.03	−0.03	ΔRES_{t-1}	−0.07	−0.07	−0.07
	−2.64	***−2.60***	***−2.55***		***−2.59***	***−2.56***	***−2.51***
ΔRES_{t-1}	1.31	1.31	1.31	$\Delta\Delta RES_{t-1}$	0.40	0.40	0.40
	10.80	*10.71*	*10.61*		*3.32*	*3.29*	*3.27*
ΔRES_{t-2}	−0.99	−0.99	−0.99	$\Delta\Delta RES_{t-2}$	−0.37	−0.37	−0.37
	−5.43	*−5.38*	*−5.31*		*−3.17*	*−3.14*	*−3.07*
ΔRES_{t-3}	0.72	0.72	0.72	$\Delta\Delta RES_{t-3}$	0.36	0.36	0.36
	3.96	*3.93*	*3.89*		*3.01*	*2.98*	*2.97*
ΔRES_{t-4}	−0.19	−0.19	−0.19	$\Delta\Delta RES_{t-4}$	0.29	0.29	0.30
	−1.66	*−1.65*	*−1.62*		*2.57*	*2.51*	*2.52*
Critical 5%	−1.95	−2.91	−3.49		−1.95	−2.91	−3.49

Notes: Dickey–Fuller test statistics are in bold italics. ^{ns} = not statistically significant.

should be rejected and, along with it, the proposition that the series are cointegrated. For the test regressions containing either an intercept or an intercept and a deterministic trend, the result is a marginal non-rejection in all cases. It would therefore be possible to argue for either the presence or the absence of cointegration. Given that neither the intercepts nor the trends are significant in either the GDP or the employment regressions, we favour the results from specifications (i) and (iv). We therefore conclude that the series do indeed form long-run relationships. The residuals of the regressions are displayed in figure 12.8.

Although the ADF tests indicate stationarity, we observe long periods when the residuals of the equations are well above or well below the zero line, and hence the very low values of the DW statistic, which imply fairly slow adjustments back to long-run equilibrium. In general, both series show similar deviations from equilibrium but of different magnitudes.

The residuals are the differences between the actual and fitted values of the regression. Using the fitted GDP equation (12.53) for illustration, we

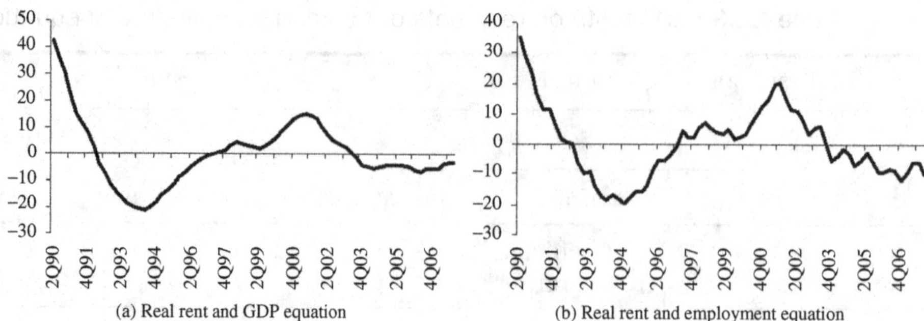

Figure 12.8 Residuals of Engle–Granger equations

could write

$$\hat{u}_t = RENT_t - \widehat{RENT}_t = RENT_t + 1.276 - 0.590GDP_t \tag{12.55}$$

At the beginning of the 1990s this residual was large in size and persistently positive, indicating that rents at that time exceeded the level that could be justified by the equilibrium relationship. This long-run association was restored via a subsequent fall in rents.

The reverse situation occurred in the period 1992 to 1996, with rental values existing below those corresponding to the long-run relationship with GDP. In this case, readjustment would have occurred via a subsequent rise in rents. By the end of our sample period, 4Q2007, rents were very close to their equilibrium relationships with both GDP and employment.

We now utilise the long-run relationships to construct the error correction models for Sydney office rents. These models can be used to explain real office rent variation in the short term and, of course, to forecast rents. We also present key diagnostics for these models.

$$\Delta\widehat{RENT}_t = \underset{(-8.8)}{-3.561} + \underset{(9.5)}{4.040}\Delta GDP_t - \underset{(-4.2)}{0.065}RESGDP_{t-1} \tag{12.56}$$

RESGDP is the residual series; Adj. $R^2 = 0.68$; DW $= 0.40$; number of observations $= 70$ (3Q1990–4Q2007). Diagnostics: normality BJ test value: 1.88 ($p = 0.39$); LM test for serial correlation (first order): 45.39 ($p = 0.00$); LM test for serial correlation (fourth order): 49.24 ($p = 0.00$); heteroscedasticity with cross-terms: 18.10 ($p = 0.00$); RESET: 5.14 ($p = 0.02$).

$$\Delta\widehat{RENT}_t = \underset{(-0.8)}{-0.230} + \underset{(1.8)}{0.441}\Delta EMP_t - \underset{(-5.1)}{0.118}RESEMP_{t-1} \tag{12.57}$$

RESEMP is the residual series; Adj. $R^2 = 0.30$; DW $= 0.21$; number of observations $= 70$ (3Q1990–4Q2007). Diagnostics: normality BJ test value: 1.02 ($p = 0.60$); LM test for serial correlation (first order): 61.31 ($p = 0.00$); LM test for serial correlation (fourth order): 63.57 ($p = 0.00$); heteroscedasticity with cross-terms: 18.48 ($p = 0.00$); RESET: 4.12 ($p = 0.04$).

There are similarities but also differences between the two error correction equations above. In both equations, the error correction term takes a negative sign, indicating the presence of forces to move the relationship back to equilibrium, and it is significant at the 1 per cent level. For the rent-GDP equation (12.56), the adjustment to equilibrium is 6.5 per cent every quarter – a moderate adjustment speed. This is seen in figure 12.8, where disequilibrium situations persist for long periods. For the rent–employment error correction equation (12.57), the adjustment is higher at 11.8 per cent every quarter – a rather speedy adjustment (nearly 50 per cent every year).

An interesting finding is that ΔGDP is highly significant in equation (12.56), whereas ΔEMP in equation (12.57) is significant only at the 10 per cent level. Equation (12.56) has a notably higher explanatory power with an adjusted R^2 of 0.68, compared with 0.30 for equation (12.57). The results of the diagnostic checks are broadly similar. Both equations have residuals that are normally distributed, but they fail the serial correlation tests badly. Serial correlation seems to be a problem, as the tests show the presence of serial correlation for orders 1, 2, 3 and 4 (results for orders 1 and 4 only are reported here). Both equations fail the heteroscedasticity and RESET tests.

An option available to the analyst is to augment the error correction equations and attempt to rectify the misspecification in the equations (12.56) and (12.57) in this way. We do so by specifying general models containing four lags of ΔGDP in equation (12.56) and four lags of ΔEMP in equation (12.57). We expect this number of lags to be sufficient to identify the impact of past GDP or employment changes on rental growth. We subsequently remove regressors using as the criterion the minimisation of AIC. The ΔGDP and ΔEMP terms in the final model should also take the expected positive signs. For brevity, we now focus on the GDP equation.

$$\begin{array}{l} \Delta RENT_t = -3.437 - 0.089 RESGDP_{t-1} + 1.642 \Delta GDP_{t-1} + 2.466 \Delta GDP_{t-4} \\ \qquad\qquad (-10.07) \quad (-4.48) \qquad\qquad\quad (2.23) \qquad\qquad\qquad (3.32) \end{array} \quad (12.58)$$

Adj. $R^2 = 0.69$; DW $= 0.43$; number of observations $= 66$ (3Q1991–4Q2007). Diagnostics: normality BJ test value: 2.81 ($p = 0.25$); LM test for serial correlation (first order): 41.18 ($p = 0.00$); LM test for serial correlation (fourth order): 45.57 ($p = 0.00$); heteroscedasticity with cross-terms: 23.43 ($p = 0.01$); RESET: 1.65 ($p = 0.20$).

Equation (12.58) is the new rent-GDP error correction equation. The ΔGDP term has lost some of its significance compared with the original equation, and the influence of changes in GDP on changes in real rents in the presence of the error correction term is best represented by the first and fourth lags of ΔGDP. The error correction term retains its significance and now points to a 9 per cent quarterly adjustment to equilibrium. In terms of diagnostics, the only improvement made is that the model now passes the RESET test.

We use the above specification to forecast real rents in Sydney. We carry out two forecasting exercises – *ex post* and *ex ante* – based on our own assumptions for GDP growth. For the *ex post* (out-of-sample) forecasts, we estimate the models up to 4Q2005 and forecast the remaining eight quarters of the sample. Therefore the forecasts for 1Q2006 to 4Q2007 are produced by the coefficients estimated using the shorter sample period (ending in 4Q2005). This error correction model is

$$\begin{aligned}\Delta \hat{RENT}_t = & \underset{(-11.40)}{-3.892} \underset{(-5.10)}{- 0.097} RESGDP_{t-1} + \underset{(1.87)}{1.295} \Delta GDP_{t-1} \\ & + \underset{(4.31)}{3.043} \Delta GDP_{t-4}\end{aligned} \tag{12.59}$$

Adj. $R^2 = 0.76$; DW $= 0.50$; number of observations $= 58$ (3Q1991–4Q2005).

We can highlight the fact that all the variables are statistically significant, with ΔGDP_{t-1} at the 10 per cent level and not at the 5 per cent level, which was the case in (12.58). The explanatory power is higher over this sample period, which is not surprising given the fact that the full-sample model did not replicate the changes in rents satisfactorily towards the end of the sample. Table 12.4 contains the forecasts from the error correction model.

The forecast for 1Q2006 using equation (12.59) is given by

$$\begin{aligned}\Delta \hat{RENT}_{1Q2006} &= -3.892 - 0.097 \times (-7.06) + 1.295 \times 0.5 + 3.043 \times 0.2 \\ &= -1.951\end{aligned} \tag{12.60}$$

This is the predicted change in real rent between 4Q2005 and 1Q2006, from which we get the forecast for real rent for 1Q2006 of 82.0 (column (ii)) and the growth rate of -2.32 per cent (quarter-on-quarter [qoq] percentage change), shown in column (vii). The value of the error correction term in 4Q2005 is produced by the long-run equation estimated for the shorter sample period (2Q1990 to 4Q2005):

$$\hat{RENT}_t = \underset{(-0.65)}{-7.167} + \underset{(7.42)}{0.642} GDP_t \tag{12.61}$$

Adj. $R^2 = 0.47$; DW $= 0.04$; number of observations $= 63$ (2Q1990–4Q2005).

Again, we perform unit root tests on the residuals of the above equation. The findings reject the presence of a unit root, and we therefore proceed to estimate the error correction term for 4Q2005. In equation (12.61), the fitted values are given by the expression $(-7.167 + 0.642 \times GDP_t)$. The error

Table 12.4 *Ex post* forecasts from error correction model

(i)	(ii) *RENT*	(iii) *GDP*	(iv) *ECT*	(v) ΔGDP	(vi) $\Delta RENT$	(vii) *RENT(qoq%)*
1Q05	83.8	151.7		0.2		
2Q05	83.9	152.1		0.4		
3Q05	84.1	152.5		0.4		
4Q05	84.0	153.0	−7.06	0.5	−0.100	
1Q06	**82.0**	153.6	**−9.40**	0.6	**−1.951**	**−2.32**
2Q06	**81.1**	154.2	**−10.77**	0.6	**−0.986**	**−1.20**
3Q06	**80.2**	154.8	**−12.01**	0.6	**−0.853**	**−1.05**
4Q06	**79.8**	155.6	**−12.95**	0.8	**−0.429**	**−0.53**
1Q07	**80.0**	156.4	**−13.24**	0.8	**0.226**	**0.28**
2Q07	**80.3**	157.2	**−13.50**	0.8	**0.254**	**0.32**
3Q07	**80.5**	158.2	**−13.86**	1.0	**0.279**	**0.35**
4Q07	**81.7**	159.2		1.0	**1.182**	**1.47**

Notes: Bold numbers indicate model-based forecasts. *ECT* is the value of the error correction term (the residual).

correction term is

$$\begin{aligned} ECT_t &= \textit{actual rent} - \textit{fitted rent} = RENT_t - (-7.167 + 0.642GDP_t) \\ &= RENT_t + 7.167 - 0.642GDP_t \end{aligned}$$

Hence the value of ECT_{4Q2005}, which is required for the forecast of changes in rents for 1Q2006, is

$$ECT_{1Q2006} = 84.0 + 7.167 - 0.642 \times 153.6 = -7.06 \tag{12.62}$$

and for 1Q2006 to be used for the forecast of $\Delta rent_{2Q2006}$ is

$$ECT_{1Q2006} = 82.0 + 7.167 - 0.642 \times 153.6 = -9.4$$

Now, using the ECM, we can make the forecast for 2Q2006:

$$\begin{aligned} \Delta RENT_{2Q2006} &= -3.892 - 0.097 \times (-9.44) + 1.295 \times 0.6 + 3.043 \times 0.4 \\ &= -0.986 \end{aligned} \tag{12.63}$$

This forecast change in rent translates into a fall in the index to 81.1 – that is, rent 'growth' of −1.20 per cent on the previous quarter. Using the forecast value of 81.1 for rent in 2Q2006, we forecast again the error correction term using equation (12.61), and the process continues. Table 12.5 provides an evaluation of the GDP error correction model's forecasts.

Table 12.5 Forecast evaluation

Measure	Value
Mean error	1.18
Absolute error	1.37
RMSE	1.49
Theil's $U1$ statistic	0.61

Table 12.6 *Ex ante* forecasts from the error correction model

(i)	(ii) *RENT*	(iii) *GDP*	(iv) *ECT*	(v) ΔGDP	(vi) $\Delta RENT$	(vii) *RENT*(*qoq* %)
1Q07	85.5	156.4		0.8		0.83
2Q07	87.5	157.2		0.8		2.34
3Q07	89.1	158.2		1.0		1.83
4Q07	89.7	159.2	−2.95	1.0		0.67
1Q08	**90.1**	**160.0**	**−2.98**	**0.8**	**0.440**	**0.49**
2Q08	**90.3**	**160.8**	**−3.34**	**0.8**	**0.115**	**0.13**
3Q08	**90.9**	**161.6**	**−3.17**	**0.8**	**0.640**	**0.71**
4Q08	**91.5**	**162.4**	**−3.02**	**0.8**	**0.625**	**0.69**
1Q09	**91.6**	**163.2**	**−3.39**	**0.8**	**0.118**	**0.13**
2Q09	**91.8**	**164.0**	**−3.72**	**0.8**	**0.151**	**0.16**
3Q09	**92.0**	**164.9**	**−4.02**	**0.9**	**0.180**	**0.20**
4Q09	**92.3**	**165.7**		**0.8**	**0.371**	**0.40**

Notes: Bold numbers indicate forecasts. The forecast assumption is that GDP grows at 0.5 per cent per quarter.

In 2007 the forecasts improved significantly in terms of average error. The ECM predicts average growth of 0.60, which is quite short of the actual figure of 1.4 per cent per quarter. We now use the model to forecast out eight quarters from the original sample period. We need exogenous forecasts for GDP, and we therefore assume quarterly GDP growth of 0.5 per cent for the period 1Q2008 to 4Q2009. Table 12.6 presents these forecasts.

For the ECM forecasts given in table 12.6, the coefficients obtained from the error correction term represented by equation (12.61) and the short-run equation (12.59) are used. The ECM predicts a modest acceleration in real rents in 2008 followed by a slowdown in 2009. These forecasts are, of course, based on our own somewhat arbitrary assumptions for GDP growth.

12.7 The Engle and Yoo three-step method

The Engle and Yoo (1987) three-step procedure takes its first two steps from Engle–Granger (EG). Engle and Yoo then add a third step, giving updated estimates of the cointegrating vector and its standard errors. The Engle and Yoo (EY) third step is algebraically technical and, additionally, EY suffers from all the remaining problems of the EG approach. There is, arguably, a far superior procedure available to remedy the lack of testability of hypotheses concerning the cointegrating relationship: the Johansen (1988) procedure. For these reasons, the Engle–Yoo procedure is rarely employed in empirical applications and is not considered further here.

12.8 Testing for and estimating cointegrating systems using the Johansen technique

The Johansen approach is based on the specification of a VAR model. Suppose that a set of g variables ($g \geq 2$) are under consideration that are I(1) and that it is thought may be cointegrated. A VAR with k lags containing these variables can be set up:

$$\underset{g\times 1}{y_t} = \underset{g\times g}{\beta_1}\underset{g\times 1}{y_{t-1}} + \underset{g\times g}{\beta_2}\underset{g\times 1}{y_{t-2}} + \cdots + \underset{g\times g}{\beta_k}\underset{g\times 1}{y_{t-k}} + \underset{g\times 1}{u_t} \tag{12.64}$$

In order to use the Johansen test, the VAR in (12.64) needs to be turned into a vector error correction model of the form

$$\Delta y_t = \Pi y_{t-k} + \Gamma_1 \Delta y_{t-1} + \Gamma_2 \Delta y_{t-2} + \cdots + \Gamma_{k-1} \Delta y_{t-(k-1)} + u_t \tag{12.65}$$

where $\Pi = (\sum_{i=1}^{k} \beta_i) - I_g$ and $\Gamma_i = (\sum_{j=1}^{i} \beta_j) - I_g$.

This VAR contains g variables in first-differenced form on the LHS, and $k-1$ lags of the dependent variables (differences) on the RHS, each with a Γ coefficient matrix attached to it. In fact, the Johansen test can be affected by the lag length employed in the VECM, and so it is useful to attempt to select the lag length optimally. The Johansen test centres around an examination of the Π matrix. Π can be interpreted as a long-run coefficient matrix, since, in equilibrium, all the Δy_{t-i} will be zero, and setting the error terms, u_t, to their expected value of zero will leave $\Pi y_{t-k} = 0$. Notice the comparability between this set of equations and the testing equation for an ADF test, which has a first-differenced term as the dependent variable, together with a lagged levels term and lagged differences on the RHS.

The test for cointegration between the ys is calculated by looking at the rank of the Π matrix via its eigenvalues.[3] The rank of a matrix is equal to the number of its characteristic roots (eigenvalues) that are different from zero (see section 2.7). The eigenvalues, denoted λ_i, are put in ascending order: $\lambda_1 \geq \lambda_2 \geq \cdots \geq \lambda_g$. If the λs are roots, in this context they must be less than one in absolute value and positive, and λ_1 will be the largest (i.e. the closest to one), while λ_g will be the smallest (i.e. the closest to zero). If the variables are not cointegrated, the rank of Π will not be significantly different from zero, so $\lambda_i \approx 0 \, \forall \, i$. The test statistics actually incorporate $\ln(1 - \lambda_i)$, rather than the λ_i themselves, but, all the same, when $\lambda_i = 0$, $\ln(1 - \lambda_i) = 0$.

Suppose now that rank $(\Pi) = 1$, then $\ln(1 - \lambda_1)$ will be negative and $\ln(1 - \lambda_i) = 0 \, \forall \, i > 1$. If the eigenvalue i is non-zero, then $\ln(1 - \lambda_i) < 0 \, \forall \, i > 1$. That is, for Π to have a rank of one, the largest eigenvalue must be significantly non-zero, while others will not be significantly different from zero.

There are two test statistics for cointegration under the Johansen approach, which are formulated as

$$\lambda_{trace}(r) = -T \sum_{i=r+1}^{g} \ln(1 - \hat{\lambda}_i) \tag{12.66}$$

and

$$\lambda_{max}(r, r+1) = -T \ln(1 - \hat{\lambda}_{r+1}) \tag{12.67}$$

where r is the number of cointegrating vectors under the null hypothesis and $\hat{\lambda}_i$ is the estimated value for the ith ordered eigenvalue from the Π matrix. Intuitively, the larger $\hat{\lambda}_i$ is, the more large and negative $\ln(1 - \hat{\lambda}_i)$ will be, and hence the larger the test statistic will be. Each eigenvalue will have associated with it a different cointegrating vector, which will be eigenvectors. A significantly non-zero eigenvalue indictates a significant cointegrating vector.

λ_{trace} is a joint test in which the null is that the number of cointegrating vectors is smaller than or equal to r against an unspecified or general alternative that there are more than r. It starts with p eigenvalues, and then, successively, the largest is removed. $\lambda_{trace} = 0$ when all the $\lambda_i = 0$, for $i = 1, \ldots, g$.

λ_{max} conducts separate tests on each eigenvalue, and has as its null hypothesis that the number of cointegrating vectors is r against an alternative of $r + 1$.

[3] Strictly, the eigenvalues used in the test statistics are taken from rank-restricted product moment matrices and not from Π itself.

Johansen and Juselius (1990) provide critical values for the two statistics. The distribution of the test statistics is non-standard, and the critical values depend on the value of $g - r$, the number of non-stationary components and whether constants are included in each of the equations. Intercepts can be included either in the cointegrating vectors themselves or as additional terms in the VAR. The latter is equivalent to including a trend in the data-generating processes for the levels of the series. Osterwald-Lenum (1992) and, more recently, MacKinnon, Haug and Michelis (1999) provide a more complete set of critical values for the Johansen test.

If the test statistic is greater than the critical value from Johansen's tables, reject the null hypothesis that there are r cointegrating vectors in favour of the alternative, that there are $r + 1$ (for λ_{trace}) or more than r (for λ_{max}). The testing is conducted in a sequence and, under the null, $r = 0, 1, \ldots, g - 1$, so that the hypotheses for λ_{max} are

$$\begin{array}{lll} \mathrm{H_0}: r = 0 & \text{versus} & \mathrm{H_1}: 0 < r \leq g \\ \mathrm{H_0}: r = 1 & \text{versus} & \mathrm{H_1}: 1 < r \leq g \\ \mathrm{H_0}: r = 2 & \text{versus} & \mathrm{H_1}: 2 < r \leq g \\ \vdots & \vdots & \vdots \\ \mathrm{H_0}: r = g - 1 & \text{versus} & \mathrm{H_1}: r = g \end{array}$$

The first test involves a null hypothesis of no cointegrating vectors (corresponding to Π having zero rank). If this null is not rejected, it would be concluded that there are no cointegrating vectors and the testing would be completed. If $\mathrm{H_0}$: $r = 0$ is rejected, however, the null that there is one cointegrating vector (i.e. $\mathrm{H_0}$: $r = 1$) would be tested, and so on. Thus the value of r is continually increased until the null is no longer rejected.

How does this correspond to a test of the rank of the Π matrix, though? r is the rank of Π. Π cannot be of full rank (g) since this would correspond to the original y_t being stationary. If Π has zero rank then, by analogy to the univariate case, Δy_t depends only on Δy_{t-j} and not on y_{t-1}, so that there is no long-run relationship between the elements of y_{t-1}. Hence there is no cointegration.

For $1 <$ rank$(\Pi) < g$, there are r cointegrating vectors. Π is then defined as the product of two matrices, α and β', of dimension $(g \times r)$ and $(r \times g)$, respectively – i.e.

$$\Pi = \alpha\beta' \tag{12.68}$$

The matrix β gives the cointegrating vectors, while α gives the amount of each cointegrating vector entering each equation of the VECM, also known as the 'adjustment parameters'.

For example, suppose that $g = 4$, so that the system contains four variables. The elements of the Π matrix would be written

$$\Pi = \begin{pmatrix} \pi_{11} & \pi_{12} & \pi_{13} & \pi_{14} \\ \pi_{21} & \pi_{22} & \pi_{23} & \pi_{24} \\ \pi_{31} & \pi_{32} & \pi_{33} & \pi_{34} \\ \pi_{41} & \pi_{42} & \pi_{43} & \pi_{44} \end{pmatrix} \tag{12.69}$$

If r = 1, so that there is one cointegrating vector, then α and β will be (4×1):

$$\Pi = \alpha\beta' = \begin{pmatrix} \alpha_{11} \\ \alpha_{12} \\ \alpha_{13} \\ \alpha_{14} \end{pmatrix} \begin{pmatrix} \beta_{11} & \beta_{12} & \beta_{13} & \beta_{14} \end{pmatrix} \tag{12.70}$$

If $r = 2$, so that there are two cointegrating vectors, then α and β will be (4×2):

$$\Pi = \alpha\beta' = \begin{pmatrix} \alpha_{11} & \alpha_{21} \\ \alpha_{12} & \alpha_{22} \\ \alpha_{13} & \alpha_{23} \\ \alpha_{14} & \alpha_{24} \end{pmatrix} \begin{pmatrix} \beta_{11} & \beta_{12} & \beta_{13} & \beta_{14} \\ \beta_{21} & \beta_{22} & \beta_{23} & \beta_{24} \end{pmatrix} \tag{12.71}$$

and so on for $r = 3, \ldots$

Suppose now that $g = 4$, and $r = 1$, as in (12.70) above, so that there are four variables in the system, y_1, y_2, y_3 and y_4, that exhibit one cointegrating vector. Then Πy_{t-k} will be given by

$$\Pi y_{t-k} = \begin{pmatrix} \alpha_{11} \\ \alpha_{12} \\ \alpha_{13} \\ \alpha_{14} \end{pmatrix} \begin{pmatrix} \beta_{11} & \beta_{12} & \beta_{13} & \beta_{14} \end{pmatrix} \begin{pmatrix} y_1 \\ y_2 \\ y_3 \\ y_4 \end{pmatrix}_{t-k} \tag{12.72}$$

Equation (12.72) can also be written

$$\Pi y_{t-k} = \begin{pmatrix} \alpha_{11} \\ \alpha_{12} \\ \alpha_{13} \\ \alpha_{14} \end{pmatrix} \left(\beta_{11}y_1 + \beta_{12}y_2 + \beta_{13}y_3 + \beta_{14}y_4 \right)_{t-k} \tag{12.73}$$

Given (12.73), it is possible to write out the separate equations for each variable Δy_t. It is also common to 'normalise' on a particular variable, so that the coefficient on that variable in the cointegrating vector is one. For example, normalising on y_1 would make the cointegrating term in the equation for Δy_1

$$\alpha_{11}\left(y_1 + \frac{\beta_{12}}{\beta_{11}}y_2 + \frac{\beta_{13}}{\beta_{11}}y_3 + \frac{\beta_{14}}{\beta_{11}}y_4\right)_{t-k} \quad \text{etc.}$$

Finally, it must be noted that the above description is not exactly how the Johansen procedure works, but is an intuitive approximation to it.

12.8.1 *Hypothesis testing using Johansen*

The Engle–Granger approach does not permit the testing of hypotheses on the cointegrating relationships themselves, but the Johansen set-up does permit the testing of hypotheses about the equilibrium relationships between the variables. Johansen allows a researcher to test a hypothesis about one or more coefficients in the cointegrating relationship by viewing the hypothesis as a restriction on the Π matrix. If there exist r cointegrating vectors, only those linear combinations or linear transformations of them, or combinations of the cointegrating vectors, will be stationary. In fact, the matrix of cointegrating vectors β can be multiplied by any non-singular conformable matrix to obtain a new set of cointegrating vectors.

A set of required long-run coefficient values or relationships between the coefficients does not necessarily imply that the cointegrating vectors have to be restricted. This is because any combination of cointegrating vectors is also a cointegrating vector. It may therefore be possible to combine the cointegrating vectors thus far obtained to provide a new one, or, in general, a new set, having the required properties. The simpler and fewer the required properties are, the more likely it is that this recombination process (called *renormalisation*) will automatically yield cointegrating vectors with the required properties. As the restrictions become more numerous or involve more of the coefficients of the vectors, however, it will eventually become impossible to satisfy all of them by renormalisation. After this point, all other linear combinations of the variables will be non-stationary. If the restriction does not affect the model much – i.e. if the restriction is not binding – then the eigenvectors should not change much following the imposition of the restriction. A statistic to test this hypothesis is given by

$$\textit{test statistic} = -T\sum_{i=1}^{r}[\ln(1-\lambda_i) - \ln(1-\lambda_i{}^*)] \sim \chi^2(m) \qquad (12.74)$$

where λ_i^* are the characteristic roots of the restricted model, λ_i are the characteristic roots of the unrestricted model, r is the number of non-zero characteristic roots in the unrestricted model and m is the number of restrictions.

Restrictions are actually imposed by substituting them into the relevant α or β matrices as appropriate, so that tests can be conducted on either the cointegrating vectors or their loadings in each equation in the system (or both). For example, considering (12.69) to (12.71) above, it may be that theory suggests that the coefficients on the loadings of the cointegrating vector(s) in each equation should take on certain values, in which case it would be relevant to test restrictions on the elements of α – e.g. $\alpha_{11} = 1$, $\alpha_{23} = -1$, etc. Equally, it may be of interest to examine whether only a subset of the variables in y_t is actually required to obtain a stationary linear combination. In that case, it would be appropriate to test restrictions of elements of β. For example, to test the hypothesis that y_4 is not necessary to form a long-run relationship, set $\beta_{14} = 0$, $\beta_{24} = 0$, etc. For an excellent detailed treatment of cointegration in the context of both single-equation and multiple-equation models, see Harris (1995).

12.9 An application of the Johansen technique to securitised real estate

Real estate analysts expect that greater economic and financial market linkages between regions will be reflected in closer relationships between markets. The increasing global movements of capital targeting real estate further emphasise the connections among real estate markets. Investors, in their search for better returns away from home and for greater diversification, have sought opportunities in international markets, particularly in the more transparent markets (see Bardhan and Kroll, 2007, for an account of the globalisation of the US real estate industry). The question is, of course, whether the stronger economic and financial market dependencies and global capital flows result in greater integration between real estate markets and, therefore, stronger long-run relationships.

We apply the Johansen technique to test for cointegration between three continental securitised real estate price indices for the United States, Asia and Europe. For the global investor, these indices could represent opportunities for investment and diversification. They give exposure to different regional economic environments and property market fundamentals (for example, trends in the underlying occupier markets). Given that these are publicly traded indices, investors can enter and exit rapidly, so it is a liquid market. This market may therefore present arbitrage opportunities to investors who can trade them as expectations change. Figure 12.9 plots the three indices.

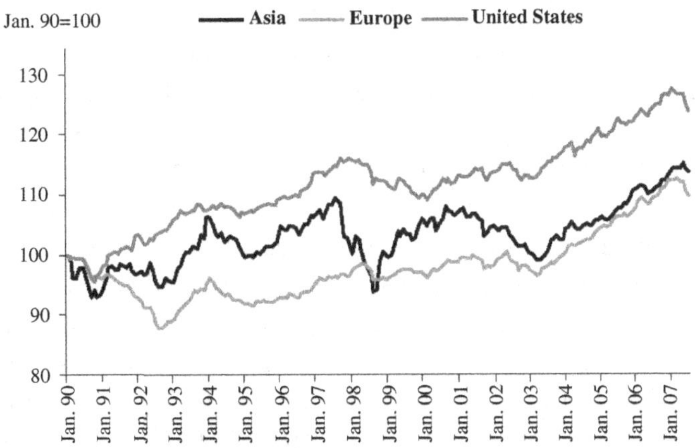

Figure 12.9
Securitised real estate indices

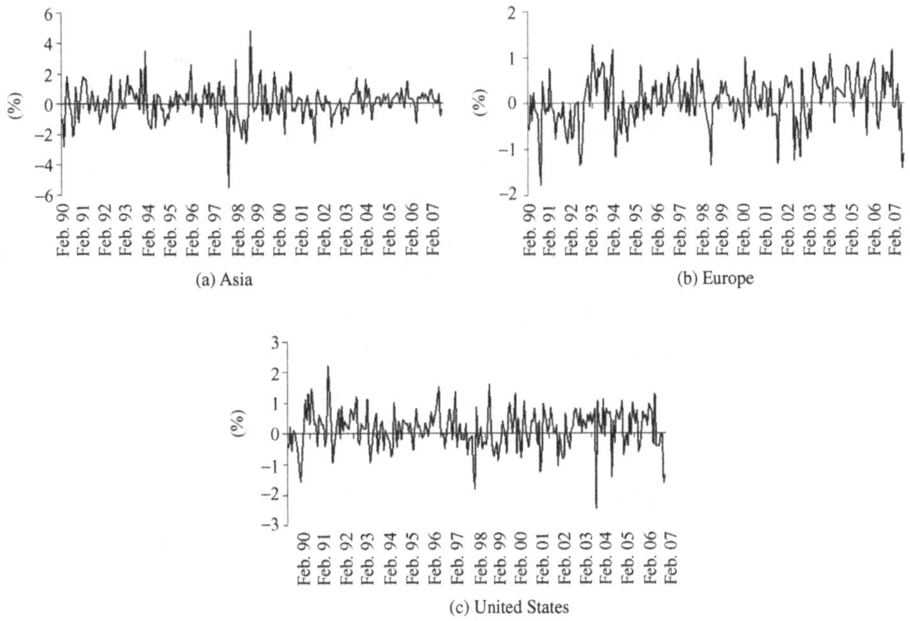

Figure 12.10
The securitised real estate returns series

The sample runs from January 1990 to January 2008.[4] In general, all indices show an upward trend. The variation around this trend differs, however. Europe showed a fall in the early 1990s that was not as pronounced in the other regions whereas the fall of the Asian index in 1998 and 1999 reflected the regional turbulence (the currency crisis). Figure 12.10 plots the returns series.

[4] The data are the FTSE EPRA/NAREIT indices and can be obtained from those sites or from online databases.

It is clear from plotting the series in levels and in first differences that they will have a unit root in levels but in first differences they look stationary. This is confirmed by the results of the ADF tests we present in table 12.7. The ADF tests are run with a maximum of six lags and AIC is used to select the optimal number of lags in the regressions. In levels, all three series have unit roots. In first differences, the hypothesis of a unit root is strongly rejected in all forms of the ADF regressions.

The Johansen technique we employ to study whether the three securitised price indices are cointegrated implies that all series are treated as endogenous. Table 12.8 reports the results of the Johansen tests. The empirical analysis requires the specification of the lag length in the Johansen VAR. We use AIC for the VAR system to select the optimum number of lags. We specified a maximum of six lags and AIC (value = 6.09) selected two lags in the VAR.

Both the λ_{max} and the λ_{trace} statistics give evidence, at the 10 per cent and 5 per cent levels, respectively, of one cointegrating equation. The maximum eigenvalue λ_{max} and λ_{trace} statistics reject the null hypothesis of no cointegration ($r = 0$), since the statistic values are higher than the critical values at these levels of significance, in favour of one cointegrating vector ($r = 1$). These tests do not reject the null hypothesis of a cointegrating vector (test statistic values lower than critical values). On the basis of these results, it is concluded that the European, Asian and US indices exhibit one equilibrium relationship and that they therefore move in proportion in the long run. The cointegrating combination is given by

$$87.76 + \text{ASIA} - 4.63\text{US} + 3.34\text{EU}$$

and a plot of the deviation from equilibrium is presented in figure 12.11.

We observe long periods when the error correction term remains well above or well below the zero line (which is taken as the equilibrium path), although quicker adjustments are also seen on three occasions. This error correction term is not statistically significant in all short-term equations, however, as the VECM in table 12.9 shows (with t-ratios in parentheses).

For both Europe and Asia, the coefficient on the error correction term is negative, whereas, in the US equation, it is positive. When the three series are not in equilibrium, the Asian and European indices adjust in a similar direction and the US index in the opposite direction. The only significant error correction term in the VECM is that in the European equation, however. Hence the deviations from the equilibrium path that these indices form are more relevant in determining the short-term adjustments of the European prices than in the other markets. The coefficients on the error correction term point to very slow adjustments of less than 1 per cent each

Table 12.7 Unit root tests for securitised real estate price indices

Unit roots in price index levels (*AS*, *EU*, *US*)				Unit roots in first differences (ΔAS, ΔEU, ΔUS)			
	Coefficient *t*-ratio				Coefficient *t*-ratio		
Asia	Dependent: ΔAS_t				Dependent: $\Delta\Delta AS_t$		
Intercept	–	2.46	6.44	Intercept	–	0.06	−0.02
	−1.45	−2.76	–		0.80	−0.13	–
Trend	–	–	0.00	Trend	–	–	0.00
	–	–	2.45		–	–	0.60
AS_{t-1}	0.00	−0.02	−0.07	ΔAS_{t-1}	−0.87	−0.87	−0.88
	0.74	***−1.41***	***−2.77***		***−12.67***	***−12.68***	***−12.68***
ΔAS_{t-1}	0.13	0.14	0.16				
	1.84	2.06	2.32				
United States	Dependent: ΔUS_t				Dependent: $\Delta\Delta US_t$		
Intercept	–	0.58	3.51	Intercept	–	0.11	0.12
	–	0.80	1.95		–	2.30	1.23
Trend	–	–	0.00	Trend	–	–	−0.00
	–	–	1.78		–	–	−0.10
US_{t-1}	0.00	−0.00	−0.03	ΔUS_{t-1}	−0.90	−0.93	−0.93
	2.43	***−0.64***	***−1.89***		***−12.91***	***−13.25***	***−13.21***
Europe	Dependent: ΔEU_t				Dependent: $\Delta\Delta EU_t$		
Intercept	–	0.37	2.82	Intercept	–	0.03	−0.09
	–	0.55	2.82		–	0.70	−1.27
Trend	–	–	0.00	Trend	–	–	0.00
	–	–	3.26		–	–	1.95
EU_{t-1}	0.00	−0.00	−0.03	ΔEU_{t-1}	−0.54	−0.55	−0.69
	0.67	***−0.52***	***−2.90***		***−5.80***	***−5.83***	***−10.23***
ΔEU_{t-1}	0.33	0.33	0.31	$\Delta\Delta EU_{t-1}$	−0.13	−0.13	
	4.70	4.72	4.42		−1.55	−1.46	
ΔEU_{t-2}	0.00	0.01	−0.00	$\Delta\Delta EU_{t-2}$	−0.13	−0.13	
	0.00	0.08	−0.02		−1.83	−1.78	
ΔEU_{t-3}	0.13	0.13	0.12				
	1.77	1.84	1.68				
Critical 5%	−1.94	−2.88	−3.43		−1.94	−2.88	−3.43

Table 12.8 Johansen tests for cointegration between Asia, the United States and Europe

Null	Alt.	λ_{max} statistic	Critical 5% (p-value)	Null	Alt.	λ_{trace} statistic	Critical 5% (p-value)
$r = 0$	$r = 1$	20.22	21.13 (0.07)	$r = 0$	$r \leq 1$	30.59	29.80 (0.04)
$r = 1$	$r = 2$	8.64	14.26 (0.32)	$r = 1$	$r \leq 2$	10.37	15.49 (0.25)
$r = 2$	$r = 3$	1.73	3.84 (0.19)	$r = 2$	$r \leq 3$	1.73	3.84 (0.19)

Notes: Lags = 2. r is the number of cointegrating vectors. The critical values are taken from MacKinnon, Haug and Michelis (1999).

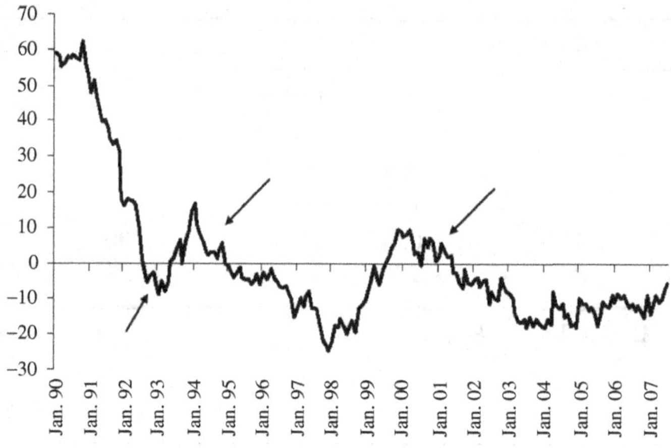

Figure 12.11 The deviation from equilibrium
Note: Arrows indicate periods when the adjustment to equilibrium has been speedier.

month in all equations. This is certainly a tiny correction each month; recall that figure 12.7 had already prepared us for very slow adjustments.

The explanatory power of the Asian equation is zero, with all variables statistically insignificant. The US equation has an adjusted R^2 of 6 per cent, with only the first lag of changes in the European index being significant. The European equation explains a little more (adjusted $R^2 = 15\%$) with, again, ΔEU_{t-1} the only significant term. It is worth remembering, of course, that the monthly data in this example have noise and high volatility, which can affect the significance of the variables and their explanatory power.

If we rearrange the fitted cointegrating vector to make Asia the subject of the formula, we obtain $\hat{ASIA} = -87.76 + 4.63US - 3.34EU$. If we again define the residual or deviation from equilibrium as the difference between

Table 12.9 Dynamic model (VECM)

	ΔAS_t	ΔUS_t	ΔEU_t
Intercept	0.0624	0.0977	0.0209
	(0.78)	(2.11)	(0.58)
ECT_{t-1}	−0.0016	0.0027	−0.0069
	(−0.37)	(1.04)	(−3.46)
ΔAS_{t-1}	0.0832	0.0216	0.0407
	(1.02)	(0.46)	(1.10)
ΔAS_{t-2}	−0.0442	−0.0229	−0.0162
	(−0.54)	(−0.48)	(−0.44)
ΔUS_{t-1}	0.0576	−0.0233	0.0326
	(0.44)	(−0.31)	(0.56)
ΔUS_{t-2}	0.0910	0.0532	0.0779
	(0.71)	(0.71)	(1.34)
ΔEU_{t-1}	0.1267	0.3854	0.2320
	(0.69)	(3.60)	(2.78)
ΔEU_{t-2}	−0.1138	−0.1153	−0.0241
	(−0.60)	(−1.05)	(−0.28)
Adj. R^2	−0.01	0.06	0.15

the actual and fitted values, then $\hat{u}_t = ASIA_t - \hat{ASIA}_t$. Suppose that $\hat{u}_t > 0$, as it was in the early 1990s (from January 1990 to the end of 1991), for example, then Asian real estate is overpriced relative to its equilibrium relationship with the United States and Europe. To restore equilibrium, either the Asian index will fall, or the US index will rise or the European index will fall. In such circumstances, the obvious trading strategy would be to buy US securitised real estate while short-selling that of Asia and Europe.

The VECM of table 12.9 is now used to forecast. Broadly, the steps are similar to those for the Engle–Granger technique and those for VAR forecasting combined. The out-of-sample forecasts for six months are given in table 12.10.

The forecasts in table 12.10 are produced by using the three short-term equations to forecast a step ahead (August 2007), using the coefficients from the whole-sample estimation, and subsequently to estimate the error correction term for August 2007. The computations follow:

$$\Delta AS_{Aug-07} = 0.0624 - 0.0016 \times (-5.44) + 0.0832 \times (-0.41) - 0.0442 \times (-0.85) + 0.0576 \times (-1.36) + 0.0910 \times (-1.62) + 0.1267 \times (-1.09) - 0.1138 \times (-1.40) = \mathbf{-0.13}$$

Table 12.10 VECM *ex ante* forecasts

	Asia	Europe	United States	ΔAS	ΔEU	ΔUS	ECT
Apr. 07	114.43	112.08	126.81				
May. 07	115.05	112.06	126.78				
Jun. 07	114.20	110.66	125.16	−0.85	−1.40	−1.62	−7.69
Jul. 07	113.79	109.57	123.80	−0.41	−1.09	−1.36	−5.44
Aug. 07	**113.66**	**109.24**	**123.58**	**−0.13**	**−0.33**	**−0.22**	**−5.66**
Sep. 07	**113.68**	**109.13**	**123.60**	**0.02**	**−0.10**	**0.02**	**−6.08**
Oct. 07	**113.77**	**109.17**	**123.67**	**0.09**	**0.03**	**0.07**	**−6.21**
Nov. 07	**113.87**	**109.25**	**123.78**	**0.10**	**0.08**	**0.11**	**−6.33**
Dec. 07	**113.97**	**109.34**	**123.89**	**0.10**	**0.09**	**0.11**	**−6.43**
Jan. 08	**114.06**	**109.44**	**124.00**	**0.10**	**0.10**	**0.11**	**−6.51**

$$\begin{aligned}\Delta EU_{Aug-07} &= 0.0209 - 0.0069 \times (-5.44) + 0.0407 \times (-0.41) - 0.0162 \\ &\quad \times (-0.85) + 0.0326 \times (-1.36) + 0.0779 \times (-1.62) + 0.2320 \\ &\quad \times (-1.09) - 0.0241 \times (-1.40) = \mathbf{-0.33} \\ \Delta US_{Aug-07} &= 0.0977 + 0.0027 \times (-5.44) + 0.0216 \times (-0.41) - 0.0229 \\ &\quad \times (-0.85) - 0.0233 \times (-1.36) + 0.0532 \times (-1.62) + 0.3854 \\ &\quad \times (-1.09) - 0.1153 \times (-1.40) = \mathbf{-0.22}\end{aligned}$$

Hence

$$\begin{aligned}AS_{Aug-07} &= 113.79 - 0.13 = 113.66 \\ EU_{Aug-07} &= 109.57 - 0.33 = 109.24 \\ US_{Aug-07} &= 123.80 - 0.22 = 123.58 \\ ECT_{Aug-07} &= 87.7559 + 113.66 + 3.3371 \times 109.24 - 4.6255 \times 123.58 \\ &= \mathbf{-5.66}\end{aligned}$$

This value for the ECT will be used for the VECM forecast for September 2007 and so forth.

If we run the VECM to January 2007 and make forecasts for Europe for February 2007 to July 2007, we get the line plotted in figure 12.12. The forecasts are good for February 2007 and March 2007, but the model then misses the downward trend in April 2007 and it has still not picked up this trend by the last observation in July 2007. Of course, we expect this model to be incomplete, since we have ignored any economic and financial information affecting European prices.[5]

[5] The full-sample estimation coefficients are employed here, but, in order to construct forecasts in real time, the model would need to be run using data until January 2007 only.

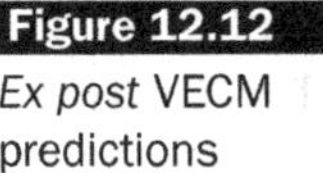
Figure 12.12
Ex post VECM predictions

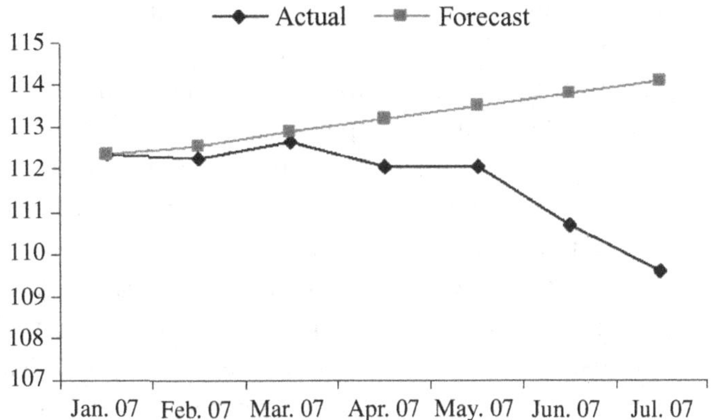

12.10 The Johansen approach: a case study

Liow (2000) investigates the long-run relationships between commercial real estate prices, real estate stock prices, gross domestic product in financial and business services and commerce, interest rates and the supply of commercial space in Singapore over the period 1980 to 1997. He uses the following framework to examine whether the variables are cointegrated,

$$cpp_t = a + b(psp_t) + c(GDP_t) + d(ir_t) + e(sos_t) + u_t \tag{12.75}$$

where cpp is the commercial real estate price, psp is the real estate stock price, ir is the interest rate and sos is the stock of space. Liow notes (p. 284) that, 'if u_t is stationary, then the five series would display a constant relationship over time although they might have diverged in certain shorter periods. This would imply that there is at least a common but unspecified factor influencing the pricing of commercial and real estate stock markets in the economy.'

The data in this study are quarterly and the sample period is 2Q1980 to 3Q1997. The variable definitions are as follows.

- Commercial real estate price index (*PPIC*). This index measures price changes in offices and shops. It is a base index published by Singapore's Urban Redevelopment Authority. The index is deflated using the consumer price index.
- Real estate stock prices (*SESP*). This is a value-weighted index that tracks the daily share price performance of all real estate firms listed on the Singapore Stock Exchange. This index is also converted into real terms using the consumer price index.
- Gross domestic product (*FCGDP*). GDP is expected to have an influence on the demand for commercial space. Since commercial real estate prices

cover offices and shops, the author aggregates financial and business services sector GDP (as the users of office space are financial institutions and business service organisations) and commerce sector GDP (which is a proxy for demand for shop space). A positive impact on commercial real estate prices is implied. The author also takes the natural logs of these first three series (denoted *LPPIC*, *LSESP* and *LFCGDP*) to stabilise variations in the series and induce normality.

- Interest rates (*PRMINT*). The prime lending rate is taken to proxy interest rates. Interest rates can positively affect the initial yield, which is used to capitalise a rent stream. Higher interest rates will lead to falls in capital values, an influence that is magnified by extensive use of borrowing for the funding of real estate investments and development. Hence the overall impact of interest rates on real estate prices is expected to be negative.
- Commercial space supply (*COMSUP*). The supply of commercial space is expected to have a negative impact on prices. The supply measure in this study is the existing stock of private sector commercial space. This series again enters the empirical analysis in logs.

The sample period for which data are available for all series is 2Q1980 to 3Q1997, giving the author seventy degrees of freedom for the analysis. ADF tests are performed for unit roots in all five variables (the study does not give information on the exact specification of the ADF regressions). The findings suggest that all variables are integrated of order 1 (I(1)).

Subsequently, Liow applies the Johansen technique to determine the presence of a cointegrating vector or vectors. The results reject the null hypothesis of no cointegrating relationship among the five variables and also establish the presence of a single cointegrating vector in the system. The cointegrating relationship is (with t-ratios in parentheses)

$$\underset{}{LP\hat{P}IC_t} = \underset{(2.74)}{1.37LSESP_t} + \underset{(1.87)}{1.73LFCGDP_t} - \underset{(-1.82)}{2.12LCOMSUP_t} - \underset{(-1.77)}{1.26LPRMINT_t} \tag{12.76}$$

An intercept is not included in the model. The author makes the following points with regard to this long-run equation.

- The respective signs for all four explanatory variables are as expected a priori.
- In absolute terms, the sum of the coefficients is above one, suggesting that real estate prices are elastic with regard to all explanatory variables.

- More specifically, the long-term real estate stock price elasticity coefficient of 1.4 per cent implies that a 1 per cent increase per quarter in the real estate stock index leads to a commercial real estate price increase of 1.4 per cent on average in the long run.

The author also undertakes tests to examine whether the explanatory variables are exogenous. These tests are not discussed here, but suggest that all explanatory variables are exogenous to commercial real estate prices. Given the exogeneity of the variables, an error correction model is estimated rather than a vector error correction model. From the cointegrating relationship (12.76), Liow derives the error correction model. A general model is first specified, with four lags of each of the independent variables, and a reduced version is then constructed. The final ECM is

$$\underset{}{\Delta LPPIC_t} = \underset{(2.74)}{0.05} - \underset{(-1.87)}{0.10ERR_{t-1}} + \underset{(1.82)}{0.48\Delta LFCGDP_{t-4}} - \underset{(-1.77)}{0.12\Delta LPRMINT_{t-4}} \tag{12.77}$$

where ERR is the error correction term derived from the coefficient estimates of the cointegrating relationship. The DW statistic is 1.96, indicating no first-order residual autocorrelation. The model also passes a range of other diagnostics. The estimated value of -0.10 for ERR_{t-1} implies that about 10 per cent of the previous discrepancy between the actual and equilibrium real estate prices is corrected in each quarter.

Key concepts

The key terms to be able to define and explain from this chapter are

- non-stationarity
- trend stationary process
- deterministic trend
- Dickey–Fuller test
- cointegration
- error correction model
- cointegration and forecasting
- random walk with a drift
- white noise
- unit root
- Phillips–Perron test
- Engle–Granger approach
- Johansen method

13 Real estate forecasting in practice

Learning outcomes

In this chapter, you will learn how to

- establish the need to modify model-based forecasts;
- mediate to adjust model-based forecasts;
- assess the contributions and pitfalls of intervention;
- increase the acceptability of judgemental intervention;
- integrate econometric and judgemental forecasts;
- conduct 'house view' forecasting meetings; and
- make the forecast process more effective.

Having reviewed econometric techniques for real estate modelling and forecasting, it is interesting to consider how these methodologies are applied in reality. Accordingly, this chapter focuses on how forecasting is actually conducted in the real estate field. We address key aspects of real estate forecasting in practice and provide useful context both for the preparer and the consumer of the forecasts, aiming to make the forecast process more effective.

There are certainly firms or teams within firms that overlook the contributions of econometric analysis and form expectations solely on the basis of judgement and market experience. In most parts of the industry, however, econometric analysis does play a part in forecasting market trends. Of course, the question that someone will ask is: 'Does the real estate industry adopt model-based forecasts at face value or does some degree of mediation take place?' The short answer to this question is that, independent of the level of complexity of the econometric or time series model, it is the convention to adjust model-based forecasts to incorporate judgement and expert opinion. In this respect, the real estate industry is no different from what really happens in other business fields. This is also the practice in economic forecasting; model-based forecasts are not adopted outright, but they are subject to alterations by field experts (see Lawrence *et al.*, 2006, and Fildes and Stekler, 2002).

The degree to which the forecast is either the result of models, a combination of models and judgement or judgement alone depends on a host of factors. There are a wealth of studies in the business economics and finance fields on judgemental forecasting and on the means to adjust quantitative forecasts. In this chapter, we draw upon selected research from this literature to provide a context for judgemental intervention in the forecast process in the real estate industry and highlight key issues, for forecasters and users alike. This discussion also benefits from the experience of the second author in this field.

Forecast adjustment in real estate occurs at the end user stage as well as at the production level. It seems that both internal end users (that is, other business units within the organisation) and external users (clients of the firm) expect experienced operators (or experts) in the market to adjust the quantitative forecasts utilising their judgement and experience.

Judgemental forecasting involves a subjective assessment by the expert, who has vision and claims a deep knowledge of a range of parameters, including how the real estate market works, ways that the external environment impacts on the market, recent trends that to the expert's mind are those that show where the market is going, and judging sentiment in the market. An expert with years of experience in the real estate market is likely to have private sources of information. Knowledge about market trends is improved through peer discussions and direct contact with market participants who hold useful pieces of information. Hence the expert benefits from regular contact with occupiers, investors, lenders, developers and other players in the marketplace.

The use of judgement in real estate forecasting raises certain issues, such as why intervention is required, the forms that this intervention can take and ways to combine statistical models and judgemental forecasting. We discuss these topics in turn.

13.1 Reasons to intervene in forecasting and to use judgement

The reasons for which intervention is required to adjust forecasts obtained from econometric models are similar to those for which this approach is practised in other industries. Key reasons include the following.

(1) *Lack of confidence in the model or poor model specification.* The forecaster has diagnostic tests at his/her disposal to assess the robustness of the model.

In this book, we have presented the conventional and most commonly used model evaluation criteria. When the forecaster has evidence that the model is not well specified or its forecasting performance in general is not satisfactory, it follows that there should be little reliance on its out-of-sample forecasts. Expert opinion is therefore a natural way to check the forecasts from this model and to adjust them. One of the tasks of the quantitative analyst is to monitor the performance of the model through time and to identify periods when model errors become larger. The forecaster may, for example, observe that the performance of a rent model is problematic towards the end of the sample. This could be a temporary phenomenon, since even a good model can experience periods when the errors become temporarily larger, but it still raises concerns about the accuracy of the immediate forecasts. In such circumstances, expert opinion could bring additional and useful information. This point also relates to (4) below.

(2) *Poor quality of inputs to the model.* The forecast team may not have confidence in the input data. For example, local economic data that drive an absorption or rent equation could be assessed as being of poor quality. Poor-quality historical data should be picked up by the model in the form of weak statistical relationships and poor diagnostics. All the same, when the quality of the historical data is assessed to be good, confidence in the forecasts for these series may be low (unless of course the model has long lags or it is a VAR, in which case forecasts of the driver series may not be required). For example, local economic data are commonly used for market (metro-level) or sub-market forecasts. Unlike forecasts for the national data, which are produced more frequently and by a larger number of forecasters, local economic forecasts are subject to more uncertainties, including historical inaccuracies that may lead to major revisions in past observations, long lags in the compilation and production of local data and a higher degree of subjectivity in the techniques used to assess local economic activity (such as shift-share analysis). The forecast team should be able to provide an assessment of the quality of the inputs and the accuracy of their forecasts by studying the past of the local economic series (for example, the degree to which both historical data and past forecasts were revised). This is a good reason to seek expert input into the real estate forecast when the accuracy of the local economic forecasts – or, indeed, of any other inputs – is doubted.

(3) *The model is unable to incorporate important information and market developments.* Any model is a simplification of the real world and it cannot incorporate all information. As we have discussed in this book, however,

assessment of the model and its residuals should tell us what the implications are (what the loss is) by excluding information not accounted for by the existing model structure. Such omitted information will affect the errors of the forecast. The team may be aware of future market developments that have not been factored into the model and that are expected to influence the forecast outcome. For example, we may know of near-future changes in planning regulation that can affect supply volumes, improvements in infrastructure that will make a location more attractive for occupiers, or tax changes that will have a bearing on investment returns. The impact of these forthcoming events will not be reflected in the forecasts. A judgemental evaluation of such developments and their impacts can be made and included in the final forecast. Goodwin (2005) suggests that experts should apply their adjustments only when they have important information about events that are not incorporated into the statistical forecasts.

(4) *Noise in the market.* The term 'noise' refers to unpredictable and usually short-lived events that result in extraordinary behaviour and adjustments in the market. Model errors are usually large when there is much noise in the market. Noise can be caused by events outside the real estate market – for instance, the economy, wider investment markets, the geopolitical environment, and so forth.

(5) *Structural breaks.* Structural breaks, which we discussed in chapter 6 and presented tests for the detection of, affect relationships permanently. A concern is always whether turbulence, in particular towards the end of the sample period, represents a structural break that sheds doubt on the model and the forecasts. Judgement to establish a structural break should be based on very deep domain knowledge. A similar case can be made for expected structural breaks – e.g. the introduction of major legislation changes – over the forecast period, which will render the forecasts redundant. If the team are indeed confident of a current or near-future structural break, judgemental forecasts should be superior to quantitative forecasts. This is important, as in the run-up period to the implementation of new legislation, for example, market behaviour and adjustments might deviate from the historical pattern that models had established.

(6) *A discrepancy between model-based forecasts and experts' expectations.* If the forecasts from the model do not match experts' expectations, the experts may be aware of trends to which they would attach more weight, and as a result they do not have confidence in the model. It could also be their own beliefs or gut feelings that differ from the quantitative forecasts. The case for intervention is stronger in fast-changing market conditions

that have been picked up by the experts but not by the inputs to the model. Of course, the experts may disagree only over the first few forecast points (say, over the next four quarters or two years) and agree with the quantitative forecasts as the horizon lengthens. It is also true that forecasts will generally not be as volatile (on account of several factors, including the smoothness of input forecasts) as the actual data; in this case, if the experts expect past volatility to be a feature of the future as well, they may intervene to increase the volatility of the forecasts.

(7) *Influence from peers and the general view.* Relating to the previous point, intervention is required to change the forecasts to conform to a consensus view or to peer belief, or to make the prediction less extreme – or, indeed, make it more volatile. Adjustment to the forecasts may be the result of a more passive attitude and a strategy of not going against the market. We mentioned the IPF consensus forecasts in the United Kingdom in chapter 9, which represent what the whole market expects. The IPF survey facilitates adjustments to the statistical forecasts by passive end users. Forecasts may be adjusted to be broadly in line with the consensus forecast.

(8) *Means of controlling the forecasts and increasing ownership of the forecasts.* Following on from the previous point, not everyone is familiar with econometric models and forecast processes, and hence it is more difficult to accept model-based forecasts. Even if the forecaster demonstrates the validity of the model, the management or the experts may not feel comfortable because of a lack of understanding of the technical aspects, and they may see the whole process as a 'black box'. By applying judgement, the individual becomes more familiar with the final forecast and controls the process, in the sense that it thereby incorporates own beliefs and today's information. The forecast is 'owned' and can be communicated more easily. As we highlight later, communicating models and forecasts in a simple way increases their acceptability.

13.2 How do we intervene in and adjust model-based forecasts?

When judgement is deployed, the intervention can be made at different stages of the forecast process and it can take a variety of forms.

(1) *Using judgement to choose the forecast model.* The forecaster may have developed models that pass the chosen diagnostic tests for model selection, but that give different forecasts. The experts' expectations about near-future market conditions can provide the basis for choosing one of the alternative models. In addition, the forecaster may have assessed

through thorough *ex post* forecast evaluation that, in periods of economic expansion, a particular form of model works better and the forecasts are more accurate than those from an alternative model (for example, by including variables capturing more readily the impact of an economic upturn).

(2) *Using judgement to select variables.* The expert can put forward variables to include in the model. Usually, theory guides the choice of variables, but sometimes theory may not be sufficient and ad hoc additions to the model may be considered. As the investment market has become more global, one suggestion is to use liquidity measures or transaction volumes in yield and capital value equations. The expert may know of different sources for such data and may also have a view of their relative quality. Another example is the use of surveys capturing business expectations in demand models. An expert may consider that such information is important to forecast demand. Furthermore, the market expert may be aware of series, such as registered enquiries by occupiers looking for space in the market in question (a term for it in the United Kingdom is *active demand*), that can act as a harbinger for absorption or take-up. The forecaster will, of course, incorporate these suggestions and assess their contributions to the model and to forecast accuracy.

In both points (1) and (2), a degree of interaction between the forecaster and an expert with good domain knowledge, helping the forecaster in building the model, is implied. To an extent, gaps in theory can be addressed, with the aim of improving the accuracy of the forecasting. Domain knowledge is also used to explain model outcomes and the impact of certain variables. For example, a declining impact of vacancy on rent growth may be due to more vacant space not really affecting rent expectations (badly specified empty buildings or a rising structural vacancy rate). The market expert will have picked up on this trend. The impact of vacancy on rents would also depend on who holds most of the vacant stock – landlords, as in the cycle of the late 1980s and early 1990s, or occupiers, as in the early 2000s in central London offices. The forecast team, with the aid of the expert, should be in a position to study the possible impacts of such market dynamics. In the context of yield models, judgement can be used to select the interest rates that valuers actually monitor when they do the valuations (e.g. the long-term government bond rate or the swap rate, and of what maturity), and this may vary between markets (countries). As such, these forms of intervention do not directly change the model-based forecast output. Judgement is incorporated in the model-building process.

We continue the discussion by focusing on situations in which judgement is used directly to change the forecasts, through intervention in the actual forecasts or ad hoc intervention to the inputs or the model itself. The acceptability of these categories of intervention varies.

(3) *Using judgement to alter the forecasts obtained from an econometric model.* This is intervention at the final output stage, which is the most common form of intervention in real estate forecasting. The forecasters and the market/sector experts meet to discuss the forecasts and come up with a final view representing the organisation's consensus (a 'house view'). It goes without saying that interventions at the final forecast output level should be made for good reasons, and, as we discuss later, they should be documented. Since this is the most common form of intervention, we discuss the stages involved in more detail in section 13.6, which looks at how the model-based and judgemental forecasts can be integrated.

(4) *Intervention at the input level.* The forecast team may change the inputs to reflect their own estimates for future values. If, for example, local output growth is an input to the model (as in our regression analysis example in chapter 7), the forecaster may change the future values of this input to reflect his/her own or someone else's judgement. In some cases, however, the forecaster may change the inputs to simulate an expected outcome; the forecaster or the expert holds a view (judgement) about future growth in, say, absorption, and therefore the future values of inputs (employment growth) are adjusted to reproduce the expected demand path. This is a highly questionable approach, and should be avoided even when there is evidence that forecasts for inputs have been inaccurate in the past. By changing the inputs, the forecast team should be required to present evidence of their greater ability to predict local economic conditions or the drivers of the forecasts.

We highlighted earlier the fact that local economic data, for example, are surrounded by imperfections and uncertainties, giving rise to a common adage: 'Rubbish in – rubbish out.' In such cases, however, the forecast team can undertake a scenario analysis by incorporating their own views. The team can demonstrate the magnitude of past errors in the economic forecasts (for example, employment forecasts used for predicting absorption) and conduct scenario analysis based on the range of these errors. This is a legitimate approach. The expert would like to see different forecast outcomes for real estate utilising alternative future paths of the inputs, which is different from changing the inputs to match expectations (the latter can be seen as a case of the real estate variables containing future information about the inputs). When real estate variables are used as inputs in modelling, the expert may hold good information. For example, the expert will have a pretty accurate picture of levels of construction in the next two to three years, which can overwrite the model's near-term forecast completion (see point (7) below). In any case, when such personal views are adopted, the forecast team must be fully transparent as to how they have generated the forecasts.

(5) *Intervention in model coefficients.* This is intervention to change either the intercept, through so-called 'added factors', or the slopes. The most common approach is the method of added factors, which impacts on the intercept but does not affect the slopes. Prior expectations about market direction and knowledge of events not accounted for by the model drive the use of added factors. The value of the intercept changes so that the forecasts now resemble prior expectations. It can apply to the whole forecast horizon or to certain periods only.

Can we also alter sensitivities to reproduce an expected trend? Changing the sensitivities (size of slope coefficients) may reflect the team's belief that, say, yields are more or less responsive now to long-term interest rates than they used to be. As in the case with intervention at the input level, such action is, again, highly questionable even if the modeller has evidence of changing slopes in recent years. It is worth pointing out that an experienced forecaster will deploy techniques at his/her disposal to allow for time-varying coefficients. For example, the forecaster can build specifications with asymmetric responses of vacancy to employment during periods of economic expansion and contraction or deploy methodologies such as state space models to allow for changing sensitivities (also see section 8.10 regarding the use of dummies).

Complications arise from the use of the sensitivity changes when one undertakes a comparative analysis. For example, how would we address the question of how responsive office yields are to long-term interest rates in the US, Asian and European markets? What betas should be used – the model-based or the modified, artificial ones? As a general observation, however, if we believe that coefficient intervention is necessary, it is legitimate to ask why the model is needed in the first place.

(6) *Using judgement to combine forecasts obtained from different approaches.* In practice, we see a tendency to combine judgemental and econometric forecasts, which raises the question of how these forecasts are combined. There is no straightforward answer to this question. There are rules that can provide the basis for combining forecasts, but judgement can be used to give more weight to one model than an alternative one. In this case, some prior expectation is, again, the criterion by which to choose the weights when combining the models.

(7) *Adjustment to the starting value of the forecast.* Judgement can be applied to the starting value of the forecast or to the initial forecast points. Once the initial values are decided, we can let the model do the rest. Take, for example, the forecast for new building development. An expert or a team of experts will know fairly well what is to be delivered in the next one to two years as building construction is under way now. They even know what is in the pipeline and possible future construction, through good knowledge of outstanding planning permissions and information from contacts as to when building construction work might start. Hence the forecasts from a model can be overwritten or adjusted on the basis of such market evidence. For given real estate series, such as new construction, this approach is more plausible than the alternatives. Moreover, since real estate markets can move slowly, the first or the first few forecast points can be fixed to the latest available observation, or there may be valuable recent information to predict the start of the forecast path. Consider forecasts made in April for the end of the year. Some trends may already be emerging that analysts have picked up. For example, the model may predict a forty basis point rise in yields, but experts may have information that this shift has already happened. An adjustment is feasible for the year-end forecast, and the model can do the rest.

13.3 Issues with judgemental forecasting

In section 13.2, we provided reasons for judgement entering the forecast process and either adjusting or largely displacing the model-based forecasts. Research work on judgement and forecasting has identified the following risks when using judgement.

(1) *Experts may see more in the data than is warranted and they may exaggerate impacts.* Noise in the market or rapidly changing trends can be seen as a structural break. It is not uncommon to talk about a structural break when it later proves to be – with the availability of more data and assessment by tests – a short-term disturbance, with the model retaining its stability.

(2) *Anchoring.* Goodwin (2005) sees anchoring as a characteristic of judgemental forecasting. This problem arises when a starting value or anchor is used that is the most recent rent or yield. This may result in adjustments that are too small, and, in periods of strong growth, for example, under-prediction is likely. The result is a tendency to underestimate both upward and downward trends. Anchoring occurs when the expert is influenced by major past events. For example the expert observes that, in

the previous cycle, absorption was negative when national employment growth was around 0 per cent. With a forecast for employment growth at 0 per cent, he/she may expect negative absorption. Even though there may have been other circumstances in the sample when employment growth was small (say 0.5 per cent) and absorption was high, this is ignored. This particular point also relates to point (7) below.

(3) *Double-counting*. As an example, confidence that there will be rent growth in the future may be based on good figures for employment and GDP growth, but such optimism may be excessive and unjustified, as these economic variables are two similar measures of business conditions (even if they do carry some different information).

(4) *Overconfidence*. Experts may tend to be overconfident. In particular, they may feel that the fact that they have full confidence in their sources of information means that they possess complete information. This confidence in their judgement may be unwarranted, but it may make it difficult for them to change their opinions even if events suggest they should do so. In the context of forecasting stock earnings, Davis, Lohse and Kottemann (1994) find that accuracy declines as confidence grows. There has been evidence in the literature in the context of the stock market, pointing to a tendency to overestimate the accuracy of the trader's information (see Daniel, Hirshleifer and Subrahmanyam, 1998). More evidence on the role of overconfidence on trading performance is provided by Biais *et al.* (2005). This empirical study shows that overconfidence reduces trading performance.

(5) *Inconsistency*. Goodwin (2005) suggests that judgemental forecasts do not make optimal use of information. Judgemental forecasts are not consistent. They are influenced by recent or easily recalled events. Big events that are rare may be given a greater weight than really should be the case; the expert may anchor his/her views, as we said in point (2). Experts tend to see systematic patterns from what in reality are random movements in the market. The general point is this: present two market participants with a similar set of information and they will come up with different answers.

(6) *Inefficient use of past relationships*. A good model will provide unbiased forecasts. Judgemental forecasts can be biased, however, as the history is either ignored or does not fully inform the view of how the market works. There is no way that an expert can make a more efficient use of prior data. As Goodwin (2005) highlights, when it comes to identifying systematic underlying relationships there is no contest: statistical methods are superior. If the past relationship is key to the forecast, a judgemental input may be unnecessary. It depends greatly on the past

forecast performance of the model. If the model does not perform well then there is little loss if we ignore or pay less attention to the historical relationship.

(7) *Domineering and opinionated individuals.* In house view meetings to agree forecasts, Goodwin (2005) highlights the problem of domineering individuals seeking to impose their judgement, which becomes a major risk if they possess information that is inferior to that of other members in the group. There may also be a general bias against statistical forecasts by these individuals, in which case an efficient combination of statistical and judgemental forecasts is blocked.

13.4 Case study: forecasting in practice in the United Kingdom

The study by Gallimore and McCallister (2004) provides evidence on how forecasts are produced and the extent to which judgement enters the forecasting process in the United Kingdom. These authors carried out nineteen interviews (in the second half of 2003) with individuals who were either producers of forecasts and/or responsible for the forecast advice that was incorporated in these forecasts. That is, the sample includes quantitative forecasters and/or the individuals overseeing the forecast view of the organisation and who might happen to be the quantitative forecasters. All nineteen main interviewees had current and prior involvement in the production of property market forecasts. Some of these forecasters also had a strong European focus.

Hardly surprisingly, this study finds plentiful evidence to suggest that adjustments to model-based forecasts are the norm. Judgement in real estate forecasting in the United Kingdom is important and widespread. The reasons that arose in the interviews were several. Uncertainty is inherent in the forecasting process and additional qualitative information may resolve some of this uncertainty. Problems with data availability and the quality of the series warrant intervention. Adjustments are also driven by users and producers recognising the limitations of econometric models – for example, the effects of structural shifts and unanticipated events. There is information about market dynamics that can be found out in a sort of qualitative way by those on the ground, who feed their information back to the forecast process. Sentiment in the market, construction information and deals that are about to be signed are all inputs into the forecast process. Some interviewees also highlighted that it is only short-term forecasts that would be changed due to feedback from those in the market. The study also establishes that forecasters themselves may be looking for input from those on the ground if they sense that the market is too volatile or the series proves difficult to predict. A forecaster working for a fund manager was quoted in this study as saying that, for a yield forecast twelve months on, someone in the market will give you a better forecast than any model.

Gallimore and McCallister also look at the role of end users in forecast adjustments. Most forecasters in the survey said that they periodically discuss their forecasts with both internal and external users prior to obtaining the final figures. This communication is aided by close relationships between the parties. The meeting could be used as a means for the forecaster to better explain the predictions to the user and, at the same time, for the forecaster to receive timely information about the market. An interesting claim was made by an individual working for a forecaster/investment adviser, who said that she had a prior view of the best-performing markets and wanted the acquisition people to focus on these markets. In order to ensure this, the rent forecasts for these markets were adjusted accordingly to show their better performance.

The authors find a wide difference of opinions about the extent to which the quantitative forecast would change before the final figures were released. In larger and more mature markets, the quantitative forecast is more resistant to qualitative modifications, the adjustment becoming more likely when a turning point is sensed in the market. It is very difficult to reach agreement on timing the turning point, however. Three interviewees made an assessment of the input of judgement into the forecast, ranging from 30 per cent to 80 per cent.

Gallimore and McAllister provide evidence of herd behaviour in the forecast process. It is safe not to be far from the consensus (for example, IPF in the United Kingdom and Europe, or some other consensus). There are no significant implications for the forecasters if the entire market is right or wrong. This is corroborated by the fact that most forecasters find it attractive to look at others' forecasts. It is, of course, interesting to find out why others' views differ from one's own, but this may be difficult, as the others' models are not known (and, indeed, one cannot even know for sure that there are any statistical models behind the forecasts). On the other hand, when the forecasts differ from others, it is not usually the practice to change the models straightaway. Of course, a forecaster whose model has passed the diagnostics will be loath to adopt a different view produced from an 'unknown' source.

The smoothing issue is highlighted in this survey. Forecasters are unwilling to release forecasts showing extreme numbers or significant shifts. There were cases in the survey when such extreme values were adjusted not only by the forecaster but also from others involved in the forecast process. The fear of getting it badly wrong provides a justification to adopt a more conservative stance. As forecasts need to be acceptable to the users, forecasters would tend not to present contentious predictions.

One would expect convergence in quantitative forecasting. One forecaster gave as reasons the same forecasting systems, inputs, series modelled and forecast education. For example, take forecasters in Europe who forecast IPD data at the national level for, say, shopping centres. The series they forecast is homogeneous. It is likely that they will use similar national economic data, such as consumer spending and forecasts of consumer spending. In relation to the position a decade ago, we now see more qualified individuals with econometric backgrounds in the real estate market. Econometric software is widely available and it is likely that similar software is used (although regression results should not depend on the software used). The quantitative forecasts will therefore tend to converge, and so perhaps bringing in judgement provides the winning formula.

13.5 Increasing the acceptability of intervention

In section 13.2, we have provided a host of reasons for which intervention and adjustments to the quantitative forecasts are required. In this section, we outline the conditions that make judgemental mediation in the forecast worthwhile and more customary. Franses (2006) says that it pays to (i) record the reasons for the adjustment of model-based forecasts, (ii) keep track of the model-based forecasts and (iii) be clear about how the model-based forecasts are adjusted. In particular, there should be the following.

(1) *Solid reasons for intervention.* A key condition for intervening is that the proposed changes to the model-based forecasts are made for good and well-understood reasons. For example, if the adjustment takes place because the rent model is not trusted, we need to have good reasons why this is so and be clear what additional information the mediation brings. If expert opinion is brought in to address noise, structural shifts or other market developments, good domain knowledge is a prerequisite before adjusting the forecasts, in particular from a robust model.

The expert should endeavour to understand the advantages of a well-specified model. We stated earlier that, when it comes to identifying systematic relationships and making efficient use of prior data, the model is superior. By understanding what information the model brings, expert opinion can focus on what the model does not capture, and in this way a positive contribution is made. Suppose that we have a forecast of rents produced by a model that incorporates an employment series. If an expert makes an adjustment to the forecast driven by future employment growth, this adjustment is based on a less efficient use of the historical relationship between rent and employment growth. The expert should direct his/her efforts towards influences that will genuinely add to the forecast. When the forecasts from a model and expert opinion bring different kinds of information and when the forecasts are not correlated, it is beneficial to combine them (Sanders and Ritzman, 2001).

(2) *Track record assessment.* Purely judgemental forecasts or adjusted model forecasts should be evaluated in a similar manner to forecasts from econometric models. The literature on this subject strongly suggests that track record is important. It is the only way to show whether expert opinion is really beneficial and whether judgement leads to persistent outperformance. It provides trust in the capabilities of the expert and helps the integration and mutual appreciation of knowledge between the quantitative team and market experts. Clements and Hendry (1998) assert that the secret to the successful use of econometric and time series models is to learn from past errors. The same approach should be followed for expert opinions. By documenting the reasons for the forecasts, Goodwin (2000a) argues that this makes experts learn from their past mistakes and control their level of unwarranted intervention in the future. It enables the expert to learn why some adjustments improve forecasts while others do not. As Franses (2006) notes, the best way to do this is to assess the forecasts based on a track record.

Do the experts look at how accurate their forecasts are, though? Fildes and Goodwin (2007) find that experts are apparently not too bothered about whether their adjustments actually improve the forecasts. This does not help credibility, and hence it is important to keep track records.

(3) *Transparency.* The way that the forecast is adjusted and the judgement is produced must be transparent. If it is unknown how the expert has modified the model, the forecast process is unclear and subjective.

13.6 Integration of econometric and judgemental forecasts

The discussion in section 13.2 has made clear that there are benefits from bringing judgement into the forecast process. As Makridakis, Wheelwright and Hyndman (1998, p. 503) put it: 'The big challenge in arriving at accurate forecasts is to utilize the best aspects of statistical predictions while exploiting the value of knowledge and judgmental information, while also capitalizing on the experience of top and other managers.' The potential benefits of combining the forecasts are acknowledged by forecasters, and this leads to the subject of how best to integrate model-based and judgemental forecasts. The integration of econometric and judgemental forecasts is a well-researched topic in business economics and finance. In summary, this literature points to different approaches to integrating econometric forecasts and judgemental views. A useful account of how the forecasts are combined is given by Timmermann (2006).

(1) *Mechanical adjustments to the statistical forecast.* The forecast team may investigate whether gains can be made by mechanical adjustments to the model's forecasts in the light of recent errors. For example, one such procedure is to take part of the error in forecasting the latest period (usually a half of the error) and add that to the forecast for the next period. Consider that a model of retail rents based on consumer spending has over-predicted rent growth in the last few periods (fitted above actual values). This could be due to intense competition between retailers, affecting their turnover, that is not captured by the model. We mechanically adjust the first forecast point by deducting half the error of the previous period or the average of the previous two periods and perhaps a quarter of the error of the following period (so that we lower the predicted rental growth). A prerequisite for this mechanical adjustment is, of course, our belief that the source of the error in the last few observations will remain in the forecast period. Vere and Griffith (1995) have found supportive evidence for this method but McNees (1986) has challenged it.
(2) *Combining judgemental and statistical forecasts produced independently.* Aside from mechanical adjustment, another approach is to combine experts' judgemental forecasts with the estimates of a statistical method produced separately. It is assumed that these forecasts are produced independently; if the parties are aware of each other's views, they might anchor their forecasts. This approach appears to work best when the errors of these forecasts take opposite signs or they are negatively correlated (note that a historical record may not be available), although it is not unlikely that a consensus will be observed in the direction of the two sets of forecasts.

    A way to combine these forecasts is to take a straightforward average of the judgemental and econometric forecasts (see Armstrong, 2001). More sophisticated methods can be used. If a record of judgemental forecasts is kept then the combination can be produced on the basis of past accuracy; for example, a higher weight is attached to the method that recently led to more accurate forecasts. As Goodwin (2005) remarks, a large amount of data is required to perform this exercise, which the real estate market definitely lacks.

Goodwin also puts forward Theil's correction to control judgemental forecasts for bias. This also requires a long series of forecast evaluation data. Theil's proposal is to take an expert's forecasts and the actual values and fit a regression line to these data. Such a regression may be

$$yield = 2 + 0.7 \times judgemental\ yield\ forecast$$

In this regression, *yield* is the actual yield series over a sufficiently long period of time to run a regression. Assume that the target variable yield refers to the yield at the end of the year. *Judgemental yield forecast* is the forecast that was made at, say, the beginning of each year. When making the out-of-sample forecast, we can utilise the above regression. If the expert predicts a yield of 6 per cent, then the forecast yield is $2\% + 0.7 \times 6\% = 6.2\%$

Goodwin (2000b) has found evidence suggesting that Theil's method works. It requires a long record of data to carry out this analysis, however, and, as such, its application to real estate is restricted. Goodwin (2005) also raises the issue of who should combine the forecasts. He suggests that the process is more effective if the user combines the forecasts. For example, if the expert combines the forecasts and he/she is aware of the econometric forecasts, then the statistical forecast can be used as an anchor. Of course, the expert might also be the user. For further reading on this subject, Franses (2006) proposes a tool to formalise the so-called 'conjunct' forecasts – that is, forecasts resulting from an adjustment by the expert once he/she has seen the forecast.

(3) *The 'house view'.* This is a widely used forum to mediate forecasts and agree the organisation's final forecasts. The statistical forecasts and the judgemental input are combined, but this integration is not mechanical or rule-based. In the so-called 'house view' meetings to decide on the final forecasts, forecasters and experts sit together, bringing their views to the table. There is not really a formula as to how the final output will be reached. Again, in these meetings, intervention can be made based on the practices we described earlier, including added factors, but the process is more interactive.

Makridakis, Wheelwright and Hyndman (1998) provide an example of a house view meeting. The following description of the process draws upon this study but is adapted to the real estate case. The house view process can be broken down into three steps.

Step 1

The first step involves the preparation of the statistical (model-based) forecast. This forecast is then presented to those attending the house view meeting, who can represent different business units and seniority.

Participants are given the statistical forecasts for, say, yields (in a particular market or across markets). This should be accompanied by an explanation of what the drivers of the forecast are, including the forecaster's confidence in the model, recent errors and other relevant information.

Step 2

The participants are asked to use their knowledge and market experience to estimate the extent to which the objective forecast for the yield ought to be changed and to write down the factors involved. That is, the participants are not asked to make a forecast from scratch but to anchor it to the objective statistical forecast. If the team would like to remove anchoring to the statistical forecast, however, individuals are asked to construct their forecast independently of the model-based one. In their example, Makridakis, Wheelwright and Hyndman refer to a form that can be completed to facilitate the process. For yield forecasts, this form would contain a wide range of influences on yields. The statistical model makes use of fundamentals such as rent growth and interest rates to explain real estate yields, whereas the form contains fields pointing to non-quantifiable factors, such as the momentum and mood in the market, investment demand, liquidity, confidence in real estate, views as to whether the market is mis-priced and other factors that the participants may wish to put forward as currently important influences on yields. This form is prepared in advance containing all these influences but, of course, the house view participants can add more. If a form is used and the statistical forecast for yields is 6 per cent for next year, for example, the participants can specify a fixed percentage per factor (strong momentum, hence yields will fall to 5 per cent; or, due to strong momentum, yields will be lower than 6 per cent, or between 5.5 per cent and 6 per cent, or between 5 per cent and 5.5 per cent). This depends on how the team would wish to record the forecasts by the participants. All forecasts have similar weight and are recorded.

Step 3

The individual forecasts are summarised, tabulated and presented to participants, and the discussion begins. Some consensus is expected on the drivers of the forecast of the target variable over the next year or years. In the discussions assessing the weight of the influences, the participants' ranks and functional positions can still play a role and bias the final outcome. All in all, this process will result in agreeing the organisation's final forecast. At the same time, from step 2, there is a record of what each individual said, so the participants get feedback that will help them improve their judgemental forecasts.

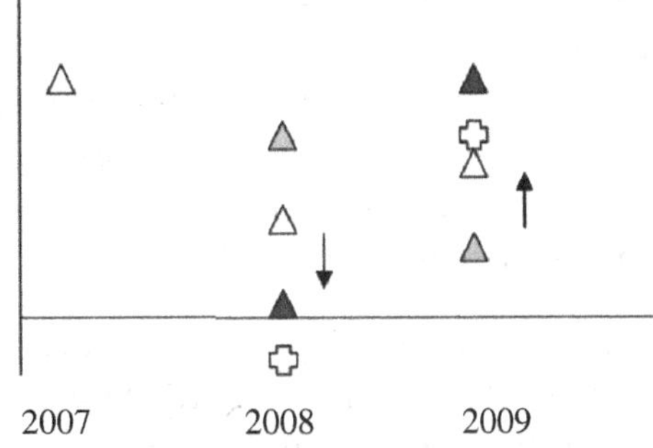

Figure 13.1 Forecasting model intervention

Under the category of 'house views', we should include any other interactive process that is not as formal as the three steps described above. Indeed, this formal process is rare in real estate; rather, there is a simpler interaction in the house view process. This informal arrangement makes it more difficult to record judgemental forecasts, however, as the discussion can kick off and participants may make up their minds only during the course of the meeting.

The outcome of the house view meeting may be point forecasts over the forecast horizon. It may also be a range of forecasts – e.g. a yield between 5.5 per cent and 6 per cent. The statistical forecast can be taken as the base forecast around which the house view forecast is made. For example, assume a statistical forecast for total returns over the next five years that averages 8 per cent per annum. The house view meeting can alter the pattern of the model forecasts but, on average, be very close to the statistical forecasts. Furthermore, point forecasts can be complemented with a weighted probability of being lower or higher. This weighted probability will reflect judgement.

Given the different ways to intervene in and adjust model-based forecasts, a way forward is illustrated in figure 13.1. The value for 2007 is the actual rent growth value. The model-based forecasts for 2008 and 2009 are given by the plain triangle. In all probability these forecasts will not be entirely accurate, as the error will incorporate the impact of random events, and the actual rent growth values for 2008 and 2009 could be either of the two shaded triangles – that is, the actual rent growth will be higher or lower than predicted by the model.

Expert judgement can come in two ways to modify this forecast.

(1) By weighting additional market information, a probability can be given as to which direction the actual value will go. In the figure, such a judgement may suggest that, based on market developments not captured by the model, there is a greater probability that rent growth will be lower

than that predicted by the model in 2008 but higher in 2009 (as shown by the black triangles).

(2) The expert intervenes to provide an absolute forecast, shown by the crosses for 2008 and 2009 in the figure. We explained earlier in the chapter how this absolute intervention can take place; it can be arbitrary or it can utilise previous errors of the model.

In any event, this chapter has highlighted two other issues: (i) the whole process should be transparent and (ii) a record should be kept so that the forecasts, of whatever origin, can be evaluated using conventional forecast assessment criteria.

13.7 How can we conduct scenario analysis when judgement is applied?

Scenario analysis is straightforward from a regression model. We can obtain different values for the dependent variable by altering the inputs to allow for contingencies. Judgemental intervention does not preclude us from carrying out scenario analysis. Some forms of judgemental mediation make it difficult to run scenario analysis, however. A prerequisite is that the final forecast is partly model-based. For the most part, we can run the scenario using the statistical model, and we then bring in the judgement we originally applied. This is an additional reason to ensure that the judgemental input is well documented when it is applied to the quantitative forecast.

With pure judgemental forecasts, scenario analysis is somewhat blurred as a process. The expert holds a view, and it is not clear how the question 'What if...?' can be answered apart from direction. The expert can, of course, give higher or lower probabilities about the outcome based on different scenarios. This is easy when the scenario is based on economic conditions, but if the expert's forecast utilises information from contacts within the industry it may be more difficult to work out the scenarios.

13.8 Making the forecast process effective

The previous sections have identified factors that will make the organisation's forecast process more efficient when statistical forecasts and judgement are combined. Bails and Peppers (1993) look into how the gap between forecasters and users (internal or external) can be bridged, and discuss the forecaster's responsibilities and how to get management to use the forecasts. Drawing on Bails and Peppers' and other studies, a number of suggestions can be made.

(1) Periodic meetings should be held between the preparers and the users of the forecasts. The meetings should involve management and experts in the forecasting process.
(2) The forecaster should explain the nature of forecasting and the problems inherent in the forecast process. What are the limits to forecasting? What can quantitative forecasts not do?
(3) The forecaster should also explain the meaning and the source of the forecast error. The aim in both (2) and (3) is to direct the attention of the experts to the gaps in statistical modelling.
(4) The forecaster should understand the user's objectives. Consumers of forecasts may be more interested in why the forecasts might not materialise.
(5) The forecaster should be prepared to test ideas put forward by experts even if these ideas are more ad hoc in nature and lack theory.
(6) The usefulness of forecasts is maximised if contingency forecasts are included. Scenario analysis is always well received.
(7) Technical jargon should be kept to a minimum. The forecaster needs to be clear about the techniques used and endeavour not to present the modelling process as a black box.
(8) Always incorporate a discussion of historical forecast accuracy and a discussion of how inaccuracies have been addressed. If there is a record of expert forecasts, the forecaster can, ideally, calculate the following metric:

$$\text{total error} = \text{model error} + \text{managerial error}$$

The error is decomposed into one portion, which is the model's responsibility, and the residual, which represents a discretionary adjustment made by management. In this way, all parties gain a perspective on the primary sources of error.

Key concepts

The key terms to be able to define and explain from this chapter are

- forecast mediation
- judgemental intervention
- domain knowledge
- reasons for intervention
- forms of intervention
- issues with forecast intervention
- acceptability of intervention
- mechanical adjustments
- 'house view'
- intervention and forecast direction

14 The way forward for real estate modelling and forecasting

Learning outcomes

In this chapter, you will find a discussion of

- the reasons for the increasing importance of forecasting in real estate markets;
- techniques that are expected to apply increasingly in real estate modelling;
- formats that forecasting can take for broader purposes; and
- the need to combine top-down with bottom-up forecasting.

Real estate modelling and forecasting constitute an area that will see notable advancements in the future, and progress is likely to be achieved in several ways. The methodologies and techniques we have presented in this book will be more widely applied in real estate analysis. We also expect to see the employment of more sophisticated approaches in real estate. Such techniques are already applied in academic work on the real estate market and could be adopted in practice.

There are several reasons why modelling and forecasting work in the real estate field will grow and become a more established practice.

- The globalisation of real estate capital and the discovery of new markets will prompt a closer examination of the data properties and relationships in these markets. Comparisons will be required with more core markets. Investors are interested in establishing possible systematic relationships and studying the sensitivities of real estate variables in these markets to their drivers. Investors would also like to know whether these markets are forecastable.
- Greater data availability will facilitate modelling in real estate markets. Real estate series are becoming longer, the data are available at

an increasingly high frequency, and data can now be found in locations that previously had very little data. New and expanding real estate databases pose challenges to analysts. Analysts will be able to test alternative theories and models with the aim of finding the best forecasting approach.

- Forecasting will also be underpinned by education trends. Larger numbers of analysts with the appropriate skills enter the industry nowadays, partly as a result of more universities including quantitative modelling streams in real estate courses. These analysts will utilise their skills, and the emphasis on rigorous forecasting should be stronger. The wealth of techniques applied in other areas of economics and finance will attract the interest of real estate modellers to assess their applicability in this field.
- There are also external pressures to undertake formal forecasting. As the real estate industry rises to the challenge to be a mainstream asset class, it should be expected that objective forecasting will be required. A characteristic of this market is that it follows economic trends fairly closely and is more forecastable (the occupier market, at least) than other asset classes. Real estate modellers will have to provide increasing evidence for it.
- There will be more sophisticated demands in real estate modelling that can be addressed only by econometric treatment, such as forecasts and simulations for the derivatives market. We describe such demands later in this chapter.

Regression analysis will remain the backbone of modelling work and will continue to provide the basis for real estate forecasts. The use of regression analysis rather than more sophisticated methods reflects the fact that, in many markets, there is a short history of data and, in several instances, the series are available only at an annual frequency. In markets and sectors with more complete databases, multi-equation specifications will offer a good alternative to single-equation regression models for forecasting and simulations. These two forms have traditionally been the most widely used forecasting techniques in real estate practice. The concepts behind these models are easy to explain to the users of the forecasts, and the process of performing scenario analysis is very straightforward. These frameworks, in particular single-equation regression models, are often taken to provide the benchmark forecast.

There is little doubt, however, that the other techniques we have presented and explained in this book will be used. Given the suitability of VARs for forecasting, these models will present a useful alternative to researchers, especially in markets with good data availability. They will provide a useful framework for forecasting quarterly and monthly series – for example, indices used for the derivatives market. ARIMA methodologies are also appealing for short-term prediction in particular, and for producing naive forecasts. Given the availability of software, such models can be constructed quickly for forecasting purposes. Cointegration is undoubtedly gaining ground as a technique for the analysis of real estate markets. More and more relationships are examined within a long-run equilibrium framework, an appealing theoretical concept, whereas the information additional to short-term adjustments from the error correction term cannot be ignored. Real estate researchers will be investigating the gains emanating from adopting cointegration analysis for forecasting.

One of the effects of globalisation in real estate has been the need to study new but data-constrained markets. A framework that researchers will increasingly be employing is *panel data analysis*. This represents a whole new area in applied real estate modelling. When time series observations are limited – e.g. when we have end-of-year yield data for six years in a location – it is worth investigating whether we can combine this information with similar series from other locations – that is, to pool the data. Assuming that we have, say, six years of data in ten other locations, pooling the data will give us around sixty observations. We can then run a panel model and obtain coefficients that will be used to forecast across the locations.

Pools of data obviously contain more information than pure time series or cross-sectional samples, giving more degrees of freedom, permitting more efficient estimation and allowing researchers to address a wider range of problems. The use of a panel can enable them to detect additional features of the data relative to the use of pure time series or cross-sectional samples, and therefore to study in more detail the adjustment process of the dependent variable in response to changes in the values of the independent variables. In some instances, it is permissible to pool the time series and cross-sectional elements of the data into a single column of observations for each variable; otherwise, either a *fixed effects* or a *random effects* model must be used. Assume we estimate a model for yields. Fixed effects will help us to control for omitted variables or effects between markets that are constant over time (reflecting certain local market characteristics). In certain markets, however, the impact of these variables may vary with time, in which case the time fixed effects model, or possibly a random effects model, should be chosen. A comprehensive treatment of panel data estimation techniques and their application is given by Baltagi (2008); an accessible discussion and examples from finance are presented by Brooks (2008, ch. 10).

Future real estate research will focus on identifying early signals in both the occupier and investment markets. The real estate industry is moving towards more timely analysis. This research will take a number of forms. We have seen a good volume of work on the relationship between direct and securitised real estate. The argument is that, due to the frequent trading of the latter, prices adjust more quickly than in the direct market. The smoothness of the direct real estate market data is partly the reason for the slow adjustments in this market. As a consequence, the securitised market can be used for price discovery in the direct market. Given the increasing number of REITs around the globe, particularly in markets in which direct real estate market data are opaque, REIT market signals will be studied closely and included in the forecast process.

Research on early signals will and should focus on leading indicators. Leading indicators are used to capture changes in direction and turning points. There is a significant amount of research being conducted in economics and finance that quantitative analysts will naturally be applying to real estate. Relating to leading indicators is the topic of predicting turning points. Again, there is a large body of work in economics on turning points, and we should expect researchers to utilise the insights of this literature for application to the real estate market.

The econometric models we have examined in this book can be augmented with leading indicators. For example, a model of rents in the United States can include consumer expectations and building permits, which are considered leading indicators of the US economy by the Conference Board. A model of rents with or without leading indicators will attempt to predict turning points through the predictions of future values of rents. The prediction of turning points is therefore a by-product of the point forecasts we make for real estate variables. There is another family of econometric models, the specific objective of which is to identify forthcoming turning points and establish probabilities for such occurrences. The difference with structural models is that the forecasts they make for, say, rents are based on the ability of these models to track past movements in rents. In the second category of models, the prediction of turning points reflects their ability to predict turning points in the past.

One such class of specifications is what are known as *limited dependent variable models*, in which the dependent variables can take only the values zero or one. This category of models includes probit and logit models. For example, we can construct a variable that specifically isolates negative returns for Tokyo, say where the values that the returns can take are $y_i = 1$ if total returns are negative and $y_i = 0$ otherwise. We can use leading indicators to assess the likelihood of a turning point in Tokyo office total returns and also evaluate the past success of the chosen models. These models are expected to show rising probabilities when turning points in total returns are about to occur. A relevant study in the real estate market is that by Krystalogianni, Matysiak and Tsolacos (2004).

The leading indicators used in models to predict the change in direction or turning points could, of course, be real estate variables themselves. For example, series of active demand, which are registered queries by occupiers for space, could be seen as a harbinger of take-up or absorption. Alternatively, surveys of expectations in the real estate market could also provide early signals. In any event, the success of these variables should be assessed within these different classes of models.

The key challenge for models focusing explicitly on turning points is the frequency and history of data. If these models are used to predict severe downturns in the real estate market, there are only three or four major downturns that can be used to train the models. Of course, the turning point can be defined more loosely, such as when returns accelerate or decline – and not necessarily when they become negative or positive. The smoothness of the real estate data can be another issue in the application of probit or logit models.

As global markets become more interlinked, we would expect future research to focus on the transmission of shocks from one market to another. This work will replicate research in the broader capital markets – for example the bond market – in which the transmission of volatility between markets is examined. Again, through the VAR and VECM techniques we studied in this book, we can trace such linkages – e.g. through impulse responses. There are of course other methodologies, such as the so-called multivariate GARCH (generalised autoregressive conditional heteroscedasticity) models, which are geared towards the study of volatility and volatility transmission. Existing work on this topic in real estate includes the study by Cotter and Stevenson (2007), examining whether bond market volatility transmits to REIT volatility, and the study by Wilson and Zurbruegg (2004), who consider how contagious the Asian currency crisis was in 1998 and the impact on real estate in the region.

Transmission can be studied to address questions such as the following.

- Do returns in Tokyo offices become negative following negative returns in New York, how severe is the impact and after how long does it dissipate?
- What is the probability of negative growth in office rents in Hong Kong if Hong Kong REIT prices fall?
- What is the impact of NCREIF and IPD capital value changes on each other?

In real estate, predictions are often expressed as point forecasts. Naturally, one should expect that the future value for rent growth will almost certainly be different from the *point forecast*. The study of uncertainty surrounding a forecast is appealing to investors, particularly in downturns. Prediction intervals can be used to show the possible size of the future error and to characterise the amount of uncertainty. In this way, the uncertainty about the model and the possible impact of a changing environment can be depicted. This *interval forecast* consists of upper and lower forecast limits and future values are expected to fall within these boundaries with a prescribed probability. At different probabilities, these boundaries can be wider or narrower around the central forecast. Interval forecasts and, more generally, estimates of the probabilities of different outcomes are valuable to underwriters, rating agencies and risk managers.

Forecast evaluation is an area that has received little attention in real estate so far, but that will change. The credibility of models is heightened if we can demonstrate their accuracy in tracking the real estate variable we seek to explain and forecast. It is also important to assess past problems, to explain what went wrong and to determine whether this could have been caused by incorrect inputs. There is more focus on demonstrating the validity of models, and users would like to know what the models do not account for. Trained producers of forecasts will be adopting forecast evaluation techniques. Based on this expectation, we have devoted a separate chapter to this subject area.

Finally, there is no doubt that judgemental forecasting will remain a feature in real estate prediction. The success and acceptance of model-based as opposed to judgemental forecasts will be evaluated, as we have discussed in the book, by an assessment of their out-of-sample forecast accuracy. Forecasters and experts will be working together more closely so that they can better understand how to combine their information.

Bottom-up forecasting has always been the main approach in real estate markets. Asset managers assess the investment with regard to the qualities of the building, the tenant characteristics and other attributes. A number of techniques are used to establish whether the building is fairly priced. We expect to see more work on bottom-up forecasting and a greater effort to combine it with *top-down* forecasting. With a greater availability of data we should see more formal forecast techniques being applied to price the risk factors at the building level and predict returns at the asset level. As we will increasingly move into situations of scenario forecasting and stress-testing our estimates, both top-down and bottom-up approaches to forecasting will be valuable to carry out these tasks at the asset level.

Key concepts

The key terms to be able to define and explain from this chapter are

- the future of real estate modelling
- panel data analysis
- limited dependent variables
- turning points
- leading indicators
- shock transmission
- interval forecasts
- bottom-up forecasts

References

Akaike, H. (1974) A new look at the statistical model identification, *IEEE Transactions on Automatic Control* 19(6), 716–23.

Amy, K., Ming, Y.-S., and Yuan, L.-L. (2000) The natural vacancy rate of the Singapore office market, *Journal of Property Research* 17(4), 329–38.

Armstrong, J. (ed.) (2001) *Principles of Forecasting: A Handbook for Researchers and Practitioners*, Norwell, MA, Kluwer Academic.

Bails, D., and Peppers, L. (1993) *Business Fluctuations: Forecasting Techniques and Applications*, Upper Saddle River, NJ, Prentice Hall.

Ball, M., Lizieri, C., and MacGregor, B. (1998) *The Economics of Commercial Property Markets*, London, Routledge.

Baltagi, B. H. (2008) *Econometric Analysis of Panel Data*, 2nd edn., Chichester, John Wiley.

Bardhan, A., and Kroll, C. (2007) *Globalization and Real Estate: Issues, Implications, Opportunities*, Research Report no. 0407, Berkeley, Fisher Center for Real Estate and Urban Economics, University of California.

Baum, A., and Crosby, N. (2008) *Property Investment Appraisal*, 3rd edn., Oxford, Basil Blackwell.

Bera, A. K., and Jarque, C. M. (1981) *An Efficient Large-sample Test for Normality of Observations and Regression Residuals*, Working Paper in Econometrics no. 40, Canberra, Australian National University.

Biais, B., Hilton, D., Mazurier, K., and Pouget, S. (2005) Judgmental overconfidence, self-monitoring and trading performance in an experimental financial market, *Review of Economic Studies* 72(2), 287–312.

Box, G. E. P., and Jenkins, G. M. (1976) *Time Series Analysis: Forecasting and Control*, 2nd edn., San Francisco, Holden-Day.

Box, G. E. P., and Pierce, D. A. (1970) Distributions of residual autocorrelations in autoregressive integrated moving average models, *Journal of the American Statistical Association* 65, 1509–26.

Brooks, C. (1997) GARCH modelling in finance: a review of the software options, *Economic Journal* 107, 1271–6.

(2008) *Introductory Econometrics for Finance*, 2nd edn., Cambridge, Cambridge University Press.

Brooks, C., Burke, S. P., and Persand, G. (2001) Benchmarks and the accuracy of GARCH model estimation, *International Journal of Forecasting* 17(1), 45–56.

(2003) Multivariate GARCH models: software choice and estimation issues, *Journal of Applied Econometrics* 18(6), 725–34.

Brooks, C., and Tsolacos, S. (1999) The impact of economic and financial factors on UK property performance, *Journal of Property Research* 16(2), 139–52.

(2000) Forecasting models of retail rents, *Environment and Planning A* 32(10), 1825–39.

(2003) International evidence on the predictability of returns to securitized real estate assets: econometric models versus neural networks, *Journal of Property Research* 20(2), 133–55.

Brown, G., and Matysiak, G. (2000) *Real Estate Investment: A Capital Markets Approach*, Harlow, Financial Times/Prentice Hall.

Chatfield, C. (1988) Apples, oranges and mean square error, *International Journal of Forecasting* 4(4), 515–18.

Clapp, J. (1993) *Dynamics of Office Markets: Empirical Findings and Research Issues*, Washington, DC, Urban Institute Press.

Clements, M., and Hendry, D. (1996) Intercept corrections and structural change, *Journal of Applied Econometrics* 11(5), 475–94.

(1998) *Forecasting Economic Time Series*, Cambridge, Cambridge University Press.

Cochrane, D., and Orcutt, G. H. (1949) Application of least squares regression to relationships containing autocorrelated error terms, *Journal of the American Statistical Association* 44, 32–61.

Collopy, F., and Armstrong, S. (1992) Rule-based forecasting: development and validation of an expert systems approach to combining time series extrapolations, *Management Science* 38(10), 1394–414.

Cotter, J., and Stevenson, S. (2007) Uncovering volatility dynamics in daily REIT returns, *Journal of Real Estate Portfolio Management* 13(2), 119–28.

D'Arcy, E., McGough, T., and Tsolacos, S. (1997) National economic trends, market size and city growth effects on European office rents, *Journal of Property Research* 14(4), 297–308.

(1999) An econometric analysis and forecasts of the office rental cycle in the Dublin area, *Journal of Property Research* 16(4), 309–21.

Daniel, K., Hirshleifer, D., and Subrahmanyam, A. (1998) Investor psychology and security market under- and over-reactions, *Journal of Finance* 53(6), 1839–85.

Davidson, R., and MacKinnon, J. G. (1981) Several tests for model specification in the presence of alternative hypotheses, *Econometrica* 49(3), 781–94.

Davis, F., Lohse, G., and Kottemann, S. (1994) Harmful effects of seemingly helpful information on forecasts of stock earnings, *Journal of Economic Psychology* 15(2), 253–67.

Dickey, D. A., and Fuller, W. A. (1979) Distribution of estimators for time series regressions with a unit root, *Journal of the American Statistical Association* 74, 427–31.

(1981) Likelihood ratio statistics for autoregressive time series with a unit root, *Econometrica* 49(4), 1057–72.

Diebold, F. (1993) On the limitations of comparing mean square forecast errors: comment, *Journal of Forecasting* 12(8), 641–2.

Diebold, F., and Kilian, L. (1997) *Measuring Predictability: Theory and Macroeconomic Applications*, Technical Working Paper no. 213, Cambridge, MA, National Bureau of Economic Research.

Diebold, F., and Lopez, J. (1996) Forecast evaluation and combination in Maddala, G. S., and Rao, C. R. (eds.) *Handbook of Statistics*, vol. XIV, *Statistical Methods' in Finance*, Amsterdam, North-Holland, 241–68.

DiPasquale, D., and Wheaton, W. (1992) The markets for real estate assets and space: a conceptual framework, *Journal of the American Real Estate and Urban Economics Association* 20(2), 181–98.

(1996) *Urban Economics and Real Estate Markets*, Englewood Cliffs, NJ, Prentice Hall.

Doan, T. (1994) *Regression Analysis of Time Series: User Manual*, 4th edn., Evanston, IL, Estima.

Dougherty, C. (1992) *Introduction to Econometrics*, Oxford, Oxford University Press.

Durbin, J., and Watson, G. S. (1951) Testing for serial correlation in least squares regression – II, *Biometrika* 38(1–2), 159–78.

Engle, R. F., and Granger, C. W. J. (1987) Co-integration, and error correction: representation, estimation and testing, *Econometrica* 55(2), 251–76.

Engle, R. F., and Yoo, B. S. (1987) Forecasting and testing in cointegrated systems, *Journal of Econometrics* 35(1), 143–59.

Fama, E., and French, K. (1988) Permanent and transitory components of stock prices, *Journal of Political Economy* 96(2), 246–73.

Fildes, R., and Goodwin, P. (2007) Against your better judgment? How organizations can improve their use of management judgment in forecasting, *Interfaces* 37(6), 570–6.

Fildes, R., and Stekler, H. (2002) The state of macroeconomic forecasting, *Journal of Macroeconomics* 24(4), 435–68.

Franses, P. (2006) *Formalizing Judgemental Adjustment of Model-based Forecasts*, Report no. 2006-19, Rotterdam, Econometric Institute, Erasmus University.

Fuller, W. A. (1976) *Introduction to Statistical Time Series*, New York, John Wiley.

Galbraith, J. (2003) Content horizons for univariate time series forecasts, *International Journal of Forecasting* 19(1), 43–55.

Gallimore, P., and McAllister, P. (2004) Expert judgement in the processes of commercial property market forecasting, *Journal of Property Research* 21(4), 337–60.

Gerlow, M. E., Irwin, S. H., and Liu, T.-R. (1993) Economic evaluation of commodity price forecasting models, *International Journal of Forecasting* 9(3), 387–97.

Gilbert, C. (1986) Professor Hendry's methodology, *Oxford Bulletin of Economics and Statistics* 48(3), 283–307.

Giussani, B., Hsia, M., and Tsolacos, S. (1993) A comparative analysis of the major determinants of office rental values in Europe, *Journal of Property Valuation and Investment* 11(2), 157–72.

Goldfeld, S. M., and Quandt, R. E. (1965) Some tests for homoskedasticity, *Journal of the American Statistical Association* 60, 539–47.

Goodwin, P. (2000a) Improving the voluntary integration of statistical forecasts and judgment, *International Journal of Forecasting* 16(1), 85–99.

(2000b) Correct or combine? Mechanically integrating judgmental forecasts with statistical methods, *International Journal of Forecasting* 16(2), 261–75.

(2005) How to integrate management judgment with statistical forecasts, *Foresight* 1(1), 8–12.

Granger, C. W. J. (1969) Investigating causal relations by econometric models and cross-spectral methods, *Econometrica* 37(3), 424–38.

Granger, C. W. J., and Newbold, P. (1986) *Forecasting Economic Time Series*, 2nd edn., San Diego, Academic Press.

Greene, W. H. (2002) *Econometric Analysis*, 5th edn., Upper Saddle River, NJ, Prentice Hall.

Gujarati, D. N. (2009) *Basic Econometrics*, 5th edn., New York, McGraw-Hill.

Hall, S. (ed.) (1994) *Applied Economic Forecasting Techniques*, Hemel Hempstead, Harvester Wheatsheaf.

Hansen, L. P. (1982) Large sample properties of generalised method of moments estimators, *Econometrica* 50(4), 1029–54.

Harris, R. (1995) *Cointegration Analysis in Econometric Modelling*, Harlow, Prentice-Hall.

Hausman, J. A. (1978) Specification tests in econometrics, *Econometrica* 46(6), 1251–71.

Hendershott, P. (1996) Rental adjustment and valuation in overbuilt markets: evidence from the Sydney office market, *Journal of Urban Economics* 39(1), 51–67.

Hendershott, P., Lizieri, C., and Matysiak, G. (1999) The workings of the London office market, *Real Estate Economics* 27(2), 365–87.

Hendershott, P., MacGregor, B., and White, M. (2002) Explaining real commercial rents using an error correction model with panel data, *Journal of Real Estate Finance and Economics* 24(1/2), 59–87.

Hendry, D. F. (1980) Econometrics: alchemy or science?, *Economica* 47, 387–406.

Hendry, D. F., and Mizon, G. E. (1978) Serial correlation as a convenient simplification, not a nuisance: a comment on a study of the demand for money by the Bank of England, *Economic Journal* 88, 549–63.

Hendry, D. F., and Richard, J. F. (1982) On the formulation of empirical models in dynamic econometrics, *Journal of Econometrics* 20(1), 3–33.

Higgins, J. (2003) *Introduction to Modern Non-parametric Statistics*, Pacific Grove, CA, Duxbury Press.

Hill, R. C., Griffiths, W., and Judge, G. (1997) *Undergraduate Econometrics*, New York, John Wiley.

Holden, K., Peel, D. A., and Thompson, J. L. (1990) *Economic Forecasting: An Introduction*, New York, Cambridge University Press.

Hollies, R. (2007) International variation in office yields: a panel approach, *Journal of Property Investment and Finance* 25(4), 370–87.

Johansen, S. (1988) Statistical analysis of cointegrating vectors, *Journal of Economic Dynamics and Control* 12(2–3), 231–54.

Johansen, S., and Juselius, K. (1990) Maximum likelihood estimation and inference on cointegration with applications to the demand for money, *Oxford Bulletin of Economics and Statistics* 52(2), 169–210.

Karakozova, O. (2004) Modelling and forecasting office returns in the Helsinki area, *Journal of Property Research* 21(1), 51–73.

Kazmier, L. J., and Pohl, N. F. (1984) *Basic Statistics for Business and Economics*, 2nd edn., New York, McGraw-Hill.

Keim, D., and Stambaugh, R. (1986) Predicting returns in the stock and bond markets, *Journal of Financial Economics* 17(2), 357–90.

Keogh, G. (1994) Use and investment markets in British real estate, *Journal of Property Valuation and Investment* 12(4), 58–72.

Koopmans, T. C. (1937) *Linear Regression Analysis of Economic Time Series*, Haarlem, Netherlands Economics Institute.

Kothari, S., and Shanken, J. (1997) Book-to-market, dividend yield and expected market returns: a time-series analysis, *Journal of Financial Economics* 44(2), 169–203.

Krystalogianni, A., Matysiak, G., and Tsolacos, S. (2004) Forecasting UK commercial real estate cycle phases with leading indicators: a probit approach, *Applied Economics* 36(20), 2347–56.

Kwiatkowski, D., Phillips, P. C. B., Schmidt, P., and Shin, Y. (1992) Testing the null hypothesis of stationarity against the alternative of a unit root, *Journal of Econometrics* 54(1–3), 159–78.

Lawrence, M., Goodwin, P., O'Connor, M., and Onkal, D. (2006) Judgemental forecasting: a review of progress over the last 25 years, *International Journal of Forecasting* 22(3), 493–518.

Leamer, E. E. (1978) *Specification Searches: Ad Hoc Inference with Nonexperimental Data*, New York, John Wiley.

(1985) Vector autoregressions for causal interference, in Brunner, K., and Meltzer, A. (eds.) *Understanding Monetary Regimes*, Cambridge, Cambridge University Press, 255–304.

Leitch, G., and Tanner, J. E. (1991) Economic forecast evaluation: profit versus the conventional error measures, *American Economic Review* 81(3), 580–90.

Ling, D., and Naranjo, A. (1997) Economic risk factors and commercial real estate returns, *Journal of Real Estate Finance and Economics* 14(3), 283–307.

Liow, K. (2000) The dynamics of the Singapore commercial property market, *Journal of Property Research* 17(4), 279–91.

Liow, K., and Yang, H. (2005) Long-term co-memories and short-run adjustment: securitized real estate and stock markets, *Journal of Real Estate Finance and Economics* 31(3), 283–300.

Lizieri, C., and Satchell, S. (1997) Property company performance and real interest rates: a regime-switching approach, *Journal of Property Research* 14(2), 85–97.

Ljung, G. M., and Box, G. E. P. (1978) On a measure of lack of fit in time series models, *Biometrika* 65(2), 297–303.

Lütkepohl, H. (1991) *Introduction to Multiple Time Series Analysis*, Berlin, Springer-Verlag.

MacKinnon, J., Haug, A. A., and Michelis, L. (1999) Numerical distribution functions of likelihood ratio tests for cointegration, *Journal of Applied Econometrics* 14(5), 563–77.

Makridakis, S., Wheelwright, S., and Hyndman, R. (1998) *Forecasting Methods and Applications*, 3rd edn., New York, John Wiley.

Matysiak, G., and Tsolacos, S. (2003) Identifying short-term leading indicators for real estate rental performance, *Journal of Property Investment and Finance* 21(3), 212–32.

McCue, T. E., and Kling, J. L. (1994) Real estate returns and the macroeconomy: some empirical evidence from real estate investment trust data, 1972–1991, *Journal of Real Estate Research* 9(3), 277–87.

(2002) A cross-sectional study of office yields in the UK, paper presented at the 18th American Real Estate Society conference, Naples, FL, 10–13 April.

McGough, T., Tsolacos, S., and Olkkonen, O. (2000) The predictability of office property returns in Helsinki, *Journal of Property Valuation and Investment* 18(6), 565–85.

McNees, S. K. (1986) Forecasting accuracy of alternative techniques: a comparison of US macroeconomic forecasts, *Journal of Business and Economic Statistics* 4(1), 5–15.

Mincer, J., and Zarnowitz, V. (1969) The evaluation of economic forecasts, in Mincer, J. (ed.) *Economic Forecasts and Expectations: Analysis of Forecasting Behavior and Performance*, New York, Columbia University Press, 1–46.

Nakamura, A., and Nakamura, M. (1981) A comparison of the labor force behavior of married women in the United States and Canada, with special attention to the impact of income taxes, *Econometrica* 49(2), 451–89.

Newey, W. K., and West, K. D. (1987) A simple positive-definite heteroskedasticity and autocorrelation-consistent covariance matrix, *Econometrica* 55(3), 703–8.

Osterwald-Lenum, M. (1992) A note with quantiles of the asymptotic distribution of the ML cointegration rank test statistics, *Oxford Bulletin of Economics and Statistics* 54(3), 461–72.

Pesaran, M. H., and Timmerman, A. (1992) A simple non-parametric test of predictive performance, *Journal of Business and Economic Statistics* 10(4), 461–5.

Phillips, P. C. B., and Perron, P. (1988) Testing for a unit root in time series regression, *Biometrika* 75(2), 335–46.

Pindyck, R., and Rubinfeld, D. (1998) *Econometric Models and Economic Forecasts*, 4th edn., New York, McGraw-Hill.

Quandt, R. (1960) Tests of the hypothesis that a linear regression system obeys two different regimes, *Journal of the American Statistical Association* 55, 324–30.

Ramanathan, R. (1995) *Introductory Econometrics with Applications*, 3rd edn., Fort Worth, Dryden Press.

Ramsey, J. B. (1969) Tests for specification errors in classical linear least-squares regression analysis, *Journal of the Royal Statistical Society B* 31(2), 350–71.

Refenes, A.-P. (1995) *Neural Networks in the Capital Markets*, Chichester, John Wiley.

RICS (1994) *Understanding the Property Cycle*, London, Royal Institution of Chartered Surveyors.

Runkle, D. E. (1987) Vector autoregressions and reality, *Journal of Business and Economic Statistics* 5(4), 437–42.

Sanders, N., and Ritzman, L. (2001) Judgemental adjustments to statistical forecasts, in Armstrong, J. (ed.) *Principles of Forecasting: A Handbook for Researchers and Practitioners*, Norwell, MA, Kluwer Academic, 405–16.

Schwarz, G. (1978) Estimating the dimension of a model, *Annals of Statistics* 6(2), 461–4.

Sims, C. A. (1972) Money, income, and causality, *American Economic Review* 62(4), 540–52.

(1980) Macroeconomics and reality, *Econometrica* 48(1), 1–48.

Sivitanidou, R., and Sivitanides, P. (1999) Office capitalization rates: real estate and capital market influences, *Journal of Real Estate Finance and Economics* 18(3), 297–322.

Stevenson, S., and McGrath, O. (2003) A comparison of alternative rental forecasting models: empirical tests on the London office market, *Journal of Property Research* 20(3), 235–60.

Stock, J. H., and Watson, M. W. (2006) *Introduction to Econometrics*, 2nd edn., Upper Saddle River, NJ, Addison Wesley.

Theil, H. (1966) *Applied Economic Forecasting*, Amsterdam, North-Holland.

(1971) *Principles of Econometrics*, Amsterdam, North-Holland.

Thompson, B., and Tsolacos, S. (2000) Projections in the industrial property market using a simultaneous equation system, *Journal of Real Estate Research* 19(1–2), 165–88.

Timmermann, A. (2006) Forecast combinations, in Elliott, G., Granger, C. W. J., and Timmermann, A. (eds.) *Handbook of Economic Forecasting*, vol. I, Amsterdam, Elsevier, 136–96.

Tong, H. (1990) *Nonlinear Time Series: A Dynamical Systems Approach*, Oxford, Oxford University Press.

Tse, R. (1997) An application of the ARIMA model to real-estate prices in Hong Kong, *Journal of Property Finance* 8(2), 152–63.

Tsolacos, S. (2006) An assessment of property performance forecasts: consensus versus econometric, *Journal of Property Investment and Finance* 24(5), 386–99.

Tsolacos, S., and McGough, T. (1999) Rational expectations, uncertainty and cyclical activity in the British office market, *Urban Studies* 36(7), 1137–49.

Tuluca, S., Myer, F., and Webb, J. (2000) Dynamics of private and public real estate markets, *Journal of Real Estate Finance and Economics* 21(3), 279–96.

Vere, D., and Griffith, G. (1995) Modifying quantitative forecasts of livestock production using expert judgments, *Journal of Forecasting* 14(5), 453–64.

Watsham, T., and Parramore, K. (1997) *Quantitative Methods in Finance*, London, Thomson Business Press.

Wheaton, W., Torto, R., and Evans, P. (1997) The cyclic behaviour of the Greater London office market, *Journal of Real Estate Finance and Economics* 15(1), 77–92.

White, H. (1980) A heteroskedasticity-consistent covariance matrix estimator and a direct test for heteroskedasticity, *Econometrica* 48(4), 817–38.

Wilson, P., and Okunev, J. (2001) Enhancing information use to improve predictive performance in property markets, *Journal of Property Investment and Finance* 19(6), 472–97.

Wilson, P., Okunev, J., Ellis, C., and Higgins, D. (2000) Comparing univariate forecasting techniques in property markets, *Journal of Real Estate Portfolio Management* 6(3), 283–306.

Wilson, P., and Zurbruegg, R. (2004) Contagion or interdependence? Evidence from co-movements in Asia-Pacific securitised real estate markets during the 1997 crisis, *Journal of Property Investment and Finance* 22(5), 401–13.

Wyatt, P. (2007) *Property Valuation*, Oxford, Basil Blackwell.

Index

Printed in the United States
By Bookmasters